EYEWITNESS TRAVEL

BRAZIL

DK

LONDON, NEW YORK,
MELBOURNE, MUNICH AND DELHI
www.dk.com

MANAGING EDITOR Aruna Ghose
EDITORIAL MANAGER Ankita Awasthi
DESIGN MANAGER Priyanka Thakur
PROJECT EDITOR Alka Thakur
PROJECT DESIGNER Mathew Kurien
EDITORS Arundhti Bhanot, Nandita Jaishankar, Vandana Mohindra
DESIGNERS Rajnish Kashyap, Baishakhee Sengupta
CARTOGRAPHY MANAGER Uma Bhattacharya
SENIOR CARTOGRAPHER Suresh Kumar
SENIOR PICTURE RESEARCHER Taiyaba Khatoon
PICTURE RESEARCHER Sumita Khatwani
SENIOR DTP DESIGNER Vinod Harish

CONTRIBUTORS
Alex Bellos, Shawn Blore, Dilwyn Jenkins, Oliver Marshall,
Christopher Pickard, Alex Robinson, Neiva Augusta Silva

CONSULTANT
Alex Robinson

PHOTOGRAPHERS
Demetrio Carrasco, Nigel Hicks, Alex Robinson, Linda Whitman

ILLUSTRATORS
Surat Kumar Mantoo, Arun Pottirayil, Gautam Trivedi, Mark Warner

Reproduced in Singapore by Colourscan
Printed and bound by L. Rex Printing Company Limited, China

First American Edition, 2007
07 08 09 10 9 8 7 6 5 4 3 2 1

Published in the United States by Dorling Kindersley Publishing,
Inc., 375 Hudson Street, New York 10014

Copyright © 2007 Dorling Kindersley Limited, London
A Penguin Company

ALL RIGHTS RESERVED UNDER INTERNATIONAL AND PAN-AMERICAN COPYRIGHT
CONVENTIONS. NO PART OF THIS PUBLICATION MAY BE REPRODUCED, STORED IN
A RETRIEVAL SYSTEM, OR TRANSMITTED IN ANY FORM OR BY ANY MEANS,
ELECTRONIC, MECHANICAL, PHOTOCOPYING, RECORDING OR OTHERWISE WITHOUT
THE PRIOR WRITTEN PERMISSION OF THE COPYRIGHT OWNER.

Published in Great Britain by Dorling Kindersley Limited.

A CATALOGING IN PUBLICATION RECORD IS
AVAILABLE FROM THE LIBRARY OF CONGRESS.

ISSN:1552-1554
ISBN 978-0-7566-2820-8

Front cover main image: Cristo Redentor, Rio de Janeiro

**The information in this
DK Eyewitness Travel Guide is checked regularly.**

Every effort has been made to ensure that this book is as up-to-date
as possible at the time of going to press. Some details, however,
such as telephone numbers, opening hours, prices, gallery hanging
arrangements and travel information are liable to change. The
publishers cannot accept responsibility for any consequences arising
from the use of this book, nor for any material on third party
websites, and cannot guarantee that any website address in this
book will be a suitable source of travel information. We value the
views and suggestions of our readers very highly. Please write to:
Publisher, DK Eyewitness Travel Guides, Dorling Kindersley,
80 Strand, London, WC2R 0RL.

CONTENTS

INTRODUCING BRAZIL

Dazzling display of an extravagant
costume at the Rio Carnaval

Statue of Dom Pedro II, Museu
Imperial, Petrópolis

◁ Vista of São Conrado with Sugar Loaf mountain in the background, Rio de Janeiro

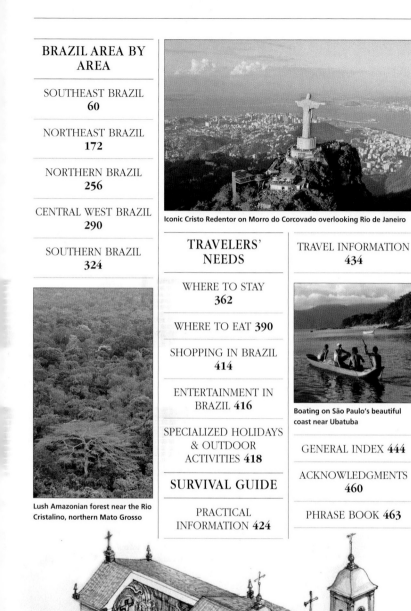

Iconic Cristo Redentor on Morro do Corcovado overlooking Rio de Janeiro

Boating on São Paulo's beautiful coast near Ubatuba

Lush Amazonian forest near the Rio Cristalino, northern Mato Grosso

Basílica do Senhor Bom Jesus de Matosinhos in Congonhas, Minas Gerais

INTRODUCING
BRAZIL

DISCOVERING BRAZIL

Brazil can be divided into five major regions, each offering a unique culture, landscape, and experience. The Southeast features two of the country's largest cities, Rio de Janeiro and São Paulo. With a distinct European character, Southern Brazil offers some breathtaking natural sights. The Northeast, with a stunning beach-studded coastline and stark interior, beautifully preserves its historic cities and a vibrant Afro-Brazilian culture. In Northern Brazil, the dense and pristine Amazon forest and tropical grasslands make up Brazil's wild frontier. Once Brazil's neglected interior, the Central West prides itself on the Modernist national capital, Brasília, and the wildlife-rich Pantanal wetlands. Below is an overview of the highlights of each region in the book.

RIO DE JANEIRO CITY

- Iconic Cristo Redentor & Sugar Loaf
- Fabulous beaches
- Sensual *samba* & Carnaval

Rio's neighborhoods and beaches need at least five days to be explored. Overlooking **Sugar Loaf** (*see pp76–7*), **Cristo Redentor** (*see pp82–3*) stands on Corcovado, surrounded by lush **Parque Nacional da Tijuca** (*see p88*). The city center is lined with museums, historic buildings, and the vast **Estádio Maracanã** (*see p84*). Just south of the center, Santa Teresa and Lapa are the nightlife hubs. Beyond these are Copacabana, Ipanema, and Leblon beaches (*see pp78–9*) with exciting shopping areas (*see pp90–91*). Rio's Carnaval (*see pp64–5*) is world-famous for its revelry and its *samba*.

RIO DE JANEIRO & ESPÍRITO SANTO

- Enchanting Palácio Imperial
- Beautiful beaches & islands
- Rainforest hikes

Combining pretty colonial towns and imperial cities with gorgeous beaches and cool mountains draped in the Atlantic rainforest, these two coastal states can be seen in a week. The national parks of **Itatiaia** (*see p111*) and the **Serra dos Órgãos** (*see p115*) offer superb birding and hiking. Between

Cristo Redentor rising through the mist at twilight, Rio de Janeiro

them is the former imperial summer retreat, **Palácio Imperial** (*see pp114–15*) at the pretty town of **Petrópolis** (*see pp112–13*). The coast is fringed with stunning beaches, such as those at the lively resort towns of **Búzios** and **Cabo Frio** (*see pp116–17*). The colonial town of **Paraty** (*see pp106–8*) lies amid fine beaches. Offshore are a number of lush islands, such as **Ilha Grande** (*see p110*), which offer good snorkeling and diving.

MINAS GERAIS

- Southern colonial towns
- Magnificent churches
- Spectacular national parks

Minas Gerais is dotted with colonial mining towns, whose cobbled streets are lined with some of the finest Baroque buildings in Brazil. Most of them can be seen in five days. The UNESCO World Heritage Sites of **Ouro Preto** (*see pp126–8*) and **Congonhas** (*see pp130–31*), in southern Minas, are famed for their haunting sculptures by Aleijadinho (*see p131*). **São João del Rei** (*see pp132–3*) has the most magnificent of all Minas churches. **Diamantina** (*see p124*) in the north is a well-preserved town. The national parks of **Serra do Cipó** (*see p125*) and **Serra da Canastra** (*see p133*) are good for trekking.

A cluster of colonial houses in Ouro Preto's historic center, Minas Gerais

◁ A painting in naïve style by Calixto Sales, depicting a market scene in Maragojipe, Bahia

Rock spurs etched against a clouded sky in the Chapada Diamantina, Bahia

SÃO PAULO CITY

- **Dining & shopping in Jardins**
- **Art at Pinacoteca & MASP**
- **Niemeyer in Ibirapuera Park**

The city's chic restaurants, bars, and shops merit at least two days. Jardins, a fashionable dining and shopping district, lies close to the museums and historical buildings in the center, which include the state art gallery, **Pinacoteca do Estado** *(see pp140–41)*. Close by, the upscale Avenida Paulista features the state gallery, **MASP** *(see p143)*, which boasts the finest collection of European paintings in the Southern Hemisphere. The vast **Parque do Ibirapuera** *(see pp146–7)* has several museums, many of which have been designed by Oscar Niemeyer.

SÃO PAULO STATE

- **Scenic beaches & rainforest**
- **Pretty offshore islands**
- **Fascinating soccer museum in Santos**

Allow up to five days for São Paulo state, which retains surprisingly large areas of wilderness and has a beautiful coastline, watched over by forest-covered mountains. The northern coast has the finest beaches, particularly around **Ilhabela** *(see p165)*. The southern coast protects the expansive coastal forest in **Estação Ecológico Juréia-Itatins** *(see p170)*. The cities

of **Santos** and **São Vicente** *(see pp168–9)* retain fine colonial buildings. Santos is also famous for its soccer club, Santos Futebol Clube *(see p169)*, for which Pelé used to play.

BAHIA

- **Afro-Brazilian Salvador**
- **Splendid beaches & resorts**
- **Scenic Chapada Diamantina**

The cultural heart of African Brazil, Bahia requires at least a week to explore. Its capital **Salvador** *(see pp184–95)* has lavish Baroque churches and colonial buildings, alongside boutique diners serving the distinctive African-influenced cuisine. *Capoeira (see p199)* is performed everywhere in the state. Bahia's coast stretches through glorious beaches and little resorts, such as the bustling **Porto Seguro** *(see p201)* and the

quieter **Trancoso** *(see p201)*. Bahia's arid interior is broken by the beautiful **Chapada Diamantina** *(see pp204–205)*.

SERGIPE, ALAGOAS & PERNAMBUCO

- **Thrilling Rio São Francisco**
- **Olinda's colonial elegance**
- **World-class diving in Fernando de Noronha**

Four days are enough for Sergipe and Alagoas, which have many pretty beaches lining the clear-blue **Rio São Francisco** *(see p213)*. Famous for its rich music scene and strong cultural identity, Pernambuco needs five days. One of Brazil's prettiest colonial towns, **Olinda** *(see pp220–22)* is known for its architecture and Carnaval. **Fernando de Noronha** *(see pp224–5)*, an hour's flight offshore, is an island famous for superb diving.

Boat floating on crystal-clear waters around Ilhabela, São Paulo state

PARAÍBA, RIO GRANDE DO NORTE & CEARÁ

- Unusual geological formations
- Festival in Campina Grande
- Beaches & dune buggies

The three states forming the heartland of the Northeast require a week. Paraíba is famous for its *sertão* desert interior, which is dotted with geological formations such as the striking boulder **Lajedo do Pai Mateus** *(see p232)* in Cariri. Fossilized dinosaur footprints can be seen at **Vale dos Dinossauros** *(see p232)* in Souza. **Campina Grande**'s Festas Juninas *(see p232)* draws almost a million people every June. Rio Grande do Norte and Ceará are renowned for their beaches. At **Genipabu** *(see p238)* and **Jericoacoara** *(see pp240–41)*, towering sand dunes can be explored by buggy.

PIAUÍ & MARANHÃO

- Magical Delta do Parnaíba & Lençóis Maranhenses
- Hills of Serra da Capivara
- Colorful São Luís

These two coastal states can be visited over four to five days. The swamps and riverine islands of the **Delta do Parnaíba** and the dunes of **Lençóis Maranhenses** *(see pp250–51)* are best explored in the wet season. The interior features the **Serra da**

Lagoon and dunes, Parque Nacional dos Lençóis Maranhenses, Maranhão

Capivara *(see p248)* mountain range. The scenic colonial city of **São Luís** *(see pp252–4)* celebrates the Bumba-meu-boi festival with great fervor.

PARÁ & AMAPÁ

- Crafts in colonial Belém
- Wildlife-rich Ilha de Marajó
- Picturesque Santarém

The principal cities and environs of the vast Amazonian states can be seen in a few days, as most parts are largely inaccessible. **Belém** *(see pp268–9)* is an attractive city of colonial buildings, craft markets, and lively nightlife. To its north is the seasonally flooded **Ilha de Marajó** *(see p270)*, once part of an indigenous empire that stretched all the way to **Santarém** *(see p274)*, a three-day boat ride away. The city lies at the meeting of the blue waters of the Rio Tapajós and the Amazon river.

AMAZONAS, RORAIMA, ACRE & RONDÔNIA

- Intriguing, wild Amazon
- Trekking in the savannas
- Chico Mendes Museum

With Brazil's largest stretch of primary tropical forest, Amazonas needs five days to visit. Most trips into the rainforest begin in its capital city, **Manaus** *(see pp280–87)*, which retains the lavish **Teatro Amazonas** *(see pp282–3)* from its rubber-boom days. Though not as accessible as Amazonas, the other three states offer attractions that can be seen in three to four days. Roraima's capital, **Boa Vista** *(see p288)*, offers trekking in the savanna, while **Rio Branco**, the capital of Acre, pays tribute to Chico Mendes in **Parque Ambiental Chico Mendes** *(see p289)*. River trips can be taken from **Porto Velho** in Rondônia *(see p289)*.

Picturesque setting of a typical stilt house on the Rio Solimões near Manaus, Amazonas

BRASÍLIA, GOIÁS & TOCANTINS

- **Modernist Brasília**
- **Colonial towns**
- **Jalapão & Ilha do Bananal**

With monumental buildings, Brasília is one of the world's finest Modernist cities. It can be seen comfortably in a day. Preserving vast *cerrado* forests, Goiás and Tocantins need at least 10 days. The spectacular **Chapada dos Veadeiros** *(see pp312–13)* and **Parque Nacional das Emas** *(see p311)* are the main attractions in Goiás. The state is dotted with colonial mining towns that are among the best preserved in South America. Tocantins features the winding sand dunes of **Jalapão** *(see pp310–11)* and the expansive river island, **Ilha do Bananal** *(see p311)*.

MATO GROSSO & MATO GROSSO DO SUL

- **Wildlife in the Pantanal**
- **Festivity in Miranda**
- **Snorkeling in Bonito**
- **Birding in Alta Floresta**

These enormous twin states preserve two extensive wilderness areas. The **Pantanal** *(see pp320–21)* is the world's largest wetland and the best place in the Americas to see wildlife. Three days in a *fazenda* (ranch house) or on a tour are enough to explore the area. **Miranda** *(see p322)*, with pretty *fazendas* in the heart of the Pantanal, is known for its *sertanejo* music and Festa do Homem Pantaneiro. The Pantanal excursion can be combined with a trip to **Bonito** *(see p323)*, which is famous for its clear rivers and dramatic caves, as well as for its snorkeling opportunities. The southern Amazon rainforest begins north of the Pantanal in Mato Grosso. The scenic Cristalino Jungle Lodge in **Alta Floresta** *(see p319)* lies on the Rio Cristalino, home to rare birds and mammals.

Jabiru storks in the northern Pantanal, Mato Grosso

SANTA CATARINA & PARANÁ

- **Majestic Foz do Iguaçu**
- **Exciting beaches & surf around Florianópolis**
- **Oktoberfest in Blumenau**

The world's most spectacular waterfalls, **Foz do Iguaçu** *(see pp340–41)* sit in their own rainforest preserve in Paraná state. They need two days to explore. The Paraná coast, which is reached via a delightful winding mountain railway, forms part of one of the largest stretches of coastal rainforest in the world. Little islands such as the low-key **Ilha do Mel** *(see p338)* offer sand and surfing. Santa

Surfing at Praia Joaquina in Florianópolis, Santa Catarina

Catarina state has some of the best beaches in Brazil. Pounded by strong surf, these beaches lie around the attractive, well-kept city of **Florianópolis** *(see pp346–7)*. Both states have a strong European influence, brought by the immigrants who began settling here in the late 19th century. The town of Blumenau still largely speaks German and has an **Oktoberfest** *(see p40)* to rival the one in Bavaria.

RIO GRANDE DO SUL

- ***Churrascarias* in Porto Alegre**
- **Hiking & wine tour**
- **Inspiring Jesuit missions**

Allow five days to visit Brazil's southernmost state, which is famous for its *gaúcho* culture *(see pp330–31)*. Its capital, **Porto Alegre** *(see pp352–3)*, is filled with *churrascarias* (steak houses) that serve fabulous steaks with *chá maté* (herbal tea). There is excellent hiking in the hills, as well as the wine tour in **Vale dos Vinhedos** *(see p355)*. Near the border with Argentina are a series of ruined Jesuit monasteries at **São Miguel das Missões** *(see p359)*, former settlements of the Guaraní, whose story inspired the 1986 film *The Mission.*

Putting Brazil on the Map

The largest country in South America, Brazil borders most other South American countries and covers over 3.3 million sq miles (8.5 million sq km), from the vast tropical Amazon region in the north to the cooler, more European-style South. It is divided into 26 states and one federal district – its political and administrative capital, Brasília. Brazil's population, now reaching over 185 million, is mostly concentrated in the Southeast *(see pp14–15)*.

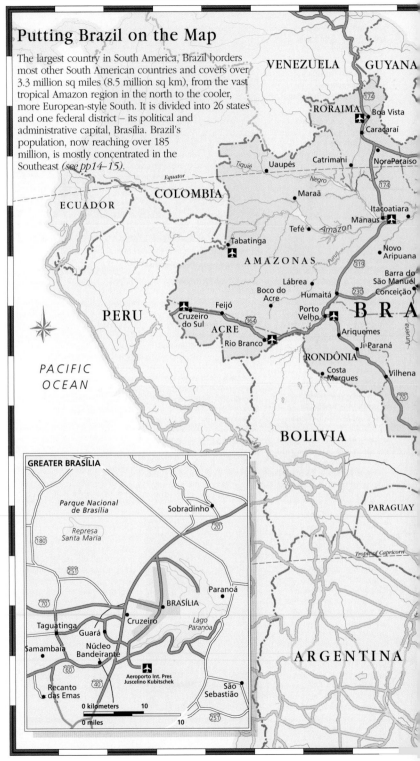

VENEZUELA   GUYANA

RORAIMA   Boa Vista

Caracaraí

Tiquié   Uaupés   Catrimani   NoraParaíso

Equator

COLOMBIA   Maraã

ECUADOR   Itacoatiara

Manaus

Tefé   *Amazon*

Tabatinga   Novo Aripuana

AMAZONAS   Barra do São Manuél

Lábrea   Conceição

Boco do Acre   Humaitá

Feijó   Porto Velho   B R A

Cruzeiro do Sul

ACRE   Ariquemes

Rio Branco   Ji-Paraná

RONDÔNIA

Costa Marques   Vilhena

PACIFIC OCEAN

BOLIVIA

PARAGUAY

Tropic of Capricorn

ARGENTINA

GREATER BRASÍLIA

Parque Nacional de Brasília   Sobradinho

Represa Santa Maria

Paranoá

BRASÍLIA

Cruzeiro   *Lago Paranoa*

Taguatinga

Guará

Samambaia   Núcleo Bandeirante

Aeroporto Int. Pres Juscelino Kubitschek

São Sebastião

Recanto das Emas

0 kilometers   10

0 miles   10

CENTRAL & SOUTH AMERICA

MEXICO   BELIZE   HAITI
GUATEMALA   HONDURAS   ATLANTIC
NICARAGUA   OCEAN
COSTA RICA
PANAMA   VENEZUELA   GUYANA   FRENCH
COLOMBIA   SURINAME   GUIANA
ECUADOR
PERU   BRAZIL
BOLIVIA
CHILE   PARAGUAY   *See pp14–15*
ARGENTINA
URUGUAY

ATLANTIC
OCEAN

PACIFIC
OCEAN

ATLANTIC
OCEAN

FRENCH
GUIANA
SURINAME
Asoenangka   AMAPÁ
Serra do
Navio   Macapá
Porteira   *Equator*
Óbidos   *Amazon*   Belém   816
Monte Alegre   *Rio do Pará*
Parintins   230   10   São
Santarém   Luís
Tapajós
Itaituba   Fortaleza
PARÁ   Caxias   CEARÁ   Mossoró
Araras   Marabá   Imperatriz   Timon   Teresina   Ilha Fernando
de Noronha
Z I L   MARANHÃO   Juàzeiro   Natal
Araguaína   do Norte   304
Cachimbo   PIAUÍ   232   PARAÍBA   João
Alta   226   Petrolina   PERNAMBUCO   Pessoa
Floresta   Peixoto de   Palmas   Recife
Azevedo   230   Juàzeiro   Paulo   101
Sinop   TOCANTINS   40   Afonso   Maceió
Jacaré   Barreiras   116
MATO   242   Feira de   Aracaju
GROSSO   GOIÁS   Santana   Alagoinhas
30   BAHIA   Salvador
Cuiabá   Ceilândia   Vitória da   Jequié
Várzea   70   Anápolis   Conquista   Itabuna
Grande   Rondonópolis   Brasília   Ilhéus
Goiânia   Gama   MINAS   116   101
MATO GROSSO   Rio   GERAIS   Montes
DO SUL   364   Verde   Uberlândia   Claros   ATLANTIC
Campo   262   Uberaba   135   Teófilo   OCEAN
Grande   São José do   Belo   Otôni
267   Rio Preto   Ribeirão   Horizonte   ESPÍRITO
Dourados   Araçatuba   Preto   Ipatinga   SANTO
Ponta Porã   SÃO PAULO   Juiz   Cariacica   Vitória
Maringá   Campinas   de Fora   Vila Velha
Apucarana   Londrina   Santo   Campos dos Goitacazes
Cascavel   277   André   São Gonçalo
Foz do   PARANÁ   São   Santos   Rio de   *Tropic of Capricorn*
Iguaçu   Guarapuava   Paulo   Janeiro
Curitiba
Joinville
SANTA
Passo   CATARINA
Fundo   Lajes   Florianópolis
785   116   Criciúma
RIO GRANDE   Caxias do Sul
DO SUL
Urugu-   Porto Alegre
aiana
Bagé   Pelotas
Rio Grande
URUGUAY   471

0 kilometers   400

0 miles   400

KEY

![International airport] International airport

Highway

Major road

Minor road

Railroad

International border

State border

Southeastern Brazil

The densely populated southeastern part of Brazil contains the country's two biggest cities. A dynamic, sprawling business center, São Paulo has nearly 9 million inhabitants in the city proper. Beautiful Rio de Janeiro, with its legendary beaches, is home to around 7 million people. With a well-developed infrastructure and economy, this region has a stunning Atlantic coastline and a wealth of historic towns.

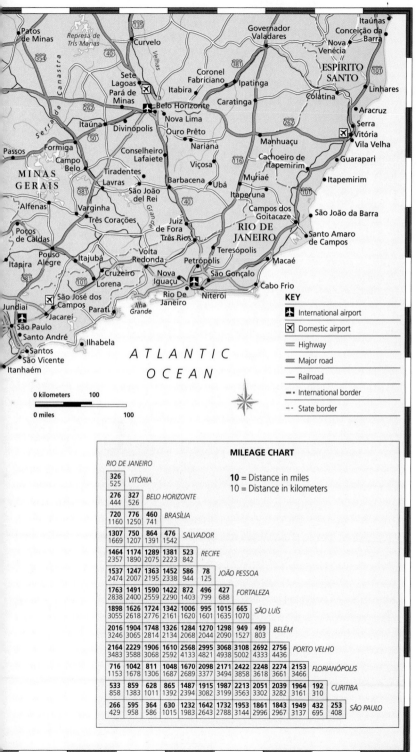

ESPÍRITO SANTO

MINAS GERAIS

RIO DE JANEIRO

ATLANTIC OCEAN

0 kilometers 100
0 miles 100

KEY

✈ International airport
☒ Domestic airport
═ Highway
━ Major road
─ Railroad
-•- International border
-- State border

MILEAGE CHART

RIO DE JANEIRO

10 = Distance in miles
10 = Distance in kilometers

326 / 525	*VITÓRIA*												
276 / 444	**327** / 526	*BELO HORIZONTE*											
720 / 1160	**776** / 1250	**460** / 741	*BRASÍLIA*										
1307 / 1669	**750** / 1207	**864** / 1391	**476** / 1542	*SALVADOR*									
1464 / 2357	**1174** / 1890	**1289** / 2075	**1381** / 2223	**523** / 842	*RECIFE*								
1537 / 2474	**1247** / 2007	**1363** / 2195	**1452** / 2338	**586** / 944	**78** / 125	*JOÃO PESSOA*							
1763 / 2838	**1491** / 2400	**1590** / 2559	**1422** / 2290	**872** / 1403	**496** / 799	**427** / 688	*FORTALEZA*						
1898 / 3055	**1626** / 2618	**1724** / 2776	**1342** / 2161	**1006** / 1620	**995** / 1601	**1015** / 1635	**665** / 1070	*SÃO LUÍS*					
2016 / 3246	**1904** / 3065	**1748** / 2814	**1326** / 2134	**1284** / 2068	**1270** / 2044	**1298** / 2090	**949** / 1527	**499** / 803	*BELÉM*				
2164 / 3483	**2229** / 3588	**1906** / 3068	**1610** / 2592	**2568** / 4133	**2995** / 4821	**3068** / 4938	**3108** / 5002	**2692** / 4333	**2756** / 4436	*PORTO VELHO*			
716 / 1153	**1042** / 1678	**811** / 1306	**1048** / 1687	**1670** / 2689	**2098** / 3377	**2171** / 3494	**2422** / 3858	**2248** / 3618	**2274** / 3661	**2153** / 3466	*FLORIANÓPOLIS*		
533 / 858	**859** / 1383	**628** / 1011	**865** / 1392	**1487** / 2394	**1915** / 3082	**1987** / 3199	**2213** / 3563	**2051** / 3302	**2039** / 3282	**1964** / 3161	**192** / 310	*CURITIBA*	
266 / 429	**595** / 958	**364** / 586	**630** / 1015	**1232** / 1983	**1642** / 2643	**1732** / 2788	**1953** / 3144	**1861** / 2996	**1843** / 2967	**1949** / 3137	**432** / 695	**253** / 408	*SÃO PAULO*

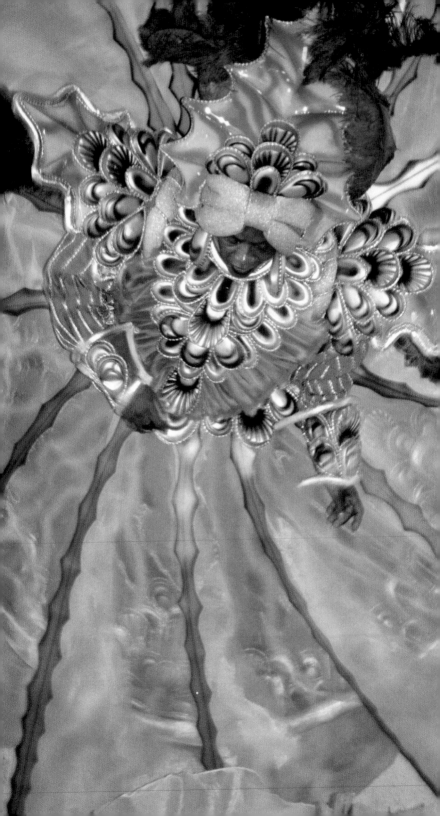

A PORTRAIT OF BRAZIL

Brazil evokes iconic images of lively Carnaval celebrations, brilliant soccer teams, bossa nova and samba performances, sensual Brazilians swaying across the sands of Ipanema and Copacabana, and the beautiful city of Rio de Janeiro. Beyond these popular images, however, there remains a lot to discover about Brazil, which is fast emerging as a global economic giant.

Covering over half of South America, Brazil is the world's fifth largest nation. The sheer size of the country helps to explain the extraordinary diversity of environments and cultures. The larger cities are known for cosmopolitan sophistication and extensive technological development, while in the Amazon region there are indigenous peoples who still use ancient agricultural techniques.

Figurine, Museu de Arte Sacra, Cidade de Goiás

The Portuguese colonization that began in the 1500s, combined with the influx of immigrants from a wide geographical and ethnic spectrum, has lent an eclectic character to the social fabric of the country. Portuguese is spoken by the vast majority of the 188 million Brazilians, although there are many commonly used words derived from indigenous and African languages.

The country's striking diversity is reflected in the major cities, each of which has its own distinctive character. The impressive Modernist architecture of the nation's capital Brasília, the ravishing cityscape of Rio de Janeiro, embraced by the gigantic statue of Cristo Redentor (Christ the Redeemer), the colonial buildings and Baroque gems of

An aerial view of high-rise concrete towers in the ultra-modern city of São Paulo

◁ A reveler dressed as a Bahian woman (Baiana), performing at Rio de Janeiro's Carnaval

Caiman and butterflies in the splendid Amazonian greenery

Minas Gerais, the historic cities of the Northeast, and the picturesque European-influenced, wine-producing towns in Southern Brazil, are just a few examples of this remarkable heterogeneity.

The diverse character of Brazil is reflected in its five distinct ecosystems – the Amazon rainforest, the semi-arid *sertão*, the central *cerrado* (savanna), the wildlife-rich Pantanal wetlands, and the lush Mata Atlântica. The varied natural attractions of the country include the spectacular falls at Foz do Iguaçu, captivating Amazônia, the splendid beaches of Rio de Janeiro and the Northeast, the luxuriant grasslands of Rio Grande do Sul, the pristine-white sand dunes of Lençóis Maranhenses, and the abundant, breathtaking flora and fauna of the Pantanal.

THE ECONOMY

The Brazilian economy is counted among the world's 10 largest, though it is riddled with contradictions – *favelas* (shantytowns) coexist with skyscrapers in the cities. The foundations for modern economic prosperity were laid, ironically, during the years of the military dictatorship from 1964 to 1984, when Brazil's rulers borrowed heavily from international banks to fund various large projects. However, it was only during the administration of Fernando Henrique Cardoso (1995–2002) that Brazil's economy became more market-orientated, a trend that has been carried forward by his successor, Luiz Inácio Lula da Silva – "Lula."

Today, Brazil's major exports feature both manufactured goods, including machinery and automobiles, as well as agricultural products, such as soya beans and coffee. In recent years, Brazil has emerged as an economic powerhouse and a strong advocate of opening up global trade to developing nations. Its vision of exploring new energy production methods is manifested by Petrobras, Brazil's largest oil-producing company. Run by the state, Petrobras is

The verdant countryside near Bento Gonçalves, a wine-producing town in the Serra Gaúcha, Rio Grande do Sul

Petrobras (Petróleo Brasileiro), Brazil's state-run gas and oil refinery, near Rio de Janeiro

a pioneer in the development of advanced technology from deep-water oil production.

Alongside Brazil's growing global significance, there still remain deep economic disparities and regional differences. It is common to see the super rich and the urban poor in Brazil's major cities, mainly Rio de Janeiro and São Paulo, two of the largest metropolises in the world. Inequitous growth is also visible not only in the undeveloped interiors, but also in the agriculture-dominated southern region where there is a rising number of landless peasants.

POLITICAL LIFE

Politicians have tremendous power in Brazil, and many start and make their way up through municipal and state politics. Some political positions outside of the capital are extremely powerful in their own right, especially that of mayor of one of the big cities, or governor of a state.

Since 1985, when the military dictatorship came to an end, Brazil has been one of the world's largest democracies. However, the

country's current political elite have immersed Brazil in a series of scandals, involving corruption, misuse of public funds, and abuse of power.

When the leftist, ex-trade union leader Lula was elected president in 2002, the Brazilians hoped for a democracy that favored the "majority of society," as promised in his Workers' Party (Partido dos Trabalhadores) manifesto. Re-elected in 2006 by more than 60 percent of the vote, Lula promises to rule on behalf of the poor, even as Brazil's underprivileged majority continues to be ruled by a wealthy minority.

Brazilians, for the most part, are united in their distrust and lack of respect for their politicians and

Supporters waving flags of Lula during his 2002 electoral campaign

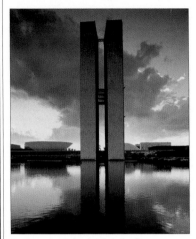

The Congresso Nacional at dusk, Brasília

people. The millions of slaves brought to Brazil from West Africa, between the 16th and 19th centuries, have also played an important role in the development of Brazil as a country and as a vibrant culture. Between the 18th and 19th centuries, the influx of immigrants from Europe, especially Italy and Germany, and also from Japan and Korea, have played their part in forming the multicultural and ethnically diverse population of Brazil.

Although Brazil has reputedly the world's largest Catholic population, its unique mix of people has given rise to many different religions and sects. The animistic beliefs of the indigenous Brazilians, ritualistic Afro-Brazilian cults, and spiritualist Kardecism, coexist with other faiths including Judaism, Islam, and Buddhism. Candomblé, a syncretic cult practiced in Bahia, is a unique amalgamation of Catholicism and African beliefs.

political parties. The average educated Brazilian resents the perceived close alliance between the politicians and their ambitious business allies.

Brazil upholds the ideal of racial harmony. However, though not blatant, racial discrimination does still exist. As well as having limited access to education and work opportunities, black people remain inadequately represented in the higher echelons of politics, academia, and business.

THE PEOPLE

Home to over half the population of South America, Brazil is the fifth most populous country in the world. The vast majority of people live in the coastal parts and major cities, and the population density grows progressively scantier toward the interior. Brazil has such a varied mix of races, nationalities, and ethnic groups that it is difficult to define a typical Brazilian. It is often argued that being Brazilian is more a state of mind than anything else.

The Portuguese, the first Europeans to explore Brazil, were followed by other colonial powers laying claim to areas along the Brazilian coast. However brief the influence of the French and the Dutch, and later the British, they all made their mark on Brazil, along with the dominant Portuguese. Their influence is still visible in its culture and its

Baianas in front of the Convento de São Francisco, Salvador

Residents of Rio de Janeiro (Cariocas) playing soccer on Ipanema beach

SPORT & CULTURE

Brazil's sporting and cultural influence has made the "Brasil" brand known throughout the world. Brazil is the world's greatest soccer (*futebol*) nation, having won the World Cup on five occasions and being the only nation to play at every World Cup. Pelé *(see p168)*, hailed as a great national hero, is the most famous soccer player of all time.

Ayrton Senna, winner of the Monaco Grand Prix in 1992

Brazil's sporting prowess has not been restricted to soccer. In Ayrton Senna, Nelson Piquet, and Emerson Fittipaldi, it has had three Formula 1 World Champions, and in tennis it saw success in the 1950s and 60s with Maria Esther Bueno and, more recently, with Gustavo Kuerten.

Culture has also played its part in establishing how the world views Brazil. The first musicians to make a mark internationally were composer Heitor Villa-Lobos and legendary performer Carmen Miranda. In literature too, writers as different in their subject matter as Jorge Armado and Paulo Coelho, have helped spread the word about their homeland. The music of Brazil, be it *samba*, *bossa nova*, or one of the many other musical styles to be found across the country, has been a powerful calling card since the 1960s. In more recent times, talented filmmakers have gone on to produce critically acclaimed works, including Walter Salles with *Central do Brasil* (*Central Station*, 1998) and Fernando Meirelles with *Cidade de Deus* (*City of God*, 2002).

Brazilians celebrate life with their colorful festivals. Carnaval, the cultural event that helped put Brazil on the map, is perceived as the biggest and best in the world, and its revelry embraces the whole country.

A group of musicians rehearsing Brazil's country music *sertanejo*, in Cidade de Goiás

The Landscapes of Brazil

Larger than the US (excluding Alaska) and bordering 10 of the 12 other South American countries, Brazil is home to a wide variety of breathtaking landscapes, from vast swamps to desert, and thick rainforest to metropolitan cityscapes. Covering over 2 million sq miles (3.5 million sq km) and embracing over 40 percent of Brazilian territory, the Amazon rainforest is the most dominant landscape in Brazil and the best known. Although massive and spectacular, the Amazon Basin is only one biome out of several in Brazil, each with its own distinct scenery, fascinating wildlife, and climate.

KEY

▦	The Amazon rainforest
▦	The Pantanal
▦	The *sertão*
▦	The *cerrado*
▦	Mata Atlântica
–•–	International border
△	Peak

The Northern Highlands in Amazônia are impressive mountains, strung along the frontier with Venezuela and Guyana.

The Amazon rainforest (see pp260–61), *one of the most complex ecosystems in the world, is characterized by vast expanses of dense forest, with a wide range of vegetation. Large areas, such as the buriti palm-dominated* igapós, *are annually flooded by the waters of the Rio Negro.*

Branco
Pico da Neblina
9,888 ft (3,013 m)
Tiquié
Negro
Japurá
Amazonas
Jutaí
Juruá
Purús
Madeira
Tapajós

The Pantanal (see pp320–21), *an immense wetland, is the largest seasonally flooded area on the planet, inundating as much as two-thirds of its total area for half the year, during the rainy season. Dotted with small, forested elevations, the southern Pantanal is used for cattle grazing during the dry season.*

THE WET & THE DRY SEASON

During the wet season, which lasts from December to March, the rising rivers inundate the flat land. This process creates *cordilhieras* (isolated islands) amid vast lakes and flowering shrubs. However, it is during the dry season (May to September), that wildlife is at its most spectacular in the Pantanal. During this time, the ponds teem with fish, and thousands of birds flock around the water holes.

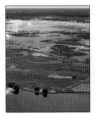

The Pantanal in the wet season, near Porto Jofre

The Pantanal with tiny forests in the dry season

The sertão (see p233) *is a semi-arid region in the interior of Brazil's northeast and parts of northern Minas Gerais. The essentially barren landscape, dominated by* caatinga, *is a uniquely Brazilian habitat. The* sertão *receives very little rainfall during the dry months, and is largely strewn with cacti and thorny shrubs. There are periods of intense drought, which makes it a harsh environment for wildlife and people alike. As a result, much of the flora and fauna have specially adapted themselves to the lack of water.*

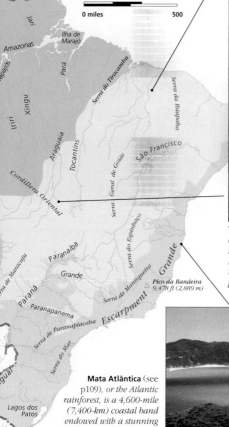

0 kilometers   500

0 miles   500

Jari

Amazonas

Ilha de Marajó

Tabajós

Pará

Xingu

Serra do Tiracambu

Serra da Ibiapaba

Iriri

Araguaia

Tocantins

São Francisco

Serra Geral de Goiás

Cordillera Oriental

Paranaíba

Serra do Espinhaço

Grande

Grande

Escarpment

Serra de Maracaju

Paraná

Serra da Mantiqueira

Pico da Bandeira
9,478 ft (2,889 m)

Paranapanema

Serra de Paranapiacaba

Serra do Mar

Uruguai

Lagos dos Patos

The cerrado (see pp296–7) *features wide expanses of open, tropical grassland scattered with small, closed canopy forests. Brazil's central plateau is the world's most biologically rich savanna with over 10,000 plant species.*

Mata Atlântica (see p109), *or the Atlantic rainforest, is a 4,600-mile (7,400-km) coastal band endowed with a stunning diversity of landscapes, from the granite peaks and sheer cliffs of the Great Escarpment to the beautiful white sands and surf of the Costa do Sol.*

Brazil's Flora & Fauna

Home to over 55,000 plant species and three of the most diverse ecosystems on the planet, the wealth of flora and fauna in Brazil is unmatched. Some of the most valuable resources of the modern world, such as rubber, originate from the rainforests of the Amazon. As a result of the relative stability of the rainforest compared to temperate areas, the fauna here has had the freedom to evolve and to adapt to very specialized local conditions. With a few of the tributaries of the Amazon river still unexplored, there are numerous species yet to be discovered. Brazil has five principal ecosystems, each with its own distinct array of plant life. From forest and swamp to desert and savanna, these stark contrasts in climate and landscape have resulted in an immensely vibrant and diverse flora, much of which is unique to the country.

Aquatic plants, *including the versatile water hyacinth, are commonly found in the Pantanal, which has the richest collection of these plants.*

AMAZÔNIA

The Amazon rainforest *(see p260–61)* possesses a wealth of flora and fauna. It is characterized by vast expanses of dense forest, extensive savannas, and other eco-systems. Vegetation and wildlife vary because of the annual flooding of large areas.

THE SERTÃO

The arid *sertão (see p233)*, which comprises 75 percent of the land area in the northeast, has its own unique wildlife including lizards, snakes, and foxes. Birdlife manages to flourish in this minimalist, unfriendly land-scape, and sheep and goats are also reared.

Blue and gold macaws *are brilliantly colored large birds that live on cliffs and high in trees in rainforests and swamps. They are considered an endangered species.*

Juazeiro, *a shrub-like tree indigenous to the sertão, is used in wine-making and medicine, as a hair tonic, and for timber.*

Aguapé *is an invasive floating plant with medicinal properties. Found in the wetlands of the Pantanal and Amazônia, it acts as a natural water filter.*

Mandacaru cactus *is a symbol of rebirth and resilience in the arid sertão. According to local legend, this tree-like cactus with fragrant blossoms originates on the site of a massacre.*

THE CERRADO

The *cerrado (see p296–7)* is a vast open savanna dotted with clusters of scattered woodlands. This is the world's most biologically rich grassland. There are over 4,000 endemic plant species. The *cerrado* is also home to maned wolves and giant anteaters.

The mutum, *or crested currasow, is a large bird which is often seen in the forested areas of the* cerrado.

Pequi, *also known as souari nut, provides sweet berries with small thorns inside. It is eaten fresh, used in food, and made into a liqueur.*

Giant anteaters *are commonly spotted in the cerrado. These solitary animals have a long tail and tongue, a bristly brown coat, and five short, sharp claws on both their paws. These animals are sometimes hunted for their meat.*

THE MATA ATLÂNTICA

The Mata Atlântica *(see p109)*, or Atlantic rainforest, is formed by remnants of Brazil's coastal rainforest. The development of cities and intensive agriculture has severely reduced this habitat, but it remains home to monkeys and exotic birds.

The piaçava *is a fibrous palm tree. Its fibers are extensively used to make brooms, thatch, mats, and cord.*

Woolly spider monkeys *are the largest primates in the Americas. This endangered species eats mainly fruits, leaves, and seeds.*

THE PANTANAL

The largest inland wetland *(see pp320–21)* on the planet is constantly abuzz with bird- and wildlife. Hundreds of birds can be heard screeching overhead or fishing in the waters while caimans bask along the river banks. The best time to visit is the dry season.

The anaconda *is a large water boa, which can grow to 32 ft (10 m) in length. It kills its prey, sometimes many times its size, by constriction as well as drowning.*

The gravatá *is a member of the* Bromeliaceae *family. Gravatá (also known as* karatas) *is a kind of fruit, similar to a pineapple, that grows on the ground.*

Peoples of Brazil

When the Portuguese arrived in 1500, the Brazilian population consisted of over 5 million indigenous people divided into at least 1,000 communities. When their numbers began depleting due to the severity of slavery, the Portuguese started shipping slaves from Africa in the mid-16th century. Many of these slaves assimilated with the white and local population. Over the centuries, Brazil's peoples were diversified further by several waves of immigration from the Middle East, Asia, and Europe. After over 500 years of immigration and integration, modern Brazil is a true ethnic mosaic, where diverse elements combine to create a vibrant nation renowned for its spirit.

Indigenous Brazilians *also include the Ticuna community, who are a large group with their own language and written literature.*

Some indigenous groups (see pp262–3) *continue to live as they had done before the arrival of the Portuguese, particularly in the forested interior.*

MULTIRACIAL BRAZIL

Brazil is unique in its assimilation of various races and ethnic groups. A white-and-indigenous Brazilian is called a *mestiço*, an Afro-Brazilian is called a *cafuzo*, while a mulatto is born of white and African parentage.

European immigrants (see pp328–9) *started moving to Brazil after slavery ended in 1888. They tended to concentrate in various parts of Southern Brazil, where people of Azorean, German, Italian, Slav, Dutch, Austrian, and other descents still thrive.*

The Portuguese, *the dominant ethnic group in Brazil today, introduced Catholicism (see p34), and have given the country its official language.*

Mulattoes, *born of black and white parentage, make up at least half the population. Prominent in music, sports, and the arts, famous Brazilian mulattoes include pop music icon Gilberto Gil (see p32) and professional soccer player Ronaldo.*

Baianas *are recognizable in their lace dresses with colorful beads that represent the various* orixás, *or Afro-Brazilian deities (see p177). Baianas play an integral role in keeping alive the Afro-Brazilian traditions that came to Brazil, especially in the slave ships from Angola and Nigeria.*

Japanese Brazilians *(see p169) are mainly descended from immigrants who came to Brazil around 1908 as laborers. There are numerous Buddhist and Shinto shrines around Brazil, and the Japanese influence can be seen in the art scene and in the popularity of its cuisine. São Paulo City's Liberdade district is home to the largest Japanese community outside of Japan.*

CARIOCAS & PAULISTANOS

Cariocas frolicking on Copacabana beach, Rio City

Residents of Brazil's two largest cities, Rio de Janeiro and São Paulo, have successfully stereotyped themselves and each other. The fun-loving Cariocas of Rio are seen as too easy-going by the Paulistanos of São Paulo, whom the Cariocas regard as workaholics with no zest for life. Paulistanos see their city as the economic force driving Brazil, while Rio is considered to be a playground for Carnaval *(see pp64–5)*. The self-image of Cariocas is that they have better music and more beautiful people. The Paulistanos, on the other hand, take pride in their diligent nature and the distinct cadence of their spoken Portuguese. The key difference really revolves around beach life. Rio's long stretch of trendy beaches forms a vital part of the city's daily life *(see pp38–9)*. The beaches around São Paulo, on the other hand, demand the weekend to enjoy, being at least 40 miles (65 km) away from the city.

Architecture

The first buildings in Brazil were made by the indigenous peoples. As these structures were made from perishable materials, little is known of them beyond early European descriptions. Colonial churches and other buildings were in spectacular form in the 18th century during the Baroque era. After independence, Brazil followed European trends until Lúcio Costa and Oscar Niemeyer developed Brazilian Modernism, most strikingly expressed in the new capital Brasília. Today, Brazil is dominated by high-rises punctuated by the occasional striking building by a contemporary architect such as Ruy Ohtake.

Avenida Atlântica at Copacabana beach, Rio de Janeiro

INDIGENOUS

Francisco de Orellana (1511–46), the first European to navigate the Amazon, described large cities created by Curucirari people extending for as much as 6 miles (10 km) and cut by large roads. These large cities no longer exist. Today, traditional indigenous villages are smaller and focus on a large communal *maloca*. Less traditional ones are made up of wattle-and-daub houses.

Dyed tree bark
Open entrance
Sloping thatched roof

Kayapó malocas, *or ocas, are communal longhouses, usually measuring 92 ft (28 m) in length and 59 ft (18 m) in width. Their shape and design influenced many of Oscar Niemeyer's buildings.*

BAROQUE

Baroque architecture began in 17th-century Europe but reached its most exuberant in Latin America. Brazilian Baroque is characterized by elaborately carved, painted interiors and ornate, florid forms set in modest, whitewash-and-raw stone façades. The style found its zenith in Salvador and Recife, and in the sculptures of Aleijadinho *(see p131)* in Minas Gerais.

Elaborately carved stone tablet

The monumental door, offset by the modest façade

São Francisco de Assis, *in Salvador, is a display of wealth and splendor. The interior of the church is covered with almost 900 lb (450 kg) of gold. Silver, gold leaf, and solid gold are coupled with stunning azulejos, or blue Portuguese tile work.*

São Pedro dos Clérigos, *in Recife, is rich in ornamental flourishes typical of the Baroque. Its second tower was left incomplete in order to avoid a tax on churches.*

NEO-CLASSICAL

Neo-Classicism is associated with Imperial Brazil and came to Brazil with the Portuguese monarchy who fled Napoleon in 1807, bringing the most fashionable European architectural ideas with them. The first Neo-Classical buildings were civic edifices in Rio de Janeiro and palaces in Petrópolis. These quickly became the norm for buildings of state in the rest of the empire.

Typical Palladian portico
Frieze in bas-relief style
Ionic column

The Museu Imperial, *in Petrópolis, marked the advent of the most popular form of Neo-Classicism. Its architect, Julius Köhler, was influenced by the English Palladian style.*

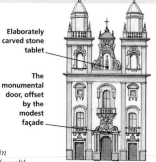
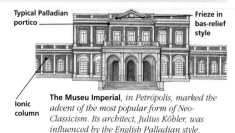

ECLECTIC

Eclecticism is an architectural style associated with 19th-century Republican Brazil. Like the styles that preceded it, it was strongly influenced by European trends, particularly French and English. Eclecticism is characterized by a combination of forms, motifs, and styles from Neo-Classical and Baroque through to Manueline, a style that fuses together in one building Portuguese Late Gothic with ornamentation in portals, windows, and arcades, along with Oriental elements.

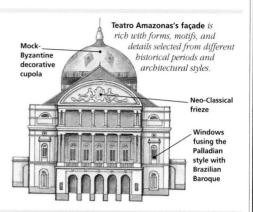

Mock-Byzantine decorative cupola

Teatro Amazonas's façade is rich with forms, motifs, and details selected from different historical periods and architectural styles.

Neo-Classical frieze

Windows fusing the Palladian style with Brazilian Baroque

MODERNIST

Modernism was shaped by architects such as Le Corbusier and Max Bill. Brazilian architects at first adhered to the strict precepts these Europeans laid down, but from the 1940s, architects such as Oscar Niemeyer developed a unique form of Brazilian Modernism, influenced by indigenous design and employing curved forms.

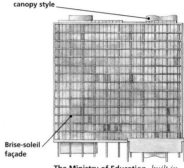

Le Corbusier canopy style

Brise-soleil façade

The Ministry of Education, built in Rio in 1943 with a striking glass brise-soleil façade, was the first Modernist building to combine civic architecture with a contemporary medium in the Americas.

Parliament buildings, *in Brasília, are a harmony of simple lines and curves incorporating water and the landscape into the design.*

CONTEMPORARY BRAZIL

Beyond Brasília and Oscar Niemeyer's continued output in Rio and Curitiba, contemporary Brazilian architecture is largely functional and not particularly inspiring. Cities are seas of identical tower-block flats broken by snaking highways. The most daring designs tend to be private homes hidden away behind high walls or corporate buildings such as Ruy Ohtake's stunning Hotel Unique *(see p374)* and Hotel Unique Garden in São Paulo.

Open-air Skye Bar   Glass set windows

Concrete pillars supporting the hotel

Landscaped garden

Hotel Unique *is a combination of bravado and functionalism. Built by Ruy Ohtake, a leading figure in contemporary Brazilian architecture, the inverted arc has 3-ft (1-m) wide windows overlooking a stunning garden. The open-air rooftop bar has a spectacular view over the city.*

Brazilian Artists & Writers

Brazil's first artists and writers were religious, and a tradition of uniquely Brazilian ecclesiastical art continued into the 20th century. Secular art in Brazil ceased to derive from Europe only in the 1920s after the emergence of the *antropofagismo* movement, which appropriated western themes into specifically Brazilian contexts. Brazil's writers found a voice in the work of 19th-century writers such as Joaquim Maria Machado de Assis and Euclides da Cunha. The explosion of Modernism in the early 20th century has left Brazil with a diverse literary output which remains largely unexplored by English-language publishers.

Ceiling painted by Dom Adelbert Gresnicht, Mosteiro São Bento, São Paulo

CHURCH ART

Brazil's first great artists were European priests. Frei Domingos da Conceição (1643–1718) was responsible for the interiors of the São Bento monasteries in Rio and Olinda. Father Agostinho de Piedade (1580–1661) and 18th-century Francisco Xavier Brito, whose works can be found in Rio de Janeiro and Minas Gerais, introduced the Baroque style, developing it as uniquely Brazilian.

Brito almost certainly taught the great artist, Aleijadinho *(see p131)*, whose statuary mocks the racist Portuguese colonists, most notably at the basilica in Congonhas and the Igreja São Francisco in Ouro Preto. The latter also preserves the finest paintings by another subtle satiricist, Mestre (Manuel da Costa) Athayde (1762–1830). Illusionism in religious art was developed by José Joaquim da Rocha (1737–1807) in Salvador, Mestre Valentim (1750–1813) in Rio,

and José Joaquim da Veiga Valle (1806–74) in Goiás. In the 19th and 20th centuries, illusionism was largely lost but for the work of Benedito Calixto (1853–1927) in Santos and São Paulo, and the Dutch artist Adelbert Gresnicht, who painted the Beuronese interior of São Paulo's Mosteiro São Bento.

SECULAR ART

Brazil's first secular art was European in theme and technique, best seen in the

Alfredo Volpi, painter known for his signature Brazilian palette

pastoral idylls of the Dutch artist Frans Post (1612–80) and the formal portraits of the Frenchman Jean-Baptiste Debret (1768–1848).

The first painting to make use of Brazil's rich tropical light was *Caipira Picando Fumo* by José Ferraz de Almeida Júnior (1850–99). However, a truly Brazilian style emerged only in the 1920s with *antropofagismo*, a movement propagating "cultural cannibalism," which adapts ideas from European art and literature and reworks them in Brazilian terms. Tarsila do Amaral (1886–1973) produced the movement's most representative paintings, and was followed by Lasar Segall (1891–1957) and Anita Malfatti (1896–1964).

Other artists pursued Modernism according to their own ideas. Emiliano Di Cavalcanti (1897–1976) turned to the masses for inspiration, producing impressionistic, erotic icons of black Brazilian women. Candido Portinari (1903–62), with a far more obvious social conscience, produced *O Mestiço* that showed the dignity of Brazilian workers, while his *Os Retirantes* portrayed their misery. The sculptor Victor Brecheret (1894–1955) offered a Brazilian take on Art Deco, while Alfredo Volpi (1896–1988) brought Brazilian colors to abstract impressionism. São Paulo's large ethnic Japanese community continues to produce artists, such as Tomie Ohtake (b.1913), who pay Brazilian homage to the styles and techniques of Japan.

Brazil's contemporary art scene is lively and diverse. Most prominently, the works of photographer Sebastião Salgado (b.1944) are rooted in the ideas of Liberation Theology *(see p34)*. Artist Siron Franco (b.1947) uses naive, surreal forms to highlight social and environmental issues.

COLONIAL LITERATURE

European Jesuits are credited with the earliest writing to come out of Brazil. José Anchieta (1534–97) chronicled his work and described the evangelization of the indigenous people. The sermons of Antônio Vieira (1608–97) are fine examples of Portuguese prose.

Gregório de Matos (1623–96), who was born in Bahia, is sometimes cited as Brazil's first celebrated homegrown literary figure. During the 18th century, poetry academies in Minas Gerais were producing writers such as Cláudio Manuel da Costa (1729–89), José Basílio da Gama (1740–95), and Tomás Antônio Gonzaga (1744–1810). They introduced revolutionary French ideas to Brazil and wrote lyric and epic poems on Brazilian themes, but in a lofty European classical style.

Legendary mulatto writer, Joaquim Maria Machado de Assis

THE EMPIRE & THE REPUBLIC

Brazil began to find its own voice in the last days of the Empire with the great 19th-century mulatto novelist, Joaquim Maria Machado de Assis (1839–1908). Starting out with traditional sentimental romances, he later became celebrated for his darkly humorous novels with their subversive social criticism. *Dom Casmurro* is considered by some to be the greatest Latin American novel of the 19th century.

After independence in 1889, Machado de Assis's social criticisms were taken a step further by a generation of Republican novelists, influenced by scientific and nascent socialist ideas from Europe. In *Triste fim de Policarpo Quaresma*, the black novelist, Afonso Lima Barreto (1881–1922), was openly critical of the corruption that characterized the Republic. Euclides da Cunha's *Os Sertões* chronicled a gory and disastrous military campaign against a messianic rebel, Antônio Conselheiro *(see p206)*, and his bandit followers in the harsh landscape of the Bahian *sertão*.

MODERNISM IN LITERATURE

Modernism proper began in Brazil with Mário and Oswald de Andrade, who sought to articulate contemporary and uniquely Brazilian styles and themes. Mário (1893–1945) traveled throughout the country, searching for a unifying traditional culture which he enunciated in his comic rhapsody *Macunaíma*. Oswald (1890–1953), together with his wife Tarsila do Amaral, formulated the ideas behind the *antropofagismo* cultural movement. The de Andrades cleared the way for the Modernist poets Carlos Drummond (1902–87) and Manuel Bandeira (1886–1968), and the greatest of all Brazilian writers, João Guimarães Rosa (1908–67), whose grand metaphysical novel, *Grande Sertão: Veredas*, invented a new syntax based on the isolated idioms of the interior of Minas Gerais.

A string of writers, including Gilberto Freyre (1900–87), Sérgio Buarque de Holanda (1902–82), and Darcy Ribeiro (1922–97), emerged from the social sciences. The 20th century also produced major popular novelists, including Jorge Amado (1902–2001) and Clarice Lispector (1920–77).

Grande Sertão exhibition, Museum of Portuguese Language, São Paulo

Vinícius de Moraes (1913–80), a seminal figure in the contemporary Brazilian music scene, was the first to plough the furrow between music and literature by writing the lyrics of many famous songs. He has since been followed by songwriter Chico Buarque (b.1944), who wrote the novel *Budapest*.

Recently, writers from Brazil's manifold ethnic communities have risen to prominence. In *Relato de um Certo Oriente*, Milton Hatoum (b.1952) probes the psyche of an Arab immigrant, while Moacyr Scliar (b.1937) explores the Jewish-Brazilian experience in his writings.

Today, Brazilian fiction accounts for about half the literary output of Latin America. Writers include Paulo Coelho (b.1947), feminist novelist and short-story writer Lygia Fagundes Telles (b.1923), and Amazonian poet Aníbal Beça (b.1946).

Leading contemporary novelist, Clarice Lispector

The Music of Brazil

The vibrant music of Brazil reflects the diversity of the cultural and ethnic backgrounds that make up the country's resident population. The music mirrors the influences of both the native and immigrant population. The rhythms of Africa are as important to the overall sound as the harmonies and melodies that were introduced from Europe. Brazil is not about one musical style, but a varied selection. Internationally, *samba* and *bossa nova* are the best-known of the country's musical styles, but regional forms, such as *frevo (see p217)*, *axé*, *forró (see p236)*, and *sertanejo (see p233)*, are just as popular within Brazil.

Heitor Villa-Lobos, one of Brazil's greatest classical composers

SAMBA

Derived from Angolan religious rhythms, *samba* has permeated virtually every other Brazilian musical form that followed it. Historically strong in Rio, São Paulo, and Bahia, *samba* made a remarkable impact throughout the country in the 1930s. *Samba* comes in many forms, and most of these have a link to dance.

Zeca Pagodinho, *who emerged in the late 1980s, is one of the most popular and best-selling artists of a new wave of samba stars.*

Clara Nunes *was one of the most prolific and popular* samba *singers of all time. Her career was tragically cut short when she died at the age of 39 in 1982.*

Gilberto Gil went from political exile to Brazilian superstar before becoming Minister of Culture in 2003. He remains an active musical force.

BOSSA NOVA

Bossa nova, a marriage of Brazilian rhythms and American jazz, has been the most exportable form of Brazilian music since international audiences first discovered it through an album, *Getz/Gilberto*, recorded by Stan Getz and João Gilberto in 1964. The album included a number of compositions from a young and unknown composer from Rio, Antônio Carlos ("Tom") Jobim. Gilberto, Jobim, and Jobim's lyricist, Vinícius de Moraes, were to become the "Holy Trinity" of *bossa nova*.

Antônio Carlos Jobim *was responsible for many of the* bossa nova *classics including "The Girl From Ipanema," one of the most played and recorded songs in popular music history.*

Sergio Mendes *and his group, Brasil '66, helped launch* bossa nova *globally in the 1960s. They have recorded with acts such as Black Eyed Peas, Erykah Badu, and Justin Timberlake.*

Caetano Veloso helped launch the *tropicalismo* movement in 1967, and is considered a Brazilian musical treasure.

Bebel Gilberto *has been the most internationally successful Brazilian artist in recent years with her hit album* Tanto Tempo, *released in 2002.*

Chico Buarque *is a composer, lyricist, performer, and author. He is as popular today as when he first performed in 1964.*

TROPICALISMO & MÚSICA POPULAR BRASILEIRA

Tropicalismo was a form of Brazilian music that arose in the late 1960s from a mix of *bossa nova*, rock and roll, Bahia folk, and African music. Many *tropicalismo* artists, led by Caetano Veloso and Gilberto Gil, were driven by political activism following the coup of 1964. Inspired in part by *tropicalismo*, *música popular Brasileira* (MPB), or popular Brazilian music, includes many Brazilian musical styles and is the most popular music played on the radio and in the clubs and bars of Brazil.

Daniela Mercury *burst on to Bahia's* axé *and reggae music scene in the 1990s. Her explosive live performances have won her a growing international following.*

REGIONAL MUSIC

Although MPB covers a multitude of Brazilian musical genres, there are a number of distinctive regional styles that include *axé, choro, forró, frevo,* and *pagode*. Bahia, one of the powerhouses of regional Brazilian music, has its own versions of jazz, reggae, hip-hop, soul, funk, rock and roll, heavy metal, electronica, and the popular homegrown country and western style known as *sertanejo*.

Carlinhos Brown, *a prolific performer, composer, drummer, and dancer, is equally popular as a solo artist or when collaborating with others.*

THE SÃO PAULO SCENE

The residents of São Paulo work hard, but they have also learnt to play hard so that the city's club scene is now considered one of the world's most exciting and innovative, with top international DJs flying in to exchange ideas and sounds with their Brazilian counterparts. Break beat, drum and bass, electronica, house, lounge, speed, garage, techno, trance, and trip hop all have a place in the Paulista scene. With a huge range of nightclubs and bars to choose from, Paulistanos can enjoy all genres of music through the week and all year round.

DJ playing in a São Paulo club

Religions of Brazil

Few countries in the world can match Brazil for religious diversity. A typical São Paulo or Rio neighborhood will be home to Catholic and Evangelical Protestant churches, Buddhist temples, synagogues, mosques, Spiritist churches, Afro-Brazilian ceremonial centers, as well as a range of smaller religious institutions. The practice of black magic is not uncommon, even in business and politics, and soothsayers and witches hand out leaflets on the streets. Only atheists are largely absent in Brazil; those who believe in nothing are looked upon with a mixture of incredulity and pity.

Igreja Nossa Senhora do Rosário dos Pretos in São Paulo

The church establishment in Brazil did little to criticize the treatment of the indigenous people, or the slaves from Africa who replaced them. Churches were divided along strict social and racial lines. The poorest churches were reserved for Afro-Brazilian slaves and were often dedicated to the black Madonna, Nossa Senhora do Rosário dos Pretos.

Latin American churches were instrumental in influencing Pope John XXIII and Pope Paul VI's groundbreaking church reforms of the mid-1960s, known as Vatican II and promoting a more egalitarian Catholic Church throughout the world. Vatican II led to the most important movement in the Catholic Church in the 20th century, Liberation Theology.

Churches in Brazil today are largely apolitical and gregarious, and are increasingly influenced by Evangelical preaching and musical styles.

CATHOLICISM

Catholicism arrived with the Portuguese, and Catholics remain Brazil's dominant religious group. Brazil has the largest number of Catholics of any country in the world.

From its earliest days, the church in Brazil, as in most colonies, was divided into an establishment linked to the Crown (and later to the Emperor and the Republican State) and factions who campaigned on behalf of the oppressed. One of these factions was the Jesuits who, while treating the indigenous people as objects of pro-selytization, nonetheless fought doggedly against their enslavement and murder by the *bandeirantes* and the settlers on the Amazon. The Jesuits began to be seen as a threat to the Portuguese Crown and were expelled from the colonies in 1757.

Evangelical Protestants at Igreja Universal do Reino, São Paulo

LIBERATION THEOLOGY

Leonardo Boff presiding over a service

In the 1970s, groups of Latin American Catholic thinkers preached what they called "a preferential option for the poor." In Brazil they were led by Leonardo Boff, Hélder Câmara, and Pedro Casaldaliga. They campaigned against the rich establishment and the dictatorships. Many of the priests involved were murdered or tortured and the movement was suppressed by the established Church.

EVANGELICAL PROTESTANTISM

The Evangelical movement emphasizes the Protestant beliefs in the authority of the Bible and of every person's right to interpret the Scriptures for themselves. Services are emotive, with pastors making use of fiery language, and often strongly encouraging their congregation to donate a *dízima* (usually 10 percent of any monthly salary) to the church. The movement has been widely criticized. Nonetheless, Evangelicalism is very popular in Brazil, so much so that populist politicians often campaign as Evangelicals in elections.

SPIRITISM
Developed by by the Frenchman Allan Kardec, Spiritism is a systematization of divergent 19th-century occult practices dealing with communication with the spirits of the dead. Kardec called Spiritism "a science which deals with the nature, origin, and destiny of Spirits, as well as their relationship with the corporeal world." Brazil has the largest number of Kardecian Spiritists of any country in the world.

Chagdud Khadro Ling temple in Tres Coroâs, Rio Grande do Sul

BUDDHISM & OTHER ASIAN RELIGIONS
The largest population of ethnic Japanese in Latin America and immigrants from many other East Asian countries live in Brazil. Consequently, there are large communities of Nichiren Daishonin Mahayana Buddhists in the country. Their beliefs are based on the teachings of a 13th-century Japanese monk who stressed the need to elevate one's state of life from being trapped within the limits of desires and instincts. The method for achieving this is through strong ethical practice and the chanting of the Nam-Myoho-Renge-Kyo mantra. The movement has proved especially successful at bridging Brazil's trenchant class divide. Yoga and

Krishna Consciousness are also popular in Brazil, though often as alternative lifestyle options.

AFRO-BRAZILIAN RELIGIONS
West African religions came to Brazil with slaves and developed into cults, such as Candomblé *(p177)*, Bautuque, and Macumba. Worship involves the invocation of *orixás* – spirits who intervene between humans and Olorun, the supreme creator. The Brazilian government legalized their practice in the mid-19th century, but followers of these religions have been persecuted by the Church.

INDIGENOUS RELIGIONS
Brazil is home to hundreds of different indigenous belief systems. These can all be loosely banded together as shamanism, which is not so much a religion as a distinct way of understanding reality. Rather than believing that we are made of material, indigenous peoples believe that material, time, and space itself are mere manifestations of a far deeper reality. Spiritual life is organized in harmony with this inner state by a shaman. A number of popular religious movements have grown up in Brazil from indigenous roots. The most widely practiced is Santo Daime, which makes use of Amazonian psychotropic plants to achieve a state of super-consciousness.

Al Iman Ali Ibn Abi Taleb mosque in Curitiba

ISLAM
Brazil has the largest Islamic community in Latin America, but Islamic fundamentalism is almost unknown. The community is private, conservative, and is generally more concerned with preserving links to Lebanese and Syrian culture and the Arabic language than it is with proselytizing. The community has produced numerous prolific writers and politicians.

JUDAISM
Brazil's Jewish community has about 150,000 members, most of whom are concentrated in São Paulo (which has the largest Ashkenazi synagogue on the continent), Recife, and Rio de Janeiro. Many are descended from the Jews who fled Europe in the 1930s. The community is active in political and cultural life. The writer Moacyr Scliar is one of the country's successful literary exports.

Santo Daime followers in Visconde de Mauá, Rio de Janeiro

Soccer in Brazil

In the first half of the 20th century, soccer went from being the private sport of Brazil's white European elite to becoming the greatest symbol of nationhood. The game united all sections of the population and, after the national team's first World Cup victory in 1958, brought about unprecedented national pride. The Brazilian way of playing *futebol* – with more emphasis on attacking, dribbling, and acrobatic ball skills – has become a benchmark for excellence, and is also known as *jogo bonito*, or "the beautiful game."

In a favela, *the main leisure activity for children is always soccer. Rough terrain helps them develop trademark ball skills such as the dribble.*

Charles Miller *is the father of Brazilian soccer. In 1894, returning to the country after attending boarding school in Southampton, UK, he brought two footballs, a pump, and a rule book. The first reported game took place a few months later.*

The 1938 national soccer team *received a joyous welcome on their return home from France. Brazil, which came third after defeating Czechoslovakia, had also won the hearts of the Europeans.*

The 1950 World Cup *was hosted in Brazil. In the fateful final game, Brazil only needed a draw against Uruguay to win the tourna-ment. Overwhelming favorites, Brazil lost 2–1 in front of a record 200,000 crowd, which caused the greatest moment of collec-tive sporting tragedy in the country's history.*

THE NATIONAL SIDE

With their iconic yellow shirts, the Brazilian national team, known as the Seleção, or Selection, is the most glamorous football team in the world. It is the only team to have taken part in every World Cup and have won it more times than anyone – in 1958, 1962, 1970, 1994, and 2002.

BRAZILIAN GREATS

Brazil has produced more soccer legends than any other country and also the greatest player of all time: Pelé *(see p168)*. The first great player was Artur Friedenreich in the 1910s. Each generation reveals new stars and the soccer factory shows no signs of stopping. Since the inauguration of FIFA's (Fédération Internationale de Football Association) World Player of the Year award in 1991, only Brazil has won it with more than one player: Romário (1994), Ronaldo (1996, 1997, 2002), Rivaldo (1999), and Ronaldinho (2004, 2005).

Leônidas da Silva, *also called "Rubber Man" for his elasticity, was the highest scorer in the 1938 World Cup.*

Garrincha, *the "Little Bird," was born with bent legs and is consi-dered to be the finest dribbler of all time.*

The Dream Team of 1970 *is considered the best soccer team of all time. Their 4–1 victory against Italy won them the World Cup for the third time.*

The torcidas, *or soccer fans, have adapted aspects of Carnaval to futebol, playing lively music at stadia, dressing up in team colors, and bringing noisemakers, colorful banners, and flags.*

MAJOR TEAMS & STADIA

There are several hundred professional clubs in Brazil. The number is impossible to calculate, since local leagues are constantly changing and teams shutting down and starting up. Brazil's best-known stadia are the Maracanã (*see p84*) in Rio, which was built for the 1950 World Cup, and the Morumbi in São Paulo.

Estádio Maracanã in Rio de Janeiro, one of the largest soccer stadia in the world

BRAZIL'S BIGGEST CLUBS & STADIA

 SOCIEDADE ESPORTIVA PALMEIRAS (1914)
Stadium: Palestra Itália, São Paulo
Capacity 35,000

 CRUZEIRO ESPORTE CLUBE (1921)
Stadium: Mineirão, Belo Horizonte, Minas Gerais
Capacity: 76,500

 CLUBE DE REGATAS DO FLAMENGO (1895)
Stadium: Gávea/Marancanã, Rio de Janeiro
Capacity: 8,000 (Gávea)/103,022 (Marancanã)

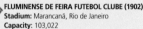 **FLUMINENSE DE FEIRA FUTEBOL CLUBE (1902)**
Stadium: Marancanã, Rio de Janeiro
Capacity: 103,022

 GRÊMIO FOOT-BALL PORTO ALEGRENSE (1903)
Stadium: Olímpico Monumental, Porto Alegre
Capacity: 54,081

 SÃO PAULO FUTEBOL CLUBE (1930)
Stadium: Morumbi, São Paulo
Capacity: 80,000

 SPORT CLUB CORINTHIANS PAULISTA (1910)
Stadium: Parque São Jorge/Pacaembu, São Paulo.
Capacity: 18,386 (P. São Jorge)/37,500 (Pacaembu)

CLUB DE REGATAS VASCO DA GAMA (1898)
Stadium: São Januário, Rio de Janeiro.
Capacity: 31,000

Pelé *was a World Cup champion at 17, and scored a record-breaking 1,283 goals in 1,367 games.*

Sócrates, *the 1982 and 1986 World Cup captain, was famous for his back heels and his political beliefs.*

Romário, *the "Baixinho" (Shorty), was the star player in the 1994 World Cup, won by Brazil.*

Ronaldo, *with two World Cup winner's medals, broke the competition's goal-scoring record in 2006.*

Brazilian Beach Culture

The beach represents a big playground for Brazilians. People living near Brazil's extensive coastline go to the beach daily to socialize and to eat and drink, while vacationers can spend all day near the sand and warm water. Brazilian music plays nonstop at the local beach stalls and, as dusk falls, beachgoers party long into the night. It is a Brazilian tradition to play soccer, beach volleyball, and footvolley, or go for a walk or bike ride along the beach or promenades. At some resorts, visitors can hire a horse or a beach buggy, or practice surfing, kayaking, paragliding, and *skibunda* (sandboarding).

Surfer at Praia Joaquina, Ilha de Santa Catarina

Urban beaches *are popular for their promenades and cycle lanes, where people go to exercise before or after work. Some beaches offer good facilities with bathrooms, showers, and gym equipment, and are illuminated at night for playing sports such as soccer and footvolley.*

Colorful food stalls *selling* coalho *cheese, corn-on-the-cob, peanuts, and shrimp sticks line the beaches. Popular local drinks include fresh coconut water, cold beer, and* caipirinha.

Brazil's beaches *can vary from calm bays to unspoilt, wild beaches accessed only by tracks through the forest. There are also exclusive resort beaches with aquatic parks and modern facilities.*

Beach sports *are very popular. Besides soccer and volleyball, people play* frescobol *(a kind of tennis). Some beaches also offer paragliding and delta-wings during holidays.*

Umbrellas in bright colors are lent for free by the food stalls to their patrons.

The *canga, a Brazilian sarong, is worn to and from the beach, and also used as a towel to lie on.*

Watersports, *such as surfing, windsurfing, kayaking, scuba diving, and snorkeling, are popular through the year due to the warm water. All equipment can be easily hired at the beach.*

Beach safety *is monitored by life-guards on buggies during holidays and at weekends. Flags offer advice on currents and deep water. Asking locals may be useful if there is no patrol.*

LOCALS ON THE BEACH

Relaxed and spontaneous by nature, Brazilians carry only the bare essentials with them to be free to walk, swim, play, or just lie on a *canga* to tan and watch the world go by.

Beach fashion *for women popularly features tiny bikinis that ensure the smallest tan line. The men, on the other hand, can be seen wearing swimming trunks under informal shorts.*

Beach parties, *or* luaus *(moon parties), are kept alive all night by typical Brazilian dance music such as* forró *(see p236) or axé. Electronic music and live concerts are also played at these parties.*

BRAZIL THROUGH THE YEAR

Brazilians are a fun-loving people. In this unique land of diverse ethnic groups and races, there is a colorful and vibrant culture, which is celebrated in the numerous parties, carnivals, festivals, rallies, and parades held through the year, but particularly in summer. The most significant events include the spectacular Carnaval and a series of

Festive silver boots with feathers

popular religious festivals related to Catholicism and a combination of syncretic traditions. The climate varies, but on average it stays warm, making it favorable to outdoor celebrations. The seasons are not so perceptible, except in Southern and Southeastern Brazil where temperatures are moderate in autumn and spring and dip sharply in winter.

SPRING

As flowers begin to decorate the landscape, Brazil prepares to display its wealth of spring flowers and gears up for festivities that last through the season. The most remarkable spring celebrations are related to the Catholic religion, but the highly charged Brazilian Grand Prix also generates great excitement.

SEPTEMBER

Expoflora *(Sep weekends)*, Holambra (São Paulo state). More than 1,000 species of flora are for sale. Dutch folk dances, music, and Dutch and Brazilian food are also featured, emphasizing the town's Dutch character.
International Fishing Festival *(2nd fortnight)*, Cáceres (Mato Grosso). Listed by the *Guinness World Records* as the biggest fishing tournament in the world, the angling event attracts more than 1,500 competitors.

OCTOBER

São Paulo International Film Festival *(2nd fortnight)*, São Paulo. Lasting two weeks, the festival screens around 350 reputed films from more than 50 countries.
São Paulo Art Biennial *(Oct–Dec, even years)*, São Paulo. The Parque do Ibirapuera is the site of an amazing display of modern visual art.
Círio de Nazaré *(2nd Sun)*, Belém. Our Lady of Nazareth procession follows the Romaria fluvial pilgrimage a day earlier.
Oktoberfest *(mid-Oct)*, Blumenau (Santa Catarina). A lively street party, second only to Munich, celebrates German music, beer, and way of life.
Brazilian Formula 1 Grand Prix *(late Oct)*, São Paulo. Organized at Interlagos Circuit, the race is usually the final round of the Formula 1 season.
Recifolia *(last week)*, Recife. A lively carnival with crowds dancing the whole week to Bahian bands.

Paying homage at Padre Cícero's towering statue, Juazeiro do Norte

NOVEMBER

Padre Cícero Pilgrimage *(Nov 2)*, Juazeiro do Norte (Paraíba). On Dia do Finados (All Souls' Day), thousands of pilgrims visit patron saint Padre Cícero's statue and the church where he is buried.
National Handicraft Fair *(late Nov)*, Belo Horizonte. A major exhibition and sale of handicrafts from all over Brazil. There are interactive workshops where many of the crafts can be learnt.

Smoke rising from the wheels of Ferrari team driver Michael Schumacher's car, Brazilian Grand Prix, São Paulo

A spectacular display of Reveillon fireworks on Copacabana beach

SUMMER

Summer is the most important time of the year for Brazilians. It marks the beginning of the year and vacation time. It rains heavily in most parts, but the sun continues to shine through. Besides a number of outdoor events to mark the advent of summer, there are trade fairs and important religious festivals. The culmination of the summer is Carnaval.

DECEMBER

Festa Santa Bárbara *(Dec 4)*, Salvador. A popular three-day Candomblé ceremony at Fonte de Santa Bárbara. The image of Santa Bárbara, called Yansã in Candomblé, is carried through the streets of the historic center.
Carnatal *(early Dec)*, Natal. Out-of-season Carnaval, where famous bands test their repertoire for the next Carnaval, with throngs of people singing and dancing through the streets.
São Silvestre Race *(Dec 31)*, São Paulo. Amateur and recreational runners join professional athletes for a 9-mile (15-km) race through the streets of São Paulo.
Reveillon at Copacabana *(Dec 31)*, Rio de Janeiro. A New Year's Eve party along Copacabana beach with performances by leading pop stars and a lavish midnight fireworks display at Forte de Copacabana and Le Meridien Hotel.

JANUARY

Processão dos Navegantes *(Jan 1)*, Angra dos Reis. A *samba* school percussion group parade across the Baía de Ilha Grande in boats of different shapes and sizes.
Processão do Bom Jesus dos Navegantes *(Jan 1)*, Salvador. Hundreds of fishing boats follow a galliot, a long ship, that carries the image of Our Lord of Navigators.
Pré Cajú *(2nd week)*, Aracaju. One of the dozens of *micaretas* (out-of-season Carnaval) before the real Carnaval in February/March.
Lavagem do Bonfim *(2nd Thu)*, Salvador. A colorful parade and ceremonial washing *(lavagem)* of the steps of the Igreja de Nossa Senhora do Bonfim.

Festas dos Ticumbi & Alardo *(Jan 19 & 20)*, Itaúnas. People in colorful clothes pay homage to São Bento and São Sebastião to the strains of traditional music.
São Paulo Fashion Week *(late Jan)*, São Paulo. Fashion shows featuring top Brazilian models and fashion designers are held.
Festa de São Lázaro *(last Sun)*, Salvador. A festival in honor of Candomblé deity Omolu, the God of Plague.

FEBRUARY

Pescadores do Rio Vermelho *(Feb 2)*, Salvador. A procession of boats carrying offerings to Yemanjá, the Goddess of the Sea, accompanied by Afro-Brazilian music.
Nossa Senhora dos Navegantes *(Feb 2)*, Porto Alegre. A boat procession on the Rio Guaíba carrying the image of Yemanjá.
Carnaval *(Feb/Mar, about 40 days before Easter)*. The most famous Carnaval takes place in the city of Rio de Janeiro. Salvador and Olinda also have fantastic celebrations.
Festa Nacional da Uva *(Feb/Mar, biennial, even years)*, Caxias do Sul. Wine production is the highlight of this festival that keeps alive the customs and traditions of the early Italian immigrants.

Carnaval performers in striking costumes, Rio de Janeiro City

Hooded torchbearers at the Procissão do Fogaréu, Cidade de Goiás

AUTUMN

In Southern Brazil and the Southeast, the autumn season is marked by steady breezes and comfortable temperatures. Religious festivals, such as the Semana Santa and Festa do Divino Espírito Santo, are celebrated with great involvement. The Hot-Air Balloon Festival is an additional attraction.

MARCH

International Book Biennial *(Mar/Apr, even years)*, across Brazil. A 10-day fair marked by book launches, interactive author sessions, lectures, and cultural performances.
Semana Santa *(Mar/Apr)*, across Pernambuco & Minas Gerais. In Nova Jerusalém, the play *Paixão de Cristo* (Passion of Christ) is staged with over 500 professional actors; the audience also participates. In the historic towns of Minas Gerais, crowds accompany the religious processions.

APRIL

Procissão do Fogaréu *(Wed before Good Friday)*, Cidade de Goiás. The city glows with lights and the streets blaze with torches during the solemn procession of the Semana Santa, when the burial of Christ and the Resurrection are re-enacted to the sound of tambours.
Festa Nacional da Maçã *(Apr/May)*, São Joaquim (Santa Catarina). Exhibitions, musical shows, and German folk performances, as well as bestowing of the "best apple producer" title.
Micarande *(late Apr)*, Campina Grande. The first *micareta* (off-season Carnaval) outside the state of Bahia. *Axé, forró (see p236),* and *frevo (see p217)* performances highlight the revelry.
Hot-Air Balloon Festival *(Easter week)*, Torres. Annual hot-air balloon event held since 1989. Other attractions include a parachute display and rodeo competition.

MAY

Festa do Divino Espírito Santo *(May/Jun, 45 days after Easter)*, Pirenópolis & Alcântara. Mock battles between Moors and Christians are enacted. *Forró* and *sertanejo* parties are held.
Festa do Bembé do Mercado *(approx May 13)*, Santo Amaro. The festival marks the abolition of slavery in 1889. Traditional Bahian music and dance performances also take place.

WINTER

With cooler climatic conditions, the southern and southeastern regions are attractive to visitors. Across Brazil, the festivities begin in June, paving the way for international music and art festivals that are a huge draw. The GLBT (Gay, Lesbian, Bisexual, and Transgender) Parade is also significant.

JUNE

Festas Juninas *(weekends through June)*, across Southeast Brazil. Homage

Women in traditional dresses performing *samba-da-roda* at the Festa do Bembé do Mercado, Santo Amaro

Elaborate headgears for the Festa do Bumba-meu-boi, São Luís

PUBLIC HOLIDAYS

New Year's Day (Jan 1)

Carnaval (Tue, 40 days before Easter)

Good Friday (Mar/Apr)

Easter Sunday (Mar/Apr)

Tiradentes Day (Apr 21)

Labor Day (May 1)

Corpus Christi (Jun)

Independence Day (Sept 7)

Our Lady of Aparecida Day (Oct 12)

All Souls' Day (Nov 2)

The Republic Proclamation Day (Nov 15)

Christmas Day (Dec 25)

is offered to St. Antony (Jun 13), St. John (Jun 24), and St. Peter (Jun 29). The festivities that take place at the *arraiá* (imitations of old country villas) are marked by traditional feasting.

Festa do Pinhão *(early Jun)*, Lages (Santa Catarina). Celebrating the edible *pinhão* (seed of the Paraná pine), the festival includes lively music performances.

GLBT Parade *(early Jun)*, São Paulo. Organized since 1999, the parade is one of the biggest events of its kind in the world.

Festa do Bumba-meu-boi *(whole month)*, São Luís. Improvised songs and dances by skilled performers tell the story of the death and resurrection of a bull.

Festa do Boi Bumbá *(Jun 28–30)*, Parintins. In Amazonas, Bumba-meu-boi is known as Boi Bumbá. Two groups, Caprichoso (in blue) and Garantido (in red), compete inside a *bumbódromo* built to hold 35,000 spectators.

São João *(Jun/Jul)*, Caruaru & Campina Grande. *Forró* is the predominant rhythm at the dance festival, which draws many leading performers.

International Puppet Theater Festival *(Jun/Aug)*, Canela. Puppeteers perform in theaters, schools, and streets over four days.

Rally dos Sertões *(late Jun)*, across Brazil. A 10-day event, when cars, truck pilots, and motorcycles drive 2,796 miles (4,500 km) through Brazil's rough interior.

JULY

Festival do Inverno *(Jul 1–30)*, Campos do Jordão (São Paulo). Begun in 1990, it is the greatest festival of classical music in Latin America.

Festival Internacional da Dança *(2nd fortnight)*, Joinville (Santa Catarina). Dance performances, workshops, and competitions take place at one of the world's largest dance festivals, featuring dance forms ranging from jazz and folk to classical ballet.

Ilhabela Sailing Week *(date varies)*, Ilhabela. Known as the sailing capital, the island is famed for competitive races and regattas, organized by the Yacht Club de Ilhabela.

Fortal *(last week)*, Fortaleza. The country's biggest *micareta*, held at Cidade Fortal, draws crowds with *axé* music and small schools of *samba*.

AUGUST

Festa da Nossa Senhora das Neves *(Aug 5)*, João Pessoa. Street celebrations for 10 days to mark the day of the city's patroness, Our Lady of the Snow. The rhythm of *frevo* defines the mood.

Festival de Gramado *(1st two weeks)*, Gramado. The most important film awards event in Brazil offers viewers the best in Brazilian and Latin American cinema.

Festa Literária Internacional de Paraty (FLIP) *(early Aug)*, Paraty. An acclaimed literary gathering of Brazilian and international writers. Literary reunions, plays, lectures, and concerts feature on the versatile program list.

Festa do Peão de Boiadeiro *(beginning on the 3rd Thu)*, Barretos (São Paulo state). The world's largest 10-day rodeo event receiving almost one million visitors every year. Concerts and food fairs.

Pinga Festival *(3rd weekend)*, Paraty. Local *cachaça* samplings *(see p391)*, also known as *pinga*, musical shows, and food stalls offering regional delicacies.

International Festival of Culture and Gastronomy *(date varies)*, Tiradentes. A 10-day international gastronomic event with workshops and exhibitions in restaurants or at public squares all over the town.

Taking the bull by the horns, Festa do Peão de Boiadeiro, Barretos

The Climate of Brazil

Brazil's climate, divided into four broad zones, varies greatly from region to region. Amazônia is hot and humid all year round, though parts experience a distinct dry season from July to October. The central band of the country is also humid, with a marked dry season, while the coastal areas enjoy pleasant tropical breezes and short seasonal downpours. High temperatures and infrequent rainfall characterize the semi-arid desert in the Northeast. In Southern Brazil, cool, wet winters contrast with humid summers. Most of Brazil can be visited at any time of the year, with the exception of the wetlands of the Pantanal during the rainy season, and the extreme south of the country during winter, when it can get very cold.

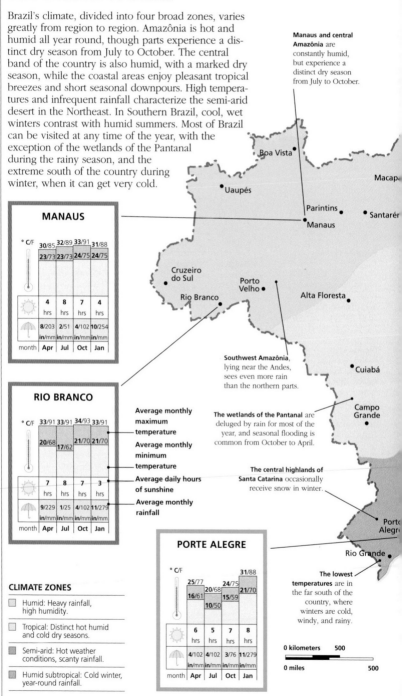

Manaus and central Amazônia are constantly humid, but experience a distinct dry season from July to October.

MANAUS

° C/F				
	30/85	32/89	33/91	31/88
	23/73	23/73	24/75	24/75
	4 hrs	8 hrs	7 hrs	4 hrs
	8/203 in/mm	2/51 in/mm	4/102 in/mm	10/254 in/mm
month	Apr	Jul	Oct	Jan

Southwest Amazônia, lying near the Andes, sees even more rain than the northern parts.

RIO BRANCO

° C/F				
	33/91	33/91	34/93	33/91
	20/68	17/62	21/70	21/70
	7 hrs	8 hrs	7 hrs	3 hrs
	9/229 in/mm	1/25 in/mm	4/102 in/mm	11/279 in/mm
month	Apr	Jul	Oct	Jan

Average monthly maximum temperature

Average monthly minimum temperature

Average daily hours of sunshine

Average monthly rainfall

The wetlands of the Pantanal are deluged by rain for most of the year, and seasonal flooding is common from October to April.

The central highlands of Santa Catarina occasionally receive snow in winter.

The lowest temperatures are in the far south of the country, where winters are cold, windy, and rainy.

PORTE ALEGRE

° C/F				
	25/77		24/75	31/88
	16/61	20/68	15/59	21/70
		10/50		
	6 hrs	5 hrs	7 hrs	8 hrs
	4/102 in/mm	4/102 in/mm	3/76 in/mm	11/279 in/mm
month	Apr	Jul	Oct	Jan

CLIMATE ZONES

- Humid: Heavy rainfall, high humidity.
- Tropical: Distinct hot humid and cold dry seasons.
- Semi-arid: Hot weather conditions, scanty rainfall.
- Humid subtropical: Cold winter, year-round rainfall.

Map labels: Boa Vista, Uaupés, Macapá, Parintins, Santarém, Manaus, Cruzeiro do Sul, Rio Branco, Porto Velho, Alta Floresta, Cuiabá, Campo Grande, Porto Alegre, Rio Grande

0 kilometers   500
0 miles   500

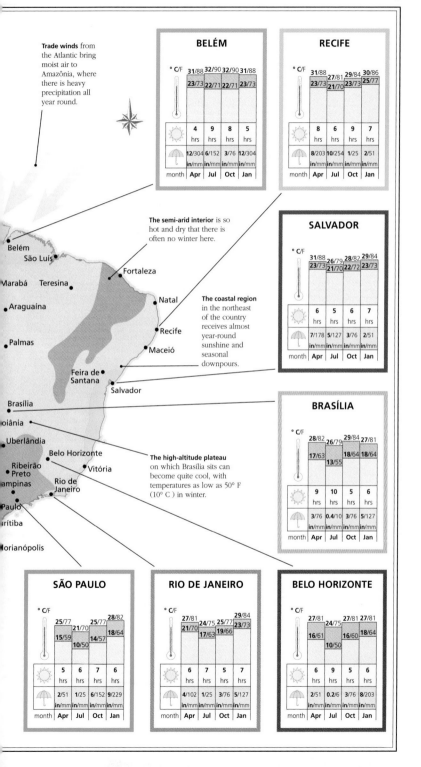

Trade winds from the Atlantic bring moist air to Amazônia, where there is heavy precipitation all year round.

The **semi-arid interior** is so hot and dry that there is often no winter here.

The **coastal region** in the northeast of the country receives almost year-round sunshine and seasonal downpours.

The **high-altitude plateau** on which Brasília sits can become quite cool, with temperatures as low as 50° F (10° C) in winter.

BELÉM

° C/F				
	31/88	32/90	32/90	31/88
	23/73	22/71	22/71	23/73
☀	4 hrs	9 hrs	8 hrs	5 hrs
☂	12/304 in/mm	6/152 in/mm	3/76 in/mm	12/304 in/mm
month	Apr	Jul	Oct	Jan

RECIFE

° C/F				
	31/88	27/81	29/84	30/86
	23/73	21/70	23/73	25/77
☀	8 hrs	6 hrs	9 hrs	7 hrs
☂	8/203 in/mm	10/254 in/mm	1/25 in/mm	2/51 in/mm
month	Apr	Jul	Oct	Jan

SALVADOR

° C/F				
	31/88	26/79	28/82	29/84
	23/73	21/70	22/72	23/73
☀	6 hrs	5 hrs	6 hrs	7 hrs
☂	7/178 in/mm	5/127 in/mm	3/76 in/mm	2/51 in/mm
month	Apr	Jul	Oct	Jan

BRASÍLIA

° C/F				
	28/82	26/79	29/84	27/81
	17/63	13/55	18/64	18/64
☀	9 hrs	10 hrs	5 hrs	6 hrs
☂	3/76 in/mm	0.4/10 in/mm	3/76 in/mm	5/127 in/mm
month	Apr	Jul	Oct	Jan

SÃO PAULO

° C/F				
	25/77	21/70	25/77	28/82
	15/59	10/50	14/57	18/64
☀	5 hrs	6 hrs	7 hrs	6 hrs
☂	2/51 in/mm	1/25 in/mm	6/152 in/mm	9/229 in/mm
month	Apr	Jul	Oct	Jan

RIO DE JANEIRO

° C/F				
	27/81	24/75	25/77	29/84
	21/70	17/63	19/66	23/73
☀	6 hrs	7 hrs	5 hrs	7 hrs
☂	4/102 in/mm	1/25 in/mm	3/76 in/mm	5/127 in/mm
month	Apr	Jul	Oct	Jan

BELO HORIZONTE

° C/F				
	27/81	24/75	27/81	27/81
	16/61	10/50	16/60	18/64
☀	6 hrs	9 hrs	5 hrs	6 hrs
☂	2/51 in/mm	0.2/6 in/mm	3/76 in/mm	8/203 in/mm
month	Apr	Jul	Oct	Jan

Belém
São Luís
Fortaleza
Marabá   Teresina
Araguaína   Natal
Palmas   Recife
Maceió
Feira de Santana
Salvador
Brasília
Goiânia
Uberlândia
Belo Horizonte
Ribeirão Preto   Vitória
Campinas   Rio de Janeiro
São Paulo
Curitiba
Florianópolis

THE HISTORY OF BRAZIL

*V*ery little is known about the history of Brazil before 1500, when Europeans first traveled there. Archaeological remains, which consist mainly of pottery, suggest a complex society that was in existence long before the colonialists arrived. After more than 300 years of Portuguese colonization, Brazil became a republic in 1889. Long periods of totalitarian rule finally led to the return of democracy in 1989.

For over a millennium, before the Europeans arrived in Brazil, Amazônia had a vast network of sophisticated societies with populations of up to 100,000. The abundance of fish in the Amazon river and its tributaries was almost certainly one of the main reasons for the wealth and rapid growth of cultures in Amazônia.

Early European depiction of the Tupinambá people

Up until the beginning of the 16th century, the middle Amazon region around Santarém was an important center for ceramic art and trading. It was home to thousands of semi-settled indigenous people who grew maize and had access to plentiful fish. Living on higher land, up above the flood plain, as well as in long houses along river banks, they left important ceramic remains. Archaeological evidence from the earth mounds near Santarém and also on the Ilha de Marajó *(see p270)* suggests that some of the shell midden mounds were part of these complex fishing societies. The most widespread of the 1,000 semi-nomadic indigenous peoples that inhabited the territory at the

time of the European conquest, were the Tupi-Guaraní Indians. While they lived off slash-and-burn farming, the Tupinambá, another large group, cultivated crops, primarily maize.

EUROPEAN DISCOVERY

The coastline was widely inhabited when Spanish explorer Vicente Yáñez Pinzón disembarked on the northeastern shore in Pernambuco, on January 26, 1500. He could not claim the newfound land for Spain, as he was officially limited by the Tordesillas meridian. The Treaty of Tordesillas, signed in 1494 between Spain and Portugal, determined that all lands discovered west of a meridian located 3 miles (5 km) west of the Cape Verde Islands would belong to Spain, and those to the east of this line could be claimed by Portugal. On April 23, 1500, Pedro Álvares Cabral landed in southern Bahia, marking the Portuguese arrival in Brazil. Portugal, which already controlled the Indian Ocean and the spice trade, bolstered its position as a mercantile power rivaled only by Spain.

TIMELINE

Detail of rock painting, dating from 2800 BC

13000 BC One of the early hunting communities flourishes near Pedra Furada, in Piauí state

1000 BC–AD 1000 Amazônian civilization, currently referred to as Patiti or Enin by archaeologists, develops a crop irrigation system

AD 1000 Hierarchical societies settled along the Amazon

20000 BC	2000 BC	1000 BC	AD 1	AD 1000

9500 BC Migration across the Pacific Ocean to mid-Amazon region

3000 BC Prehistoric cultural developments in Marajoara and Santarém have been dated to this time

AD 500–1300 Period of major growth and expansion of Marajoara culture

AD 1500 Pedro Cabral of Portugal lands in Bahia

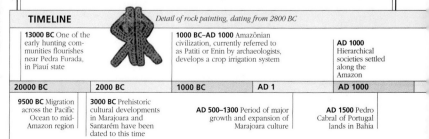
◁ Detail of a meeting of Portuguese sailors and natives of Brazil, a 1592 line engraving by Theodor de Bry

The Portuguese Conquest

When the Portuguese reached Brazil in 1500, their period of maritime expansion was at its peak. In 1501, Emperor Manuel I ordered Amerigo Vespucci to explore the new territory further, leading to the settlement of Guanabara Bay (Rio de Janeiro). In 1530, an expedition led by Martim Alfonso de Sousa resulted in the first colonial towns – São Vicente and São Paulo. Preoccupied with Africa and the Far East, Portugal neglected Brazil until 1532, when João III divided the land into 15 captaincies. The early settlers mainly comprised impoverished Portuguese peasants and nobles, who were expected to explore and govern these captaincies.

Armillary sphere, a globe used by early navigators

Manuel I (1469–1521)
An illuminated Portuguese manuscript features the royal coat of arms, as well as armillary spheres symbolizing Emperor Manuel's reign as a golden age of exploration.

Priests also joined the expedition, hoping to spread Christianity in the New World.

Cabral erected a cross and held a Catholic service to signify the ownership of Brazil.

PEDRO ÁLVARES CABRAL

The commander of the fleet sent to India by Emperor Manuel I, Cabral accidentally landed at Porto Seguro in southern Bahia on April 23, 1500. The Portuguese navigator baptized the bay, where they anchored for 10 days, Terra de Vera Cruz, or "Land of the True Cross." His onward voyage to India was beset with calamities, and Cabral finally drowned in a shipwreck a few months later.

Indigenous People meeting the Portuguese
Initial Portuguese fleets were received by friendly indigenous people. Gradually, these confrontations and meetings became more hostile in nature.

THE NAMING OF BRAZIL

Early Brazil map, showing a couple under brazil wood

Officially, the land was named for *pau-brasil*, or brazil wood, a tree yielding a valuable red dye. However, the name "Brazil" appeared in the Irish legend of St. Brendan as Hy Brazik (Blessed Land in Gaelic). It became part of European maritime folklore, designating a hypothetical land located somewhere in the Atlantic. When Cabral found a new land in that general area, he may have identified it with Brendan's Brazil. The tree might have been named after the land, rather than the other way around.

Botocudos Man
Still surviving in some parts of Brazil, the Botocudos were hunter-gatherers.

Woodcut Showing Tupinambá People
Ritually practicing cannibalism, the Tupinambá were some of the first Brazilians to make contact with the Portuguese. They soon died from diseases carried by the Europeans, and from the conditions of their capture and enslavement.

João III (1502–57)
King João III ascended to the throne while the Portuguese Empire was at the height of its mercantile and colonial power. Unable to directly govern Brazil, King João III divided the land into 15 capitanias, or captaincies. Settlement was focused mainly on the long coastline. Only São Vicente and Pernambuco immediately prospered. In 1548, the king repossessed the captaincies and brought Brazil under his direct control.

Skilled captains accompanied Cabral in his explorations to discover new territories.

A Jesuit Admonishing Indigenous People
The influence of the Jesuits accompanied this early period of colonization. The first missionaries had arrived in 1549 and acquired great power in Brazil through their influence on the Portuguese court. A zealous missionary movement began, aimed at converting the local people.

Painting showing a group of indigenous Brazilian slaves at work in a sugar plantation

COLONIZATION & EXPANSION

King João III conferred special colonial privileges to the *donatários*, the aristocrats and minor gentry, who were expected to develop and govern the *capitanias* on behalf of the Crown. The *donatários*, however, met with adverse climatic conditions and hostile indigenous people. Some of the *capitanias* were attacked by the indigenous Brazilians. In 1549, the Crown was forced to send Tomé de Sousa as the first governor, who was assigned the task of protecting the few remaining captaincies.

SUGAR & THE SLAVE TRADE

Introduced to Brazil in 1532, sugar replaced the country's first major export, brazil wood, which was nearly wiped out as a result of over-exploitation. Setting up his capital in Salvador, Tomé de Sousa enlisted the support of the Jesuits. The indigenous people who did not convert to Christianity were enslaved and sent to work in sugar plantations. As a result of the high demand for sugar in Europe, sugar cane grown in

engenhos (plantations) along the northeastern coast soon became the base of the Brazilian economy. Salvador and Olinda emerged as key centers for the sugar trade.

The hunting-gathering indigenous people, however, were found to be unsuitable slaves for the plantations. They were better suited for the brazil wood trade, and were made to log and transport timber instead. From the 1550s, the landowners turned to Africa, importing millions of slaves.

COLONIAL WARS

While the Portuguese Crown was still struggling to consolidate its hold on Brazil, the Dutch and French forces continued to encroach on its territories. In 1555, the French had made inroads into the bay of Guanabara, establishing their own colony, French Antarctic. Portuguese forces seized the colony in 1565, and founded a new city, Rio de Janeiro.

Throughout the first half of the 17th century, French and Dutch privateers continued to plunder the coastal cities. With a powerful fleet, the Dutch offered a greater challenge. In 1624, the Dutch captured Salvador and laid siege to the city, until the combined

African slaves in a sugar mill, using an early form of grinder for refining sugar

TIMELINE

1532 King João III divides the land into 15 *capitanias*	1550 African slaves shipped to Brazil to work sugar plantations	1572 Construction of Salvador's Catholic cathedral completed	*Slave ship*	
		1554 Jesuits found São Paulo		1630 The Dutch occupy Olinda
1500		**1550**		**1600**
1532 Sugar cane is introduced to Brazil	1549 Salvador founded by Tomé de Sousa		1565 French Antarctic destroyed and Rio de Janeiro founded	1624 The Dutch capture Salvador, laying the city to seige for the next nine months

An engraving depicting naval combat between French and Portuguese ships off the coast of Brazil

fleet of the Portuguese and Spanish expelled them. The Dutch occupied Olinda in 1630 and, by 1641, controlled a vast stretch of coastline, ending Portugal's monopoly of the sugar trade. During 1648 and 1649, two battles were fought at Guararapes, in Pernambuco, where the Dutch were routed and their territory reduced to an enclave around Recife. Following several years of open warfare, the Dutch formally withdrew in 1661.

THE DISCOVERY OF GOLD
The decline of the sugar industry coincided with the discovery of gold. In 1695, gold was first discovered in Sabara, Minas Gerais, by the *bandeirantes* (paramilitary adventurers), who faced grueling conditions as they pressed inland toward the Andean foothills. Gold was also found in Cuiabá, Mato Grosso, in 1719. Both events led to further development and

expansion of the country's interior. Traffic to São Paulo and Rio de Janeiro rapidly increased and new communities drew people away from the Northeast coast. The focus of power in Brazil moved from the Northeast to the Southeast, and Rio de Janeiro was made the new capital in 1763.

STRUGGLE FOR INDEPENDENCE
The gold rush lasted not more than 70 years. The decline of gold in the 18th century led to high taxes, as Brazil was forced to meet the quota set by the Crown for the minimum annual gold production. This, coupled with the Brazilian resentment at their exclusion from administration and the Portuguese dominance of foreign trade, culminated in the 1789 Inconfidência Mineira rebellion. Led by Tiradentes *(see pp126–7)*, who was eventually executed, the uprising was aimed at Brazilian independence from Portuguese rule.

1661 The Dutch formally withdraw from Portuguese territories

1719 Gold discovered in Cuiabá, Mato Grosso

1763 Rio de Janeiro made the new capital city of Brazil

1789 Inconfidência Mineira uprising is quelled, and the leader, Tiradentes, is hanged

1700   1750   1800

1695 Gold discovered in Sabara, Minas Gerais

Portrait of Tiradentes

Dom Pedro proclaiming "Independência ou Morte!" at the Rio Ipiranga, on September 7, 1822

THE FIRST EMPEROR OF BRAZIL

The advance of French Emperor Napoleon, in 1808, forced King Dom João VI, who was ruling from Lisbon, to relocate his government to Brazil. In 1821, the royal family were forced to return to deal with rebels back home. Dom João's son, the Prince Regent, who had stayed back in Brazil, proclaimed independence from Portugal on September 7, 1822. In a famous scene at the Rio Ipiranga, he tore the Portuguese insignia from his uniform, drew his sword, and declared, "Independência ou Morte!" (Independence or Death). Three months later, he crowned himself Emperor Dom Pedro I.

Although the assumption of independence had been easy, Dom Pedro soon realized that organizing the new government was riddled with challenges. His own autocratic nature proved to be the biggest hurdle in winning the confidence of his subjects. The new consitution he proposed, based on his own unlimited power, was strongly opposed by the assembly. When Dom Pedro dismissed his assembly in 1831, demonstrators demanded its reinstatement.

PROVINCIAL UNREST

Dom Pedro I was forced to abdicate in favor of his five-year-old son, Dom Pedro II. From 1831 to 1840, three appointed regents ruled the country in the young emperor's name during a period of turmoil, in which local factions struggled to gain control of their provinces and to keep the masses in line. The regency in Rio de Janeiro gave considerable power to the provinces in 1834, when Brazil became a federation of locally autonomous regional powers, with loose allegiance to the center. The rebellions, riots, and popular movements that marked these years did not spring from economic misery, but from attempts to share in the prosperity stemming from the North Atlantic demand for Brazil's exports.

THE COFFEE INDUSTRY

Coffee, which was introduced to Brazil in the early 1800s, filled the void left by the collapse of the sugar industry and the waning gold rush. An army officer, Francisco de Mello,

A formal portrait of Brazil's Emperor Dom Pedro II (1825–91), depicting him in full regalia

TIMELINE

Dom Pedro I

1808 Napoleon's advance forces Dom João to flee Portugal, and relocate to Brazil

1831 Pedro dismisses the Constituent Assembly after a draft constitution is proposed

1837–38 The Sabinada Rebellion in Salvador

1842 Rebellions in Minas Gerais and São Paulo

| 1810 | 1820 | 1830 | 1840 |

1822 The Prince Regent proclaims independence from Portugal, crowning himself Emperor Dom Pedro I

1825 Britain and Portugal sign a treaty recognizing Brazilian independence

1834 Brazil becomes a federation of autonomous regional powers

1838–41 The Balaiada Rebellion in Maranhão

was believed to have brought the first coffee beans into Brazil, from his journey to French Guiana. The coffee industry began to flourish, mainly in Minas Gerais and São Paulo. Expanding coffee production in the 1850s and 1860s attracted British investment in railroads to speed transport of the beans to the coast. The coastal Santos–São Paulo Railroad (1868) was followed by a series of railroads that linked the northeastern coast to the interior.

The Surrender of Uruguaiana, painted during the war

THE WAR OF THE TRIPLE ALLIANCE

From 1864 to 1870, Paraguay and the allied countries of Argentina, Brazil, and Uruguay fought one of the bloodiest conflicts on the American continent. Also known as the Paraguayan War, it has been widely attributed to the expansionist ambitions of Paraguayan dictator Francisco Solano Lopez, and the Brazilian and Argentinian meddling in internal Uruguayan politics. The outcome of the war was the devastating defeat of Paraguay by the Triple Alliance, but at the cost of over 100,000 casualties.

SLAVERY ABOLISHED

As coffee exports rose steadily, so did the numbers of imported slaves. In Rio de Janeiro alone, they soared from around 26,000 in 1825 to 44,000 in 1828. While slave owners argued that slavery was not demoralizing, others were in favor of replacing slavery with free European immigrant labor. Eventually, a contract system that was little better than slavery was established by the Parliament. New laws and decrees, unacceptable to slave owners, were simply not enforced, such as the 1829 order forbidding slave ships to sail for Africa. The failure to enforce these orders caused regional slave rebellions throughout the 19th century. In 1850, British and domestic pressure finally forced the Brazilian government to outlaw the

An 1857 portrayal of black slaves on a plantation

African slave trade. Over the next five years, even clandestine landings stopped, ending the transAtlantic trade. In 1875, the cabinet in Rio Branco approved a law freeing newborn slaves and requiring masters to care for them until they were eight years old. Between 1875 and 1887, 156,000 immigrants arrived in São Paulo to work as free laborers and fill the void created by the gradual decline in the slave population. By the 1880s, the slave population was reduced to half its size. In 1888, the Golden Law was passed, finally abolishing slavery.

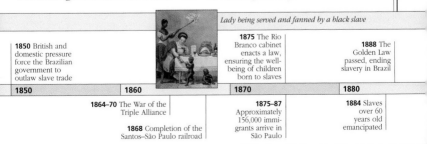

Lady being served and fanned by a black slave

1850 British and domestic pressure force the Brazilian government to outlaw slave trade		**1875** The Rio Branco cabinet enacts a law, ensuring the well-being of children born to slaves	**1888** The Golden Law passed, ending slavery in Brazil
1850	**1860**	**1870**	**1880**
	1864–70 The War of the Triple Alliance	**1875–87** Approximately 156,000 immigrants arrive in São Paulo	**1884** Slaves over 60 years old emancipated
	1868 Completion of the Santos–São Paulo railroad		

THE FIRST REPUBLIC

In 1889, the monarchy was overthrown by a military coup, which was led by Marechal Deodoro da Fonseca and supported by Brazil's coffee barons. Dom Pedro II was exiled in Paris, where he died two years later. A republic was born, with Deodoro as the first president. The Constituent Assembly that drew up the 1891 constitution was a confrontation between the São Paulo coffee oligarchy that sought to limit executive power and the radical authoritarians who wanted to expand presidential authority. The growing opposition culminated in a navy revolt, forcing Deodoro to step down only a few months later. It was recognized that

The funeral of King Dom Pedro II in Paris, reported in a French journal

the central government could exercise control only through the local oligarchies, or *patrias*. The constitutional system was offset by the *coronelismo*, or the real system of unwritten agreements among these local bosses, by which local oligarchies chose the state governors, who in turn selected the president.

The informal distribution of power emerged as the result of armed struggles and bargaining. In order to check the nationalizing tendencies of the army, the oligarchic republic strengthened the navy and police, turning them into small armies in the larger states.

Scooping coffee beans for shipment after drying, on a São Paulo plantation

"CAFÉ COM LEITE" REPUBLIC

The early years of the republic were called *café com leite* (coffee and milk) by its opponents. Brazilian politics was dominated by an oligarchy that comprised São Paulo coffee barons and Minas Gerais cattle ranchers. These groups controlled electoral politics, and the presidency alternated between the two wealthy states of coffee and milk.

THE STRUGGLE FOR MODERNIZATION

At the turn of the 19th century, Brazil lacked an integrated economy. Domestic consumption was largely neglected, and the middle class was not yet active in political life. The economy was organized around large agricultural estates, or *latifundia*. Brazil had lost its sugar market to Caribbean producers, while the rubber boom in Amazônia was beginning to lose its primacy to more efficient Southeast Asian plantations. The outbreak of World War I was the turning point for the dynamic urban sectors. Industrial production doubled, and agricultural diversity received an impetus, as the growing demand by the Allies for staple products sparked a new boom for goods other than sugar and coffee. The old order gave way to the political aspirations of the

TIMELINE

1889 Military officers rebel against Dom Pedro II, establishing a republic

1897 Belo Horizonte founded in Minas Gerais, as Brazil's first modern planned city

Train station, Belo Horizonte

1916 A civil statute formally enshrines hierarchical and patriarchal view of family and sexual relations

1890	1900	1910	1920

1891 The first president of Brazil, Deodoro Fonseca, ousted by a navy revolt

1896 Teatro Amazonas (*see pp282–3*) opens in Manaus

1902 Euclides da Cunha writes *Os Sertãos (see p206)*

1908 The first Japanese immigrants arrive in Santarém

1915 Southeast Asian rubber elbows out Brazil from the market

new urban groups – government, white-collar workers, professionals, bankers, merchants, and industrialists. Increasing support for industrial protectionism marked Brazilian politics in the 1920s. Disparate social reform movements cropped up during this period. Between 1922 and 1926, junior military officers staged a revolt against the landed elite, demanding socio-economic modernization.

Brazilian army confronts rebels during the 1930 coup

THE NEW STATE

A bloodless coup by the military installed Getúlio Vargas as provisional president in 1930. Between the World Wars, he built a corporatist, centralized state along fascist lines, although he did advocate some liberal reforms. The collapse of the old order had created a vacuum, which was filled by the fascist Integralistas and communists. The former had once enjoyed Vargas's support, but later turned against him when they realized that creating a strictly fascist state was not on his agenda. They were bidding to seize power in the 1938 election, which the Constitution barred Vargas from contesting. Months before the election, Vargas declared a state of emergency to avert an alleged communist plot. He dissolved the Constitution and established the Estado Nôvo (New State), which used repressive political tactics and rejected free-market liberal capitalism. Vargas's promise of a "post-war era of liberty" could not save the fall of the Estado Nôvo in 1945, when he was ousted by General Eurico Dutra. His return to presidency in 1951 was marred by inflation, corruption, and a political scandal involving an attack on a journalist by the President's body-guard. Faced with the ultimatum to resign, Vargas ended his life in 1954 by shooting himself.

Citizens of Rio de Janeiro welcoming rebel troops upon the success of the 1930 coup

Poster, World Cup, 1950

1932 Young army officers lead their units against the old order in Minas Gerais and Rio

1938 Vargas establishes the Estado Nôvo, or the "New State"

1950 World Cup soccer held in Rio de Janeiro

1954 Vargas commits suicide with a bullet to the heart

1930 **1940** **1950**

1930 A military coup installs Getúlio Vargas as provisional president

1937 Vargas assumes dictatorial powers under a new constitution

1945 The Estado Nôvo collapses, Eurico Dutra comes to power

1951 Vargas re-elected president

The Vargas Era (1930–54)

Spanning the creation of Brazil as a modern nation-state, the long political career of Getúlio Vargas exemplifies the various contradictions at the heart of the Brazilian national character. His rise to power in 1930 marked the resurgence of a generation of young, dynamic administrators, but also marked the beginning of an authoritarian rule. During his first term, he assumed absolute power to overthrow the old order, and established the Estado Nôvo. Forced to step down after World War II, he remained popular and was re-elected in 1950.

Getúlio Dornelles Vargas
A pro-industry nationalist and virulent anti-communist, Vargas possessed an authoritarian streak. The hero of the newly-emerged urban working class, he favored capitalism and liberal reforms to some extent.

Crowd Cheering Vargas's Victory
A bloodless coup in 1930 ended the reign of President Washington Luis, and brought Vargas into power.

NATIONALIZED FASCISM

Exploiting communist paranoia, Vargas assumed dictatorship in 1937, abolishing opposition parties and imposing censorship. He tolerated anti-Semitism, initially encouraging the fascist Integralistas *(see p55)* until they decided to contest the elections against him in 1938.

Vargas, diminutive in stature, emulated Hitler and Mussolini in some ways.

Ties with Mussolini
In January 1938, two Italian aircraft, one of them piloted by Mussolini's son, were received in Brazil with great applause.

Integralistas in Rio de Janeiro, 1938
A group of Integralistas led a short-lived revolt against the corrupt Vargas regime. They attacked the Palácio Guanabara, and made a bid for Vargas's life, but government forces promptly suppressed the uprising.

Carmen Miranda (1909–55)
During the Vargas era, the Portuguese-Brazilian singer-actress charmed post-World War USA and the world.

1950 World Cup
Brazil was confident of winning the World Cup in the first tournament to be held after World War II. The final was played on home ground at Rio's Estádio Maracanã. However, in a surprise victory, Uruguay defeated Brazil 2–1. With slighted pride, the humiliated nation plunged into mourning.

New Ministry of Education
Vargas was responsible for the erection of a sky-scraping new Ministry of Education, whose cutting-edge design was emphasized by its incongruous location behind a colonial church in Rio de Janeiro.

Toward the Future
Vargas recognized that Brazil's strength lay in its vast natural resources. He created Petrobras, the state oil company, and invested in road and air transport.

Daily Life
Under Vargas's rule, modern tramways were constructed to carry white-collar employees to their various offices in the capital city of Rio de Janeiro.

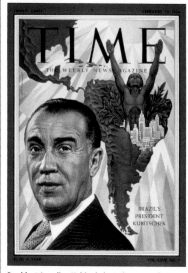

President Juscelino Kubitschek on the cover of *Time* magazine dated January 13, 1970

INTO MODERNITY

The reign of Juscelino Kubitschek, Vargas's successor, lasted from 1956 to 1961, ushering Brazil into modernity. Campaigning on a platform of "Fifty years of progress in five," Kubitschek tried to achieve this progress with generous incentives for foreign investors, such as low taxes, privileges for the importation of machinery, and donations of land. All this gave impetus to the economic growth rate, which paved the way for the economic boom in the next decade. The most notable manifestation of Kubitschek's

Trans-Amazon Highway construction near Altamira Brazil, July 1971

nationalistic aspirations was the creation of Brasília *(see pp294–5)* as the new capital of Brazil.

Despite instilling national confidence, Kubitschek's era was also beset with massive inflation. Also, the influx of foreign capital rapidly captured domestic industry, and the urban bourgeoisie found state control threatening rather than protective. Mild structural reforms took place under President João Goulart (1961–64), but the increasing political infighting between left and right culminated in the 1964 military junta.

THE ERA OF MILITARY RULE

A period of right-wing military dictatorship followed. In a bid to appease the hard-liners, the new president, Marshal Humberto Castelo Branco, recessed and purged Congress, and decreed the expansion of the president's powers at the expense of the legislature and the judiciary. His gamble curbed the populist left, but gave his successor, Artur da Costa e Silva (1967–69), a basis for authoritarian rule. Despite their victory, the hard-liners were still unable to institutionalize their agenda politically. They did not give up their liberal constitutionalism as they feared damage to their alliance with the US, the citadel of anti-communism. In 1969, the democratic mask fell off when General Médici came to power and continued to rule an authoritarian regime without popular support. An extremely

TIMELINE

1960 Brasília inaugurated as the new capital of Brazil

1970 Brazil wins the soccer World Cup in Mexico

1977 *Dona Flor and Her Two Husbands* brings international fame to Brazilian cinema

1979 General Figueiredo is sworn in as president

| 1960 | 1965 | 1970 | 1975 | 1980 |

1961 Janio Quadros elected president, replaced by João Goulart in the same year

Jules Rimet trophy

1974 Ernesto Giesel's rule begins, marking a slow return to democracy

1980 Film *Bye Bye, Brazil* brings more recognition to Brazilian cinema

1984 Benedita d Silva becomes th first black woma in Congres

oppressive government apparatus hounded political opponents. Yet the Médici administration cloaked itself in the green and gold flag when Brazil won the Jules Rimet trophy for its third consecutive victory in the soccer World Cup in 1970. From 1968 to 1974, during the darkest days of dictatorship, the military-civil alliance took shape as the economy boomed, reaching annual GDP growth rates of 12 percent. During this period, the Trans-Amazon Highway was built, and the Rio Paraná was dammed.

President Luiz Inácio Lula da Silva, victorious after his re-election

Geisel's accession in 1974 signaled a move toward democratic rule. He attempted to restrain the growing strength of the opposition parties by creating an electoral college that would approve his selected replacement. He allowed the return of exiles, restored *habeas corpus*, and installed General João Figueiredo as his successor in 1979. A 1981 bombing incident at Rio City's RioCentro, confirmed direct military involvement in terrorism. The Figueiredo regime's inaction in punishing the guilty strengthened the public's resolve to end military rule, as Brazil faced inflation and mounting foreign debt.

THE RETURN TO DEMOCRACY

In 1985, civilian Tancredo Neves was voted into office as president. However, he died before taking office. Brazil completed its transition to a popularly elected government in 1989, when Fernando Collor de Mello won 53 percent of the vote. The democratization of the government was visible in the impeachment of the corrupt de Mello regime, forcing him to resign in 1993. The 1994 elections brought to power Fernando Cardoso, who served two terms but failed to match the growth of the country's wealth and power with better living conditions. Socio-economic contradictions helped usher Lula da Silva in 2003 as Brazil's first elected left-wing president. His Workers' Party (Partido dos Trabalhadores) government declined to nationalize private companies or collectivize land. This disappointed his most radical allies, but restored investor confidence in the country that underwrote strong economic growth and employment expansion. Despite an unfulfilled promise of economic and social revolution for Brazil, Lula was re-elected to power in October 2006 and has returned with a strong mandate to reduce poverty in Brazil.

A 1997 demonstration by landless farm workers, demanding jobs, justice, and land reform

1985 Civilian Tancredo Neves is elected to presidency	*Brazilian President Fernando Collor de Mello*	1995 Fernando Cardoso takes office as president	2001 Congress approves a civil code, giving equal rights to men and women	
			2002 Brazil wins its fifth World Cup title defeating Germany	
1985	**1990**	**1995**	**2000**	**2005**	**2010**
	1994 Brazil defeats Italy to win the World Cup title	2000 UNESCO declares the Atlantic rainforest a World Heritage Site	2006 Lula da Silva is re-elected in a landslide victory, returning as Brazil's president	

SOUTHEAST BRAZIL

Introducing Southeast Brazil

The four states of Rio de Janeiro, Espírito Santo, Minas Gerais, and São Paulo constitute Brazil's economic heartland. The giant metropolises – Rio de Janeiro, Belo Horizonte, and São Paulo – burst with energetic cultural life. Rio de Janeiro holds the greatest attractions with its Carnaval and breathtaking mountains and beaches. Beyond the urban hubs, nature and rural life exist undisturbed. Wild islands lie a short boat ride away. Inland, in the folds of the rugged Minas hills, are colonial towns whose cobbled streets, colorful Portuguese town houses, and ornate Baroque churches remain little changed since imperial times.

Parque Nacional Serra da Canastra (see p133), *one of the protected areas dotting the region, preserves pristine rainforest and* cerrado, *as well as rich fauna.*

São Paulo City (see pp134–59), *the capital of São Paulo state, is relentlessly urban and frenetic, but has Brazil's best restaurants, shops, and nightlife.*

SÃO PAULO STATE
(see pp160–71)

SÃO PAULO CITY
(see pp134–59)

São Paulo's coast (see pp164–71), *stretching across 250 miles (400 km), features beaches and islands that serve as the weekend playground for the city.*

◁ **Rio de Janeiro at sunset, with a view of the Botofogo Bay and the dazzling Sugar Loaf mountain**

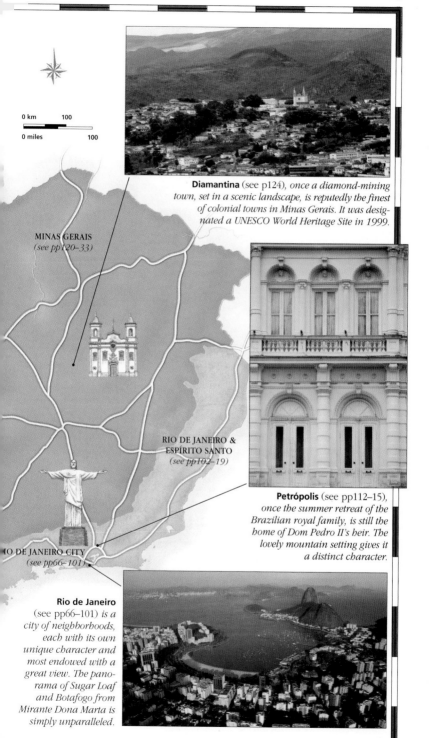

0 km 100

0 miles 100

Diamantina (see p124), *once a diamond-mining town, set in a scenic landscape, is reputedly the finest of colonial towns in Minas Gerais. It was designated a UNESCO World Heritage Site in 1999.*

MINAS GERAIS
(see pp120–33)

RIO DE JANEIRO &
ESPÍRITO SANTO
(see pp102–19)

RIO DE JANEIRO CITY
(see pp66–101)

Petrópolis (see pp112–15), *once the summer retreat of the Brazilian royal family, is still the home of Dom Pedro II's heir. The lovely mountain setting gives it a distinct character.*

Rio de Janeiro
(see pp66–101) is a city of neighborhoods, each with its own unique character and most endowed with a great view. The panorama of Sugar Loaf and Botafogo from Mirante Dona Marta is simply unparalleled.

Carnaval in Rio

One of the world's most spectacular festivals, Carnaval is celebrated all over Brazil, but the celebrations in Rio are justly famous. They remain unmatched for their sheer scale and splendor. Falling in the first days of February or March, Carnaval derives its origin from religion, and it is linked to the calendar of the Catholic Church. Traditionally, Carnaval is the last celebration of excess and joy before the austerity and fasting of the Lenten period. Its key elements include street celebrations, carnival balls, and the world-famous parade of top *samba* schools, which tradition-ally takes place at the Sambódromo in downtown Rio.

CARNAVAL DATES

2008 February 3
2009 February 22
2010 February 14
2011 March 6
2012 February 19
2013 February 10
2014 March 2
2015 February 13

Porta bandeira is the school's standard bearer, dressed in lavish 18th-century formal wear, regardless of the school's theme.

Samba schools *are large social clubs found in Rio's poorer communities and neighborhoods, often linked to the local favelas. Mangueira, one of the most prominent schools, was founded in 1928, and Portela, which began in 1923, has won the most Carnaval titles. Many top schools date from the 1940s and 50s, while Grande Rio formed as late as 1988.*

Giant puppets *are put together to decorate the floats and fascinating costumes are created for the participants. Craftspeople work throughout the year, as Carnaval is a year-round industry. Much of the work can now be seen at close quarters in the Cidade de Samba in downtown Rio.*

Street carnivals *take place wherever there is a band that can strike up a samba and move around the streets. Bands attract a large following who dance and sing through the neighborhoods.*

Party-loving Cariocas *consider Carnaval more important than any other event in the calendar, and that includes both Christmas and New Year. It is a week-long holiday for partying around the clock and a sign that summer is finally coming to a close.*

TIPS FOR VISITORS

Transport: Take the metro. Use Central Station if your ticket is for an uneven numbered sector and Praça Onze for an even one.
Winner's Parade: Those who missed the event can see part of the parade by winning schools on the Saturday after Carnaval.
Tickets: Book your tickets in advance (Maracanã stadium box office, (021) 2568 9962).

A different theme *is chosen by every school, and conceptualized by the* carnavalesco *(director). The history of Espírito Santo, represented by the state colors, pink, blue, and white, was the theme of the Caprichosos de Pilares school in 2006. This float shows* antropofagismo, *the concept of "cultural cannibalism," putting foreign art, music, and literature in a Brazilian context.*

The central display is the focal point of the float, and is often the most elaborately designed aspect, with the most creative costumes on display.

Passistas, or participants, numbering a minimum of 2,500, join each float with at least 200 in the *bateria* (percussion section).

THE PARADE

Each of the 12 main *samba* schools will have around 4,000 participants who must cover the Passarela do Samba in not less than 65 minutes and not more than 80 minutes. In that time, they will put on a performance every bit as complex and visually exciting as any musical showing on Broadway or in London's West End. Six schools parade each night.

Mestre sala is the school's dance master who, along with the *porta bandeira*, performs a complex series of dance steps as they move along the route.

Sambódromo, *or Passarela do Samba, was inaugurated in 1984. Designed by Oscar Niemeyer, it can accommodate over 60,000 spectators at any one time. The end square is used for Carnaval, outdoor concerts, and festivals.*

RIO DE JANEIRO CITY

*R*io de Janeiro is quite simply one of the world's most beautiful and vibrant cities, and is the number one destination for visitors coming to Brazil. Its unique setting, with dramatic mountains and beaches at its very center, sets it apart from the other great cities of the world. In addition, Rio's flamboyant Carnaval, samba, and bossa nova *make for a heady mix that is impossible to ignore.*

Rio de Janeiro was first discovered by European explorers on January 1, 1502. They mistook the huge Guanabara Bay for the mouth of a river (*rio*) and called the site "River of January," thus giving the city its name. Evidence of the city's colonial past can still be seen in downtown Rio, with buildings and artifacts dating from the 16th to the 19th centuries, including the imposing Paço Imperial and Palácio Tiradentes. In 1763, the city became the capital of Brazil's Vice-Royalty and in 1808, the Portuguese royal family and court abandoned Lisbon for Rio, making it the capital of both Brazil and the Portuguese Empire. It remained home to the Brazilian monarchy until 1889 and the capital of the Brazilian Republic until 1960, when the title was awarded to the newly-built Bauhaus-style Brasília.

Today, Rio is an international metropolis and a spectacular tropical resort. It has several iconic sights, including the enormous statue of Christ that looms protectively over the city from Corcovado mountain, the easily recognizable Sugar Loaf mountain at one end of Urca Bay, and the famous stadium, Estádio Maracanã, which opened for the 1950 World Cup and has hosted crowds of up to 200,000 people.

Rio's residents, affectionately called "Cariocas," are a laid-back, friendly people who love to go out. Visitors will be spoiled for choice in this hedonistic city, and can visit Lapa for its extravagant clubs, Gávea for its bars, and Ipanema and Leblon for their boutiques and restaurants. Rio's beaches provide ample opportunity for all manner of watersports and are a great meeting place for the city's residents, both rich and poor.

The colorful Copacabana beach, lined with palm trees

◁ Cristo Redentor (Christ the Redeemer) on Corcovado mountain, with Sugar Loaf in view

Exploring Rio de Janeiro City

Rio de Janeiro covers a vast area of 473 sq miles (1,225 sq km) and is home to 6 million people, making it Brazil's second largest and second most populous city. It has two main zones – Zona Norte (North Zone), encompassing miles of poor housing, known as *favelas*; and Zona Sul (South Zone), with plush neighborhoods and famous beaches such as Ipanema and Copacabana. Centro is Rio's main business district, and has a concentration of historic buildings, museums, and churches.

SIGHTS AT A GLANCE

Historic Buildings, Streets, Neighborhoods & Townships

Barra pp86–7 31
Confeitaria Colombo 5
Docks & Avenida Rio Branco 3
Morro do Corcovado & Cristo Redentor pp82–3 26
Lapa 8
Niterói 34
Palácio Itamaraty 30
Praça XV & Centro pp70–71 1
Quinta da Boa Vista 28
Sambódromo & Cidade do Samba 29
Theatro Municipal & Cinelândia 6

Churches & Monasteries

Catedral Metropolitana 7
Igreja de São Francisco da Penitência 4
Igreja Nossa Senhora da Glória do Outeiro 12
Mosteiro de São Bento 2

Parks & Gardens

Jardim Botânico 22

Beaches & Lagoons

Baía de Guanabara 33
Copacabana p78 17
Ipanema p79 18
Lagoa Rodrigo de Freitas 20
Leblon p79 19

Museums

Museu Carmen Miranda 14
Museu Casa de Rui Barbosa 25
Museu de Arte Moderna 11
Museu Histórico Nacional 10
Museu do Índio 23
Museu Nacional de Belas Artes 9
Museu da República 13
Museu do Rio 15
Museu Villa-Lobos 24

National Parks

Parque Nacional da Tijuca 32

Football Clubs & Stadiums

Jóquei Clube Brasileiro 21
Estádio Maracanã 27

Areas of Natural Beauty

Sugar Loaf Mountain pp76–7 16

SEE ALSO

- ***Street Finder*** pp96–101
- ***Where to Stay*** pp366–9
- ***Where to Eat*** pp394–6

KEY

- Street-by-Street area: *see pp70–71*
- International airport
- Domestic airport
- Train station
- Ferry service
- Metro station
- Post office
- Tourist information
- Highway
- Main road
- Other road
- Railroad

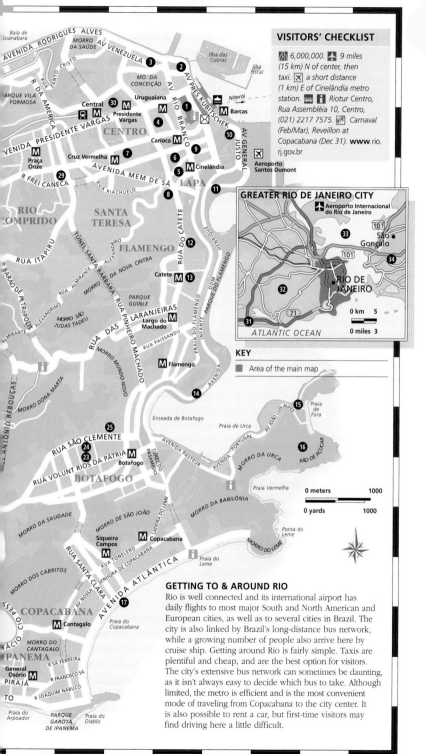

VISITORS' CHECKLIST

6,000,000. 9 miles (15 km) N of center, then taxi. a short distance (1 km) E of Cinelândia metro station. Riotur Centro, Rua Assembléia 10, Centro, (021) 2217 7575. Carnaval (Feb/Mar), Reveillon at Copacabana (Dec 31). www.rio.rj.gov.br

GREATER RIO DE JANEIRO CITY

Aeroporto Internacional do Rio de Janeiro

RIO DE JANEIRO

ATLANTIC OCEAN

0 km 5

0 miles 3

KEY

Area of the main map

0 meters 1000

0 yards 1000

GETTING TO & AROUND RIO

Rio is well connected and its international airport has daily flights to most major South and North American and European cities, as well as to several cities in Brazil. The city is also linked by Brazil's long-distance bus network, while a growing number of people also arrive here by cruise ship. Getting around Rio is fairly simple. Taxis are plentiful and cheap, and are the best option for visitors. The city's extensive bus network can sometimes be daunting, as it isn't always easy to decide which bus to take. Although limited, the metro is efficient and is the most convenient mode of traveling from Copacabana to the city center. It is also possible to rent a car, but first-time visitors may find driving here a little difficult.

Street-by-Street: Praça XV de Novembro & Centro **1**

Originally called the Largo do Paço, Praça XV de Novembro is the historic heart of Rio, even if it was only so named after the declaration of the republic on November 15, 1889. The Praça witnessed the arrival of Dom João VI of Portugal in 1808 as he fled with his court from Napoleon. The House of the Viceroy became the Paço Imperial, and for a time the square was the center of Brazil's political and commercial power. Today, Praça XV and the surrounding area is packed with historic buildings and streets. The square was given a new lease of life in the late 1980s with the restoration of the palace, which has acted as a catalyst in bringing culture and life back to the city center.

Statue of General Osório
General Manuel Luís Osório defended the Empire in the War of the Triple Alliance between 1864 and 1870 (see p53).

Nossa Senhora do Monte do Carmo once served as the royal chapel.

★ Arco do Telles
Today a pedestrian exit, Arco de Telles dates from 1757 and is all that remains of the old Senate House that was destroyed by a fire in 1790. It is Rio's only surviving colonial arch.

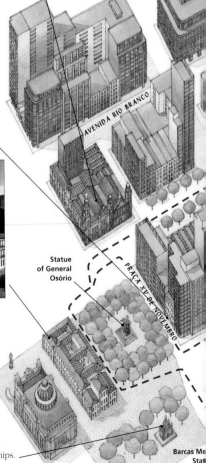

AVENIDA RIO BRANCO

PRAÇA XV DE NOVEMBRO

Statue of General Osório

★ Paço Imperial
The Paço Imperial has been the backdrop for many key events in Brazilian history, including the signing of the Lei Aurea in 1888, abolishing slavery in Brazil.

STAR SIGHTS

★ Arco do Telles

★ Paço Imperial

★ Nossa Senhora da Candelária

Chafariz da Piramide was built in 1789 to distribute fresh water to the city and to visiting ships.

Barcas Me... Stat...

★ Nossa Senhora da Candelária
One of Rio's earliest churches was built on this site in 1630. The current impressive structure dates from 1775.

0 meters 25

0 yards 25

VISITORS' CHECKLIST

Rio de Janeiro. **M** *Barcas.*
≕ *Estação de Barcas.* **Paço
Imperial** Praça XV de Novembro
48. **Map** 5 E3. *Tel* (021) 2533
4491. ◯ *noon–6pm Tue–Sun.*
Nossa Senhora da Candelária
Praça Pio X, Centro. **Map** 5 D2.
Tel (021) 2233 2324. ◯ *7am–
noon & 2–4:30pm Mon–Fri.*
Espaço Cultural da Marinha
Av Alfredo Agache, Centro.
Map 5 E2. *Tel* (021) 2104 6025.
◯ *noon–5pm Tue–Sun.*

Casa França-Brasil (Franco-Brazil Center) was opened in 1990. It is located in an 1820 customs house.

Travessa do Comércio
This photogenic pedestrian street beyond Arco do Telles is lined with bars and restaurants. Carmen Miranda lived at No. 13 as a small girl. The street is lively at lunch and in the evening when the bars fill up.

Espaço Cultural da Marinha, the Navy's cultural center, was inaugurated in 1996. Located in the old docks, the center is the starting point for tours of Baía de Guanabara.

KEY

— — — Suggested route

Detail of the gilded Baroque interior of Mosteiro de São Bento

Mosteiro de São Bento ❷

Rua Dom Gerardo 68 (entrance by elevator at No. 40), Centro. **Map** 5 D2. **Tel** *(021) 2206 8100*. Ⓜ *São Bento.* ◯ *7–11am, 2–6pm daily.* 🕮 ♿ ✝ *7:15am Mon–Sat; 8am, 10am & 6pm Sun.* **www**.osb.org.br

Benedictine monks from Bahia founded the São Bento Monastery in 1590 and much of the historic building, located on the hills of São Bento, has remained structurally untouched since it was built between 1617 and 1641. The exterior of the main building reflects the simplicity of the time of its construction and gives no hint of the opulence of the gilded Baroque interior.

A number of the works on display were carved by one of the monks, Frei Domingos da Conceição (1643–1718). They include the main altar of the monastery's church. The painting displayed on it, which was created around 1676, is dedicated to Nossa Senhora de Montserrat (Black Virgin).

São Bento is still very much a working monastery. The Benedictine monks are protective of the monastery and their work and have tried hard to keep the church from becoming simply a tourist attraction. Many areas, such as the beautiful cloisters, remain out-of-bounds except on special occasions. Mass for the public is said daily, with a full Gregorian chant at 10am on Sundays.

Visitors should dress appropriately if they wish to view the interior of the monastery.

Docks & Avenida Rio Branco ❸

Praça Mauá, Centro. **Map** 5 D2. Ⓜ *Carioca.* ♿

Though not as thriving as they once were, Rio's docks remain one of the most important in South America. The terminal in the old Touring Club do Brasil in Praça Mauá is the first port of call for visitors who arrive in Rio by ship. The docks are situated at the top end of Avenida Rio Branco, one of Brazil's important business streets. The street dates from 1904, when 590 buildings were demolished to make way for a modern central avenue, the spine of Rio's financial district. A handful of early 20th-century buildings survive, among them the glorious Theatro Municipal.

Igreja de São Francisco da Penitência ❹

Largo de Carioca 5, Centro. **Map** 5 D4. Ⓜ *Carioca.* **Tel** *(021) 2262 0197*. ◯ *9am–noon, 1–4pm Tue–Fri.* 🕮 ✎

Restored to its former glory in 2001, the church of São Francisco da Penitência is considered one of the richest and most beautiful examples

of Baroque art in Brazil. Built between 1657 and 1772, the church exhibits various works of the Portuguese artist Francisco Xavier de Brito. His art heavily influenced the Brazilian artist Aleijadinho *(see p131)*, whose own work spectacularly adorns many of the Baroque churches of Minas Gerais. One of the church's highlights is the 1738 painting of the glorification of St. Francis by Caetano da Costa Coelho, the first Brazilian painting to be done in perspective.

The neighboring Convento de Santo Antônio, dating back to 1615, is one of Rio's oldest structures. Its Baroque interiors contain priceless colonial art and *azulejos* (Portuguese tiles).

Confeitaria Colombo ❺

Rua Gonçalves Dias 32, Centro. **Map** 5 D5. **Tel** *(021) 2232 2300*. Ⓜ *Carioca.* ◯ *9:30am–8pm Mon–Fri, 9am–5pm Sat.* ♿ *limited.* **www**.confeitariacolombo.com.br

The Colombo Tearoom dates from 1894 and remains a wonderful mix of Art Nouveau and Belle Époque. Located in what was then the very heart of Rio, it was a meeting point for intellectuals, artists, and politicians. Regulars included politician Ruy Barbosa, President Getúlio Vargas, and composer Heitor Villa-Lobos.

The mirrors were shipped in from Belgium and the marble from Italy, while

Lavish interior of the historic Confeitaria Colombo

much of the original furniture is made of Brazilian jacaranda wood. Visitors can savor the atmosphere of Rio's past by eating a snack in the Bar Jardim, or a meal at the restaurant.

Theatro Municipal & Cinelândia 6

Av Rio Branco, Centro. **Map** 5 D4. **Tel** (021) 2262 3935. M Cinelândia. 🆗 🛦 www.theatromunicipal.rj. gov.br

Rio's Municipal Theater, built between 1905 and 1909, is the main venue for the city's ballet, opera, and orchestra (including the Brazilian Symphony Orchestra), and continues to attract the very best talent from both Brazil and abroad. Illustrious names include Nijinsky, Sarah Bernhard, Anna Pavlova, and Luciano Pavarotti, to name just a few.

Farther south along Avenida Rio Branco is the heart of Cinelândia or "cinema land," the area around which the city's movie houses sprang up in the 1920s. Many are still in operation, most notably the Cine Odeon BR which opened in 1926 and closed in 1999 to be renovated. It reopened a year later as the headquarters of the Rio Film Festival. Other buildings in the area include the Museu Nacional de Belas Artes *(see p74)*, Biblioteca Nacional, and Palácio Pedro Ernesto.

Stained-glass window at the Catedral Metropolitana

Catedral Metropolitana 7

Av República do Chile 245, Centro. **Map** 5 D4. **Tel** (021) 2240 2669. M Cinelândia. ◯ 7:30am–6pm daily. 🛦 ✝ 11am Mon–Fri, 10am Sat & Sun. **Museu Arquidiocesano de Arte Sacra** ◯ 10am–4pm Wed, Sat & Sun (other days by appt only). 🛦 www.catedral.com.br

Rio's striking Metropolitan Cathedral, with its truncated conical shape, was conceptualized by Ivo Calliari (1918–2005), a Catholic priest.

The cathedral's first stone was laid on January 20, 1964, and the inauguration of the still unfinished building was held 12 years later, in 1976, marking the 300th anniversary of the Diocese of Rio.

Standing 248 ft (75 m) high with no interior columns, this huge cathedral has a seating capacity of 5,000 and can accommodate up to 20,000 people standing. The interior is dominated by four magnificent stained-glass windows that stretch 197 ft (60 m) to the ceiling. They represent the apostolic (yellow), Catholic (blue), ecclesiastical (green), and saintly (red) traditions.

The **Museu Arquidiocesano de Arte Sacra** (Sacred Art Museum) in the basement includes historical items in its collection, such as the baptismal fonts used for christening the Brazilian royal family, the golden rose gifted to Princess Isabel by Pope Leo XIII to celebrate her signing the abolition of slavery, and the throne of Dom Pedro II.

Lapa 8

Lapa, Centro. M Carioca.

The most famous image of the area known as Lapa is the **Arcos da Lapa**, an aqueduct built in 1724 to bring water down from the Santa Teresa forest to the public fountain in Largo da Carioca. In 1896, it became the base for the viaduct that carries streetcars to and from the city center.

Lapa has always had a slightly bohemian feel and during the first half of the 1900s was the center of Rio's alternative nightlife. The area still boasts a vibrant nightlife, attracting people from all over the city who come looking for the best of Brazilian music. Key hot spots include Rio Scenarium, Carioca de Gema, and Dama da Noite. In 2004, the area saw the return of the **Circo Voador** (Flying Circus), now held in a purpose-built music venue that replaced the earlier tent of the 1980s and early 1990s. Many of the leading names in contemporary Brazilian music – most recently, Seu Jorge – got their first break at the Circo Voador.

🎪 **Circo Voador**
Rua dos Arcos, Lapa. **Tel** (021) 2533 0354. ◯ for shows only. 🖼 🛦

Opulent façade of the Theatro Municipal

A Batalha do Avaí (1877) by Pedro Américo, Museu Nacional de Belas Artes

Museu Nacional de Belas Artes ❾

Av Rio Branco 199, Centro.
Map 5 E4. *Tel (021) 2240 0068.* Ⓜ
Cinelândia. ☐ *10am–6pm Tue–Fri, 2–6pm Sat, Sun & public hols.* 🅿 *free on Sun.* 🚻 ♿ www.mnba.gov.br

The National Museum of Fine Arts is one of the most important permanent art collections in Latin America. The building in which it is housed dates from 1908.

The collection, which has over 16,000 pieces in its archive, features Brazilian artists from the colonial period as well as from the 19th and 20th centuries. Artists include Frans Post, who painted Brazilian landscapes in classical Dutch style, the Frenchman Jean Baptiste Debret, who painted the immortal *Battle of Guararapes* (1879), Vitor Meireles, and Pedro Américo, whose *A Batalha do Avaí* (1877) is one of the largest paintings in the world painted on an easel. There is also a gallery for contemporary exhibits.

The gallery has an extensive collection of non-Brazilian works and a particularly fine selection of Baroque Italian art dating from the 17th and 18th centuries. The museum was created on the basis of a prized art collection, brought to Brazil from Europe by Portugal's King Dom João VI and his court when they fled Napoleon in 1808 *(see p52).*

Sculpture, Museu Nacional de Belas Artes

Museu Histórico Nacional ❿

Praça Marechal Âncora. **Map** 5 F4.
Tel (021) 2550 9224. Ⓜ *Cinelândia.* ☐ *10am–5:30pm Tue–Fri, 2–6pm Sat, Sun & public hols.* 🅿 🚻 ♿ *restricted.* www.museuhistoriconacional.com.br

Founded in 1922, the country's leading history museum recounts the history of Brazil up to 1889. Its collection of 287,000 pieces includes everything from paintings and coins to carriages and rarities such as the pen used by Princess Isabel to sign the decree abolishing slavery. Apart from displaying period furniture, 19th-century firearms, and locomotives, the museum also traces Brazil's colonial past in its charts and written declarations. The building is one of the oldest in Rio, with a portion belonging to Santiago Fort, dating from 1603.

Museu de Arte Moderna ⓫

Av Infante Dom Henrique 85, Centro. **Map** 5 F5. *Tel (021) 2240 4944.* Ⓜ *Cinelândia.* ☐ *noon–6pm Tue–Fri, noon–7pm Sat, Sun & public hols.* 🅿 🚻 ♿ www.mamrio.org.br

Rio's Modern Art Museum (MAM) has one of the best collections of 20th-century art in Brazil, surpassed only by MASP in São Paulo *(see p143).* The museum also houses one of the largest archives of Brazilian films.

The strikingly modern building that houses the MAM was far ahead of its time in its design and architecture when it was built in 1958. In 1978, a major fire destroyed many of its irreplaceable exhibits, including the works of Miró, Picasso, Salvador Dalí, Max Ernst, and René Magritte. It has taken time and the generosity of collectors in Brazil and abroad to rebuild the collection. Today, the MAM is once more a highly regarded institution, not only for its own archive but also for the visiting exhibitions from around the world that it stages through the year.

Located close to its gardens is a monument to the victims of World War II. Inaugurated in 1960, it represents two arms raised with hands outstretched in prayer. In 1980, Pope John Paul II said mass from the steps of the monument to a crowd of more than 2 million people. Below the monument is a museum describing Brazil's participation in the Allied operations, known as the Italian Campaign, in and around Italy between 1944 and 1945.

Entrance to the Museu de Arte Moderna (MAM)

Igreja Nossa Senhora da Glória do Outeiro rising above tree tops

Igreja Nossa Senhora da Glória do Outeiro ⑫

Praça Nossa Senhora da Glória 135, Glória. **Tel** (021) 2557 4600. Ⓜ Glória. ⬭ 8am–5pm Tue–Fri, 8am–noon Sat & Sun. ➕ 8:30am Sat, 9–11am Sun. **www.** outeirodagloria.org.br

Most visitors to downtown Rio cannot help but notice the beautiful octagonal church of Our Lady of Gloria, as it sits majestically on top of a hill beside the freeways cutting through Flamengo Park.

The spot where the church was built, in 1714, was first used as a place of worship in 1608, when the image of Our Lady of Gloria was placed in a grotto. The land was donated to the church in 1699 by the nobleman Cláudio Gurgel do Amaral.

The church, which was completed in 1739, came to national attention when it became the favorite place of worship for Dom Pedro VI and his family after their arrival from Portugal in 1808. Known for its hand-painted tiles dating from the 1730s, it was declared a national monument by President Vargas in 1937.

The church can be reached either by car, or by foot up the steps known as Ladeira de Nossa Senhora. It is also possible to take a small cable car that starts from Rua do Russel 312. There are views across the bay and there is also a small sacred art museum.

Museu da República ⑬

Rua do Catete 153, Catete. **Tel** (021) 2558 6350. Ⓜ Catete. ⬭ noon–5pm Tue, Thu & Fri; 2–5pm Wed; 2–6pm Sat, Sun & public hols. ⬚ ⬚ **www.**museudarepublica.org.br

The story of Brazil's history, as told by the Museum of the Republic, picks up where the Museu Histórico Nacional left off. It begins with the Proclamation of the Republic in 1889, and covers events until 1960, when the capital and the then President Kubitschek moved from Rio de Janeiro to Brasília. What makes the museum particularly special is that its building, constructed between 1858 and 1866, was the presidential residence from 1897 until 1954.

A portrait of Carmen Miranda

In that year, President Getúlio Vargas (see pp56–7), Brazil's most influential statesman who was president for 24 years, committed suicide in his bedroom. The third floor is dedicated to an exhibition about the life and work of Vargas. His bedroom has been preserved exactly as it used to be when he lived here. In total, the palace was home to 18 Brazilian presidents, all of whom feature in the museum's various exhibits.

Apart from the historical museum and palace, there is also an attractive garden on the grounds.

Attractive garden outside the Museu da República

Museu Carmen Miranda ⑭

Av Rui Barbosa, Flamengo. **Tel** (021) 2299 5586. Ⓜ Flamengo. ⬭ 11am–5pm Tue–Fri; 2–5pm Sat, Sun & public hols. ♿ **www.**sec.rj.gov.br/webmuseu/mcm.htm

Fans of Carmen Miranda will not want to miss this small museum tucked away in Flamengo Park. One of the most famous Brazilians of all time, Maria do Carmo Miranda da Cunha was born in Portugal in 1909, but moved to Rio with her family when she was a baby. Carmen cut her first record in 1929. However, it was the big screen that would make her a global star. Her first film in 1932 shot her to international stardom, and in 1941, she became the first South American to be honored with a star on the Hollywood Walk of Fame. After her death on August 5, 1955, her body was returned to Rio where a crowd of almost 500,000 watched her burial.

The museum exhibits iconographic costumes and artifacts belonging to Carmen, as well as many of her records and films.

Museu do Rio ⑮

Av João Luiz Alves 13, Urca. ⬭ due to open in 2007. ♿

The Museum of Rio is a new undertaking that aims at giving the city its very own museum. Located on Urca beach in the looming shadow of the spectacular Sugar Loaf mountain, the museum is housed in the historic Cassino da Urca – the city's main showhouse between 1933 and 1946.

Between 1950 and 1980, the Cassino served as a television studio. Work began in 2005 to restore and adapt it into a museum covering the history of Rio and the advent of television in the city.

Sugar Loaf Mountain ⑯

Guarding the entrance to Guanabara Bay, the monolithic granite and quartz Sugar Loaf rises 1,300 ft (396 m) above the waters of the southern Atlantic Ocean. From the summit, it is easy to understand why the early explorers believed that they had sailed into the mouth of a great river they christened Rio de Janeiro. The Sugar Loaf experience takes in two mountains, Morro do Urca and Pão de Açúcar (Sugar Loaf). It is possible to scale both these mountains via organized climbs on most weekends. Demanding less effort, the cable car, originally opened in 1912, stops at the 705-ft (224-m) high Morro da Urca before ascending to the summit.

The original 1912 cable car, a remarkable feat of its times

The summit provides unforgettable views out over Copacabana, Ipanema, and the scenic Corcovado and Tijuca.

Pão de Açúcar
The name of Sugar Loaf, adopted in the 19th century, is assumed to have been derived from the mountain's shape, which resembles conical clay molds used earlier to refine sugar. The Tupi Indians, however, called it "Pau-nh-Acucua" (high, pointed, or isolated hill).

A scene from the film *Moonraker*

JAMES BOND'S MOONRAKER

In 1979, Sugar Loaf and the cable car formed the backdrop for a main action sequence in *Moonraker*, with Roger Moore playing James Bond. In real life, the Great Train Robber, Ronald Biggs, was kidnapped in 1981 by a group of British mercenaries from a restaurant, which was then located next to the cable car station. Ironically, during a first kidnap bid in 1979, the kidnappers had claimed to be part of the *Moonraker* crew.

Rock Climbing
Since British nanny Henrietta Carstairs made the first recorded solo ascent in 1817, climbing the smooth Sugar Loaf has become a popular sport, with over 60 known routes to the towering summit.

Cable Car Ride

The current Italian cable system carries as many as 1,360 passengers every hour. The glass walls of the cable car allow sweeping views of the city.

VISITORS' CHECKLIST

Av Pasteur 520, Praia Vermelha,
Urca. 🚌 107, 500, 511 & 512.
🖼 🍴 🛍 www.bondinho.
com.br **Helisight** *Tel* (021)
2511 2141. **Cable Car** Praia
Vermelha. 🕐 8am–10pm.

Helisight, with a heliport base at Morro da Urca, offers flights around Sugar Loaf and Corcovado *(see pp82–3).*

Morro da Urca

The flat summit of Morro da Urca has restaurants, bars, and a theater that hosts popular shows, concerts, and even Carnaval balls.

Wooded Trails

A series of trails that lead to a number of good climbing locations wind their way up to the summit. The trails are also an ideal place to spot marmosets.

Cable car station at Praia Vermelha

Boats can be hired at many key locations for an enjoyable ride in the calm waters to the base of Sugar Loaf.

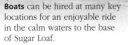

Rio City at Night

The city of Rio de Janeiro boasts a stunning nightscape. The magnificent Sugar Loaf remains illuminated, even in the dead of the night, by powerful 1,000-watt projectors.

Bustling Copacabana beach, popular with locals and holiday-makers

Copacabana ⑰

M *Siqueira Campos.* **ℹ** *Av Princesa Isabel 183, (021) 2542 8080.*

One of the world's most celebrated beaches, Copacabana is the center of Rio's tourist trade. On New Year's eve, the neighborhood becomes Rio's spiritual and festive heart, as millions of Cariocas and visitors take to the beach to celebrate, party, and honor Yemanjá, Goddess of the Sea.

The name Copacabana, or "Copa Caguana" (Luminous Place) in Quechua, an ancient language still spoken in Peru, was given by the Incas to a lovely site by the Lagoa Titicaca, where they built a temple. In the 17th century, the captain of a Spanish galleon erected a chapel in honor of Our Lady of Copacabana, who came to his aid during a shipwreck.

Built in 1914, on the promontory of the chapel as Rio's defense against attack, the **Forte de Copacabana** offers scenic views of the entire sweep of Copacabana.

The main attraction of Copacabana is the beach which, along with Leme, constitutes a magnificent 3-mile (5-km) stretch from Le Meridien hotel in the north on the corner of Avenida Princesa Isabel, to the Forte de Copacabana and Sofitel Rio in the south. Until 1892, it had been a leading trek for those from the city to reach Copacabana. In that year, a tunnel was cut through from Botafogo to Copacabana, followed by a second tunnel in 1904 that allowed the trams to reach the beach. The real turning point, however, was the creation of the Neo-Classical **Copacabana Palace** hotel *(see p368)*, a part of the fabric of Rio life since its

opening in 1923. It has hosted both authentic royalty and the royalty of the entertainment world, including Queen Elizabeth II and Marlene Dietrich. The hotel continues to draw celebrities, as well as gays and transvestites.

The beachfront kiosk bars lining Avenue Atlântica – the road that runs the length of the beach – are popular. The entire length of Copacabana is divided into stations *(postos)*. Postos 5 and 6 attract older residents and *favela* youngsters. The fresh catch of the day can be bought at Posto 7 – at the southern end – known as the *posto de pescadores* (fisherman's post).

🏛 Forte de Copacabana
*Praça Eugênio Franco 1. **Tel** (021) 3201 4049.* ◯ *10am–8pm Tue–Sun.* 🎟 📷 👟

The imposing exterior of the Copacabana Palace Hotel

MAP OF COPACABANA, IPANEMA & LEBLON

Key to Symbols *see back flap*

Exterior of an upmarket jewelry store in Ipanema

Ipanema ⑱

Ⓜ *General Osório.* **Feira Hippie de Ipanema** Praça General de Osório. ☐ *8am–6pm Sun.* **www**. feirahippie.hpg.ig.com.br

Almost as famous as Copacabana, Ipanema shot into the limelight in the 1960s with the globally-famous song written by Antônio Jobim and Vinícius de Moraes, "The Girl from Ipanema."

The actual name of this fashionable area is credited to the native Tupi-Guaraní who called the area Y-panema, or "rough water." The first non-native residents moved into the area around 1884, and today Ipanema and

THE GIRL FROM IPANEMA

One of the most played and recorded songs in popular music history, "The Girl from Ipanema," or "A Garota de Ipanema" was written in 1962, by Antônio Carlos Jobim and Vinícius de Moraes. The duo are said to have been inspired by a sensual girl from Ipanema, Helô Pinheiro. A year later, the recording of the song's most famous version took place in New York's A&R Studio, featuring João

Astrud Gilberto

and Astrud Gilberto, in the Portuguese and English versions, respectively. In 1964, Stan Getz, Jobim, and the Gilbertos took *bossa nova* to a global audience with the release of *Getz/Gilberto*. With "The Girl from Ipanema" as the opening track, the album stayed on the US charts for 96 weeks and won four Grammys.

neighboring Leblon are considered the most desirable places to live in Rio. More residential than Copacabana, Ipanema is also more stylish, with its back streets dotted with chic boutiques, bars, restaurants, and nightclubs.

The most prestigious address in Rio is Avenida Vieira Souto, while running parallel, two streets back, is Rua Visconde de Pirajá, the backbone to the Ipanema shopping experience. At the Copacabana end is Praça General Osório, the public square that plays host to Rio's popular **Feira Hippie de Ipanema** (Hippie Fair), every Sunday. The fair has been a part of life in Ipanema and Rio since opening in 1968.

The mile-long stretch of Ipanema beach runs from Leblon in the west, up to Arpoador in the east. Arpoador extends the beach by another half mile, and is popular with the surf set.

Leblon ⑲

▥ *Copacabana.*

For many years, Leblon sat in the shadow of Ipanema. But today it is considered as fashionable and desirable as its neighbor, with perhaps an even greater density and mix of bars, clubs, and restaurants.

Rua Dias Ferreira, at the most westerly point, boasts a particularly eclectic mix. Like Ipanema, there are only a few hotels along the beachfront Avenida Delfim Moreira.

While the beaches of Copacabana and Leme flow seamlessly into each other, Leblon and Ipanema are separated by Jardim de Alá and the canal that links the Lagoa Rodrigo de Freitas with the sea. The 1-mile (2-km) long Leblon is said to have been given its name in honor of a blond foreigner, one of its first residents in the area. The nationality of "Le Blond" is debatable. Some scholars say that he was French, while others surmise he was Dutch.

Leblon is the headquarters of Clube de Regatas Flamengo, of which the most famous is the Flamengo Football Club, the World Club Champions in 1981.

MORRO DE SÃO JOÃO

Ⓜ Siqueira Campos

Ⓜ Arcoverde

AV. PRINCESA ISABEL

COPACABANA

Copacabana Palace Hotel ★

ⓘ

▨ Praia do Copacabana

0 meters 500
0 yards 500

The exclusive Leblon neighborhood and its fashionable beach

View of Lagoa Rodrigo de Freitas and Jóquei Clube Brasileiro from Corcovado

Lagoa Rodrigo de Freitas 🄴

Lagoa. **Map** 2 A3. 🚻 ♿
www.lagoarodrigodefreitas.com.br

The picturesque Lagoa Rodrigo de Freitas, or Lagoa (lagoon) as it is often called, sits at the foot of Corcovado peak and separates the Serra da Carioca from Ipanema and Leblon. A full circuit of the lagoon is about 5 miles (8 km), and is popular with joggers, cyclists, and parents with children in prams. There are plenty of halts en route, with kiosks selling everything from coconut water to full meals. Some kiosks even offer live music in the evenings.

The Lagoa is also bordered by more conventional restaurants and bars, especially along the Ipanema stretch. One of Rio's most traditional places, **Bar Lagoa** *(see p396)* opened here in 1934. Along the northern shore, highlights include **Mistura Fina** *(see p93)*, a top-notch venue for jazz and Brazilian music, and Claude Troisgros' **Olympe** *(see p396)*, which, despite a change in name since it opened in 1983, is still one of Rio's best restaurants.

Several sports clubs are also located here. Among the most famous are the Jockey Club Brasileiro, the **Sociedade Hípica Brasileira**, the city's main equestrian center, and the headquarters of the Clube Regatas do Flamengo. Flamengo, along with Vasco da Gama, Fluminense, and Botafogo, is one of Brazil's top soccer teams and has

won the National and South American titles on many occasions. All clubs have rowing divisions as the Lagoa is Brazil's main rowing center. Several international regattas have been held here.

Visitors can go boating, as *pedallos* and other craft are available for rent. It is also possible to hire bicycles.

The **Fundação Eva Klabin** is one of Rio's prolific cultural centers and museums. Its exhibits are part of the private collection of Eva Klabin, whose family made a fortune in paper in the mid-20th century.

The scenic **Parque da Catacumba** around Lagoa is interspersed with sculptures by artists Roberto Moriconi, Bruno Giorgi, and Caribé.

> 🏛 **Fundação Eva Klabin**
> Av Epitácio 2480. **Tel** *(021) 2523 3471.* ◯ *9am–6pm Mon–Fri, visits by appointment only.*

> 🌿 **Parque da Catacumba**
> Av Epitácio Pessoa 3000. **Tel** *(021) 2521 5540.* ◯ *8am–5pm daily.*

> 🏛 **Sociedade Hípica Brasileira**
> Av Borges de Medeiros 2448. **Tel** *(021) 2156 0191.* ◯ *only for events.* ♿ ♿

Jóquei Clube Brasileiro 🄵

Rua Jardim Botânico 1003, Gávea. **Map** 1 A2. **Tel** *(021) 2512 9988.* Ⓜ *Botafogo.* 🚌 ◯ *6:30pm onward Mon, 3:30pm onward Fri, 1:30pm onward Sat & Sun.* ♿ ♿
www.jcb.com.br

With a great view of the Lagoa and the Corcovado mountain, the Jockey Club has one of the most spectacular

settings of any racecourse in the world. Races are held four days a week, all year round, so it is easy to catch the action. The club will allow even non-members and visitors into the members' stand to enjoy the race.

The track first opened in 1926, with the main stand designed in a Louis XV style. In total, there are five stands, a paddock, a turf track, two sand tracks, and an equestrian village. The biggest race of the year – and one of South America's most important – is the Grande Prêmio Brasil do Turfe, that was first run in 1933. It traditionally takes place in August each year.

Jardim Botânico 🄶

Rua Jardim Botânico 920 & 1008, Gávea. **Map** 1 A1. **Tel** *(021) 3874 1808.* 🏠 ◯ *8am–5pm daily.* ◐ *Dec 25 & Jan 1.* 🎫 📷 ♿ *restricted.* www.jbrj.gov.br

One of the most fascinating gardens in the world, Rio's Jardim Botânico was founded in 1808 by the Prince Regent, Dom João VI. Originally meant to acclimatize plants and spices coming in from the Orient and the East Indies, it later became the Royal Garden, and opened to the public in 1822. Among its many illustrious visitors were Charles Darwin in 1832, and Albert Einstein in 1925.

Today, Jardim Botânico includes 205 acres (83 ha) of natural rainforest, and is

A track lined with palm trees in Jardim Botânico

home to many species of plants, as well as innumerable types of birds and animals. However, the garden's signature are the 200 imperial palms that line its main avenues.

Jardim Botânico has other attractions within its grounds. These include Rio's original gunpowder factory dating from 1808, the old gates of the Fine Arts Academy, and the Empress's Mansion, which became the headquarters of the National School of Tropical Botany in 2001.

Museu do Índio ㉓

Rua das Palmeiras 55, Botafogo.
Tel (021) 2286 8899. M *Botafogo.*
◷ 9am–5:30pm Tue–Fri; 1–5pm Sat, Sun & public hols. 📷 📷 **www.**
museudoindio.org.br

Founded in 1953, the Museum of the Indian is run by the National Indian Foundation (Funai) with the aim of giving people an insight into the lives of Brazil's Indian and indigenous groups. Housed in a 19th-century mansion, this dynamic institution has over 14,000 indigenous artifacts, 50,000 photographs, and over 200 films. With 16,000 books and magazines, it also has one of the most complete libraries covering topics related to indigenous peoples.

There are several permanent exhibits in the gardens, including a Guaraní house and farm field, a Xingu kitchen and house, and Kuarup ritual tree trunks. There is also a well-stocked store that sells genuine indigenous artifacts.

Museu Villa-Lobos ㉔

Rua Sorocaba 200, Botafogo.
Tel (021) 2266 1024. M *Botafogo.*
◷ 10am–5:30pm Mon–Fri. 📷
www.museuvillalobos.org.br

With over 1,000 compositions to his credit, Heitor Villa-Lobos (1897–1959) is considered one of the greatest composers in Latin America (*see p32*). It is believed that it was through his work that Brazilian music first became popular abroad, eventually gaining universal appeal with the advent of *bossa nova*.

The Villa-Lobos Museum, which moved to a stately 19th-century mansion in Botafogo in 1986, helps organize the Villa-Lobos Festival that begins on the anniversary of his death, November 17, each year. His second wife, Arminda Neves d'Almeida, set up the museum in 1960, one year after his death. Its aim is to preserve the composer's personal collection of artifacts and keep his work alive. Exhibits include his books, music scores, photographs, and instruments.

Villa-Lobos's best-known work is his cycle of the nine *Bachianas Brasileiras*, which pays homage to both Bach and Brazilian folk music. Such was his versatility that he wrote a variety of music from *choros* (an upbeat waltz or polka), concertos, symphonies, and orchestral works, to chamber music, operas, and ballets, as well as guitar and solo piano pieces.

Stately building housing the Museu Casa de Rui Barbosa

Museu Casa de Rui Barbosa ㉕

Rua São Clemente 134, Botafogo.
Tel (021) 3289 4600. M *Botafogo.*
◷ 10am–5pm Tue–Sun. 📷 📷
www.casaruibarbosa.gov.br

A renowned politician, diplomat, and jurist, Rui Barbosa de Oliveira (1849–1923) helped shape several important Brazilian policies, including those pertaining to direct elections and the abolition of slavery. He made his mark internationally during the 1907 Peace Conference at the Hague, where he argued that all countries should be treated equally. Barbosa contested twice for the Brazilian presidency – in 1910 and 1919 – but lost on both occasions.

Barbosa was also a great essayist and was one of the founders of the Brazilian Academy of Letters. He later became its second president. He was eventually elected as a judge to the International Court of Justice at the Hague.

The 1850 building that houses the Rui Barbosa Museum was the statesman's home from 1895 until his death in 1923. When it opened to the public in 1930, it was the first private residence in Brazil to be turned into a museum. The museum showcases a collection of Barbosa's personal possessions, such as furniture and art, and a library, containing 200 of his own works.

Indigenous roundhouse on the grounds of Museu do Índio

Morro do Corcovado & Cristo Redentor 26

Cog train logo

The 2,316-ft (706-m) Corcovado mountain derives its name from *corcova* (hunchback), which describes the physical appearance of the mountain itself. On the summit, the iconic Cristo Redentor statue towers over Rio, and is Brazil's most recognizable landmark. It was officially inaugurated in 1931 to mark the centenary of Brazil's independence. The enormous statue sits in the center of the gorgeous tropical jungle of Parque Nacional da Tijuca.

Making the Head
Work on the statue began in Paris in 1926, with French sculptor Paul Landowski working on the head and hands. The head alone weighs 30 tons.

THE STATUE
Having been shipped from France to Brazil, the 98-ft (30-m) statue was faced in limestone and hauled up the mountain by rail to be assembled and attached to supporting pillars.

Wide Open Arms
The entire Rio City is embraced by Christ, and the statue's open arms are seen as a testament to the warmth of the Brazilians.

MORRO
FORMIG

ESTR DO

ALTO DA
BOA VISTA

CORCOVADO

MORRO
CORCOVA

Cr
Reder

Famous Visitors
Pope John Paul II, Pope Pius XII, and Albert Einstein are some of the famous people to have visited Corcovado.

The chapel at the base of the statue can accommodate 150 people.

Escalators link the base to the train station and car park.

The pedestal, on which the statue stands, is 26 ft (8 m) high.

STAR FEATURES

★ Museu Internacional de Arte Naïf

★ Stunning Views

★ **Museu Internacional de Arte Naïf**
The museum has one of the largest collections of naive art in the world, featuring more than 6,000 works, dating from the 15th century to the present.

VISITORS' CHECKLIST

Morro do Corcovado. 🚌 513 from Rua Cosme Velho, 8:30am–8pm daily. 🚌 180, 184, 583 & 584. 🅿 at the base of Cristo Redentor. 🛈 Corcovado, (021) 2492 2252. ◯ 8:30am–6:30pm daily (entrance at Parque Nacional da Tijuca). **www**.corcovado.com.br

Largo do Boticário is a lovely square surrounded by seven private houses. Colonial in appearance, the houses date from around 1920.

CENTRO RIO
DE JANEIRO

Largo do
Boticário

COSME
VELHO

Estação da Estrada
de Ferro Corcovado

Museu
Internacional
de Arte Naïf

ENTRO RIO
E JANEIRO

ALMIRANTE

MORRO DONA MARTA

SILVESTRE

ESTR MIRANTE DONA MARTA

R DAS PAINEIRAS

PARQUE
NACIONAL
DA TIJUCA

Mirante Dona Marta offers splendid views of Rio City.

TÚNEL ANTÔNIO/REBOUÇAS
TÚNEL ANDRÉ REBOUÇAS

Cog Train
Passing through the dense Atlantic rainforest, the train ride up the summit is a plus. Originally built in 1882 by Dom Pedro II, the current Swiss train dates from 1979.

PARQUE NACIONAL DA TIJUCA
The statue of Christ sits in this scenic national park, which contains the world's largest urban forest – Floresta da Tijuca. Dotted with natural springs, the park is home to more than 200 species of birds and several small mammals. It draws regular crowds of resident Cariocas, especially at the weekend *(see p88)*.

0 km   2
0 miles   2

KEY

▬▬ Major road

══ Other road

══ Minor road

▬ Cog train route

= = Tunnels

‒ ‒ Park boundary

🚩 Cog train station

☀ Viewpoint

★ **Stunning Views**
Corcovado is located right in the center of Rio and can be seen from most areas of the city. The views over and across Rio from the summit offer a sweeping aerial panorama.

Estádio Maracanã  ㉗

Rua Prof. Eurico Rabelo (gate 18), Maracanã. *Tel* *(021) 2299 2936.* M *Maracanã.* ⬜ *9am–5pm for tours (not on game days).* 🎥 📷 ♿ www.sec.rj.gov.br/webmuseu/ me.htm

Rio's Maracanã Stadium is one of the most famous soccer grounds in the world. It is also the largest, having hosted crowds of up to 200,000 people.

The stadium, which was refurbished for the 2007 Pan-American Games, was built for the 1950 World Cup and inaugurated on June 16, the same year, with a game between Rio and São Paulo.

The first game played by the Brazilian team took place on June 24, 1950, with Brazil beating Mexico 4–0. A month later, a crowd of almost 200,000 tested the stadium's capacity to see Brazil play Uruguay in the final game. Brazil lost 2–1, and thus began its eternal rivalry with Uruguay.

It is not only soccer that has set stadium records. Big artists have attracted massive crowds to the Maracanã, including Frank Sinatra, Paul McCartney, Kiss, Madonna, the Rolling Stones, Sting, Tina Turner, and the second "Rock in Rio" Festival. Pope John Paul II's public appearances in 1980 and 1997 were also attended by thousands.

The Maracanã Stadium can be visited on the days of soccer matches and concerts *(see p94),* or as part of a daily guided tour that takes visitors behind the scenes and onto the pitch.

Rio Zoo's main gate, gifted to Dom Pedro I by an English aristocrat

Quinta da Boa Vista ㉘

Av Pedro II (between Rua Almirante Baltazar & Rua Dom Meinrdo, São Cristóvão). M *São Cristóvão.* **Museu Nacional** *Tel (021) 2568 8262.* ⬜ *10am–4pm Tue–Sun.* ⬤ *Dec 25, Jan 1, Carnaval & Good Friday.* 🎥 📷 **Jardim Zoológico** *Tel (021) 2569 2024.* ⬜ *9am–4:30pm Tue–Sun.*

The Quinta da Boa Vista, the landscaped grounds of a former royal estate, includes the **Museu Nacional** and the **Jardim Zoológico** (Rio Zoo). Founded by Dom João VI in 1818, the Museu Nacional is the country's oldest scientific institution, which started out as the House of Birds before becoming the Royal Museum, the Imperial Museum, and, finally, the National Museum.

Its permanent exhibits cover a variety of fields from archaeology, biodiversity, and botany to ethnology, geology, and palaeontology. A part of the collection belonged to Emperor Pedro II, a botanist, and his wife, the Empress

Teresa Cristina, who was an archaeologist. The museum's gardens and the former royal palace are an attraction in their own right, and their lakes and grottos are a big draw on the weekends. They were landscaped by the French architect Auguste Glaziou in 1869 and cover an area of 38 acres (15 ha).

The Jardim Zoológico is considered one of the best in the world and is Brazil's oldest zoo, having been founded in 1888. Covering 30 acres (12 ha), it is home to approximately 350 species and more than 2,100 animals, including one of the most complete collections of Brazilian mammals and butterflies. The zoo also boasts an excellent aviary and an aquarium that houses a variety of fascinating Brazilian river species.

The zoo's beautiful main entrance was a wedding gift, presented to Dom Pedro I and the Empress Leopoldina by an English aristocrat in the early 19th century.

Sambódromo & Cidade do Samba ㉙

Av Marquês de Sapucaí, Centro. **Map** 4 A4. *Tel (021) 2563 9000.* M *Praça XI.* ♿ **Cidade do Samba** Rua Rivadávia Correa 60, Gamboa. *Tel (021) 2213 2503.* ⬜ *9am–5pm Wed–Mon; shows: 9am–11pm Thu.* ♿ www.cidadedosambarj.com.br

The Sambódromo, or Passarela do Samba, is where Rio's famous *samba* schools parade each February during Carnaval *(see pp64–5).*

Before Carnaval was as popular as it is today, the schools simply paraded on the streets and people stood on the sidewalk, and later, on specially built stands. As the crowds got bigger, the disruption caused by the building of the stands each year meant another solution had to be found.

The renowned Brazilian architect, Oscar Niemeyer *(see p295),* came up with a permanent solution. He built what is today the Sambódromo, which was inaugurated in

Aerial view of the spectacular Estádio Maracanã

The Sambódromo, venue of Rio's annual Carnaval

time for the 1984 Carnaval. In order to complement the Sambódromo, a large complex, known as the **Cidade do Samba** (City of Samba), was established in 2005. This space is used by the main *samba* schools to build their floats and make their vibrant costumes.

Throughout the year, visitors are allowed in to watch the preparations and see how a *samba* school puts on its parade.

Palácio Itamaraty ㉚

Av Marechal Floriano 196, Centro. **Map** 4 B3. *Tel (021) 2253 2828.* Ⓜ *Palácio Itamaraty.* ☐ *1–4pm Mon, Wed & Fri.* ☒ *2pm, 3pm & 4pm daily.*

The Itamaraty Palace, a rare example of Neo-Classical architecture in Rio, was built between 1852 and 1853. It acted as the headquarters of the Brazilian Foreign Service from 1899 until 1970, when

the department finally moved to Brasília. The palace was named for the man who built it, the Baron of Itamaraty. Its close links with the Foreign Service over a period of six decades has made the name "Itamaraty" synonymous with the Brazilian Foreign Office.

The palace's most notable resident was a foreign minister, José Maria da Silva Paranhos (1845–1912), the Baron of Rio Branco, an outstanding statesman who helped shape South America as we know it today.

Presently, the Itamaraty Palace houses the Museu Histórico e Diplomático (Diplomatic and Historical Museum), established in 1955. Tours of the palace and the museum reveal some of the Foreign Service's most important treasures, many of which, including furniture and paintings, date from the 19th century. There is also an archive of historic documents, as well as the Foreign Office's prized collection of maps.

RIO'S FAVELAS

As much a part of the city's landscape as Corcovado and Sugar Loaf, Rio's *favelas* are famous, lately due to their prominence in Fernando Meirelles' 2002 film, *Cidade de Deus* (City of God). They are often erroneously referred to as slums, and while some are, the majority are simply Rio's main areas of poor housing. What started as one or two shacks on a hillside has slowly grown into cities in their own right. Estimates suggest that there are now as many as 800 *favelas* in Rio, and up to 20 percent of the city's population may now live in these areas. Some *favelas* have grown to giant communities, such as Rocinha in São Conrado, with over 150,000 residents. Others, such as Pavão, Cantagalo, Vidigal, and Chapéu Mangueira, are strategically located in hilly Zona Sul areas offering breathtaking views.

Favelas are complex and vibrant communities, deriving their name from the hardy *favela* plant. Many still have drug lords who run *boca de fumos*, where narcotics are openly sold and violence is not uncommon. However, people's conceptions that these ghettos are dangerous warrens full of criminals simply is not true, as the majority of people who live here are law-abiding citizens working in low-paying jobs. That said, it is still advisable only to visit these areas as part of a guided tour. There are now several good tours on offer. The most traditional tour is organized by Marcelo Armstrong, who was brought up in an apartment block adjoining the Vila Canoas *favela*. He and his team have been escorting visitors around Vila Canoas and Rocinha since 1992. The tours offer valuable insights into the lives of thousands of Rio's less privileged citizens.

Rocinha, located in São Conrado, one of Rio's largest and most complex *favelas*

Barra ㉛

The fastest growing suburb of Rio, Barra da Tijuca houses the RioCentro, Latin America's largest convention and exhibition center, and the Sítio Roberto Burle Marx, one of the best collections of tropical plants around the world. Besides Barra Shopping Center, the largest shopping mall in South America, Barra boasts many other modern malls and supermarkets. There are also Rio City's most modern multiplex cinemas and an ever-growing number of restaurants, bars, clubs and hotels. Barra is bordered by the city's longest beach, Praia da Barra da Tijuca.

Barra Shopping Center, the largest shopping mall in Latin America

MAP OF BARRA DA TIJUCA

SERRA DO NOGUEIRA
Projac-TV Globo ⑥
JACAREPAGUÁ
SERRA DOS TRES RIOS
Rio Water Planet
Centro de Conveções RioCentro ⑤
④ Nelson Piquet
Autódromo Internacional
ITANHANGÁ
Sítio Roberto Burle Marx (2km) ⑦
Lagoa de Jacarepaguá
Barra Shopping Center
BARRA DA TIJUCA
③ ②
Las Palmas
Cidade da Musica Roberto Marinho
Downtown
RECREIO DOS BANDEIRANTES
Lagoa de Marapendi
①
Casa do Pontal ⑧
Lagoina
Praia da Barra da Tijuca
Praia dos Bandeirantes
ATLANTIC OCEAN
⑨
Praia do Pontal
Praia Prainha & Grumari
0 kms 3
0 miles 2

Key to Symbols *see back flap*

⛱ Praia da Barra da Tijuca ①

Av Sernambetiba.

Stretching for over 11 miles (18 km), Praia da Barra da Tijuca is Rio's longest beach. The first 4 miles (6 km) are the most built-up, a modern-day Copacabana, with large condominiums.

There are different hot spots along the length of the beach, the most famous of which is Barraca do Pepê, a tremendously busy food outlet that has been a favorite with the surfing and hang-gliding crowd, with a kiosk that served organic food long before people had heard of it.

Crowds from all over Rio are drawn to this beach at weekends, but farther along the beach it becomes less crowded and unspoilt. During the week, when schools are in session, it is even possible to find large isolated stretches of the beach.

The long stretch of Praia da Barra da Tijuca

🛍 Barra Shopping Center ②

Av das Américas 4666.

Tel *(021) 3089 1100.*

Drawing shoppers from all over Rio City, this massive shopping center features an impressive range of shops. There are also eight movie theaters and a medical center, as well as a bowling alley and many coffee shops.

🏛 Cidade da Música Roberto Marinho ③

Trevo das Palmeiras. ♿

Although not expected to open until 2008, this cultural center will house one of the largest concert halls in Latin America and become the new home for the Brazilian Symphony Orchestra.

With the main building suspended 33 ft (10 m) above the ground, this cultural center will have a 1,800-seater main hall, smaller halls with 800 and 500 seats, a four-screen cinema, and many shops, bars, and restaurants.

For hotels and restaurants in this region see pp366–9 and pp394–6

Fascinating collection of tropical plants at Sítio Roberto Burle Marx

Autódromo Internacional Nelson Piquet ④

Av Embaixador Abelardo Bueno, Jacarepaguá. ***Tel*** *(021) 3410 6850.* 🕒 *race days only.* 💳

Named after Nelson Piquet, the only Brazilian to win a Grand Prix in Rio, this circuit opened in 1978 and held the Brazilian Formula One Grand Prix that year. Thereafter, the race returned to São Paulo before coming back to settle in Rio from 1981 until 1990. A favorite with the drivers, it became one of the most glamorous events on the motor racing calendar. In 1991, Rio lost out to São Paulo and it has not held a Grand Prix since.

🏛 Centro de Conveções RioCentro ⑤

Av Salvador Allende 6555. ***Tel*** *(021) 2442 1300.* 💳 ♿

Latin America's largest exhibition and convention center, RioCentro received tremendous global attention when it hosted the 1992 United Nations Conference on Environment and Development. The event, better known as the Earth Summit, was unprecedented for its magnitude and the scope of its concerns.

The large, well-equipped complex has five pavilions, and includes a heliport, lawns, gardens, a natural lake, and parking facilities for up to 7,000 vehicles.

Projac – TV Globo ⑥

Estrada dos Bandeirantes 6700, Jacarepaguá. ***Tel*** *(021) 2540 4444.*

Globo is one of the world's largest television networks and produces most of its own prime time programing, including its famous soap operas, called the *novelas*, three of which are screened daily. A complete entertainment factory, Projac includes four studios, two auditoriums, scenery and costume workshops, a restaurant, and the production offices.

🌳 Sítio Roberto Burle Marx ⑦

Estrada Burle Marx 2019. ***Tel*** *(021) 2410 1412.* 🕒 *9:30am–1:30pm by appointment.* 💳

This private garden belonged to Roberto Burle Marx *(see p295)*, one of the most important landscape architects of the 20th century. In 1949, Burle Marx bought a 90-acre (36-ha) plantation and started to organize his private collection of amazing plants. He moved here in 1973 and stayed there until his death. In 1985, he donated the entire estate to the National Institute for Cultural Heritage (IPHAN).

With around 3,500 plant species, the garden is considered one of the most important collections of tropical and semitropical plants in the world. This horticultural paradise also displays the works of Burle Marx, from the designs for his landscape projects to his paintings and sculptures. The garden also has a small Benedictine chapel dating from the 17th century, dedicated to St. Anthony.

🏛 Casa do Pontal ⑧

Estrada do Pontal 3295. ***Tel*** *(021) 2490 3278.* 🕒 *9:30am–5pm Tue–Sun.* 💳 ♿

Almost the entire collection in this charming museum is based on the private collection by the Frenchman, Jacques Van de Beuque.

VISITORS' CHECKLIST

Rio de Janeiro. 👥 *30,000.* [M] *Botafogo.* 🚌 *from Copacabana (No. 523).* ℹ *Rua da Assembléia 10, (021) 2217 7575.* **www**.rio.rj.gov.br/riotour

Approximately 200 artists from every region of Brazil have had their works represented here.

The superb collection at the Casa do Pontal consists of more than 8,000 works of Brazilian folk art including sculptures, wood carvings, models, and mechanized sets. These are made from a variety of materials including clay, wood, cloth, sand, iron, aluminium, straw, wire, and even bread dough.

🏖 Praia Prainha & Grumari ⑨

Av Estado da Guanabara.

Prainha and Grumari are the city's most unspoilt beaches, and are deserted during the week as they are only accessible by car. Prainha, just 164 yards (150 m) long, is particularly popular with the surf crowd, while Grumari is larger and attracts couples and families. Some scenes from the 1984 Hollywood comedy *Blame It on Rio* were filmed along the road to Grumari.

The restaurant and bar, Point de Grumari, on the top of the hill to the west, offers spectacular views along the coast to the west.

A surfer at the picturesque and secluded Praia Prainha

The lush setting of the Mayrink Chapel, Parque Nacional da Tijuca

Parque Nacional da Tijuca ❷

Tel (021) 2492 2253. 🚌 ⬜ 8am–6pm daily. ♿ 🛈 *Terra Brasil,* (021) 2492 2252.

Covering 15 sq miles (39 sq km), the Tijuca National Park encompasses the last remaining tracts of Atlantic rainforest that once surrounded Rio de Janeiro. It includes the Floresta da Tijuca (Tijuca Forest), Serra da Carioca (Carioca Mountains), and the monoliths of Pedra da Gávea and Pedra Bonita. The park's most famous landmark is the towering statue of Cristo Redentor atop Corcovado peak *(see pp82–3)*. Other well-known viewpoints are the Dona Marta, the Vista Chinesa (with a Chinese-style pavilion), and the Mesa do Imperador (Emperor's Table), all of which offer spectacular but varied views over the city.

Sights within the Floresta da Tijuca include **Cascatinha do Taunay**, a waterfall near the main gate named after the French painter Nicolau Taunay (1755–1830); the 19th-century **Mayrink Chapel**, featuring the work of Candido Portinari (1903–62), one of the most important Brazilian painters; the lovely Os Esquilos restaurant *(see p395);* and the hundreds of species of plants, birds, and mammals that live here.

Many of the park's 150-odd trails, originally made by Brazil's indigenous people, exist even today. One of them, dating from the 19th century, takes walkers up from Largo do Bom Retiro, a picnic spot in the Floresta da Tijuca, to the 3,940-ft (1,201-m) high Tijuca Peak. It is easy to get lost in the dense foliage, so stick to the main trails and do not go without a guide if planning on trekking. Book in advance if a guide is required.

Tiled map of park routes in Alto da Boa Vista

Another attraction near the Floresta da Tijuca is the **Museu Açude**, a museum housed in the Neo-Colonial building that once served as the residence of the successful businessman, Raymundo Ottoni de Castro Maya (1894–1968). The museum is known for its French, Dutch, Spanish, and Portuguese tiles from the 17th and 18th centuries, and for Castro Maya's personal collection of Oriental art.

🏛 **Museu Açude**
Estrada da Açude 764, Alto da Boa Vista. *Tel* (021) 2492 2119.
⬜ 11am–5pm Wed–Mon. 🎟 *free on Thu.* 📷 ♿

Cascatinha do Taunay, one of Parque Nacional da Tijuca's many waterfalls

Baía de Guanabara ❸

Without Baía de Guanabara, Rio de Janeiro would probably have been known by a different name. On January 1, 1502, the navigators André Gonçalves and Amerigo Vespucci became the first Europeans ever to sail into the bay. Assuming it was the mouth of a great river, they called it Rio de Janeiro or "River of January." Guanabara, meaning "Lagoon of the Sea," was the name given to the dominant bay by indigenous Brazilians and is rather more accurate.

The bay is flanked by Rio to its west and Niterói to its east, and encompasses countless islands. As well as the ferry services that begin at Praça XV, boats can be hired from the **Marina da Glória** in Flamengo Park, the center of all nautical activities in Rio. One of the more pleasant ways to enjoy the bay is by taking the special cruise that starts from the **Espaço Cultural da Marinha** (Navy Cultural Center) in Centro. Centro has a number of fine nautical exhibits, including an Imperial Barge built in Salvador in 1808, and also offers a cruise on the historic tugboat, *Laurindo Pitta,* which was built in England in 1910 and took part in World War I. The cruise lasts an hour and a half and passes several interesting sights along the way.

The Tom Jobim International Airport is located on the largest of the islands in the bay, **Ilha do Governador**, while the tiny **Ilha Fiscal** houses a palace built in 1889 at the request of Emperor Dom Pedro II in the style of a 14th-century French castle. The castle's highlights include its exceptional carved stone work and cast-iron work, and the turret's mosaic floor, which is made from different species

For hotels and restaurants in this region see pp366–9 and pp394–6

Museu de Art Contemporârnea (MAC-Niterói), hovering like a flying saucer above Boa Viagem

of hardwood. Also noteworthy are the wall paintings by 19th-century Dutch artist Frederico Steckel, and the tower clock and stained-glass windows, which were imported from England.

Ilha Paquetá, north of the bay, is an oasis of calm where no cars are allowed. Ferries and hydrofoils cruise up the bay to the island from the Estação das Barcas in front of the historic Praça XV. Crossing the bay is the Rio-Niterói Bridge (officially the Presidente Costa e Silva Bridge), which is one of the longest in the world at 9 miles (13 km). The project was financed by Britain, and construction began in 1968 in the presence of Queen Elizabeth II.

Espaço Cultural da Marinha
Av Alfredo Agache, Centro.
Tel (021) 2104 6025. noon–5pm
Tue–Sun.

Ilha Fiscal
Baía de Guanabara. *Tel* (021) 2233 9165. only for tours at 1pm, 2:30pm & 4pm Thu–Sun.

Marina da Glória
Av Infante Dom Henrique, Glória.
Tel (021) 2205 6716.

Niterói ❸

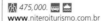
475,000.
www.niteroiturismo.com.br

Cariocas like to joke that the best thing about Niterói is its view across the bay to Rio de Janeiro, and it is true that the city's popularity has shown a decline due to its proximity to Brazil's first city. Both cities, however, developed simultaneously, and as the ferries got faster and more reliable, Niterói became a popular residential option for people working in downtown Rio.

The British preferred Niterói to Rio, and in 1872, founded the Rio Cricket and Athletic Club that is still active there today. Praia de São Francisco in Guanabara Bay is the city's answer to Copacabana beach, but for the most part, is not ideal for swimming. Niterói's better beaches – **Camboinhas**, **Itaipu**, and **Itacoatiara** – lie on the Atlantic coast, and are very popular on weekends.

The two most popular sights in the city are the imposing **Fortaleza de**

Santa Cruz and the **Museu de Art Contemporârnea** (MAC-Niterói). The Fortaleza de Santa Cruz (Santa Cruz Fort) sits on a rocky outcrop just outside the city, and guards the entrance to Guanabara Bay. Parts of the fort date from the 16th century, when the French built an improvised fortification to protect the city. The structure grew until it became the most important fortress in Brazil. It helped protect Niterói from two invasions, the first of which came from the Dutch in 1599, and the second from the French in 1710.

The stunning Museu de Art Contemporârnea (Contemporary Art Museum) appears to hover above the neighborhood of Boa Viagem. The illusion comes from its slender base pillar, which is only 30 ft (9 m) in diameter. Inaugurated in 1996, it was the brainchild of the acclaimed Brazilian architect, Oscar Niemeyer *(see p295)*. Its exhibits are based on the 1,000 pieces of Brazilian art donated by the eminent art collector, João Sattamini. The most enchanting spectacle, however, is the view from inside the museum at dusk, when Rio's lights twinkle from across the bay.

Fortaleza de Santa Cruz
Estrada Gaspar Dutra, Jurujuba.
Tel (021) 2711 0462. noon–5pm
Tue–Fri, 9am–5pm Sat & Sun.

Museu de Art Contemporârnea
Mirante da Boa Viagem, Niterói.
Tel (021) 2620 2400. 10am–6pm Tue–Sun.

A panoramic view of the Marina da Glória, Baía de Guanabara

SHOPPING IN RIO

Resident Cariocas have turned shopping into something of an art form and use it as an alternative form of entertainment when they are bored with the beach. Visitors will be pleased to find out just how far their money goes in Rio's stores, especially when it comes to buying items that have been manufactured in Brazil. This includes top fashion clothing, beach and sportswear, leather goods, jewelry and numerous other items. Until the 1980s, the best place to shop was along Visconde de Pirajá in Ipanema. Although the area is still considered to have the

Handy bag and matching flip-flops

hippest boutiques, Rio's residents have fallen in love with the experience of shopping in the larger malls, such as Rio Sul and Barra Shopping Center, the largest shopping and entertainment complex in Latin America. The historic districts of Centro and Copacabana (mainly the area along Avenida Nossa Senhora de Copacabana) cannot be overlooked, as it is here that most of Rio's quirky, special interest shops are found. The Hippie Fair is the best place to buy arts and crafts items, trinkets, curios, and souvenirs to take home as gifts.

Rio Sul, one of the two giant malls dominating Rio's shopping scene

OPENING HOURS

Most stores in Rio open from 9 or 10am in the morning until 6 or 7pm in the evening Monday to Friday, and between 9 or 10am until 1pm on Saturday. The big shopping malls, such as Barra Shopping and Rio Sul, stay open from 10am to 10pm Monday through Saturday and from 3 to 9pm on Sunday.

Most supermarkets are open from 8am to 10pm Monday to Saturday, with a limited selection remaining open on Sunday. There are also several 24-hour supermarkets scattered throughout the city.

SHOPPING MALLS

Two giant malls have dominated Rio's shopping scene since the 1980s and offer just about anything people could want under one roof. The closest and most convenient for visitors staying

in Copacabana and Ipanema is the **Rio Sul** mall, which is located on the main artery linking the Sugar Loaf end of Copacabana to Botafogo and the city. Rio Sul has more than 400 stores, plus restaurants and cinemas. It also runs a free bus service that picks up shoppers from all the main hotels along the beachfront and drops them back with their purchases. Of course, there are always plenty of taxis at Rio Sul.

Barra Shopping Center (see p86), the largest shopping and entertainment complex in Latin America, can almost be treated as a tourist attraction in its own right. At last count, the mall had close to 700 stores. It also has a good selection of bars and restaurants, and entertainment that includes a modern bowling alley, an 18-screen multiplex cinema, and a gaming area known as Hot Zone. Both Rio Sul and Barra Shopping

Center have branches of virtually all the top Brazilian retailers as well as some familiar international names. The two giants malls are not the only shows in town, and malls in every shape and size can be found all over Rio, including the popular **Fashion Mall** in São Conrado.

JEWELRY

Brazil has huge deposits of precious and semi-precious gemstones, and in some cases, holds more than 90 percent of the world's total supply. This has turned Brazil into one of the most important manufacturers of jewelry, both traditional and modern, and has made Rio de Janeiro into one of the jewel capitals of the world.

The two market leaders, **H. Stern** and **Amsterdam Sauer**, have stores in most of the city's major hotels, and at the airport. They also organize special jewelry tours at the Ipanema headquarters.

H. Stern, offering a wide range of traditional and modern jewelry

The famous **Blue Man** line of beachwear

BIKINIS & BEACHWEAR

The girls from Ipanema, Copacabana, and Barra have helped make the bikini a symbol of the city's lifestyle. Shops specializing in bikinis, swim, surf, and beachwear can be found all over Rio, especially in Copacabana, Ipanema, and all the big malls. Famous names in bikiniwear include **Blue Man**, **Bum-Bum**, and **Kitanga**.

What you wear to the beach is a fashion statement in Rio, so designs, shapes, and colors change with every season. Many stores offer a special line for visitors who find Brazilian fashions a bit daring.

FASHION WEAR

Brazil features prominently in the international fashion scene, and Brazilians like to keep up with the latest trends. Walk around Ipanema

or any of the large malls to get an idea of what is available. Items on display are usually of high quality and are also well priced.

SHOES

Brazil is one of the largest manufacturers of shoes and footwear in the world. Even the local supermarket is likely to stock fashionable flip-flops, and the two most famous brands are Havaianas and Grendha. The most popular stores that manufacture well-made and reasonably priced leather shoes, are part of the **Mr. Cat** chain. Other stores worth checking include **Andarella** and Datelli.

MUSIC

While no one music chain dominates in Rio, some music stores are better than others. **FNAC** mega store in Barra Shopping Center has a very good selection. **Modern Sound** in Copacabana is Rio's most traditional and famous store, and has a wide selection. Another top name is **Saraíva**, which has a large store in Rio Sul. Leading supermarkets, especially Lojas Americanas, sell cheap CDs.

ARTS & CRAFTS MARKETS

The best and most famous arts and crafts market in Rio is the Hippie Fair, taking place every Sunday in and around Praça General Osório in Ipanema. The fair, which first began in 1968, runs from 8am to 6pm and is the perfect place to pick up souvenir paintings or Brazilian arts and craft works.

Flip-flops

There are a number of specialized arts and crafts stores throughout the city, including those found in the Rio Sul and Barra Shopping Center malls. There is also a good selection in Copacabana, mostly along the historic Avenida Nossa Senhora de Copacabana, situated behind Copacabana Palace Hotel. In Ipanema, the H. Stern store has a good selection, as does **Brasil & Cia**.

Ipanema's Hippie Fair, a great place for souvenir shopping

DIRECTORY

ENTERTAINMENT IN RIO

As a major world city, Rio offers a wide variety of high-quality entertainment. However, these are targeted more toward the local residents than the casual tourists. The big local and international acts perform mainly for the Brazilians, and the same is true of what is presented at the theater, in the movie houses, clubs, and bars. Though

Elaborately dressed samba dancer

some clubs give a watered-down take on Brazilian culture, on the whole, visitors can enjoy a scintillating nightlife. The trendiest and most fashionable choices are found in Ipanema and Leblon, and around the Lagoa. Downtown Rio is also back in fashion, with Lapa being particularly popular when it comes to clubs and bars that play upbeat Brazilian music.

INFORMATION

For details of entertainment in Rio, check with the daily newspapers or their web sites, most notably *O Globo* and *Jornal do Brasil*. For an update on on-going events, check *Veja Rio*, the special Rio supplement in Brazil's leading weekly news-magazine, *Veja*. It normally offers an accurate guide to the current scene. The concierge at any big hotel would also be of help.

BOOKING TICKETS

Brazilians traditionally only buy their tickets at the very last moment. Even for the biggest events, tickets may go on sale only a few days ahead. In many cases, the tickets will be sold at the venue itself, or through an

agency. Large ticket agencies, such as **Ticketmaster**, **Ticketronics**, and **Ingresso**, operate countrywide, and offer tickets to both events and particular venues.

MAJOR VENUES

Rio is an important venue and tour stop for not only the top names in Brazilian music, but also for all the leading international acts. The major Brazilian acts tend to prefer to play in one of two big show houses in Rio, **Canecão** in Botafogo and the **Claro Hall** in Barra da Tijuca. Opened in 1967, Canecão has hosted many major concerts and a number of classic live Brazilian albums have been recorded here. Claro Hall, a purpose-built state-of-the-art facility, opened for business in 1994, with a show by Diana Ross.

Vivo Rio in the Modern Art Museum in Flamengo is expected to soon open for shows, while 2008 will see the opening of the **Cidade da Música** in Barra with a spacious main concert hall.

Smaller bands, or big names looking for a more intimate setting, also use the **Circo Voador** in Lapa and other smaller venues such as the **Teatro João Caetano** in Centro, **Ballroom** in Humaitá, and even **Noites Carioca** on the half-way stage of Sugar Loaf *(see pp 76–7)*.

The open-air venues of **Praça de Apoteose** and **Cidade do Rock** stage large acts. Even the Copacabana and Flamengo beaches occasionally hold free concerts.

Rio also hosts a number of festivals during the year that cover all genres. The

Colorfully costumed *samba* performers in the floor show at Plataforma 1

largest and most famous festival is Rock in Rio, though this is not an annual event.

Over the years, Rio has offered a number of shows that primarily target the visitor who might want a quick, though somewhat over-simplified, version of the vast range of Brazilian culture.

The glitziest show to outlast them all takes place daily at Leblon's **Plataforma 1**. The kitschy variety show features *samba*, *bossa nova*, and other Brazilian sounds.

The Pe de Moleque group playing at the Carioca de Gema bar in Lapa

SAMBA, BOSSA NOVA & GAFIEIRA

Most visitors to Rio will hope to catch a little live music and dance action when they are in town. While the big Brazilian acts will be found at Canecão and Claro Hall, there will also be a lot of artistes performing in smaller, more intimate venues, many of which are also bars and clubs.

On the Jardim Botanico side of the Lagoa, Rio's most popular and successful music bar **Mistura Fina** has offered an eclectic mix of jazz, instrumental, and MPB *(see pp32–3)* for over 25 years. Many top names started here and still return to perform.

Fans of *bossa nova* flock to **Vinícius** in Ipanema and **Bar do Tom** in Leblon. Celebrated for its outstanding music and a lively bar, the tiny **Bip Bip** in Copacabana is a well-frequented haven for MPB.

Since the end of the 1990s, the reinvigorated nightlife in the city center has given a special boost to *samba* and *choro* (an upbeat waltz or polka). Lapa remains the main hub, with places such as **Carioca da Gema**, **Dama da Noite**, and **Rio Scenarium**. Close by, in Praça Tiradentes, the **Centro Cultural Carioca** is known to host Brazilian music.

Even when the center of Rio was not in fashion, two clubs prospered there and still hold sway as the city's authentic ballrooms, or *gafieiras*. **Estudantina**, in Praça Tiradentes, dates from 1928, while the 1918 **Cordão da Bola Preta** in Cinelândia is the oldest carnival *bloco*.

For those who wish to learn the basics of dance, there are a number of schools in Rio. The Centro Cultural Carioca offers beginner classes for *samba*, *forró*, and *gafieira*.

SAMBA SCHOOLS

The number of shows and opportunities increase the closer it gets to Carnaval *(see pp64–5)*, with the "high season" for *samba* from December through February. However, those who are not visiting the city during this time can watch the *samba* schools in action. Any good hotel will be able to organize a visit to the **League of Samba Schools (LIESA)** as part of the schools' own official tours, or to the technical rehearsals that take place at the Sambódromo.

The *samba* schools are also known to host programs featuring performances and other events at the new **Cidade de Samba** that opened in Centro at the beginning of 2006.

People dancing to a live *gafieira* show in Rio Scenarium

BARS & CLUBS

Rio enchants visitors with its unique range of bars and clubs. Bars go through every degree of sophistication, from periodically-changing hot spots, to those specializing in *cachaça* and *caipirinhas*, such as the popular **Academia da Cachaça** in Leblon and Barra. Enhancing the variety are several pub-like venues, the most famous of which is **Lord Jim** in Ipanema, while sophisticated bars in the top hotels offer a more formal elegance. Then there are the traditional *botequins*, or the corner bars, with plenty to eat and drink, well into the early hours. **Bar Luiz** in Centro, **Lamas** in Flamengo, **Cervantes** in Copacabana, **Hipódromo** in Gavea, and **Bar Lagoa** on the Lagoa, have been drawing a steady clientele. Favored by visitors, **Garota de Ipanema** was where Tom Jobim and Vinícius de Moraes are said to have written the song "A Garota de Ipanema." Trendy **Barril 1800**, an Ipanema landmark, attracts local celebs and tourists alike. **Caneco 70**, on the Leblon beachfront, is another well-known club.

The line between bars, DJ bars, and clubs can get blurred in Rio, with a surfeit of bars offering dancing and music as the night goes on. The "in" venues change extremely quickly in terms of popularity and name. Therefore, it is always a good idea to ask a resident or the concierge at the hotel about the places that may be currently in vogue.

GAY & LESBIAN

Rio has a very active gay and lesbian scene, much of which simply blends into the everyday life of the city. Among the most traditional gay and lesbian clubs are the upbeat **Le Boy** and **La Girl**, at the Ipanema end of Copacabana. **Dama de Ferro** is as popular.

A good starting point is Ipanema beach. The block running back from the beach also has a number of gay and lesbian friendly bars.

EATING OUT

For many Cariocas, eating out *(see p390–91)* is an entertainment in its own right. Foreign visitors get the best value from dining at the *churrascaria rodizios*, the large barbecue houses with a fixed-price menu.

In Rio, trying traditional Brazilian cuisine normally means a *feijoada (see p392)*, a sumptuous feast usually served for lunch on Wednesday or Saturday.

THEATER

Theater in Rio de Janeiro is of a high quality, but a majority of the productions will be in Portuguese. The main theaters, generally small and intimate, are found in Copacabana, Ipanema, and Leblon. In Centro, the **Centro Cultural Banco do Brasil** is a major venue. For listings, check *O Globo* and *Jornal do Brasil*.

CINEMA

Brazil is one of the world's biggest cinema-going markets. However, the latest multiplex operations all tend to be in

A football match in progress at the Estádio Maracanã

Barra, such as the 18-screen **Cinemark**. Smaller and older theatres can be found in Copacabana and Ipanema.

International films quickly make their way into Brazil, and unless they are aimed at children, will be left in their original language with subtitles added. At least one new Brazilian film is released each week, a few of which will go on to international acclaim. Independent world cinema takes over the city each September and October, when the city's main film festival, Festival do Rio, holds public screenings.

CLASSICAL MUSIC, OPERA & DANCE

Rio de Janeiro has a healthy and vibrant music, opera, and dance scene that is currently focused in the **Theatro Municipal** in Centro. From 2008, however, it is likely to share the spotlight with the new **Cidade da Música** in Barra. Small concerts and recitals also use the **Sala Cecília Meireles** in Lapa.

Rio has its own music, opera, and dance companies, but also attracts the very best from the rest of Brazil and the world.

HELICOPTER TOURS

One of the most popular tours with visitors to Rio, a helicopter ride takes people over the city and beaches, or around Sugar Loaf and Corcovado mountains.

Since 1991, **Helisight** has been offering eight different tours that vary from eight minutes to an hour. The most popular tours are those that circle Corcovado and the statue of Christ the Redeemer.

Helisight has modern heliports at Dona Marta, Morro da Urca, and the Lagoa. It also operates from Pier Maua when the cruise ships are in. Prices are much less than most people imagine.

SOCCER

The mecca of soccer-lovers, Rio is world-renowned for its abiding passion for the game. Matches take place all through the year, and are usually held on Wednesday evenings or Sunday afternoons. The city's four big clubs are Flamengo, Fluminense, Vasco da Gama, and Botafogo.

Almost synonymous with Brazil's legendary sport, the **Estádio Maracanã** is widely acclaimed for hosting some of the best soccer matches.

HORSE RACING

Unusual as it may seem to list it among the entertainment options, horse racing at the **Jóquei Club Brasileiro** on the Lagoa takes place four times a week. On Monday and Friday evenings, one can enjoy drinks or dinner in the members' stand, and watch the racing go on under the floodlights.

An aerial view of the Helisight heliport at Morro da Urca

DIRECTORY

INFORMATION

Jornal do Brasil
www.jbonline.terra.com.br

O Globo
www.oglobo.globo.com

BOOKING TICKETS

Ingresso
www.ingresso.com.br

Ticketmaster
www.ticketmaster.com.br

Ticketronics
www.ticketronics.net

MAJOR VENUES

Ballroom
Rua Humaitá 110.
Tel (021) 2537 7600.

Canecão
Av Venceslau Braz 215,
Botafogo. *Tel (021) 2105 2000.*

Cidade da Música
O Trevo das Palmeiras,
Barra.

Cidade do Rock
Av Salvador Allende,
Barra da Tijuca.

Circo Voador
Rua dos Arcos, Lapa.
Map 5 D5. *Tel (021) 2533 0354.*

Claro Hall
Av Ayrton Senna 3000,
Barra da Tijuca. *Tel (0300) 789 6846.*

Noites Carioca
Av Pasteur 520, Praia
Vermelha, Urca. *Tel (021) 2546 8400.*

Plataforma 1
Rua Adalberto Ferreira 32,
Leblon. *Tel (021) 2274 4022.*

Praça da Apoteose
Rua Marques de Sapucai,
Cidade Novo. **Map** 4 A5.
Tel (021) 2217 7575.

Teatro João Caetano
Praça Tiradentes, Centro.
Map 4 C4. *Tel (021) 2221 1223.*

Vivo Rio
Av Infante Dom Henrique
85, Flamengo.
Tel (021) 2240 2303.

SAMBA, BOSSA NOVA & GAFIEIRA

Bar do Tom
Rua Adalberto Ferreira 32,
Leblon. *Tel (021) 2274 4022.*

Bip Bip
Rua Almirante Gonçalves
50, Copacabana.
Map 2 C4.
Tel (021) 2267 9696.

Carioca da Gema
Rua Mem de Sá 79, Lapa.
Map 5 D5. *Tel (021) 2221 0043.*

Centro Cultural Carioca
Rua do Teatro 37, Praça
Tiradentes, Centro.
Map 4 C4. *Tel (021) 2252 6468.*

Cordão da Bola Preta
Rua Treze de Maio 13,
Cinelândia. **Map** 5 D4.
Tel (021) 2240 8049.

Dama da Noite
Rua Gomes Freire 773,
Lapa. **Map** 4 C5.
Tel (021) 2508 6219.

Estudantina
Praça Tiradentes 79,
Centro. **Map** 4 C4.
Tel (021) 2232 1149.

Mistura Fina
Av Borges de Medeiros
3207, Jardim Botanico.
Map 1 C1. *Tel (021) 2537 2844.*

Rio Scenarium
Rua do Lavradio 20, Lapa.
Map 4 C4. *Tel (021) 2233 3239.*

Vinícius
Rua Vinícius de Moraes
39, Ipanema. **Map** 2 B4.
Tel (021) 2287 1497.

SAMBA SCHOOLS

Cidade do Samba
Rua R. Correa 60,
Gamboa. *Tel (021) 2247 2330.*

League of Samba Schools (LIESA)
Av Rio Branco 4.
Map 5 D2. *Tel (021) 2253 7409.*

BARS & CLUBS

Academia da Cahaça
Rua Conde Bernadotte
26, Leblon.
Tel (021) 2239 1542.
Av Armando Lombardi
800, Barra.
Tel (021) 2492 1159.

Barril 1800
Av Vieira Souto 110,
Ipanema. **Map** 2 B5.
Tel (021) 2523 0085.

Bar Lagoa
Av Epitácio Pessoa 1674,
Lagoa. **Map** 2 A4.
Tel (021) 2523 1468.

Bar Luiz
Rua da Carioca 39,
Centro. **Map** 5 D4.
Tel (021) 2262 6900.

Caneco 70
Av Delfim Moreira 1026,
Leblon. **Map** 1 A5.
Tel (021) 2294 1180.

Cervantes
Av Prado Júnior 335,
Copacabana. **Map** 3 F1.
Tel (021) 2275 6147.

Garota de Ipanema
Rua Vinícius de Moraes
49, Ipanema. **Map** 2 A5.
Tel (021) 2523 3787.

Hipódromo
Praça Santos Dumont
108, Gávea.
Tel (021) 2274 9720.

Lamas
Rua Marques de
Abrantes 18, Flamengo.
Tel (021) 2556-0799.

Lord Jim
Rua Paul Redfern 63,
Ipanema. **Map** 2 C4.
Tel (021) 2259 3047.

GAY & LESBIAN

Dama de Ferro
Rua Vinícius de Moraes
288, Ipanema.
Map 2 B4.
Tel (021) 2247 2330.

Le Boy
Rua Raul Pompéia 92,
Copacabana. **Map** 2 C4.
Tel (021) 2513 4993.

La Girl
Rua Raul Pompéia 102,
Copacabana. **Map** 2 C4.
Tel (021) 2247 8342.

THEATER

Centro Cultural Banco do Brasil
Rua Primeiro de Março
66, Centro. **Map** 5 E3.
Tel (021) 3808 2020.

CINEMA

Cinemark
Av das Americas, Barra
da Tijuca. **Map** 5 D5.
Tel (021) 2494 5007.

CLASSICAL MUSIC, OPERA & DANCE

Sala Cecília Meireles
Largo da Lapa 47.
Map 5 D5. *Tel (021) 2224 3913.*

Theatro Municipal
Av Rio Branco. **Map** 5 D4.
Tel (021) 2299 1711.

HELICOPTER TOURS

Helisight
Rua Conde de Bernadotte
26. **Map** 1 A4. *Tel (021) 2511 2141 (weekdays),
(021) 2542 7895 (Sat,
Sun & public hols).*

SOCCER

Estádio Maracanã
Rua Eurico Rabelo, São
Cristóvão.

HORSE RACING

Jóquei Clube Brasileiro
Rua Jardim Botânico
1003. **Map** 1 A2, 1 A3,
1 B2, 1 B3. *Tel (021) 2512 9988.*

RIO DE JANEIRO CITY STREET FINDER

Map references given in this guide for entertainment venues and other attractions in Rio City refer to the Street Finder maps on the following pages. Map references are also provided for Rio City restaurants (see pp394–6) and hotels (see pp366–9). The first figure in the map reference indicates which Street Finder map to turn to, and the letter and number which follow refer to the grid reference on that map. The map below shows the different areas of Rio City – Leblon, Copacabana, Ipanema, and Centro – covered by the five Street Finder maps. Symbols used for sights and useful information are displayed in the key below. An index of street names and important places of interest marked on the maps can be found on page 68.

KEY

◼	Place of interest
◼	Other building
🚉	Train station
🚢	River-boat terminal
Ⓜ	Metro
🅿	Parking
ℹ	Visitor information
✚	Hospital
🚓	Police station
✝	Church
⊠	Post office
══	Railroad
▬	Pedestrian street

SCALE OF MAPS 1 & 2–3

0 meters 400
0 yards 400

SCALE OF MAP 4–5

0 meters 200
0 yards 200

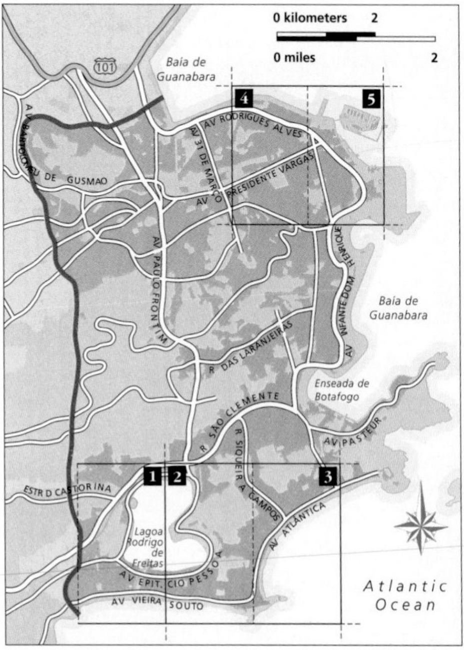

STREETWISE IN RIO

Though street crime is prevalent in Rio, a few precautions could help to prevent it from happening.

Contrary to general belief, it is probably best to avoid taking a stroll on the deserted streets of Centro on Sundays. Praça Mauá, just to the north of Centro, is best avoided after nightfall. Lapa, a popular nightspot in Rio, must be explored with great caution. It is advisable not to wander unaccompanied around the darker corners of the Parque do Flamengo, or to walk between Cosmo Velho and Corcovado late at night. Robbery and assault in these areas are common.

Passengers taking a bus are easy targets for thieves, and need to be vigilant. Taxis are plentiful and inexpensive, so avoid walking along empty and unfamiliar streets. Make sure the driver turns on the meter and ask for an estimate of the average fare to your destination.

Various instances of bag-snatching are common on the crowded beaches of Copacabana and Ipanema, especially during the weekends, so visitors must keep a keen eye on their belongings. Again, do not go down to the water after dark. Stay on the well-lit, busy sidewalks.

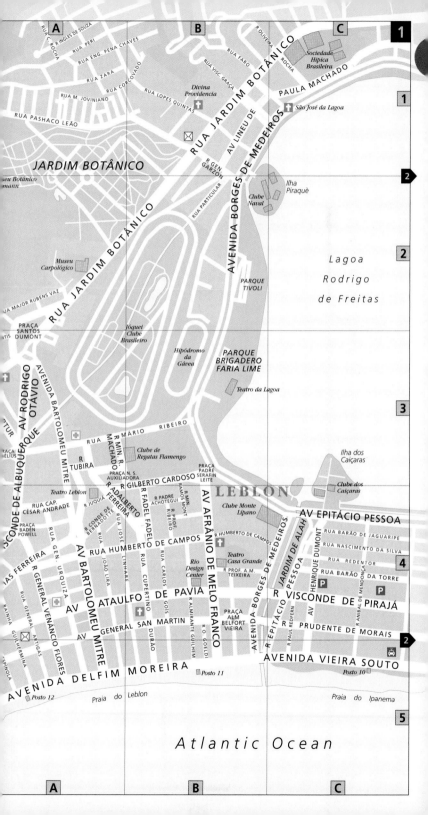

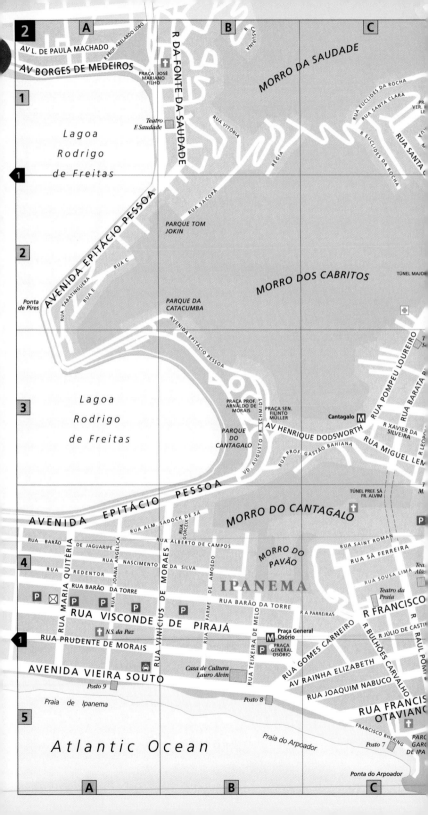

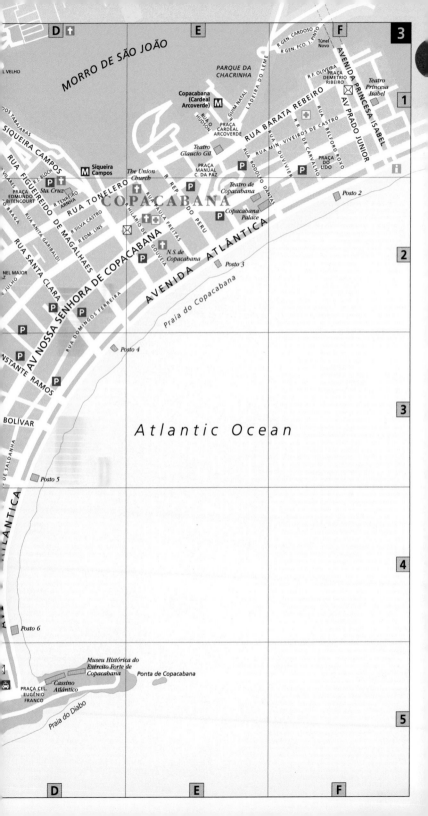

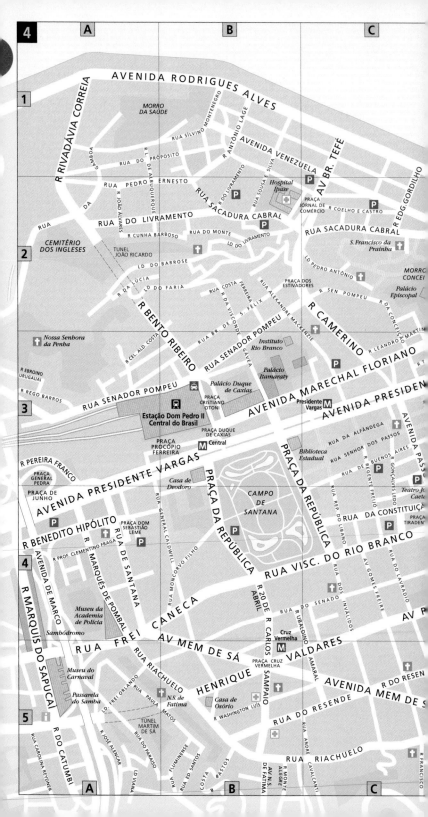

RIO DE JANEIRO & ESPÍRITO SANTO

eyond the capital cities of Rio and Vitória, the magnificent scenery dominating the cities continues unchecked by rapid modernization. Along the coast are giant boulder-strewn mountains, while farther inland are the steep, lushly-forested ridges of the Mata Atlântica. Spectacular beaches, picturesque islands, and several resort towns are among the area's other attractions.

Stretching north and south of Rio City are long strands of beaches and half-moon coves lapped or pounded by a bottle-green Atlantic and visited by troops of sea turtles. Some surround the popular resort towns of Búzios, "discovered" by Brigitte Bardot in the 1960s, and Cabo Frio, while others lie close to the colonial port of Paraty, which once lay at the end of the mule route from the gold mines of Minas Gerais. Its cobbled streets are better preserved than others on the southeastern coast.

Inland, the steep ridges of the Mata Atlântica begin to rise vertiginously towards Minas Gerais and São Paulo, protecting a string of national and state parks, including Itatiaia and the Serra dos Órgãos, in their folds. Considered one of the world's biodiversity hot spots, an astounding 950 species of birds are found here and 40 percent of the plants are unique, including the cattleya orchid, referred to as the "Queen of Flowers." The largest among the islands, Ilha Grande has no roads. Steep walking trails leave its only town Abraão, to cut through the forest to still more beaches deserted but for surfboards and fishing shacks.

The Espírito Santo coast is equally beautiful with its mountains, beaches, and small towns. One of them, Itaúnas, is backed by sand dunes large enough to swallow it. A stunning sight here is Pedra Azul, a granite monolith which changes from slate gray to fiery orange with the passage of the sun.

Pedra Azul, a spectacular granite monolith in Espírito Santo

◁ Rolling hills and calm waters of the untouched coast of Costa Verde, Rio de Janeiro state

Exploring Rio de Janeiro & Espírito Santo

Several towns pepper the coast of Rio de Janeiro state. Among these, Búzios draws the most visitors and has the best hotels and restaurants, while the colonial town of Paraty, nestled between the coastal mountains and an island-strewn sea, is emerging as a center for the arts. North of Rio is the imperial city of Petrópolis. Brazil's oldest national park, Itatiaia, lies just off the interstate between Rio and São Paulo. Ilha Grande, off the coast of Rio, and the resorts of northern Espírito Santo are relatively untouched. Vitória, the state's capital, dates to the 1550s. To its south is the beach town of Guarapari, while inland is the dramatic peak of Pedra Azul.

Statue of King Dom Pedro II, the founder of the magnificent city of Petrópolis

Lush Mata Atlântica in Parque Nacional do Itatiaia, Rio de Janeiro

SIGHTS AT A GLANCE

Towns & Cities

SEE ALSO

• **Where to Stay** pp370–72
• **Where to Eat** pp396–7

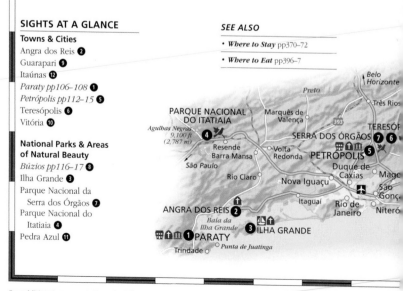

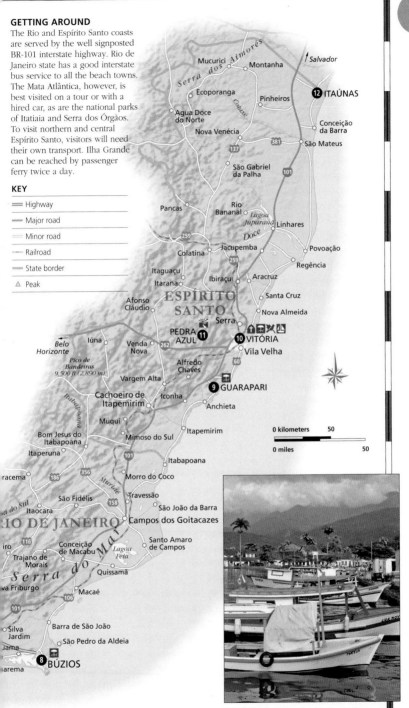

GETTING AROUND

The Rio and Espírito Santo coasts
are served by the well signposted
BR-101 interstate highway. Rio de
Janeiro state has a good interstate
bus service to all the beach towns.
The Mata Atlântica, however, is
best visited on a tour or with a
hired car, as are the national parks
of Itatiaia and Serra dos Órgãos.
To visit northern and central
Espírito Santo, visitors will need
their own transport. Ilha Grande
can be reached by passenger
ferry twice a day.

KEY

▬▬▬ Highway

▬▬ Major road

▬▬ Minor road

▬ ▬ Railroad

▬▬ State border

△ Peak

Salvador

Mucurici
Montanha

Serra dos Aimorés

Ecoporanga
Pinheiros
12 ITAÚNAS

Agua Doce
do Norte

Conceição
da Barra

Nova Venécia
São Mateus

Cauaxi

137
381

São Gabriel
da Palha

101

Pancas
Rio
Bananal
*Lagoa
Juparanã*
Linhares

Doce

259

Colatina
Jacupemba
Povoação

259
Regência

Itaguaçu

Itarana
Ibiraçu
Aracruz

**ESPÍRITO
SANTO**

Afonso
Cláudio
Santa Cruz

Nova Almeida

Serra

*Belo
Horizonte*
Iúna
Venda
Nova
262
PEDRA
AZUL **11**
10 VITÓRIA

Vila Velha

Pico de
Bandeiras
9,500 ft (2,890 m)

Alfredo
Chaves
60

Vargem Alta

Itabapoana

Cachoeiro de
Itapemirim
Iconha

Anchieta

Muqui

Bom Jesus do
Itabapoana
Mimoso do Sul
Itapemirim

0 kilometers   50

0 miles   50

Itaperuna

101

Itabapoana

...racema
186
356

Muriaé

Morro do Coco

São Fidélis
158
Travessão

...a do Sul
Itaocara
São João da Barra

RIO DE JANEIRO
Campos dos Goitacazes

...iro
116

Santo Amaro
de Campos

Conceição
de Macabu
*Lagoa
Feia*

Trajano de
Morais

Serra do Mar

...va Friburgo
Quissamã

106
Macaé

*...Silva
Jardim*
Barra de São João

...ama
São Pedro da Aldeia

8 BÚZIOS

...arema

Colorful boats anchored on the Paraty shore

Paraty ●

One of the most photographed colonial towns on the Brazilian coast, Paraty has been a UNESCO World Heritage Site since 1958. Though settled by the Portuguese in the 16th century, it was developed a century later as an important port from where gold was shipped to Europe. Extremely charming, the whitewashed churches and

Shop window in Paraty

terra-cotta roofs offset the lush green of the rainforest-clad mountains, and the placid bay whose emerald waters lap at the town's quay. Paraty has an impressive literary tradition; the annual Festa Literária Internacional de Paraty (FLIP) is a big draw. It is also an ideal base for exploring the dazzling Brazilian coastline, and boasts lovely *pousadas* (exclusive hotels).

Statue of St. Benedict, Nossa Senhora do Rosário e São Benedito

Sturdy iron bars of the Casa de Cadeia, a former prison

🏛 Casa de Cadeia

Rua Travessa Santa Rita. **Tel** (024) 3371 1056. ☐ 9am–5pm daily. 🏞🎥🚫

The 18th-century Casa de Cadeia served as the town's prison until 1890. Retaining its original iron prison bars, this building now serves as the public library, besides housing the Casa do Artesão (Artisan's House).

🏛 Nossa Senhora dos Pardos Libertos

Largo da Santa Rita. ☐ 10am–noon & 2–5pm Wed–Sun. 🏞🚫

The façade of Paraty's oldest church now graces travel brochures of the city. It was built in 1722 by, and for, all those considered not white enough to attend the church of the ruling elite. These would have included the illegitimate offspring of the aristocracy, their children in turn, indigenous people, and freed slaves. In design the church is typically Jesuit, with three windows in the upper chancel and a curvilinear door. Except for the beautifully worked altarpiece in the sanctuary and fine woodwork on the doorways, its interior is plain. Deconsecrated in the 20th century, the church now serves as the sparse **Museu de Arte Sacra**. Displayed religious artifacts include gold and silver remonstrances.

⛪ Nossa Senhora do Rosário e São Benedito

Rua Tenente Francisco Antônio. ☐ 1–5pm daily. 🏞🚫

Slaves worshipped at Nossa Senhora do Rosário e São Benedito, which was built in 1725. The interior of this humble church is almost entirely free of embellishment, except for heavy gilt on the altarpiece. However, it retains a simple dignity and a sacred atmosphere. Its design resembles the Minas Gerais chapels of the same period. Every November, locals celebrate A Festa dos Santos (Feast of All Saints) here, where they remember some of the building's historical past. Mass is followed by a procession where churchgoers carry figures of a king and queen, recalling the Maracatú monarchs of Pernambuco, and icons of the various saints.

Paraty's whitewashed buildings reflected in the placid waters at the quay

Nossa Senhora dos Remédios

Praça Monsenhor Helio Pires.
8am–noon & 2–5pm Mon, Wed, Fri, Sat & Sun.
Originally meant for the white elite, this stately church took 100 years to build, owing to financial constraints. When it was near completion in 1873, the architects discovered that Paraty's soil was too muddy to support the planned twin towers. It was left in its current squat state, slowly subsiding to the left. Today, it serves as a parish church.

Cannons resting outside Forte Defensor Perpétuo

Nossa Senhora das Dores

Rua Fresca at Rua Beco da Capela.
8am–noon & 2pm–5pm Thu.
The colonial aristocracy also attended the graceful chapel of Nossa Senhora das Dores. Built in 1800, it was renovated in 1901, and administered by the nuns of the convent of Our Lady of Sorrows. Just as the rest of Paraty's churches, it has an unembellished interior, although there is some fine carving on the balustrades in the upper chancel. A catacomb-like cemetery adjoins the chapel.

VISITORS' CHECKLIST

Rio de Janeiro. 30,000. Rua Jango Pádua. Av Roberto Silveira, (024) 3371 1897. Carnaval (Feb), Festas Juninas (Jun), Festa Literária Internacional de Paraty (Aug), Festival da Pinga (Aug), Festa da Nossa Senhora dos Remédios (Sep), Festa de Divino Espírito Santo (Dec). **www.**paratyvirtual.com.br

Forte Defensor Perpétuo

Morro do Forte. 9am–noon & 2–5pm Wed–Sun. **Centro de Artes e Tradições Populares**
10am–5pm Tue–Sun.
On the northern headland, just outside town, the Forte Defensor Perpétuo is a 19th-century fort that looks more like an elongated squat town house. Rusted cannons and remnants of a thick wall sit in front of it. The **Centro de Artes e Tradições Populares** (Center for Popular Art), an interesting museum and gallery, now occupies its principal room, displaying local handicrafts and items related to the traditional way of life of the local people.

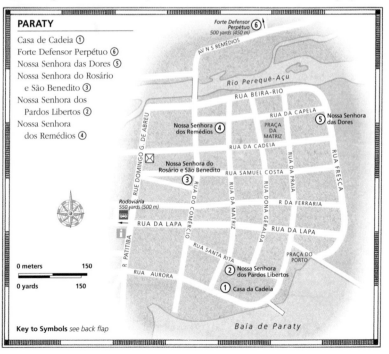

PARATY

Forte Defensor Perpétuo ⑥
500 yards (450 m)

AV N S REMÉDIOS

Rio Perequé-Açu

RUA BEIRA-RIO

RUA DA CAPELA

Nossa Senhora ⑤ das Dores

RUE DOMINGO G. DE ABREU

Nossa Senhora ④ dos Remédios

PRAÇA DA MATRIZ

RUA DA CADEIA

Nossa Senhora do Rosário e São Benedito ③

RUA SAMUEL COSTA

RUA DA PRAIA

RUA FRESCA

Rodoviária 550 yards (500 m)

RUA DO COMÉRCIO

RUA DA MATRIZ

RUA DONA GERALDA

R DA FERRARIA

RUA DA LAPA

RUA DA LAPA

PRAÇA DO PORTO

R PATITIBA

RUA SANTA RITA

② Nossa Senhora dos Pardos Libertos

RUA AURORA

① Casa da Cadeia

0 meters 150
0 yards 150

Baía de Paraty

Key to Symbols see back flap

Beaches Around Paraty

Paraty, with its forest-swathed spurs of the coastal mountains, lies at the heart of a beautiful stretch of coastline. A short way offshore are a string of islands. Until only a few decades ago, this area was little-known even to Brazilian holiday makers. Much of the area, surrounded by a wealth of exotic flora and fauna, is protected by national and state parks. The islands can be reached by boat from Paraty town, or the nearby Paraty-Mirim.

A surfer with board

VISITORS' CHECKLIST

Rio de Janeiro state.
Paraty Tours, Av Roberto Silveira 11, (024) 3371 1327.
to islands from Paraty pier. from Paraty (every 45 minutes for Paraty-Mirim & Trindade). www.paratytours. com.br *Praia do Jabaquara, Praia do Pontal, Paraty-Mirim, Trindade.*

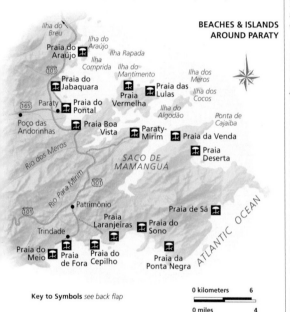

BEACHES & ISLANDS AROUND PARATY

Ilha do Breu
Praia do Araújo
Ilha do Araújo
Ilha Rapada
Ilha Comprida
Ilha do Mantimento
Praia do Jabaquara
Praia das Lulas
Ilha dos Meros
Ilha dos Cocos
Paraty
Praia do Pontal
Praia Vermelha
Ilha do Algodão
Poço das Andorinhas
Praia Boa Vista
Paraty-Mirim
Praia da Venda
Ponta de Cajaiba
Rio dos Meros
SACO DE MAMANGUÁ
Praia Deserta
Rio Para Mirim
Patrimônio
Praia de Sá
Trindade
Praia Laranjeiras
Praia do Sono
Praia do Meio
Praia de Fora
Praia do Cepilho
Praia da Ponta Negra
ATLANTIC OCEAN

Key to Symbols see back flap

0 kilometers   6
0 miles   4

Exploring Around Paraty

The bays and islands off Paraty are a favorite playground for Brazil's rich elite, who moor their expensive yachts in the Paraty Marina and fly in to the adjacent airport in their private jets for a weekend cruise.

Paraty's city beach, close to the historic center, **Praia do Pontal** lies across the Rio Perequê-Açu. The water is not very clean, but the *barracas* (restaurants) are pleasant. A shallow and spacious beach, **Praia do Jabaquara** is within walking distance of Paraty town. A glorious long beach, **Paraty-Mirim** lies 17 miles (27 km) east of town, and can be reached by a bumpy dirt road. Just south, **Saco de**

Mamanguá is lined with old fishing villages and plush holiday homes. A deep sleeve of water, it is good for snorkeling. **Ilha dos Meros**, 9 miles (14 km) northeast of Paraty, is another snorkeling spot, though marine life is limited to large shoals of sheepshead bream and the occasional turtle.

The small town of **Trindade**, 13 miles (21 km) south of Paraty, is popular with surfers from São Paulo. It offers a choice of simply-appointed *pousadas* and some pretty beaches connected by footpaths. The scenic beach running south of Trindade, **Praia de Fora**, is backed by forest-covered hills. **Praia do Meio** is a long stretch of fine sand, washed by waves perfect for body surfing. **Laranjeiras**, a small distance downhill, is the hideaway for Rio's super-rich who flock to its private condominium. Trails lead from here through the forest to a string of pristine beaches to the south. **Praia do Cepilho** is one of the best surfing spots along this stretch of coast.

Located 21 miles (34 km) from Paraty, **Ilha do Breu** is a tiny private island dominated by a single *pousada*. The owner breeds rare golden lion tamarins, which he lets run free on his island. He also maintains a small aviary, and has planted trees to attract Atlantic rainforest birds. **Poço das Andorinhas**, one of the many waterfalls in the region, is a popular spot for bathing.

Secluded scenic Praia de Fora near Trindade

For hotels and restaurants in this region see pp370–72 and pp396–7

Mata Atlântica

The Atlantic coastal forest, or Mata Atlântica, is one of the best bird-watching sites in the world, with 950 resident species, almost 200 of which are endemic. It once covered the lowlands and coastal mountains from Rio Grande do Norte to Rio Grande do Sul. Today, less than 5 percent remains, concentrated mainly in Rio de Janeiro, Minas Gerais, São Paulo, and Paraná. Its proximity to the Atlantic blesses it with heavy rainfall. The vegetation is thick with epiphytic plants, and the forest is particularly rich in breathtaking orchid species. There are many rare mammals too, including the most endangered primate in the world, the woolly spider monkey, as well as several striking species of uniquely colored marmosets and tamarins.

Black jacobin

Epiphytes *are plants encrusting every available nook and cranny of the larger trees, drawing moisture directly from air.*

Clearwater streams cut across the thick forest, which receives heavy rainfall, especially in the Southeast.

Vegetation at the water's edge tends to consist of fast-growing species that quickly replenish their numbers after floods.

BRAZIL

LOCATOR MAP

▢ Mata Atlântica

BIODIVERSITY

Mata Atlântica is one of the world's most biodiverse regions, with some 20,000 plant species, 40 percent of which are endemic, and one of the highest numbers of threatened or endangered vertebrates in the world.

The seven-colored tanager *is one of the local species listed as endangered or threatened by CITES.*

The cattleya orchid, *the world's most famous orchid genus, was discovered by Englishman William Cattley in 1818.*

The woolly monkey, *among South America's largest primate, can weigh more than 13 lb (6 kg).*

The golden lion tamarin, *one of the three lion tamarin species, lives on a few islands and in the Atlantic forest.*

Ocelots, *the third largest of Brazil's eight indigenous big cats, are most abundant in southern São Paulo.*

The Costa Verde

The Costa Verde (Green Coast) stretching south of Rio, past Paraty and Trindade *(see pp106–107)*, deserves its name. Rainforests swathe the coastal mountains, which reach almost 9,143 ft (2,787 m) in the alpine meadows and the forests of Parque Nacional do Itatiaia. From here, they plunge down into steep ridges to meet an emerald ocean, tinged with turquoise at numerous long sandy beaches. Beyond are a scattering of breathtaking islands set in aquamarine and sitting in the deep, bottle-green Atlantic. The largest, Ilha Grande, is particularly lush, with trees covering its rocky mountains and sheltering its spectacular strands of fine white sand. The island is also the playground for the rich, who host extravagant parties in the Antipodean summer.

Angra dos Reis ❶

Rio de Janeiro. 🏚 *114,000.* 🚌 *from Rio.* 🛈 *Rua Caravelas, (024) 3364 4759.* **www**.angra-dos-reis.com

This unprepossessing port is today mainly a jumping-off point for the islands of Ilha Grande and Ilha da Gipóia. It was once a charming colonial town and vestiges of its once dignified past are hidden among the ever-expanding *favelas.* Angra dos Reis was once as pretty a town as Paraty. The main church, **Nossa Senhora do Conceição**, was built in 1626 in front of the docks, while the nearby **Nossa Senhora do Carmo** dates from 1593. The colonial naval complex lies some 2 miles (3 km) north of the town center towards the Praia do Bonfim.

Environs
Ilha da Gipóia, an hour's boat ride off the port of Angra dos Reis, is the second largest island in the bay after Ilha Grande, and is known for its stunning white sand beaches such as Jurubaíba, Praia do Dentista, and Norte. Most of the beaches here are bustling with bars floating offshore, which can be reached by the yachts and boats that ply the waters of the bay.
The forested **Serra do Mar** lies 25 miles (40 km) inland from Angra. On weekends and holidays, visitors can take a picturesque train journey there. Train tickets should be booked a day in advance from the tourist office.

Town church in Vila do Abraão, Ilha Grande, against a lush backdrop

Ilha Grande ❸

Rio de Janeiro. 🏚 *3,000.* 🚤 *from Angra dos Reis.* 🛈 *Rua da Praia, Vila do Abraão, (024) 3361 5508.* 🛥 *Vila do Abraão.* **www**.ilhagrande.com

The most romantic and pretty of southeastern Brazil's numerous islands, Ilha Grande remains unspoilt by development and heavy tourism. The only settlement of any size is the two-street **Vila do Abraão**, the port town and main village on the island. Tour operators and hotels in Abraão offer a range of trips around the island, many of them on pretty, painted wooden fishing boats. The most popular trip is to the sheltered cove at **Palmas**, to the east of the village, from where a trail leads to **Lopes Mendes** to the east, one of Ilha Grande's longest beaches, washed by powerful surf. Other trips include snorkeling in the clear waters of the Saco do Céu or visits to the 18th-century **Igreja de Santana** at Freguesia de Santana.

Self-guided trails from Abraão lead throughout the island. Many of them are steep and rocky, but offer wonderful views out over the Atlantic. The most challenging is to the 3,248-ft (990-m) high peak of Pico do Papagaio.

Although most of the 75-sq mile (193-sq km) island now forms part of the Parque Estadual da Ilha Grande, Ilha Grande's pristine state owes more to its long isolation than to efforts at conservation. From the earliest colonial days the island was a notorious pirate lair. It then became a landing port for slaves destined for Rio and in the late 20th century an infamous prison for political prisoners. Ruins of the prison buildings remain, covered in thick vegetation.

Pristine beach alcove surrounded by lush green forest, Ilha Grande

Steep mountain ridges in Parque Nacional do Itatiaia, Brazil's oldest national park

Parque Nacional do Itatiaia ❹

Rio de Janeiro. ▦ *from Resende, then taxi.* ▯ *Centro Excursionista Brasileiro, Av Almirante Barroso 2, (021) 2252 9844, Rio.* ▨ *Ralph Salgueiro, (021) 3351 1823.* ▨ ◔ *Hotel Donati, (021) 3352 1110.* **www**.hoteldonati.com.br

Brazil's oldest national park, Parque Nacional do Itatiaia, was founded in 1937. It was established to protect the high alpine meadows and the gradations of thick Atlantic rainforests that cover its steep mountain ridges. It is the only part of Rio de Janeiro state ever to see snow, albeit rarely.

The scenery here is magnificent. The highest regions of the park are capped with giant boulders, eroded into strange organic shapes by millions of years of rain and wind. They sit on expansive grassland coursed by babbling brooks, which become fast-flowing, clear-water rivers once they reach the warmer forested areas below. Here they tumble, roar, and fall over waterfalls and rapids.

The trees around them are busy with primates. Curious brown capuchin monkeys are a common sight on the numerous trails. Scarcer are the beautiful and shy black-faced titi monkeys, a threatened species. Birdlife, too, is prolific in the park, which is home to 350 species, many of which are endangered. The park plays a crucial role in their conservation. Dusky-legged guans wander along the park's few paved roads, brilliant seven-colored and black and gold cotingas flit about with toucans, and the early morning air buzzes with the sound of dozens of different hummingbirds.

The park can be crowded on weekends when Brazilian families romp in the numerous waterfalls and wildlife makes itself scarce. But during the week the various trails are deserted and quiet. The ranger station provides rather poor walking maps but the trails are fairly clear. Hotel Donati, which is the best hotel in the park, can organize walking tours, and with advance notice, wildlife guides.

Trail through the verdant rainforests of Parque Nacional do Itatiaia

Petrópolis ❺

Medal on display at Casa de Santos Dumont

Located in the mountains near Rio, Petrópolis owes its creation to the Brazilian royal family. Dom Pedro I's dream of building a summer residence here was fulfilled by his son, Dom Pedro II, who was equally taken by the charms of the region. In 1843, before construction of the palace began, he decreed the creation of Petrópolis as the summer seat of his government. The city soon rose in importance, as trappings of royalty made their mark. Today, Petrópolis is popular for its royal attractions, as well as for its mountain scenery and the national park of Serra dos Órgãos *(see p115)*.

Palácio Imperial

See pp114–15.

Palácio Rio Negro

Av Koeller 255, Centro. ***Tel*** *(024) 2246 9380.* 🕒 *9:30am–5pm Wed–Sun, noon–5pm Mon.* 📷 📹

Built in 1889 by Barão do Rio Negro, a wealthy coffee baron, the palace acted as the seat of the state government between 1894 and 1902, when Petrópolis was the capital of Rio de Janeiro state.

Between 1903 and 1960, the palace served as the summer residence of the presidents of the Republic. While Vargas converted a wine cellar in to a Roman-style bathhouse, Kubitschek added built-in closets. All the original rooms are in excellent condition.

Detail on the façade of Palácio Rio Negro

Exterior of French-Gothic Catedral de São Pedro de Alcântara

Catedral de São Pedro de Alcântara

Rua São Pedro de Alcântara 60, Centro. ***Tel*** *(024) 2242 4300.* 🕒 *8am–noon Mon, 8am–6pm Tue–Sun.* ♿

Though the cathedral's first stone was laid in 1884 by Dom Pedro II, much of its current structure dates from 1925. Built in French-Gothic style, it has a striking interior decorated in Carrara marble. The walls here depict detailed scenes from the Crucifixion.

The Imperial Chapel, to the right of the main entrance, contains the mortal remains of King Dom Pedro II, Princess Regent Dona Teresa Cristina, their daughter Isabel, her husband Count d'Eu, and several other members of the royal family. Statues of the royal family are also featured inside the chapel. The 1848 baptismal font is the original.

Palácio de Cristal

Rua Alfredo Pachá, Centro. ***Tel*** *(024) 2247 3721.* 🕒 *9am–6:30pm Tue–Sun.* ♿

The metal structure and glass enclosure of the Palácio de Cristal (Crystal Palace) were made in France in 1879 and shipped to Brazil. Inaugurated on February 2, 1884, the palace is a fine example of the architectural style that emerged during the French industrial revolution.

Although it was originally planned as a greenhouse for growing orchids, the Palácio de Cristal was later meant to be an exhibition hall for hosting regular displays of local products. However, it ended up as the imperial ballroom, and has been the sight of many spectacular parties. Most momentous were the extravagant balls hosted by Princess Isabel and Count d'Eu, who is believed to have conceived the palace's basic design. It was during one such event in 1888 that Isabel signed an order liberating 103 slaves. On May 13 of the same year, Isabel went on to sign the Lei Aurea (Golden Law), the decree that, in theory, abolished slavery in Brazil.

The metal-and-glass exhibition hall at the Palácio de Cristal

VISITORS' CHECKLIST

Rio de Janeiro. 🚗 287,000.
🚌 Rua Porciúcula. 🛈 Petrotur,
Praça Dom Pedro, (0800) 3241
516. **www**.petropolis.rj.gov.br

Although most of its former glory is lost, the palace today serves as an exhibition hall. It occasionally hosts art shows and cultural events.

⚜ Casa de Santos Dumont

Rua do Encanto 22, Centro.
Tel (024) 2247 3158. ⬤ 9:30am–5pm Tue–Sun. 📷

In 1918, the great Brazilian aviator and inventor of the wristwatch, Alberto Santos Dumont (1873–1932), designed and built his summerhouse in the style of a French alpine chalet and named it "A Encantada," or enchanted. The three floors contain a workroom, a lounge-cum-dining room, a bedroom, and an office. The alcohol-heated shower in the bathroom was the first of its kind in Brazil. There is no kitchen because Dumont had all his meals sent in by the then Palace Hotel.

The fascinating personal collection of this delightful inventor includes everyday objects, such as furniture, photographs, and various artifacts, including beautiful vases and lamps.

⚜ Quitandinha

Av Joaquim Rolla 2. **Tel** (024) 2237 1012. ⬤ 9am–5pm Tue–Sun. 📷 ♿

An imposing palace built in Norman style, Quitandinha is located southwest of the town center. Entrepreneur Joaquim Rolla built it in 1944 to be the largest casino complex in South America. For the exterior, Rolla copied the large casinos that were popular at the time along the Normandy coast, while the interior was by Dorothy Drape, a famous Hollywood set designer.

Quitandinha's glory ended in 1946, when President Dutra banned gambling. Remarkably well preserved, today it is mainly used for conventions and other events. Its interior still recalls the glamorous days of the 1940s when the guests were kings, queens, and Hollywood stars.

[Map of Petrópolis showing streets including Casa de Rui Barbosa, Catedral de São Pedro de Alcântara, Avenida Ipiranga, Palácio de Princesa Isabel, Praça Princesa Isabel ③, Rua de Leon, Avenida Tiradentes, Palácio de Cultura, Palácio Rio Negro, Quitandinha Avenida Koeler, Palácio Amarelo, Praça Visconde de Maua, Salão das Viaturas, Rua da Imperatriz, Rua D Pedro I, Palácio Imperial ①, Praça Dom Pedro II, Rua 16 de Março, Rua 13 de Maio, Rua Tamandaré]

Key to Symbols *see back flap*

| 0 meters | 500 |
| 0 yards | 500 |

PETRÓPOLIS

The Norman-style architecture of the Quitandinha palace complex

Petrópolis: Palácio Imperial

Statue of Dom Pedro II

Built by Dom Pedro II between 1845 and 1864, the Neo-Classical Imperial Palace was used by the Emperor as his summer residence every year from 1848 until the end of the monarchy and declaration of independence in 1889. In that year, the palace was leased out as a college, and continued to function as such until President Vargas passed a decree in 1943 creating the Imperial Museum. Among the highlights of the museum, which faithfully reflect the daily life of the Brazilian royal family, are the Imperial Crown Jewels, as well as other artifacts, paintings, and furniture that belonged to the Emperor and his family.

★ Crown Jewels
The Imperial Crown of Dom Pedro II is the most valuable piece in the collection and was made for his coronation on July 18, 1841, when he was just 15 years old.

Sala do Primeiro Reinado
This room features the last painting of Dom Pedro I in Brazil prior to his abdication on April 7, 1831.

★ Cetro
The Imperial Scepter, depicting an open-mouthed dragon with outstretched wings, was made in 1822 for the coronation of Dom Pedro I.

Entrance

Ground floor

MUSEUM GUIDE
The ground floor displays royal exhibits, and prominently features the Crown Jewels. The first floor houses the State Room, as well as the royal bedrooms. The museum is set in a pretty garden designed by Jean Baptiste Binot, a French landscape artist.

STAR EXHIBITS

★ Crown Jewels

★ Cetro

★ Sala de Estado

Elegant Neo-Classical façade of the Palácio Imperial

Gabinete
The study features Brazil's first telephone, presented to Dom Pedro II in 1876 by Alexander Graham Bell.

VISITORS' CHECKLIST

Rua da Imperatriz 220, Petrópolis. *Tel (024) 2237 8000.*
⬤ *museum: 11am–6pm Tue–Sun; sound & light show: 8pm Thu, Fri & Sat.* 🎫 *free entry to the garden from 8am–5pm on Sun.* 💻 🏨
www.museuimperial.gov.br

★ Sala de Estado
The throne on show in the State Room came from the palace in São Cristovão.

—— **First floor**

Sala do Senado
features the 1872 *Fala do Trono* (Speech from the Throne), a portrait of Dom Pedro II in full regalia.

Sala de Música
Besides a rare triangular spinet built by Mathias Bosten in 1788, the music room also has a beautiful harp.

KEY

☐ The Dining Room	☐ Dom Pedro I's Room
☐ The Music Room	☐ Room of His Majesty
☐ The Royal Costumes & Scepter	☐ Princesa Isabel's Room
☐ The Imperial Throne	☐ Lobby
☐ Dom Pedro II's Study	☐ The Empress's Sewing Room
☐ The Princesses's Room	☐ The Empress's Piano Room
☐ Imperial Brazilian Jewelry	☐ Saleta
	☐ Senate Room
	☐ Other Exhibition Space
	☐ Non-Exhibition Space

Teresópolis ❻

Rio de Janeiro. 🏠 140,000. 🚌 from Rio de Janeiro City. 🛈 Centro Turístico, (021) 2644 4095.

Set amid pretty countryside, Teresópolis is known for its artisan fair in Praça Higino da Silveira, which is lined with more than 700 stands at weekends. Just 3 miles (5 km) south of the town center, the **Orquidário Aranda** is one of Brazil's best orchid farms, with over 3,000 varieties on display.

🌸 **Orquidário Aranda**
Rua João Daudt de Oliveira s/n.
Tel (021) 2742 0628.
📅 9am–4:30pm Mon–Fri.

Parque Nacional da Serra dos Órgãos ❼

Rio de Janeiro. 🚌 from Rio de Janeiro. 🛈 (021) 2152 1100.
⬤ 8am–5pm Tue–Sun. 🎫 🛈 ⛺

Created in 1939, this national park covers an area of approximately 46 sq miles (105 sq km) that stretches from Teresópolis across to Petrópolis. The park offers good climbing and treks, including a spectacular three-day guided trek of 26 miles (42 km) between the two towns. Among the park's most notable peaks are the 7,425-ft (2,263-m) Pedra do Sino, the highest in the mountain range, and the more famous Dedo de Deus (God's Finger), which stands 5,512 ft (1,680 m) high.

Of the many entrance points to the park, the most popular and best equipped is located 3 miles (5 km) south of Teresópolis.

Dedo de Deus (God's Finger), Parque Nacional da Serra dos Órgãos

Búzios ❽

Rio de Janeiro. 🚌 *from Cabo Frio.*
ℹ️ *Praça Santos Dumont, (024) 2633
6200.* 🌐 www.buzios.com.br

Since Brigitte Bardot's visit to
Búzios in 1964 with her then
boyfriend, Brazilian actor
Bob Zagury, this peninsula
has developed from a quiet
string of isolated fishing
villages lost in semi-
tropical *maquis*, into one
of the country's most
stylish low-key resorts.
Private homes,
designer boutiques,
and little *pousadas*
cling to its hills or
watch over the
numerous beaches.
Beach buggies driven
by holiday-makers

**Statue of Brigitte
Bardot on the
Orla Bardot**

buzz along the scruffy roads.
Yachts bob in the bay in front
of Búzios town, which is little
more than a cluster of
cobblestoned streets lined
with smart boutiques and
restaurants. During high
season, the resort buzzes
with cruise-ship passengers
and middle-class Brazilian
tourists who shop by day
on **Rua das Pedras**, the
town's main thoroughfare,
sip cocktails in the
evening at one of the
oceanfront *pousadas*,
and then dance the
night away in the
Ibiza-style clubs
and beachside bars.
Búzios's *raison d'être*
is its beaches,
which range from
half-moon bays to

**One of the souvenir shops
lining Rua das Pedras in Búzios**

long stretches of fine white
sand. The best way to see
them is to hire a beach buggy
and explore, armed with one
of the ubiquitous free maps

Beaches of Costa do Sul

The southern coast, extending between Niterói and
Búzios, is best known for its landscape, outstanding
beaches, and upmarket resorts. Attractive beaches and
sparkling waters make it ideal for a lazy stretch on the
sand, or a dip in the clean waters. With its crashing
waves and a steady breeze, this stretch is popular for
wind-surfing. It is easy to find accommodation here,
both in busy resorts and isolated fishing villages.

**SOUTHEAST
BRAZIL**

RIO DE
JANEIRO
&
ESPÍRITO
SANTO
Rio de
Janeiro ●

LOCATOR MAP

☐ Costa do Sul

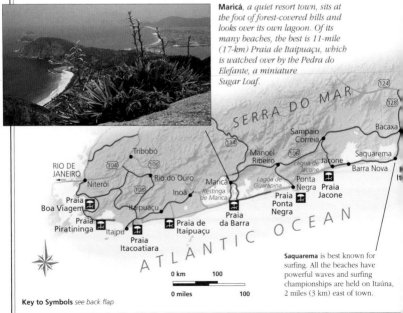

Maricá, *a quiet resort town, sits at
the foot of forest-covered hills and
looks over its own lagoon. Of its
many beaches, the best is 11-mile
(17-km) Praia de Itaipuaçu, which
is watched over by the Pedra do
Elefante, a miniature
Sugar Loaf.*

SERRA DO MAR

RIO DE
JANEIRO

Niterói · Tribobó · Rio de Ouro · Inoã · Maricá · Restinga de Marica · Manoel Ribeiro · Sampaio Correia · Lagoa de Jacone · Jacone · Saquarema · Barra Nova · Bacaxa

Praia
Boa Viagem · Itaipuaçu · Praia da Barra · Lagoa de Guarapina · Ponta Negra · Praia Ponta Negra · Praia Jacone

Praia
Piratininga · Itaipu · Praia de Itaipuaçu

Praia
Itacoatiara

ATLANTIC OCEAN

Saquarema is best known for
surfing. All the beaches have
powerful waves and surfing
championships are held on Itaúna,
2 miles (3 km) east of town.

0 km   100
0 miles   100

Key to Symbols *see back flap*

For hotels and restaurants in this region see pp370–72 and pp396–7

of the peninsula available from every other hotel reception. The peninsula is extremely well-signposted, and since it is only 4 miles (6 km) long and 2 miles (4 km) wide, it is difficult to get lost here.

Many of the beaches, including the two sets of twin sheltered coves – at **Praia João Fernandes**, **Praia João Fernandinho**, **Praia Azeda**, and **Praia Azedinha** – are within half an hour's walk of town. Others are a beach buggy ride away. **Praia da Ferradura**, on the opposite side from Búzios, is one of the most beautiful beaches near town, and one of the least spoilt by hotel development. Fishermen still work from here at dawn and dusk.

Praia Brava, at the peninsula's eastern extreme, is washed by the fiercest waves and is a popular surf beach. **Olho de Boi**, which can be reached only via a rocky trail that runs from Brava's southern end, is surrounded by rocky hills on all sides, and is an unofficial nudist beach. **Ferradurinha**, at the peninsula's southern extreme, has clear, calm waters and natural swimming pools, good for a dip.

The small, isolated Praia Azeda, known for its tranquil waters

Cabo Frio is a triumph of concrete over natural beauty. The region's busiest resort, it overflows with locals at weekends. There is good surf on the numerous beaches and dune-boarding at Praia do Peró, 5 miles (8 km) north.

VISITORS' CHECKLIST

Rio de Janeiro. 🚌 from Rio. **Cabo Frio** 🛈 *Av Américo Vespúcio 200, (022) 2647 1689.* **Arraial do Cabo** 🛈 *Av do Liberdade 50, (024) 2622 1650.* **Araruama** 🛈 *Av Brasil 655 (022) 2665 4145.* **Saquarema** 🛈 *Secretaria de Turismo, Rua Coronel Madureira 77, (022) 2651 2123.* **Maricá** 🛈 *Av Ver Francisco Sabino da Costa 945, (021) 3731 5094.*

Praia da Tartaruga — Armacão de Búzios
106 — 178 — Praia de Tucuns
104 — Praia do Peró
138 — Iguaba Grande — Sáo Pedro da Aldeia — Praia das Conchas
Iguaba Pequena — Porto do Carro — Cabo Frio
Araruama — Lagoa de Araruama
Praia Seca — Figueira — 132 — Praia Grande — Arraial do Cabo
Ilha — Praia Massambaba — Praia do Cabo Frio — ILHA DO CABO FRIO

Araruama, one of the largest lakes in Brazil, is ringed by myriad long white-sand beaches. A constant breeze makes for good windsurfing. It is also famous for its medicinal mud and high salinity.

Arraial do Cabo *town itself is uninspiring but the confluence of currents around the cape provides the best diving in southeastern Brazil and a wealth of magnificent beaches.*

Terceira Ponte Bridge connecting Vila Velha to Vitória

Guarapari ❾

Espírito Santo. 🏚 2,000. 🚌 from Vitória. 🛈 Praça Jerônimo Monteiro, (027) 3361 2322 (ext: 273). www. guarapari.com.br

Espírito Santo's busiest beach resort is fringed by dozens of long, white beaches. People from Minas Gerais rush down on weekends to bask on the sandy beaches of Guarapari, said to have mildy radioactive healing properties. The best beach is **Praia do Morro**, north of the city. **Praia do Meio**, also to the north, has rock pools filled with clear water, and is good for snorkeling.

Guarapari offers light adventure activities, such as rappeling, rafting, and some of the best diving in the Southeast. The town also has a lively nightlife scene.

Vitória ❿

Espírito Santo. 🏚 292,000. ✈ 🚌 from Rio. 🛈 Av Nossa Senhora de Penha 714, (027) 3380 2232. 🎭 Carnaval (Dec).

The capital city of Espírito Santo is dominated by an expansive bay with sheltered crescent coves, and surrounded by a bottle-green open ocean. Vitória was originally made up of 36 distinct islands, but landfills have now reduced these to just a handful, connected by five grand bridges. **Praia do Camburi**, the main beach south of the city is a busy 4-mile (6-km) stretch, dotted with restaurants and hotels.

Across the river, **Vila Velha** (Old Town), the most interesting part of the city, is reached by the majestic bridge, **Terceira Ponte**. Although few colonial buildings remain, it is home to the architectural symbol of the city, **Convento da Nossa Senhora da Penha**. Sitting high on a lush palm-covered hill overlooking Vitória Bay, its thick fortified walls beautifully reflect both the sunrise and sunset. The monastery was founded in 1558 and preserves fine 16th-century wood carvings and one of Brazil's first paintings, *Nossa Senhora das Alegrias*, by an unknown early 16th-century Iberian artist. At the base of the hill is the simple Igreja Nossa Senhora do Rosário, the oldest church in the state, dating from 1551.

South of Vila Velha, **Praia de Costa** is not as busy a beach as Camburi, but is a good place to go bodysurfing.

Manguezal de Vitória, situated northeast of Vitória, is the largest stretch of urban mangroves in South America. The mangroves are an important nursery for marine life and can be visited by boat alongside a number of the bay's wilder islands.

🛅 **Convento da Nossa Senhora da Penha**
Vila Velha, Vitória. **Tel** (027) 3329 0420. ⬚ 5:30am–4:45pm Mon–Fri, 4:30am–4:45pm Sun.

🌿 **Manguezal de Vitória**
Santuário de Santo Antônio. 🚗 Av Dario Lourenço de Souza, (027) 3222 3810.

Sunbathers on Praia do Morro in Guarapari

Pedra Azul **⓫**

Espírito Santo. 🚌 *from Vitória.*
🏨 *Parque Estadual da Pedra Azul,
(027) 3248 1156.* ⬜ *8am–5:30pm
daily.* 📷 ✅ *9am & 1:30pm onward
daily.* **www**.pedraazul.com.br

Sitting in a tiny island of
remnant Mata Atlântica forest,
the 500-m (1,640-ft) high
Pedra Azul (Blue Stone) rises
in the middle of the Parque
Estadual da Pedra Azul,
forming a stunning center
piece. Its natural color is an
almost polished blue-grey,
but shifts in hue and shade
depending on the light, coal-
black and brooding under a
dark cloud, burning orange
with the setting sun, or silvery
white under a full moon.

There is a small visitors'
center at the foot of the stone
which is a good place to
collect a detailed map of the
park. A park ranger will also
point out the trail leading up
to the stone – a fairly easy
but long walk punctuated by
nine natural pools where
visitors can take a refreshing
dip. The trail is closed during
and after heavy rains. Serious
climbers are permitted to
camp in the park for free.

The forest surrounding
Pedra Azul is small but it
is the nesting ground for a
diverse variety of wildlife.
Hummingbirds, tanagers, and
tiny tufted-eared marmosets
are a common sight.

Dramatic Pedra Azul, a granite monolith

Itaúnas **⓬**

Espírito Santo. 🏠 *2,500.* 🚌 *from
Vitória.* 🎭 *Festa de Forró (Jul).*

This sleepy little fishing town
lies tucked away in the far
north of Espírito Santo on
the border with Bahia. Long
strands of beaches stretch to
the north and south of the
town. These have drifted into
dunes so large that the first
Itaúnas lies submerged, the
remains of the original church
tower occasionally appearing
from the sand after a strong
wind. The town lies next to
the Rio Itaúnas which spreads
into broad marshy meadows
behind the sea. Ocelots,
caimans, and capybaras live
here, along with an impressive variety of rare waterbirds
and small mammals.

The smattering of hotels
in town offer dune buggy
tours, crossing dozens of
towering dunes and empty
turtle-nesting beaches, eventually reaching the sandy cliffs
on the state border with Bahia.

Itaúnas itself is surprisingly
lively for a town so small. It
is famous, particulary among
students, for its exuberant
samba and *axé* parties, which
continue from December to
March, and exciting *forró*
dance festival in July.

Sand dunes flanking the sleepy fishing town of Itaúnas along the Rio Itaúnas

MINAS GERAIS

The state of Minas Gerais is dotted with pretty colonial towns, set in a stunning landscape of rugged hills. Of these, Ouro Preto, Congonhas, and Diamantina are UNESCO World Heritage Sites. Beyond the towns is pastoral country broken by wilderness, much of which has been protected by a series of national and state parks, where several rare species of animals, birds, and plants can be seen.

Minas's old mining towns are laid out along the Estrada Real, once Brazil's first great wagon trail and now one of its major tourist routes. The most famous is Ouro Preto, named after the black gold that was discovered here in the late 17th century by an itinerant adventurer (*bandeirante*), who came through the vast interior in search of slaves. Gold brought a rush of speculators and new discoveries and by the mid-18th-century ramshackle mining camps had grown into prosperous towns. Today, Ouro Preto, Tiradentes, Mariana, São João del Rei, Congonhas, and Diamantina preserve some of the finest ecclesiastical buildings and Baroque carvings in the Americas.

The state's spectacular parks are home to the maned wolf, as well as a plethora of endemic birds and plants. The Serra do Cipó and the Serra da Canastra lie on the tablelands of the Brazilian shield. Their *cerrado* forests are cut by several rivers that plunge dramatically over the edges of the *mesetas* (tabletop mountains), forming some of the world's highest waterfalls. The mountains of the Serra do Caparaó protect a swathe of the Mata Atlântica, dripping with orchids and the habitat of one of the few remaining populations of woolly spider monkey – the Americas' largest and rarest primate.

The state capital, Belo Horizonte, is a modern industrial city with a lively café life. President Juscelino Kubitschek's favorite architect, Oscar Niemeyer, adorned the city's Pampulha neighborhood with several structures before building the nation's capital, Brasília. Minas is also well known for its distinct cuisine and its rich literary and musical heritage.

A breathtaking view of mauve *ipê* flowers in full bloom outside Diamantina

◁ Enchanting Igreja de Nossa Senhora do Carmo, towering above the colonial town of Ouro Preto

Exploring Minas Gerais

Belo Horizonte, the capital of Minas Gerais, is the focus of life here. Most colonial mining towns, including Ouro Preto and Congonhas, lie immediately to its south. Mariana, another colonial city south of Belo Horizonte, is still a working mining center. Farther south, and a day's drive from the capital is the hilly Serra da Canastra National Park. Northern Minas is much wilder, with large tracts of *cerrado* forest in the Serra do Cipó and around Diamantina. The extreme north is arid, dominated by the *sertão*, a region of scrub and grassland, whose distinct culture and language was mythologized in the most famous of all Brazilian novels, *Grande Sertão: Veredas*, by João Guimarães Rosa *(see p31)*.

Painting inside Igreja Nossa Senhora do Carmo, Diamantina

SIGHTS AT A GLANCE

Towns & Cities
Belo Horizonte ❸
Diamantina ❶
Mariana ❺
Ouro Preto pp126–8 ❹
São João del Rei ❽
Tiradentes ❼

National Parks & Areas of Natural Beauty
Parque Nacional Serra da Canastra ❾
Parque Nacional Serra do Cipó ❷

Historic Buildings
Basílica do Senhor Bom Jesus de Matosinhos, Congonhas pp130–31 ❻

KEY

▭▭	Highway
▬▬	Major road
▭▭	Minor road
▭▭	Railroad
▭▭	State border
△	Peak

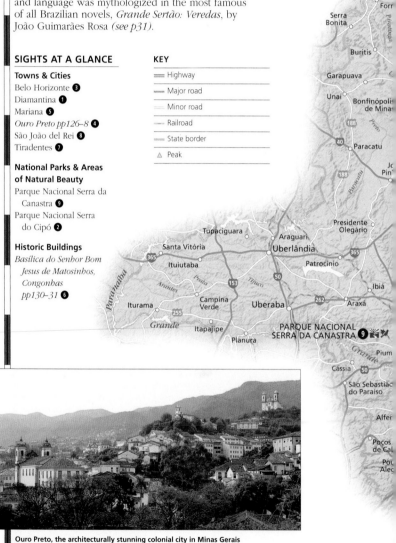

Ouro Preto, the architecturally stunning colonial city in Minas Gerais

Map labels:
Forr
Serra Bonita
Buritis
Garapuava
Unaí
Bonfinópoli de Minas
Paracatu
Presidente Olegário
Tupaciguara
Santa Vitória
Araguari
Uberlândia
Ituiutaba
Patrocínio
Ibiá
Campina Verde
Uberaba
Araxá
Iturama
Itapajipe
Grande
Planura
PARQUE NACIONAL SERRA DA CANASTRA ❾
Pium
Cássia
São Sebastião do Paraíso
Alfer
Poços de Cal
Pou Alec

SEE ALSO

- **Where to Stay** pp372–3

- **Where to Eat** pp398–9

Sunset in the *cerrado* landscape of Serra da Canastra

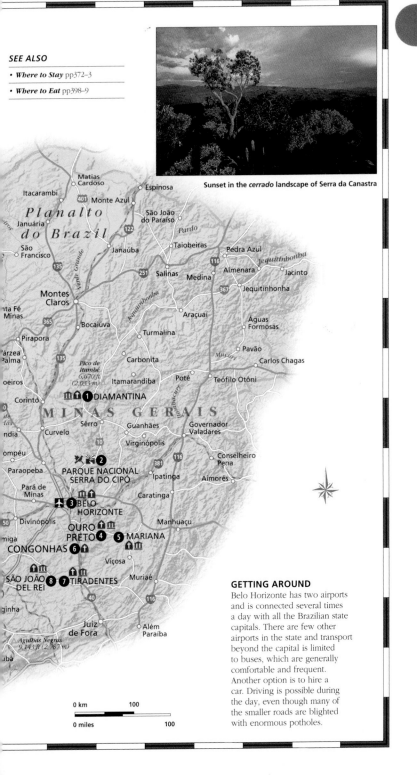

Planalto do Brazil

Matias Cardoso
Itacarambi
Monte Azul
Espinosa
São João do Paraíso
Januária
Pardo
São Francisco
Janaúba
Taiobeiras
Pedra Azul
Jequitinhonha
Salinas
Medina
Almenara
Jacinto
Montes Claros
Jequitinhonha
nta Fé Minas
Bocaiúva
Araçuaí
Águas Formosas
Pirapora
Turmalina
Muc...
Pavão
árzea Palma
Carbonita
Carlos Chagas
oeiros
Pico de Itambé 6,670 ft (2,033 m)
Itamarandiba
Poté
Teófilo Otôni
Corintó
🏛🏠❶ DIAMANTINA

MINAS GERAIS

Sêrro
Guanhães
Governador Valadares
ndia
Curvelo
Virginópolis
ompéu
⚔🚣❷
Conselheiro Pena
Paraopeba
PARQUE NACIONAL SERRA DO CIPÓ
Ipatinga
Aimorés
Pará de Minas
🏛🏠❸ BELO HORIZONTE
Caratinga
✈
Divinópolis
Manhuaçu
OURO PRETO 🏠🏛❹ ❺ MARIANA 🏠🏛
miga
CONGONHAS ❻ 🏠
Viçosa
SÃO JOÃO DEL REI 🏠🏛❽ ❼ TIRADENTES 🏠🏛
Muriaé
ginha
Agulhas Negras 9,143 ft (2,787 m)
Juiz de Fora
Além Paraíba
iba

0 km   100

0 miles   100

GETTING AROUND

Belo Horizonte has two airports and is connected several times a day with all the Brazilian state capitals. There are few other airports in the state and transport beyond the capital is limited to buses, which are generally comfortable and frequent. Another option is to hire a car. Driving is possible during the day, even though many of the smaller roads are blighted with enormous potholes.

Old *fazenda* in the beautiful village of Biribiri near Diamantina

Diamantina ❶

🏠 *48,000.* 🚌 *Largo Dom João 134, (038) 3531 9176.* 🚉 *Praça Juscelino Kubitschek 25, (038) 3531 8060.* **www.**diamantina.com.br

Nestled in rugged hills and shrouded with *cerrado* forest, Diamantina is the prettiest and best preserved of all the colonial cities in the state, and also a UNESCO World Heritage Site. Diamonds were discovered here in 1728, when the city was a small settlement called Arraial do Tijuco. Within a few decades the mud huts and encampments transformed into one of the wealthiest towns in Brazil.

The city is tiny and most of its historic buildings and churches lie within easy walking distance of the main square, Praça Guerra. This is an obvious point of orientation as it is dominated by the twin towers of the largest building in the city – the Catedral Metropolitana de Santo Antônio, built in the 1930s. Just south of this in the adjacent Praça Juscelino Kubitschek is a small **Museu Casa do Diamante**, which houses a handful of the stones, together with iron collars once fitted onto slaves.

South again is the **Museu de Juscelino Kubitschek**, the modest former home of the Brazilian president, Juscelino Kubitschek (1902–76), who built Brasília *(see pp302–303).* Two blocks west is the city's most beautiful landmark, the

Casa da Gloria, consisting of two houses on opposite sides connected by an enclosed, brilliant blue, second-storey passageway. The building is not open to the public.

There are several churches in Diamantina. The oldest is the **Nossa Senhora do Rosário**, in the square of the same name, a short distance to the northeast of the Praça Guerra. It was built and used by the enslaved black community and the city's poor. Next to it is an original 18th-century fountain whose waterspouts are bas-reliefs of African heads.

A block south is the spectacular **Nossa Senhora do Carmo**. Built between 1760 and 1784, it was the town's richest church and attended by the elite white community. It is remarkable chiefly for the interior paintings by José Soares de Araujo, from Braga, Portugal. Araujo's works lie in many of the town's churches but those here are his finest. The ceiling paintings are very striking. Near the back of the church is a portrait of the Prophet Elijah ascending to heaven in a chariot of fire.

The **Casa de Chica da Silva**, a smart town house one block south of the Nossa Senhora do Carmo, is famous far more for its former

owner than it is for its small collection of period furniture. During the 18th century, Francisca (Chica) da Silva was a mulatta slave who became one of the few black people to become accepted by high colonial society through sheer force of personality.

Environs
A string of stunning natural locations lie within easy reach of Diamantina, the most impressive of which is **Biribiri**, located 7 miles (12 km) north of town. A historical village, Biribiri is home to many *fazendas* and is surrounded by waterfalls and mountains. Next to Biribiri is a winding black water river and the Parque Rio Preto, a good location for bird-watching.

🏛 **Casa de Chica da Silva**
Praça Lobo Mesquita 266.
🕐 *noon–5:30pm Tue–Sat, 9am–noon Sun.*

🏛 **Museu Casa do Diamante**
Rua Direita 14. **Tel** *(038) 3531 1382.* 🕐 *noon–5:30pm Tue–Sat, 9am–noon Sun.* 📷

🏛 **Museu de Juscelino Kubitschek**
Rua São Francisco 241. **Tel** *(038) 3531 3607.* 🕐 *8am–noon & 2–6pm Tue–Sat, 9am–noon Sun.* 📷

⛪ **Nossa Senhora do Carmo**
Rua do Carmo. 🕐 *8am–2pm & 2–6pm Tue–Sun, 9am–noon Sun.*

⛪ **Nossa Senhora do Rosário**
Largo do Rosário. 🕐 *8am–noon & 2–6pm Tue–Sat, 9am–noon Sun.*

Nave, Igreja de Nossa Senhora do Carmo

Magnificent waterfall at Parque Nacional Serra do Cipó

Parque Nacional Serra do Cipó ➋

from Belo Horizonte to Jaboticatubas, or Santana do Riacho. Secretária do Turismo, (031) 3718 7228. **Tel** (031) 3718 7129. 8am–5pm daily. Cipó Veraneio Hotel, Rodovia MG-10, Serra do Cipó, (031) 3718 7000. **www**.cipoveraneiohotel.com.br

Just northeast of Belo Horizonte, the state capital, this 131 sq-mile (338 sq-km) national park lies in high rugged country in the Serra do Espinhaço mountains, which run through the middle of northern Minas Gerais. Cipó protects some pristine areas of *cerrado* as well as the watersheds of many of the tributaries of the São Francisco and the Doce rivers. Waterfalls, plants, rare animals, and birds are abundant, making this one of the most beautiful national parks in Minas Gerais.

It is particularly lovely in May and June when the skies are invariably blue, the rivers full, and many of the numerous wildflowers in bloom. This is also a good time to go on a guided tour, at dawn or dusk, to spot pumas, giant anteaters, ocelots, maned wolves, and howling monkeys on the quieter trails.

The park is a popular location for ecotourism – particularly rock climbing, with excellent facilities and accommodation options.

Belo Horizonte ➌

3,000,000. Aloturismo (Belotur's hotline), (031) 3277 9777. Carnaval (Feb/Mar). **www**.pbh.gov.br

The capital city of Minas Gerais was laid out in the 1890s and resembles a mini-São Paulo. Clusters of seemingly endless skyscraper apartment blocks sit in a broad valley under lush hills. Belo Horizonte is known worldwide for its visionary architecture. Its architectural highlights lie in the suburb of Pampulha, often regarded as the blueprint for Brasília. The buildings are set in expansive gardens designed by Roberto Burle Marx (1909–94), gathered around a large, beautiful artificial lake. All were commissioned by the then Minas governor, Juscelino Kubitschek, and designed by the renowned architect Oscar Niemeyer in the 1940s.

The most impressive of all the buildings is the **Igreja de São Francisco de Assis**, which was built in 1943 as a series of parabolic arches in concrete, and has a wonderful sense of light and space. On the outside walls are a series of *azulejos*, or Portuguese blue tiles, depicting scenes from the life of St. Francis and painted by Brazil's foremost Modernist artist, Candido Portinari (1903–62). Other important buildings in the Pampulha complex include the dance hall **Casa do Baile**,

Azulejos on the outside walls of São Francisco de Assis

with its sweeping curved walkway that functioned as a ballroom till 1946 and the twin sports stadia, which are a clear precursor to the gymnasium Niemeyer designed for Brasília.

In the inner city, the **Museu Mineiro** preserves some fine colonial era religious art, including a number of paintings attributed to Mestre Athayde (1762–1830). Beyond this, Belo Horizonte's main attractions are the lively restaurant and nightlife scene around the inner city neighborhoods of Lourdes and Savassi. These areas have many chic restaurants, which often have live music playing during the weekends *(see p398)*. The Lourdes and Savassi neighborhoods are easily explored on foot, and make a pleasant walk.

Environs
The colonial towns of Sabará, Caeté, and Santa Luiza, to the east of Belo Horizonte, lie less than half an hour's drive away. All preserve fine Baroque churches and streets of 18th-century town houses.

> **Igreja de São Francisco de Assis**
> Av Otacilio Negrão de Lima, Pampulha. **Tel** (031) 3427 1644. 9am–5pm Mon–Sat, 9am–1pm Sun.

> **Museu Mineiro**
> Av João Pinheiro 342. **Tel** (031) 3269 1168. 10am–6pm Tue–Fri, 10am–4pm Sat & Sun.

Igreja de São Francisco de Assis in Pampulha, Belo Horizonte

Street-by-Street: Ouro Preto ❹

Ouro Preto, or "Black Gold," earned its name shortly after its founding in 1698, from tarnished gold nuggets mined in the surrounding areas. It still resembled a boom town when it was given city status in 1711. By the mid-18th century, however, the gold rush had turned Ouro Preto into a wealthy town with fine buildings. It nurtured a gene-ration of some of Latin America's finest artists and craftsmen, including the eccle-siastical painter Mestre Athayde and the great sculptor Aleijadinho among others. Ouro Preto became the base of the Inconfidência rebellion led by Tiradentes against Portuguese colonists.

Christ, Nossa Senhora do Pilar

Casa dos Contos
Once the gold exchange, then a prison, the building is now a small museum dedicated to money and finance.

A cluster of colonial buildings in hilly Ouro Preto town

★ Matriz de Nossa Senhora do Pilar
Exquisite artwork is showcased in this opulent Brazilian Baroque church, resplendent in gold. The carvings in the chancel are breathtaking.

STAR SIGHTS

- ★ Matriz de Nossa Senhora do Pilar

- ★ Matriz de Nossa Senhora da Conceição

- ★ Igreja de São Francisco de Assis

RUA S. ROCHA LAGOA

RUA DIREITA

RUA COR ALVES

RUA PARANÁ

RUA DO PILAR

Museu do Oratório

| 0 meters | 100 |
| 0 yards | 100 |

★ **Matriz de Nossa Senhora da Conceição**
Manuel Francisco Lisboa transformed this once-rustic church into one of the city's most magnificently decorated cathedrals.

VISITORS' CHECKLIST

Minas Gerais. 65,000.
from Belo Horizonte.
Praça Tiradentes 41, (031)
3559 3269. Carnaval (Feb/
Mar). **Casa dos Contos** Rua São
José 12. **Tel** (031) 3551 1444.
**Igreja de Nossa Senhora de
Carmo** Rua B. Mosqueira.
Tel (031) 3551 3282.

Statue of Tiradentes
The leader of the Inconfidentes was the only rebel against the Portuguese colonizers to be executed. He is a cult figure in Brazil, mainly for the poor.

Portrait of Aleijadinho
This likeness, which was painted long after the sculptor's death, is housed in the Museu Aleijadinho. The museum preserves a small collection of Aleijadinho's works.

KEY

– – – Suggested route

Museu da Inconfidência
features relics related to the Inconfidentes, as well as drawings by Aleijadinho.

Igreja de Nossa Senhora do Carmo
The Rococo font (in the sacristy), door-case the altars, and the statue of Santa Helena in this church are all attributed to Aleijadinho.

★ **Igreja de São Francisco de Assis**
One of Latin America's most important Rococo buildings, the church combines the finest work of Aleijadinho and Mestre Athayde.

Exploring Ouro Preto

Carving by Francisco Xavier de Brito

One of the first gold towns in Minas Gerais and a former state capital, Ouro Preto is built on a series of hills. Steep, curving streets lined with 18th-century residences, many of which have now been converted into restaurants, bars, and shops, link the hills. Within the town, the streets lead to pretty little squares dominated by Baroque churches and stately town houses. These include the churches of São Francisco de Assis and the Nossa Senhora do Pilar, whose interiors bear the stamp of some of Latin America's finest artists and craftsmen.

⛪ Igreja de São Francisco de Assis

Largo de Coimbra. *Tel (031) 3551 4661.* ☐ *8:30am–noon & 1:30–4pm Tue–Sun.* 🔲

This understated, elegant little church was constructed between 1766 and 1802 and seems modest next to many of Latin America's grand Baroque churches. It is characterized by gentle curves, from the elegant S-shaped balustrades of its façade to the exquisitely unified, undulating lines of its interior. The quality of the church's beauty lies in the mastery of its art, created by two of Brazil's greatest artists, Aleijadinho *(see p131)* and his long-term partner Manuel da Costa Athayde (1762–1830). The tablet on the church's façade

showing St. Francis receiving the stigmata is believed to have been Aleijadinho's first great carving. It was followed by others, including the ornately carved door-case and the front of the sacristy at the rear of the church.

⛪ Matriz de Nossa Senhora do Pilar

Praça Mons Castilho Barbosa. *Tel (031) 3551 4736.* ☐ *9–10:45am & noon–4:45pm Tue–Sun.* ✝ *7am Mon–Fri, 7am & 7pm Sat & Sun, 7pm 1st Fri of the month.* 🔲 📷

Commissioned by two of the wealthiest ecclesiastical orders in Ouro Preto, this church was intended as a showpiece of their influence. Pomp and circumstance surrounded its inauguration in 1731, which witnessed

grand processions of clergy in opulent vestments and horses in velvet mantles mounted by knights in diamond-studded robes.

Nearly half a ton each of gold and silver were used to gild its interior, which is largely the work of 18th-century sculptor Francisco Xavier de Brito, an expatriate Portuguese. The gilt carving of Christ on the Cross on the door-case to the *capela-mor* (apsidal chapel) and the Resurrection scene on the tabernacle are regarded as de Brito's finest work.

Façade of Matriz de Nossa Senhora da Conceição

⛪ Matriz de Nossa Senhora da Conceição

Praça Antônio Dias. *Tel (031) 3551 3282.* ☐ *8–11:45am & 1:30–4:45pm Tue–Sat, noon–4:45pm Sun.* 🔲

Built by Manuel Francisco Lisboa, this church was constructed between 1727 and 1770. It is most celebrated for its harmonious proportions – the unity of curves and straight lines on the façade and the sense of space generated by what is in reality a modest nave and chancel. Manuel Francisco only added the finishing touches to the heavily gilt interior, and the sculptors of the elaborate interior remain largely unknown. Both Lisboa and his son Aleijadinho are buried in the church.

There is a small museum devoted to the life and times of Aleijadinho in the basement of the church, containing only very few of his pieces.

Ceiling painting by Athayde in Igreja de São Francisco de Assis

Praça Gomes Freire in Mariana, lined by fine 18th-century houses

Mariana ❺

🏘 47,000. 🚌 ℹ Praça Tancredo Neves, (031) 3558 2762. **www.** mariana.mg.gov.br.

The oldest colonial town in Minas Gerais, Mariana, which was also a significant mining town, was the capital of the state in the first half of the 18th century and far more important than its immediate neighbor, Ouro Preto.

The simple 18th-century **Basílica de São Pedro dos Clérigos** stands on top of the city's only hill. From here, there are spectacular views of Mariana's small colonial center.

The main focus of the old town is the **Praça Gomes Freire**, a lovely garden square surrounded by 18th-century town houses. A short distance west of Praça Gomes Freire are the twin churches of **São Francisco de Assis** and **Nossa**

Unique window in Mariana

Senhora do Carmo. Both date from the late 18th century and sit next to each other in front of the colonial building, the Casa de Camara.

The church of São Francisco de Assis is decorated with ceiling paintings by Manuel da Costa Athayde, who was buried in the church.

Especially worth seeing are the evocative scenes of the death of St. Francis, showing the saint in serene contemplation in an Italian pastoral landscape, combined with the Brazilian landscape.

The Nossa Senhora do Carmo also has striking paintings by Athayde. Although damaged by fire in 1999, the church is still remarkable for its delicately balanced and very Portuguese exterior. Known for its gentle curves and round towers, it also has exquisite lozenge-shaped key windows. The city's other famous

church is the **Basílica de Nossa Senhora da Assunção**, which dates from 1760. Its exterior is modest, but the interior has some of the finest ceiling paintings by the 16th-century Portuguese artist, Manuel Rabello de Sousa. It also contains an exquisite 17th-century German organ and altarpieces by Francisco Xavier de Brito, and a portal and *lavebo* attributed to Aleijadinho. The organ was a gift to the diocese when Mariana was the foremost city in inland Brazil. Restored in 1984, it can be heard during regular weekend organ recitals.

Just around the corner to the south of the basilica is the most interesting of the civic buildings, the **Museu Arquidiocesano de Arte Sacra**. This preserves paintings by Athayde, *objets d'art* by Aleijadinho, and antique liturgical objects. Its façade is crowned with a medal by Aleijadinho.

🔒 **Basílica de Nossa Senhora da Assunção**
Rua Direita. **Tel** (031) 3557 1216.
◯ 6am–8pm Tue–Sun.

🏛 **Museu Arquidiocesano de Arte Sacra**
Rua Frei Durão. **Tel** (031) 3557 2516. ◯ 8:30am–noon & 1:30–5pm Tue–Sun. 🖼

🔒 **Nossa Senhora do Carmo**
Praça Gomes Freire. ◯ 1–4pm daily (timings may vary depending on the curator).

🔒 **São Francisco de Assis**
Praça Gomes Freire. ◯ 9am–4pm daily.

View of Mariana and the twin churches from Basílica de São Pedro dos Clérigos

Basílica do Senhor Bom Jesus de Matosinhos, Congonhas ❻

Completed in 1771, the Baroque church of Bom Jesus de Matosinhos was built by the diamond miner Feliciano Mendes, who, after recovering from the brink of death, vowed to build a church in homage to "Bom Jesus." At the entrance of the church, 12 soapstone statues of prophets from the Old Testament overlook a gently sloping garden, where six chapels containing life-size figures commemorate episodes from the Passion of Christ. The church is famous for preserving the most impressive ensemble of statues in Latin America, carved by Aleijadinho between 1780 and 1814.

Painted Ceiling
Painted by Bernardo Pires da Silva in 1776, the artwork on the ceiling is regarded as the finest Rococo church painting in Brazil.

Oséias

Joel

Na

Ezequie

Daniel

Jonas

Amós

Baruc

Abdias

Jeremias

Carved Altar
Designed by sculptor Aleijadinho, the altar was beautifully carved by his disciple, João Antunes de Carvalho.

Isaías
The sculpture of Isaías has narrow shoulders and disproportionately short arms, and is thought to have been carved by Aleijadinho's students.

The Crucifixion
is particularly grisly, depicting smiling soldiers hammering nails into a spread-eagled Christ, his face contorted in agony.

★ **The Prophet Habacuc**
Aleijadinho's sculptures are celebrated for having an air of theatricality and accentuated characteristics, both striking in his statue of Habacuc.

STAR SIGHTS

★ The Prophet Habacuc

★ The Capture of Christ

★ The Last Supper

Façade of the church inspired by and modeled on the Santuário do Bom Jesus in Braga, Portugal, with the prophets at the entrance

VISITORS' CHECKLIST

Basílica do Senhor Bom Jesus de Matosinhos, Congonhas. Basílica from Av Júlia Kubitschek 1892. FUMCULT, Praça Presidente Juscelino Kubitschek 135, (031) 3713 3100 (ext: 114). 8–11am Mon–Fri, 8am–9pm Sat, 7am–10pm Sun. 9am–1pm Sun. Jubileu do Senhor Bom Jesus do Matosinhos (Sep 7–14). www.cidadeshistoricas. art.br/congonhas

ALEIJADINHO

Aleijadinho (1738–1815) meaning "Little Cripple," was nicknamed due to the disfigurement he suffered from leprosy. When he carved the statues at Bom Jesus de Matosinhos, he could no longer walk and had completely lost the use of his hands. His students carried him up the hill each day and strapped hammers and chisels to his arms. The figure watching the Crucifixion and hiding his hands is reputed to be a self-portrait by Aleijadinho. The statues are, without doubt, his masterpieces, and his final works of art.

Statue of Aleijadinho (standing, right) witnessing the Crucifixion

The Flagellation of Christ and the Coronation with Thorns depicts a prelude to the Crucifixion.

★ The Capture of Christ
Jesus is captured by Herod's soldiers, led to him by his disciple, Judas Iscariot, in the Garden of Gethsemane.

Christ carrying the cross, a sculpture portraying one of the stations in the Passion of Christ.

The Angel
The figure of an angel carrying a cup filled with Faith for Christ is in the chapel of the Mount of Olives.

★ The Last Supper
The figures are so life-like that when they were completed, some pilgrims are said to have greeted them as if they were real people.

Colonial Portuguese houses lining the cobbled streets of Tiradentes

Tiradentes ⑦

🏛 6,000. 🚌 🚖 Largo dos Forros, Rua Resende Costa 71, (032) 3355 1212. 🎭 Festival de Cinema (Jan), Carnaval Mardi Gras (Feb/Mar). www.portaltiradentes.com.br

Like Ouro Preto and Mariana, Tiradentes became rich on gold, producing some of the most lavish Baroque church interiors and façades in all of Brazil. The town takes its name from the nickname "Tiradentes" (Tooth-puller) of José da Silva Xavier (1746–92), an erstwhile resident who became a martyr of the Inconfidência Mineria, the first movement in Brazil towards independence from Portugal.

Tiradentes is a delightful colonial town. Its multi-colored Portuguese cottages and miniature Baroque churches flank the cobbled roads on the steep, low São José hills around the Rio Santo Antônio. There is a craft shop, an arty little café or gourmet restaurant on every other corner. Pretty horse-drawn carriages gather in Largo das Forras, the town's main plaza, and a narrow gauge steam train, Maria Fumaça (see p440), with wooden Pullman coaches, puffs and heaves its way to and from neighboring São João del Rei on weekends and public holidays.

The center of Tiradentes is tiny and best seen on foot. Rua da Praia runs west from Largo das Forras following the course of the Rio das Mortes. Rua Direita runs parallel to it and a series of smaller streets

cross the two. The most important of these is Rua da Câmara, whose steep cobbles rise to the town's most imposing church, the **Matriz de Santo Antônio**, built between 1710 and 1752. This is one of the finest Baroque churches in Brazil, with wonderful woodcarvings and gilt interiors. Parts of the façade are attributed to Aleijadinho (see p131).

The **Museu Padre Toledo**, just east of the Matriz on the street by the same name, is the former house of another martyr from the Inconfidência, Padre Toledo. It is now a museum preserving art, documents, and furniture from the 18th century.

There are various other small churches scattered throuogut the town and these are all worth a visit. The best of these churches is **Igreja Nossa Senhora do Rosário dos Prestos**, on Rua Direita, which features some elegant statues and painted panels.

Gilt altar and interior of Matriz de Santo Antônio, Tiradentes

Tiradentes has a magnificent 18th-century public fountain, the **Chafariz de São José**, just across from Rua da Camara. It features an oratory with an image of São Jose de Botas and three faces representing love, good fortune, and health. The water comes from a spring in the São José hills over-looking the town, which offer excellent hiking.

🔒 **Matriz de Santo Antônio**
Rua da Camara. ⏰ 8am–5pm daily. 🎟 🚫 📷 Dec–Mar: 8pm Fri & Sun, 8:30pm Sat (sound & light show).

🏛 **Museu Padre Toledo**
Rua Pedro Toledo. Tel (032) 3355 1549. ⏰ 9am–4pm Tue–Sun. 🎟 🚫

Chafariz de São José, an 18th-century fountain in Tiradentes

São João del Rei ⑧

🏛 79,000. 🚂 Maria Fumaça (only between São João del Rei & Tiradentes). Fri, Sat, Sun & public hols, (032) 3371 8485. 🚌 from Tiradentes. 🚖 Rua Padre José Maria, Praça Frei Orlando (032) 3372 7338. 🎭 Carnaval Mardi Gras (Feb), Semana de Inconfidência (Apr). www.saojoaodelreisite.com.br

The largest of the historic towns of Minas Gerais, São João del Rei did not suffer from the decline of the gold boom in the 1800s. Today, it remains a bustling town, less than 19 miles (30 km) from Tiradentes, and boasts some beautiful churches, old mansions, and an attractive colonial center.

Façade, Igreja de São Francisco de Assis, São João del Rei

The principal reason for visiting São João is to see the magnificent **Igreja de São Francisco de Assis**, whose unusual curved façade, turtle-back roof and intricately carved medal overlook a beautiful square lined with towering palms. The square is in the shape of a lyre and at sundown the shadows of the palms form the instrument's strings. Together with the Santuário do Bom Jesus do Monte Sítio in Braga, Portugal, and the church of São Francisco in Ouro Preto (see p126–8), this church is one of the jewels in the crown of Baroque architecture.

The town has a handful of other interesting sights. The **Museu Regional do Sphan**, a colonial mansion built in 1859, is full of antique furniture and sacred art, and is one of the best in Minas Gerais. The **Museu Ferroviária**, at the Maria Fumaça railway station, is a tiny locomotive museum housing an old, Philadelphia-built, narrow gauge steam train. It sits alongside the Pullman carriages used by Emperor Dom Pedro II when he traveled to Minas Gerais from Rio by train in the 19th century.

🔒 **Igreja de São Francisco de Assis**
Praça Frei Orlando. **Tel** (032) 3372 3110. ☐ 8am–5:30pm Mon–Sat, 7am–4pm Sun. 🖾

🏛 **Museu Ferroviária**
Estacão Ferroviária, Rua Antônio Rocha. **Tel** (032) 3371 8485. ☐ 9–11am & 1–5pm Tue–Sun. 🖾

🏛 **Museu Regional do Sphan**
Praça Severino Resende s/n. **Tel** (032) 3371 7663. ☐ noon–5pm, Tue–Sun, 9am–noon Sat & Sun. 🖾

Parque Nacional Serra da Canastra ⑨

🚌 from Belo Horizonte. 🚹 Av Tancredo Neves, São Roque de Minas, (037) 3433 1452. ☐ 8am–6pm daily. 🖾

The extensive Parque Nacional Serra da Canastra, tucked away in the far southwest of Minas Gerais, protects the head-waters of one of South America's largest rivers – the Rio São Francisco. This great waterway flows 1,963 miles (3,160 km) through the rippling hills of Minas, and the bone-dry deserts of the northeastern interior. But in the Serra da Canastra, it is little more than a large mountain

Giant anteater in the Parque Nacional Serra da Canastra

stream cutting through rugged terrain. Bare granite peaks rise to almost 4,920 ft (1,500 m). Sparse *cerrado* forest sprinkled with boulders gathers at their feet. Around the numerous waterfalls and along the wild rivers are stretches of lush, gallery forest. The most famed of the falls is the **Cachoeira d'Anta**. Here the river's ice-cold waters form a series of pools before plunging 186 m (610 ft) off an escarpment. The park's most famous trail, the **Trilha Casca d'Anta**, begins in front of the waterfall and offers a spectacular view out over the park to the denuded pasture land beyond.

There is plenty of wildlife in the Serra da Canastra, though it can be hard to see. Maned wolves and giant anteaters are relatively common here, as are the pig-sized giant armadillos. The park is especially rich in birdlife, and is one of the few places in the world where it is possible to see the endangered Brazilian Merganser duck.

Granite peaks looming over the *cerrado* and pasture land beyond, Parque Nacional Serra da Canastra

SÃO PAULO CITY

*B*ristling concrete towers extend interminably over São Paulo, an expansive, vibrant city located on a high plateau. The impressive number of immigrants settled in its many districts makes it the world's second largest metropolis. Its immense cultural diversity has blessed it with the liveliest and most creative artistic, musical, and gastronomic scene in the country.

São Paulo was founded in 1554 by Manuel da Nóbrega and José de Anchieta, and established as a Jesuit missionary outpost. The 17th century saw the town become the headquarters for *bandeirantes*, or slave-trading pioneers. São Paulo became a major stopover point for explorers and pioneers, lured by the prospect of gold mines and slave trading in the interiors. The expansion of the sugar and coffee industries in the late 18th and 19th centuries attracted immigrants from the Middle East, Spanish America, the Russian republics, Central Asia, Europe – including Spain and Portugal – and Japan.

Internal migrants from every corner of the nation came to São Paulo in the mid-20th century. Among them was an impoverished metal-worker from Pernambuco, Luíz Inácio da Silva, who by a wave of public support went on to become Brazil's President in 2002, and again in 2006. Regional festivals from all over the country are celebrated with great enthusiasm in the city's enormous *favelas* (shanty towns).

São Paulo's vastness and complex character can be intimidating to an outsider. The greatest pleasures of this magnificent city are to be found behind closed doors – in museums, galleries, concert halls, and in a wealth of restaurants and shops. A true haven for gourmets, São Paulo is known to serve the best food in South America. The city center offers a host of attractions, such as the 17th-century Igreja de São Francisco and the 20th-century Mosteiro São Bento. The city's finest museum, Museu de Arte de São Paulo (MASP), is one of the highlights of the famed Avenida Paulista.

Carnaval dancers participate in the final night of the São Paulo parade

◁ Avenida Brigadeiro Faria Lima, one of the important commercial and financial centers of São Paulo

Exploring São Paulo City

Brazil's largest city covers an area of 6,332 sq miles (10,190 sq km). The conurbation of São Paulo, which includes the cities of São Bernardo de Campo, Guarulhos, and Sorocaba, is home to about 29 million people, making it the largest urban area in the world. There are three city centers – the old center preserves the few remaining historical buildings, including the Catedral Metropolitana. A short distance to the southwest is Avenida Paulista, home to the famous Museu de Arte Contemporânea (MAC). The commercial districts of Itaim and Brooklin lie south, on the banks of the Rio Tietê. The city's posh neighborhood, Jardins, is lined with South America's finest shops and restaurants. Another upscale area, Vila Mariana is home to Parque do Ibirapuera, a green oasis among the relentless high-rises.

SIGHTS AT A GLANCE

High-rise modern buildings dominating the skyline, central São Paulo

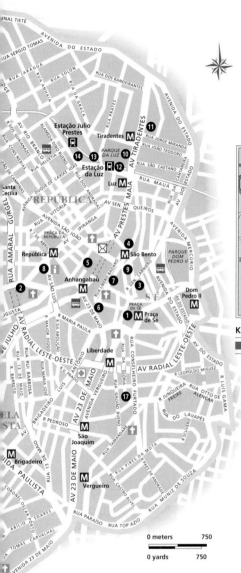

VISITORS' CHECKLIST

🎎 9,000,000. ✈ 19 miles
(30 km) NE of center. ✈ 9 miles
(4 km) S of center. 🚌 ℹ Praça
Antônio Prado 9, (011) 3104
6898. 🎭 Festas Juninas (Jun),
Bienal Internacional de São
Paulo (Sep–Nov), Festa da
Primavera (Sep). **www**.
cidadedesaopaulo.com

KEY

🟦 Area of the main map

SEE ALSO

KEY

✈ International airport

✖ Domestic airport

🚉 Train station

Ⓜ Metro station

🚌 Bus station

✚ Hospital

♦ Church

✖ Post office

ℹ Tourist information

━ Major road

═ Minor road

GETTING AROUND

São Paulo is well connected, with daily international flights to most
major European and North, and South American cities. Most of
these depart from Cumbica airport in Guarulhos, 19 miles (30 km)
northeast of the city. Domestic flights leave from Congonhas
Airport, just south of Ibirapuera Park in the main urban center.
There are buses to every corner of Brazil and beyond to Bolivia,
Argentina, Paraguay, and Uruguay. There is an extensive network
of taxis and buses within the city. The metro and urban railway
are clean, fast, and efficient. Cars can be rented at both the
airports, although the city's numerous one-way systems and
choking traffic make driving a little daunting.

Catedral Metropolitana ●

Praça da Sé, Centro. **Map** 1 C3.
Tel (011) 3107 6832. **M** Praça da Sé.
◔ 8am–1pm & 3–6pm daily. **▨**
✝ 8:30am, 2pm & 6pm Mon; noon
Tue–Sat, 9am, 11am & 5pm Sun.

At the heart of old downtown
São Paulo, the towering
Catedral Metropolitana (also
known as Catedral da Sé)
watches over the large
pebbled **Praça da Sé**, shaded
by tropical fig and palm trees.
Built between 1912 and 1954,
the cathedral gained its full
complement of 14 turrets only
recently, in 2002.

Built by Maximiliano Hell,
the exterior is a fusion of
Neo-Gothic and Renaissance,
with an overly narrow nave
squeezed between two enormous 318-ft (97-m) high
spires and a bulbous copper
cupola. The cavernous
interior, said to seat up to
8,000 people, looks starkly
European. The only obvious
local influences are visible in
the capitals, delicately carved
with distinctly Brazilian flora
and fauna. The stained-glass
windows were designed
in Germany and Brazil.

The cathedral's façade has
watched over the country's
largest public protests, when
crowds gathered in the square
outside the cathedral in the
late 1980s to demand the
end of military rule.

**Exterior of São Paulo Catedral
Metropolitana, Praça da Sé**

**Carved altar in the interior of Igreja
de São Francisco de Assis**

Igreja de São Francisco de Assis ●

Largo de São Francisco 133. **Map**
1 A3. **Tel** (011) 3106 0081. **M** Praça
da Sé. **◔** 7:30am–8pm daily. **ȹ**

Immediately to the
west of Catedral
Metropolitana is
the Igreja de São
Francisco de Assis,
one of the city's
oldest churches.
Parts of the modest
Baroque interior,
featuring an intric-
ately carved altar
and ornaments, date
from the mid-1600s.
The church is often
referred to as O Convento São
Francisco after the exquisite
Baroque convent that stood
here until the 1930s, when it
was demolished along with
parts of the colonial center.

Pátio do Colégio ●

Praça da Sé. **Map** 2 D3. **M** Praça da
Sé. **◔** 9am–5pm Tue–Sun. **✝**
noon–2pm Mon–Fri, 10am–noon
Sun. **Museu Padre Anchieta**
Tel (011) 3105 6899. **▨ ȹ**

Within easy walking distance
from the Praça da Sé, the Pátio
do Colégio has an interesting
history behind it. On January
25, 1554, the Jesuits inaugurated the Colégio de São Paulo
de Piratinga on a small bluff

overlooking an extensive
forest. The original wattle-
and-daub shack, built for
them by their Guaraní
cohorts, eventually became
a school. That school became
a church, and around the
church arose the buildings
that formed the core of the
original city of São Paulo.

In 1760, the Jesuits were
expelled from the city, but
the college and chapel they
founded remained and came
to be known as the Pátio do
Colégio. In 1886, the tower of
the original church collapsed
and the whole building
was demolished.

Upon their return in 1954,
the Jesuits immediately set
about building an exact replica
of their original church and
college, which is what stands
today as Pátio do Colégio.

Most of the buildings are
occupied by the **Museu Padre
Anchieta**, named after the
Jesuit captain who led the
first mission. The collection
features a Modernist portrait
of the priest, by the Italian
artist Menghini, some
of the priest's rem-
ains, a 17th-century
font used to baptize
indigenous people,
as well as a collection
of Guaraní artifacts
from the colonial era.
A model reprod-
uction of São Paulo
in the 16th century
is also on display.

**Visão de Anchieta
by Menghini**

Mosteiro São Bento ●

M São Bento. **Map** 1 C2. **◔** 7am–
6pm Mon–Fri, 7am–noon Sat & Sun.
✝ 7am, 1pm & 6pm Mon–Fri, 6am
Sat, 8:30am & 10am Sun. **www.**
mosteiro.org.br

Brazil is the only South
American country where the
Benedictine order gained a
foothold, arriving in São
Paulo on this site in 1598. The
current building, however,
dates from the 1920s and was
designed by Munich-based
architect Richard Bernl.

The monastery has a
beautifully painted Beuronese
interior. This style is named
after techniques developed in

the late 19th and early 20th centuries by Benedictines in the monastery of Beuron in southwest Germany. It is characterized by a compressed perspective and vivid colors. The finest representation of Beuronese art in Latin America is visible inside this beautiful Blessed Sacrament chapel. Scenes from the life of St. Benedict are depicted on the stained-glass windows and the ceiling.

The church has a large organ, which is the centerpiece of a festival held in November and December every year. There is also a shop selling delicious sweets and cakes made by the monks in their bakery.

The 1920s interior of Mosteiro São Bento, with its painted ceiling

Theatro Municipal ❺

Praça Ramos de Azevedo.
Map 1 C2. **Tel** (011) 3223 3022.
Ⓜ *Anhangabaú*. ✗ www.
theatromunicipal.com.br

Located near the Parque Anhangabaú, São Paulo's largest central park with some pretty fountains, the Theatro Municipal overlooks the Praça Ramos. The theater is one of the continent's most important venues. Opera and theater were very popular among the elite in turn-of-the-19th-century São Paulo and Rio de Janeiro. The theater was modeled on the Paris Opera and the city waited in fevered anticipation for its inaugural

View of the exterior of Theatro Municipal

night. It opened on September 12, 1911, with a production of *Hamlet*, starring the Italian baritone Titta Ruffo. Nijinski, Caruso, and Toscanini have all performed here.

Igreja da Consolação ❻

Rua da Consolação 585.
Map 1 C3. **Tel** (011) 3256 5356.
Ⓜ *Anhangabaú*. ○ 7am–8pm. ✗

Designed by Maximiliano Hell, the architect of the Catedral Metropolitana, the Igreja da Consolação is a similar fusion of European styles. Some of the 19th-century master Benedito Calixto's *(see p30)* best religious paintings adorn the Blessed Sacrament chapel.

Centro Cultural Banco do Brasil ❼

Rua Álvares Penteado 112.
Map 1 C3. **Tel** (011) 3113 3651.
Ⓜ *São Bento/Anhangabaú*. ○ 10am–9pm Tue–Sat, 10am–8pm Sun. ✗ www.bb.com.br/appbb/portal/bb/ctr/sp/index.jsp

An early 20th-century building with a lovely Art Deco glass ceiling houses the Centro Cultural Banco do Brasil. Inside, there are a series of spaces devoted to showing contemporary arts – from photography, installation works, and fine art to cinema and theater. The exhibition spaces are contained within the bank's original vaults, some of which retain their massive iron doors.

Edifício Itália ❽

Av Ipiranga 344. **Map** 1 B2, 1 B3.
Tel (011) 3257 6566. ○ 8am–10pm daily. Ⓜ *República*.

The Edifíco Itália, one of São Paulo's tallest buildings, was built in 1965 to honor the thousands of Italian immigrants to the city. The famous postcard shot of Oscar Niemeyer's Edifíco Copan with the vast environs of São Paulo behind was taken from the **Terraço Itália** restaurant *(see p399)* and viewing deck on the 45th floor of the building. People do not usually come for the food – most come for the unbeatable view of this incredible city. The view from here is second only to that from the Edifício Banespa.

Edifício Banespa ❾

Rua João Bricola 24. **Map** 1 C3.
Tel (011) 3249 7180. Ⓜ *São Bento*.
○ 10am–5pm Mon–Fri.

The best panoramic view of São Paulo is from the observation deck on the 36th floor of the Edifício Banespa – a miniature version of New York's Empire State Building. Built in 1939, the building was inaugurated in 1947.

Every morning, a helicopter hovers through the thick smog to report on traffic conditions from here. Blocks of high-rise concrete towers crowd together as far as the eye can see, but the wonder of São Paulo is captured around late afternoon, when the lights start coming on in all the high-rises and the city takes on a different life.

Pinacoteca do Estado ⑩

The Pinacoteca is a significant repository of Brazilian art, with an archive of over 5,000 paintings and sculptures representing all major Brazilinan artists and artistic movements. The galleries trace the evolution of Brazilian styles, which began as mock-European naturalism and gradually diversified into social realist, naive, and abstract forms. In the mid-1990s, the Pinacoteca was magnificently renovated by the noted architect Paulo Mendes de Rocha, who filled the original Neo-Classical building with carefully positioned partitions and capped it with a translucent roof. The magical sense of space and light perfectly complements the intensity of color and tone which characterizes Brazilian art.

★ Composição
This Brazilian Constructivist composition by Alfredo Volpi (1896–1988) fuses European style with tropical colors.

Serie Bahia Musa da Paz
Belonging to an infuential group of Paulista artists, José Pancetti (1902–58) rejected a European academic approach to art and strove to return to a more naive style.

Entrance

Octagonal exhibition hall

Façade
The Pinacoteca was tastefully refurbished in the 1990s, leaving only the shell of the original building.

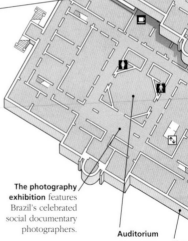

The photography exhibition features Brazil's celebrated social documentary photographers.

Auditorium

First floor

STAR FEATURES

- ★ Composição
- ★ Tropical
- ★ Caipira Picando Fumo

GALLERY GUIDE

The Pinacoteca's permanent collection is on the first floor, with galleries housing the Modernist collection, just above the main entrance. Brazilian 19th-century paintings and the more recent works flank this gallery, while sculptures by French artists, such as Aristide Maillol, occupy a prominent display. The ground floor is devoted to temporary exhibitions and also has a bookshop and a café.

★ Tropical
Portraying a caboclo woman in a tropical setting, this painting by Anita Malfatti (1889–1964) is a fine example of Brazilian Modernism.

VISITORS' CHECKLIST

Praça da Luz 2, Jardim da Luz.
Map 1 C1. **Tel** *(011) 3229 9844.*
M *Luz.* 🚌 ⃝ *10am–5:30pm Tue–Sun.* 🚻 📷 **www.** saopaulo.sp.gov.br

Third floor

Formal portraits of Portuguese colonial dignitaries are the most European of the Brazilian paintings.

★ Caipira Picando Fumo
Almeida Júnior (1850–99) was one of the first to paint Brazil's rich tropical light and everyday Brazilians.

Second floor

Génio do Repouso Eterno
This statue is regarded by many to be one of the most beautiful works of legendary French sculptor, Auguste Rodin (1840–1917).

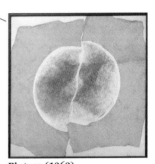

Pintura (1969)
Brazilian artist Tomie Ohtake (b.1913), mother of the famous architect Ruy Ohtake, has introduced Japanese elements into Brazilian art.

First floor, with a temporary exhibition area

KEY

- ☐ Brazilian Painting
- ☐ Landscapes (1850–1930)
- ☐ French Sculpture Yard
- ☐ Brazilian Contemporary Art
- ☐ Brazilian Constructivism
- ☐ Brazilian Sculpture
- ☐ Art by European Visitors
- ☐ Temporary Exhibition Gallery
- ☐ Photography Exhibition
- ☐ Non-Exhibition Space

Elegant façade of the Mosteiro da Luz, housing the Museu Arte Sacra

Museu Arte Sacra ⓫

Av Tiradentes 676. **Tel** (011) 3227 7687. Ⓜ Tiradentes. 🚋 ◯ 11am–7pm Tue–Sun. 📷 **http://**artesacra.sarasa.com.br

Often overlooked by visitors, this small museum boasts one of the finest collections of religious artifacts in the Americas. The exhibits are housed in a large wing of a distinguished colonial building, the early 19th-century Mosteiro da Luz. Restful and serene, the entire complex is a peaceful haven from the frenetic chaos of São Paulo.

The museum's priceless objects and artifacts include lavish monstrances (ceremonial vessels), ecclesiastical jewelry, and church altarpieces. Of particular note is the statuary, with pieces by many of the most important Brazilian Baroque masters such as Aleijadinho, Mestre Valentim, and Frei Agostinho da Piedade. One of the gems is the 18th-century *Mary Magdalene* by Francisco Xavier de Brito, which displays an effortless unity of motion and melancholy contemplation. Among the sculptures, mostly by anonymous Brazilian indigenous artists, two pieces stand out – a majestic African-Brazilian São Bento (with blue eyes) and an exquisitely detailed 18th-century Neapolitan nativity crib comprising around 2,000 pieces, which is the most important of its kind outside Naples.

The collection also features works by 18th-century

São Bento with baby, Museu Arte Sacra

masters such as Benedito Calixto and Mestre Athayde. Of special significance is the one that depicts Padre Anchieta taming a wild ocelot with the cross, a symbol of the Jesuit founder of São Paulo's mission to the indigenous Brazilians.

Estação da Luz ⓬

Praça da Luz 1. **Tel** (0800) 550 121. Ⓜ Luz. 🚋

One of modern Brazil's prominent symbols of industrial progress, São Paulo's railway station was built in 1901. The design of the Estação da Luz is a homage to the English railroad, and imitates the Victorian eclectic style.

Just like all of São Paulo's railways, Estação da Luz was the creation of Brazil's first industrialist, the Visconde de Mauá. After a visit to London in the 1840s, Mauá was convinced that Brazil's future lay in rapid industrialization. He founded an ironworks, employing some 300 workers from England and Scotland. In 1854, Mauá opened his first railway, which was designed and run by the British. It linked Jundiaí, in the heart of São Paulo's coffee region, with Santos on the coast. Today, the Estação da Luz serves only the São Paulo city area. Romanesque red-brick arches and stately cast-iron pillars support a single vault that covers four tracks and platforms.

Estação Pinacoteca ⓭

Largo General Osório 66. **Map** 1 C1. **Tel** (011) 3337 0185. Ⓜ Luz. 🚋 ◯ 10am–6pm Tue–Sun. 📷 free admission on Sat.

Located in an attractive early 20th-century Neo-Classical building, the annex of the Pinacoteca do Estado (see pp140–41) is one of the city's best contemporary exhibition spaces. Some of Brazil's finest Modernist paintings, taken from the archive of the Fundação José e Paulina Nemirovsky, are displayed here.

An important milestone in Brazilian Modernism is *Antropofagia* by Tarsila do Amaral (1886–1973), the founder of the vital *antropofagismo* movement (see pp30–31). There are also key pieces by Candido Portinari, Anita Malfatti, and Lasar Segall. International art is represented by Marc Chagall, Pablo Picasso, and Georges Braque, among others.

Sala São Paulo ⓮

Praça Júlio Prestes. **Map** 1 B1. **Tel** (011) 3337 5414. Ⓜ Luz. 🚋 ◯ 10am–6pm Mon–Fri. 🎫 1–4:30pm Mon–Fri, 2pm Sat. 🌐 www.salasaopaulo.art.br

Known for the finest acoustics in Latin America, this concert hall was inaugurated in 1997. It is the city's premier classical music venue and the home of Brazil's top orchestra, the Orquestra Sinfônica do Estado de São Paulo (OSESP).

The orchestra's artistic director John Neschling, who studied conducting under Hans Swarowsky and Leonard Bernstein, is also a composer of film music. He most famously composed the sound track for *Kiss of the Spider Woman* (Brazil/USA, 1985).

The grand railway building, the Estação Júlio Prestes, in which the hall is housed, was designed in 1938 by Brazilian architect Cristiano Stockler. Largely inspired by New York, it contrasts strongly with the English Estação da Luz.

Museu de Arte de São Paulo (MASP) ⓯

One of Brazil's finest museums, MASP preserves a vast collection of European old masters and early Modernist paintings. Pietro Maria Bardi, a Brazilian of Italian origin, scouted around Europe between 1947 and 1953. He bought the now priceless works of Degas, Van Gogh, Velázquez, Rembrandt, Turner, Titian, Bellini, and Raphael at absurdly low prices. By the 1960s, the works had become so important that Bardi persuaded the São Paulo authorities to build a gallery to house them.

The extensive collection is constantly rotating, as paintings are taken in and out of the archive. The works are loosely grouped by country.

VISITORS' CHECKLIST

Av Paulista 1578. **Map** 4 F2.
Tel (011) 3251 5644.
Ⓜ *Trianon-Masp.* ◯ 11am–
6pm Tue–Sun. 🈯 free admission
on Thu. 🅿 🍴 **http://**masp.uol.
com.br

Resurrection of Christ (1501/1502)
by Raphael, Italian collection

The Schoolboy by Van Gogh (1888),
Northern European Collection

ITALIAN ART

Of the museum's three dozen pre-19th-century Italian paintings, 17 date from the early Renaissance, prior to 1510. These include a series of iconographic religious works from Florence and Modena, a particularly haunting painting of a penitent St. Jerome in the desert by Andrea Mantegna, and *Resurrection of Christ* by Raphael. There are also 10 paintings of impeccable

quality, covering the 150 years of Venetian Renaissance and Baroque painting between Bellini and Saraceni. A Titian and a Tintoretto are prominently featured, besides Bellini's beautiful *Madonna and Child*.

FRENCH ART & PARISIAN SCHOOL

With more than 300 paintings, from the 18th to early 20th century, France dominates the museum. The collection has a wonderful chronological consistency. A few notable exceptions apart, including David, Millet, Seurat, and Braque, all the major artists are represented. Also showcased here are those who drew influence from late 19th- to early 20th-century Paris, such as Van Gogh, Chagall, and Picasso. Many of the works are among the artists' greatest masterpieces, especially those by Manet and Cézanne. Another gem is Toulouse-Lautrec's *Paul Viaud Dressed as an 18th-century Admiral* (1901).

ART FROM THE IBERIAN PENINSULA & NORTHERN EUROPE

The rest of Europe is represented as a chronological mishmash of glorious paintings. Of particular note are very fine Spanish pieces by Velázquez, El Greco, and a magnificent series of etchings and portraits by Goya, the best of which is that of Cardinal Luís María de Borbón y Vallabriga (1800). Central Europe has some fine works by Bosch, Holbein, Memling, Rembrandt, Rubens, and Franz Hals. There are also a few paintings by Frans Post, depicting Dutch colonial Pernambuco. England is represented by a group of respectable works by Constable, Gainsborough, Joshua Reynolds, and Turner.

BRAZILIAN ART

Though not as vast as Rio de Janeiro's Museu Nacional de Belas Artes *(see p74)*, or the Pinacoteca do Estado *(see pp140–41)*, MASP contains works by Almeida Junior, Brecheret, Di Cavalcanti, Tomie Ohtake, and Candido Portinari, among others.

The room displaying works from MASP's French collection

Aerial view of the exclusive Avenida Paulista

Avenida Paulista ⑯

Map 4 E2, 4 F2, 4 F3.
Ⓜ Brigadeiro/Trianon-Masp/
Rebourças. Ⓡ Gay Pride (Jun).

Modern São Paulo's first symbol of prosperity, Avenida Paulista and its crowded skyscrapers continue to attest to Brazil's status as South America's major economic power. Though often compared to New York's Fifth Avenue, it is actually a corporate valley, business-like and functional.

In the 19th century, when a Uruguayan named Joaquin Eugenio de Lima first set up house here, Paulista was a hill on the outskirts of a small colonial town surrounded by pastoral land and forest. Around this time, São Paulo was growing rich on trains and coffee. Others followed de Lima and began to build large houses here.

By the turn of the 19th century, the avenue had become São Paulo's most desirable address, and was lined with large, opulent mansions owned by extremely wealthy Brazilian moguls, or the coffee barons. Each mansion reflected the architectural predilections of the owner, be it Neo-Classical, Rhineland, or even

mock-Tudor. Having suffered large-scale demolition after World War II, the avenue had lost its splendid character by the 1960s. Today, only one mansion remains, the French-style **Casa das Rosas**, which is now a cultural center managed and run by São Paulo state. Interesting art shows are occasionally held here, but the 1935 mansion itself is well worth visiting for its pretty rose garden and Art Nouveau stained-glass window.

There are a few other sights of interest along the street. The **Instituto Itaú Cultural**, near Brigadeiro metro station, hosts a range of concerts and exhibitions, all of which are free of charge. It also houses the largest currency museum in the country, the Itaú Numismática. The **Centro Cultural FIESP**, at Trianon-Masp, is a business headquarters with a small Centro Cultural that presents free live theater and hosts occasional art shows.

Immediately to its north and opposite MASP is the **Parque Trianon**, the only green respite from the concrete. It was named in homage to the gardens of the Palace of Versailles, to which it bears no resemblance. However, in the quiet of the early morning, small mammals, including agouti and marmosets, can be

seen foraging here, and in the heat of the day, the trees provide welcome shade. There are plenty of cinemas in and around Paulista, along the avenue itself, in the Shopping Paulista Mall, near Brigadeiro metro, and dotted along Rua da Consolação, near Paulista's northern end.

Together with the Praça da Sé *(see p138)*, Paulista is one of the city's most important venues for protests and celebrations. Brazil's World Cup soccer victories see the avenue packed with millions of cheering, shirtless fans.

In June, the world's largest Gay Pride *(see p43)* march takes place there. During this prominent public event, as many as 2 million Brazilians and foreigners dance *samba* behind enormous decorated floats that are topped with outlandishly dressed transvestite dancers.

For a taste of Avenida Paulista as it once was, head a few blocks south, across the chic shopping streets of the Jardins and into Jardim Europa. Here, along Avenida Brasil and Avenida Groenlandia, the stately homes of the city's current rich can be seen.

🏛 **Casa das Rosas**
Av Paulista 37. **Tel** (011) 3285 6986.
◯ 10am–6pm Tue–Sun.

🏛 **Centro Cultural FIESP**
Av Paulista 1313.
Tel (011) 3146 7406.

🏛 **Instituto Itaú Cultural**
Av Paulista 149. **Tel** (011) 2168 1775. ◯ 10am–9pm Tue–Fri, 10am–7pm Sat & Sun. ⌀

🌿 **Parque Trianon**
Rua Peixoto Gomide.
◯ 6am–6pm daily.

Parque Trianon, with its lush greenery, on Avenida Paulista

Liberdade ⑰

Praça da Sé, via Av da Liberdade.
Ⓜ *Praça de Sé/Liberdade.*
🚌 *Liberdade Rodoviária.*

São Paulo has more ethnic Japanese than any other city outside Japan. Liberdade, located just south of the city center, is the hub of the Japanese community. The neighborhood, small and easily manageable on foot, is best explored during the afternoon. Streets are lined with shops and restaurants selling everything, from woks and manga comics, to sushi and sashimi. On Sundays, there is a lively market in the **Praça de Liberdade**, where stalls serve up steaming lacquer bowls of miso soup and yakisoba noodles.

Liberdade's main thoroughfare, Rua Galvão Bueno, runs south from this square, lined with the bulk of the shops and decorated with red Japanese arches, or *torii*. Many of Liberdade's most traditional Japanese restaurants are located on, and around, Rua Tomaz Gonzaga, which cuts across Galvão Bueno, south of the square.

At the corner of Galvão Bueno and Rua São Joaquim, an undistinguished block houses the **Museu da Imigração Japonesa** (Japanese Immigration Museum). The museum was opened in 1978 by the erstwhile prince, now Emperor Akihito of Japan. It has two floors of artifacts and displays devoted to telling the story of the Japanese immigrant community, their origins, and their lives in early 20th-century Brazil. These include a replica of the *Kasato-Maru* – the ship which brought the first immigrants in 1908 *(see p169)*, a complete early Japanese-Brazilian agricultural cottage, and a memorial to the Dekasseguis – the Japanese Brazilians who returned to Japan to fight in World War II. The building also features a lovely rooftop garden.

One of São Paulo's many Buddhist temples, built only recently in 1995, the **Templo Busshinji** lies west of the

Shrine Gate at Oriental Quarter Japanese Town, Liberdade

Museu da Imigração Japonesa on the same street. Its traditional Japanese-style architecture comprising wood is topped with a pyramid-shaped roof. Visitors are welcome to attend the various ceremonies, the most impressive of which is the monthly Cerimônia de Kannon. The rituals, paying homage to the Buddha's compassionate nature, are accompanied by traditional Japanese instruments.

🏛 **Museu da Imigração Japonesa**
Rua São Joaquim 381. **Tel** *(011) 3209 5465.* ⏰ *1:30–5:30pm Tue–Sun.* ♿

🛕 **Templo Busshinji**
Rua São Joaquim 285. **Tel** *(011) 3208 4515.* ⏰ *9am–5pm daily.* ♿ *by prior appointment.*

SÃO PAULO FASHION WEEK

With Rosa Chá and Havaianas among its brands, and supermodels Gisele Bundchen and Ana Beatriz Barros, Brazil has rapidly risen to the upper echelons of the fashion world in recent years. Established only in 1996, São Paulo's fashion week is now Latin America's most important fashion event. All of the top Brazilian names and faces are showcased here, together with supermodels from around the world. While the show is on, the city erupts into a fashion frenzy. During this time, the fashion fraternity can be spotted in fashionable bars and boutiques throughout the wealthy corners of the city. Over 100,000 people visit the show itself, which takes place twice a year – usually in January and June – in Oscar Niemeyer's Bienal building in Parque do Ibirapuera *(see pp146–7)*. More column inches are devoted to the event than to any other activity in Brazil, except for soccer and political scandals. The event generates an estimated $45 million through the media alone, with more than 2,500 newspaper and magazine pages and almost 200 hours of television coverage.

A fashion show in full swing, with models displaying a collection

Parque do Ibirapuera ⑱

**Statue of
Pedro Álvares
Cabral**

Parque do Ibirapuera is the largest green space in central São Paulo, and its native Brazilian woodlands and lakes are a welcome respite from the city's urban sprawl. Opened in 1954, it houses several museums and exhibition spaces, as well as a complex of buildings by the country's celebrated architect, Oscar Niemeyer (b.1907). These stage major exhibitions such as the Terracotta Warrior exhibition from China and the Rodin retrospective.

Monumento ás Bandeiras
Completed in 1950, this tribute to explorers or bandeirantes, who opened up Brazil's interior, is one of the more severe works by Brazil's foremost sculptor, Victor Brecheret.

★ Hotel Unique
Hotel Unique (see p374), the intriguing, half-melon structure on stilts is the most famous work of Brazil's leading contemporary architect, Ruy Ohtake, son of the artist, Tomie Ohtake.

A son et lumière fountain show is held here on weekends.

The newly restored, state-of-the-art planetarium is one of the most impressive in Latin America and is very popular with children. All shows are in Portuguese.

Pavilhão Japonês
This pavilion and its gardens were built in strict accordance with traditional Japanese design, using only Japanese materials. There is also an exhibition space and a Japanese tearoom.

STAR SIGHTS

★ Hotel Unique

★ O Obelisco aos Heroís de 32

★ MAM

The small vivarium houses a few species of native subtropical trees.

The Bosque da Leitura or "reading wood" is the place to head for on Sundays. Visitors can borrow a book and read in the shade of the trees.

0 meters   25

0 yards   25

The lush expanse of Lago do Ibirapuera (Ibirapuera Lake) in the park

VISITORS' CHECKLIST

Av Pedro Álvares Cabral.
Map 4 E5. ⬜ *6am–9pm daily.*
**Museu de Arte Moderna
(MAM)** *Tel (011) 5549 9688.*
⬜ *noon–6pm Tue, Wed & Fri;
noon–10pm Thu; 10am–6pm Sat
& Sun.* 🅿 **Museu Afro Brasil**
Tel (011) 5579 8542. ⬜ *10am–
6pm Tue–Sun.* **Bosque da
Leitura** ⬜ *10am–4pm Sun.*

**The Monumento do Pedro Álvares
Cabral** honors the Portuguese
explorer who first set foot on
Brazilian soil in 1500.

Museu Afro Brasil is devoted to
celebrating Afro-Brazilian
culture. It hosts films,
exhibitions, dance, music, and
theater events.

**Ibirapuera
Auditório**

★ O Obelisco aos
Heroís de 32
*This giant Cleopatra's
needle was built to honor
the Paulistano rebels who
died in 1932 when
President Vargas crushed
resistance to his Estado
Nôvo regime (see p55).*

Oca do Ibirapuera
*Designed by Oscar
Niemeyer, this dome
pays homage to the
indigenous Brazilian
roundhouse. It hosts
the city's major
international art
exhibitions.*

The Bienal Building, also by Niemeyer,
stages the city's flagship fashion, art, and
other premier events – São Paulo fashion
week and the Art Bienal, among others.

★ Museu de Arte Moderna (MAM)
*The best of Brazilian contemporary art is
showcased here. This work,* Cristo de
Rapadura *by Caetano Dias, is a sculpture of
Christ made from raw cane sugar. The idea is
that it will gradually be consumed by visitors,
thus symbolizing the lives of African slaves
who died working in Brazil's sugar industry.*

Façade of the imposing Museu Paulista do Ipiranga in the Parque de Independência, Ipiranga

Museu Paulista do Ipiranga ⑲

Parque da Independência s/n, Ipiranga. **Tel** (011) 6165 8000. 🚌 ⬜ 9am–5pm Tue–Sun. 🏛 📷 www.mp.usp.br

In 1822, Dom Pedro I declared the famous "Grito de Ipiranga," or call for independence from Portugal (Independência ou Morte, or Independence or Death), on the banks of the Rio Ipiranga (see p52). This large palace, built in 1890, was one of the earliest monuments of independent Brazil.

The Museu Paulista is housed in the palace at the top of extensive formal gardens in the Parque da Independência. The museum is devoted to the nation's history, containing a collection of exhibits which includes old maps, traditional colonial furniture, carriages, rare documents, old coins, clothing, and paintings. The artist Pedro Américo's monumental canvas *Independência ou Morte* (1888), depicting the young prince shouting his *grito* (cry), sits in the building's most handsome room, the Salão Nobre.

The mock French Renaissance gardens are dotted with sculptures and monuments. These include an an enormous bronze sculpture to the nation's independence, *Monumento a Independência*, made by the Italian sculptor Ettore Ximenes in 1921. In the

chapel at the base of the monument, a tomb contains the remains of Dom Pedro I and Empress Leopoldina. Also in the grounds is the **Casa do Grito**, a replica of the simple adobe house depicted by Pedro Américo in his painting.

Museu de Arte Contemporânea ⑳

Rua da Reitora 109a, Cidade Universitária. **Tel** (011) 3091 3538. 🚇 ⬜ 10am–6pm Mon–Fri, 10am–4pm Sat & Sun. 📷 by appointment. 🏛 📷 www.macvirtual.usp.br/mac/

A treasure trove of modern and post-modern European and Brazilian art lies tucked away in the campus of São Paulo's most distinguished university. The collection at the Museu de Arte Contemporânea (MAC) is an amalgamation of donations given by wealthy individuals since the early 20th century and prizes from São Paulo's Art Biennials.

***Estrada de Ferro Central do Brasil** by Tarsila de Amaral at MAC*

The collection comprises some 8,000 works of art. Prominent among these are important, little-seen European works by Amadeo Modigliani, Pablo Picasso, Max Ernst, and Henri Matisse, which sit alongside the cream of Brazil's artists. Brazilian Modernists, such as Anita Malfatti, Vitor Brecheret, and Candido Portanari, are well represented. MAC also holds three of the most celebrated works by Tarsila do Amaral – *A Negra, Estrada de Ferro Central do Brasil*, and *A Floresta*. Tarsila was the founder of *antropofagismo* (see pp30–31) – a movement which paved the way for many important artistic trends within post-War Brazil.

Instituto Butantã ㉑

Av Vital Brazil 1500, Cidade Universitária. **Tel** (011) 3726 7222. 🚌 ⬜ 9am–4:30pm daily. 🏛 📷 by appointment. www.butantan.gov.br

The Instituto Butantã is a biomedical research center affiliated to the Cidade Universitária, the University of São Paulo. Founded in 1901 by Vital Brasil to conduct research into venomous animals, the institute is now one of the leading producers of anti-venoms and sera in the world. It is also one of the city's principal tourist attractions, as it is located in a pretty forested garden full of hummingbirds.

Pits alongside the center and an adjacent museum house many of South America's more exotic snakes and arachnids. Smaller but even deadlier creatures can be seen through microscopes in the institute's newly opened **Museu de Microbiologia**. This bright, modern space also includes excellent interactive displays which are particularly popular with children.

Jardim Botânico ㉒

Av Miguel Stéfano 3031. *Tel* (011) 5073 6300. 🚍 ⬜ 9am–5pm Wed–Sun. 🖼 ♿

Other than the Serra da Cantareira mountains on the city's western fringe, the Jardim Botânico is the largest area of green in São Paulo's metropolitan area. It combines formal gardens, laid out around a series of lakes with areas of forest large enough to support several resident troops of red howler monkeys. Their guttural calls can be heard here at dawn and dusk and sometimes the monkeys themselves can be seen in the trees. There is plenty of other wildlife too, including agoutis, pacas and tufted-eared marmosets. The latter often loiter about in the trees around the lawns of the sculpture garden hoping to grab a fruity morsel.

The entrance to the park is through an avenue of magnificent royal palms, surrounded by tropical and subtropical trees. Most are labeled with their common and scientific names (the former in Portuguese only). The avenue leads to the **Jardim Lineu**, inspired by the gardens in Uppsala, Sweden, and, like them, are laid out in homage to 18th-century biologist Carl Linnaeus. Glass houses here contain a number of Atlantic rainforest plants and a botanical museum preserves a bank of Brazilian seeds from flowering plants and important fruit species.

Beyond the Jardim Lineu are areas of ponds and lawns popular with picnickers on the weekends. These are

Pond with a tropical forest glade at the Jardim Botânico

fringed with tropical forest cut by short trails and little running streams. Walkers should be wary of snakes.

Parque Burle Marx ㉓

Av Dona Helena Pereira de Morais 200. *Tel* (011) 3746 7631. 🚍 ⬜ 9am–7pm daily. 🖼

Roberto Burle Marx (1909–94) was South America's greatest landscape architect and one of the three core designers of Brasília (see pp294–5). His designs were strongly influenced by Modernist ideas inspired by his studies in Germany, and his early work

with the architect Lucio Costa who had worked with Le Corbusier. Burle Marx was one of the first architects to combine sculptural and painting techniques with landscape design.

His gardens in the Parque Burle Marx have been compared to abstract paintings, utilizing simple shapes, some curvilinear and rectilinear patterns to create blocks of color and texture, broken by paths and areas of woodland. Marx was a keen ecologist and promoted the use of Brazilian native species, the park is surrounded by a small area of forest, comprising various Mata Atlântica species.

Although Marx contributed to Parque Ibirapuera (see pp146–7), the park is the only exclusive example of his work in his home city. The gardens were originally private, commissioned for the millionaire industrialist "Baby" Pignatari in the 1940s.

As well as landscaping, Burle Marx was allowed to experiment and place abstract structures in the gardens. These include mirrors of water and rectangular blocks reminiscent of the low Mixtec buildings in Mitla, Mexico. The constructions near the avenue of palms at the park's entrance are by Oscar Niemeyer.

Abstract rectangular structures, Parque Burle Marx

SHOPPING IN SÃO PAULO

Shopping in São Paulo is like shopping in a large North American city. It is largely mall- and boutique-based and the best items to buy are high-end luxury goods. However, more interesting are markets and fairs that take place around town on weekends, selling traditional goods. Unlike many big cities in South America, São Paulo has no exclusive craft markets or traditional artisanware of note, but there are a few arts and craft specialist shops. São Paulo is Latin America's fashion capital and the

Cachaça bottles on display

districts of Jardins, Pacaembu, and Vila Madalena are bursting with smart little fancy boutiques. Many others can be found in the city's numerous opulent malls, which are large, air-conditioned, and filled with restaurants, entertainment areas, and shops housing international brands and leading Brazilian designers. The city's other good buys, including CDs, books, coffee, and *cachaça* can be bought from malls. High-quality household items can be found on Rua Gabriel Monteiro Silva in Jardins.

Designer shops lining Rua Oscar Freire

SHOPPING HOURS

Shops in São Paulo are open from 8am to 6pm. Street shops tend to open from 8 or 10am to 6pm. They are closed on Brazilian public holidays. Most shopping centers and malls are open from 10am to 10pm and on weekends (including Sunday) from 10am to 8pm. They often do not close on public holidays.

FASHION

The domestic fashion market in Brazil is flourishing, with almost all Brazilian labels coming from São Paulo. The market is strongest for women's clothing and the best place to begin a browse is in Jardins. Here hundreds of tasteful little shops sell colorful, beautifully cut clothes. Many of the latest generation of young Paulistana designers, such as **Adriana Barra** and **Cris Barros**, have their showrooms in Jardins. These labels are

particularly strong on dresses and evening wear. More established names can be found here too. **Rosa Chá** stocks the world's sexiest and most fashionable bikinis (by Amir Slama).

Other designers, such as rising star **Santa Paciência**, celebrated for her elegant and original use of light, flowing fabrics, are based in Pacaembu, a short taxi drive away from central São Paulo.

MUSIC & FILM

Bossa nova, samba, frevo, forró, axé, choro – it is difficult to think of a country with as many homegrown musical genres as Brazil. São Paulo is the best place in the country either to begin an acquaintance with this diversity or to explore its variety.

Many of the larger stores give customers the chance to listen to CDs before buying.

Brazilian music CDs

Such shops are to be found in many of the larger malls but the best in the city is probably **FNAC**, which also stocks an excellent selection of Brazilian DVDs. Its selections of Latin American arthouse films are particularly strong.

Grandes Galerias or the **Galeria do Rock** has a large choice of rock CDs and DVDs. This arcade has around 100 different small shops selling every manner of CD and DVD. However, only a few stores offer the desirable option of listening before buying.

BEVERAGES

The raw ingredient for the *caipirinha* cocktail, Brazilian *cachaça* or sugar cane rum is sometimes difficult to find outside of Brazil. But in São Paulo, bottles are on sale in any corner shop at a reasonable price. The **Cachaçaria Paulista**, however, is a bar and shop for connoisseurs, selling more than 300 different *cachaças*, the best of which are said to be from Minas Gerais.

Very fine coffee beans and grounds can be bought here. **Santo Grão** in Jardins and boutiques in the various malls have shops selling gourmet and quality blends. Some of the very best are to be found in the shop of the Museu do Café in Santos *(see p168)*.

BOOKS & MAGAZINES

Large bookshops can be found in the malls and are usually well-stocked with English language novels. The greatest variety is to be found in FNAC, **Saraíva**, and **Livraria Cultura**. The bookshops attached to the **MASP** and **MAM** galleries are well worth a browse. Brazilian art books are of a very high international standard and much of the material, including reproductions of European art kept in Brazil, can only be found here. Particularly interesting are the gorgeous photographic books. Brazilian art and social photography is excellent and well-represented in the gallery souvenir shops.

Overpriced international papers and magazines can also be bought at the larger bookshops. There are no English language publications in Brazil. Portuguese readers will find newsstands or *bancas* dotted throughout the city with a bewildering variety of glossy reading material to choose from.

Household knick-knacks on display at Jacaré do Brasil

ARTS, CRAFTS & DESIGN

Although arts and crafts are best bought regionally, particularly in centers such as Manaus, Palmas, or Caruaru, there are a few specialist shops in São Paulo. The **Casa das Culturas Indígenas** sells indigenous jewelry and household goods. **Jacaré do Brasil** stocks indigenous and regional items from household decoration to textiles.

Paulistanos adore decor. **Etel Interiores** has exquisite top-end home furnishings from furniture to small decorative items. The most interesting pieces are made from sustainable materials in Acre in the Brazilian Amazon. **Firma Casa** stocks the best of Brazil's furniture makers.

SHOPPING MALLS

There are shopping malls throughout the city, many of which stock similar items and brands, making it difficult to choose between them. The best design names are to be found in South America's oldest mall, **Iguatemi**, which still looks as if it was built yesterday. **Ibirapuera Shopping** has the most shops and perhaps the greatest middle-brow choice.

São Paulo has only one department store, **Daslu**, but it is internationally famous and attracts élite and wealthy clients from around the continent. Many international and Brazilian big design names are sold here, together with Daslu's own brand.

DIRECTORY

FASHION

Adriana Barra
Rua Peixoto Gomide 1801, Casa 5. **Map** 4 E3.
Tel (011) 3064 3691.
www.adrianabarra.com.br

Cris Barros
Rua Oscar Freire 295.
Map 3 C2.
Tel (011) 3082 3621.

Rosa Chá
Rua Oscar Freire 977.
Map 3 C2 *Tel* (011) 3081 2793. www.rosacha.com.br

Santa Paciência
Rua Girassol 170, Vila Madalena. **Map** 3 A1.
Tel (011) 3814 9188.

MUSIC & FILM

FNAC
Av Paulista 901.
Map 4 F3. *Tel* (011) 2123 2000.

Galeria do Rock
Rua 24 de Maio 62 & Av São João 439.
Map 1 B2.

BEVERAGES

Cachaçaria Paulista
Rua Mourato Coelho 593, Vila Madalena. **Map** 3 A3.
Tel (011) 3815 4756.

Santo Grão
Rua Oscar Freire 413.
Map 4 D3.
Tel (011) 3082 9969.

BOOKS & MAGAZINES

Livraria Cultura
Av Paulista 2073.
Map 4 E2. *Tel* (011) 3170 4033.

MAM
Parque do Ibirapuera, Portão 3. **Map** 4 E5.
Tel (011) 5549 9688.
www.mam.org.br

MASP
Av Paulista 1578.
Map 4 F2.
Tel (011) 3251 5644.
www.masp.art.br

Saraíva
Morumbi Shopping, Av Roque Petroni Jr., Morumbi. *Tel* (011) 5181 7574.

ARTS, CRAFTS & DESIGN

Casa das Culturas Indígenas
Rua Augusta 1371, loja 107. **Map** 4 E1.
Tel (011) 3283 4924.

Etel Interiores
Al Gabriel Monteiro da Silva, 1834.
Map 3 A4. *Tel* (011) 3064 1266.
www.etelinteriores.com.br

Firma Casa
Al Gabriel Monteiro da Silva 1487. **Map** 4 B4.
Tel (011) 3068 0377.
www.firmacasa.com.br

Jacaré do Brasil
Rua Dr. Melo Alves 555.
Map 4 D2. *Tel* (011) 3081 6109. www.jacaredobrasil.com.br

SHOPPING MALLS

Daslu
Av Chedid Jafet 131.
Tel (011) 3841 4000.
www.daslu.com.br

Ibirapuera Shopping
Av Ibirapuera 3103.
Tel (011) 5095 2300.

Iguatemi
Av Faria Lima 2232.
Map 3 A5.
Tel (011) 3816 6116.

ENTERTAINMENT IN SÃO PAULO

São Paulo has an incredible nightlife with a bewildering choice of activities on offer. Live music, in diverse styles, is performed every night by the most distinguished artists from the country. Brazil's finest orchestra, theater, and concert halls are also located in São Paulo. The city boasts myriad dance clubs offering *samba*, *forró*, and a dozen other traditional styles, alongside ubiquitous international club music, often with a Brazilian twist. A

Veja São Paulo, a listings magazine

wide range of films can be viewed as well, with arthouse theaters showing the latest blockbusters from Europe, Latin America, or Asia and state-of-the-art multiplexes offering popular national cinema. A progressive city, São Paulo has the largest Gay Pride parade in the world, which takes place in June. Children are welcome everywhere – even in bars and restaurants, and the largest theme park in South America, Playcenter, lies on the city's doorstep.

GUIDES & LISTINGS

The **Tourist Information Desk** at Guarulhos International Airport offers important information in English about what's on in the city. The Friday edition of the *Folha de São Paulo* and *Estado do São Paulo* newspapers and *Veja* magazine's cultural insert, *Veijinha*, have comprehensive listings in Portuguese.

The central ticket-selling office in São Paulo is **Ticketmaster**, which sells tickets through the Saraíva and FNAC bookshops *(see p151)*.

LIVE MUSIC

A plethora of small venues in the *bairros* of Vila Madalena, Pinheiros, and Vila Olímpia play host to all manner of live acts. Almost all have a small restaurant area, a dance floor, and a sitting area. All have bars and serve beer and excellent cocktails. Musical performances may vary from week to week – from *samba* to Brazilian funk, *bossa nova*, or the latest post-*mangue* beat sounds from the state of Pernambuco. The best venues include **A Marcenaria**, the **Urbano Club**, the **Bourbon Street Music Club** that features jazz and Dixieland, and the **Villaggio Café** for acoustic music. Funk acts such as Tutti Baê and others regularly play in these venues.

The more popular performers, such as João Bosco or Otto, play in the **SESC**s – cultural centers with

Sergio Dias, Ceumar, and Rebecca Matta performing at SESC Pompéia

excellent concert halls. The best are in Vila Mariana and Pompéia. Legendary singers such as Milton Nascimento, who won a Grammy in 1994, and Caetano Veloso play in numerous concert halls such as the **Via Funchal**. The most popular national and international musical groups, such as Ivete Sangalo and U2, play in the Pacaembu stadium.

CLASSICAL MUSIC & DANCE

Brazil's most reputable orchestra, the São Paulo State Symphony Orchestra, has its home in Latin America's best 1,500-seat concert hall, the **Sala São Paulo**. The acoustics here are almost perfect. The Sala São Paulo regularly advertises its upcoming programs on its website. The city's other key music venue for opera and classical concerts is the distinguished **Theatro Municipal**. The **Teatro Alfa** specializes in ballet.

DANCE BARS & CLUBS

Dance bars and clubs are concentrated in two areas of the city – Vila Madalena and Pinheiros, southwest of the center, and the contiguous *bairros* of Vila Olímpia, Itaim, and Moema in the south. The former is more lively, with live *forró* and *samba* bands playing to bars filled with

Popular Vila Madalena Club in São Paulo

university students. The **Bambú** and the **Canto da Ema** are always packed at weekends. Vila Olímpia, Itaim, and Moema are generally livelier and are home to the bulk of clubs such as the **Lov.E**, which host big name DJs, such as Marky and Patiffe, and play techno and trance music.

CINEMA & THEATER

The city has some 250 cinema houses and hosts several important film festivals. Almost all the shopping malls have large multiplexes showing not only the latest films from Hollywood but also national releases. There are more than 20 arthouse cinemas, including the **Cine SESC** and the **Cinearte** off Avenida Paulista. Non-Portuguese films are subtitled rather than dubbed.

São Paulo has more than 100 theaters with shows almost exclusively in Portuguese. Most of the theaters are found in Bela Vista and Bixiga. The **Cultura Inglesa** features English language films and shows.

Fans cheer during a championship match at the Estádio Morumbi

CHILDREN

São Paulo's urban environment makes outdoor attractions for children few and far between, although there are some popular amusement and theme parks scattered across the city. However, the biggest attraction, the largest theme park in Latin America, the **Playcenter**, is 50 miles (80 km) from the city. The city also boasts the **Fundação Parque Zoológico de São Paulo** (São Paulo Zoo), set in a state preserve of coastal rainforest.

SOCCER

Soccer is an obsession in São Paulo, as it is throughout the country, and the city has the most prestigious soccer teams in Brazil. There are three First Division teams based in São Paulo who play in the impressive Morumbi and Pacaembu stadiums. **Estádio Morumbi** is the home ground of São Paulo Futebol Clube. Matches are generally held on Wednesday and at the weekend. To watch a game check the schedules in ticket offices.

DIRECTORY

SÃO PAULO STREET FINDER

Map references given in this guide for entertainment venues, shopping areas, and other attractions in São Paulo City refer to the Street Finder maps on the following pages. Map references are also provided for São Paulo City restaurants *(see pp399–401)* and hotels *(see p374)*. The first figure in the map reference indicates which Street Finder map to turn to, and the letter and

number that follow refer to the grid reference on that map. The map below shows the different areas of São Paulo City – Centro, Bela Vista, Jardins, and Jardim Paulista – covered by the five Street Finder maps. Symbols used for sights and useful information are displayed in the key below. An index of street names and important places of interest marked on the maps can be found on page 136.

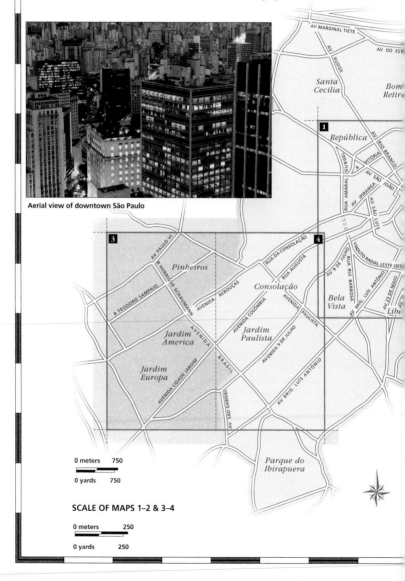

Aerial view of downtown São Paulo

0 meters   750
0 yards   750

SCALE OF MAPS 1–2 & 3–4

0 meters   250
0 yards   250

STREETWISE IN
SÃO PAULO

São Paulo has one of the highest crime rates of any city in the world. However, most of the violence is restricted to the isolated areas dominated by the *favelas* (shanty-towns), which lie on the periphery of the city far from the upmarket areas more frequented by visitors. Though you are unlikely to meet with serious trouble in São Paulo, it is important nonetheless to take all adequate precautions. Visitors are required to carry their identification documents at all times.

Visitors must exercise greater caution while traveling in certain parts of the city, including the district of Luz, areas around the city's main train station, Praça da Sé, Praça da República, and Praça Roosevelt. Be careful in the city center late at night, as well as in the cheap accommodation area around Rua Santa Efigênia.

Cameras, credit cards, and cash should be kept out of sight, preferably in a money belt, with a few notes left in a pocket or handbag. It is wise to withdraw cash only during the day and use ATMs that are within the bank premises rather than in a crowded street.

The metro is safe for commuting during the day, but it is recommended to use taxis after dark. These can be booked through a hotel or rented at one of the many taxi stands.

Driving and navigation in São Paulo is difficult. Carjacking and red-light robberies are common after dark. The new traffic law allows drivers to slow down

Policia Militar booth in São Paulo, responsible for traffic checks

at red lights and continue driving without stopping if there is little or no traffic on the roads.

If held up or driven at gunpoint to an ATM machine, avoid any provocation that could prove fatal.

There have been many incidents in recent years of organized violence by the PCC (Primeiro Comando da Capital) against public servants and police. In the unlikely event of PCC activity, it is advisable to stay in your hotel.

Y	
▊	Place of interest
	Other building
▊	Train station
▊	Metro
▊	Bus station
	Parking
	Visitor information
	Hospital
	Police station
	Church
	Post office

Crowded shopping street lined with a selection of stores, São Paulo

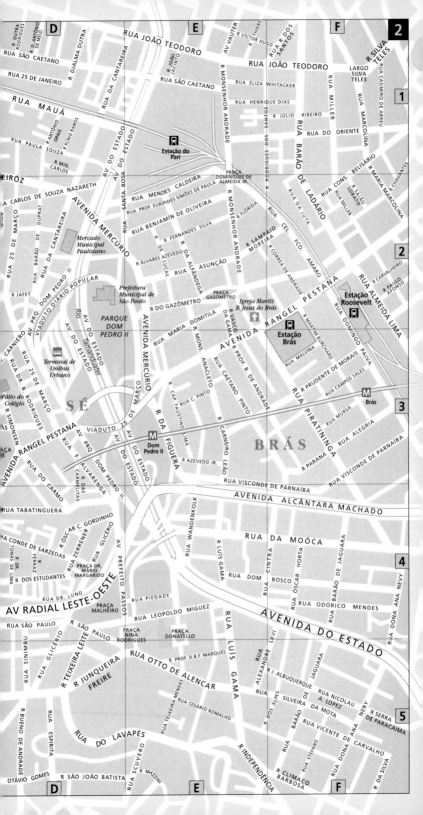

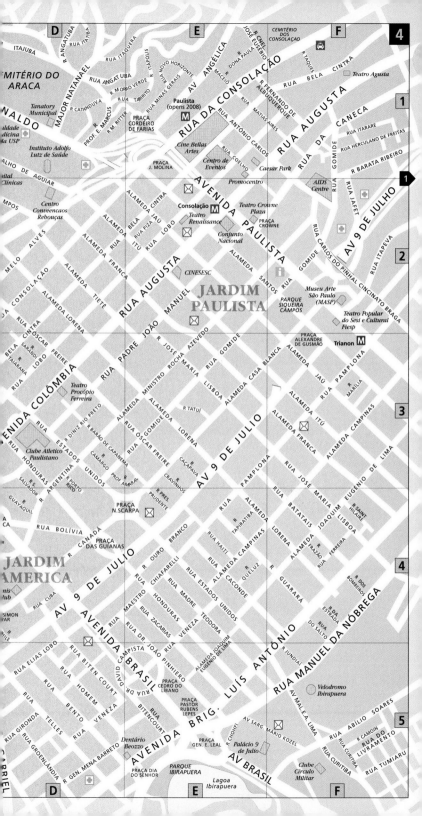

SÃO PAULO STATE

*S*ão Paulo is famous for its beaches, pristine island resorts, spectacular surf, and majestic rainforests. Divided into Litoral Norte and Litoral Sul, the state's coastline is one of the most incredible in the southern half of Brazil. São Paulo's agricultural hinterland is the reason it is Brazil's economic powerhouse. It is also home to a diverse range of immigrant communities.

The colony of Brazil was officially established in São Vicente (present-day Santos) in 1532 by Martim Afonso de Souza. The handful of sailors that remained formally named the beach São Vicente, and as pioneers, had to fend for themselves in a new land, coping with assaults launched by the local Tamoio Indians. Settlements followed shortly after in nearby Santos and in São Sebastião, opposite the island of Ilhabela, now a beautiful resort. All towns in the region preserve interesting sights and legacies dating from their early colonial days.

Most visitors, however, come to the São Paulo coast not for history but for sand, surf, and rainforest. Ilhabela, Brazil's largest tropical island, Ubatuba, whose 70 beaches stretch to the state's far north, and Guarujá, similar to Copacabana in Rio City, with similar amounts of high-rise buildings facing the ocean, are the most popular destinations. All three have beaches that have consistently been rated among the nation's top ten by the country's tourist magazines. Puma and ocelot still hunt in the wild Atlantic mountain forests which lie only a short distance behind them.

The full majesty of the Atlantic coastal forest, the Mata Atlântica, unfolds around Estação Ecológico Juréia-Itatins, and Cananéia in the Litoral Sul. Lush ridges, waterfalls, and abundant plant life are its main attractions. The forest is also home to a wide array of animals, birds, and brilliantly colored butterflies. One of the loveliest spots is Ilha do Cardoso, a boat-ride from Cananéia, where caimans can be seen basking in the sun on the beaches.

Stream flowing through the lush Mata Atlântica near Ubatuba

◁ White sand beach on São Paulo's coast in the Ubatuba region

Exploring São Paulo State

The São Paulo coast is divided into the Litoral
Norte, which stretches towards Rio in the northeast
from the port city of Santos, and the Litoral Sul,
which stretches from Santos towards Paraná state.
The Litoral Norte is one of the most heavily visited
coastlines in southeastern Brazil. Beaches on the
Ilhabela, Brazil's largest tropical island, and the
resort of Ubatuba, are magnificently backed by
towering spurs swathed in tropical rainforest. The
sands of the Litoral Sul are darker and siltier than
those of the Litoral Norte. Around Cananéia and
Juréia, and stretching into Paraná, are the largest
tracts of lowland coastal forest outside the Amazon.
The beautiful beaches of the Ilha do Cardoso are
just a boat ride away from Cananéia.

KEY

█ Area illustrated

SIGHTS AT A GLANCE

Towns & Cities
Cananéia ❾
Iguape ❽
Santos ❺
São Sebastião ❷
São Vicente ❻
Ubatuba ❶

**State Parks & Areas of
Natural Beauty**
Estação Ecológico Juréia-Itatins ❼

Islands
Ilhabela ❸
Ilha do Cardoso ❿

Beaches
Maresias ❹

SEE ALSO

• *Where to Stay* p375

• *Where to Eat* p401

KEY

═══ Highway

─── Major road

═══ Minor road

╌╌╌ Railroad

═══ State border

△ Peak

0 km   25

0 miles   25

The beautiful Praia das Toninhas in Ubatuba

Rio de Janeiro →

Socorro
Amparo
Belo Horizonte
agança Paulista
Piracaia
Atibaia
São José dos Campos
Franco da Rocha
Jacareí
ulhos Itaquaquecetuba
Santo André Moji das Cruzes
São Paulo
São Bernardo do Campo
Cubatão
VICENTE ❻❺ SANTOS
a Grande Guarujá
anhaém

Piquete
Campos do Jordão
Lorena
Guaratinguetá
Bairro dos Macacos
Areias
Bananal
Serão da Bocaina
Taubaté
Cacapava
Lagoinha
Pindamonhangaba
Cunha
São Luís do Paraitinga
Paraibuna
Salesópolis
Caraguatatuba
MARESIAS ❹
❷ ❸ ILHABELA
SÃO SEBASTIÃO
Ilha do São Sebastião
❶ UBATUBA
Serra do Mar
Paraitinga
Ponta do Boi
Ilha de Alcatrazes
Ilha do São Sebastião

GETTING AROUND

There are two large airports – international and domestic – in São Paulo City. Regular bus services ply between São Paulo City and the major towns on the coast, but reaching the best of the beaches requires a car. The main routes to the coast are the Anchieta and Imigrantes highways between São Paulo City and Santos. From Santos, the route north follows the Rio–Santos (SP-055), which passes through all the major beach towns and heads into Rio de Janeiro state. The Litoral Sul can be reached by SP-055, which reaches only as far as the northern part of Juréia State Park. Towns farther to the south can be reached off highway BR-116.

Verdant Mata Atlântica (Atlantic rainforest) in São Paulo

Piçinguaba beach in Ubatuba with Serra do Mar mountains in the distance

Ubatuba ❶

🏠 *65,000.* ✈ 🚌 ℹ️ *Av Iperoigi 306, (012) 3832 4255.*

Lying at the northern extreme of São Paulo state and sitting at the feet of the Serra do Mar mountain range, Ubatuba is a little beach resort with a small colonial center lined with terraced houses. Glorious beaches surround the resort.

The most popular beaches, especially those south of the town center such as **Praia Grande**, have an excellent infrastructure, including play areas for children. Buses running along the coastal road pass other nearby beaches, such as **Enseada**, **Piçinguaba**, and **Flamengo**. Even in high season it is easy to find a quiet stretch of sand or lonely cove tucked away along the coast to the south of Ubatuba.

Projeto Tamar signboard

The **Aquário de Ubatuba** in the center of the town contains some of the largest tanks and most diverse range of tropical marine life in all of Brazil. The office of the **Projeto Tamar**, a Brazil-wide organization that monitors and preserves turtle nesting beaches, is also located in town. Visitors are permitted to witness turtle hatchings under supervision.

The Serra do Mar rises in a vertiginous green wall only a short distance north of Ubatuba and an easy drive away from the town. Carpeted in thick primary forest, the Serra is home to many endangered endemic species. Birdlife, too, is prolific in this picturesque mountainous area.

Environs
The twin beaches of **Domingas Dias** and **Lazaro**, whose crystal-white sands curve gently on either side of a forest-clad promontory, are located 11 miles (18 km) south of Ubatuba. The **Peninsula da Ponta da Fortaleza** lies just south of Domingas Dias and is fringed with dozens of quiet beaches, including **Praia Vermelha do Sul**. Surfers head to **Praia Vermelha do Norte**, just north of Ubatuba, which has the best waves on the Litoral Norte.

🐠 **Aquário de Ubatuba**
Rua Guaraní 859. **Tel** *(012) 3832 1382.* ⏰ *10am–8pm Sun–Tue, 10am–10pm Fri & Sat.* 📷

🐢 **Projeto Tamar**
Rua A. da Silva 273. **Tel** *(012) 3832 6202.* ⏰ *10am–6pm Mon, Tue, Thu & Sun; 10am–8pm Fri & Sat.*

São Sebastião ❷

🏠 *58,000.* 🚌 ℹ️ *Av Doutour Altino Arantes 174, (012) 3892 2620.* 🎉 *Festas do 20 de Janeiro (Jan).* **www**.*saosebastiao.com.br*

São Sebastião was founded in the early 17th century, when Brazil's coastline was cloaked in a forest larger than the Amazon. North of Guanabara Bay was Tamoio indigenous country, and São Sebastião became the northernmost Portuguese outpost for the indigenous slave trade. As it grew, the city became one of the country's first sugar growing centers and the thirst for slave labor became unquenchable. The city was also among the first to receive Africans in the slave trade.

Although most people who come to São Sebastião do so merely to pass through on their way to Ilhabela, the town has a colonial center of historical importance which merits at least a couple of hours' leisurely stroll before departing.

São Sebastião's colonial streets lie in the few blocks between the shoreline and the Praça Major João Fernandes at the heart of the city, easily recognizable by the imposing 17th-century church, the **Igreja Matriz**, which watches over it. This is largely a 19th-century reconstruction devoid of much of its original church art. However, the newly refurbished **Museu de Arte Sacra** housed in the 17th-century chapel of São Gonçalo, a block to the south of the church, preserves a number of beautiful, delicate

Façade of Igreja Matriz, São Sebastião

images of Christ.
Dating from the 16th century, these images were found within cavities in the wall of the Igreja Matriz during its restoration in 2003.

There are also a few streets lined with Portuguese houses and a number of civic buildings, the most impressive of which is the **Casa Esperança** on the waterfront. Built from stone and wattle and daub congealed with whale oil, the exterior is whitewashed with lime made from thousands of crushed shells. The Casa contains some faded but original 17th-century ceiling paintings and statuary.

🏠 **Casa Esperança**
Av Altino Arantes 144. ◯ 9am–5pm Mon–Fri, 7–10am Sat & Sun.

⛪ **Igreja Matriz**
Praça Major João Fernandes.
Tel (012) 3892 1110. ◯ 9am–noon & 1–8pm daily.

🏛 **Museu de Arte Sacra**
Rua Sebastião Neves 90. **Tel** (012) 3892 4286. ◯ 1–6pm daily. ♿ 📷

Ilhabela ❸

🏝 28,000. ⛴ from São Sebastião to Perequê. ℹ Rua Doutor Carvalho s/n, (012) 3896 3777. 🎭 Festa de Camarão (Aug). **www**.ilhabela.com.br

One of Brazil's largest islands, Ilhabela rises steeply out of the Atlantic, a short distance offshore from São Sebastião. With a coastline sculpted by dozens of bays and beaches, it is covered in rainforest, much of it cut by fast-flowing mountain streams. Visitors from São Paulo throng here during weekends, but during the week (outside of holiday season), the island is all but deserted. Much of the forest is protected as part of the **Parque Estadual de Ilhabela** and there is plenty of wildlife, including ocelots and several species of primates. Biting flies, or *borrachudos*, on the island make insect repellent essential.

Ilhabela has just two roads. One is paved and runs the entire length of the western, leeward coast. Most of the numerous *pousadas* and guesthouses lie here, as do the villages of **Perequê** (where

Waterfront at Vila Ilhabela with 18th-century cannon

the ferry arrives), **Borrifos**, **São Pedro**, and **Vila Ilhabela**. The latter has a few colonial remains. Rusting 18th-century cannons adorn its waterfront and there is a little avenue of Portuguese buildings, including a 16th-century church, the Matriz de Nossa Senhora d'Ajuda.

The island's other road is a dirt track, usable only by four-wheel drives, which cuts across the interior from Perequê into the park and to the windward beaches. The most spectacular of these is the **Baía de Castelhanos**, a perfect half-moon of sand backed by rainforest covered slopes. The island's longest beach, and the best for surfing, is **Bonete** which is 9 miles (15 km) south from Borrifos village, along a rough forest trail.

Ilhabela's forests are dripping with waterfalls, but many are either completely

Visitors relaxing outside a café in Vila Ilhabela

inaccessible or reachable only by trail. A short distance inland from Perequê beach, **Cachoeira da Toca** waterfalls plunge in a series of little cascades into swimming pools, replete with water slides. **Cachoeira da Água Branca** is larger with more swimming pools. It is an hour's walk along a trail which begins at the entrance to the state park, a short distance beyond the turn-off to Cachoeira da Toca.

Numerous shipwrecks off Ilhabela also make it a popular scuba diving destination, despite the murky water.

💦 **Cachoeira da Toca**
Estrada Baía de Castelhanos.
◯ 24 hrs daily. 📷

Maresias ❹

🏝 3,000. ℹ Praça Pordo Sol, in Boiçucanga, 4 miles (7 km) W of Maresias, (012) 3865 4335.

South of São Sebastião lie a number of beautiful beach resorts. Maresias, the liveliest of the lot, is busy with young, hip Paulistanos at weekends and holidays. **Praia de Maresias** is famous for its powerful surf, which has been the site for many international surfing competitions. **Toque Toque Grande** and **Toque Toque Pequeno**, 6 miles (9 km) southeast, are smaller, quieter beaches, sheltered by rainforest-covered spurs. There are plenty of *pousadas* and restaurants on, or just off, the São Sebastião road, which runs along the coast.

The archipelago of Ilha dos Alcatrez near São Sebastião, São Paulo ▷

Stained-glass skylight, depicting a representation of Brazil, the *Mãe Douro*, Bolsa e Museu do Café, Santos

Santos ❺

🏚 *418,000.* 🚏 ℹ *Setur, (0800)*
173 887. **www**.santos.sp.gov.br

When Santos was founded in 1535, it was one of Portugal's first New World settlements. Since the mid-16th century, when neighboring São Vicente was established, Santos had been a port. First it dealt with sugar, and then with African slaves. However, it grew rich on coffee, which was brought out of the mountains on Brazil's first trains, built by the British in the late 19th century.

Unlike São Vicente, Santos has preserved vestiges of its historical legacy, and under recent enlightened municipal governance, is reinventing and refurbishing itself. Once decrepit, the city center is undergoing a spruce-up and is

Scottish tram

now very attractive. Scottish trams in British racing green run through its streets, taking visitors on a whistle-stop tour of the various attractions. The city center is also small enough to stroll around and have a closer look at these sights on foot.

The jewel in the city's crown is the Art Nouveau **Bolsa e Museu do Café**. Its modest Victorian exterior hides an opulent marble-floored turn-of-the-19th-century stock exchange and museum, together with a café shop serving excellent coffee and desserts. The Bolsa was once open only to wealthy (and exclusively male) coffee barons who plied their wares and trade here. When it was built, coffee was the most important and coveted commodity in Brazil.

The auction room is crowned by a magnificent stained-glass skylight, with an arresting representation of Brazil, the *Mãe Douro*; crowned with a star and rising from flames in a landscape thick with tropical animals and startled-looking indigenous people. The skylight and the beautiful Neo-Renaissance painting of Santos that adorns the walls of the stock exchange are by Brazil's most celebrated mid-19th-century artist, Benedito Calixto *(see p30)*.

A number of Calixto's paintings are displyed in the **Fundação Pinacoteca Benedito Calixto**, which is housed in one of the few remaining coffee baron mansions. The landscapes shown here give an idea of the city's once breathtaking natural beauty.

Santos has a handful of interesting churches, but the only one open to the public is the **Santuário Santo Antônio do Valongo**. The church's mock-Baroque interior dates from the 1930s. The fine original 17th-century altarpiece remains preserved in the Franciscan chapel to the left of the main entrance. The statue of Christ is particularly striking. Next door to the church is the British-built terminus of the now defunct Santos–São Paulo railway. Built between 1860 and 1867, the station is vaguely reminiscent of London's Victoria.

The once-filthy city beaches are now much cleaner and are lively with bustling bazaars, and people playing volleyball and football, every evening and weekend.

FOOTBALL LEGEND PELÉ

Pelé during Champions World Series 2003, New York

Regarded as the world's most famous sportsman, Pelé was born in Tres Corações, Minas Gerais. He started his career in Santos when, in 1956, the Santos Futebol Clube signed him. Soon, he was offered a place in the Brazilian national team, and went on to play in three of Brazil's five World Cup winning teams. Since his retirement in 1977, Pelé has worked as a charity patron Goodwill Ambassador for UNICEF. In 1992, he became the UN Ambassador for Ecology and Environment. In 1995, he was appointed Minister of Sports, a post he resigned after becoming caught up in one of the rumored, or real, corruption scandals that blight Brazilian politics.

A monument to the thousands of Japanese-Brazilians who arrived in São Paulo state in the early 20th century sits here, together with the small but popular **Aquário de Santos**. In addition to a stunning range of tropical marine life, it displays three of the five species of sea turtles found in Brazil. The beaches lying farther out in the Baía de Santos (Bay of All Saints) bustle with activity at the weekends.

For all its history, it is for football that Santos is most famous outside Brazil. Pelé played here for almost all his professional life. The Santos Football Club has an excellent museum, the **Memorial das Conquistas**, devoted to the club's illustrious history.

🐟 **Aquário de Santos**
Av Bartolomeu de Gusmão, Ponta da Praia. *Tel (013) 3236 9996.*
🕐 *8am–6pm Tue–Fri, 8am–8pm Sat & Sun.* 🖼

🏛 **Bolsa e Museu do Café**
Rua 15 de Novembro 95. *Tel (013) 3219 5585.* 🕐 *9am–5pm Tue–Sat, 10am–5pm Sun.* 🖼 🚫

🏛 **Fundação Pinacoteca Benedito Calixto**
Av Bartolomeu de Gusmão 15. *Tel (013) 3288 2260.* 🕐 *2–7pm Tue–Sun.* 🚫

🏛 **Memorial das Conquistas**
Rua Princesa Isabel 77, Vila Belmiro. *Tel (013) 3257 4000.* 🕐 *9am–7pm Tue–Sun, 1–7pm Mon.* 🖼 🖼 *prior booking required.* 🚫

⛪ **Santuário Santo Antônio do Valongo**
Marquez de Monte Alegre 13.
🕐 *8am–6pm Tue–Sun.* 🚫

JAPANESE IMMIGRATION

Brazil has the largest number of ethnic Japanese outside Japan, and almost all their ancestors arrived at Santos. Immigration began in earnest after the Russo-Japanese War (1904–5). Although Japan emerged victorious, the penalty was high, leaving the poorer Japanese population with a bleak future. São Paulo seemed to offer hope, as the state was rich in coffee and workers were in short supply.

The first Japanese ship to land was the *Kasato Maru*, which brought 165 families to Santos on June 18, 1908. They left for the coffee plantations in the Mogiana region. By the beginning of World War II, almost 150,000 Japanese had arrived. After freeing themselves from their labor contracts, communities began to grow in metropolitan São Paulo *(see p145)* and other parts of Brazil.

Japanese Immigration Monument, Santos

São Vicente ❻

🏘 *418,000.* 🚆 **www**.saovicente. sp.gov.br

The pleasant, laid-back port town of São Vicente is known more for its historical significance than the usual tourist attractions.

In 1532, Martim Afonso de Sousa established a small settlement on the eastern shores of South America. Thus Brazil was born, in the words of Afonso's brother, with "each man as lord of his own property, and private injuries redressed, and all the other benefits of a secure and sociable life." São Vicente is the scene of that noble beginning, though only a handful of relics belonging to that distinguished past can be found today.

First capital of the Captaincy of São Vicente, as São Paulo state was formerly known, São Vicente won the epithet of "Cellula Mater" (Mother Cell) for being Brazil's first organized town. The 18th-century Baroque parish church, the **Igreja Matriz de São Vicente Mártir**, is one of the very few historical buildings in the city to have survived the ravages of time. A tidal wave destroyed the first church, built close to this site by Martim Afonso shortly after his arrival. The second parish church was built inland on this present site. However, it fared no better, and was ransacked by pirates. The current bulding, standing on its ruins, is named in honor of the Spanish saint who is patron of the city.

Also in the city center are the remains of Martim Afonso's former home, and the first brick building in Brazil. These are housed inside the impressive late 19th-century **Casa Martim Afonso**, along with a few other interesting pieces of colonial bric-a-brac.

🏛 **Casa Martim Afonso**
Rua Martim Afonso 24, Centro. *Tel (013) 9134 7602.* 🕐 *9am–5pm Tue–Fri; 10am–6pm Sat, Sun & public hols.*

⛪ **Igreja Matriz de São Vicente Mártir**
Praça João Pessoa s/n, Centro
🕐 *irregular timings.*

Proud display of trophies at the Memorial das Conquistas, Santos

Striking hills in the Estação Ecológico Juréia-Itatins

Estação Ecológico Juréia-Itatins ❼

🚌 to Iguape, then taxi. 🏠 Av São Pedro 189, Barra do Ribiera, Iguape, (013) 3849 1293. 📷 ✔

Brazil's coastal rainforest stretches in a series of rippling mountains and lowland forests cut by broad rivers, mangrove wetlands, and pristine beaches all the way through from Peruíbe in southern São Paulo state to Paranaguá in Paraná. The Estação Ecológico Juréia-Itatins sits at the northern end of this rainforest, protecting 316 sq miles (820 sq km) of Mata Atlântica.

Access to the ecological station is restricted to daytime visits only, and must be arranged through the park authorities in Iguape, just south of Juréia-Itatins. Only certain areas are open to the public, and most of these areas require prior permission before entering. Iguape is a good base for information on organized tours.

This is one of the most important breeding grounds for marine species in the southern Atlantic and the myriad forest types growing here protect one of the world's greatest diversities of vascular plant, vertebrate and invertebrate species. There is a unique range of birds, butterflies, and mammals. Many larger animals, such as jaguars and tapirs, which have all but disappeared from coastal Brazil, live in healthy numbers here.

Juréia itself protects a wide variety of habitats, as a result, the scenery is magnificent. Lush green forest swathes the high slopes of the Serra do Itatins in the eastern extremity of the park and continues all the way through to the lowland coastal areas, mixing with mangrove wetlands and perfuming the park's extensive beaches. These beautiful stretches of fine sand, many of which are cut by clear rivers or washed by waterfalls, are so deserted that caimans can occasionally be seen basking in the sun at dawn.

Iguape ❽

🏘 28,000. 🚌 🏠 Preifetura Rua 15 de Novembro 272, (013) 3841 3009. www.guiadeiguape.com.br

This pretty little colonial town sits in a pocket of the Brazilian coastal rainforest, the Complexo Estuarino Lagunar de Iguape-Cananéia-Paranaguá, in the midst of breathtaking scenery. The verdant Serra do Mar mountains rise up behind the town which is surrounded by pristine mangrove wetlands and lowland subtropical forest on all sides including the wilds of the Estação Ecológico Juréia-Itatins to the north. The **Mirante do Morro do Espio** is a lookout point with a fabulous view of the port and surrounding area.

Iguape was founded in 1538 by the Portuguese. No buildings remain from that time but the city center preserves the largest collection of post-17th-century colonial architecture in the state. Most are civic buildings and town houses painted in thick primary colors and clustered around **Praça São Benedito**, a sleepy central square watched over by a towering 18th-century basilica.

There are also two small museums in the city center. The **Museu Histórico e Arqueológico** is housed in a 17th-century building which was once the first gold foundry in Brazil. It showcases a mixed bag of historical material, from pre-Columbian remains found in nearby middens to artifacts from the slaving era, and early

Rio Ribeira do Iguape estuary and Igreja do Rosário rising over Iguape town

photographs. The **Museu de Arte Sacra** in the 18th-century Igreja do Rosário houses some 100 ecclesiastical objects, most of which date from the 18th and 19th centuries.

Environs
Just across the Rio Ribeira do Iguape estuary, east of the town center, are extensive stretches of fine white sand beaches which make up the island of **Ilha Comprida**. They are accessible by road, or a 5-mile (8-km) walk across the estuary and sand flats via the pedestrian bridge.

Boqueirão Norte, located immediately across the town, and **Praia do Viareggio**, 6 miles (10 km) south, are popular in high season and lined with holiday homes. Farther south still and reach-able by dune buggy or by car is the far quieter **Praia das Pedrinhas**.

🏛 **Museu de Arte Sacra**
Igreja do Rosário, Rua 15 de Novembro s/n. ⬜ 9–11:30am & 1–5:30pm Mon–Sat. 🖼

🏛 **Museu Histórico e Arqueológico**
Rua das Neves 45. **Tel** (013) 841 1626. ⬜ 9–11:30am & 1–5:30pm Mon–Fri. 🖼 📷

Cananéia ⑨

🏚 14,000. 🚌 📍 Av Beira Mar 247, (013) 851 1473. **www.**cananeia.net

Cananéia is the farthest south of São Paulo's small colonial seaside towns, and like the others, it lies nestled at the feet of the Serra do Mar mountains overlooking stretches of mangrove and an open ocean dotted with forest-covered islands. Outside of the high season few visitors ever make it here and the town's crumbling colonial streets and fig tree-filled central square often have a sleepy feel to it.

The most compelling reason to come to Cananéia is to take a boat trip out to the beaches and islands; preferably with plenty of time to spare. Fishing boats and launches can be chartered

Stuffed great white shark, Museu Municipal, Cananéia

from the docks in Cananéia to **Ilha do Cardoso** that lies in the Lagomar bay. Car and passenger rafts take 10 minutes to ferry across the estuary in front of the town to the southern reaches of the **Ilha Comprida**, east of Iguape, and do so several times per day. The beaches here lie a short distance beyond the island's ferry port along a sandy road, which is lined with a handful of tumble-down *pousadas*.

While in Cananéia, it is worth visiting the tiny town museum, **Museu Municipal**, which preserves bits of nautical miscellany. Pride of place among the exhibits goes to what is reputed to be the largest great white shark ever, weighing a hefty 7,716 lb (3,500 kg), now stuffed, painted, and hanging safely from the museum ceiling.

🏛 **Museu Municipal**
Rua Tristão Lobo 78. **Tel** (013) 3851 1753. ⬜ noon–6pm Mon–Fri, 10am–4pm Sat & Sun. 🖼

Ilha do Cardoso ⑩

🚤 from Cananéia. 📍 Núcleo Perequê, Cananéia, (013) 3815 1108. **www.**cananeia.net

Just a two-hour boat ride south of Cananéia, Ilha do Cardoso, a rugged 37,000-acre (15,000-ha) island, rises dramatically out of the Atlantic Ocean. The island is primarily an ecological preserve which also has beautiful deserted beaches and walking trails. Together with Juréia-Itatins and Superagüi (see p339) across the border in Paraná, it forms the core protected area of the Brazilian coastal rainforest. Wetlands, man-groves, extensive beaches, coastal dunes and all of the numerous forest types associated with the Mata Atlântica are found here. Several species of turtle nest on the island, caimans live in the rivers and estuaries and jaguars and pumas still hunt in the forests that cover the upper reaches. The island is also rich in birdlife.

Pre-Columbian shell middens, or *sambaquis*, dot the park's beaches and six traditional *caiçara* fishing communities live within the park, preserving a semi-indigenous way of life which has so far largely resisted the pressures of urbanization. *Caiçara* tidal fish traps can be seen in the shallows of the various little rivers and bays, attesting to the strong indigenous heritage the com-munities preserve to this day. Many of the *caiçaras* act as guides and boatmen.

Virgin beach on Ilha do Cardoso, near Cananéia

NORTHEAST
BRAZIL

Northeast Brazil at a Glance

Comprising the nine states of Bahia, Sergipe, Alagoas, Pernambuco, Paraíba, Rio Grande do Norte, Ceará, Piauí, and Maranhão, the Northeast is truly a tropical paradise. Most of the states have three distinct areas – the fertile coastal strips with idyllic sand beaches giving way to the intermediate hilly areas with lush Atlantic rainforests, also home to a variety of fauna, and finally the vast semi-arid interiors. The beaches here range from the fascinating Canoa Quebrada beach in Ceará, to Genipabu and its sand dunes in Rio Grande do Norte, Porto de Galinhas in Pernambuco, and the Fernando de Noronha archipelago, among many others. The legacy of the Northeast's colonial history can still be seen in numerous, impressive historic monuments in Salvador, Olinda, and São Luís.

São Luís (see pp252–5), *capital of Maranhão, was founded by the French. It is a town with a beautiful historic core, Centro Histórico, with cobbled streets and 3,500 pastel-colored colonial buildings, which have recently been renovated. A UNESCO World Heritage Site, it is one of Brazil's finest examples of Portuguese architecture.*

PIAUÍ & MARANHÃO
(see pp244–55)

Teresina
(see p248)

BAHIA
(see pp180–207)

Lençóis (see p204), *in Bahia, is the perfect starting point to explore the Chapada's caves and waterfalls, or to hike up the 3,937-ft (1,200-m) surrounding peaks. Miners flocked to this area during the gold and diamond rush.*

0 km	100
0 miles	100

◁ **A panoramic view of Lençóis Maranhenses**

FERNANDO DE NORONHA

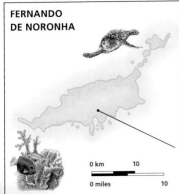

0 km   10

0 miles   10

Fernando de Noronha (see pp224–5), *part of Pernambuco, comprises 21 islands. The warm, clear waters here offer Brazil's best scuba diving and snorkeling experience.*

PARAÍBA, RIO GRANDE DO NORTE & CEARÁ
(see pp226–43)

SERGIPE, ALGOAS & PERNAMBUCO
(see pp208–25)

Recife *(see pp216–19)*

Natal (see p236), *capital of Rio Grande do Norte, is a popular sunshine destination. The beaches around Natal, with huge moving dunes, shaped by the shifting wind, create fascinating landscapes of snowy white sand.*

Salvador (see pp184–95), *capital of Bahia, has beautifully restored complexes of Baroque churches and palaces, built during the 18th-century sugar boom. Its historic center, Pelourinho, a UNESCO World Heritage Site, offers a unique glimpse into Brazil's history and is the crown jewel of Portuguese architecture.*

Afro-Brazilian Culture

A direct legacy of three centuries of slavery, the presence of African culture in the Northeast makes the region distinctly different from the rest of Brazil. Throughout the slavery period in colonial Brazil, there was little or no sanction on miscegenation. Over the years, masters, slaves, former slaves, and their descendants integrated into the new society of Brazil, creating an interesting blend of cultures and bloodlines with Portuguese, Dutch, West African, and Indian elements. This has uniquely resulted in what is now called Afro-Brazilian culture, visible in the people, clothing, food (see pp178–9), religion, and music of the Northeast.

Colorful ribbons, bringing luck if tied around the wrist

MUSIC

Africans brought along their fine command of percussion. Bahia's characteristic brand of Afro-Brazilian music grew in many forms, with *axé* becoming the signature sound of Salvador's Carnaval. In Pernambuco, as many as 13 distinct rhythms developed, including Recife's signature beat, *frevó (see p217)*. During the 20th century, African music became part of the mainstream. *Samba* won acceptance in the 1930s.

Pop star Carlinhos Brown *is one of the traditional singers who have become world-famous with their percussion-heavy rhythms. This noted advocate of Afro-Brazilian culture hails from Bahia.*

CAPOEIRA

A rhythmic, dance-like form of martial arts, *capoeira* was once practised only by slaves and former slaves. Over the years, it came to put less emphasis on fighting and more on the cooperative elements of dance and display, with rhythmic, graceful moves (see p199).

Traditional instruments *used in capoeira* mainly constitute berimbau, *a single-stringed percussion instrument featuring a steel string and a hollowed-out gourd;* atabaque, *a large drum, and the* pandeiro, *which resembles a tambourine.*

Capoeira *was a way for the slaves to continue practising martial arts, with kicks disguised as fluid body movements. Increasingly popular, today it is taught and performed all over the region, and indeed the world.*

RELIGION

Of West African origin, most of Brazil's original slave population believed in a pantheon of deities, or *orixás (see p194)*. Each *orixá* was endowed with its own personality and unique powers, and was associated with a particular set of natural elements. The Portuguese, however, insisted that all new arrivals be forcibly converted to Catholicism. The struggle gave rise to Candomblé, a blending of Catholicism and the African beliefs *(see p35)*.

Festive celebrations, *such as the Lavagem do Bonfim (see p195), can be experienced in and around Salvador. The day is meant to honor Yemanjá, the Goddess of the Sea. The ceremonies blend Catholic-style processions with African beats and music.*

ARTS & CRAFTS

Many of the Bahian arts and crafts are strongly influenced by Afro-Brazilian traditions. The Mercado Modelo *(see p192)* in Salvador is a good place for souvenirs. Look for *berimbaus* and percussion instruments, sometimes painted in bright colors, as well as masks and pottery.

Wooden masks *are intricately carved and decorated with stones, shells, and beads. The northeastern masks are allegoric representations of the* orixás.

Colorful figurines *are produced by local artisans as part of the rich pottery tradition in the Northeast. Drawn from popular folklore, these figurines are sold throughout the region.*

DRESS

The most striking sartorial examples of African influence are the Baianas, the women in turbans and long white dresses, often seen on the streets of Salvador selling *acarajé (see p179)*. The ensemble is believed to be derived from the traditional dress of women in Nigeria. While their dresses are often similar, each Baiana wears a different set of jewelry to pay homage to her particular *orixá* (deity).

Colorful beads and trinkets *can be bought from the Baianas. Every color is known to denote a specific* orixá; *the blue is for Oshun, while red represents Yansã.*

A young Baiana *can be seen in layers of starched lace skirts, a shoulder cloth, high turban, and yellow and white beads and accessories.*

The Flavors of Northeast Brazil

Northeast Brazil has two distinct regional cuisines, a reflection of both culture and climate. The narrow, densely populated coast, rich in fresh fruit and sugar cane and bordered by a generous sea, is home to an African-descended population who flavor their food with coconut milk and red *dendê* (palm) oil. The interior, or *sertão*, is arid semi-desert, given over to cattle tended by the cowboy descendents of Portuguese immigrants. The interior cuisine consists of sober, simple dishes, whose staples include sun-dried meat, manioc (cassava) root, rice, and black beans.

Spicy cayenne pepper

Distinctive *caju* fruit of the cashew tree, showing the nut

COZINHA NORDESTINA

When Brazilians refer to *cozinha nordestina* (north-eastern food) they usually mean the dishes of the hot, dry hinterland. Fresh ingredients are few here, and refrigeration virtually non-existent. Ingredients include the more resilient vegetables such as beans, corn and, especially, manioc. Meat –

beef or, just as often, goat – in the Northeast is usually either sun-dried (*carne de sol*) or air-dried and heavily salted (*carne seca*). Both are served in small portions, often shredded, and mixed in with either beans, rice, or manioc. Manioc, indeed, is a centerpiece of northeastern cooking. Sliced into strips and fried, the sweeter version of this versatile root is known as *macaxeira*. Plain ground manioc flour (*farinha*) is often served as a side dish; locals put it in their morning coffee. Pan-fried with a little oil, the manioc flour becomes another common side dish, *farofa*. Finally, the lighter parts of the manioc root are made into tapioca, the base ingredient of desserts and breakfast pancakes. Desserts in the Northeast are usually simple mixtures of sugar and tapioca or cornflour, often covered in condensed milk. Also popular are small and

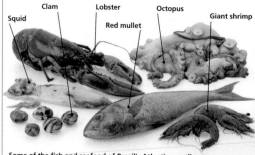

Squid   Clam   Lobster   Octopus   Giant shrimp   Red mullet

Some of the fish and seafood of Brazil's Atlantic coastline

REGIONAL DISHES & SPECIALTIES

Bahian cuisine is the most popular and sophisticated in all of the Northeast. The cooking is characterized by the use of coconut milk, hot peppers, and, importantly, *dendê* oil, which gives the dishes their deep orange color. This oil is extracted from a palm tree that was brought to Brazil by African slaves.

Dendê oil

Signature Bahian dishes include *moqueca*, *vatapá*, and *bobó de camarão*. All are variations on a tasty seafood stew. Traditionally, a *moqueca* is cooked in a large clay pot and served with white rice and a serving of *pirão*, a manioc paste. Both *bobó de camarão* and *camarão na moranga* (see p393) feature large, juicy prawns cooked in coconut milk. The *camarão na moranga* comes served in a hollowed-out pumpkin shell, its broth thickened with the addition of fresh, sweet pumpkin, locally called *jerimum*.

Bolinho de bacalhau *is a Portuguese snack made from mashed potatoes and shredded salt cod.*

Baiana woman in traditional all-white costume, selling *acarajé*

ACARAJÉ

Acarajé is one of the most popular snacks, especially in Bahia. Cooked only by Baianas, it was originally served as an offering to Yansã, the Goddess of Tempests. Balls of mashed black-eyed beans are fried in *dendê* oil, then cut open and served with dried shrimp, *vatapá* (shrimp paste), *caruru* (okra stew), and hot sauce. *Abará* is another kind of *acarajé*, steamed and served on a banana leaf with the same toppings.

intensely sweet portions of dried and concentrated fruits, such as *caju* (cashew), *jaca* (jackfruit), *goiaba* (guava), and banana, usually consumed together with a small, very sweet cup of coffee.

FISH & SEAFOOD

The long Atlantic coastline from Bahia to Maranhão yields a wealth of fish, shellfish, and crustaceans. Everywhere on the coast, the *guaiamu*, a small, blue-shelled crab with tasty meat, is usually steamed and served up as an appetizer. Larger, soft-shelled crabs are also popular, served steamed and eaten whole, including the shell. Another crustacean is the *cavaquinha*, a small lobster known for its sweet and tender meat, but the full-size south Atlantic

lobster is also found to the north, around Ceará. Large and succulent shrimp are another regular menu item. However, the tastiest northeastern shrimp, the *pitu*, is a freshwater variety. Spicy *pitu moqueca* is among the best featured on any menu.

Grated manioc root ready to be processed into tapioca

ON THE MENU

Baião de dois Made with rice, beans, cheese, and garlic, this dish is often served with sun- or air-dried meat.

Caldo de sururu A rich broth made from tiny clams with coconut milk, *dendê* oil, coriander, and spices.

Carne de sol Goat meat or beef is sun-dried to seal in moisture. It may be served grilled or sautéed.

Casquinha de siri A savory appetizer of shredded crab-meat flavored with coriander, coconut milk, and spices.

Tapioca Small pancakes made with tapioca, served stuffed with sweet or savory fillings.

Xinxim de galinha Chicken sautéed in *dendê* oil with ginger, dried shrimp, and cashew nuts. Served with white rice and manioc flour.

Moqueca *is a rich fish dish made with coconut milk,* dendê *oil, cayenne pepper, and coriander (cilantro).*

Ensopado *is a seafood and coconut milk stew made without* dendê *oil, making it lighter in flavor.*

Cocada *is a sweet made with sugar and coconut. The darker variety is sweetened with dried sugarcane juice.*

BAHIA

The largest state in the Northeast, Bahia is known for its endless stretches of stunning beach along the Atlantic coast. The idyllic white-sand coast is dotted with laid-back resorts along its length. Beyond the gorgeous beaches and plains, where most of Bahia's population lives today, lies the sertão, *an arid semi-desert covered in* caatinga, *small trees used for cattle grazing.*

When the Portuguese first arrived in Bahia in 1500, the entire 621-mile (1,000-km) coastline was covered in a swathe of lush green Atlantic rainforest. Today, only a few pockets of the rainforest remain along the coast in isolated patches. Inland from the coast, the Portuguese successfully established the cultivation of sugar cane, and later cotton and cocoa in the Recôncavo, a narrow, flat, well-watered plain, which they called the *agreste*.

Bahia played a key role in the history of Brazil. Salvador, its capital, was founded in 1549, and served for over two centuries as the administrative and political center of colonial Brazil. The legacy of that period is on display in Salvador's colonial core, Pelourinho, a jewel of colonial Baroque churches, cathedrals, and palaces.

Bahia was also the key point of entry for the thousands of slaves brought to Brazil from ports in Africa. The legacy of that trans-Atlantic trade can be seen in Bahia's cultural diversity. The state has Brazil's highest percentage of Afro-Brazilian residents. Bahia's percussion-driven music, the fast fight-dance known as *capoeira*, and the spiritualist Yoruban Candomblé religion all have their roots in Africa.

In addition to these legacies, visitors to Bahia can experience one of Brazil's longest and most beautiful coastlines. Fine beach resorts such as Praia do Forte and Costa do Sauípe lie to the north of Salvador. To the capital's south, there are small villages such as Morro de São Paulo and Itacaré. Inland, Bahia provides unique hiking amid the mesas and valleys of the Chapada Diamantina.

A view of the Parque Nacional Marinho dos Abrolhos, comprising an archipelago of five islands

◁ A Baiana walking on a cobblestoned street, past a tree in full bloom in the colonial town of São Félix

Exploring Bahia

Living up to its official motto, *Sorria, você está na Bahia* (Smile, you're in Bahia), Bahia offers a diverse range of sights. The extensive coastline varies from fine Linha Verde resorts to sleepy villages with stunning unspoilt beaches such as Trancoso. Salvador and the historic towns of the Recôncavo provide fascinating glimpses into Brazil's history. The Chapada Diamantina is a highland region that resembles the mesas of Arizona and New Mexico in Southwest USA. Lençóis, founded during the area's 19th-century gold and diamond rush, boasts caverns, waterfalls, and some of Brazil's best hiking.

SIGHTS AT A GLANCE

Towns & Cities
Cachoeira ❹
Canudos ❺
Ilhéus ❾
Itacaré ❽
Lençóis ❸
Porto Seguro ❿
Salvador pp184–95 ❶
Santo Amaro ❸
São Félix ❺
Trancoso ⓫

National Parks
Parque Nacional de Chapada Diamantina pp204–205 ⓮
Parque Nacional Marinho de Abrolhos ⓬

Areas of Natural Beauty
Ilha de Itaparica ❷
Morro de São Paulo ❻
Peninsula de Maraú ❼

Beaches & Resorts
Linha Verde p207 ⓰

0 kilometers 100
0 miles 100

Paçarrão
Sento Sé
Barragem de Sobradinho
Del
Umburanas
Xique-Xique
Central
Capixaba
Irecê
Morro do Chapéu
Morpara
Ipupiara
B A H I A
Brotas de Macaúbas
Ibotirama
Uting
Brasília
Wagner
LENÇÓIS ⓭ ❶
PARQUE NACIONAL DE ⓮
Paratinga
CHAPADA DIAMANTINA
Macaúbas
Ia
Brasília
Bom Jesus da Lapa
Piatã
Iram
Paramirim
Barra da Estiva
Riacho de Santana
Ituaçu
Caetité
Carinhanha
Brumado
Guanambi
Aracatu
Caculé
Verde Pequeno
Urandi
Vitóri
Conq

Belo Horizonte,
Rio de Janeiro

A white-sand beach resort near Itacaré, with palm trees lining the shore

KEY

— Highway
— Major road
— Minor road
— Railroad
— State border
△ Peak

KEY

■ Area illustrated

A Baiana under the towering cross outside Salvador's Memorial das Baianas

SEE ALSO

- **Where to Stay** pp376–8

- **Where to Eat** pp401–403

GETTING AROUND

Bahia is large, and the roads are mostly precarious. However, the Linha Verde (BA-099), which runs north along the coast from Salvador to the border with Sergipe, provides easy, quick access to the beach towns. Traveling south from Salvador, the BR-101 runs parallel to the coast, about 37 miles (60 km) inland. Access to beach towns on the southern coast is via secondary roads. The best way to get around is to fly to one of the major destinations, such as Salvador, Ilhéus, or Porto Seguro, and proceed by bus to explore the surrounding regions. The main destination inland, the Chapada Diamantina, is a drive from Salvador on the BR-324, BR-126, and BR-242 highways. Lençóis in the Chapada Diamantina can be reached by road and plane.

Salvador ❶

Founded by the Portuguese in 1549 on the protective shores of the Baía de Todos os Santos (Bay of All Saints), Salvador is Brazil's third largest city, after São Paulo and Rio de Janeiro. Modern Salvador offers a fascinating blend of old and new. In the colonial heart, Pelourinho, the cobblestoned streets are lined with the restored 17th- and 18th-century palaces and Baroque churches. The city's recent growth has been northward along the beaches that face the Atlantic Ocean. The city's vibrant community of musicians draws from the region's African and Portuguese heritage, blending these into a unique Bahian sound.

***Azulejos* in the cloisters of Igreja e Convento de São Francisco**

Imposing buildings in Pelourinho, the heart of Salvador

SIGHTS AT A GLANCE

Historic Buildings, Streets, Towns & Neighborhoods

Elevador Lacerda ⑨
Forte de Santo Antônio ⑭
Fundação Casa de Jorge Amado ②
Mercado Modelo ⑩
Palácio Rio Branco ⑧
Pelourinho pp186–7 ①
Praça da Sé ⑦

Churches, Cathedrals & Monasteries

Catedral Basílica ⑤
Igreja e Convento de São Francisco pp190–191 ⑥
Nosso Senhor do Bonfim ⑮

Museums

Museu Afro-Brasileiro ④
Museu de Arte da Bahia ⑬
Museu de Arte Sacra ⑪
Museu Tempostal ③
Solar do Unhão ⑫

RUA DA POLÔNIA
RUA CONDE
AVENIDA DA FRANÇA
AVENIDA ESTADOS UNIDOS
R DA ARGENTINA
RUA MIGUEL CALMON
RUA CONS. DANTAS
RUA CONS. SARAIVA
RUA F. GONÇALVES
RUA OURIVES
RUA ALGIBERES
RUA PINTO MARTINS
RUA PORTUGAL
CIDADE BAIXA
R FRED. REBELO
RUA SANTOS DUMONT
RUA LOPES CARDOSO
Terminal da França
R VISC. DO ROSARIO
RUA DA BELGICA
PRAÇA DO MERCADO
10
Terminal Marítimo Turístico
LADEIRA DA MONTANA
9
Baía de Todos os Santos
AVENIDA DAS NAUS
AVENIDA DE CONTORNO
LADEIRA DA PREGUIÇA
LAD DA CONCEIÇAO
CIDAD
ALTA
LAD PAU DA BANDEIRA
PRAÇA CASTRO ALVES

For additional map symbols *see back flap*

GETTING AROUND

Most of the attractions in Salvador are
concentrated in Cidade Alta (Upper City),
linked to the Cidade Baixa (Lower City) by
a furnicular railway and the Carlos Lacerda
elevator. The historic neighborhood of Pelourinho
is located downtown, on top of a bluff overlooking the harbor. The main sights outside
Pelourinho are within walking distance of the
bustling waterfront. Bus services easily connect
to every part of the city. Travelers coming from
the south can take BR-101 around the Baía de
Todos os Santos and connect to the BR-324.
Those arriving from the north can follow the
BR-009, called the Linha Verde.

VISITORS' CHECKLIST

2,400,000. ✈ 22 miles
(35 km) from city center. Av
Antônio Carlos Magalhães 4362,
Pernambués, (071) 3450 3871.
Av Oscar Pontes 1051, (071)
3254 1020; across from
Mercado Modelo, (071) 3241
2893. Rua Gregório de
Matos 12, Pelourinho, (071)
3321 2463. Lavagem do
Bonfim (Jan), Carnaval (Feb).
www.emtursa.ba.gov.br

GREATER
SALVADOR

BAIA DE
TODOS OS
SANTOS

Bonfim

São
Caetano

Terminal da
Estação
Marítima

Quintas

Barris

Rio
Vermelho

Pituba

Barra

Ondina

ATLANTIC OCEAN

Amaralina

KEY

Area of the main map

RUA PE. A.
GOMES

DO TABOÃO

RUA A. FERRAZ

RUA L. DE
CARVALHO

RUA ALFREDO DE BRITO

RUA J. C.

SOUZA

RUA JOÃO DE DEUS

ROBELA

RUA GREGÓRIO DE

LADEIRA DE SÃO MIGUEL

R INÁCIO ACCIOLE

R SANTA
ISABEL

RUA LARANJEIRAS

TERREIRO
DE JESUS

RUA DR.

RUA MONTE ALVERNE

RUA SALDANHA DA GAMA

R TRES DE MAIO

DA ORAÇÃO

R GUEDES DE BRITO

RUA

RUA SÃO

FRANCISCO

GONÇALVES

JOSÉ

R VINTE E OITO SETEMBRO

RUA DA GRAÇA

LADEIRA DA PRAÇA

BAIXA DOS SAPATEIROS

CHAPEU

A

TESOURO

RUA RUY BARBOSA

RUA DR. JOAQUIM SEABRA

VISCONDE

DE ITAPARICA

BARROQUINHA

KEY

Street-by-Street area: *see pp186–7*
Train station
Bus station
Post office
Tourist information
Church
Highway
Major road
Minor road
Railroad

0 meters   200

0 yards   200

SEE ALSO

• **Where to Stay** p377

• **Where to Eat** pp402–403

Street-by-Street: Pelourinho ①

Detail on church façade

The crown jewel of Salvador is the restored historic center, Pelourinho, which means whipping post. This originally described only the small triangular plaza in the heart of the city where slaves were publicly flogged. Located on a high bluff overlooking the commercial city below, Pelourinho was built by the Portuguese in the boom years of the 18th and 19th centuries as a residential and administrative center. Abandoned for a greater part of the 20th century, Pelourinho was designated a UNESCO World Heritage Site in 1985. Today, visitors can explore its magnificent colonial houses, Baroque churches, and museums.

★ Museu Afro-Brasileiro
The large wood carvings of the Candomblé deities by renowned artist Carybé are the highlights of this museum of Afro-Brazilian culture ④

Catedral Basílica
Built in 1657, the renovated cathedral has a cedar wood altar, and two smaller side altars, both covered in thin layers of gold ⑤

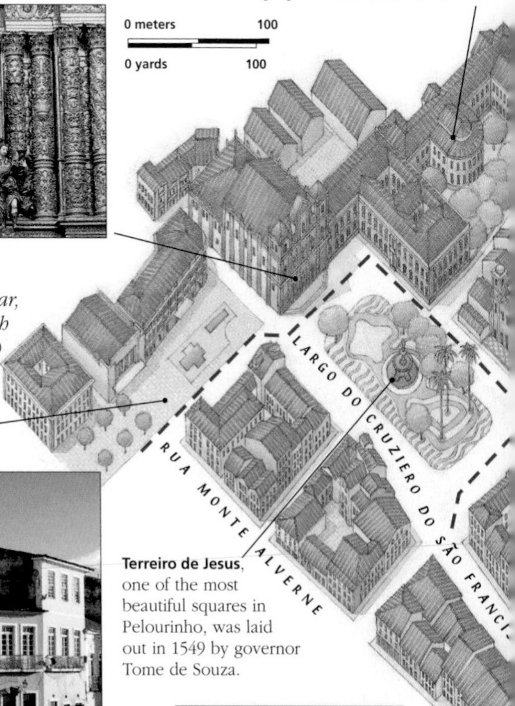
0 meters 100
0 yards 100
LARGO DO CRUZIERO DO SÃO
RUA MONTE ALVERNE

Praça da Sé offers views across the Baía de Todos os Santos ⑦

Terreiro de Jesus, one of the most beautiful squares in Pelourinho, was laid out in 1549 by governor Tome de Souza.

Pastel-hued buildings along the slope of Pelourinho

STAR SIGHTS

- ★ Museu Afro-Brasileiro
- ★ Igreja e Convento de São Francisco
- ★ Fundação Casa de Jorge Amado

★ Igreja e Convento de São Francisco
A silver chandelier weighing 176 lb (80 kg) hangs over the ornate carvings of this richly embellished church ⑥

For hotels and restaurants in this region see p377 and pp402–403

Igreja Nossa Senhora do Rosário dos Pretos

Built by slaves in the 18th century, the church remains the center of Afro-Brazilian traditions in Pelourinho.

VISITORS' CHECKLIST

Bahia. ▥ *Barra from Praça da Sé.* ▯ *Rua Laranjeiras 12, (071) 3321 2463.* ◯ *8:30am–9pm daily.* ▨ *Terça da Benção (every Tue).* **Igreja Nossa Senhora do Rosário dos Pretos** *Praça José de Alencar s/n.* ◯ *9am–6pm daily.* ▯ *6pm Tue, 10am Sun.* **Igreja da Ordem Terceira de São Francisco** *Rua Inácio Accioli.* **Tel** *(071) 3321 6968.* ◯ *8:30am–5pm daily.* ▯ *8:30am Wed & Sun.* ▨

★ Fundação Casa de Jorge Amado
The lovely café inside Foundation House, which is dedicated to the life of one of Brazil's most famous authors, is decorated with hundreds of book jackets from Amado's novels published around the world ②

Museu Abelardo Rodrigues
One of Brazil's largest private collections of sacred art is housed in this impressive museum.

KEY

– – – Suggested route

Igreja da Ordem Terceira de São Francisco
The fine 18th-century sandstone façade of this church was rediscovered only in the 1930s. Craftsmen chipped away at plaster for nine years to reveal this marvelous building.

Fundação Casa de Jorge Amado ②

Largo do Pelourinho s/n. ***Tel*** *(071) 3321 0122.* 🕒 *9am–6pm Mon–Sat.*

Although Brazilian author Jorge Amado (1912–2001) never lived in Pelourinho, many of his beloved novels were set in this neighborhood *(see p200)*. Opened in 1987, the Casa de Jorge Amado is a small museum housed in a pretty blue colonial building located at the top end of Largo do Pelourinho. It is one of the main monuments dedicated to Bahia's most famous author. Its four floors comprise the entire archive of his work and include a research center.

The collection on display consists mostly of covers of his books and personal belongings that tell the story of his life. A mural on the ground floor shows the languages into which his works have been translated; over 60 in total, including Chinese and Hungarian.

Covers of Amado's books exhibited at Fundação Casa de Jorge Amado

Museu Tempostal ③

Rua Gregorio de Matos 33, Pelourinho. ***Tel*** *(071) 3117 6383.* 🕒 *1–6pm Tue–Sat.* ♿

Housed in a beautiful colonial building in the heart of Pelourinho, this museum displays only a fraction of founder Antônio Marcelino's collection of 30,000 postcards and photographs. Most date from the 19th and 20th centuries. Antique postcards comprising the main display tell the history of Salvador as it has developed and grown. Some cards are enlarged to give visitors a better view of the photographic details. A smaller exhibit of Belle Époque postcards showcases some elaborate samples of postcard "art," some adorned with embroidery, others painted like aquarelles.

Antique postcard displayed at the Museu Tempostal

Museu Afro-Brasileiro ④

Terreiro de Jesus s/n, Pelourinho. ***Tel*** *(071) 3321 2013.* 🕒 *9am–6pm Mon–Fri, 10am–5pm Sat & Sun.* ♿

This small museum in the former Faculty of Medicine building houses a collection of photographs, artwork and artifacts all related to the African diaspora in Brazil. The main exhibit displays objects and crafts from the original African cultures of regions such as Angola and Nigeria where Brazil-bound slaves were captured. The highlight of the collection are the 27 life-sized wood carvings of the *orixás (see p177)* by Bahian artist Carybé (1911–97), depicting their characteristic weapons and regalia, together with the animals or domain over which they are thought to rule. Yemanjá, the Goddess of the Sea, is shown with a fish and seashells and the mirrors and trinkets offered to her by supplicants, and the warrior Ogun is shown with his sword and metal armor.

Yansã, Candomblé Goddess of Tempests, at Museu Afro-Brasileiro

Catedral Basílica ⑤

Terreio de Jesus, Praça XV de Novembro s/n. ***Tel*** *(071) 3321 4573.* 🕒 *8:30–11:30am & 1:30–5:30pm Mon–Sat.* ✝ *11am–noon Sun. Baroque concert held every Sun at 11am.* ♿

Salvador's main cathedral, built between 1657 and 1672, is considered to be one of the richest examples of Portuguese Baroque architecture. The cathedral's façade is made of Portuguese *lioz,* a type of limestone. The interior walls and tall pillars are also covered with the pale-colored stone, giving the church a bright and spacious feel.

The vaulted ceiling of the main nave is made from wood. The decorations are carved in relief and stand out from the ceiling with an almost three-dimensional effect. The main altar and two smaller side altars are also carved out of wood and covered in gold leaf.

Dedicated to St. Francis, the altar contains a silver-plated statue of Nossa Senhora das Maravilhas (Our Lady of Miracles), which is said to have inspired Father Antônio Vieira, a 17th-century Jesuit priest who fought against the enslavement of indigenous people. His fiery, anti-slavery sermons did not sit well with the Inquisition, who subsequently ordered his arrest. The former Jesuit library now holds a small museum of religious art. The collection includes silver and gold religious artifacts such as chalices and candleholders. The most modern piece in the cathedral is the powerful German organ with more than 500 pipes, 18 registers, and two keyboards.

Altar of Catedral Basílica, the main cathedral of Salvador

Igreja e Convento de São Francisco ⑥

See pp190–91.

Praça da Sé ⑦

Memorial das Baianas ☐ *9am–7pm daily.*

Pelourinho's Praça da Sé blends the modern with the historic. The square is a transition point between the Terreiro de Jesus and the Praça Tomé de Sousa. Recent

renovations have added fountains and benches, so people can linger and enjoy the *capoeira* presentations or other cultural events often held in the square. There is a lookout point, the Belvedere, on the north side of the square which provides a beautiful view of the Lower City and the Baía de Todos os Santos (Bay of All Saints).

Just to the left and down a few steps from the Belvedere is the **Memorial das Baianas**. This small kiosk-like building pays homage to the women who have become such a symbol of Salvador. The memorial shows and explains the ceremonial clothing and accessories worn by Baianas *(see p177)*, and often showcases the works of modern Bahian artists. There are also photographs of famous Baianas from days gone by.

Palácio Rio Branco ⑧

Praça Tomé de Sousa s/n. ☐ *10am–noon & 2–6pm Tue–Fri.*

The original Palácio Rio Branco has nothing in common with the building that currently goes by that name. The first palace was built on this site in 1549 to house Bahia's first governor, Tomé de Sousa. The Portuguese queen and later the prince regent resided in this palace temporarily in

1808, when the entire Portuguese court relocated to Rio de Janeiro in order to escape Napoleon's invasion of Portugal *(see p52)*. The building survived until 1900, when the whole structure was leveled and then rebuilt from scratch in Renaissance style.

A fire in 1912 forced another major overhaul, giving the building the eclectic look it still has today. Used as an official government building until 1979, the Palácio Rio Branco was rededicated in 1986 as a cultural foundation, the Centro Memoria da Bahia. The former reception hall on the ground floor now tells the history of Bahia's 40 governors through paintings, historic documents, and their personal belongings.

Art Deco Elevador Lacerda with market stalls below

Elevador Lacerda ⑨

Praça Tomé de Sousa s/n. ☐ *24 hrs daily.*

Built by merchant Antônio Francisco de Lacerda in 1873 from the original Jesuit-installed manual pulley, the Elevador Lacerda connects Praça Tomé de Sousa in the Upper City with Praça Cairu in the Lower City.

The Elevador Lacerda is a popular site in Salvador, used by more than 30,000 people daily. The elevator's current Art Deco look dates from a 1930s restoration. Four elevators make the 236-ft (72-m) trip up vertical shafts in just 30 seconds, where the view across the bay on a clear day is simply stunning.

Preparations for a cultural show outside Palácio Rio Branco

Igreja e Convento de São Francisco ⑥

The complex of the Church and Convent of St. Francis is one of Brazil's most impressive Baroque monuments. The complex was constructed between 1708 and 1750. The convent's church stands out for its rich and opulent interior. The inner walls and the ceiling are largely covered in gold leaf. The main altar and the large side altars are magnificently carved out of wood and in typical Baroque style, ornately decorated with angels, birds, mermaids, fruits, and leaves. An enormous silver chandelier hangs above intricate wooden carvings, and hand-painted blue-and-white Portuguese tiles.

Statue of St. Francis

★ **Franciscan Shield**
Featuring the crossed forearms of Jesus and St. Francis, the shield represents the bond between the two.

São Pedro de Alcântara
The altar of São Pedro de Alcântara, carved by Brazilian artist Manuel Inácio da Costa, is a particularly fine example of Brazilian Baroque.

Façade
The church façade dominates the Largo de São Francisco with imposing twin bell towers.

Doors and windows in bright tones adorn the outer walls of the church.

Oil Painting of St. Francis
The oil painting depicting an event in the life of St. Francis in the church entryway is one of the classic examples of Brazilian Baroque Illusionism.

STAR SIGHTS

★ Franciscan Shield

★ Main Altar

★ Azulejos

★ Main Altar

A statue of Jesus on the cross with St. Francis by his side graces the main altar. The blue-and-white tiles behind the main altar tell the life story of the saint. The gold-and-white motif is offset by dark jacaranda wood handrailings.

VISITORS' CHECKLIST

Largo Cruzeiro de São Francisco, Praça Anchieta, Pelourinho. **Tel** (071) 3322 6430. ⬜ 8am–5pm Mon–Sat, 8am–4pm Sun. 🖼 🎫 ♿
Sound & Light Show ⬜ 11:30am & 4pm Mon & Wed–Sat. **Igreja Terceira Ordem de São Francisco** Rua Inácio Accioli. ⬜ 8:30am–5:30pm Mon–Sat, 1–5pm Sun. 🖼

Detailing of pure gold leaf decorates the church interior.

Cloisters
These secluded interior arcades are where the monks of St. Francis would gather for prayer or quiet contemplation.

Black Saint São Bento
Two of the side altars are dedicated to black saints such as Santa Efigênia, an Ethiopian princess, and São Bento, the son of African slaves.

★ Azulejos

Brought over from Portugal in 1743, the decorative tiles are based on the etchings by Flemish painter Otto van Veen in his book of moral emblems.

IGREJA TERCEIRA ORDEM DE SÃO FRANCISCO

The ornately carved and detailed soapstone façade of the church of the Third Order of St. Francis next door is the only one of its kind in Brazil. The façade remained hidden for many years behind a layer of plaster, only to be uncovered accidentally when wiring was being installed in the 1930s. The church also has a museum and a room of Franciscan tombs.

Soapstone exterior of the church

Pretty lace hammocks displayed in the stalls outside the Mercado Modelo

Mercado Modelo ⑩

Praça Visconde de Cairu, Comércio. **Tel** (071) 3241 2893. ☐ 9am–7pm Mon–Sat, 9am–2pm Sun.

The Mercado Modelo was built in 1861 as a customs building. The square behind the market, now used by *capoeiristas (see p199)*, was where boats would dock to unload their merchandise for inspection. The building was transformed into an indoor craft market in 1971, and renovated after a major fire in 1984. Nowadays, the Mercado's two floors house 259 stalls that offer a variety of northeastern arts and crafts. Popular items include naive art paintings of Pelourinho, *berimbaus* (a stringed instrument), embroidered lace tablecloths, hammocks, and colorful hats, as well as spices and sweets.

Museu de Arte Sacra ⑪

Rua do Sodré 276. **Tel** (071) 3243 6310. ☐ 11:30am–5:30pm Mon–Fri.

One of Brazil's best collections of religious art can be found in this museum, which is housed in a former Carmelite convent. The serene and beautiful structure was built between 1667 and 1697, and serves as the perfect backdrop for the varied exhibits, which include statues, icons, paintings, *oratorios* (portable altars), and numerous finely-wrought silver crosses, candlesticks, chalices, censors, and other artifacts from the 16th to 19th centuries.

The Museu de Arte Sacra, housed in a 17th-century convent

Solar do Unhão ⑫

Av do Contorno s/n. **Tel** (071) 3329 0660. **Museu de Arte Moderna** ☐ 1–6pm Tue–Sun. **Tel** (071) 3117 6130.

A renovated colonial sugar mill, the Solar do Unhão beautifully blends the old and the new. The original design is typical of the 17th century – a chapel, a big house with slave quarters on the lower floor, and a large mill where cane was transformed into sugar.

During the sugar boom of the 18th century, the owners added a courtyard fountain and a full-size church, Nossa Senhora da Conceição. After the sugar trade collapsed in the 19th century, the Solar was used variously as a factory, a warehouse, and naval barracks. Finally, in the 1940s it was designated a National Historic Monument and chosen as the site for the **Museu de Arte Moderna**. A series of renovations restored the buildings to their former glory, while upgrading the facilities to include eight exhibit rooms, a theater, and a library.

The complex also houses an excellent restaurant, besides displaying paintings, etchings, and sculptures by some of Brazil's best-known modern artists. In the evenings, it hosts a presentation of traditional Bahian dance and folklore, held in the former slave quarters.

Exterior of the Solar do Unhão, once a colonial sugar mill

Museu de Arte da Bahia ⑬

Av 7 de Setembro 2340, Vitória.
Tel *(071) 3117 6902.* ☐ *2–7pm Tue–Sun.* 🖾

Also referred to as the Palacete de Vitória, the Museu de Arte da Bahia offers a glimpse of the opulent lifestyle of Salvador's colonial elite. The collection includes paintings, *azulejos*, furniture, silverware, glass, china, and crystal used by the local ruling families during the 18th, 19th, and early 20th centuries. Many of the large dressoirs, canopy beds, desks, and other pieces of furniture are made from exquisite tropical hardwoods. The highlight of the China collection is the 17th- and 18th-century Qing dynasty ceramic vases and dishes, imported by Portuguese traders via Macau.

The south wing has a small group of landscape paintings by artists, such as the 18th-century master José Joaquim da Rocha, depicting everyday life in colonial Bahia.

The Forte de Santo Antônio, topped by the lighthouse

Forte de Santo Antônio ⑭

Praça Almirante Tamandaré, Largo do Farol s/n, Barra. **Tel** *(071) 3264 3296.* ☐ *8am–7:30pm Tue–Sun.* 🖾

One of Salvador's best-known landmarks, the Forte Santo Antônio was erected in 1535. The fort was strengthened in the early 17th century, in response to Dutch attacks on the coast, and upgraded to its present star shape at the beginning of the 18th century.

A lighthouse atop the fort was originally built in 1698, and is still used by boats navigating the entrance to the bay.

Inside the fort, the Museu Hidrográfico (Museum of Hydrography) shows historic navigation instruments and a variety of charts. There is also a notable collection of coins and China from a Portuguese galleon that foundered in 1668, off Rio Vermelho beach.

The fort also boasts a café with an outdoor terrace offering sweeping views of Salvador's skyline.

CARNAVAL IN SALVADOR

Salvador's signature event, the Carnaval is celebrated during February or March. The center-piece is the *trio elétrico*, a giant flatbed truck carrying a massive array of speakers, topped by a rectangular stage. The tradition was started in the 1950s with Dodó and Osmar, two local musicians who took their music to the street on top of a 1929 Ford. Running out from behind the *trio elétrico* truck, a large roped-off area serves as a movable dance floor. Access to this area is restricted to those in an *abadá*, or uniform-style tank top. Revelers outside the roped-off area are called *pipoca*, or popcorn, as they pop up everywhere.

Blocos parade along one of three routes – Pelourinho, mostly for smaller and more traditional groups, while Campo Grande runs through the narrow streets of downtown Salvador, and Ondina goes through the beachside neighborhoods of Barra and Ondina. Performers at the Carnaval include major Brazilian artists such as Daniela Mercury, Caetano

Costumed dancers at the Salvador Carnaval

Veloso, Gilberto Gil, Carlinhos Brown, and popular groups such as Olodum, Ara Ketu, and Chiclete com Banana. In addition to these name-brand performers, there are Afro-Brazilian *blocos* such as Ilê Aye, which only allows people of black heritage in their parade. The queen of the Carnaval is Ivete Sangalo, a noted exponent of *axé*, Bahia's unique rhythm that combines pop with *samba* and Afro-Brazilian beats.

The grand finale occurs in the wee hours of Ash Wednesday. All the various *blocos* make their way to Praça Castro Alves for the Encontro dos Trios, a last late-night jam that marks the closure of the Carnaval.

Exquisite Portuguese *azulejo* (tile work) at Nosso Senhor do Bonfim

Nosso Senhor do Bonfim ⑮

Largo do Bonfim s/n. **Tel** *(071) 3316 2196.* ◯ *7–11am & 2–5pm daily.* 🔹 *7am, 8am & 5pm Tue–Sun.*

Nosso Senhor do Bonfim (Our Lord of Good Success) stands atop a small hill on the Bonfim Peninsula, a strip of land jutting out into the Baía de Todos os Santos

about 6 miles (10 km) north of Pelourinho. The church was built between 1746 and 1754 by Captain Rodrigues de Faria in fulfilment of a pledge he made in the midst of a fierce Atlantic storm. While the hilltop setting is picturesque, what sets the church apart is not its architecture but the role it plays in Bahia's Afro-Brazilian religion. The church is dedicated to God the Father, but it also honors

Oxalá, the supreme deity in the Candomblé religion *(see p177)*.

On Fridays, worshippers dress in white and dedicate their prayers to Oxalá. On other days, in a small chapel just to the right of the main altar, one can visit the Sala dos Milagres (Chamber of Miracles). Believers come here to offer items made of wax, wood, or even gold. The item represents a miracle that has been bestowed upon them. The room is packed with replicas of hearts, lungs, livers, and breasts, as well as babies, houses, and even cars.

Outside, visitors are besieged with offers of *fitas*, little colored ribbons purchased as a good luck charm. The ribbon is meant to be tied around the wrist with three knots, and a wish is made for each knot. The ribbon is then worn until it falls off in order for the wishes to be granted.

Salvador's Atlantic Coast

The tip of Porto da Barra is the beginning of a string of ocean beaches. The best beaches for swimming and sunbathing are close to the southern edge of the city. The best beach close to the city center is Porto do Barra. Farther out, Amaralina's food stalls and *acarajé (see p179)* kiosks are popular on weekends. Itapoã is known for its calm waters and reefs that form natural pools at low tide.

Ondina's beautiful beach *is lined with many of Salvador's biggest and best hotels that look out over the foamy waves.*

Rio Vermelho *is the starting point of a procession honoring Yemanjá (see p41).*

Porto da Barra *is the closest swimming beach to Salvador's historic center. The lighthouse here is a great place from which to watch a spectacular sunset over calm waters.*

Historic Center

Porto da Barra — BARRA
AV. OCEANICA
AV. 7 GARIBALDI

Praia do Farol da Barra
Ondina
Praia de Ondina
Rio Vermelho
Praia do Rio Vermelho
AV. J. MAGALHÃES JUNIOR
AV. CARIOS
SANTA CRUZ
PARQUE DA CIDADE JOVENTINO SILVA
PI'
Amaralina
Praia de Amaralina
P

The impressive 16th-century **Forte de São Felipe** is located to the church, in the neighborhood of Boa Viagem. Just below the fort is the popular beach, **Praia de Boa Viagem**, which is usually bustling with locals and lined with busy stalls selling a variety of trinkets and snacks on weekends.

🏯 **Forte de São Felipe**
Monte Serrat, Boa Viagem.
Tel (071) 313 7339. ⏰ *8am–4pm Mon–Thu, 8–11:30am Fri.* 📷

Colorful ribbons on the railing outside Nosso Senhor do Bonfim

A group of colorfully dressed women during Lavagem do Bonfim

LAVAGEM DO BONFIM

Salvador is home to some of the largest celebrations of the Candomblé religion. One event that occurs each year at the Nosso Senhor do Bonfim is the Lavagem do Bonfim (Washing Ceremony), which takes place on the third Thursday of January. A procession of thousands of devotees makes its way from Salvador city center to the church. Once the procession has reached the church, women in traditional white lace dresses wash the church steps with perfumed water in honor of Oxalá. The tradition is said to stem from the days when the slaves were not allowed inside the church and had to worship outside. The Catholic church does not entirely approve of the ceremony, and keeps its doors shut throughout the festival.

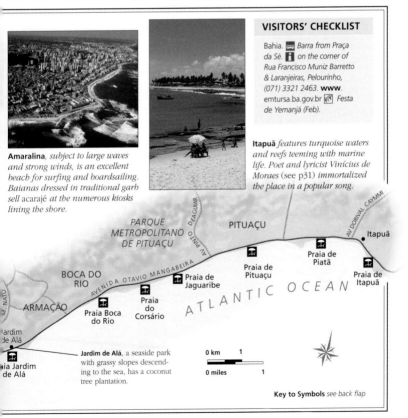

VISITORS' CHECKLIST

Bahia. 🚌 Barra from Praça da Sé. 🛈 on the corner of Rua Francisco Muniz Barretto & Laranjeiras, Pelourinho, (071) 3321 2463. **www. emtursa.ba.gov.br** 🎭 Festa de Yemanjá (Feb).

Itapuã *features turquoise waters and reefs teeming with marine life. Poet and lyricist Vinícius de Moraes (see p31) immortalized the place in a popular song.*

Amaralina, *subject to large waves and strong winds, is an excellent beach for surfing and boardsailing. Baianas dressed in traditional garb sell acarajé at the numerous kiosks lining the shore.*

PARQUE METROPOLITANO DE PITUAÇU

PITUAÇU

Itapuã

AV DORIVAL CAYMMI

Praia de Piatã

Praia de Pituaçu

Praia de Itapuã

BOCA DO RIO

AVENIDA OTAVIO MANGABEIRA

Praia de Jaguaribe

ARMAÇÃO

M. NATO

Praia Boca do Rio

Praia do Corsário

ATLANTIC OCEAN

Jardim de Alá

ia Jardim de Alá

Jardim de Alá, a seaside park with grassy slopes descending to the sea, has a coconut tree plantation.

0 km 1

0 miles 1

Key to Symbols *see back flap*

Ilha de Itaparica, one of the tropical islands in the Baía de Todos os Santos

Ilha de Itaparica ❷

🏠 18,000. 🚢 from Salvador.
🚤 Zimbo Tropical, (071) 638 1148.

The largest island in the Baía de Todos os Santos (Bay of All Saints), with summer-houses lining its shore, Itaparica is a popular week-end refuge for the residents of Salvador.

Located on the northern tip of the island, the main city is guarded by the Forte de São Lourenço, which was built by the Dutch in 1711. Among the island's main attractions are some historic buildings, including the 1622 Nossa Senhora da Piedade (Chapel of Our Lady of Piety) and the 1610 Igreja de São Lourenço.

The island is connected to the mainland by a bridge at its narrow southern tip. The **Praia da Penha**, 10 miles (6 km) south, is a lovely beach with views of Salvador. The region's biggest resort, **Club Med**, lies on the Praia da Conceição, 12 miles (19 km) south of town.

Santo Amaro ❸

🏠 60,000. 🚌 from Salvador.
🎭 Bembé do Mercado (May 13–18).

The laid-back town of Santo Amaro lies in the Recôncavo, the fertile zone at the top end of the Baía de Todos os Santos, which has formed the backbone of Salvador's colonial economy for almost 300 years. The region's high humidity, abundant rainfall,

and rich soils were condusive to growing tobacco, and more signicantly, sugar cane. Until the crash of the sugar economy in the 19th century, Santo Amaro remained the focus of Recôncavo's sugar industry. Dilapidated mansions of the erstwhile sugar barons can still be seen along the old streets. Nowadays, this unpretentious town is known for its paper industry. It is also famous as the home town of Caetano Veloso and Maria Bethânia, two of Brazil's most popular singers.

Many of the slaves, who were brought from Africa to work on plantations, remained in the Recôncavo after slavery was abolished in 1888. The region still has a very high percentage of Afro-Brazilian residents, and Santo Amaro plays a key role in preserving their distinct traditions. Every year, the city commemorates the abolition

Lush hillsides in the Recôncavo, covered with sugar cane

of slavery with a five-day festival of the Bembé do Mercado. During this time, offerings are made to Yemanjá, Goddess of the Sea, to celebrate freedom of religion. In the main square in front of the town market, local groups put on *capoeira* performances. Theater performances of pieces, such as *Nego Fugido* (Runaway Slave), recount the story of slaves fleeing their masters to join *quilombos*, independent communities set up by runaway slaves.

In an effort to keep folkloric traditions alive, the Afro-Brazilian community also organizes presentations of the lesser-known *maculelê* sword dance, an African fight-dance, and *samba de roda* dances performed by women.

Cachoeira ❹

🏠 30,000. 🚌 🛈 Praça da Aclamação 4. 🎭 Festa da Boa Morte (Aug 13–15).

Historically more powerful than the other two main towns in the Recôncavo – Santo Amaro and São Félix – Cachoeira was also the most prominent. Its strategic location, between the Baía de Todos os Santos and the roads leading inland, made it an important crossroads between Salvador and the rest of the state.

The city once had a busy river port on the Paraguaçu. Boats sailed upstream from Salvador to load up with

For hotels and restaurants in this region see pp376–8 and pp401–403

Cobblestoned streets lined with colorful houses in Cachoeira

sugar and tobacco produced in the Recôncavo region. The town's privileged position as a commercial center is reflected in its imposing colonial architecture. However, with the creation of road access to Salvador, Cachoeira lost its key position and its port gradually faded away.

In the old city center, many of the city's churches and wealthy merchants' houses are still standing, although in a dilapidated condition. Only recently has the city begun to renovate and preserve its historic center. As a cultural hub of the Recôncavo region, Cachoeira celebrates the Festa da Boa Morte, one of the most important features of the Candomblé religion. Today, the city is as much celebrated for its robust wood-sculpting tradition, as its production of the best tobacco in Brazil.

Coronas cigar box, São Félix

São Félix ❺

🚋 from Cachoeira.

Regarded as the twin of Cachoeira, São Félix lies just across the Rio Paraguaçu, on a hillside overlooking the river. The railway bridge connecting the two towns was commissioned by Dom Pedro II, and built by British engineers in 1895. Cars, trains, and foot traffic all share the rickety railway bridge. Several times a day, São Félix comes to a standstill as freight trains roll right through the town center.

Larger in size, though not as impressive as Cachoeira, São Félix used to earn a living in its own right as a producer of fine *charutos* (cigars). The heart of this industry was the Dannemann cigar factory, founded in 1873

by German cigar-maker, Gerhard Dannemann. Blessed by optimum conditions for growing and processing tobacco, the Dannemann factory quickly became one of the region's finest cigar producers. The region still produces Dannemann cigars, but the original factory has now been converted into a cultural center, known as the **Centro Cultural Dannemann**. A small exhibit of old machinery tells the story of the early factory days. On weekdays, it is possible to watch the factory workers rolling cigars.

🏛 **Centro Cultural Dannemann**
Av Salvador Pinto 29. *Tel* (075) 3425 2208. ⬜ 8am–5pm Tue–Sat, 1–5pm Sun.

Market scene in São Félix, with a vendor selling fruit

Members of the Sisterhood of the Good Death in festive regalia

FESTA DA BOA MORTE

Celebrated from August 13 to 15, the Festa da Boa Morte (Festival of the Good Death) is one of the most important events of Candomblé *(see p35)*, a blend of African spirituality and Catholicism. The ceremonies are held by members of the Sisterhood of the Good Death, a religious and self-help organization composed entirely of women of African descent. The festival honors both the *iyás* (female spirits of the dead), and the Assumption of the Virgin Mary. A Catholic mass is followed by a large procession through the historic streets of Cachoeira. The women come dressed in multilayered lace skirts and blouses, white turbans, and traditional accessories in honor of various *orixás* (deities). At the head of the procession, they carry a statue of the Virgin Mary. At the end, the women prepare an all-white meal of rice, fish, potatoes, onions, and other white-colored foods. Samba de Roda, a dance based on the African circle dances, marks the end of the ceremonies. Women take turns dancing in the circle to the pounding rhythm of the drums. Onlookers may also be called on to dance.

The ruins of Fortaleza do Tapirando in Morro de São Paulo

Morro de São Paulo ❻

🏠 50,000. ✈ from Salvador. ⛴ from Salvador. ℹ (075) 3652 1104. www.morrodesaopaulo. com.br

Although within easy reach of Salvador, the coast immediately south of the state capital does not have many large, developed tourist destinations, apart from Morro de São Paulo. Now a picturesque beach destination, Morro de São Paulo, on the northern tip of Ilha da Tinharé, once played a key role in the coastal defences of Bahia. In 1630, Governor General Diego Luiz de Oliveira ordered **Fortaleza do Tapirando** to be strategically built here where it could control the Itaparica channel, one of the main approaches to Salvador. The ruins of the fort have been designated a National Heritage Site. The view of the sunset from the fort's crumbling walls is spectacular, and dolphin sightings are quite common.

Still accessible only by boat or plane, Morro maintains much of its original charm. No cars are allowed in the village. Lined with *pousadas*, boutiques, and restaurants, the "streets" are made of sand, and wheelbarrows and bicycles are the primary means of transportation. In the evenings, the village square transforms into a craft market, the small stands often lit only by candlelight, making for a very cozy atmosphere.

Morro's beaches are famous in Brazil for their parties. During high season, there are parties every night and the beaches are packed. Most nights start around midnight, when **Primeira** beach fills with locals and visitors, who dance *axé* and drink fruity cocktails. As you move away from the village, the beaches get wider and less developed. **Segunda** and **Terceira** beaches feature progressively more scattered *pousadas*. From **Quarta** beach onwards, the coast remains blissfully undeveloped, offering long stretches of white sand backed by waving groves of coconut palms.

Environs
Just south of Morro, **Ilha de Boipeba** offers a quiet, idyllic island getaway, with pristine, deserted beaches. Ponta de Castelhanos is especially known for diving. Travelers can get here via boat from Morro de São Paulo. Visitors coming from Salvador can access Boipeba by road, heading down the BA-001.

Peninsula de Maraú ❼

⛴ from Itacaré or Camamu to Barra Grande. ℹ Barra Grande, (075) 3255 2228.

The main destination at the northern tip of the Peninsula de Maraú is **Barra Grande**, a delightful, remote fishing village. Beautiful beaches are scattered along the entire length of the peninsula, but it is difficult to get around without a car. Four wheel drives ferry passengers from *pousadas* to various beaches around the peninsula. Alternatively, the 31-mile (50-km) walk across various palm-fringed beaches along the coastline is spectacular.

Most of the peninsula is covered in native Mata Atlântica rainforest, which has been relatively well preserved. The Baía de Camamu, one of Brazil's largest bays, separates the peninsula from the mainland. The long dirt road heading down the peninsula (often impassable after rains) leads to some of the best beaches facing the open ocean. **Praia Taipús de Fora**, 4 miles (7 km) south of Barra Grande, is considered one of Brazil's most beautiful beaches. At low tide, the coral reefs form a clear, natural pool, perfect for snorkeling and swimming.

There are also a handful of small fishing villages scattered along the coast. Local fishermen offer excursions to **Lagoa Azul** (Blue Lagoon), scenic view points such as Lagoa do Cassange, bay islands and down the Rio Maraú.

Peninsula de Maraú, overlooking the Baía de Camamu

Capoeira

Bahia, the birthplace of *capoeira*, offers visitors plenty of opportunities to see this dazzling and mesmerizing mixture of dance, gymnastics, and martial arts. Evolving from the martial rituals practiced in what is now modern day Angola, the dance and acrobatic aspect of *capoeira* came to predominate in Brazil because Brazilian slave owners banned slaves from practicing martial arts. Outlawed in 1890 and forced underground, the sport made a

slow comeback over the next few decades as white Brazilians began to accept and celebrate the African aspects of Brazil's culture. *Capoeira* was fully rehabilitated in the 1930s, when President Vargas, calling it "the only true Brazilian sport," invited one of the most renowned *capoeiristas* of the day, Mestre Bimba, to perform in the presidential palace. Today, Mestre Bimba's school in Pelourinho is run by his son, Mestre Nenel, and is the best in Brazil.

A berimbau

Berimbau, a single-string instrument that produces a metallic droning sound, sets the *capoeira* beat.

African drums are the additional instruments used in *capoeira*.

The roda, *or the circle in which* capoeira *is always performed, is created by participants who sit or stand and clap to the beat of a single-stringed* berimbau. *The people who form the* roda *will take turns, usually with no predefined order, to go inside the circle and participate.*

CAPOEIRA MOVES

Capoeiristas exhibit incredible muscle control, strength, and flexibility as they carry out acrobatic moves, while keeping their opponent at bay. The *capoeira* moves are carried out at lightning speed, but with a dance-like fluidity, where each move is a combination of skill, balance, and beauty.

Escorpião, *or the scorpion move, is a combination of back flips and cartwheels. Both opponents try to create a beautiful performance.*

Au malandro *starts like a cartwheel, but only one hand goes down while the opposite leg kicks up in the air in a swift, fluid move.*

The esquiva (escape), *a low ducking move, is a very common one since* capoeiristas *primarily attack with kicks and sweeps.*

The beautiful and unspoiled Prainha beach in Itacaré

Itacaré ⑧

🏠 *18,000.* ✈ *Ilhéus.* 🚌 ℹ *Itacaré Ecotourismo, (073) 3251 3666.*

The small fishing town of Itacaré is part of Brazil's famous Discovery Coast. Portuguese explorer Pedro Álvares Cabral *(see p48),* who was the first European to officially "discover" Brazil, landed in Porto Seguro, close to Itacaré, in 1500.

Large areas of protected Atlantic rainforest, which were given World Heritage status by UNESCO in 1999, meet the sea along the coast of Itacaré. Relatively isolated, the town is favored by nature lovers. Itacaré is also known for its relaxed lifestyle and typical Afro-Brazilian culture.

The beaches in this town have enormous waves, making it a popular surfing destination. Most are surrounded by lush forest and can only be accessed on foot. **Prainha**, Itacaré's main attraction, is considered to be one of Brazil's most beautiful beaches, and is accessible only by a trail through the rainforest from Ribeira beach, just south of town.

Environs

Known as the **Estrada Parque** (the Park Drive), the road that connects Itacaré to Ilhéus traverses a well-preserved strand of Atlantic rainforest. Care has been taken not to disrupt the ecosystem and to protect animals crossing the highway. In places, nets have been strung from tree to tree to provide safe passage for monkeys crossing the road. The scenic 49-mile (80-km)

drive follows the coastline and allows access to a string of beautiful, secluded beaches, many of which have little or no facilities.

Ilhéus ⑨

🏠 *221,000.* ✈ 🚌 ℹ *Ilhéustur, (073) 3634 3510.*

When farmers began growing cocoa trees imported from the upper Amazon basin in the early 20th century, Ilhéus, the largest city on Bahia's southern coast, established itself as a major cocoa growing region. A disaster of epic proportions struck in 1989, when a parasite infected most of the plantations and destroyed the entire crop. The industry has yet to recover, but several of the old plantations have been converted into museums.

Ilhéus is best known as the setting for several novels by Bahia's most beloved author, Jorge Amado. One

of his best books, *Gabriela, Clove and Cinnamon,* takes place in the city's historic core at the height of the 1920s cocoa boom. Today, visitors can stroll along the promenades and see the famous Bar Vesúvio and Bataclã Cabaret that feature in his novel. The author's childhood home has been opened to visitors as the **Casa de Cultura Jorge Amado**.

Among the city's other sights is the 16th-century **Igreja de São Jorge**. There are several fine beaches to the north and south of town and **Cururupe**, near the village of Olivença, is a favorite.

🏛 Casa de Cultura Jorge Amado
Rua Jorge Amado 21. **Tel** *(073) 3634 8986.* ⏰ *9am–noon & 2–6pm Mon–Fri, 9am–1pm Sat.* ♿

🏛 Igreja de São Jorge
Praça Rui Barbosa. ⏰ *irregular hrs.*

Casa de Cultura Jorge Amado, childhood home of the famed author

---

JORGE AMADO (1912–2001)

Life-like statue of Jorge Amado, Ilhéus

The son of a cocoa plantation owner, Jorge Amado was born near Ilhéus in 1912. In 1931, Amado moved to Rio to study law, but his heart was already given to literature. That very year, he published his first novel, *O País do Carnaval.* He based his 1958 novel, *Gabriela, Clove and Cinnamon,* on the warring cocoa barons of his native Ilhéus, but infused it with a sense of humor that won him acclaim in Brazil and around the world. *Dona Flor and her Two Husbands* (1966), *Tieta do Agreste* (1977), and *Gabriela, Clove and Cinnamon* were later turned into popular and successful films. Armado published 21 novels, which were translated into 49 languages. He died in 2001.

Main square and the Matriz Nossa Senhora da Pena, Porto Seguro

Porto Seguro ⑩

🏠 *96,000.* ✈ 🚌 ℹ *Visconde de Seguro Square, (073) 3288 4124.*

Porto Seguro (Safe Port) is officially recognized as the site of the first Portuguese landing in 1500, where Pedro Cabral and his fleet arrived and said mass on Brazilian soil. The city's small historic center (Cidade Histórica) has several stately old buildings, including the **Matriz Nossa Senhora da Pena**, built in 1535. Its altar has an image of Saint Francis of Assisi, which was the first religious statue to be brought to Brazil in 1503. On the same square, the former jail built in 1772 is now home to the **Museu de Porto Seguro**, which holds a small collection describing the early colonization of the region.

Today, Porto Seguro is best known for its buzzing nightlife, beach parties, music festivals, and the notorious "Passarela do Alcool" (alcohol boardwalk), the nickname for the city's main street where dozens of vendors set up kiosks selling freshly mixed fruit cocktails with a heavy alcoholic kick. Visitors looking for a more tranquil holiday experience usually head farther south to the lovely neighboring villages of Arraial d'Ajuda and Trancoso.

South of town are a few beaches that mainly attract backpackers. Less developed, but serene, these beaches can be accessed from Porto Seguro airport, which receives daily flights from all over Brazil. Road access can often be challenging, as distances are long and the coastal highways are in a state of disrepair.

🏛 **Museu de Porto Seguro**
Praça Pero Campos Tourinho s/n.
Tel (073) 3288 5182.
⬭ 9am–5pm daily.

Trancoso ⑪

✈ *Porto Seguro, then bus.* 🚌

Though just a short drive from Porto Seguro, Trancoso has a sense of tranquility that sets it apart from the nearby party town. Set on a high bluff overlooking the ocean, the town center or *quadrado* is a long, grassy space, anchored by a small church and framed by houses, many of which have turned their gardens into tasteful little cafés. Trancoso offers sophisticated services focusing on high-end travelers – upscale B&Bs, fine dining, and music. The beaches are backed by red sandstone cliffs, and remain largely secluded and unspoiled.

Parque Nacional Marinho de Abrolhos ⑫

🖼 ℹ *Ibama, Av Juracy Magalhães Junior 608, Salvador, (071) 240 7322.*

Remote and uninhabited, the archipelago of Abrolhos, discovered by Amerigo Vespucci in 1503, offers excellent opportunities for viewing wildlife. The five islands are located off the coast of southern Bahia. In 1983, the islands, together with 351 sq miles (909 sq km) of surrounding ocean, were declared a National Marine Park, the first such park in Brazil. Known for its rare formations of south Atlantic coral, the park teems with sea turtles, squid, and a rich assortment of fish. A variety of bird species come to feed and lay eggs on the islands, which are otherwise dry and covered in grasslands. The best time for spotting humpback whales is between July and November, when the archipelago becomes a calving ground for these gentle giants.

Only one of the five islands, Siriba, can actually be visited. Guided tours to the marine park should only be made with an operator accredited by Brazil's environmental agency, IBAMA. Visitors can also book a day or overnight excursion to the islands and surrounding coral reefs from the town of **Caravelas** on the mainland. For snorkeling and diving enthusiasts, underwater visibility is best between January and March.

Birds nesting on Siriba island, Parque Nacional Marinho de Abrolhos

Crystal-blue water of Poço Azul (Blue Pool), Chapada Diamantina ▷

A view of the old diamond mining town of Lençóis

Lençóis ⓫

🏠 9,000. ✈ 16 miles (25 km) E of town. 🚌 🛈 Sectur, (075) 3334 1380. 🎉 Festa de Senhor dos Passos (Jan), Festa de São João (Jun). www.guialencois.com

The town of Lençóis sprang up almost overnight, as diamond fever struck in these interior highlands in the late 19th century. Unlike many other mining boomtowns, however, Lençóis has a colonial air, with small Baroque churches, and tiny houses and shops painted in pastel colors. The town's distinguished main square, Praça Horácio de Matos, consists of 19th-century houses, characterized by high, arched windows. Another town landmark, Praça Otaviano Alves, lined with gracious colonial homes, is farther south of the main square.

In recent years, Lençóis has reinvented itself as the base camp for ecotourists venturing out to explore the caves, waterfalls, and isolated mountain tops of the surrounding highlands. The town's pretty colonial homes now house trekking equipment stores, Internet cafés, and tasteful photo galleries. The **Calil Neto Fotografia** gallery displays stunning photographs of the panoramic Chapada Diamantina.

🏛 **Calil Neto Fotografia**
Rua do Siriaco s/n. **Tel** (075) 9984 1093. ◔ 7–10pm daily.

Parque Nacional de Chapada Diamantina ⓮

Established in 1985, towering red rock formations, interspersed with lush vegetation, characterize this 587-sq mile (1,520-sq km) park in the hinterland of Salvador. Numerous small rivers crisscross the highlands, cascading over waterfalls, carving through canyons, and tumbling down waterslides. Countless trails lead to caves and caverns. These undefined paths are best navigated with a guide.

Rio Santo António
Morro do Pai Inácio
3,675 ft (1,120 m)
SALVAL
Rio Mucugezinbo
Gruta do Lapão
Rio Lençóis
Lençóis
Cachoeira da Fumaça
Caeté-Açú
Rio Capivara
Rio Ca
Rio
SERRA DA GARAPA
Vale do Paty
Rio Preto
Rio Capãzinho

★ **Morro do Pai Inácio**
The striking mesa is the park's signature mountain formation. The 3,675-ft (1,120-m) plateau offers breathtaking views of the northern half of the park.

Cachoeira da Fumaça, or the Waterfall of Smoke, wears a veil of mist as the water plunges down the 1,150-ft (340-m) precipice.

★ **Vale do Paty**
The multiday hike up this scenic valley offers extraordinary views of the highlands from Morro do Castelo. Other attractions include abandoned miners' settlements and waterfalls with natural swimming pools at Cachoeira dos Funis, as well as the sound of Barbado monkeys that inhabit this vast wilderness.

Rappeling in the Chapada Diamantina
The Chapada's main adventure sport is rappeling down a cliff face or into a cavern. Tour companies in Lençóis offer thrilling rappeling alongside amazing waterfalls.

VISITORS' CHECKLIST

Bahia. ✈ 🚌 ℹ *Fundação Chapada Diamantina, Rua Pe de Ladeira, (075) 3334 1305.* 📷 *Cirtur (day trips & treks): Rua da Baderba 41, Lençóis, (075) 3334 1133. Andrenalina (adventure sports & treks): Rua das Pedras 121, Lençóis, (075) 3334 1689.* Ⓐ *in Chapada Diamantina (free, no permit required for camping and sleeping in the park's abundant caves).*

KEY

Ⓐ	Campground
▬	Major road
═	Minor road
- -	Trail
▬ ▬	Park boundary
△	Peak

Poço Encantado
At the bottom of a deep cavern, the cobalt-blue Enchanted Pool is accessible by a steep trail. Between April and September, sunlight streaming through an aperture makes the pool and cavern glow.

★ Cachoeira do Buracão
Near the park's southern edge, this waterfall plunges 394 ft (120 m) into a vast pool. The river then carves its way through a deep gorge of sedimentary rock. Strong swimmers can swim downstream towards the trailhead.

STAR SIGHTS

★ Morro do Pai Inácio

★ Vale do Paty

★ Cachoeira do Buracão

0 kilometers 25

0 miles 15

Church and colorful houses in the small town of Canudos

Canudos ⑮

🏛 55,000. 🚌

Traveling through the sleepy town of Canudos, it is hard to imagine that this was once the staging ground for a year-long rebellion in 1897. Led by Antônio Conselheiro, the war wound up costing the lives of more than 20,000 people and almost destroyed the future of the Brazilian Republic.

An eyewitness account at the end of the Canudos War was written by journalist Euclides da Cunha, who was on the scene to cover the events for a São Paulo newspaper. He went on to write a book based on his coverage of the war. Published in 1902, *Os Sertões* (*Rebellion in the Backlands*) is one of the most important works of Brazilian literature. In 1997, the University of Bahia turned the site of the 19th-century Canudos War into a state park, **Parque Estadual de Canudos**. To access the park, visitors should get permission from the Memorial de Canudos.

The original settlement of Canudos now lies at the bottom of the Lagoa Cocorobó, which flooded the area in 1970. However, many of the original battle-fields escaped the deluge and have been made into an open-air museum which is part of the park, just on the outskirts of the town. The principal museum sites include Morro do Conselheiro (Counsellor Hill), Vale da Morte (Valley of Death), the Estrada Sagrada (Holy Road), and the Vale da Degola (Valley of Beheadings). The dry *sertão* landscape is quite striking – vegetation consists of *caatinga* bushes, cacti, bromeliads, *umbu* trees and *favelas*, a small thorn-covered shrub. After the April rains, the landscape briefly turns lush and animals such as deer, hyacinth macaws, and armadillos can be spotted frequently.

In the Canudos region during the war, Republican soldiers were camped in the hills that were covered by *favela* trees, a very common shrub in the dry interior of Bahia. Upon their return to Rio, the soldiers never received the land which they had been promised. They ended up squatting on the hills, naming their new-found community *favela* after the trees in the *sertão*. Hence, the name *favela (see p85)* that is now used to refer to the urban ghettos traces its origins to the Canudos War.

🌺 **Parque Estadual de Canudos**
Tel (075) 3494 2241. 📷 🎫 tours arranged by Memorial de Canudos.

Statue of Antônio Conselheiro

ANTÔNIO CONSELHEIRO

Part Robin Hood, part religious fanatic, Antônio Conselheiro, the leader of Brazil's 1897 Canudos War, was born Antônio Vicente Mendes Maciel in 1830 in Ceará. Conselheiro traveled the dry *sertão* for decades, first as a salesman and legal *conselheiro* (counselor), then as a preacher and reformer, raging against the plight of the peasants. In 1893, Conselheiro, outraged at the newly imposed taxes on an already starving population, settled in the tiny upland town of Canudos and began creating what was, in effect, an independent state. Conselheiro began implementing an early form of socialism, heavily tinged with religious values. The poor of the region flocked to Conselheiro and Canudos quickly grew to a community of more than 8,000 people. With the prestige of the new Republican government at stake, the army sent three large forces against Canudos. All were destroyed. Finally, in November of 1897, the army mounted a full-scale invasion. Conselheiro died during the battle and all the residents of Canudos were slaughtered.

Linha Verde 16

Projeto
Tamar logo

The Linha Verde (Green Line) is the 152-mile (252-km) stretch of coast that runs north from Salvador all the way to Mangue Seco on the Sergipe border. It is often referred to as the Estrada do Côco, or Coconut Highway, because of the thick stands of palm trees that line the beaches. This part of the coast offers several popular holiday destinations and well-developed resorts. The most favored destinations are Praia do Forte and Costa do Sauípe. Farther north, the beaches are pristine and beautiful.

VISITORS' CHECKLIST

Bahia. 🚌 from Salvador.
📍 Odara, Av ACM s/n, Praia do Forte. **Tel** (071) 3676 1080.
www.odaratours.com.br;
Centrotour, Av ACM s/n, Praia do Forte. **Tel** (071) 3676 1091.
www.centrotouristico.com.br
Projeto Tamar Av ACM s/n, Praia do Forte. **Tel** (071) 3676 1020. ⏰ 9am–6pm daily.
📷 🖼 www.projetotamar.com.br

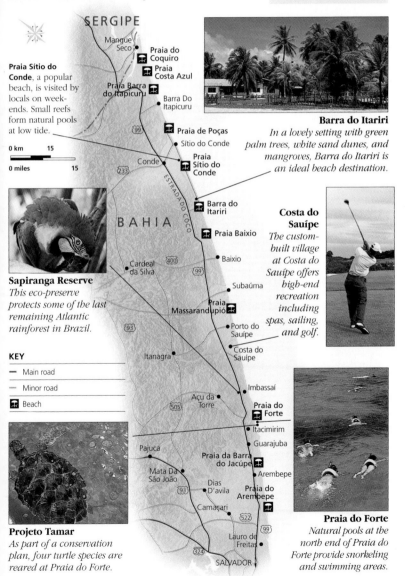

Praia Sítio do Conde, a popular beach, is visited by locals on weekends. Small reefs form natural pools at low tide.

Barra do Itariri
In a lovely setting with green palm trees, white sand dunes, and mangroves, Barra do Itariri is an ideal beach destination.

Sapiranga Reserve
This eco-preserve protects some of the last remaining Atlantic rainforest in Brazil.

Costa do Sauípe
The custom-built village at Costa do Sauípe offers high-end recreation including spas, sailing, and golf.

KEY

— Main road

— Minor road

🏖 Beach

Projeto Tamar
As part of a conservation plan, four turtle species are reared at Praia do Forte.

Praia do Forte
Natural pools at the north end of Praia do Forte provide snorkeling and swimming areas.

SERGIPE, ALAGOAS & PERNAMBUCO

Long stretches of white beach bathed by a warm, blue-green ocean comprise the magnificent coastline of Sergipe, Alagoas, and Pernambuco. In contrast, much of the interior of this region is dry sertão, *where the landscape is barren and harsh. Despite, or perhaps because of their material poverty, these northeastern states are culturally rich in music and folklore.*

The states of Sergipe, Alagoas, and Pernambuco in the Northeast were among the first parts of Brazil to be colonized by Portugal, and for centuries afterward they were the richest region of colonial Brazil. The wealth of the region came from sugar. With slave labor, sugar cane could be cultivated in abundance, and sugar sold in the burgeoning markets of Europe. In 1654, the Portuguese reclaimed Pernambuco after a brief Dutch takeover, but opted to keep the new city, Recife, as the capital instead of Olinda.

Sugar still dominates the economy, but the beaches make this region one of Brazil's hottest tourist destinations. These states have also developed a rich culture and penchant for lively festivals. Popular musical styles such as *forró* and *frevo* began or culminated in the Northeast.

All three states have pretty, historic towns, stunning coastlines, and picture-perfect beaches. Reefs of stone and coral provide natural habitats for fish, sea turtles, sharks, and other tropical marine life. The island archipelago of Fernando de Noronha, a municipality of Pernambuco, is one of Brazil's prime marine habitats and a preferred destination of scuba divers. The Rio São Francisco, the longest river in Brazil, passes through the beautiful scenery of Sergipe and Alagoas in the last leg of its journey before finally meeting the Atlantic Ocean.

Dois Irmãos (Mount of the Two Brothers), Parque Nacional Marinho de Fernando de Noronha

◁ The serene Igreja Nossa Senhora dos Remédios, Vila dos Remédios, Fernando de Noronha

Exploring Sergipe, Alagoas & Pernambuco

Year-round warm weather makes this region a popular sunshine destination. The island archipelago of Fernando de Noronha in Pernambuco is Brazil's top scuba diving destination, and it also offers a fascinating ecosystem rich in wildlife. Recife and Olinda provide a captivating impression of 17th- and 18th-century Brazil, a legacy of Dutch and Portuguese colonization. São Cristóvão and Penedo, located on the border between the two states, are both charming Baroque colonial towns. Penedo has the added advantage of offering a spectacular view of the Rio São Francisco.

Rio São Francisco, the largest river in Northeast Brazil

CANION XINGÓ **5**

Stunning blue sky and pastel-colored colonial houses in the picturesque town of Olinda

SIGHTS AT A GLANCE

Towns & Cities
Aracaju **1**
Caruaru **12**
Maceió **7**
Marechal Deodoro **6**
Olinda pp220–22 **10**
Penedo **3**
Recife pp216–19 **9**
São Cristóvão **2**

Beaches, Islands & Areas of Natural Beauty
Canion Xingó **5**
Porto de Galinhas **8**
Fernando de Noronha pp224–5 **13**
Ilha de Itamaracá **11**
Rio São Francisco **4**

GETTING AROUND

Recife, Aracaju, Maceió, and Fernando de Noronha have good flight connections to the rest of Brazil. However, only Recife has an international airport. Cities on the coast are easily accessible by bus or car. Bus connections are fast and convenient through the region. Highway BR-101 connects Aracaju, Maceió, and Recife, while smaller coastal destinations are only a short drive east on secondary roads off the main highway. However, roads in the interior require a bit more patience as they are often in poor condition, making night driving hazardous. Gas stations and services become scarce in the sparsely populated interior; drivers should be prepared with a full tank of gas, snacks, and plenty of water.

SEE ALSO

• *Where to Stay* pp378–9

• *Where to Eat* pp403–405

FERNANDO DE NORONHA ⓭

Fortaleza

Mossoró

Natal

Campina Grande

João Pessoa

Caruaru   Recife

0 km   200
0 miles   120

José Egito

Campina Grande nia

Pesqueira rcoverde

Timbaúba   Goiana

João Pessoa

ILHA DE ITAMARACÁ ⓫ 🏯🏛✗
Limoeiro   Carpina   Paulista
Sta. Cruz do Capibaribe
Vitória de Sto. Antão   🏛🏠 ⓾ OLINDA
Nova Jerusalém   ✈🚍 ⓽ RECIFE
🏯🏛🏠
⓬ CARUARU   Jaboatão
Escada   Cabo de Santo Agostinho
Lajedo   🚍🏛 ⓼ PORTO DE GALINHAS
Quipapá   Palmares   Rio Formoso
Garanhuns   Una   Barreiros
Porto Cavlo   Maragogi
Águas Belas   União dos Palmares
almeira dos Índios   São Luis do Quitunde
ALAGOAS   Rio Largo   🏛🚍
Arapiraca   Atalaia   ⓻ MACEIÓ
🚍🏛🏠 ⓺
MARECHAL DEODORO
⓸ RIO SÃO FRANCISCO   Coruripe
pria   🏯🏠 ⓷ PENEDO
RGIPE   Piassabussu
Maruim
anjeiras
ARACAJU
O CRISTÓVÃO 🏛

KEY

— Major road
— Minor road
— Railroad
— State border

0 kilometers   50
0 miles   50

Sailboats near Fernando de Noronha with Morro do Pico at a distance

The wide boulevards of Sergipe's capital, Aracaju

Aracaju ❶

Sergipe. 🏙 492,000. ✈
🛈 Centro de Turismo, (079) 3179
1933. 🎭 Festa de São João (Jan),
Forró Caju Music Festival (Jun), Festa
de Yemanjá (Dec).

Sergipe's original capital was
São Cristóvão, located inland
from the Atlantic Ocean. A
burgeoning trade in sugar,
however, made a sizable port
necessary, and in 1855, the
capital transferred to Aracaju,
situated at the mouth of the
Rio Sergipe. By 1901, the
sleepy fishing village soon
transformed into a stately
capital, with a horse-drawn
street-car and a movie theater.

Today, Aracaju is a small
city with a commercial downtown area along the south
riverbank. Sea-life enthusiasts
visit **Oceanário** with its models
of various marine habitats.

➤ Oceanário
Av Santos Dumont. **Tel** (079) 3243
9214. ☐ 2–8pm Tue–Fri, 9am–9pm
Sat & Sun. 🖼

Environs
Aracaju's lively beach
neighborhoods lie 6 to 12
miles (10 to 20 km) south of
the city center. The most
popular suburban beach is
Atalaia, with sports and
recreation facilities,
stages for cultural
events, as well as
good seafood joints.
The other favorite is
Praia Atalaia Nova, on
the Ilha de Santa Luzia,
an island just off the
coast. It is accessible
by boat from the
ferry station in the
city center.

**Detail from Convento
de São Francisco, São
Cristóvão**

São Cristóvão ❷

Sergipe. 🏙 73,000. 🚌 from
Aracaju. 🛈 Centro de Turismo, (079)
3214 8848. 🎭 Festival de Arte de
São Cristóvão (Oct).

A designated National Historic
Heritage Site, São Cristóvão
was founded in 1590, and is
considered one of the oldest
cities in Brazil. It served as
the capital of Sergipe in the
17th and 18th centuries, but
when the capital shifted to
Aracaju, it soon dwindled to
the sleepy interior town it is
today. Its change in status,
however, was the reason
why many of São Cristóvão's
churches and colonial
buildings were spared the
pressures of modern development, and still survive intact.

The town's charming
historic center is a panoply of
colonial squares and buildings, and is also a hub of
commerce. The most beautifully preserved square, **Praça
de São Francisco**, is easily
identified by the large
Franciscan cross at its center.
Flanking the square are
the Santa Casa Hospital,
the former Governor's
Palace, and the
Convento de São
Francisco, which now
houses the **Museu de
Arte Sacra** (Museum
of Sacred Art). The
museum has a fine
collection of silver
chalices and
crosses, and a few
beautifully sculpted
statues of saints. The ceiling
of the convent chapel was
painted by the Bahian artist,
José Teófilo de Jesus (1758–
1847). The annual Festival
de Arte de São Cristóvão
hosts popular art and music.

🏛 Museu de Arte Sacra
Praça de São Francisco. **Tel** (079)
3261 1385. ☐ 9:30am–5pm Tue–
Fri, 9am–5pm Sat & Sun. 🖼

Franciscan cross in front of Convento de São Francisco in São Cristóvão

Streets and historic buildings by the Penedo waterfront

Penedo ❸

Alagoas. 🏠 60,000. 🚌 from Maceió. 🏢 Diretor do Turismo, (081) 9931 3440. 🎉 Bom Jesus dos Navegantes (2nd Sun in Jan).

The oldest settlement in Alagoas, Penedo was founded in 1565 by Duarte Coelho Pereira on a strategic bluff overlooking the Rio São Francisco, about 19 miles (30 km) upstream of the delta. Invading Dutch forces conquered the town in 1637, and after eight years, the Portuguese managed to regain control. Today, Penedo's historic center has been designated a National Historic Monument. Particularly noteworthy is the complex housing the **Convento de São Francisco** and **Igreja de Santa Maria dos Anjos**, built over a period of 100 years.

The **Igreja Nossa Senhora da Corrente** (Church of Our Lady of Chains), built in 1765 by the Lemos de Gonzaga family, was used as a refuge for runaway slaves, who the family often provided with forged certificates of freedom. It has a fine Rococo-style main altar.

🏛 **Convento de São Francisco & Igreja de Santa Maria dos Anjos**
Rua 7 de Setembro 218.
⏰ 8am–5pm Mon–Fri, 8–11am Sat.

🏛 **Igreja Nossa Senhora da Corrente**
Praça 12 de Abril. ⏰ 8am–5pm Mon–Sun. 🅿

Environs

The **Rio São Francisco Delta** is easily accessed from the town of Piaçabuçu, 9 miles (15 km) east of Penedo. The delta, situated on the Sergipe side of the river, is rich in lagoons and mangrove forests, and is home to turtles and migrating seabirds. The riverbank in Alagoas features low rolling sand dunes.

Rio São Francisco ❹

Sergipe, Alagoas, Pernambuco & Minas Gerais.

The largest and most important river in the region, the Rio São Francisco has long served as the main transport and irrigation lifeline, for the people in the small towns of the arid northeastern interior to the bigger cities along the coast. Considered a symbol of national untiy, Brazilians revere the São Francisco, and it is the subject of many myths and fables. Nicknamed Velho Chico (Old Chico), the 1,963-mile (3,160-km) river meanders through five states. Originating in the Serra da Canastra mountains in Minas Gerais, it flows north through Bahia, crosses briefly into Pernambuco before continuing east, toward the Atlantic, marking the border between Sergipe and Alagoas in its final run to the sea.

LAMPIÃO & MARIA BONITA

In the 1920s and 30s, bandit leader Lampião and his wife Maria Bonita led a band of 40 outlaws, nicknamed *cangaceiros* (*cangaço* means badlands), on a 15-year spree of robberies, hold-ups, rapes, and shoot-outs across the Northeast. As their raids continued, Lampião and Maria Bonita became notorious figures throughout Brazil. The duo even introduced their own style of clothing, with the round leather *cangaceiro* hat, the front brim turned upward and decorated with stars or coins. The police and militia searched for them endlessly, but were unable to capture them. Finally, in 1938, Lampião, Maria Bonita, and nine *cangaceiros* were ambushed and killed by the police in Sergipe. Their story has inspired numerous songs, plays, and different versions on film and TV.

Lampião and Maria Bonita clay statues

Canion Xingó [5]

Sergipe. 🚌 *from Aracaju.* ℹ *Reservatório de Xingó, (079) 9972 1320.* 📋 *trips to the dam at 8am, 11:30am & 3pm.* $

Standing on the Rio São Francisco, the Xingó Dam in Sergipe is one of the largest in Brazil. When it was completed in 1994, the dam blocked off the São Francisco canyon at a point about 155 miles (250 km) from the ocean, causing the river to rise and create the Xingó Reservoir. This artificial lake is now a popular destination.

Catamarans and schooners depart from the dam and travel upstream, crossing the reservoir and re-entering the main part of the river. Several rock passageways that previously lay at the top of the canyon are now open to exploration by boat.

Situated 2 miles (3 km) from the dam, the **Museu de Arqueológia de Xingó** displays numerous archaeological objects from nearby sites that were flooded when the dam was created. Artifacts from the earliest sites, dating from around 5000 BC, include arrows, rock paintings, primitive stone mortars, and fish cleaning tools. Later sites reveal a variety of items including bone jewelry, decorative ceramics, and clay containers and dishes.

🏛 Museu de Arqueológia de Xingó
2 miles (3 km) from Xingó dam at Rodoviaria Canindé-Piranhas. 🕐 *9am–4pm Wed–Sun.* $ 📋 ♿

Igreja de Santa Maria Madalena in Marechal Deodoro's historic center

Marechal Deodoro [6]

Alagoas. 👥 *30,000.* 🚌 *from Maceió.* ℹ *Alseturs, (082) 315 1503.*

The capital of Alagoas until 1839, Marechal Deodoro was founded in 1611 as Vila Madalena. The city was renamed in honor of its native son, Marshall Manuel Deodoro da Fonseca (1827–92), elected as Brazil's first president in 1891. Fonseca's childhood home is now a small museum, displaying much of the original furniture and family memorabilia.

The city's small 18th-century colonial center features the Rococo **Igreja de Santa Maria Madalena**. Adjoining the church, the **Convento do São Francisco** houses a small museum.

Just a 15-minute bus ride from the city is the **Praia do Francês**, with powdery sand and deep blue water. It has enormous waves for surfing at one end, while the other end is protected by a large reef. The authorities are working toward removing the restaurants that have been built right on the sand.

View of Praia de Francês, one of the popular beaches of Marechal Deodoro

⛪ Convento do São Francisco
Praça Pedro Paulinho. ***Tel*** *(082) 3551 2279.* 🕐 *8–11:30am & 2–5pm Mon–Fri, 8–11am Sat & Sun.*

⛪ Igreja de Santa Maria Madalena
Praça João 23. ***Tel*** *(082) 3263 1623.* 🕐 *9am–5pm Mon–Sun.*

Maceió [7]

Alagoas. 👥 *885,000.* ✈ 🚌 *(082) 221 4615.* ℹ *Rua Antônio Cansanção 1268, Ponta Verde, (082) 2121 0978.* 🎉 *Maceió Fest (Nov).*

The capital of Alagoas, Maceió is known for its many beautiful urban beaches. The best known ones, from north to south, are **Jatiúca**, **Ponta Verde**, **Sete Coqueiros**, and **Pajuçara**. Protected by reefs, the beaches have little or no surf, warm water, and a Caribbean turquoise-green color. The shores are lined with thick groves of coconut palms, especially dense at Ponta Verde.

About 1 mile (2 km) offshore from Pajuçara, a series of large coral reefs are partially exposed at low tide, forming sizable natural pools that can be explored with a mask and snorkel. Small single-sail rafts known as *jangadas* depart daily at low tide from Ponta Verde and take about 20 minutes to reach the pools.

In addition to the beaches, Maceió has a small historic core. The neighborhoods of Jaraguá and Centro, just inland from the port, have a large number of well-preserved historic buildings which convey some of the atmosphere of the city's 19th-century sugar boom. One of the loveliest mansions on the waterfront has been beautifully restored and now houses the **Museu Théo Brandão**. Named after a local writer who wrote about Alagoan folk art and anthropology, the small museum has a good collection of native art. It also

Jangadas, small sailboats, on the beach at Ponta Verde in Maceió

has some wonderfully creative displays that use local crafts to depict the region's religious festivals, typical foods, the sugar cane industry, and folklore.

The southern end of the city borders the **Lagoa Mundaú**, one of the many lagoons that have given Alagoas its name. The lagoon encompasses several mangrove islands teeming with crustaceans and other marine-life. Boats make excursions into the lagoon's channels.

The **Pontal da Barra** neighborhood on the lagoon's shore is a small fishing village. There are several rustic restaurants overlooking the water, which serve the catch of the day. Dishes with *sururu* (a small type of clam) and crab are especially popular. In Pontal da Barra, visitors will find highly skilled *rendeiras*, or lace-makers, working on a variety of laces.

The one most typical of the neighborhood is known as *filé*, a loose weave that is often brightly colored.

🏛 **Museu Théo Brandão**
Av da Paz 1490, Centro.
Tel (082) 3221 2651. ⬜ 9am–noon & 2–5pm Tue–Fri, 3–6pm Sat & Sun. 🎫 🈯

Environs
Praia do Gunga is a pretty, palm-fringed beach located 9 miles (15 km) south of Maceió. Access to the beach is gained via a private road cutting across one of the region's largest coconut plantations. Permission to enter must be obtained at the gate, but beaches in Brazil are public property and access cannot be denied. One side of the beach faces the lagoon, while the other side looks toward the ocean, offering the option of fresh or salt water swimming, as well as kayaking.

Porto de Galinhas ❽

Pernambuco. 🏠 10,000. ✈ Recife Guararapes International Airport, 38 miles (60 km) N of town, then bus. ℹ (081) 3552 1480.

Porto de Galinhas is one of the most popular tourist destinations in Northeast Brazil, and deservedly so. There are no high-rises dwarfing the beach here, just low-scale *pousadas* and bungalows. The star attraction of the area, in addition to the beach, are the natural tide pools that form in the reefs just a short distance offshore. Colorful *jangada* rafts take swimmers and snorkelers out to swim in the clear shallow waters teeming with tropical fish.

Porto de Galinhas also offers a lively atmosphere with excellent restaurants and shopping, and better still, it does not take much effort to get away from the bustle. The main mode of transportation is the dune buggy, allowing for easy transit along the dirt and sand roads that lead to local beaches. A short distance south along the beach leads to **Ponta de Maracaípe**, a beautiful spot with a large white sand bar, where the Rio Maracaípe runs into the ocean. The mangroves in the estuary are home to several species of sea horse that live amid the roots of the mangrove.

QUILOMBOS

In the African Yorubá language, *quilombo* means dwelling place. In Brazil, the term was used to describe a community of runaway slaves. Brazil's most famous *quilombo*, Quilombo dos Palmares in Alagoas, grew to the size of a small city, with 30,000 residents. In the late 1600s, Zumbi, the *quilombo*'s second leader, successfully defended it from repeated Portuguese attacks. However, the Portuguese were relentless, and finally, in 1694, Palmares fell. Zumbi was beheaded and the community destroyed. A number of such places escaped Palmares' fate and survive even today. There are now 1,000 *quilombos* registered in Brazil. Zumbi's legacy is remembered every year on November 20, when Zumbi dos Palmares Day, or Black Awareness Day, is celebrated.

Portrait of Zumbi

Clearwater rock pools offshore from Porto de Galinhas

Recife 9

The Portuguese, who had built Olinda on a hillside, ignored the swampy islands below. The site of present-day Recife was only a fishing village when the Dutch took over Pernambuco in 1630. Count Maurice of Nassau commanded the draining and dyking of the flat islands at the mouth of the Rio Capibaribe. The islands of Santo Antônio, Boa Vista, and Recife Antigua (Old Recife) were connected to each other and the mainland with an ingenious system of bridges. This early Dutch urban planning forms the basis of downtown Old Recife today, where some of the attractions are located.

Marco Zero in Praça Rio Branco, the founding point of Old Recife

Exploring Recife Antigua

In the heart of downtown Old Recife is the **Marco Zero** and the surrounding square, which marks the official point where the city was founded. The site of the original pier, it controlled all arrivals and departures taking place in the bay. Largely deserted until a few years ago, the now bustling district of the city makes for a pleasant walk during the day. It is possible to take a boat from the square across to the **Parque das Esculturas**, which features an imposing collection of tall, exotic sculptures made by the ceramic artist Francisco Brennand *(see p219)*.

The most interesting street in the historic quarter is **Rua do Bom Jesus**. During the brief period of Dutch rule, the street was known as Rua dos Judeus (Street of the Jews). The Jewish community thrived under Dutch rule, but once the Catholic Portuguese re-established their control, most fled, converted, or went underground. A large number of the buildings on this street have been restored to their original 17th-century condition. Every Sunday, the street comes alive, as an art and crafts fair, live music, and outdoor festivities take place.

🏛 Paço da Alfândega

Rua da Alfândega 35. ***Tel*** *(081) 3419 7500.* ⏰ *10am–10pm Mon–Sat, noon–9pm Sun & public hols.* ♿ **www**.pacoalfandega.com.br

Just on the edge of the historical quarter, the Paço da Alfândega brings together the old and the new elements of the city. Overlooking the Rio Capibaribe, the former customs building dates back to 1826, when Recife was one of Brazil's major ports. The renovated building houses restaurants, an art gallery, and a shopping and entertainment center.

🏛 Kahal Zur Israel Synagogue

Rua do Bom Jesus 197. ***Tel*** *(081) 3224 2128.* ⏰ *9am–5pm Tue–Fri, 3–7pm Sun.* 📷

Built in 1637, during the city's brief period of Dutch rule, this synagogue recounts the history of the Jewish community in Recife. It was the first synagogue anywhere in the Americas. Many of the Jews, who immigrated to Dutch-controlled Recife, had

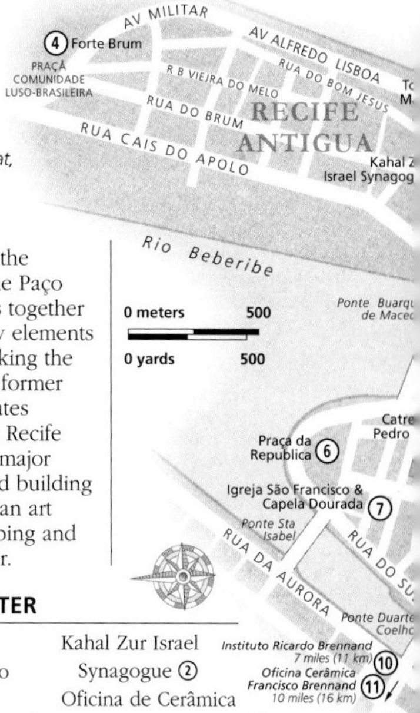

RECIFE CITY CENTER

Casa da Cultura 9
Catedral de São Pedro dos Clérigos 8
Forte das Cinco Pontas 5
Forte do Brum 4
Igreja São Francisco & Capela Dourada 7
Instituto Ricardo Brennand 10
Kahal Zur Israel Synagogue 2
Oficina de Cerâmica Francisco Brennard 11
Paço da Alfândega 1
Praça da República 6
Torre de Malakoff 3

Key to Symbols *see back flap*

The well-preserved old buildings on Rua do Bom Jesus

The rebuilt Kahal Zur Israel Synagogue

VISITORS' CHECKLIST

Pernambuco. 🏠 1,500,000.
✈ Aeroporto dos Guararapes,
7 miles (11 km) S of city center.
🚌 9 miles (14 km) SW of city
center. ℹ Empetur, (081) 3427
8000. 🎭 Carnaval (Feb/Mar).
www.recife.pe.gov.br

originally come from Portugal, fleeing the Inquisition. At the height of Dutch rule, about half of Recife's white population was Jewish. Unfortunately, the period of religious tolerance was short-lived, and when

Recently, archaeologists confirmed the exact location of the original synagogue after digging up part of a *mikveh* (ritual bath). The current synagogue has been rebuilt from the ground up, based on these findings, historical data, and other sources. The museum presents an excellent documentary and display on the history of the Jews in Recife.

🏛 Torre de Malakoff

Praça do Arsenal da Marinha, Rua do Bom Jesus.
Tel (081) 3424 8704.
◻ 3–8pm Tue–Sun.
A relative newcomer to the Rua do Bom Jesus, the Malakoff Tower was built in 1845 as South America's first astronomical observatory, which is still functional. Visitors can climb to the top terrace for a splendid view of the city with the LX 200 telescopes.

🏛 Forte do Brum

Praça Comunidade Luso-Brasileira.
Tel (081) 3224 4620. ◻ 9am–
4:30pm Tue–Fri, 2–5pm Sat & Sun.
One of the few constructions to pre-date the Dutch, Forte Brum is located at the far end of Avenida Militar. Built by the Portuguese in 1629, it was taken over by the Dutch in 1630, and strengthened and expanded. A military museum today, the new design was kept by the Portuguese when they reclaimed it in 1654.

🏛 Forte das Cinco Pontas

Praça das Cinco Pontas. **Tel** (081)
3224 8492. ◻ 9am–6pm Tue–Fri,
1–5pm Sat & Sun. 🎟 🎫
Somewhat deceptively, the Forte das Cinco Pontas (Five-Pointed Fort) actually only has four points. The original Dutch fort, built in 1630 to protect the new Dutch-Brazilian capital of Mauritsstad, had five. When the Dutch withdrew in 1654, the Portuguese leveled the unique shape, and put up a more traditional four-pointer. Wonderfully restored, the fort now houses the city museum and contains an impressive collection of maps, paintings, and artifacts that tell the history of Dutch rule.

the Dutch surrendered to the Portuguese in 1654, the Jews were given three months to liquidate their assets and leave. Many members of the Recife community set sail to New Amsterdam and helped found New York.

The synagogue was dismantled, and its role as a temple and meeting place of the Jewish community was completely forgotten. The building was eventually torn down at the beginning of the 20th century.

FREVO

Recife's signature beat is *frevo*. Fast, upbeat, almost polka-like, the rhythm is particularly popular during Carnaval (*see p41*). This distinct musical genre is reputed to have derived its name from the verb *ferver* (to boil), which refers to the frenetic beat of the brass bands. One of the accessories of a *frevo* dancer is the brightly colored hand-held parasol that

A dancer performing *frevo* with a colorful parasol

is used in the choreography. First recorded in the 1930s, the rhythm made its way into the repertoire of mainstream Brazilian musicians by the 1950s and 60s.

Exploring Modern Recife

Though modern Recife stretches onto the mainland, its center comprises the islands of Santo Antônio, Boa Vista, and Recife Antigua. Skyscrapers exist alongside a handful of old colonial buildings and crowded markets, lending the city a striking character. The area north of the center is as appealing, with leafy suburbs and a few museums and parks. The squares, dotted with impressive churches, retain much of their old-world charm.

The courtyard of Igreja São Francisco with a graceful, colonnaded arcade

🏛 Praça da República

Palácio do Campo das Princesas
Tel (081) 3425 2416. ☐ *9am–5pm Mon–Fri.* **Teatro Princesa Isabel** *Tel* (081) 3224 1020. ☐ *Check for performance timings.* **Palácio da Justiça** *Tel* (081) 3419 3222.
Modern Recife's main civic square, Praça da República, is located at the tip of Santo Antônio island. Some of the city's finest public buildings can be found here.

The **Palácio do Campo das Princesas** (Governors' Palace) building was built in the 1840s. Over the years, renovations and additions have somewhat altered the original Neo-Classical design and made the building more eclectic. The lovely interior garden was designed by Brazil's premier landscape artist Roberto Burle Marx. Unfortunately, the only view available to the public is the one through the wrought-iron fence posts.

The **Teatro Princesa Isabel**, a recently renovated pink theater, hosts many of Recife's prime cultural productions.

The building is an elegant example of classic imperial architecture, marked by its symmetric forms and French and Italian decorative styles.

With a dome-shaped cupola, the **Palácio da Justiça** was constructed in 1930 to mark the presidency of Getúlio Vargas (*see pp56–7*).

🔒 Igreja São Francisco & Capela Dourada

Rua do Imperador, Santo Antônio.
Tel (081) 3224 0530. ☐ *8–11am & 2–5pm Mon–Fri & Sun.* 🖼
One of the major attractions in Recife, Igreja São Francisco served as the convent of the Third Franciscan Order. It was built in 1606, when the island of Santo Antônio only had 200 inhabitants. The initial convent was small and rather plain. During the Dutch occupation of Recife (1630–54), it was used as army barracks. Renovations began after the return of the Franciscans. The courtyard was added with a surrounding arcade of delicate and ornate Tuscan columns. Blue-and-

white Portuguese tiles (*azulejos*) were used to decorate the main altar and the walls of the small, charming cloister.

However, the *pièce de résistance* is the **Capela Dourada** (Golden Chapel), added in 1695, in an annex of the main church. All of the wood in the chapel is jacaranda and cedar and is covered in gold leaf or paint. The intricately carved altars, arches, and beams showcase some outstanding Portuguese Baroque art. Each altar consists of various arches, adding a depth of field to the statues on display. One of the walls in the church is adorned with a painting that depicts the Crucifixion of a group of Franciscan saints.

🔒 Catedral de São Pedro dos Clérigos

Rua São Pedro s/n, Santo Antônio.
Tel (081) 3224 2954.
☐ *8am–noon & 2–4pm Mon–Fri.*
Dating back to 1728, Catedral de São Pedro dos Clérigos is one of the most impressive churches in Pernambuco. Its striking façade is dominated by a statue of St. Peter, which was added only recently, in 1980. While from the outside the walls of the church look perfectly square and straight, on the inside the church nave is octagonal. The best features of the church are its stunning wood carving and the illusionistic ceiling. The main altar, balconies, and most of the remaining interior elements were renovated in the 19th century in the Rococo style. The only original pieces that remain are the two gold-painted wooden pulpits.

The square in front of the church, **Pátio de São Pedro**, is one of Recife's most popular public squares. The beautifully restored area hosts a number of cultural events. The most important, Terça Negra (Black Tuesday), takes place every Tuesday night. It is widely known for showcasing typical regional Afro-Brazilian musical styles, such as *afoxé*, *maculelê*, and *coco*.

Eye-catching ceramic figures and souvenirs on sale, Casa da Cultura

⊞ Casa da Cultura

Rua Floriano Peixoto s/n, São José.
Tel (081) 3224 7626.
⏱ 9am–7pm Mon–Fri, 9am–6pm Sat, 9am–2pm Sun.

Used as a jail until 1973, the former penitentiary now houses the Casa da Cultura, the city's largest arts and craft market. Each of the old jail cells holds a shop showcasing some of the finest leather, lace, and ceramic crafts of this region. Built in 1850, the jail was modeled after US prisons in New Jersey and Pennsylvania. The four wings are in a cross shape, allowing a view of all four corridors from one vantage position in the center of the cross. The center brings out the monthly *Agenda Cultural*, an excellent listing of cultural events.

🏛 Instituto Ricardo Brennand

Av Antônio Brennand, Várzea.
Tel (081) 2121 0352. ⏱ 1–5pm Tue–Sun. ♿

Founded by the cousin of ceramic artist Francisco Brennand, the Instituto Ricardo Brennand includes a small castle, the Castelo São João, with a large collection of European art, an impressive collection of medieval armory and weapons, and an extensive archive of paintings and documents from the years of the Dutch conquest of Brazil.

Also worth seeing is the Pinacoteca gallery that features a large collection of 17th-century paintings and drawings by landscape artists Frans Post and Albert Eckhout, both of whom were hired by Dutch count Maurice of Nassau to portray Brazil's fauna and flora, as well as scenes from everyday life. Over the years, Brennand has amassed the world's largest collection of Post's work. The exhibit also includes many antique maps and documents that recount the brief, but eventful, history of the Dutch in Brazil.

Ceramic tiles by Francisco Brennand

🏛 Oficina de Cerâmica Francisco Brennand

Access via Av Caxangá, Várzea.
Tel (081) 3271 2623. ⏱ 8am–6pm Mon–Thu, 8am–6pm Fri.

Acclaimed as the most unusual cultural attraction in Recife, the Oficina de Cerâmica Francisco Brennand is the famed artist's personal gallery. Brennand (b.1927) is best known for his large collection of phallic-shaped ceramic sculptures, nearly all of which are striking, potent, and larger than life. His collection is creatively displayed inside a ceramic-covered brick factory and its surrounding gardens, beautifully landscaped by Burle Marx, a renowned landscape architect of the 20th century.

In addition to Brennand's superb ceramic art, the collection also showcases thousands of playfully designed ceramic tiles, as well as some of his paintings and drawings. The bold mix of stylized imagery, embellishment, and erotic motifs, visible in all his works, led one critic to define Brennand's art as "tropical sensual Baroque."

Gardens in Oficina de Cerâmica Francisco Brennand, adorned with ceramic sculptures

Olinda ❿

One of the best-preserved colonial cities in Brazil, Olinda was founded in 1535 by the Portuguese. Much of it was burned down during the Dutch occupation in 1631, and later beautifully restored to its former glory. Magnificent colonial buildings, gardens, Baroque churches, and numerous small chapels mark Olinda, which was designated a UNESCO World Heritage Site in 1982. Although much of this historic city lies on a steep hillside, it is only a short walk up, and the views of the Atlantic Ocean are splendid. Its narrow cobblestone streets are perfect for exploring on foot. The highlight of the walk suggested here is the Praça da Sé, which features historic churches and sweeping views of Recife *(see pp216–19)*, only 6 miles (10 km) to the south.

The view of Olinda from Alto da Sé, with the sea in the background

① **Praça do Carmo**, the prominent city square, faces the splendid Igreja Nossa Senhora do Carmo, resting on a small hill above.

ATLANTIC

AVENIDA MARCOS FREIRE

RUA DO SOL

TRAVESSA DO PORTINO

RUA DO SÃO FRANCISCO

LIBERDADE

RUA DO BON...

TRAVESA J. ALFRE...

RUA DA PALHA

LADEIRA DA SÉ

RUA DAS B...

R. DO BISPO COUTINHO

② **Convento de São Francisco**
Brazil's oldest Franciscan convent was built in 1585. When the Dutch invaded Olinda in 1630, the convent was abandoned, and rebuilt in the 18th century. The cloister walls, decorated with Portuguese tiles, depict the life of St. Francis.

③ **Igreja da Sé**, which was built in 1535, is the oldest parish church in Northeast Brazil. The church has undergone many renovations over the centuries. The last, in 1984, restored the building almost to its original 16th-century state.

KEY

••• Walk route

TIPS FOR WALKERS

Starting point: Secretaria de Turismo, Praça do Carmo.
Walking time: 2–3 hours. Flat, non-slippery footwear is best.
Best days: Tue–Sat. Museums are only open in the morning.
Places to eat: Oficina do Sabor, Rua do Amparo 335; Olinda Sorvetes e Sucos, Rua São Bento 358.

④ **Alto da Sé**
The Alto da Sé is one of the highest points in Olinda and offers a magnificent view of Recife in the distance. In the evenings, locals gather here to browse the crafts market, and eat tapioca and pancakes made from manioc.

⑤ Mercado Ribeira

Originally the building where slaves were bought and sold, this 18th-century structure is now one of Olinda's busiest craft markets. Especially popular are naïve art ceramics, carnival masks, and frevo *umbrellas (see p217).*

VISITORS' CHECKLIST

Pernambuco. 🏠 *380,000.*
✈ *Recife International Airport.*
🚌 ℹ *Largo do Amparo, (081) 3439 9434.* 🎭 *Carnaval (Feb/ Mar); Olinda Arte em Toda Parte, open house event of artists' studios (late Nov–early Dec).*
www.olindaarteemtodaparte. com.br

⑥ Igreja e Mosteiro São Bento

Founded in 1582, this church holds a magnificent gold altar. It took more than a year and 30 professionals to fully restore the altar in 2001. Gregorian chanters add a special touch to the Sunday morning mass.

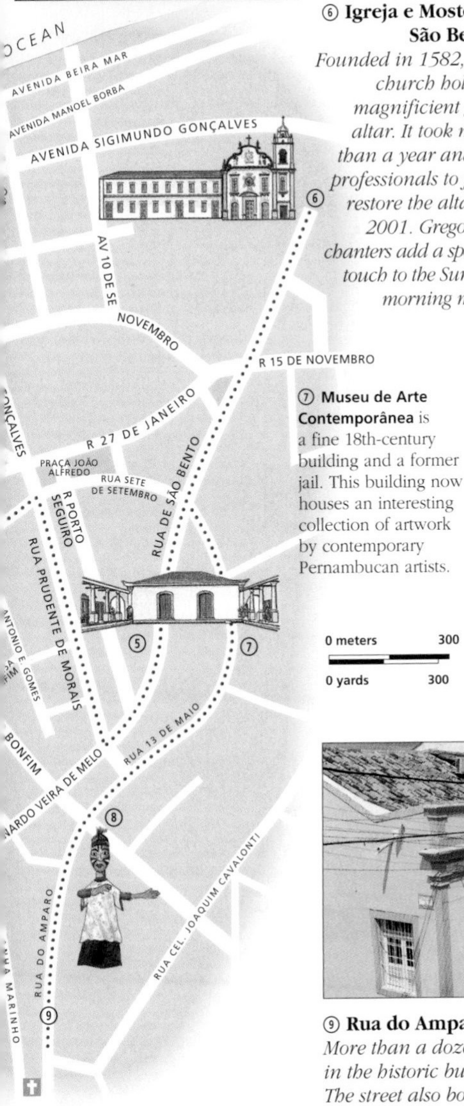

⑦ Museu de Arte Contemporânea is

a fine 18th-century building and a former jail. This building now houses an interesting collection of artwork by contemporary Pernambucan artists.

0 meters	300
0 yards	300

⑧ Museu do Mamulengo displays

a large collection of puppets from all over the Northeast. Unique to Olinda's Carnaval, the giant puppets, carried by revelers along the parade route, are true works of art.

⑨ Rua do Amparo

More than a dozen artists have set up their studios in the historic buildings along Rua do Amparo. The street also boasts several excellent restaurants, cafés, and B&Bs.

Key to Symbols *see back flap*

Exploring Olinda

A calm, colonial city, Olinda grew to be the capital of the rich sugar-growing region of Pernambuco. Reconstruction started in earnest only after Dutch forces were expelled in 1654. The city has maintained its 17th-century architectural fabric intact. Olinda is also home to a vibrant community of artists, musicians, and liberal professionals. The scenic city, though, is most renowned for its lively Carnaval.

Ceramic doll, Olinda

The exterior of Igreja e Mosteiro de São Bento in Olinda

🛡 Convento de São Francisco

Rua de São Francisco 280. **Tel** (081) 3429 0517. ⏰ 7am–noon & 2–5pm Mon–Fri, 7am–noon Sat. 📷

The Convento de São Francisco was the first convent built by the Franciscan order in Brazil. The complex includes a 1585 church, Nossa Senhora das Neves (Our Lady of the Snow), and the adjacent chapels of St. Anne and St. Roque, built in 1754 and 1811, respectively. The highlight of the convent is the beautiful arcade surrounding the cloister. The tiled walls tell the story of St. Francis of Assisi. The sacristy's beautiful Baroque furniture, carved from dark jacaranda wood, is as impressive.

🛡 Igreja e Mosteiro de São Bento

Rua São Bento. **Tel** (081) 3429 3288. ⏰ 9–11am & 2–5pm Mon–Sat. 🕍 6:30am Mon–Sat, 10am & 6pm Sun (with Gregorian chants).

Built in 1582, this monastery was destroyed by the Dutch along with most of the city, and rebuilt in the late 18th century. It is acclaimed for its Baroque altar in the chapel and intricate wood carving, which features the image of São Bento (St. Benedict) himself. In 2001, the original wood altar was repainted with gold leaf. The sacristy's three large paintings, by 18th-century artist José Eloy da Conceição, portray scenes from the life of the saint.

🏛 Museu de Arte Contemporânea

Rua 13 de Maio. **Tel** (081) 3429 2587. ⏰ 9am–noon Tue–Fri, 2–5pm Sat & Sun.

Housed in a fine 18th-century building that originally served as an *ajube*, or jail working in conjunction with the Catholic church, the Museum of Contemporary Art displays both permanent and temporary exhibits. During the Inquisition, religious prisoners were brought here to pray and confess their sins. Today, the place holds some interest for those looking for serious modern art. Works by local contemporary artists are regularly displayed in front of the stairs.

🏛 Museu do Mamulengo

Rua do Amparo 59. **Tel** (081) 3429 6214. ⏰ 8am–5pm Tue–Fri, 10am–5pm Sat & Sun.

One of the region's unique gifts to the cultural scene in Brazil, *mamulengo*, or puppetry, is showcased in this fascinating museum. Nearly 1,000 puppets are featured here, with a portion of the collection dating from the 1800s. Having performed before political figures, royalty, and luminaries through the ages, these puppets are today used as popular entertainment. During folk festivals, the puppets can be seen enacting comedies, skits, and Pernambucan folk legends. For those interested in the puppets' historical background, there is a curator who can explain it by asking the puppets themselves.

THE OLINDA CARNAVAL

Revelers filling a street in Olinda, with larger-than-life papier-mâché puppets

Every year during Carnaval, the cobblestoned streets of Olinda become the stage for a week-long street party. The meeting place is the square, known as *quarto cantos* (four corners), on the corner of Rua do Amparo and Rua Prudente de Moraes. Here, *blocos* (neighborhood groups) begin their parades through the streets, playing music, singing, and dancing as they go. The *blocos* often have themes or names such as "Virgins," "Elephant," or "Midnight Man." Dominating the festivities are enormous papier-mâché puppets that *bloco* members proudly carry along the parade route. The music varies from *frevo*, an upbeat, almost frenetic beat unique to Pernambuco, to *maracatu*, a much more African beat.

For hotels and restaurants in this region see p378–9 and p403–405

Ilha de Itamaracá ⓫

Pernambuco. 🏠 *16,000.* 🚌 *from Recife.* **www**.itamaraca.pe.gov.br

The island of Itamaracá played an important strategic role during the Dutch interregnum in Brazil. In 1631, the Dutch built the **Forte Orange** here, to protect their new domain from invading forces. The Portuguese destroyed the Dutch-built adobe when they took over in 1654. However, the location was so unique that the Portuguese created a new fort in stone on the site. During recent renovations, artifacts dating back to the Dutch period were found. Just across from the fort is a small island, Coroa do Avião, which has natural reef pools. Boat tours to the island leave from the beach in front of the fort.

Itamaracá is also home to the **Projeto Peixe Boi**, a manatee research and rehabilitation center. Manatees live along the Brazilian coast from Alagoas to Amapá, but are threatened by loss of habitat, as well as by speedboats and their often-lethal outboard propellers. Scientists estimate that there are only around 400 animals in the wild along this coast. The center works to rehabilitate injured manatees, and to study those that cannot be released. A natural history exhibit on the manatee is offered along with a host of interactive learning activities for children. Visitors are only allowed to observe those animals that cannot be

Pottery on display at a craft shop in Caruaru

released into the wild. The eastern part of Itamaracá, with its lovely ocean beaches, is also a popular weekend destination.

🏰 **Forte Orange**
Estrada do Forte. ⏱ *9am–5pm Mon–Sat, 8am–5pm Sun.* 📷

🐋 **Projeto Peixe Boi**
Estrada do Forte Orange.
Tel *(081) 3544 1835.*
⏱ *10am–4pm Tue–Sun.* 📷 ♿

Caruaru ⓬

Pernambuco. 🏠 *300,000.* 🚌 *from Recife.* 🎉 *Festa do Forró (Jun–Jul).* **www**.caruaru.pe.gov.br

Located 100 miles (160 km) on the mainland southwest of Itamaracá, Caruaru is a market town whose fame rests on its marvelous ceramic *figurinhas* (figurines). Artist Vitalino Pereira dos Santos (1909–63) made many of these brightly painted sculptures, and his hometown, Alto de Moura, a community of potters located 4 miles (6 km) west of Caruaru,

still specializes in producing figurines. **Casa Museu Mestre Vitalino** in Alto do Moura is dedicated to this great artist, and displays his tools and some personal possessions.

Caruaru's open market is the largest in the Northeast, and is a very popular tourist attraction. Besides figurines, leather bags, straw baskets, and ceramic pots are also sold at some of the best prices in Brazil. Apart from a bustling market scene, Caruaru, known as the capital of *forró* (see p236), hosts Brazil's largest month-long *forró* festival. The **Museu do Barro** pays tribute to Luis Gonzaga, the father of *forró* music.

Figurine, Casa Museu Mestre Vitalino

Environs
Situated 17 miles (30 km) northwest of Caruaru, **Nova Jerusalém** is an intriguing re-creation of Jerusalem. In the week before Easter, thousands of people flock to watch an epic performance of the *Paixão de Cristo* (*Passion of Christ*). Local tour operators offer all-inclusive packages to the town and its annual play.

🏛 **Casa Museu Mestre Vitalino**
Praça Cel. José de Vasconcelos 100, Centro, Caruaru. ⏱ *8am–5pm Tue–Sat, 9am–1pm Sun.*

🏛 **Museu do Barro**
Praça José de Vasconcelos.
Tel *(081) 3721 0012.*
⏱ *8am–5pm Tue–Sat, 9am–1pm Sun.*

Rehabilitated manatees at the Projeto Peixe Boi, Ilha de Itamaracá

Fernando de Noronha ⑬

Discovered in 1503 by Amerigo Vespucci, the 21-island archipelago of Fernando de Noronha was fought over for the next two centuries by the French, Dutch, and Portuguese, who built forts on strategic lookout points. The island was used in a variety of ways, including as a political prison during World War II. In 1988, the Parque Nacional Marinho de Fernando de Noronha was created in order to protect the fragile marine and island ecology of the archipelago. Today, a combination of crystal-clear water, fascinating wildlife, diverse marine life which includes multicolored fish, turtles, sharks and whales, and stunning beaches make Fernando de Noronha one of the most beautiful destinations in Brazil.

KEY

--- Park boundary

Surfing on Praia do Boldró
Fernando de Noronha offers some of Brazil's best surfing, but only between December and March.

★ Baía do Sancho
The most beautiful and isolated beach on Noronha, Baía do Sancho is also a snorkelers' paradise with its clear, turquoise waters and myriad tropical fish.

★ Spinner Dolphins
Hundreds of dolphins gather at sunrise to leap and spin at Dolphin Cove in the Baía dos Golfinhos.

Praia do Boldró

Praia Cacimba do Padre

Praia da Baía do Sancho

Praia da Baía do Porcos

MO

BAÍA DOS GOLFINHOS

FERNAN

MORRO BRANCO

MORRO DA QUIXABINHA

Praia do Leão

ILHA MORRO DO LEÃO

Ponta Capim Açu

STAR SIGHTS

★ Baía do Sancho

★ Spinner Dolphins

★ Turtle Hatchlings

★ Praia da Atalaia

★ Turtle Hatchlings
Ilha Morro do Leão is a prime hatchery for green sea turtles. Between December and May, around sunset, scores of tiny turtle hatchlings break out of their shells and make a dash for the sea.

For hotels and restaurants in this region see pp378–9 and pp403–405

Morro do Pico
The sharp basalt finger of Morro do Pico, a testament to the island's volcanic heritage, stands 1,053 ft (321 m) above sea level.

VISITORS' CHECKLIST

Pernambuco. ✈ *from Recife.*
🏠 2,500. ℹ *Divisão de Turismo, Palácio São Miguel, Vila dos Remédios (081) 3619 1352, or Projecto Tamar, Alameda do Boldró (081) 3619 1171.*
🎫 *environmental tax assessed on all visitors to the island; to be paid on arrival at the airport. License required for scuba diving in national parks.* **www. fernandodenoronha.pe.gov.br**

ILHA DO RATA

Renting a buggy is one of the best ways to explore Fernando de Noronha.

ILHA DO MEIO

Praia do Meio is located close to the ruins of Forte Nossa Senhora Conceição.

ILHA RASA

Ponta de Santo Antônio

Praia de Santo Antônio

Forte dos Remédios 🏛

Buraco da Raquel

🏖 Praia do Meio • Vila dos ℹ Remédios

Vila do Trinta

NORONHA

MORRO DO FRANCÊS

DE

ORRO DO BAO VISTA

🏛 Praia da Atalaia

★ Praia da Atalaia
A shelf of volcanic rock extends out into the surfline. At low tide, tropical fish take refuge in the natural pools.

Baía do Sueste is the site for the Projecto Tamar *(see p207)*, and it is possible to swim with the turtles.

```
0 kilometers     1
0 miles          1
```

DIVING & MARINE-LIFE

Protected as a marine national park, Fernando de Noronha offers the best scuba diving in Brazil. Greatly suited for diving, its water temperature is a constant 28° C (82° F) and the depth of underwater, visibility is almost 98 ft (30 m). Underwater there is an astounding variety of marine-life – rays of all types, green sea turtles, and the even rarer hawksbill turtle, monk fish, lemon sharks and reef sharks, clownfish hiding in anemones, surgeon fish, and parrotfish are just some varieties. As a result of the island's volcanic heritage, there are also numerous swim-throughs.

KEY

—	Major road
—	Minor road
- -	Trail
-- -	Park boundary
✈	Airport
🏖	Beach
🏛	Fort

A school of surgeon fish in the coral reefs of Fernando de Noronha

PARAÍBA, RIO GRANDE DO NORTE & CEARÁ

A combination of pristine beaches, lively beach towns, and massive shifting sand dunes are the main attractions of these three states. Natal, the capital of Rio Grande do Norte, and João Pessoa are pleasant, historic cities with good urban beaches. However, this part of Northeast Brazil is best experienced along its coast, and in its quiet, relaxed fishing villages and beautiful, isolated beaches.

In 1532, Paraíba, Rio Grande do Norte, and Ceará were among the first states in the Northeast to be colonized by the Portuguese. However, these states never grew as rich or settled as their more southerly neighbors because sugar cane did not thrive here.

In recent years, the three states have taken advantage of the constant sunshine and beautiful beaches and have developed tourism as the mainstay of the economy.

Ceará is famous for its beaches, with their warm, turquoise waters, set against a backdrop of red sandstone cliffs. The most popular include Morro Branco and the lively beach town of Canoa Quebrada, both located to the southeast of Fortaleza, and the isolated beach of Jericoacoara, north and west of Fortaleza. Parque Nacional de Ubajara lies in western Ceará and comprises caves, eco trails, and magnificent waterfalls.

Rio Grande do Norte lies in the extreme northeast corner of Brazil. The real growth industry here is tourism. Natal, the capital city, has become one the Northeast's main points of entry for tourists from Western Europe. Nearly all come here for the sunshine and beaches.

Wedged in between Pernambuco and Rio Grande do Norte, Paraíba boasts some of Brazil's least spoilt beaches. Agriculture plays an important role in the state economy. The capital, João Pessoa, is a pleasant city with a small historic center. The city of Campina Grande is famous for its June festival, the Festas Juninas.

View of the Rio Branco and João Pessoa, Paraíba

◁ *Jangadas* (fishing boats) and fishing nets, Canoa Quebrada, Ceará

Exploring Paraíba, Rio Grande do Norte & Ceará

Most visitors to the states of Paraíba, Rio Grande do
Norte, and Ceará focus on the natural beauty of the
beaches and the coastline. The most popular gateway
destinations are Natal in Rio Grande and Fortaleza
in Ceará, with easy access to most of the region's
attractions. Paraíba's capital, João Pessoa, with its
colonial buildings, parks, and beaches, is a pleasant
place to visit. In the interior of Paraíba, the monster
rock formations in Cariri offer an almost other-worldly
experience. Dinosaur fossils, discovered in
Souza, have made the place archaeo-
logically important. The harsh, arid
interior landscape of these states
has a unique, stark beauty.

SIGHTS AT A GLANCE

Towns & Cities
Campina Grande ❷
Fortaleza pp242–3 ⓬
Genipabu ❼
João Pessoa pp230–31 ❶
Mossoró ❿
Natal ❺
Souza ❹

National Parks
Parque Nacional de Ubajara ⓮

Areas of Natural Beauty
Canoa Quebrada ⓫
Cariri ❸
Costa Branca ❾
Jericoacoara ⓭
Maracajaú ❽

Beaches & Resorts
Rota do Sol Beaches p237 ❻

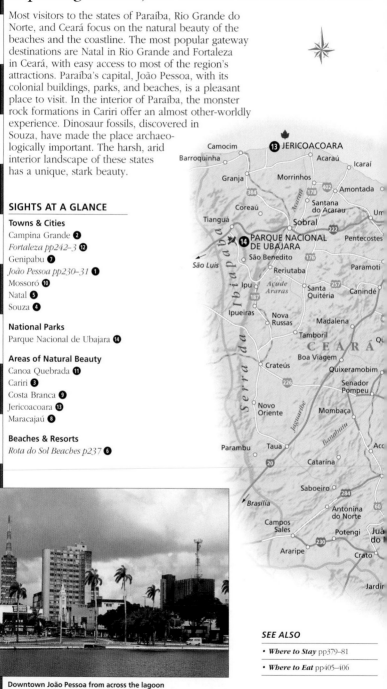

Downtown João Pessoa from across the lagoon

SEE ALSO

• *Where to Stay* pp379–81

• *Where to Eat* pp405–406

Colorful old buildings in the historic center of Fortaleza

KEY

— Highway
— Major road
— Minor road
— Railroad
— State border

GETTING AROUND

All major cities and some smaller destinations, such as Campina Grande in Paraíba, can be reached by domestic flights. There are regular buses between all towns and cities. However, roads in this part of Brazil are in poor condition and are very badly maintained. The BR-101 connects João Pessoa to Natal. From Natal, travelers continuing north to Fortaleza take the BR-304, which veers west and cuts inland across Rio Grande do Norte to Ceará. The stretch of the BR-230 towards Souza is in rough shape. Ensure that the vehicle, preferably a 4WD, is in good condition. Be sure to carry extra gas, water, and supplies.

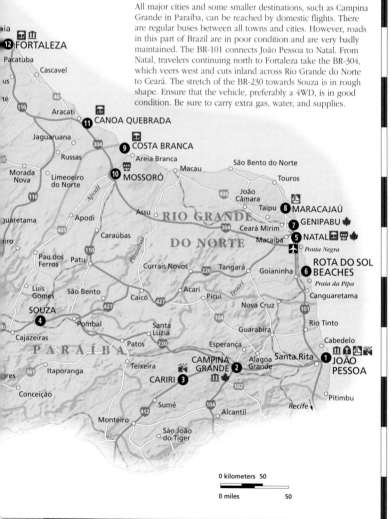

0 kilometers 50

0 miles 50

João Pessoa ❶

Founded in 1585 as Nossa Senhora das Neves, the city derives its present name from a former governor of Paraíba. Brazil's third oldest city, João Pessoa maintains an air of old-world charm, with a host of well-restored colonial churches, convents, and monasteries. Local visitors, however, flock here mainly for the easy atmosphere of its great white sandy beaches along the coastline. The dense tropical forest that once covered the coastal strip of Paraíba now thrives only in patches, one of which lies within João Pessoa, forming one of the largest areas of natural wilderness in any city in the world.

Rococo-style painting on Igreja de São Francisco's ceiling

Old majestic colonial buildings lining a street, Centro Histórico

Exploring João Pessoa

One of the oldest and less developed cities in Brazil, João Pessoa has a small historic core, which remains little changed despite the modernization drive. It is located a bit inland, on a small hill overlooking the Rio Sanhauá and Rio Paraíba. Modern João Pessoa, with fast emerging skyscrapers, gravitates towards the beaches. Due to a state law restricting the height of buildings within 490 ft (150 m) of the shoreline to four stories or less, the waterfront is free of the curtain wall of concrete highrises that afflict some other Brazilian beachfronts.

🔒 Basílica de Nossa Senhora das Neves

Rua General Osório, Centro. *Tel (083) 3221 2503.* ◯ *2–5pm Mon–Fri, 5–7pm Sat.* 🕆 *5pm Mon–Fri; 7:30pm Sat; 6am, 9am & 7:30pm Sun.* 📷

After four major renovations, little remains of the original cathedral built in 1586. The interior maintains a striking harmony, unlike many of the elaborate Rococo-style churches in Brazil.

🔒 Igreja de São Francisco

Praça São Francisco, Centro Histórico. *Tel (083) 3218 4505.* ◯ *9am–noon & 2–5pm Tue–Sun.* 📷 📹

One of the most spectacular churches in the city sits majestically atop a hill that bears the same name. The most striking feature of this impressive 18th-century church is the tower topped with an oriental dome. The altar contains an 18th-century statue of St. Benedict, one of the few black saints. The beautiful Rococo-style

Façade of Igreja de São Francisco, João Pessoa's celebrated church

painting on the ceiling of the church depicts various images of St. Francis. Even older than the church by a few decades is a stone cross across the courtyard. The church is part of the larger Centro Cultural de Sao Francisco complex, which also includes the Convento de Santo Antônio, chapels, and a museum of popular and sacred art, the result of grand-scale reforms carried out in 1718 and 1788.

♨ Mosteiro de São Bento

Rua General Osório, Centro Histórico. ◯ *on request Mon–Sat.* 🕆 *7am.*

Built in the 17th century, this working monastery is a shining example of simplicity. Its unembellished, well-restored interior features a curved wooden ceiling.

🏖 Praia de Tambaú

4 miles (7 km) E of city center.

João Pessoa's most popular urban beach is Praia de Tambaú, a 4-mile (7-km) long stretch of sand lined with restaurants, cafés, and interesting food and craft stalls. In the evenings, locals stroll the seawall, enjoying the cool breeze.

🏖 Praia do Cabo Branco

S of Praia do Tambaú.

Better suited for swimming than Tambaú, Cabo Branco is a residential beach area looking out over the eastern-most point in the Americas, **Ponta do Seixas** (Seixas Point). The point juts out into the ocean, and is topped by a small lighthouse, with a monument marking the spot.

🏊 Ilha de Picãozinho

N of Praia de Tambaú.

Actually a large coral reef, Ilha de Picãozinho is a popular spot. At low tide, boats depart from Praia do Tambaú, and take visitors over to swim and snorkel in the natural tide pools. Fish and starfish can be easily observed in the crystal-clear water. Check the tide table for specific times daily before taking a dip. For a few days every month, the tide is too high for the reef to be visited.

🏊 Ilha de Areia Vermelha

12 miles (20 km) N of town.

Another low-tide attraction is Ilha de Areia Vermelha (Island of Red Sand). For approximately 25 days every month, low tide exposes a beautiful beach of striking red-orange sand, a short distance off the coast of João Pessoa. With a choice of floating bars, it makes a perfect spot for swimming, snorkeling, or sunbathing. The temporary island is accessible from Praia da

Camboinhas, 8 miles (13 km) north of Tambaú. Trips to this island can be arranged by travel agencies.

🏖 Praia Tambaba

19 miles (30 km) S of town. Tambaba is a beautiful, secluded nude beach with lush vegetation, small reefs, and tidepools. Two coves make up this splendid beach. Clothing is optional on one of the coves. The other cove,

VISITORS' CHECKLIST

Paraíba. 🏠 650,000.
✈ 7 miles (11 km) W of city center. 🚌 Rodoviária at Rua Francisco Londres, Varadouro.
ℹ Sectur, Centro do Turismo, (083) 3218 9852.

which is exclusively a nudist beach, is closed off by a gate and allows men only if accompanied by women.

Low tide at the expansive Ilha de Areia Vermelha

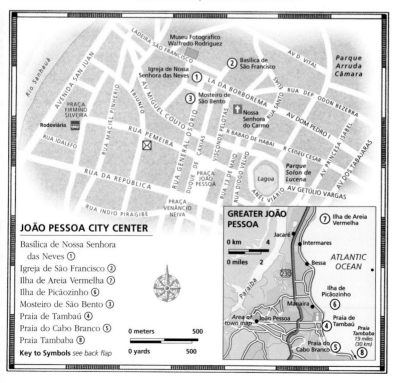

JOÃO PESSOA CITY CENTER

Basílica de Nossa Senhora
  das Neves ①
Igreja de São Francisco ②
Ilha de Areia Vermelha ⑦
Ilha de Picãozinho ⑥
Mosteiro de São Bento ③
Praia de Tambaú ④
Praia do Cabo Branco ⑤
Praia Tambaba ⑧
Key to Symbols see back flap

Campina Grande ❷

Paraíba. 🏠 400,000. ✈
🚌 from João Pessoa. ℹ Praça
Clementino Procópio, (083) 3251
7717. 🎭 Festas Juninas (Jun),
Micarande (late Apr).

Ideal for experiencing the
unique *sertão* culture,
Campina Grande is a large
market town with some
degree of industrial growth.

The autumn harvest festival,
Festas Juninas, although
celebrated everywhere in
the Northeast, is biggest in
Campina Grande. The vast,
purpose-built fairground,
Parque do Povo, includes
several smaller theme parks
such as the Sítio São João, a
reproduction of a traditional
ranch where visitors can
observe the rural *nordeste*
lifestyle, and the Arraial
Hilton Motta, a replica of
a small interior town.

The **Museu de Arte Assis
Chateaubriand** has a striking
collection of modern works,
with a focus on the work of
artists from the Northeast.

🏛 **Museu de Arte
Assis Chateaubriand**
Parque do Açude Novo. ⏰ 9am–
noon & 2–10pm Mon–Fri.

Parque do Povo
Tel (083) 3310 6100. ⏰ only during
Festas Juninas. 🎭 ♿

The Lajedo do Pai Mateus rock formation, Cariri

Cariri ❸

Paraíba. 🚌 from Campina Grande.
🎫 Cariri Ecotours, (084) 3234 4046.

Situated in the Cariri
Paraíbano, a large plateau in
the Serra da Borborema,
Cariri is the point at which
the *sertão* proper begins.
Tours in this area of abori-
ginal rock carvings and huge
rock formations can be
organized by Cariri Ecotours,
based in Ponta Negra, Natal.

One of the formations, the
Lajedo do Pai Mateus, sits on
the private grounds of a
fazenda. A vast slab of bare
granite, it is littered with
boulders bigger than houses,
as if a giant had scattered his
collection of pebbles. Hence
the local epithet, "Devil's
Marbles." The most
remarkable of these granite
monsters is the Pedra do
Capacete (Helmet Stone),
a 20-ft (6-m) high boulder
that is open in the front and
hollow underneath, resemb-
ling a huge war helmet.

From the plateau, there
are breathtaking views of
the expansive Borborema
valley. The diverse landscape
consists of small trees,
bushes, cacti, and bromeliads.
Sightings of emu birds,
an ostrich-like avian, are
common in this area.

Souza ❹

Paraíba. 🏠 60,000. 🚌 from
Campina Grande. 🎫 Manary
Ecotours, (084) 2192 900.

Brazil's most important
prehistoric site, Souza is
located deep in the Paraíba
interior, almost on the border
with Ceará. It was a large
shallow lake where hundreds
of dinosaur species roamed,
130 million years ago. Today,
the dry riverbed of the Rio de
Peixe, also known as the **Vale
dos Dinossauros**, contains one
of the world's best collections
of dinosaur tracks. The largest
and best track forms a perfect
164-ft (50-m) long trail across
the meandering riverbed.

Scattered throughout the
valley are numerous other
tracks, most of which have
not yet been catalogued or
protected. Some, indeed, have
yet to be discovered. Manary
Ecotours can combine trips in
this area with visits to Cariri.

A night scene of Campina Grande, lit up during the Festas Juninas

FESTAS JUNINAS

One of the most popular folklore traditions of the
Northeast, the Festas Juninas began as a peasant celebration of the corn harvest and the June solstice, the longest
night of the year in the Southern Hemisphere. June also
coincided with the feasts of St. Anthony, St. John, and
St. Peter. Over the years, the pagan rituals and Catholic
events were melded together. The atmosphere is burlesque,
as partiers dress up in peasant outfits and perform square
dances to the sounds of *forró (see p236)*. Bonfires are lit
and fireworks sent aloft to safeguard the harvest and ward
off evil spirits, as well as to bring light to the long night.

The Sertão

The *sertão* is a geographic region that encompasses almost half the territory of the Northeast. Aridity is its single most important characteristic. Rainfall is sparse, and the vegetation is primarily *caatinga,* which consists of small trees and bushes. Agriculture is difficult in the *sertão,* which makes it one of Brazil's poorest regions.

Clay figurine of a *nordestino*

Traditionally, *sertanejos* have made a living herding goats or cattle. One of the country's original cowboy regions,

the *sertão* has also seen the largest outflow of people in Brazil. Hard climatic conditions forced *en masse* immigrations either to the coast, or to the big cities such as São Paulo and Rio de Janeiro. Not just the dislocated northeasterners, or *nordestinos,* but all Brazilians have an affinity for the *sertão* way of life. While *forró* music is loved throughout the country, Brazil's popular culture abounds with *sertanejo* stories and images.

After a sudden rain, the dry land will turn green and lush for a short period.

Palma cactus is often the only food available to livestock. The tough, chewy leaves are ground into a paste and used as cattle feed.

Caatinga, *the vegetation growing in this arid landscape, consists of cacti, bromeliads, and scrubby trees and bushes. These plant species are suitable to the challenging conditions of the* sertão.

The goat *is the most important livestock in the* sertão. *More adaptable than other animals, it thrives in the dry and hot conditions. It is an important source of meat, milk, and leather.*

Rio São Francisco *is one of the main water sources in the* sertão. *Large irrigation projects are using the water to make agriculture possible. Many areas in Pernambuco grow fruits and vegetables.*

Nordestino markets *are where homesick communities of migrants from the Northeast meet, listen to* forró, *and eat some of their favorite foods. São Paulo and Rio de Janeiro have the largest* sertanejo *immigrant communities.*

Luiz Gonzaga *(1912–89), Brazil's most famous "Son of the* Sertão," *was a* forró *musician. Most of his songs celebrated or lamented the life of those living in the* sertão.

Aerial view of a palm-lined beach resort in Natal ▷

View of the small chapel in the central courtyard of the Forte dos Reis Magos

Natal [5]

Rio Grande do Northe. 👥 *710,000.* ✈ 🚌 ℹ *Centro de Turismo, (084) 3211 6149.* 🎉 *Carnatal (Dec).* www.natal.rn.gov.br

Natal is a pleasant, modern, and safe city, increasingly sought out as a sunshine destination for winter-weary Europeans. Natal has several attractions, including beautiful beaches, dune buggy rides, unusual sand art, and an incredible nightlife.The city and its most famous landmark, **Forte dos Reis Magos**, date back to December 25, 1598, when the Portuguese established a fort and settlement at the mouth of the Rio Potengi. In honor of the season, the city was named Natal, the Portuguese word for Christmas. The fort was named after the three wise kings of the east who had traveled to Bethlehem bearing gifts. The Dutch occupied the fort in 1633, upgrading it into its current five-pointed formation before turning it back over to the Portuguese in 1654. Access to the fort is via a narrow pedestrian walkway. At high tide, the fort is cut off from land by the waves. Visitors have the full run of the fort, from garrisons and mess hall to the high ramparts, which offer terrific views of the city skyline.

Natal was never a large trading center, and there are few historic buildings. The city's 19th century penitentiary has been converted into the **Centro de Turismo**, a showcase for regional arts and crafts. Each of the dozens of prison cells have been transformed into a shop selling leatherwork, lace, and figurines from northeastern folk festivals. On Thursday evenings, the courtyard of the old prison becomes an outdoor dance hall, as the center plays host to *forró com o turista*, an evening of *forró* dancing, with live music and instructors won hand to help shy and left-footed foreigners with the dance steps. Most visitors to Natal stay in **Ponta Negra**, a waterfront neighborhood in a modern part of the city featuring a lovely long beach with good waves for surfing. At the far end of the beach the Morro do Careca, a towering 390-ft (120-m) sand dune, is now off-limits to climbers because of the danger of erosion.

Sand art in bottle

On the coast between the old downtown and the modern parts of Natal there stands the **Parque das Dunas**, a 12-sq mile (6-sq km) reserve of coastal dunes. The park has several trails, but can only be visited with a guide.

FORRÓ

Couples dancing to the lively music of *forró*

According to local legend, the musical style known as *forró* is said to have been inspired by visiting foreigners. In the early days of World War II, the Americans created a massive air base near the city. Locals invited the American airmen to their parties, and to make sure they felt welcome they put up signs proclaiming that simplified dances with a two-step rhythm, were "for all." The label stuck to the musical style, though in common speech "for all" became *forró*.

Centro de Turismo
Rua Aderbal de Figueiredo 980.
Tel *(084) 3211 6149.* 🕐 *9am–7pm daily.* ♿

Forte dos Reis Magos
Praia do Forte. ***Tel*** *(084) 3502 1099.*
🕐 *8am–4:30pm daily.* 💲

Parque das Dunas
Av Alexadrino de Alencar s/n.
Tel *(084) 3201 3985.* 🕐 *8am–6pm Tue–Sun.* 💲 📷

Rota do Sol Beaches [6]

Heading south from Natal on the Rota do Sol (Route of the Sun), there are beaches and more beaches, stretching from the edge of the city to the far southern border of the state. Variety is the key feature of this golden stretch of coast. There are beaches with small reefs and little surf, and others with strong and steady waves, much loved by avid surfers. There are deserted beaches surrounded by tall dunes, accessible only by dune buggy or 4WD, far from the hustle and bustle of even the smallest fishing village. Other beaches, particularly Pipa, are full to bursting with energetic young Brazilians.

Mãe Luiza lighthouse north of Ponta Negra

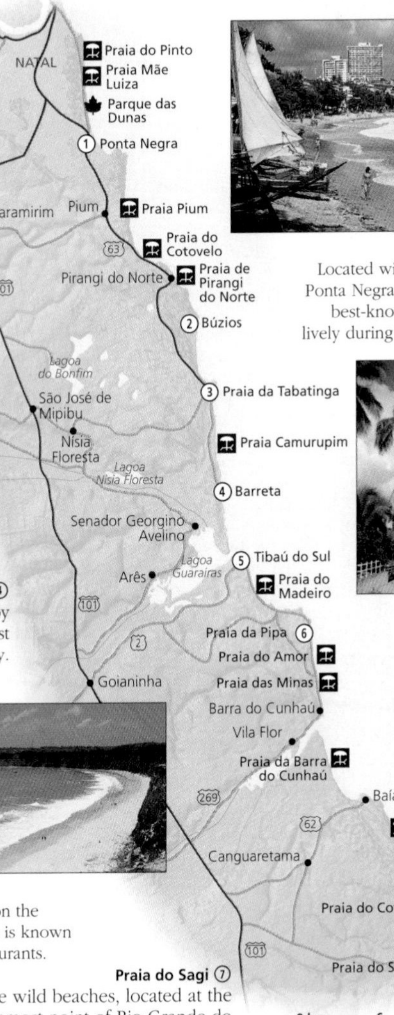

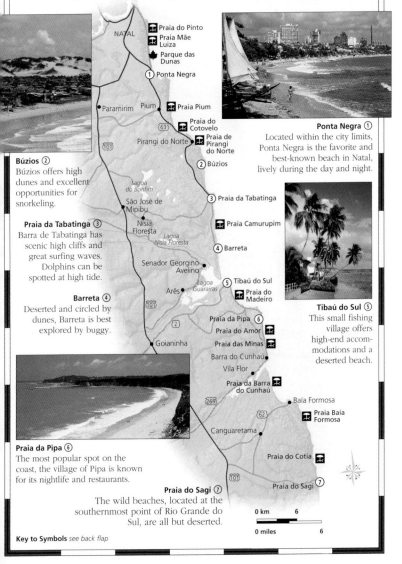

Ponta Negra (1)
Located within the city limits, Ponta Negra is the favorite and best-known beach in Natal, lively during the day and night.

Búzios (2)
Búzios offers high dunes and excellent opportunities for snorkeling.

Praia da Tabatinga (3)
Barra de Tabatinga has scenic high cliffs and great surfing waves. Dolphins can be spotted at high tide.

Barreta (4)
Deserted and circled by dunes, Barreta is best explored by buggy.

Tibaú do Sul (5)
This small fishing village offers high-end accommodations and a deserted beach.

Praia da Pipa (6)
The most popular spot on the coast, the village of Pipa is known for its nightlife and restaurants.

Praia do Sagi (7)
The wild beaches, located at the southernmost point of Rio Grande do Sul, are all but deserted.

Key to Symbols *see back flap*

Snorkeling in the coral reefs, Maracajaú

Genipabu ❼

Rio Grande do Norte. ▓ 5,000.
✈ Natal Airport. ▦ ℹ *Associação
dos Bugueiros do Rio Grande do
Norte, (084) 3225 2077.*

The main reason to visit
Genipabu is to experience
the magnificent dunes. This
small town is located north
of Natal, close to the edge of
an impressive landscape of
shifting sands that pile up into
high dunes and plunge down
to the edge of the Atlantic
Ocean. Though it is possible
to ride a camel through the
dunes or sand-board down
them, the best way to enjoy
these enormous ridges of
sand is behind the roll bar
of a dune buggy with an
experienced driver at the
wheel. The **Parque Dunas**
de Genipabu is the perfect
place to start. This area of
164-ft (50-m) tall shifting
dunes is off-limits to all but
licensed buggy drivers who
know their way around every
hump and dip. Passengers
have the option of requesting
a ride "*com ou sem emoção*"
(with or without the thrills
and heart palpitations). Well
worth requesting, the thrill-
ride is an amazing roller-
coaster of maneuvers up
and down along the slippery
front faces of the dunes,
descending at almost 90-
degree angles before zooming
straight up another dune
on the far side.
   The best time of day to visit
the Parque das Dunas is in
the afternoon, to enjoy the
lovely golden sunset over
the dunes after the ride.

Maracajaú ❽

Rio Grande do Norte. ▦ ◯ *at low
tide only.*

Maracajaú's coral reefs
offer one of the best spots
for snorkeling along the
whole of Brazil's north coast.
The reefs lie approximately
4 miles (7 km) offshore. At
low tide, the receding ocean
leaves the reefs from just 3
to 9 ft (1 to 3 m) underwater,
and forms natural pools,
called *parrachos*, which
combine the beauty of the
tranquil water with a spectacular array of marine-life.
They are shallow enough for
snorkelers and swimmers to
observe dozens of species of
colorful, tropical fish trapped
inside the reefs. The water is
crystal clear and warm round
the year, making it a popular
destination for scuba divers
and swimmers alike. Tour
operators offer scuba diving
trips, but the water is so
shallow, it is hardly worth
the effort or expense.
   The best way to reach
Maracajaú is by a dune
buggy, departing from Natal
(or Genipabu) and traveling
north along the white, sandy
beaches. Check the tide tables
to time the journey in order
to arrive in Maracajaú at, or
a few hours before, low tide.
The large **Manoa Water Park**,
replete with slides and swimming pools, en route to the
coral reefs in Maracajaú, is an
enjoyable stop for children.

Tourists enjoying a buggy ride on the white sand dunes in Genipabu

For hotels and restaurants in this region see pp379–81 and pp405–406

Sailboats, known as *jangadas*, on Tibaú beach, one of the beach-villages along Costa Branca

Costa Branca ❾

Rio Grande do Norte.
🚌 *Catavento Turismo Mossoró, (084) 3433 6999.*

The Costa Branca lies in the extreme northwest of Rio Grande do Norte. Starting at **Porto do Mangue**, it stretches across the villages of **Areia Branca** and **Grossos** and ends at **Tibaú**. The name "Costa Branca" refers to both the white dunes and the salt works found along this coast. The region has not yet been discovered by mass tourism, and its beaches, mangroves, dunes, and lagoons are blissfully devoid of crowds. **Praia do Rosado**, just west of Porto do Mangue, is famous for its pinkish sand dunes. The red soil underneath the shifting dunes mixes with the white sand of the beach giving the dunes an unusual and distinctly soft, pink hue.

The largest village on this coast, Areia Branca has around 20,000 residents and offers the best tourist facilities for those wanting to spend a few days exploring the region. Tibaú is the last village in Rio Grande do Norte, right on the border with Ceará. Its beach is mostly used by residents of the inland city of Mossoró. Local artisans use sand from the colored dunes to make artistic and pretty designs inside small glass bottles.

Sand design in glass bottle

Mossoró ❿

Rio Grande do Norte. 👥 *225,000.*
✈ 🚌 *Secretaria de Turismo (084) 3315 4820.* 🎉 *Batalha do Mossoró (Jun).*

Located 34 miles (55 km) inland from the coast, Mossoró is, in many ways, the archetypal *sertão* town of the northeastern interior. The main places of interest in Mossoró are connected to a glorious moment in history in 1924, when the townspeople fought off an attack by the legendary bandit leader Lampião and his gang of outlaws. The event is still commemorated every June 13 with great ceremony.

Mossoró is an ideal jumping-off point for visiting the **Lajedo de Soledade**, an archaeological site. Its limestone rocks were formed more than 90 million years ago. Tours begin at the visitors' center, at the Museu de Soledade. From here, visitors can depart on a guided walk featuring 10,000-year-old rock paintings, and impressive fossils containing the remains of extinct animals, including sabertooth tigers.

🏛 **Lajedo de Soledade**
Tel (084) 3333 1017. 🕐 *7am–5pm Tue–Sun.* 🎫 📷

REPENTISTAS

Repentista is a popular form of entertainment in the interior of the Northeast. Its singers engage in a two-man musical duel, making their rhymes up on the spot, trying to score points off their opponent. Singers sometimes accompany themselves with a tambourine or the melodious *viola nordestina*, developed from the Portuguese seven-string guitar. The singing duelists take turns singing out a stanza, trying to win the favor of the audience by making fun of their opponent, preferably with a clever bit of rhyme. The adversary's manhood, sexual prowess, and ancestry are common topics, but

Repentistas performing

politics and day-to-day events also play into the mix. In big cities with significant *nordestino* populations, such as São Paulo and Rio de Janeiro, *repentistas* make money on the downtown streets by creating impromptu songs to entertain homesick migrants.

Canoa Quebrada ⓫

Ceará. 👥 65,300. 🚌 from Fortaleza. 🛈 Secretaria de Turismo, (088) 3446 2451. **www.** canoaviagem.com.br

In just over three decades, Canoa Quebrada has transformed from a sleepy fishing village to a popular hippy hangout in the 1970s, and now a mainstream beach resort. According to a legend, the name Canoa Quebrada, meaning "Broken Canoe," originated with a Portuguese skipper who wrecked his ship close to shore and donated the useless craft to local fishermen. Never having seen such a craft before, locals named it a broken canoe.

The beaches of Canoa Quebrada, featuring red cliffs, fine sand, and offshore reefs, attract many visitors today. The village itself is a bustling place, known for its cafés and restaurants, and for the bars and clubs lining the main cobblestone street. It is also famous for its lacework. Even at the busiest times, however, it is not difficult to get away from the crowds and find a spot on one of the more deserted beaches or high sand dunes surrounding Canoa Quebrada. Buggy tours are a popular way to get out of town. The tour to Ponta Grossa, 18 miles (30 km) southeast, travels along miles of empty beaches framed by high red sandstone cliffs. Other activities include kitesurfing, riding, and sailing on a *jangada* (sailboat).

Beach along the fishing village of Jericoacoara

About 6 miles (10 km) northwest is the small town of **Aracati**. It is one of the few historic towns in this part of Northeast Brazil. An important center for the 18th-century cattle industry, Aracati has several buildings dating back to this time. Most noteworthy is the Mercado Central (Central Market), dating back to the 1700s, still used as the town's daily open-air market on Rua Pompeu.

Fortaleza ⓬

See pp242–3.

Jericoacoara ⓭

Ceará. 👥 2,000. 🚌 from Fortaleza. www.jericoacoara.com

The isolated village of Jericoacoara is a beach lover's paradise. Although no longer the sleepy fishing community it once was, it preserves much of its original charm. The village consists of five streets made of sand, and houses and apartments are simple, even rustic. In 2002, the entire region was declared a national park, putting a complete halt to the construction of new buildings.

Red sandstone cliffs in and around the beaches of Canoa Quebrada

The spectacular Ubajara Cave in Parque Nacional de Ubajara

Surrounded by dunes and lagoons, Jeri (as locals call it) is a place for those who like water, waves, and wind. From June to January, the winds pick up and kite-surfers, windsurfers, and sailors from around the world flock to Jeri.

Dune buggies are used to explore the surrounding beaches and dunes and visit the various lagoons. The most beautiful are **Lagoa Azul** and **Lagoa Paraíso**, located about 12 miles (20 km) east of the village. Jeri's postcard view is that of **Pedra Furada**, a basalt outcrop, on the edge of the sea with a 13-ft (4-m) hole in the middle. It sits on the beach at Praia Malhada, about 2 miles (3 km) east, a 15-minute walk from the village. The red rock glows in the late afternoon light and from June to September, the aperture lines up perfectly with the tropical setting sun. Another beautiful spot is **Pôr do Sol** (Sunset Dune).

Parque Nacional de Ubajara ⓮

Ceará. 🚌 from Fortaleza.
ℹ️ Secretaria de Turismo, (088) 3634 2288; Park Headquarters, (088) 3634 1388. ⭕ 9am–2:30pm Tue–Sun.
🐾 📷

Located almost exactly halfway between Fortaleza and Teresina, the Parque Nacional de Ubajara is the smallest national park in Brazil.

Located close to the small town of Ubajara, the park features the **Ubajara Cave**. The entrance to the cave can be reached either by cable car or via a steep, marked trail through the forest. The 3,937-ft (1,200-m) long cave is filled with stalactites and stalagmites, the work of several patient centuries of erosion and calcium deposition.

Fifteen chambers totaling 3,674 ft (1,120 m) have been mapped, of which 1,182 ft (360 m) are open to visitors. Eight galleries are lit up to display some of the amazing formations that have taken shape inside the cave. The main formations seen inside are Pedra do Sino (Bell Stone), Salas da Rosa (Rose Rooms), Sala do Cavalo (Horse Room), and Sala dos Retratos (Portrait Room). The cave is also home to 14 different types of bat.

The elevation gain is just over 1,640 ft (500 m), and the trail leading up to the cave, though rather strenuous, offers some spectacular views of the Serra da Ipiapaba and several waterfalls and beautiful natural pools. The hike takes about two hours, one way. There are also many local guides available here to show visitors around the park's eco trails, caves, and waterfalls.

BUGGIES

Dune buggies are found everywhere on Brazil's northeastern coast. Essentially a Volkswagen Beetle chassis with a fiberglass body and soft, fat tires, the Brazilian dune buggy is the perfect vehicle for exploring the endless beaches and towering sand dunes that characterize Northeast Brazil.

Popular places to buggy here are Genipabu (see p238), just north of Natal, and Cumbuco and Canoa Quebrada, respectively north and south of Fortaleza. They all feature towering mountains of sand, and dune buggy drivers are trained to make the most of them.

High speed runs up, down, and along the sheer, steep face of sand dunes are among the most hair-raising maneuvers one can expect from such a tour.

Multiday buggy expeditions include tours from Natal to Fortaleza, nearly 311 miles (500 km) of untouched sand.

Dune buggy in Canoa Quebrada

Fortaleza ⑫

With pretty urban beaches, a pleasant year-round climate, and a constant cooling breeze coming off the ocean, Fortaleza has an appealing resort-like atmosphere. Though founded in the early 1500s, Fortaleza remained a small town until after Brazilian independence in 1822. Fortaleza quickly developed into one of Brazil's largest ports, exporting vast amounts of cotton to England in particular. There is a small historic section near the old port, now renovated as a nightlife area called Praia de Iracema, but beyond that Fortaleza has a rather modern feel, with apartment high-rises, beach boulevards, and appealing outdoor cafés.

Brightly painted colonial buildings lining the streets

🎭 Teatro José de Alencar
Praça José de Alencar s/n. **Tel** (085) 3101 2583. ◯ 8am–5pm Mon–Fri, 8am–noon Sat. 🖼 🛗 🔗
Named after one of Brazil's famous novelists, the Teatro José de Alencar was built in 1908. The theater's high-Victorian cast-iron structure was imported straight from Glasgow. Additional elements, such as the stained-glass windows and interior furnishings, were done in the Art Nouveau style.

Iron-work, Teatro José de Alencar

🏛 Centro de Turismo
Rua Senador Pompeu 350. **Tel** (085) 3488 7411. ◯ 7am–6pm Mon–Sat, 7am–noon Sun. 🔗
This formerly grim Victorian prison has been transformed into a bustling market, with a different shop in each of the old jail cells. The market specializes in local handicrafts, including fine lace, leather, and figurines. The market is a good place to stock up on top-quality cashew nuts.

🏛 Museu do Ceará
Rua São Paulo 51. **Tel** (085) 3101 2606. ◯ 8:30am–5pm Tue–Sun. 🖼 🛗
The museum possesses a vast archive of things relating to the history of Ceará – coins, medals, paintings, furniture, indigenous artifacts, folk art, and more. Its most prized exhibit is the dagger belonging to notorious outlaw Lampião *(see p213).*

🏰 Forte Nossa Senhora da Assunção
Rua Maestro Alberto Nepomuceno 250. **Tel** (085) 3255 1600. ◯ 8am–4:30pm Mon–Sat, 8am–noon Sun. 🖼 🔗
Fortaleza's oldest fort was built by the Dutch in 1649 as Fort Schoonenborch. The Portuguese captured and re-christened it in 1654. The five-pointed fort remains an active military post to this day.

🏛 Mercado Central
Rua Maestro Alberto Nepomuceno 199. **Tel** (085) 3454 8586. ◯ 8am–7pm Mon–Fri, 8am–5pm Sat, 8am–noon Sun. 🔗
Fortaleza's central market is the cheapest place in town to pick up some fine leatherwork, lace, or textiles. The market is also an excellent place to sample local ice cream made from regional fruits.

FORTALEZA
Centro de Turismo ②
Forte Nossa Senhora da Assunção ④
Mercado Central ⑤
Museu do Ceará ③
Praia de Cumbuco ⑨
Praia de Iracema ⑥
Praia de Meireles ⑦
Praia do Futuro ⑧
Teatro José de Alencar ①

Statue of Iracema waiting for her lover

THE STORY OF IRACEMA

Written by José de Alencar in 1865, the story of Iracema tells of the love that a Tabajara princess bore for Martim, a white Portuguese settler. Iracema uses magic to make Martim fall in love with her, and is ostracized by her community. Away from her people, she loses her magical powers and her lover. A statue of Iracema on Meireles beach is located where, according to legend, she stood awaiting the return of her beloved.

VISITORS' CHECKLIST

Ceará. 2.3 million. 4 miles (6 km) S of town. (085) 3256 2100. Secretaría do Turismo, Centro Administrativo Virgílio Távora, (085) 3101 4672. daily craft market at Meireles beach. Fortal (Jul), Regata de Jangadas (Jul), Semana do Folclore (Aug). www.fortaleza.ce.gov.br

Praia de Iracema

Just east of the city center lies the Praia de Iracema. Though called a beach, it is actually the very urban former port, now renovated and transformed into the city's most popular nightlife and restaurant area. The centerpiece of the area is a long ocean pier called Ponte dos Ingleses (Englishman's Pier), first built in 1920, and modeled on the piers of Brighton. Many restaurants occupy other original turn-of-the-19th-century buildings in the area. Locally famous nightlife spots include Piratas (open Mondays), and Lupus Bier, known for its Wednesday-evening folklore and variety show.

Praia de Meireles

The city's prettiest urban beach is lined with thick groves of coconut palms and waterside cafés, although the water is not considered good for swimming. Meireles is a great place for strolling,

Visitors at a waterside café, Praia de Meireles

shopping, sun-bathing, or people-watching while sipping on fresh cashew juice. Home to what has become the city's prime residential and hotel neighborhood in Fortaleza, Meireles' pedestrian boulevard, running beside the beach, becomes a night market every evening.

Praia do Futuro

Praia do Futuro is one of the best beaches in the city for swimming, and a bustling nightlife destination in its own right. The 7-mile (11-km) long beach southeast of the center is lined with restaurants and beach shacks that serve local cuisine. There are several discos on the beach that are popular on weekends. On Thursday nights, Fortalezans head to Barraca Chico do Caranguejo to feast on fresh crab and listen to popular live *forró (see p236)* music.

Praia de Cumbuco

21 miles (33 km) W of town. Cumbuco is the city's favorite beach playground. The Lagoa da Banana offers a wide variety of watersports, including jet-skiing, boating, banana boating, and kayaking. Lagoa do Parnamirim, just south of Cumbuco, is surrounded by tall dunes, making it the perfect spot for "ski-bunda" (bum-skiing), where skiers sit on a wooden board and slide down the side of the dune into the lagoon. Other sport activities on offer here include horseback riding and sailing on *jangadas*, or single-sail rafts.

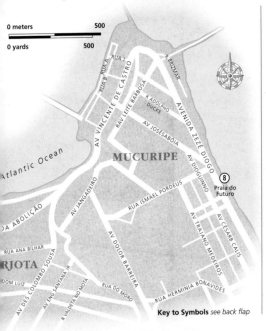

0 meters 500
0 yards 500

RUA RUA J

AV VICENTE DE CASTRO
RAV LEITE BARBOSA
R BRIZMAR
ADOLPHO DUCKE
AVENIDA ZEZÉ DIOGO
AV JOSÉ SABÓIA

Atlantic Ocean

MUCURIPE

AV JANGADEIRO
AV DIOGUINHO
RUA ISMAEL PORDEUS
AV ISMAEL PORDEUS
⑧ Praia do Futuro

DA ABOLIÇÃO
RUA ANA BILHAR
RJOTA
AV DOLOR BARREIRA
AV DES COLOMBO SOUSA
AVENG SANTANA JR
R VALDETANO MOTA
RUA DO MORO
AV TRAJANO MEDEIROS
AV CÉSAR B CALS
RUA HERMINIA BONAVIDES

Key to Symbols *see back flap*

PIAUÍ & MARANHÃO

Although part of the Northeast, Piauí and Maranhão are different from the rest of the region culturally and geographically. Both states have violent histories. Piauí was the site of many skirmishes between the indigenous population and cattle herders, and Maranhão was forcibly settled in 1612 by the French. Today, the area is abundant in natural and cultural riches.

Unlike its southern neighbors, Piauí was settled by ranchers on horseback pushing northwards from the sugar plantations of Bahia in the late 1700s.

Largely visited in transit, Piauí is sparsely populated and possibly the poorest state in Brazil. The economy here is greatly dependent on agriculture and livestock. The only significant industry revolves around the *carnaúba* palm, which yields a wax that is an important ingredient of shellac. However, Piauí boasts a few fascinating natural attractions. The state capital, Teresina, located more than 186 miles (300 km) inland, is the only capital in Northeast Brazil which is not on the ocean, and has some interesting sights.

For many years after they first came to Brazil, the Portuguese showed little interest in the area that now forms Maranhão. Taking advantage of the Portuguese neglect of the Maranhão coast, the French, in 1612, landed a sizable force and founded São Luís, named in honor of King Louis XIII. Portuguese forces laid seige for four years to drive the new French colony out.

Maranhão's golden age came in the 19th century, with a rich agricultural export economy based on cotton and sugar. Ports such as São Luís and Alcântara grew wealthy. When slavery was abolished in 1888, Maranhão sugar and cotton industries collapsed, causing an economic slump that lasted for most of the 20th century.

Maranhão is today an exciting destination, both in terms of natural and cultural treasures. The state's main festival, Bumba-meu-boi, celebrates the indigenous, Portuguese, and African cultures.

Mesmerizing sand dunes of Lençóis Maranhenses in Maranhão

◁ Festa do Divino celebrations in Alcântara, Maranhão

Exploring Piauí & Maranhão

Most of Piauí's attractions are a long way from the coast. The Serra da Capivara is one of the largest archaeological sites in the world, containing more than 30,000 prehistoric rock paintings. The only important destination on Piauí's tiny 41-mile (66-km) coastline is the town of Parnaíba. It sits at the edge of the Delta do Parnaíba, one of the largest deep-water river deltas in the world, and a new ecotourism destination. Most of the delta itself lies in Maranhão. Its capital, São Luís, rivals Salvador for its collection of restored colonial homes and heritage buildings. Outside of São Luís, the biggest draw is a spectacular region of stark beauty in the form of coastal sand dunes known as Lençóis Maranhenses.

SIGHTS AT A GLANCE

Towns & Cities

National Parks & Areas of Natural Beauty

KEY

— Major road

═ Minor road

— Railroad

═ State border

Pedra do Elefante at the Parque Nacional de Sete Cidades

The beautiful pristine Caburé beach at Lençóis Maranhenses

DELTA DO PARNAÍBA &
4 PARQUE NACIONAL DOS
LENÇÓIS MARANHENSES

GETTING AROUND

The São Luís airport in Maranhão has international flights, and Piauí's capital city Teresina can be reached by flights en route to São Luís. There are buses linking almost every town in this region, but roads are in very poor condition. It is also possible to rent a car. The inland attractions of Piauí are far from Teresina, and from each other, so travel well equipped with plenty of gas, water, and supplies.

Most of Maranhão's highlights are on the coast. The Lençóis Maranhenses are best accessed from Barreirinhas, located just on the edge of the Lençóis Maranhenses National Park. From São Luís, it is a 45-minute flight in a single-engine plane, or a four-hour drive. Once there, most excursions are by boat or in a 4WD, as there are no paved roads in the region.

Colonial-style houses and Ponte José Sarney, São Luís

0 kilometers 100

0 miles 100

SEE ALSO

Church exterior, Nossa Senhora do Amparo

Teresina ❶

Piauí. 🏠 775,000. ✈ 🚌
ℹ Piemtur, (086) 3221 7100.
www.teresina.pi.gov.br

Founded in 1852, Teresina was named in honor of the Empress Teresa Cristina, wife of Brazilian Emperor Dom Pedro II. Teresina has the dubious honor of being one of Brazil's hottest cities, although Rio Parnaíba and Rio Poty, as well as several large, tree-shaded squares scattered throughout Teresina, moderate the worst of the city's scorching heat.

Most historic buildings date back only to the end of the 19th century. One of the oldest buildings is the cathedral, **Nossa Senhora do Amparo**. Construction was started in 1851, but completed only in 1952. More modern but interesting is the Palácio Karnak, Piauí's new state legislature. Built in 1926, the palace's façade was modeled on an ancient Egyptian temple. The former state legislature is now home to the **Museu do Piauí**. Its small collection provides a good overview of regional history, including both prehistoric artifacts and folk art.

Environs
Easily reached by bus, the **Parque Ambiental Encontro dos Rios** is located just north of Teresina, where the Poty and Parnaíba rivers join up. This pleasant park offers walking trails, fishing spots, gardens, two lookouts, a floating restaurant, a store with regionally made crafts and a statue of Crispim, the Bowl Head.

🏛 **Museu do Piauí**
Praça Marechal Deodoro da Fonseca, Centro. **Tel** (086) 3221 6027. ◯ 8am–5pm Tue–Fri, 8am-noon Sat & Sun.

Parque Nacional de Serra da Capivara ❸

Piauí's most compelling park is the Serra da Capivara, located in the far south of the state. The park's impressive canyons, plateaux, and rock formations also form one of Brazil's most important prehistoric sites, one that was designated a UNESCO World Heritage Site in 1991. Over 30,000 rock paintings have been discovered within the park. The paintings portray aspects of prehistoric life such as the hunt, dances, and other rituals.

Andorinhas
Every evening, thousands of swifts (andorinhas) perform amazing aerial acrobatics before retiring to a nearby cave to spend the night.

Rock Painting
Scientists estimate that many of these rock paintings were created between 6,000 and 12,000 years ago. The oldest drawings may date to as far back as 29,000 years.

KEY

ℹ	Visitor information
▬	Major road
═	Other road
─	Minor road
– –	Trail
▬ ▬	Park boundary

TERESINA ↑

SERRA BOM JESUS DA GURGUEIA

Riacho Nova Olin

324

Portaria Terra Vermelha

Baix And

↓ PETROLIN

Trails leading up to rock formations at Parque Nacional de Sete Cidades

Parque Nacional de Sete Cidades ❷

Maranhão. 🚌 from Teresina.
🛈 Ibama Office, Centro de Visitantes, (086) 3343 1342.
🕐 8am–5pm daily. 🎟 ⌘ Parque Hotel Sete Cidades, (086) 3223 3366.

The name Sete Cidades (Seven Cities) refers to seven distinct and unusual rock formations, spread out in the park along 7 miles (12 km) of trails. Only the first six

are accessible to the public. Sculpted by rain, wind, heat, and erosion, the rocks resemble animals, people, mythological beings, and even man-made structures. Among the shapes are **Mapa do Brasil**, a backward facing map of Brazil and **Biblioteca** (Library) in Quarta Cidade (Fourth City). Segundo Cidade, the second of the seven "cities" has a 147-ft (45-m) tall lookout with views out over five of the cities of stone. There are also more than 2,000

prehistoric rock paintings, some 6,000 years old. The most impressive painting, **Pedra de Inscrição** (Inscribed Rock), said to be marked with cryptic Indian runes, can be seen at Quinta Cidade (Fifth City). Other formations include **Pedra do Elefante** (Elephant Rock) at Sexta Cidade (Sixth City), and lookout points such as the **Arco de Triunfo** (Triumphal Arch), a 59-ft (18-m) tall arch-shaped rock, which lies between Quarta Cidade and Quinta Cidade.

CRISPIM, THE BOWL HEAD

A popular Piauí legend tells the story of Crispim, a fisherman who lived by the banks of the Rio Parnaíba. He came home one day frustrated after not having caught any fish. Outraged with the meager lunch of beef bone soup, Crispim took up a large bone and beat his mother. As she lay dying, she cursed him, condemning him to live in the river as a bowl-headed monster. The curse would be lifted

Rio Parnaíba, reputedly haunted by Crispim

when he devoured seven virgins named Maria. Locals still tell of spotting Crispim in the river, looking for virgins to eat.

Caldeirão dos Rodrigues, a walk through Baixão da Pedra Furada, leads to archaeological sites with rock paintings.

Desfiladeiro da Capivara is a 2- mile (4-km) long trail, leading to many rock-painting sites.

Baixão do Sítio Meio is the site where a pottery shard nearly 9,000 years old was found. It is the oldest in the Americas.

VISITORS' CHECKLIST

Coronel José Dias, Piauí. 🚌 from Teresina to São Raimundo Nonato, then taxi. 🛈 Museu de Homem Americano, Bairro Campestre, São Raimundo Nonato, (089) 3582 1612. 🕐 7am–5pm daily. Best time to visit is from March to June. 🎟 valid for three days. 🎫 tour groups up to a maximum of 10 people. ⌘ Hotel Serra da Capivara, Santa Luiza, (089) 3582 1389.

Baixão da Pedra Furada
The trail leading to the large unusual-shaped rock, known as Pedra Furada (Pierced Rock), leads to 10 different archaeological sites.

Delta do Parnaíba & Parque Nacional dos Lençóis Maranhenses ❹

The Delta do Parnaíba stretches roughly from the Piauí border some 56 miles (90 km) farther up the coast in Maranhão, where the Rio Parnaíba runs into the sea. Shaped like a hand, the river breaks into five fingers, meandering through some 83 islands. Small villages thrive on sea salt, cashews, and crabs. Tourism is still in its infancy. Straddling Piauí and Maranhão, the Parque Nacional Lençóis Maranhenses offers over 600 sq miles (1,555 sq km) of spectacular white sand dunes created by strong coastal winds. From May to August, rain collects in the basins between dunes, forming countless crystal-clear freshwater lagoons. In June, when the water levels are at their highest, the Lençóis dunes look like an array of white stripes, interspersed with sparkling ribbons of blue, turquoise, and green.

★ Queimada dos Britos
Deep inside the park is an oasis, surrounded by sand dunes. It can be visited by 4WD from Sucuruju.

★ Scarlet Ibis
Born gray, these birds obtain their distinct red color from eating tiny crustaceans found in tide flats in the estuary of the Rio Preguiças.

ATLANTIC OCEAN

Lagoa Travosa

Lagoa de Santo Amaro

Queimada dos Britos

Santo Amaro do Maranhão

PRIMEIRA CRUZ

Provoado de Sucuruju

Alegre

Lagoa de Santo Amaro
This beautiful clear-water lake near the tiny village of Santa Amaro do Maranhão sits isolated amid sand dunes.

KEY

✕	Domestic airport
▬	Major road
═	Minor road
- -	Trail
▬ ▬	Park boundary

STAR SIGHTS

★ Queimada dos Britos

★ Scarlet Ibis

★ Lençóis

★ Lençóis
On foot, visitors can only access a small portion of the park. To appreciate the size and scale of the dunes, it is worth taking a sightseeing flight from São Luís. The views of the large dunes and lagoons are breathtaking.

THE VERSATILE BURITI PALM TREE

The delta area's dense vegetation is dominated by the multipurpose buriti palm tree. The fruit can be eaten or used for wine. The trunk is used for house poles, while the fronds make thatch roofs and baskets. Buriti fiber is crucial for the strong but limber pouch used to squeeze the poison from manioc root. The twigs make good placemats. The seeds can be fashioned into jewelry, and the bark can be spun into twine.

Buriti palm tree with its hanging fruit

VISITORS' CHECKLIST

Piauí/Maranhão. ✈ 🚌 from Teresina to Delta do Parnaíba & Lençóis Maranhenses. 🚤 from Lençóis Maranhenses to Barreirinhas, then to Caburé. 🛈 Casa do Turismo, Porto das Barcas, Parnaíba, (086) 3321 1969; Ecotrilha, Av Joaquim de Cavalho 682, Barreirinhas, (098) 3349 0372. 🗓 **Giltur** Rua Montanha Russa 22, São Luís. **Tel** (086) 231 7065. 🛥 Barreirinhas. **www**. parquelencois.com.br

Caburé

Sitting on a sandpit a short distance from the Atlantic Ocean, this tiny settlement is a good starting point for reaching the northeastern part of the Lençóis Maranhenses by ferry.

Baixa Grande oasis can be reached by hiking across the dunes.

0 km 5

0 miles 5

Caburé
Atins
Mandacaru
Praia Pequenos Lençóis
Baía Tutóia
DELTA DO PARNAÍBA
Tutóia
Paulino Neves
34
Preguiças
Barreirinhas
SÃO LUÍS 225

Pequenos Lençóis

This small desert of dunes rises out of Rio Preguiças. Ropes assist in hiking to the Boi hill.

Barreirinhas is a small town, and the main access point to the park.

Delta do Parnaíba

Formed where the Rio Parnaíba meets the Atlantic Ocean, the Parnaíba delta, comprising 83 islands with immense beaches, is one of the richest habitats for birdlife in the Northeast.

Street-by-Street: São Luís ❺

Detail of a tile, São Luís

One of Brazil's finest examples of Portuguese colonial architecture, São Luís was ironically founded by the French in 1612, and later taken over by Dutch invaders. In 1644, the city was finally settled under Portuguese rule, serving as the export point for sugar and cotton. Expensive houses and buildings covered with brightly colored Portuguese tiles were built in the city's urban center. By the late 1800s, with slavery at an end, São Luís went into a decline. At the end of the 1970s, the state government began to invest in preserving the city's historic center. In 1997, the historical core of São Luís was designated a UNESCO World Heritage Site.

A row of colorful houses along one of the streets in São Luís

★ Palácio dos Leões
Built in 1766 on the site of the original French Fort St. Louis, the Palácio dos Leões is now home to the Maranhão state government.

Beco Catarina Mina
This picturesque 18th-century alley connects the lower lying streets of the historic center with Avenida Dom Pedro II.

Museu de Arte Visuais is covered in elaborate Portuguese tiles.

STAR SIGHTS

★ Palácio dos Leões

★ Casa das Tulhas

★ Centro de Cultura Popular

Casa do Maranhão
The former 19th-century customs building now houses a fine collection of Bumba-meu-boi folklore. Guides walk visitors through the colorful exhibits.

Matriz da Sé
*The cathedral little
resembles the original 1699
structure. Extensive renovations were carried out in
1922, including the addi-
tion of a Neo-Classical
façade, giving the cathedral
its imposing look.*

VISITORS' CHECKLIST

Maranhão. ☐ *Central de
Serviços Turísticos, (098) 3212
6211.* www.turismo.ma.gov.br/
en/ **Casa das Tulhas** Rua de
Estrela. **Tel** *(098) 231 6766.*
☐ *8am–6pm daily.* **Palácio
dos Leões** *Av Dom Pedro II.* ☐
3–6pm Mon, Wed & Fri. 📷 ✈

KEY

– – – Suggested route

Praça Benedito Lete
is framed by historic,
beautifully tiled houses.
The statue in the center
of the square is of for-
mer senator and state
governor, Benedito Leite.

0 meters	100
0 yards	100

Rua de Estrela is
one of the live-
liest streets in the
historic center of
São Luís.

RUA 28 DE JULHO

RUA DE ESTRELA

TRAV. M. ALMEIDA

RUA 14 DE JULHO

TRAV. BOAVENTURA

RUA DA ESTRELA

BECO DA PRENSA

★ Casa das Tulhas
*Regional delicacies, such as
cashew nuts and dried
shrimp, are on sale in the
food stalls of this 19th-
century market building.*

★ Centro de
Cultura Popular
*This center exhibits
costumes, artifacts,
and photographs of the
Festa do Divino, one of
Maranhão's most popular
religious festivals.*

José Sarney Bridge connecting the historic district to São Francisco, São Luís

Exploring São Luís

The rich and diverse historical center of São Luís makes it ideal for touring on foot. This is the oldest part of the city, known interchangeably as the Praia Grande, the Reviver, and the **Centro Histórico**. All the city's museums and beautifully preserved historic sites are located here.

The **Casa do Maranhão** is one of the city's most interesting museums, offering two floors of colorful exhibits that elaborately explain the Festa do Bumba-meu-boi.

The **Centro de Cultura Popular** (also known as the Casa da Festa) is dedicated to showcasing the traditions and customs of the Festa do Divino Espírito Santo. The highlights of the museum are the poster-size photographs of the actual celebrations, including some compelling black-and-white images of the elderly women who have served as festival queens.

The building that once housed the city slave market is now home to the **Cafua das Mercês**, also known as the Museu do Negro. This small museum contains numerous artifacts from the slave era, including musical instruments and tribal artwork, and sinister tools of the slave trade, such as shackles and instruments of torture. One of the more poignant monuments is the Pelourinho, or the whipping post, on display in the museum's central courtyard.

Cazumba figure, Casa do Maranhão

The **José Sarney** Bridge leads from the Centro Histórico into the newer parts of the city. Across the bridge lies São Francisco, the city's small central business district. Just beyond São Francisco, there is a large freshwater lake, the Lagoa de Jansen, circled by a boardwalk with a number of bars and restaurants. Much calmer than the Centro Histórico, it is a very popular place to stroll in the evenings. São Luís is blessed with a string of excellent beaches, all of which can be easily accessed by bus from the Terminal de Integração in the city center.

Farther south, beyond the Lagoa de Jansen, the popular beaches are Ponta d'Areia, São Marcos, Praia do Calhau, **Calhau**, and Olho d'Agua. Calhau, located 6 miles (10 km) from São Luís, is considered by many to be one of the nicest beaches around the city. Many busy kiosks and restaurants line the beachside boulevard. The quiet far end of the beach, where the water is calm and restaurants fewer, is known as Caolho.

🏛 **Cafua das Mercês**
Jacinto Maia 43. ◯ 9am–6pm Mon–Fri.

🏛 **Casa do Maranhão**
Rua do Trapiche s/n. **Tel** (098) 3231 1557. ◯ 1–7pm Mon–Fri, 9am–6pm Sat & Sun.

🏛 **Centro de Cultura Popular**
Rua do Giz 221. **Tel** (098) 3318 9924. ◯ 9am–7pm Tue–Sun.

Alcântara ❻

Maranhão. 🏠 6,000. 🚢 from São Luís. 🛈 Casa Municipal de Turismo, (098) 3212 6205. 🎉 Festa do Divino Espírito Santo (May).

Just across from São Luís, Alcântara lies on the other side of the Baía de São Marcos. The city was founded by the Portuguese in the 1640s, and used as a temporary capital and base during the campaign to drive the Dutch away from São Luís. Alcântara reached its zenith in the 19th century as

BUMBA-MEU-BOI

A unique folklore event endemic to Northeast Brazil, the Festa do Bumba-meu-boi revolves around a legendry folktale about the life, death, and resurrection of a magical Brazilian bull. Over the centuries, the celebration has grown into a huge carnival-esque festival, with different neighborhood groups competing to put on the best re-enactment of the story. In São Luís alone, more than 100 groups take to the streets. A papier-mâché bull is created each year and displayed in raucous parades, where participants take on the roles of medicine men, Indians, peasants, and cowboys. The largest celebrations take place in the second half of June. The music is upbeat and lively, with different groups using different rhythms and instruments.

A colorful celebration of the Bumba-meu-boi festival

Pillory, restored mansions, and ruin of a church in Alcântara

the regional center for the surrounding sugar and cotton plantations. It was the place where wealthy slave-owning aristocrats built their splendid city mansions. When slavery was abolished in 1888, the local economy crashed, the white upper class departed, and many of the fine mansions stood abandoned.

Appreciation of Alcântara's heritage value began as early as the 1950s, but restoration has been slow and quite a few of its churches and mansions remain as ruins, giving the city its own charm. These ruins are now the town's main tourist attractions. Day-trippers from São Luís come here to stroll the quiet cobblestoned streets, peer among the ruins, and admire the often brightly-tiled mansions of this former colonial capital.

The Brazilian Heritage Institute, Iphan, has restored several of the old mansions as museums. The best is the **Casa Histórica do Iphan**, featuring period furniture and glassware. Informative wall plaques and well-trained guides make getting around easy in the museum.

Another attraction to Alcântara is the Festa do Divino Espírito Santo, a vibrant religious festival held in May every year.

🏛 **Casa Histórica do Iphan**
Praça de Matriz s/n. 🕐 9am–5pm
Tue–Sun. 🚫

Reentrâncias Maranhenses ⑦

Maranhão. 🚌 from São Luís to Cururupu. 🚢 from Cururupu.
🛈 Sematur, Praça Joao Lisboa 328, São Luís, (098) 3232 2098.

One of the world's largest wetlands, the Reentrâncias Maranhenses is also one of Maranhão's more off-the-beaten-track natural attractions. The small town of **Cururupu** to the north of São Luís offers the best access to the Reentrâncias Maranhenses, with boats departing regularly.

Spread over an area of 10,350 sq miles (26,800 sq km), the Reentrâncias Maranhenses forms an important habitat for shore-birds such as scarlet ibis, spoonbills, whimbrels, egrets, willets, ruddy turnstones, and black-bellied plovers, as well as an array of marine-

Scarlet ibis, one of the shorebirds found in Reentrâncias Maranhenses

life, including sea turtles and manatees. Many species of fish and crustaceans are also found in the Reentrâncias. The region is geographically diverse and consists of a complex riverine system of extensive bays, coves, and rugged coastline covered mainly by mangrove forest. Many low-lying islands are also found here.

In order to protect the flora and fauna of this region, the Reentrâncias Maranhenses was designated an Area de Proteção Ambiental (Area of Environmental Protection) and was also made a Ramsar site (a wetland site listed under the Convention on Wetlands of International Importance) in 1993.

One of the more popular destinations here is the **Ilha dos Lençóis**, to the northeast of Cururupu. The island's geography somewhat resembles the Lençóis Maranhenses *(see pp250–51)*, with its endless landscapes of dunes and lagoons.

A small community of 300 people live here and still practice subsistence fishing. Some of them are descendants of the Filhos da Lua (Sons of the Moon), an albino community that settled here in the beginning of the 20th century. The isolation and flooding was harsh on the residents, and not many survived. Some of the fishermen work as local tour guides for a small fee.

NORTHERN BRAZIL

Introducing Northern Brazil

The six states of Pará, Amapá, Amazonas, Roraima, Acre, and Rondônia cover almost half of Brazil. Northern Brazil was relatively quiet until the rubber boom in the late 19th century. With expansive savannas to the north, and a rich diversity of flora and fauna in the east, today the region's economy is sustained by traditional forest products. Belém, Manaus, Santarém, Rio Branco, and Porto Velho, cities created by the rubber industry, are growing fast, connecting Amazônia to the outside world.

Boa Vista's Monte Roraima (see p288), *with its massive uplifted plateau, inspired Sir Arthur Conan Doyle's book* The Lost World.

Rio Branco (see p288) *was founded during the rubber boom. Today, it is better known for its sustainable rubber-tapping forest reserves.*

AMAZONAS, RORAIMA, ACRE & RONDÔNIA
(see pp276–89)

Madeira-Mamoré Museu Ferroviário (see p289), *in Porto Velho, houses several impressive locomotive steam engines, antique carriages, and other railway paraphernalia.*

0 km	100
0 miles	100

◁ Lush vista of the Amazon rainforest flanking the Rio Amazon

The river scenery of Santarém (see p274), *known for its serene beauty, is the primary reason for visiting this popular Amazon port town.*

Ilha de Marajó *(see p270)* is the world's largest inland river island. Its eastern half is savanna dotted with small woodland copses.

The old port of Belém (see pp268–9) *possesses more character than any other sector of the city. Attractive fishing boats bob up and down in the harbor, with the large old white fort on one side and the colorful Ver o Peso market on the other.*

PARÁ & AMAPÁ
(see pp264–75)

The Amazon river *(see pp284–7)*, known as Rio Solimões in its upper reaches, was first identified by Vicente Yáñez Pinzón. Its lower reaches are called Rio Negro.

Teatro Amazonas (see pp282–3), *in Manaus, exudes the opulence of its rubber-boom architects. It took the finest of materials and the most skilled of craftsmen to re-create an Italian Renaissance-style edifice, with a steel structure from Scotland and marble imported from Italy.*

The Amazon Ecosystem

Tree frog perched on log

Brazil has over 1.3 million sq miles (3.5 million sq km) of rainforest, the largest in the world. This massive river system contains a fifth of the world's fresh running water at any moment. The Amazon is home to a variety of plant, bird, fish and insect species. From the air, its magnificent canopy hides a variety of eco-systems, many with dramatic seasonal changes. Between December and April, visitors explore the flooded forest swamps and creeks that offer access to the fascinating flora and fauna.

ECOLOGICAL CONCERN

An estimated 208,495 sq miles (540,000 sq km) of the rainforest is reported to have been destroyed by indiscriminate felling. Stringent measures being taken to save this eco-logical treasure include expansion of protected areas and sustainable use of forest resources.

Rubber trees (Hevea brasiliensis) *growing on river banks are the source of valuable latex, which is later transformed into rubber.*

The ceiba tree (Ceiba pentandra), *with elegant buttress roots that surround the trunk's base, is the biggest tree in the Amazon, with an average height of 120 ft (37 m).*

Walking palms appear to migrate across the forest floor due to their characteristic stilt roots loosely attached to the ground.

Flowering bromeliads *are epiphytes that gather water and nutrients from raindrops on leaves as well as from dew.*

Amazon river winding through dense rainforest

FAUNA

One of the world's most diverse ecosystems, the Amazon harbors an infinite variety of animal life. There are plenty of remote areas that provide habitats for jaguars, tapirs, and wild pigs. However, spotting these elusive creatures is difficult. Monkeys, sloths, and alligators are more commonly sighted.

The emerald tree boa *is not venomous, but feeds on rodents and small animals of the forest.*

Hoatzins, *one of the most primitive of birds, live in flocks and build their nests in low canopy trees.*

The three-toed sloth *inhabits the forest canopy, moving incredibly slowly in search of its vegetarian diet of fruits, leaves, and sprouting plants.*

Buriti palm

The upper canopy, *about 131 ft (40 m) above the ground, is active with reptiles, mammals, tropical birds, and other wildlife.*

The guamo tree, found all across the Amazon, grows very fast to an average height of 30 ft (10 m).

Pau-d'arco-amarelo bears bright yellow flowers from August to November, while shedding all its leaves.

The black water owes its color to its source in low-lying forests where rotting vegetation is absorbed into the river system.

Tapirs, *the largest of all Amazon mammals, can weigh up to 661 lb (300 kg). These vegetarians take refuge in water to escape danger.*

Freshwater river dolphins, *both gray and pink, live in the main rivers and lakes of the Amazon basin.*

Piranhas *are known for their razor-sharp teeth. Only a few species pose a threat to larger animals.*

The People of Amazônia

Approximately 345,000 indigenous people, distributed among 215 groups, live in Brazil. Each group has its own unique dialect, mythology, arts, and culture. A majority of them are semi-nomadic, and live by hunting, gathering, fishing, and migratory farming. These indigenous people live in close harmony with the rhythms of the rainforest, and conservation and sustainability are an integral part of their life. The degree of exposure to western society varies greatly. Some people, such as the nomadic Maku, are incredibly isolated, while others, such as the literate Ticuna *(see p26)*, are heavily reliant on modern Brazilian society.

Man peering through a *cokar* (headgear) of blue macaw feathers

YANOMAMI PEOPLE

The Yanomami live in the rainforests of southern Venezuela and Northern Brazil. One of the most recently contacted tribes in Amazônia, they number around 20,000 today. Considered fierce warriors, the tribe consists of four subdivisions, each with its distinct language.

The patterns painted on a Yanomami adult *have an aesthetic, as well as magical and religious significance.*

During Rehao, *a yearly ceremony of paying obeisance to the dead, the Yanomami decorate their arms and shoulders with colorful feathers.*

Hammocks, slung under palm leaf roofs *along the inside perimeter of the circular hut, are commonly used by old and young alike.*

TUKANO PEOPLE

The name Tukano is used for a number of ethnolinguistic subgroups living in northwestern Brazil along the Rio Uapés. The individual groups live in communal houses. These are spaced out along the river at a distance of several hours by canoe. The Tukano grow bitter manioc and cultivate sweet potato, peanut, and plantain.

Tukano handicrafts *are sold in local markets, or used as trade items favored by non-indigenous people in the area.*

The traditional flute, *played by male initiates, is characterized by a piercing echo. The flute is believed to be the earthly manifestation of spirits which dominate the magical and religious world of the Tukano.*

The maloca, *a hut made from wood and palm leaves, provides shelter to the whole village.*

IMPACT OF GLOBALIZATION

The need for national development, fueled by globalization, is prompting the government of Brazil to enforce economic policies that are inimical to the tribal way of life. Pipelines to expand fuel production, and highway projects for transporting goods for global enterprises, are opening up indigenous lands to loggers, miners, ranchers, and colonists. The positive impact of globalization may be easier access to the modern world, including medicines, education, and tools.

Women gaining access to modern tools

KAYAPÓ PEOPLE

Around 7,000 Kayapós live in the Amazon River Basin in an area the size of Austria, with villages along the Rio Xingú. Circles are one of the tribe's main symbols, representing the course of the sun and moon. Body paint, which is worn at all times, is equally symbolic. The Kayapó also wear ear plugs and lip discs, according to which their social status can be determined, particularly their right to speak and be heard.

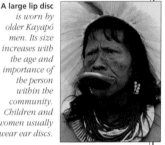

A large lip disc *is worn by older Kayapó men. Its size increases with the age and importance of the person within the community. Children and women usually wear ear discs.*

Ritual communal dancing *constitutes a crucial part of the Kayapó celebration of important events in the year. This is the time when Kayapó men and women show off their interesting headdresses – usually made from macaw and parrot feathers – and other ritual adornments.*

Beautiful bead bracelets, *created by Kayapó women, bear geometric designs with symbolic meanings. These are similar to the brightly colored patterns painted on their bodies with vegetable dyes.*

ASHANINKA PEOPLE

Originally from Peru, the Ashaninka fled to parts of Brazil to escape the rubber boom from 1839 to 1913. Still possessing a fairly traditional material culture, the Ashaninka wear long *cushmas* that the women weave from cotton grown in small forest gardens. They make a living from hunting, fishing, and small-scale gardening. Rice, coffee, and chocolate supplement their way of life with bought-in goods including metal tools and soaps.

Small dugout canoes or balsawood rafts *are regularly used by the riverine Ashaninka for traveling on the rivers along with their families.*

Red face paint *is traditionally applied by most of the Ashaninka people. The strong color comes from seeds of the garden-grown annatto bush.*

Ashaninka women weave cotton cloth *on primitive back-strap looms, almost every day, to make the men's pretty robes.*

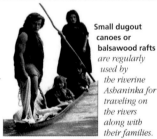

PARÁ & AMAPÁ

The states of Pará and Amapá in the eastern Amazon are the gateway to the world's largest river basin. In many ways, they are different from one another. Pará covers an enormous surface area, and has benefited from the natural wealth of the Amazon rainforest. Much smaller than Pará, Amapá is relatively poor. Both states rely on the mineral extraction industry.

It is the Amazon river itself that brings most visitors to this part of Brazil. Pará stretches west as far as the straits of Óbidos, where the river suddenly becomes narrow. This happens due to a geological meeting of the Guyana Shield from the north and the Brazilian Shield from the south. North of the Amazon, Amapá occupies an isolated region, stretching from the Amazon delta all the way to the borders of French Guyana and Suriname.

Pará has many places of cultural and ecological interest. The capital city, Belém, has been a vital Atlantic port since the colonial era, and still boasts many extravagant period buildings. Santarém, another sizeable city, is a busy and attractive river port replete with fascinating beaches. The massive island, Ilha de Marajó, which has vast areas of mangrove swamps, some splendid beaches, and a scattering of resorts, is located in the heart of the Amazon river delta.

Pará is also known for large modern iron ore mines, such as Grande Carajás and the older gold mine of Serra Pelada, once infamous for the vast scale of human labor used for extraction. In southern Pará, the rainforest transforms into *caatinga*, a scrubby savanna landscape.

Once exploited for its natural resources, Amapá is now making concerted efforts towards sustainable development. More than half of the state is under environmental protection. Macapá, the state capital of Amapá, lies on the equator. The English, Dutch, and French clamored for a base in this part of Amazon, before the Portuguese settled at Macapá in 1738.

Fishing boats moored at the old harbor near Ver o Peso market, Belém

◁ A view of the magnificent interior of Basílica de Nossa Senhora do Nazaré, Belém

Exploring Pará & Amapá

Even with their widespread rainforest canopy, which can only be seen clearly from the air, it is ocean and river travel that have long been the hallmark of Pará and Amapá states. The sights include the tasteful, recently restored historic buildings of Belém in Pará, along the verdant forest-edged Amazon river, as well as splendid riverine beaches such as Alter do Chão, close to Santarém, and those found on the Ilha de Marajó. Macapá, the capital of Amapá, with its refreshing sea breeze, was founded around the Forte de São José. It lies on the equator in a strategic position on the north side of the Amazon river estuary. More than half of the state is under environmental protection.

Corner tower, Fortaleza de São José de Macapá, Macapá

SIGHTS AT A GLANCE

Towns & Cities

Areas of Natural Beauty

SEE ALSO

Ferries moored on the shore of Rio Tapajós, Santarém, Pará

Kapiting

Asoenangka   Serra do Tumuvur

Merirumã

Maloca

Manaus   Mapireme

Arere

Porteira

Cuminá   Arapari
ÓBIDOS **6**   **7** MC
AL
Juruti   Curuai   SANTAR **5**
Alter do Chão
Boim   P A R

Boa Vista

Vila Braga   Porto

Itaituba
Lua Nova   Sem Tripa
Bacabal   Tucuparé
São Martinho   Entre Rios

Jacareacanga   Araras
Uari
*Porto
Velho*   Serra do Cachimbo

Manuelzin

Usina

Teles Pires

Cachimbo

0 km   50

0 miles   50

Mountains of fresh fruit at Ver o Peso market, Belém

GETTING AROUND

Rivers are the transport arteries of Pará, where virtually every village has some form of riverboat service. There are regular riverboat services connecting Belém, Macapá, and Santarém. While there are very few bus routes in Pará, most access is by road in Amapá. However, the roads are mainly unsurfaced, and bus travel during the rainy season can be treacherous in both states. Air services are widespread. Belém and Macapá can be reached from most cities in Brazil by air. There are daily flights from Belém to most places in the Amazon.

KEY

— Major road

═ Minor road

— Railroad

▬ International border

〰 State border

A creek near Araruna beach, Ilha de Marajó

Belém ❶

The attractive city of Belém was founded by the Portuguese in 1616 to guard the mouth of the Amazon river against other European powers. As the Amazon region's resources, mainly spices, were exploited, the city soon became a major trading port. It was ravaged during the 1835 Cabanagem Rebellion, when the poor settlers attacked the wealthy local elite. By the end of the 19th century, Belém had more than recovered its economic position, largely due to the rubber boom. It is still the most important port in Northern Brazil, and a fascinating place from which to explore the wealth of colonial and republican architecture.

Cannon on display at the 17th-century Forte do Castelo

Ships docked on the waterfront at the Ver o Peso market

🚢 Ver o Peso

Av Castilhos França.
⏱ 6am–2pm daily.
Incredibly hectic early in the morning, Ver o Peso, or "See the Weight," was originally a colonial customs point (Posto Fiscal), where goods were assessed for taxation purposes. These days, its most obvious feature is the harborside iron-built fish market, the Mercado de Ferro, which was designed and manufactured in England and assembled here in the late 19th century. The variety of seafood inside this elegant building is staggering. Outside, the main market expands into numerous stalls that can be explored at leisure. They sell everything from jungle fruits and *farinha* (manioc, or cassava-root, flour) to medicinal herbs and aromatic oils. The market extends along the promenade where there are further stalls and kiosks selling craft goods from the region, including cotton clothing, tribal jewelry, and wooden carvings. It is also a good place to try local

delicacies, such as *tacaca*, a delectable soup made with manioc and dried shrimp, inspired by indigenous Brazilian cooking.

🏛 Forte do Castelo

Praça Frei Caetano Brandão 117, Cidade Velha. **Tel** (091) 3219 1134.
⏱ 10am–6pm Tue–Fri, 10am–8pm Sat & Sun. 🎟
Sitting at the confluence of Rio Guamá and the Baía do Guajará, this fort was first built of wood and mud plaster by the Portuguese

colonists in 1616. It was rebuilt six years later, and again in 1878. It now houses the Museu do Encontro, a small historical museum presenting the city's history and the early conquest of the Amazon.

🏛 Palácio Antônio Lemos

Praça Dom Pedro II. **Tel** (091) 3219 8217. ⏱ 9am–6pm Tue–Fri, 9am–1pm Sat & Sun. 🎟
This splendid palace housed the municipal authorities between 1868 and 1883. It still has offices for the Prefeitura, but much of the building is open to the public, with some furnished period rooms upstairs. The palace is home to the Museu de Arte de Belém, which houses a fine collection of Brazilian 20th-century paintings.

🏛 Teatro da Paz

Praça da República. **Tel** (091) 3224 7355. ⏱ 9:30–11am, 12:30–2:30pm & 4–5pm Tue–Fri; 9:30–12:30pm Sat. 🎟
This grand Neo-Classical opera house was built in 1878, along the very Parisian

---

TRANSAMAZÔNICA

Until the middle of the 20th century, river boat or mule trail were the only viable forms of travel across Amazônia and Northern Brazil. With the ambitious construction of Highway BR-230, during the late 1960s, the Atlantic port of Belém was effectively connected all the way to the Peruvian border. Known as the Transamazônica, this road is in a poor state of repair along much of its length. In 2005, a river bridge to Peru was opened in the remote jungle state of Acre, completing the Brazilian end of the Transamazônica.

Unpaved section of the Transamazônica

---

mosaics and supporting a breathtaking red cedar roof. It was completed in 1909, to house the miraculous Virgin image of Nossa Senhora de Nazaré, which is traced back to early Christian Nazareth.

Linked to the icon, the Círio de Nazaré, or the Festival of Candles, attracts over a million visitors to the city every October. In one of the main symbolic acts, hundreds of local people work together, dragging an enormous rope from the mud and water of the port, through the streets of the city to the Basílica de Nossa Senhora de Nazaré. For those who participate, their sins are purged, and their

Elegant interior of the Neo-Classical Teatro da Paz

Avenida Presidente Vargas. Inspired by La Scala in Milan, the furnishings are still largely original. Legendary Russian ballerina Anna Pavlova was one of the great artists to have performed here.

🔒 Basílica de Nossa Senhora de Nazaré
Praça Justo Chermont. *Tel (091) 3241 8894.* ⬜ 6:30–11:30am & 3–6pm daily. **Museu Círio de Nazaré** ⬜ 9am–6pm Tue–Fri.
The basilica's spectacular interior makes it one of the most stunning churches in Brazil. Partially modeled on St. Peter's in Rome, it stands on 16 major arches, each ornately covered in stone

VISITORS' CHECKLIST

Pará. 🏘 1,387,000. ✈ 7 miles (12 km) N of town. 🚍 Av G. José Malcher, (091) 3266 2625. 🚢 from Macapá, Manaus & Santarém. 🚕 Radiotaxi Aguia, (091) 3276 4000. 🛈 Belémtur, Av G. José Malcher, (091) 3282 4852; Paratur, Praça Waldemar Henrique, (091) 3212 0669. 🎉 Círio de Nazaré (Oct, 2nd Sun).

hopes and wishes for the year are granted. The basilica also houses the **Museu Círio de Nazaré**, devoted to the cult of the Círio which exhibits over 500 pieces relating to the religious festival.

Nave of the Basílica de Nossa Senhora de Nazaré

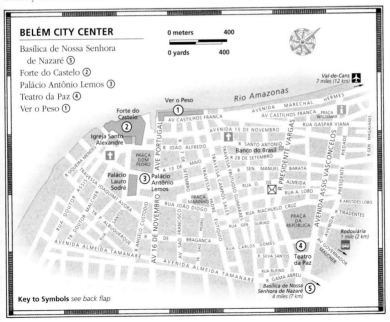

BELÉM CITY CENTER

Basílica de Nossa Senhora de Nazaré ⑤
Forte do Castelo ②
Palácio Antônio Lemos ③
Teatro da Paz ④
Ver o Peso ①

Key to Symbols see back flap

Salinópolis ❷

Pará. 🏠 40,000. ✈ Belém Val de Caes Airport, 110 miles (180 km) SE of town, then bus. 🚌 Av Miguel Santa Brigada. 🛈 Paratur (091) 3423 2203.

The town of Salinópolis, locally known as Salinas, is just about as far east as the Amazon river delta reaches. Very much the traditional summer resort for city folk, Salinas has plenty of beaches fringed with beach huts and second homes. The busiest beach is the central **Praia do Macarico**, with several bars and restaurants. More pleasant still, there is the **Praia do Atalaia**, not far from the center of town, backed by sand dunes and well provided with *barracas* (tents) for food and drink. A continuation of this beach, the **Praia do Farol Velho**, is thickly lined with beach houses, and is most popular during July, when it can often get rather crowded.

Environs
About 19 miles (30 km) west of Salinópolis is the relatively sleepy fishing settlement and beach resort of **Algodoal**. The resort lies on the western edge of Ilha de Maiandeua, just a 40-minute boat ride

A secluded beach near Souré, Ilha de Marajó

away. There are no motorized vehicles in the village or on Maiandeua island, adding to the remote and idyllic feel. Electricity only reached the island in 2004, so facilities are improving.

The main beach for the village is the **Praia da Vila do Algodoal**. More popular, however, is the palm-fringed **Praia da Princesa do Farol**, a superb stretch of sand secluded from the main beach by a short walk at low tide or a canoe ride. There are trails on the island, offering the opportunity to spot wildlife and explore the area around an inland freshwater lake. It is advisable to carry adequate cash to visit the island, since there are no banks or ATMs.

Ilha de Marajó ❸

Pará. 🏠 250,000. 🚢 from Belém to Porto Camará. 🛈 Trapiche Municipal, Rua 1, Souré, (091) 3741 2223.

The world's largest river island, Ilha de Marajó covers over 18,533 sq miles (48,000 sq km), mostly dedicated to cattle ranches, or *fazendas*. The island is famous for having the biggest and finest buffaloes in Brazil. Their meat, leather, and dairy products are widely available to purchase. Ilha de Marajó was also the ancient home to the indigenous culture of the Marajoaras, notable for their exquisite ceramic burial and ceremonial urns.

The unofficial capital of the island is **Souré**, which has the most shops, restaurants, and other facilities, but the ferry port is **Porto Camará**, some 16 miles (27 km) south of Souré. Located between Porto Camará and Souré, the best and most secluded beach is at the small town of **Joanes**, some 3 miles (5 km) off the main road. There are good beaches at the other town on the island, **Salvaterra**, where there are also several hotels and *pousadas*. The Praia Grande beach in Salvaterra is well served with beach chairs, snack *barracas*, and refreshment stands.

During the peak rainy season (February–May) many of the roads are inaccessible for long periods; this includes the road to Joanes and Salvaterra at times. Boats for moving around the island can be found easily at Souré, Salvaterra, and Porto Camará.

POTTERY ON ILHA DE MARAJÓ

Marajó pottery displayed in Museu Goeldi, Belém

In 1948, anthropologists Betty Meggers and Clifford Evans discovered a large, painted anthropomorphic vessel on Ilha de Marajó. The ancient inhabitants, the Marajoaras, left behind not only burial mounds, some almost 3,000 years old, but also some very fine ceramics, leading archaeologists to believe that between the 5th and 13th centuries, there were sophisticated societies living along the banks of the Amazon river.

Excavations reveal that the dead were buried in line according to their social ranking, with larger urns indicating higher status. Most of these ceramics, representing abstract feminine figures, demonstrate the matrilineal nature of this early Amazonian society. As well as funerary ceramics, there were also bowls, vases, spindle whorls, and stools. The larger urns generally took three main forms: humanoid, cyclindrical, and round; and around 15 different finishing techniques are known to have been utilized. Some excellent examples of the urns can be found in the Museu Goeldi in Belém.

Macapá ❹

Amapá. 🏙 325,000. ✈ 🚢 from
Belém. 🚌 Bairro São Lázaro, (096)
3251 2009. 🛈 Detur, Rua Vinga
Uchôa 29, Centro, (096) 3251 1275.
🎭 O Marabaixo (May).

Split in two by the equator,
Macapá is hot and humid all
year round. The city occupies
its position as Amapá's capital
sitting on the northern bank
of the Amazon river, very
close to the giant river's
mouth. It is rather isolated,
with mostly air and boat
transportation, rather than
road connections.

The history of the city is rich
and varied. Several European
countries, including England
and France, attempted to take
it over from the Portuguese,
but the Portuguese established
their hold here by completing
the grand **Fortaleza de São
José de Macapá** in 1782, after
almost 20 years of construction
by black and Indian slave
labor. The bricks used were
brought over from Portugal
as ballast on the ships.

Just to the north of the fort,
there is an attractive pier, the
Trapiche Eliezer Levy, dating
back to the 1930s. The pier
stretches far out into the
water and it is an enjoyable
stroll to the end of it, especially on a breezy evening.
The charming Trapiche
Restaurante *(see p407)*, also
located at the end of the pier,
has a breathtaking view
overlooking the river.

A replica of a typical indigenous home, Museu SACACA, Macapá

These days, Macapá is the
capital of a progressive state.
Following the election of
the environmentalist João
Capiberibe as state governor
in 1995, successive governors
have kept the
spirit of environ-
mentalism alive.
One present
project is to
connect all the
state's protected areas
with wildlife or bio-
diversity corridors. The **Museu
SACACA**, or the Museum of
Sustainable Development,
just a short distance south
of the town center, offers
fascinating guided tours of
replica *ribeirinho* (river-
dweller) houses.

Wooden artifact,
Museu SACACA

The **Mercado dos Produtos
da Floresta** offers a wide
range of local art and craft
goods, ranging from *balata*
(ceramics) dusted with man-
ganese ore to indigenous

crafts, leather goods, carved
wooden statues and all-
natural medicines.

The Marco Zero monument,
a large obelisk-cum-sundial,
4 miles (6 km) southwest of
the city center,
marks the
equatorial line
on Avenida
Equatorial. A sports stadium
and *sambódromo*
also form part of
the same complex.

🏰 **Fortaleza de
São José de Macapá**
Av Candido Mendes. **Tel** (096) 3212
5118. ⏰ 9am–6pm Tue–Sun. 📷

🛍 **Mercado dos
Produtos da Floresta**
Rua São José 1500. **Tel** (096) 9961
0913. ⏰ 8am–6pm Mon–Fri.

🏛 **Museu SACACA**
Av Feliciano Coelho, 1509.
Tel (096) 3212 5361. ⏰ 9am–6pm
Tue–Sun. 📷

Buildings inside the Fortaleza de São José de Macapá

Wooden house on stilts, with a horse standing in the water-logged paddock in front, Ilha de Marajó, Pará ▷

Santarém ❺

Pará. 🏙 200,000. 🛬 🛩 ⛴ from Docas do Pará (W of center). ℹ Amazon Planet, (093) 3527 1172; Santarém Tour, (093) 3522 4847.

Amazônia's fourth largest city, Santarém sits at the mouth of the Rio Tapajós, surrounded by brilliant white sandy beaches. Modern Santarém began in 1661 as a Jesuit mission, following 30 years of military action in the area to subdue the fierce, indigenous Tapuiçu Indians.

In 1867, there was an influx of ex-Confederates from the USA, a handful of whose descendants still survive. However, it was the rubber boom and Santarem's strategic position as a pit stop en route along the Amazon river that turned the town into a buzzing commercial center.

In the late 19th century, Henry Wickam, an English settler in Santarém, smuggled rubber tree seeds out to establish rubber plantations in Asia. Within 40 years, and just in time for World War I, Asian rubber plantations majorly outproduced the Brazilian Amazon.

The local economy is today based on rubber, logging, soya, brazil nuts, and tourism. Colorful boats

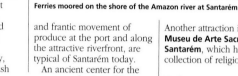

Ferries moored on the shore of the Amazon river at Santarém

Burial urn, Museu de Santarém

and frantic movement of produce at the port and along the attractive riverfront, are typical of Santarém today.

An ancient center for the production of fine ceramics, the town showcases its distinct Santarém Phase Pottery in a striking museum, the **Museu de Santarém**. The exhibits prominently feature burial urns, reputed to be among the oldest in South America. Also known as Centro Cultural João Foua, the museum has a striking interior, painted by João Foua, an artist from Pará.

Another attraction is the **Museu de Arte Sacra de Santarém**, which has a decent collection of religious art.

Environs

Located 20 miles (33 km) west of Santarém, the river-beach town of **Alter do Chão** has fine sandy beaches set against a calm bay on the Rio Tapajós. Canoes ferry visitors across the bay to climb the low lying hills offering breath-taking views. Closer to the main beach, another prom-inently shaped hill resembles a church altar. **Fordlândia**, 62 miles (100 km) south of town, was Henry Ford's first rubber

Belterra, a rubber plantation set up by John Ford in the 1930s

THE RUBBER STORY IN BRAZIL

In the mid-1700s, Charles-Marie de la Condamine was presented with latex syringes from the *Hevea brasiliensis* tree by the Omagua people living in Amazônia. He returned to France with samples, and rubber became known to the world. Soon it was being used for everything from insulation to tyres, and *Hevea brasiliensis* had become the oil of its day. In Amazônia, where the rubber tree grew in abundance, foreign banks and companies began to set up plantations. The rubber boom ushered Manaus and Belém into the Belle Époque era, with electric lights, lavish opera houses, and mansions for the rubber barons. Brazil emerged as the world's largest producer of natural rubber. The euphoria lasted until 1910, when the British colonies in Asia – Malaya, Ceylon, and Singapore – outproduced the Brazilian rubber. Unprepared for competition, Brazil was elbowed out of the rubber market by 1914. The indigenous Brazilians, who had been rounded up and forcibly settled to work on the plantations, returned to relative freedom. Today, much of Brazil's rubber is imported from Asia.

For hotels and restaurants in this region see p382 and p407

plantation founded in the 1920s to produce rubber for the Ford Motor Company. In the 1930s, he also established **Belterra**, 12 miles (20 km) south. Both ventures failed, and Ford had to sell them to the Brazilian government in 1945. These towns are accessible by boat from Alter do Chão.

🏛 Museu de Arte Sacra de Santarém
Rua Siqueira Campos 439, Centro. *Tel* (093) 3523 0658. ⬜ 8am–5pm Mon–Fri.

🏛 Museu de Santarém
Rua do Imperador, Praça de Santarém. ⬜ 8am–5pm Mon–Fri. 🖼 donation expected.

Óbidos ❻

Pará. 🏠 47,000. 🚢 from Santarém. 🛈 Rua Guiamarães, (091) 3547 1766.

The real gateway to the deeper Amazon, Óbidos marks the narrowest section of the Amazon river valley. It was created 40 million years ago, when a massive inland lake burst through to the Atlantic at this point, where the Guyanan Shield meets the Brazilian Shield.

The pretty waterfront has some beautifully tiled buildings and the 17th-century Forte Pauxias. There is also a free-admission museum featuring, among other exhibits, luxury items from the rubber-boom days. The museum can be opened on request.

A surfer catching the "Pororoca" tidal wave

POROROCA WAVE

A rage with surfers, the Pororoca is a legendary wave, over 16 ft (5 m) tall, that regularly rolls up the Amazon river. The name Pororoca comes from a local Tupi Indian phrase which means "great destructive noise." Predicted to happen twice daily during full moons between January and April every year, the wave comes in from the Atlantic causing some devastation along the river banks. Following a low tide in the rainy season, the force of the mighty river against the turning tide creates the large and powerful wave that rolls, literally unstoppable, up the Amazon. The surfing record so far is 27 minutes in time and 7 miles (12 km) in distance, while the tidal waves are known to travel over 12 miles (20 km) per hour at times.

Monte Alegre ❼

Pará. 🏠 23,500. 🚢 🛈 Rua do Jaquara 320, (091) 3533 1430.

Located impressively on top of a small hill beside the Amazon river, the town of Monte Alegre was one of the first places on the river to be colonized by Europeans. A band of English and Irish sailors were the earliest to settle here in the 1570s, soon to be expelled by the Portuguese. Over the last 200 years, Monte Alegre has benefitted from ranching and the rubber industry. It is best known for the rock paintings of **Serra Paytuna** and **Serra Ererê**, located 19 miles (30 km) out of town. Estimated to be 10,000 years old, they feature abstract patterns, mostly geometric in form, and some stylized representations of human and animal figures. It is obligatory to hire a guide and a vehicle to visit them. Monte Alegre is also renowned for scenic waterfalls and its wealth of birdlife, for which a local guide and a canoe will be required.

Boats moored along the waterfront in Óbidos, with rows of houses in the background

AMAZONAS, RORAIMA, ACRE & RONDÔNIA

*T*he states of Amazonas, Roraima, Acre, and Rondônia form the heartland of the vast Amazon rainforest region, which is drained by the world's largest network of freshwater lakes and rivers. Despite hundreds of years of European presence and the deforestation ravages of the 20th century, the region continues to be home to some of the world's last indigenous peoples.

Amazonas is larger than the other three states put together. Manaus, its capital, is the most popular place for exploring the jungle. The city sits at the confluence of two of the world's largest rivers – the Solimões (as the Amazon river is called in this section) and the Rio Negro. The vast Rio Madeira lies downstream of Manaus.

Roraima, which literally juts up into Venezuela and Guyana, is best known for its superb plateau-topped mountains, lakes, and substantial rainforest. A host of indigenous groups live here, tenaciously holding on to their land and culture. Roraima also boasts open savannas that have been transformed into cattle ranches. The state capital, Boa Vista, is a well-planned city on the banks of the Rio Branco.

Acre and Rondônia, in the very southwest corner of the Brazilian Amazon, possess some fantastic protected areas of biodiversity, home to many indigenous communities. Acre, the rubber-tapping center of the Amazon, is known for its lush beauty. Environmental destruction has been met with equally forceful conservation movements here. Its capital, Rio Branco, was where activist Chico Mendes fought to defend the forest in the late 1980s.

Rondônia, an area which has developed beyond recognition, still retains some of Brazil's best flora and fauna. It also offers fascinating gems in terms of heritage, such as the Madeira-Mamoré railway museum in the state capital, Porto Velho.

Village huts surrounded by tall palm tree plantations in Acre

◁ Virgin forests and a meandering tributary of the Rio Negro, Amazonas

Exploring Amazonas, Roraima, Acre & Rondônia

This region offers the ultimate rainforest experience. Most people travel here to explore the dense forests, picturesque river islands, and tranquil waterways. The sights include Manaus, the legendary capital city of Amazonas, which offers much architectural and cultural interest. Also located in Amazonas is the Mamirauá Reserve, Brazil's first sustainable development reserve. The secluded and beautiful mountains of Roraima are worth a visit, as is Acre, with its natural beauty, history, and *seringueiro* (rubber-tapping) culture. Porto Velho, the capital of Rondônia, overlooking the Amazon's longest tributary, the mighty Rio Madeira, is a lively place to visit. Riverboat excursions on the Rio Madeira are a good way to idle away a few hours and spot a few pink dolphins.

Caimans peering above the water of Rio Amazonas near Manaus

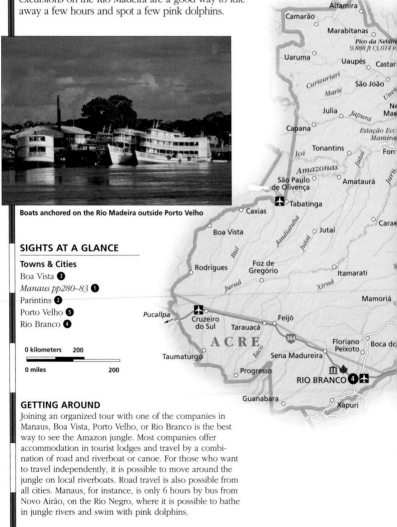

Boats anchored on the Rio Madeira outside Porto Velho

SIGHTS AT A GLANCE

Towns & Cities
Boa Vista ❸
Manaus pp280–83 ❶
Parintins ❷
Porto Velho ❺
Rio Branco ❹

0 kilometers   200

0 miles   200

Map labels:
Altamira
Camarão
Marabitanas
Pico da Neblina 9,888 ft (3,014 m)
Uaruma
Uaupés
Castar
Curicuriari
São João
Marié
Une
Julia
Japurá
Ne
Ma
Capana
Estação Eco Mamira
Içá
Tonantins
Jutaí
Fon
Amazonas
São Paulo de Olivença
Amatauá
Juru
Tabatinga
Caxias
Jandiatuba
Jutaí
Cara
Boa Vista
Inui
Jutaí
Rodrigues
Foz de Gregório
Itamarati
Juruá
Xiruá
Mamoriá
Pucallpa
Cruzeiro do Sul
Tarauacá
Feijó
ACRE
364
Floriano Peixoto
Boca do
Taumaturgo
Iaco
Sena Madureira
RIO BRANCO ❹
Progresso
Guanabara
Xapuri

GETTING AROUND

Joining an organized tour with one of the companies in Manaus, Boa Vista, Porto Velho, or Rio Branco is the best way to see the Amazon jungle. Most companies offer accommodation in tourist lodges and travel by a combination of road and riverboat or canoe. For those who want to travel independently, it is possible to move around the jungle on local riverboats. Road travel is also possible from all cities. Manaus, for instance, is only 6 hours by bus from Novo Airão, on the Rio Negro, where it is possible to bathe in jungle rivers and swim with pink dolphins.

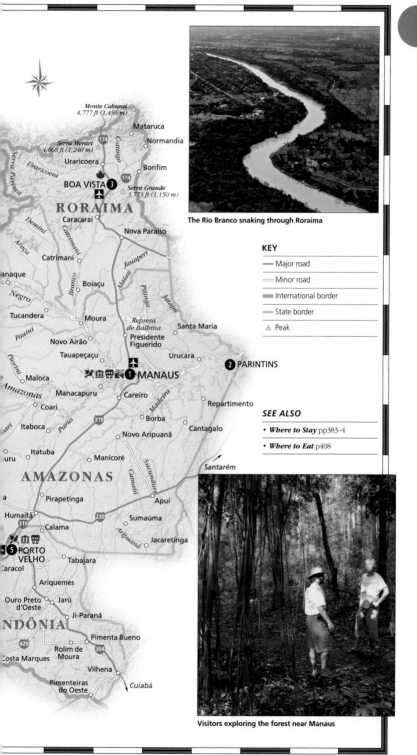

The Rio Branco snaking through Roraima

KEY

— Major road
— Minor road
— International border
— State border
△ Peak

SEE ALSO

• *Where to Stay* pp383–4

• *Where to Eat* p408

Visitors exploring the forest near Manaus

Manaus ❶

Fountain detail, Praça São Sebastião

Manaus is a legendary city, located at the heart of the Amazon forest on the banks of the Rio Negro, close to where this massive river blends with the even larger Amazon river, or Rio Solimões as it is known along this section of its course. With a slightly decaying cityscape, Manaus is a busy city bringing together the hectic pace of a modern port with the hot, laid-back feel of a jungle town. The fancy European buildings of the port and the even more splendid

Teatro Amazonas are the only real signs left of the economic boom in rubber exploitation which catapulted Manaus into wealthy city status between 1888 and 1912.

🏠 Mercado Municipal Adolfo Lisboa

Rua dos Bares 46. ◯ *5am–6pm Mon–Sat, 5am–noon Sun.*
The municipal market of Manaus was built in 1902, very close to the port. It is a joy to behold for the variety of fish on display alone. Tropical fruits and vegetables, many usually unfamiliar to the visitor's eye, are also piled high. Several stalls sell some of the most interesting and least expensive indigenous handicrafts. The market is an amazing building in its own right. Looking up to the elegant ceiling and structure of the building, it is not difficult to see that Gustave Eiffel himself had a hand in its design, which is said to be inspired by the Les Halles market in Paris.

🏛 Alfândega

Rua Marquês de Santa Cruz. ◯ *8am–1pm Mon–Fri.*
Constructed in 1906 at the height of the rubber boom, the Alfândega (Customs

Bananas for sale in the Mercado Municipal Adolfo Lisboa

House), like many of the well-engineered features of Manaus from this period, was entirely pre-fabricated in England. The stone used for the building was brought from Scotland. The tower used to be a lighthouse. Much of this refined building's glory can be seen from the Praça Adalberto Valle opposite.

🏛 Teatro Amazonas

See pp282–3.

🏛 Museu do Homen do Norte

Av 7 de Setembro 1385. **Tel** *(092) 3232 5373.* ◯ *8am–noon & 1–5pm Mon–Fri.* 🈺
An anthropology and ethnology museum, the Museu do Homen do Norte (Museum of Northern Man) displays the way of life of the people of Northern Brazil. It is particularly dedicated to the *caboclos* (copper-colored), or the mixed descendants of the indigenous people and Portuguese who live along the riverbanks. Cultural, social, and economic aspects of life in Northern Brazil are detailed with photographs, documents, artifacts, and everyday objects. The museum also contains an interesting collection of indigenous weapons, including the infamous *furador de olhos* (eye piercer).

🏛 Palácio Rio Negro

Av 7 de Setembro 1570. **Tel** *(092) 3232 4450.* ◯ *10am–5pm Tue–Fri, 2–6pm Sat & Sun.*
A remarkably well-preserved rubber boom mansion, the almost garish Palácio Rio Negro was built in 1913. It was originally home to an eccentric German rubber baron, Waldemar Scholz. In later years, it housed the local government. These days, much of it has been opened to the public as a cultural center. The palace hosts art exhibitions and screens films. The annex houses a couple of small museums – the Museu Numismatica (Numismatic Museum) and the Museu da Imagem e do Som (Museum of Images and Sound).

The Rio Negro with the Porto Flutante (Floating Port) and the Catedral Metropolitana in the background

🏛 Museu do Índio

Rua Duque de Caxias 356.
🕐 8am–noon & 2–5pm Mon–Fri,
8am–noon Sat. 📷

An excellent ethnographic museum, the Museu do Índio was established by Salesian nuns and is based on their work as missionaries in the Rio Negro area. There are many feather work exhibits and some weapons and tools,

as well as household and sacred objects on display, along with musical instruments and artworks. The Tukano people (see p262) are particularly well represented here. Explanations of the displays are in Portuguese, English, and German. The museum has a good craft shop, with a wide range of handicrafts on sale.

Traditional indigenous longhouse at the Museu do Índio

VISITORS' CHECKLIST

Amazonas. 🏠 1,593,000. ✈
✕ 🚌 Rua Recife 2784, (092)
642 5805. 🚢 Porto Flutuante.
🎭 Festival Folclórico de
Amazonas (Jun); Manaus Opera
Festival (Apr/May).
www.manausonline.com

🐾 Zoológico do CIGS

Estrada Ponta Negra 750. **Tel** (092)
3625 2282. 🕐 9am–4:30pm Tue–
Sun. 📷

One of the few places around Manaus where you might get to see a jaguar at close quarters, the Zoológico do CIGS is a great place to take children. Located 8 miles (13 km) from Manaus toward Ponta Negra in the army jungle training center, this small zoo is home to over 300 animals including many caimans, monkeys, exotic birds, and an unforgettable large pit full of anacondas.

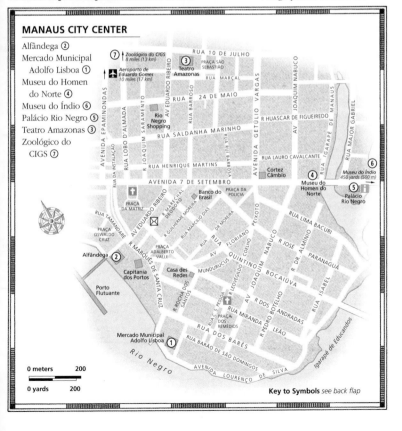

MANAUS CITY CENTER

Alfândega ②
Mercado Municipal
  Adolfo Lisboa ①
Museu do Homen
  do Norte ④
Museu do Índio ⑥
Palácio Rio Negro ⑤
Teatro Amazonas ③
Zoológico do
  CIGS ⑦

0 meters 200
0 yards 200

Key to Symbols see back flap

Manaus: Teatro Amazonas

Built at the end of the 19th century during the Belle Époque, when fortunes were made from the extraction of rubber in Manaus, the Teatro Amazonas remains one of the jewels of the Amazon region. This grand state-of-the-art, Renaissance-style opera house was designed by Gabinete Português de Engenharia de Lisbon (Portuguese Engineering Academy of Lisbon). Inaugurated on December 31, 1896, it was two more years before construction was completed and the prominent landmark with a glistening dome appeared above the port.

The Teatro façade, restored to pink at the close of the 20th century

The theater's roof, made of red tiles, keeps out the tropical rain.

★ The Painted Curtain

The main stage curtain was created by Manaus-based artist Crispim do Amaral (1845–1911) to depict the Meeting of the Waters (see p285), and also a local river goddess, Iara. The curtain is pulled up into the specially designed cupola at the start of each performance.

The Wooden Floor

The opera house floor, laid with thousands of pieces of Amazon timber, is a masterpiece of craftsmanship. The light and dark patterns represent the meeting of the Negro and Amazon rivers (see p285).

Events
Regular musical events and operas include those of the relatively new Companhia de Dança and the resident Orquestra Filarmônica do Amazonas.

STAR FEATURES

- ★ The Painted Curtain
- ★ The Cupola
- ★ The Four Painted Pillars

★ The Cupola
The impressive cupola was created using 36,000 colorful ceramic tiles, imported from Alsace on the Franco-German border.

VISITORS' CHECKLIST

Praça São Sebastião, Manaus.
Tel (092) 3622 2420. ⬜ 9am–4pm Mon–Sat. 🚫 🎭 **Shows**
Opera, theater & dance performances through the year.

The columns are made from Italian Carrara marble.

★ The Four Painted Pillars
A key feature of the main auditorium is a ceiling rosette whose four pillars were painted in Paris and reassembled in Manaus. The pillars create the impression of gazing up from underneath the Eiffel Tower.

Lobby
The lobby is furnished with Murano chandeliers made with Venetian glass and French bronze work.

Outside balconies are built in finely cut Portuguese stone.

Main Auditorium
Designed in the shape of a harp, the theater can seat almost 700 people. Like the main columns and the three curving balconies, the seats are made from English cast iron. The polished wooden armchairs are made from local jacaranda. The lower columns bear the names of many classical composers.

Amazon Excursions from Manaus

Manaus is well located as a base from which to explore the rainforest. The main destinations include the Rio Negro, Lago Mamori, Rio Juma, Lago Manaquiri, Presidente Figueiredo, and, farther west, the splendid reserve at Mamirauá. Operators run tours, offering everything from basic accommodation to four- or five-star luxury lodges and boats. It is good to have at least half a day out of Manaus for a reasonable chance at seeing a wide range of tropical birds and mammal wildlife such as agoutis, monkeys, deer, or wild boar.

The Rio Urubuí and Cachoeira Iracema near Presidente Figueiredo

Presidente Figueiredo

62 miles (100 km) N of Manaus. 🚌
🛈 *Centro Turístico, (092) 3321 1158.*
Presidente Figueiredo is a small town linked to Manaus by a relatively good road. There are more than 100 waterfalls dotted around the town, as well as some caves. Tours in and around the area can be booked from Manaus or directly with local guides through the tourist information office located at the bus stop. One of the best waterfalls is the **Pedra Furada**, where the waterfall gushes out of a hole in the rocks. The waterfalls **Cachoeira Iracema**, **Pedra da Lua Branca**, and **Natal** are on the **Rio Urubuí** and only accessible by boat. The **Caverna Araras** is on a trail bordering the Rio Urubuí. Another attractive cave is **Caverna Maruaga**, which has a a shallow river running over its floor. Permission for the caves has to be obtained from the tourist information office in Manaus.

🎋 Rio Negro & Ilha de Anavilhanas

60 miles (90 km) NW of Manaus.
🚌 🛈 *Amazonastur, Rua H. de Figueiredo, Manaus, (092) 3233 1095.*
One of the least visited regions of South America, the Rio Negro area possesses distinctive flora created by its acidic waters and soil type. There is a lower density of wildlife here than any other area along the Rio Negro. There are few towns and even fewer tourist facilities along the river, which stretches right up to the Colombian and Venezuelan borders.

Ilha de Anavilhanas is a biological reserve and the largest group of freshwater islands in the world. Tours to visit these islands are offered from Manaus. There are over

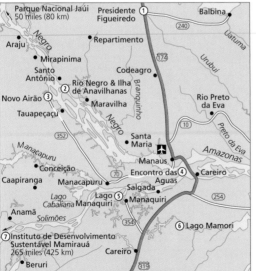

SIGHTS AT A GLANCE

0 kilometers 60

0 miles 60

KEY

✈ International airport

▬ Main road

= Other road

Aerial view of the Rio Negro winding through the Amazon

250 uninhabited islands stretching for more than 187 miles (300 km). Depending on the season and time of day, it is possible to see caimans, sloths, snakes, frogs, and a wide range of bird species. Sprawled across an area of 1,350 sq miles (3,500 sq km) of protected rainforest on the left bank of the Rio Negro, the Estação Ecológica de Anavilhanas (Ecological Station of Anavilhanas) is part of the Anavilhanas islands. Created in 1998 and named after the Archipelago dos Anavilhanas, it boasts several species in great danger of extinction, including jaguars and night monkeys.

Toco toucan in Amazonas

A day-and-a-half's journey from Ilha de Anavilhanas, Barcelos, the only town of any size along the river, is an interesting place to start a jungle expedition for intrepid adventurers. Another two days upriver, the town of São Gabriel Da Cachoeira is a beautiful place deep in the Amazon with stunning jungle scenery and wildlife.

Visitor feeding fish to pink dolphins at El Delfin in Novo Airão

Novo Airão

71 miles (115 km) W of Manaus.
🚌 from Manaus. 🚤 from Manaus.
Ibama Rua Ministro João Gonçalves de Souza s/n, Manaus. *Tel (092) 3613 3080*. **Parque Nacional Jaú** *Tel (092) 3613 3277*.

The small town of Novo Airão is located on the western side of the Rio Negro, opposite the Archipelago dos Anavilhanas. Pleasant, yet laid-back, with only a handful of attractions, the town draws tourists mainly for the pink dolphins that come to a platform behind the **El Delfin** restaurant at Novo Airão's small port. The restaurant owner has been feeding dolphins from the restaurant for several years. They now appear to be friendly and swim with visitors who feed them. Along with its standard fare, the restaurant also sells raw fish to offer the dolphins from the wooden platform.

The area neighboring Novo Airão is home to a number of interesting sights, such as **Airão Velho**, the overgrown ruins of the old town center, with prehistoric spiral and figure-like petroglyphs. The beautiful and peaceful **Igarapé do Mato Grosso**, a forested section of a tributary river nearby, makes a great place for a walk or a swim in fresh water. The **Parque Nacional Jaú** is a two-day trip from Novo Airão, and is a wonderful opportunity to visit virgin Amazon rainforest. A permit is required from the **Ibama** office in Manaus.

🏞 Encontro das Aguas

🚤 from Manaus.

One of the main tours offered from Manaus, the Encontro das Aguas (Meeting of the Waters) is where the Rio Solimões joins the Rio Negro. The relatively creamy and alkaline light brown or "white" water of the Solimões (Amazon) river takes several miles to absorb the dark, acid water coming in from the Rio Negro. The Solimões is light because it starts mainly in the Andes and brings plenty of silt with it. The Rio Negro wells up primarily in the swamplands and smaller hills of the northeastern Amazon and contains much more decomposed plant life than it does soil or silt.

Small boats go out from Manaus allowing tourists to take photographs and see the clear line between light brown and black running down the middle of the river. It is a two-hour return trip from Manaus, and the best time to visit is between 7 and 10am.

Meeting of the Rio Solimões and Rio Negro at Encontro das Aguas

Limpid blue sky mirrored in the clear waters of Lago Mamori

🏞 Lago Manaquiri

40 miles (64 km) SW of Manaus.
www.amazonastur-en.am.gov.br

A five-hour boat ride from Manaus, the backwater lake of Manaquiri is best entered first via the Rio Solimões, then upstream to a tributary that leads to the lake. Its waters rise and fall with the seasons. Relatively isolated, the Lago Manaquiri is usually a good spot for seeing water birds, including the great egret (*Casmerodius albus*) and fish eagles. It is not unusual to see caimans and large Amazonian alligators basking on the sandy shore.

The lake provides sustenance to the small fishing town of Manaquiri. Local economy depends more on fishing than on tourism. In 1995, however, both were hit by the worst drought in over 40 years, when the lagoons evaporated, and thousands of dead fish lay on the bed of the dried-up lake. The changed climatic conditions continue to deplete fish in the

area. Nonetheless, fishing remains the main activity, and there are many tour operators based in Manaus, offering budget fishing packages.

It is always best to go through a travel company registered with the Brazilian Tourism Bureau (Embratur) (*see p425*). Some of the tour agencies provide typical Amazon riverboats, which may come fully equipped with kitchen, dining area, canopied sundeck, bathroom, and shower. Fishing is best in the dry season, which usually lasts from August to December or January.

🏞 Lago Mamori

60 miles (96 km) SE of Manaus.
Gero's Tours Rua 10 de Julho 632, Manaus. **Tel** (092) 3232 9416.
Nature Safaris Rua Flavio Espiritu 1, Manaus. **Tel** (092) 3656 6033.

Easily accessible by road and boat from Manaus, the elongated and breathtaking Lago Mamori is located in a lush rainforest setting. Much of it is surrounded

by narrow creeks, hidden among forests full of sloths, monkeys, and colorful, noisy tropical birds. The river and lake offer the opportunity to see both pink and gray river dolphins, as well as go piranha fishing. Nearby, the Lago Arara is great for fishing, and home to a pink dolphin-feeding ground. The local people, known as *caboclos*, have been here for generations and live in scattered riverside communities, occasionally coming together for celebrations. They earn their living by making *farinha* (manioc flour), rearing cattle, and fishing. Visits to the *caboclo* homes can be organized by **Gero's Tours**. Run independently by English-speaking Gero Mesquita, it can book hotels, arrange transport, and meticulously plan tours.

Farther upstream and deeper into the forest from here, the Rio Juma region offers better access to wild life, but requires expedition-type preparation and several days.

Nature Safaris, a tour company based in Manaus, can arrange expeditions in Amazônia, offering short package tours, as well as longer safaris. It is possible to stay either in a floating lodge, or one of the many jungle lodges along the Rio Juma. Most of them offer jungle hikes, piranha fishing, and caiman spotting at night.

Caimans luxuriating on the sandy riverbank of Manaquiri, with a great egret in the foreground

Cormorants and great egrets in the Mamirauá Reserve

✗ Instituto de Desenvolvimento Sustentável Mamirauá

280 miles (450 km) W of Manaus.
www.mamiraua.org.br **Programa de Ecoturismo** *Tel (092) 3343 4160.*

Located at the confluence of two rivers, the Rio Solimões and Rio Japurá, the Mamirauá Sustainable Development Reserve covers an area of 3.65 million acres (1.25 million ha). Since 1990, when it was declared an ecological station, the Mamirauá Reserve has been one of Brazil's most prized ecotourism spots.

Splendid and luxuriant, its *várzea* (seasonally flooded) vegetation offers plenty of opportunity for spotting abundant wildlife, including endemic species such as the white uakari monkey and black-headed squirrel monkey. The annual flood transforms the life of the whole region. During the high water season, fish invade the flooded forest and disperse seeds as they move about. More than 300 species of fish have already been catalogued in the reserve. Mamirauá is also home to pink river dolphin, great egret, and the rare scarlet macaw. The Neotropic cormorant, whose diet consists mainly of fish, can be spotted swimming and feeding in large, noisy flocks.

In the dry season, which lasts from September to December, one can walk on trails, or paddle almost silently through them on canoes. The preserve's ecotourism program features a range of activities, which also including guided nature expeditions in the lakes and trails in the forest.

The preserve also offers comfortable and ecologically sound accommodation at the Uakari Floating Lodge *(see p383)* close to forest trails, pretty jungle lakes, and *caboclo* communities. Book through a Manaus tour company, or directly with the **Programa de Ecoturismo** in Tefé, 16 miles (25 km) south.

Parintins ❷

Amazonas. 🕋 *105,000.* 🛥 *from Manaus.* 🚼 *(092) 3533 4400.*
🎭 *Festa do Boi Bumbá (Jun); Festa das Pastorinhas (Dec–Jan).*

A large jungle town, Parintins was originally the refuge of a community of indigenous riverine people, known as *caboclos,* who were escaping Portuguese slave traders. Today, Parintins is best known for its popular Festa do Boi Bumbá. The festival is celebrated in June, when the town gets so packed that visitors often stay on boats.

Though there is little else to see, besides the well-preserved colonial architecture, Parintins is known for its rich indigenous culture. The local handicrafts make unique souvenirs. The flea markets sell everything from masks, trinkets, lace, bead-work, and mahogany carvings. During the dry season, boat trips can be taken to nearby lakes and river beaches.

FESTA DO BOI BUMBÁ

The vibrant festival, Festa do Boi Bumbá, is centered around a ritualistic dance recounting the death and rebirth of a legendary *boi* (ox). Originating on the 18th-century Northeast plantations, the festival arrived in Parintins almost 100 years ago with the Cid brothers from Maranhão. They brought with them the Bumba-meu-boi *(see p43)* musical influence, steeped in the vibrant rhythms of the Northeast. The last few decades saw the festival gaining in prominence. Every June, at least 35,000 people crowd into Bumbódromo, a purpose-built stadium in the town center, to join in the revelries. The fantastic procession incorporates dazzlingly dressed participants, including mythological beasts. The rivalry between the two competing camps, the red Garantido and the blue Caprichoso groups, is expressed in traditional songs. Over the years, this competitive spirit, which goes right down to who wears the most outlandish costume, has brought forth some radical and electrifying spectacles.

Garantido in bright red headgear, gearing up for the contest

Tranquil waters of the Rio Branco, flowing past Roraima's capital Boa Vista

Boa Vista ❸

Roraima. 🏘 237,000. ✈ ⊠ 🚍
🛈 Centro Turismo, (095) 3623 2365.
www.roraima-brasil.com.br

Created in 1991, Roraima
is one of Brazil's newest
states, and Boa Vista is its
capital city. While the savannas surrounding it are an
important cattle ranching
territory, the gold rush of
the 1980s continues to drive
development in the region.

The Praça Civica forms the
heart of the town's arch-
shaped street layout. The
modern Palácio Municipal is
here beside the Monumento
ao Garimpeiro, a local monument honoring the gold
miners who have brought
significant wealth to this state.

There are good swimming
beaches on the Rio Branco,
only 15 minutes by bus from
Boa Vista. The sandy beaches
right in the town center,
opposite the Orla Taumanam,
offer excellent swimming
when the river is low.

Environs

Boa Vista is blessed with lush
tropical rainforest, endless
stretches of savanna plains,
and pretty river beaches,
which make the surrounding
region well worth exploring.
Though ecotourism is still in
its initial stages, organized
tours are fairly developed.

A significant staging port
en route south to Manaus
or north to Guyana and
Venezuela, Boa Vista is easily
connected by bus to the
Venezuelan town of **Santa
Elena de Uairén**, located 147
miles (237 km) north. The
route from Boa Vista to

Santa Elena is dotted with
some interesting sights. The
ecological island preserve of
Ilha do Maracá, 62 miles
(100 km) north of Boa Vista,
is known for its species
preservation and biodiversity.
Fringed with groves of
cashew trees, the enchanting
Lago Caracaranã is located
112 miles (180 km) north.

Santa Elena de Uairén
offers the best access to the
**Parque Nacional de Monte
Roraima**. The park is ideal
for trekking through a variety
of eco-niches with changing
vegetation to climb **Monte
Roraima**, a point where Brazil,
Guyana, and Venezuela meet.
At 8,970 ft (2,734 m) above
sea level, good camping
equipment and preparation
is essential.

Several Boa Vista-based
companies offer excellent
week-long packages.
International visitors require
a Venezuelan tourist card,
which can be obtained at
the Venezuelan consulate
in Boa Vista.

Rio Branco ❹

Acre. 🏘 255,000. ✈ ⊠ 🚍
🛈 Av Getúlio Vargas 91,
(068) 3222 7661.

Another relatively new state,
Acre was annexed from
Bolivia in the early 20th
century by a pioneering army
of Brazilian rubber-tappers.
It was founded in 1904, under
the name of a rubber com-
pany, Seringal Empressa, by
Newtel Maia from Ceará.

The newly created Parque
de Maternidade has magically
transformed a small town
water canal into a long,
green city walk. In the town
center, just a couple of blocks
north from the Rio Acre,
which cuts the town in half,
stands the **Palácio Rio Branco**.
Though newly restored, the
building maintains its original
Neo-Classical façade with four
columns at the entrance.
It was built in the 1930s as
headquarters for the state
government, and retains a
good collection of period

An aerial view of Rio Branco city with Rio Acre

furniture from the 1940s and 50s. A main feature of the palace, the largest painting in Brazil, depicts a scene in homage to the revolutionary heroes who liberated Acre from Bolivia. The palace also contains several large rooms dedicated to the prehistory and history of the region. The main focus is on the 20th-century history of Acre, and there is a superb room dedicated to indigenous culture, displaying some stupendous feather headdresses. Artifacts relating to local history and tribes are also displayed in the palace.

A few blocks north, the **Museu da Borrachá** (Rubber Museum) focuses on the fascinating local ethnic cultures, rubber-tappers, and *ayahuasca* churches, known for their ceremonial use of hallucinogenic herbs.

Rio Branco is transforming the city's south bank of the Rio Acre, which was the focal point during the rubber boom, and until the new north-based commercial center emerged in mid-20th century. The municipality is restoring many of the buildings, which once served the river port as hotels, bars, a splendid movie theater, as well as merchants' stores. A new promenade, La Gameleira, makes a perfect riverside walk.

The **Parque Ambiental Chico Mendes** (Chico Mendes Environmental Park) is located in the former rubber plantation at Itucumã near Vila Acre, 6 miles (10 km) south of Rio Branco. It contains virgin forest areas, some replica *malocas* (indigenous longhouses) and rubber-tapper dwellings, as well as a zoo and the Chico Mendes memorial.

🏛 **Museu da Borrachá**
Av Ceará 1441. *Tel (068) 3223 1202.* ◯ *8am–6pm Mon–Fri.*

🏛 **Palácio Rio Branco**
Praça E. Gaspar Dutra s/n. *Tel (068) 3223 9241.* ◯ *8am–6pm Tue–Fri, 4–9pm Sat & Sun.* 🎥 ♿ ⌀

🔀 **Parque Ambiental Chico Mendes**
Rodovia AC-40 Km 7, Vila Acre. ◯ *7am–noon & 2–5pm Tue–Sun.*

Visitors walking through the ruined Forte Principe da Beira, Guajará-Mirim

Porto Velho ❺

Rondônia. 🏘 *381,000.* ✕ 🚌 📧 🛈 *Departamento do Turismo, (069) 3221 1499.*

A very fast growing jungle city, Rondônia's capital, Porto Velho, has grown out of a few streets beside the giant Rio Madeira in the last 100 years. River trips to the nearby beach of Santo Antônio are popular for freshly-cooked fish at a waterside restaurant.

The star attraction, however, is the **Madeira-Mamoré Museu Ferroviário**, where several steam locomotives, some under cover, still defiantly symbolize a rusting industrial vision in the middle of the Amazon jungle. In the main museum shed, there are interesting exhibits from the turn of the 19th century, when the railway was being built. Unfortunately, its

inauguration in 1912 was just in time to witness the collapse of Brazil's rubber industry.

Environs
Guajará-Mirim on the Bolivian border is accessible by road. From here, it is possible to visit the lonely jungle fort, the **Forte Príncipe da Beira**, built by the Portuguese in 1773.

The **Reserva Biologica do Guaporé** near Costa Marques town, which is located 12 miles (20 km) east of Príncipe de Beira town, is known for its diverse bird species. The Ibama in Porto Velho can arrange trips.

🏛 **Madeira-Mamoré Museu Ferroviário**
Praça Madeira-Mamoré. ◯ *8am–noon & 2–6pm Mon–Fri.* 🎥 ♿

🔀 **Reserva Biologica do Guaporé**
Av Cabixi com Limoeiro 1942. *Tel (069) 651 2315.*

Environmentalist Chico Mendes

CHICO MENDES (1944–88)

A rubber-tapper union leader and environmental activist, Chico Mendes helped establish the National Council of Rubber Tappers. His design for extractive rainforest preserves won him recognition by the UN in 1987, with a Global 500 award. He received another award from the Better World Society, before his assassination by hired men employed by the ranchers on December 22, 1988. His untimely death brought international attention, for the first time, both to the plight of the rainforest and the positive solution offered simply by harvesting the rainforest's fruits and sustainable products. Many leading Brazilian human rights activists, environmental campaigners and church organizations came together to establish the Chico Mendes Committee, which successfully dedicated itself to seeing his murderers brought to justice.

CENTRAL WEST
BRAZIL

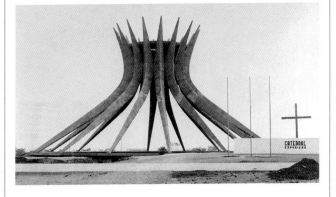

Introducing Central West Brazil

The Federal District of Brasília and four other states make up Brazil's Central West. Goiás and Tocantins in the east of the region and Mato Grosso and Mato Grosso do Sul in the west, are areas where the expansive wilderness of craggy *cerrado*-covered plateaus, vast wetlands, rainforests, and deserts are beginning to give way to industrialization. The slow pace of life in colonial mining towns such as Cidade de Goiás and Pirenópolis is being eclipsed by the urban attractions of cities such as Campo Grande and Brasília. However, the Central West remains one of the best regions in which to savor Brazil's traditional rural way of life as well as spot amazing wildlife.

Cristalino Jungle Lodge (see p319) *is situated on the banks of the Rio Cristalino, in Alta Floresta. This region is rich in the Amazon flora and fauna, and has a number of splendid birding trails. Guided hiking tours are also on offer.*

MATO GROSSO & MATO GROSSO DO SUL *(see pp314–23)*

Bonito (see p323), *a small, quiet town located at the southern edge of the Pantanal, offers visitors light adventure activities such as snorkeling in clear-water rivers, visiting caves, and hiking along short wildlife trails.*

◁ Elusive jaguar stretching on isolated lakeshore, Mato Grosso do Sul

Ilha do Bananal (see p311), *one of the world's largest river islands, contains rivers that extend up to 155 miles (250 km), and is home to several indigenous peoples. A bird-watcher's paradise, the island's wild interior is not easily accessible.*

BRASÍLIA, GOIÁS & TOCANTINS
(see pp298–313)

Brasília (see pp302–305), *the country's capital, is renowned for its Modernist buildings, many of which were designed by the noted architect Oscar Niemeyer.*

0 km	150
0 miles	150

Pirenópolis (see pp308–309), *a picturesque former mining town with colonial buildings and impressive restaurants, is a popular weekend retreat. It is also a base for exploring the cerrado and the region's numerous waterfalls.*

Creation of a Capital

President Juscelino Kubitschek and his team of designers, planners, and architects, led by Oscar Niemeyer, envisaged Brasília not only as a city, but also as a monument to the national motto – Order and Progress. In creating this, they turned to European Modernism, following the doctrine of Charles-Edouard Jeanneret (1887–1965), or "Le Corbusier," for their inspiration. The concept stated that modern cities should be zoned functionally with separate areas for housing (in high-rise blocks), recreation, and administration, broken by green belts and roads.

Juscelino Kubitschek *was the president of Brazil between 1956 and 1961. He was responsible for the creation of Brasília as the new, modern capital of the country.*

The Missão Cruls *was commissioned by President Floriano Peixoto in 1892 and led by the Belgian scientist Luiz Cruls. It sought to find a possible site for a new capital in the Brazilian interior to make a more regionally neutral federal capital where resources could be equally divided.*

Superquadra 309, a residential neighborhood, was built in one of the "wings" of Brasília.

The candangos *were workers from the Northeast brought to Brasília in vast numbers to build the city. Homes for their descendants were not included in the grand plan and today Brasília is ringed with the slum cities of their children.*

BRASÍLIA

Located at the heart of the country, Brazil's capital city is today on UNESCO's list of World Heritage Sites, and is famous for its innovative urban planning and daring architecture.

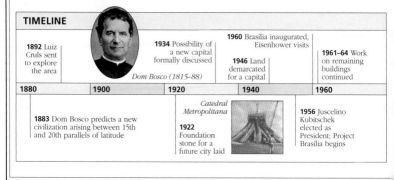

TIMELINE

1892 Luiz Cruls sent to explore the area

1934 Possibility of a new capital formally discussed

1960 Brasília inaugurated, Eisenhower visits

1946 Land demarcated for a capital

1961–64 Work on remaining buildings continued

Dom Bosco (1815–88)

| 1880 | 1900 | 1920 | 1940 | 1960 |

1883 Dom Bosco predicts a new civilization arising between 15th and 20th parallels of latitude

Catedral Metropolitana

1922 Foundation stone for a future city laid

1956 Juscelino Kubitschek elected as President; Project Brasília begins

Lúcio Costa and Roberto Burle Marx, *the urban planner and landscape designer behind Brasília, intended that every element, from the layout of the residential and administrative districts to the symmetry of the buildings, should be in harmony with the city's overall design.*

OSCAR NIEMEYER

Born in Rio de Janeiro in 1907, Niemeyer went on to become one of the most important names in modern architecture. His first job was with Le Corbusier and Lúcio Costa on Rio's Ministry of Education in 1936. After this he went on to design a series of landmark buildings such as the Contemporary Museum of Art in Niterói *(see p89)*. Niemeyer's socialist beliefs led to his exile under the coup of 1964. He returned to Rio in the 1980s, where he continues to work.

Oscar Niemeyer at his office in Rio de Janeiro

Ministerial buildings were built to flank Praça dos Três Poderes and Eixo Monumental *(see pp302–303)*.

Original pen and ink drawings *submitted by Lúcio Costa in 1956 in the competition for a new capital city show Brasília's distinctive shape, which has been variously interpreted as an airplane, a bird in flight, and a bow and arrow.*

Eixo Rodoviária Sul is one of the main roads in the "wings" connecting Brasília from one end to the other.

American President Dwight D. Eisenhower, *on an official visit to Brazil, inaugurated the new capital city of Brasília with great fanfare on February 23, 1960. He also visited Rio de Janeiro and São Paulo.*

The inauguration of Brasília *by President Juscelino Kubitschek and President Eisenhower was attended by thousands of people. The new capital saw the installation of the three powers of the republic – parliament, judiciary, and presidency.*

Flora & Fauna in the Cerrado

The Brazilian *cerrado* (meaning inaccessible in Portuguese) is a biome unique to South America and is the tropical world's largest woodland savanna. The *cerrado* landscape is made up of scattered woods and vast swathes of grassland along riverbanks and in small valleys. One of the richest ecosystems in the world, the *cerrado* is home to almost every species of large mammal found in South America, together with an enormously prolific birdllife. The *cerrado* landscape is home to some 10,000 plant species, of which 4,400 are endemic to the region.

KEY

☐ The cerrado

☐ The Pantanal

Hyacinth macaws *are an endangered species due to overcollection for the caged-bird trade. They are also hunted by the Kayapó people (see p262), who use their bright blue feathers in their headdresses.*

The cerrado, a sprawling 1.2-million sq mile (3-million sq km) mix of forest and savanna, covers 75 percent of Brazil.

Capybaras, *abundant in the* cerrado, *are semi-aquatic, herbivorous rodents. They live in herds and spend most of their time feeding on riverbanks, where they are easily spotted during mornings and evenings.*

The marsh deer *is generally a solitary animal, or lives in herds of less than six. It has webbed feet which help it walk on flooded land.*

The rhea *is a large, flightless bird native to South America. Because rheas will eat almost any crop plant, farmers sometimes kill the birds. This, along with egg gathering and habitat loss, has led to a significant drop in their numbers. The species is listed among the wildlife of "special concern."*

The maned wolf *is the only large canid in the world that does not form packs. The animal, now endangered, was hunted by poachers for its body parts, notably the eyes, which were believed to be good-luck charms.*

Buriti palms often grow over subterranean water. They are an important source of food for many large parrots and primates.

Savanna formations in the *cerrado* are not homogenous. Hilly areas have denser, more varied flora than the grasslands.

CONSERVATION OF THE CERRADO

Central Brazil's ancient *cerrado* forests are rapidly being cleared for soya plantations and cattle ranches. Since the late 1990s, steps have been taken to identify conservation-priority areas and better manage protected areas. Recently, private reserves, established under the Private Natural Heritage Reserve system, have become an important component of biodiversity protection in the *cerrado*. There have also been more intensive faunal and floral surveys of the region.

Tractors paving the way for a new farm in the *cerrado*

Ipê tree *is a large canopy tree. Its vibrant trumpet-shaped flowers bloom in spectacular yellow, pink, and mauve throughout the* cerrado.

FLORA IN THE CERRADO

The *cerrado* is characterized by its vast expanses of grassland, scattered forests, and palm groves. The landscape varies between the "open *cerrado*," predominantly grassland, without trees and shrubs, and "closed *cerrado*," the more forested areas.

FLORA & FAUNA OF PANTANAL

Although the world's largest wetland forms part of the southern extreme of the *cerrado*, the Pantanal *(see pp320–21)* comprises habitats most associated with the Amazon. Many *cerrado* species live here, as well as marsh deer, capybara, caimans, waterbirds, and monkeys.

The white-necked heron *is a common sight in the Pantanal, especially along riverbanks, where it feeds. This graceful bird builds its nest on a platform on trees close to the river.*

Caiman *numbers in the Pantanal have increased after a ban on hunting them for their skin and teeth (considered charms against witchcraft) took effect.*

Guira cuckoos *are slightly scruffy-looking birds that nest, roost, and feed in groups, eating insects, frogs, and eggs off the ground.*

BRASÍLIA, GOIÁS & TOCANTINS

The capital of Brazil since 1960, Brasília is the region's only metropolis. Its striking city plan and futuristic architecture makes it vastly different from any other city in the country. Goiás and Tocantins make up Brazil's heartland. Northern Goiás and Tocantins are mostly wilderness areas of mountains and dry savanna, while in the south are the colonial towns of Pirenópolis and Goiás Velho.

Until the mid-20th century, only *bandeirante* slavers and gold hunters had ventured into the wilderness of central Brazil, a land of *cerrado* (savanna) woodland, *mesetas* (tabletop mountains), and giant winding rivers, peopled by bands of valiant indigenous groups such as the Xavante. Some gold prospectors stayed on, building a handful of colonial towns near their mines. Cidade Goiás and Pirenópolis in central Goiás are very well preserved, so much so that the former is now a UNESCO World Heritage Site. Pirenópolis is famous for its festivals, the liveliest of which, the Festa do Divino Espírito Santo, re-enacts the battles between the Christians and the Moors. The city is also a center for ecotourism, and a favorite watering hole for nearby Brasília's middle class. The Utopian, but impersonal, capital city sits on an exposed plain under an expansive sky. Its brave new domes, churches, and steel-reinforced monoliths, now ringed with *favelas*, should not be missed.

Northern Goiás and Tocantins remain frontier lands, where fields of soya are fast encroaching upon the foothills of the *mesetas* in Chapada dos Veadeiros National Park, the dune-filled expanses of the Jalapão *cerrado*, and indigenous lands on the world's largest river island, Ilha do Bananal. The scenery here is spectacular, and adventure activities, such as canyoning and rappeling, are developing rapidly.

The Palácio de Itamaraty (Palace of Arches), one of the most impressive modern buildings in Brasília

◁ Sculpted rock formations creating a lunar landscape, Vale da Lua, Parque Nacional Chapada dos Veadeiros

Exploring Brasília, Goiás & Tocantins

Cidade de Goiás and Pirenópolis in Goiás remain
pleasant colonial towns, while the spectacular
Chapada dos Veadeiros National Park in northern
Goiás showcases the unique flora and fauna of high-
altitude *cerrado*. Brasília, the capital city of Brazil
from 1960 onward, was built from the dust and scrub
of the central western *cerrado*, and is a Modernist
marvel. In Tocantins state, the Ilha do Bananal, one of
the largest islands in Brazil, is also the point at which
three ecosystems converge – rainforest, *cerrado*, and
wetland. The dune deserts of Jalapão in Tocantins are
fringed by dry *sertão*, vast horizons of soya farms,
waterfalls, crystalline rivers, and forests inhabited by
the Xavante and Xingú indigenous groups.

**Bust of Juscelino
Kubitschek, Museu
Historicó de Brasília**

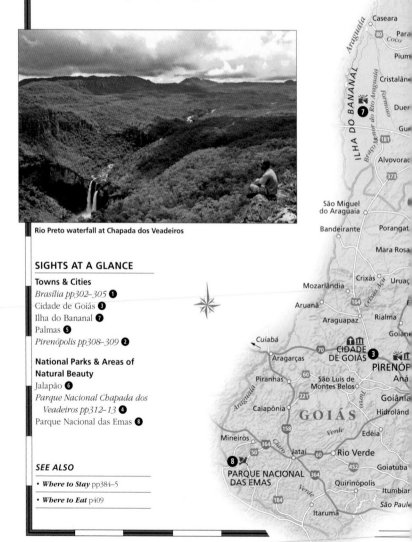

Rio Preto waterfall at Chapada dos Veadeiros

SIGHTS AT A GLANCE

Towns & Cities

Brasília pp302–305 **1**
Cidade de Goiás **3**
Ilha do Bananal **7**
Palmas **5**
Pirenópolis pp308–309 **2**

**National Parks & Areas of
Natural Beauty**

Jalapão **6**
*Parque Nacional Chapada dos
Veadeiros pp312–13* **4**
Parque Nacional das Emas **8**

SEE ALSO

Pon
Garir
Aragua
Caseara
Para
Coco
Pium
Cristalân
Duer
Gu
Alvovorac
São Miguel
do Araguaia
Bandeirante   Porangat
Mara Rosa
Crixás   Uruaç
Mozarlândia
Aruanã
Araguapaz   Rialma
Cuiabá   Goiân
CIDADE
Aragarças   DE GOIÁS **3**
PIRENÓP
Piranhas   São Luís de   Aná
Montes Belos
Goiânia
Caiapônia   GOIÁS   Hidrolând
Verde
Mineiros   Edéia
Jataí   Rio Verde
PARQUE NACIONAL   Goiatuba
8 DAS EMAS   Quirinópolis
Itumbiar
São Paul
Itarumã

ILHA DO BANANAL   **7**

Araguatins

io Novo   *Teresina*
ocantins

ioa   Tocantinópolis

ana

derlândia

Araguaína

Piaca

Craolândia

Itacajá

ra dos parecis

Pedro Afonso

perdida

acema do   Lizarda
antins

TOCANTINS

Sono

PALMAS

JALAPÃO

nal   Ponte Alta   *La Trís*
do Norte   *Ríos*

Natividade   Dianópolis

anuel Alves   Salvador

palma

Paranã   Tagu
atinga

Paranã

onte Alegre   Campos Belos
de Goiás

São
Domingos

**ARQUE NACIONAL
ADA DOS VEADEIROS**

Paraíso   Iaciara
e Goiás

ândia   Mambai

São João
da Aliança

Formosa

BRASÍLIA

Gama

Luziânia

Cristalina

polis

es
Rio   *Belo*
Horizonte

Catalão

*Represa de
Emborcação*

São Paulo

Ministry buildings, Catedral Metropolitana, and Museu Nacional, in Brasília

GETTING AROUND

Travel inevitably begins in Brasília. There is an international airport, and flights connecting with most larger Brazilian cities, including frequent flights to Goiânia in Goiás and Palmas in Tocantins. Roads radiate out from these cities to other towns and states cutting through the harvest land and the stunning scenery. Pirenópolis, a weekend getaway from Goiânia, is reached from Brasília via a filigree of small roads and regular buses. There are daily buses to Cidade de Goiás from Goiânia via the BR-070. The Chapada dos Veadeiros, which, together with Pirenópolis, boasts the best ecotourism infrastructure, is reached from the little towns of São Jorge or Alto Paraíso in northern Goiás. These are connected to Brasília via the GO-118. Apart from the main north–south artery, the BR-153, transportation in Tocantins is difficult. Ilha do Bananal in the west and Jalapão in the east are remote and best visited on tours.

0 km   100

0 miles   100

KEY

— Major road

═══ Minor road

═══ State border

Sweeping sand dunes in Jalapão

Brasília ❶

Brasília is the embodiment in concrete of erstwhile President Juscelino Kubitschek's promise of "fifty years of economic and social development in five," and of the national motto – Order and Progress. The city was built by vast teams of *candangos*, workers from the Northeast, who carved it from the *cerrado* at breakneck speed. They were led by urban planner Lúcio Costa, architect Oscar Niemeyer, and landscape engineer Roberto Burle Marx *(see p295)*. The capital of Brazil shifted from Rio de Janeiro to Brasília on April 21, 1960. Brasília was added to UNESCO's list of World Heritage Sites in 1987 as an example of daring urban planning and modern architecture. Today, Brasília is a stately, organized city, albeit a little quiet.

View of the Eixo Monumental from atop the TV Tower at dusk

Memorial dos Povos Indígenas is fashioned like a *maloca*, a traditional longhouse. It is a tribute to Brazil's indigenous peoples.

TV Tower is the best place to get a bird's-eye view of the city. The observation deck is on top of the 426-ft (75-m) high building.

Quartel General do Exército

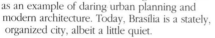

VIA N-1 OESTE

VIA S-1 OESTE

VIA S-1 OESTE

PARQUE SARA KUBITSCHEK

VIA S-2

0 meters   250

0 yards   250

EIXO MONUMENTAL

The Eixo Monumental, Brasília's main thoroughfare, forms the centerpiece of the city. Kubitschek stands at one end of the Eixo, waving from his towering Modernist column to the seat of government, the Congresso Nacional and Palácio do Planalto, which sit around the Praça dos Três Poderes. Many of Brazil's most famous architects and sculptors were involved in its construction.

Memorial Juscelino Kubitschek

Built in honor of the president responsible for the construction of Brasília, this monument contains his mausoleum, with photographs of, and documents about, the construction of the city.

Quartel General do Exército

This fusion of curves, straight lines, and jagged waves echoes the Congress complex and is the headquarters of the Brazilian army – at times the key player in affairs of state.

Esplanada dos Ministérios
Tall ministry buildings, 19 in all, are lined up in disciplined rows along Esplanada dos Ministérios.

VISITORS' CHECKLIST

Brasília Distrito Federal.
2,200,000. Presidente Juscelino Kubitschek International Airport, (061) 3364 9000. Tourist Office, Presidente Juscelino Kubitschek International Airport, (061) 3364 9488, or Adetur, Centro de Convenções, (061) 3429 7600.
www.infobrasília.com.br

Congresso Nacional e Anexos
Oscar Niemeyer's most famous and celebrated group of Modernist buildings at the heart of Brasília is also Brazil's seat of government.

Os Candangos
Artist Bruno Giorgio's Os Candangos was built in homage to the thousands of migrant workers from Northeast Brazil who went by this nick-name and who helped build Brasília.

Teatro Nacional,
a set of four theaters, is the most important in the city.

Esplanada dos Ministérios

Palácio do Planalto,
or the President's Office, is one of Niemeyer's best examples of Modernist architecture.

VIA N-1 OESTE

VIA N-2

VIA L2 NORTE

 Rodoviária

VIA S-1 OESTE

VIA S-2

VIA L2 SUL

Estação Galaria dos Estados

Palácio de Justiça,
the building of the Ministry of Justice, has a beautiful internal garden.

Catedral Metropolitana Nossa Senhora Aparecida
Niemeyer's iconic cathedral with its curved columns and stained-glass interior is flanked by haunting sculptures of the four apostles.

Supremo Tribunal Federal
The highest court in the country, the Supremo Tribunal Federal is the seat of Brazil's judicial power.

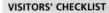

Exploring Brasília

The capital of Brazil, Brasília, is shaped like an airplane in homage to what was then the incipient jet age. While to its north and south lie the residential wings, the Eixo Monumental *(see pp302–303)* forms the body of the jet, with the city's major attractions.

Praça dos Três Poderes

Eixo Monumental. **Congresso Nacional e Anexos** ☐ *9–11:30am & 3:30–4:30pm Mon–Fri, 10am–2pm Sat & Sun.* 🚹 **Palácio do Planalto** ☐ *9:30am–1:30pm Sun.* **Palácio de Itamaraty** ☐ *3–5pm Mon–Fri, 10am–3pm Sat & Sun.* **Palácio da Justiça** ☐ *9–11am & 3–5pm Mon–Fri.*

This vast square is flanked by buildings that form the locus of the Brazilian government. The axis of the federal state, the **Congresso Nacional e Anexos** is a harmonious fusion of lines and curves, creating the most monumental and timeless architecture in the city. On the other side of the square are the seats of two other branches of power – the **Palácio do Planalto**, which is the executive office of the presidency, and opposite it, the **Supremo Tribunal Federal**, the Supreme Court headquarters. The latter is not open to the public.

Immediately below this group of buildings are the **Palácio de Itamaraty** and the **Palácio da Justiça**, two of Brasília's few buildings that are more aesthetic than monumental. The latter's Modernist columns seem to rise gently from the lily pond

Palácio da Justiça with lily pond in the foreground

The interior of Santuário Dom Bosco, bathed in blue light

lying at its feet to form smooth arches. Inside is a vast hall decorated with some fine sculpture and paintings. The main highlight is 19th-century artist Pedro Américo's *O Grito de Ipiranga*, depicting the moment when Dom Pedro I proclaimed Brazilian Independence *(see p52)*.

🏛 Catedral Militar de Nossa Senhora da Paz

Canteiro Central do Eixo Monumental Oeste. ☐ *8am–7pm daily.* **Tel** *(061) 3323 3858.*

This brilliant white triangular church, with its jagged windows and vast gable, echoes the French Notre Dame du Haut, designed by Niemeyer's mentor, Le Corbusier. It was completed in 1991, and was built to house the papal altar used by John Paul II on his visit to Brasília in 1980.

Quartel General do Exército

Setor Militar Urbano.

At the northeastern end of the Eixo Monumental, this vast complex of imposing buildings is set in a sea of lawns and watched over by a towering obelisk. It was built during the military dictatorship and was intended to show the presence of military power in the government, which was notably absent from the Praça dos Três Poderes. The intimidating stature of the buildings conveys Niemeyer's objective of constructing something grand for the generals. He was determined that the monumentalism of these generals should not be eclipsed by that of President Juscelino Kubitschek *(see p58)*.

🏛 Santuário Dom Bosco

Av W3 Sul, Quadra 702. **Tel** *(061) 3223 6542.* ☐ *7am–7pm daily.* 🚫

The city's finest church honors the 19th-century Italian visionary saint and founder of the Salesian order. His proclamation that a new civilization would arise in the third millennium between the 15th and 16th parallels of latitudes, inspired Kubitschek to build Brasília on the edge of an artificial lake. The stunning interior features an almost seemless panoply of glass, which ranges from light to dark blue and indigo, as it ascends. In the late afternoon, shafts of light penetrate the building, illuminating the marble statue of the Virgin and the vast cross whose vertical was carved from a single piece of tropical cedar. The church was blessed by John Paul II on his 1980 visit.

Templo da Boa Vontade

Setor Garagem Sul 915. **Tel** *(061) 3245 1070.* ☐ *24 hrs daily.*

Many religions, some orthodox, some decidedly alternative, thrive in and around Brasília. This marble pyramid with open sides was built to reflect the ecumenical attitude towards spirituality which characterizes the city. The building's geometry is based on multiples of seven in accordance with sacred numerology. The sides rise to 69 ft (21 m), the cavernous nave spans 92 ft (28 m), and spiral steps wind around the interior. The central portion of the temple is illuminated by light, filtering through an enormous and priceless rock crystal found at Cristalino in Goiás.

Catedral Metropolitana Nossa Senhora Aparecida

Designed by Oscar Niemeyer to resemble a crown of thorns, this cathedral features 16 soaring curved pillars spread like an open hand. Between them, a filigree of glass windows is united by a fluid series of color. The main altar and the altarpiece was given by Pope Paul VI in 1967, who also blessed the metal cross sitting on top of the building. The statues of the evangelists outside the cathedral are by the Mineiro sculptor Alfredo Ceschiatti, who also sculpted the archangels suspended from the ceiling inside.

VISITORS' CHECKLIST

Esplanado dos Ministérios.
Tel (061) 3224 4073. ☐ 8am–5pm Mon & Sat, 8am–6pm Tue–Fri & Sun. ● during masses: 12:15pm & 6:15pm Tue–Fri; 5pm Sat; 8:30am, 10:30am & 6pm Sun. **www**.catedral.org.br

The Catedral Metropolitana, etched against a cloudy Brasília sky

Subterranean Entrance
The remarkable entrance was intended to recall the catacombs where Christ was interred, with visitors emerging out of darkness into the cathedral's light.

Curved concrete pillars, all 16 of them, are held together at their apex by a high-tensile steel ring.

São Mateus
Designed by sculptor Alfredo Ceschiatti (1918–89), this 10-ft (3-m) high bronze figure of St. Matthew is one of the four sculptures that stand in front of the cathedral.

Stunning Interior
Archangels hover over the central altar, while the light marble and ample daylight infuse the entire building with a transcendent glow. The glass panels in the interior reflect sunlight from the rippling water outside.

Striking interior of Catedral Metropolitana Nossa Senhora Aparecida with glass roof panels, Brasília ▷

Pirenópolis ②

The picturesque town of Pirenópolis is gathered around the Rio das Almas, surrounded by verdant *cerrado* woodlands, and tucked away at the feet of low ragged hills. Pirenópolis skilfully balances the old and the new, the traditional and the contemporary. Crowned by Portuguese Baroque churches, the cobbled streets clatter to the sound of cowboys on horseback. They are lined with chic little restaurants, housed in rustic 18th-century bungalows, or designed in low-key 20th-century Art Deco style. The entire historical center can be walked around in less than two hours. There are only a few streets – the principal ones being Rua Direita, Rua da Aurora, Rua do Bonfim, and Rua do Rosário, which has the bulk of the restaurants. At weekends, a bustling crowd from Brasília fills up the streets.

Display of costumes from the Festa do Divino, Museu das Cavalhadas

Souvenir shops selling traditional handicrafts on Rua Rui Barbosa

🏠 Igreja Nosso Senhor do Bonfim

Praça do Bonfim. ◯ *check with tourist office before visiting.*
This simple but elegant little church on Rua do Bonfim was built between 1750 and 1754. One of the best-preserved churches in Goiás, this modest Baroque church is architecturally similar to Matriz de Nossa Senhora do Rosário and has a plain white

The well-maintained Igreja Nosso Senhor do Bonfim

façade. The image of Nosso Senhor do Bonfim, in the main altarpiece, was brought here from Salvador by a convoy of 250 slaves.

🏠 Igreja Matriz de Nossa Senhora do Rosário

Rua Do Rosário. ◯ *check with tourist office before visiting.*
This parish church, founded in 1728, is the largest and the oldest ecclesiastical building in Goiás. Until 2002, when the entire attractive colonial edifice was gutted in a fierce fire, it also had one of the finest Baroque interiors in the state. The church boasted an altarpiece decorated with motifs taken from the flora of the surrounding *cerrado*, and an impressive ceiling painted by the Brazilian artist, Inácio Pereira Leal, in 1864. The church was restored and opened anew in 2006, but a shortage of funds has left it with a plain interior.

🏛 Museu das Cavalhadas

Rua Direita 39. ◯ *8am–8pm daily.* 🖾
This small museum contains an incredible display of Carnaval masks, ornate metal armor costumes, photographs, and folklore relating to the hugely popular Festa do Divino Espírito Santo. The festival was originally Portuguese but the court costumes and the animal masks are uniquely Brazilian, originating from Afro-Brazilian and indigenous customs. The collection occupies the ground floor of a home belonging to a family which has for generations played a central role in performances at the festival.

🏛 Museu da Família Pompeu

Rua Nova 31. *Tel (062) 3331 1299.* ◯ *call ahead to arrange a visit.*
Set up in a corridor inside a large 18th-century house, this tiny museum displays regional historical items, including an odd collection of colonial bric-a-brac, furniture, Dickensian shelves of old documents, municipal newsletters, an old printing press, and silver jewelry. The museum preserves the most comprehensive and well-maintained records of the early

Museu da Família Pompeu

years of the colonial town of Pirenópolis, including pictures and documents from its gold-mining days. The Pompeu family does not reside here. There is a proposal to turn this treasure-house into a public municipal museum.

FESTA DO DIVINO ESPÍRITO SANTO

Also known as Cavalhadas, the festival is based on Iberian lore dating from the Crusades and Catholic Whitsuntide celebrations. The festival begins 15 days before Pentecost Sunday, with a gathering of riders, known as the Folia do Divino, at the Matriz. They then proceed out of Pirenópolis into the surrounding countryside. Masked dancers, parades of horsemen dressed as Crusaders, Moors, or Cavalhadas, and many cultural and musical events follow. The festival culminates on Pentecost Sunday in the recently built stadium, the Cavalhadodrómo.

Cavalhadas parade costume

Teatro de Pirenópolis

Praça da Matriz s/n. *Tel* (062) 3331 2029 (box office). ◻ box office open all day on show days.

This delightful, newly-restored miniature 19th-century theater, commemorating the centenary of its foundation, is one of the town's hidden treasures. The Teatro de Pirenópolis is best visited during one of the regular plays, performances, and shows. One of the most interesting small acts in the past has featured the popular Mato Grosso do Sul-born guitarist Almir Sater. The Goiás singer-songwriter, Maria Eugenia, and the Tocantins Forró singer, Dorivã, regularly play here. Just around the corner, on the Rua do Direita, is the little Art Deco **Cine Pireneus Art Cinema**, with an impressive eclectic program.

The Art Deco façade of Cine Pireneus Art Cinema

VISITORS' CHECKLIST

Goiás. 🏛 23,000. ✈
🚌 Rodoviária, Av Neco Mendonça, (062) 3331 1080.
ℹ Central de Atendimento ão Turista, (062) 3331 2633. 🎭
Festa do Divino Espírito Santo (Feb). **www**.pirenopolis.com.br

🏞 Santuário de Vida Silvestre Fazenda Vagafogo

7 miles (12 km) NW of Pirenópolis. *Tel* (062) 3335 8515. 🚗
◻ 8am–6pm daily. 📷

A beautifully preserved patch of forest lined with streams and exquisite trails, Santuário Vagafogo makes for a good excursion into the countryside. This stunning nature preserve of *cerrado* and gallery forests (forests along a river or stream) is home to a number of animal species such as brown capuchins, armadillos, as well as many bird species. At weekends and on holidays, a small restaurant at the visitors, center serves fantastic fare using homegrown ingredients. Visitors can hire one of the many motorbike taxis from pick-up points in town – an inexpensive way to get to the sanctuary – or hire a cab.

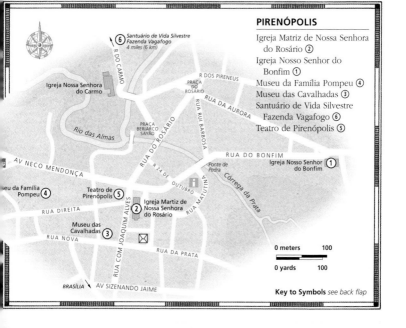

PIRENÓPOLIS

0 meters 100

0 yards 100

Key to Symbols *see back flap*

A cobbled street lined with townhouses in Cidade de Goiás

Cidade de Goiás ❸

Goiás. 🏠 28,500. ✈ 🚌
🛈 Secretaria de Turismo, (062) 3201
8122. 🎭 Semana Santa (Apr),
Festival International de Cinema
Ambiental (Jun). **www.**
cidadeshistoricas.art.br/goias

Like most colonial towns in
Brazil's interior, Cidade de
Goiás grew rich on gold. Until
the middle of the 20th
century, it was the capital of
what was once the largest
Brazilian state apart from
Amazonas. Also known as
Goiás Velho, or just Goiás,
Cidade de Goiás is a magical
little city nestled at the foot of
the rugged Serra Dourado
hills. Winding cobbled streets
lined with 18th-century town
houses lead to hills capped
with churches, leafy squares
and little markets. Life here
seems to trot along as it has
done for centuries.

While historic, Goiás is far
from being lost in a bygone
age. The city's busy social
calendar is a testament to its
successful fusion of the old
with the new. There is something happening almost every
weekend through the year
in Goiás, from thoroughly
traditional hooded parades
in Semana Santa (Holy Week)
to some of the best world-
cinema festivals and classical
music concerts in Brazil.

Many buildings and
museums testify to the city's
illustrious past, and Goiás is
small enough to see them all
leisurely on foot. The best
place to begin a tour is at
Praça Brasil Caiado, the large
square which graces the
town's southern end. There

are a number of museums
and monuments here. These
include the **Museu das
Bandeiras**, the former seat of
government, which preserves
a forbidding dungeon and
a set of rooms with period
furniture, a magnificent
Baroque public fountain,
Chafariz de Cauda, and the
Quartel do Vinte, an 18th-
century barracks, which now
houses the tourist office.

Immediately north of Praça
Brasil Caiado and capped
with an attractive, though
modest, Baroque church is
another square, **Praça do
Correto**. The most interesting
of all the city's museums,
Museu de Arte Sacra in the
Igreja de Boa Morte, is
located here, preserving a
series of hauntingly lifelike
religious effigies by José
Joaquim da Veiga Valle (1806–
74), a self-taught sculptor.
Opposite this museum is the
Palácio Conde dos Arcos,
complete with 18th-century
furniture and still used by the
governor on city visits.

🏛 **Museu de Arte Sacra**
Praça do Correto. **Tel** (062) 3371
1207. ◯ 8am–5pm Tue–Fri,
9am–1pm Sun. 🎟

🏛 **Museu das Bandeiras**
Praça Brasil Caiado. **Tel** (062) 3371
1087. ◯ 8–11am & 1–5pm
Tue–Fri, noon–5pm Sat. 🎟

🏛 **Palácio Conde dos Arcos**
Praça Dr. Tasso de Camargo.
Tel (062) 3371 1200. ◯ 8am–5pm
Tue–Sat, 8am–noon Sun. 🎟

Chapada dos Veadeiros ❹

See pp312–13.

Palmas ❺

Tocantins. 🏠 137,500. ✈ 🚌 (063)
3228 5600. 🛈 Embratur, Secretaria
da Industria, Comercio e Turismo,
Praça Girossóis, (063) 3218 2357.
🎭 Carnaval (Feb/Mar).

Built in 1989, Brazil's newest
state capital sits at the base
of a range of forested low
hills. It is a pleasant, but
sprawling, modern city.
Most visitors come to Palmas
as it is a good jumping-off
point for the numerous
attractions that lie within the
interior of Tocantins state,
most notably Jalapão and the
Ilha do Bananal.

Aside from the vast Palmas
lake formed by the dam on
the Rio Tocantins, Palmas'
most interesting area is its
vast, grassy main square,
Praça Giróssois, which is
lined by grandiose public
buildings and various
monuments to its founder,
José Wilson Siqueira Campos,
and his legacy.

**The sparkling Rio Tocantins in
Palmas at sunset**

Jalapão ❻

Tocantins. 🚩 Korubo, (011) 3667
5053, **www.**korubo.com.br; or
Bananal Ecotour (063) 3219 4200.
www.bananalecotour.com.br

A journey through Brazil's
interior would be incomplete
without a visit to Jalapão.
Located deep within eastern
Tocantins, this breathtaking
area is one of South America's
great wilderness destinations.
Jalapão, stretching across
13,130 sq miles (34,000 sq
km), is made up of a state
park, three private protected

areas, and an ecological station, Estação Ecológica. The best time to visit is the dry season between June and September.

Beyond the inaccessible reaches of southern Piauí, the arid *cerrado* forests and incipient *caatinga* thornlands are more pristine here than anywhere else. Many fast-flowing rivers cut through spectacular canyons and thunder over myriad water-falls throughout Jalapão. A number of rivers are born in limpid glassy springs that bubble forth from the sands of Jalapão. Others wind their way through groves of buriti palms called *veredas*. These are visited by Spix's macaws and Brazilian Merganser ducks, two of the extremely rare birds lost to the rest of the continent but still found in Jalapão.

Towering over Jalapão's seemingly interminable plains and striding out to the endless horizons are stands of monolithic tabletop mountains, winding yellow sand dunes, and craggy rock pinnacles. The air is so clear that even when these are far in the distance, they appear close enough to touch. Trails running across the mountain summits range from moderate to difficult, depending on the experience of the hiker.

The views from the top of the mountains and dunes are mesmerizing. But for the whistling breeze, it is so silent that the infrequent pick-ups running across the very few dirt roads can be heard clearly even when they are

Dark waters of the Rio Javaés, one of Ilha do Bananal's rivers

Ilha do Bananal 🐾

Tocantins. 👥 *3,500.* 🚌 *Bananal Ecotour Quadra 103-S, Loja 28, Palmas, (063) 3219 4200.* **www.** bananalecotour.com.br

The Rio Araguaia runs from southern Goiás across Tocantins state to join the Rio Tocantins before draining into the Amazon. In the middle of this river sits the Ilha do Bananal, an island so vast that it has its own rivers running through it and contends with Ilha de Marajó *(see p270)* for the title of the world's largest river island. Access to the island's wild interior is not easy. Visits here are only possible with a licensed tour operator.

Three ecosystems converge on the island – rainforest, wetland, and *cerrado*. Bananal's southern extremes are mostly Terras Indígenas (indigenous territories), where tourists are not welcome. Its center and north are

impenetrable without a guide. Indigenous communities, including the Javaés and the Karajás, inhabit the island, some of whom produce carved wooden animals and pottery figurines. The southern part of the island also comprises seasonally flooded forests, lakes, and swamps filled with wildlife. This is a wonderful area for bird-watching, particularly waterbirds. There are also black caimans, which grow to an immense size in the dark, fish-filled waters.

Parque Nacional das Emas 🐾

Goiás. 🚌 *Drena, Rua Aurora 21, Centro Histórico Pirenópolis, (062) 3331 3336.* 🛏 *Fazenda Santa Amélia, (064) 3634 1380.* **www.** drena.tur.br

Tucked far away in the southwest corner of Goiás and surrounded by a sea of soya, Emas National Park is a 500-sq mile (1,300-sq km) island of grassland and sparse *cerrado,* dotted with millions of termite hills and cut by blackwater rivers. The park is considered the best preserved *cerrado* in the country. In 2001, it was designated a UNESCO World Heritage Site.

Populations of larger mammals, particularly the armadillo, maned wolf, and puma, are so healthy here that the park is a favorite location for film crews from the BBC Natural History Unit. It is also an important destination for bird-watchers from around the world, with the greatest concentration of blue-and-yellow macaws outside Amazônia.

Although there is no compulsion to go on a guided tour, it is a good idea to organize a trip through a tour operator in Pirenópolis, or through the tourist office in the nearby town of Chapadão do Céu, east of the park. Facilities at the park are minimal. Accommodation is limited to very rustic, simply-appointed **Fazenda Santa Amélia** in Chapadão do Céu.

A breathtaking view of Tocantins landscape from a dune, Jalapão

Parque Nacional Chapada dos Veadeiros ❹

Beautiful hummingbird

Named for the marsh deer that inhabit the area, this national park sits on the edge of the *cerrado*, one of the largest areas of wild country in the interior of Brazil. Most easily accessed from the small town of Alto Paraíso, the park is set in a stunning landscape. The surrounding area is just as magical; sprawling forest is broken up by rushing waterfalls and meadows, and dotted with stands of buriti palms. This remarkably isolated destination offers spectacular walks and pretty trails for nature-lovers as well as exciting outdoor adventure activities, such as rappeling and canyoning.

Buriti palm groves, widely scattered in the Chapada

0 kilometers 10

0 miles 6

Morro da Chapéu 3,300 ft (1,000 m)

COLINAS

Rio Ronca

SERRA DE SANTANA

Rio Preto

SERRA RIO PR

239

Cachoeira Cariocas · Cânion I
· Cânion II
Cachoeira do Rio Preto ·
Salto do Rio Preto ·

São Jorge
VALE DA LUA

Rio São Miguel

★ **Cânion Rio Preto**
The narrow gorges of the Rio Preto, which runs through the middle of the park, cut into the sandstone cliffs. The most stunning precipice has waterfalls gushing down the cliffs.

Giant Anteater
One of the larger mammals in the Chapada, the giant anteater is a common sight.

Vale da Lua
The light in this shallow canyon is particularly beautiful at sunset. The rocks have been sculpted into strange Daliesque shapes by the Rio São Miguel.

STAR SIGHTS

★ Cânion Rio Preto

★ Cachoeira Almeçegas

Chuveirinho Flower
The cerrado has thousands of endemic plants and one of the highest numbers of species found in a single area. One such indigenous plant is this unusual meadow flower.

VISITORS' CHECKLIST

Goías. 🚐 *from Brasília to Alto Paraíso, then bus.* 🛈 *Av Ari Valadão, (061) 3446 1201, Alto Paraíso.* 🍴 *in Alto Paraíso.* 🕐 *8am–5pm Tue–Sun. Best time to visit is April–October.* 📷 👣 *visits are permitted only with a guide, available at the park entry station. Only 450 visitors may enter the park at any one time and for day trips only.*

KEY

🛈	Visitor information
▬	Highway
═	Minor road
- -	Trail
– –	Park boundary
▲	Peak

Adventure Sports
The Chapada is one of the most popular places in Brazil for outdoor adventure sports such as abseiling and canyoning.

★ Cachoeira Almeçegas
A picturesque many-tiered waterfall drops over 260 ft (80 m) into deep pools, which are good for swimming. Access is along a rather tortuous trail.

Trekking
The Chapada is home to several forest trails, which are perfect for avid hikers and nature-lovers.

MATO GROSSO & MATO GROSSO DO SUL

O nce a destination for explorers and gold hunters, today Mato Grosso and Mato Grosso do Sul attract avid nature-lovers. The world's largest wetland and a vital ecosystem, the Pantanal straddles both states. Blessed with crystalline rivers and spectacular national parks, and dotted with ranches and farms, this vast region is still home to a large population of indigenous groups.

Explorations of Mato Grosso were limited to nature expeditions and Jesuit missionaries until the discovery of gold in the 18th century. The gold rush led to clashes between Europeans and indigenous groups. Many of these groups, such as the Bororo and Kayapó, still live in this state.

The building of Brasília as the new capital of Brazil brought waves of migrant workers to the Central West in the mid-20th century. In 1979, the state was split into Mato Grosso and Mato Grosso do Sul, divided by the star attraction of the region, the wetlands of the Pantanal.

Very few places in the world can boast such enormous numbers of large birds as the Pantanal. While wildlife can be difficult to see in the closed forests of the Amazon, it is visible in abundance here. In July and August, storks, ibis, herons, and huge, colorful parrots swarm the Pantanal, and can even be seen while driving along dirt roads. The wetlands are home to a diverse range of wildlife, including the anaconda, the elusive jaguar, and giant otter.

Outside the Pantanal, large tracts of farmland are broken by low mountains and giant, sluggish rivers. Amazon forests cling on in places such as Alta Floresta, Chapada dos Guimarães, and Bonito despite the expansion of the soya industry. The entire region offers prime opportunities for bird-watching, angling, and snorkeling.

Capybara, the largest rodent in the world, frequently spotted in water ponds of the Pantanal

◁ Limestone rock formations and transparent blue waters, Gruta do Lago Azul, Bonito

Exploring Mato Grosso & Mato Grosso do Sul

Both Mato Grosso and Mato Grosso do Sul are regions of enormous plains with a handful of mountain ranges. The main attraction of this region is the Pantanal, the world's largest wetland. This harbors an important ecosystem with varied fauna such as caimans, jaguars, and a profuse variety of birds. Cuiabá, Corumbá, and Campo Grande are good springboards for ecotourists who wish to travel into or through the Pantanal. Alta Floresta, in the extreme north of Mato Grosso, is considered one of the best places for spotting rare birds and mammals. Bonito, in Mato Grosso do Sul, is an area of plunging waterfalls, caves, and crystal-clear rivers – ideal for walks through mountains and forests, and rafting and snorkeling. Flowing from central Mato Grosso, the Rio Xingú has indigenous peoples from nine distinct ethnic groups living along its banks.

SIGHTS AT A GLANCE

Towns & Cities
Bonito ❾
Campo Grande ❽
Corumbá ❻
Cuiabá ❶
Miranda ❼

National Parks & Areas of Natural Beauty
Alta Floresta ❹
Chapada dos Guimarães ❷
Pantanal pp320–21 ❺
Xingú ❸

SEE ALSO

• *Where to Stay* pp385–6

• *Where to Eat* pp409–10

Recreio
Panelas
Barracão do Barreto
Theodore Roosevelt
Branco
Juruena
ALTA FLOREST
Aripuanã   Juruena   Itapulu
Moreru   *Apiacá*   *Peixes*
Juara
Juina   Porto dos Gaúchos Óbid
Porto Velho   Brasnorte
Camararé   Juruena
Comodoro   Utiariti   MATO
Serra de Santa Bárbara   *Juruena*   *Verde*   GROS
Parecis
174
Faz. Itanorte   Nob
Pontes-e-Lacerda   Barra do Bugres
Porto Esperidião   Cáceres   CUIA
Corixa Grande   *Bento Gomes*   Po
Porto Jofre
Amolar   ✠
Paiaguás   P
⌂🏛 ❻⚡   A
CORUMBÁ ❻   N
Porto Esperança   Barra   T
MIRAND   A
BONIT
Porto Murtinho   J
26
Bela Vi

Jabiru storks, also known as *tuiuiú*, gather to feed in the Pantanal

↑ *Santarém*

Peixoto de
Azevedo

de Azevedo

Xingu

Liberdade

Villa Rica

S. José
do Xingu

Tapirapé

Porto Alegre
do Norte

nissuú Missu

XINGÚ ❸

322

Suiá Missur

Arraias

Culuene

Querência

Verentes

Jatobá   Gaúcha do
Norte   Garapu

Rio das Mortes

Mariembero

Araguaia

Planalto do   Canarana

Mato Grosso   158

Areões   Cocalinho

argão   Paranatinga   Nova
Xavantino

PADA DOS   General
VARÃES   70   Carneiro *Goiânia*

Poxoréu
Guiratinga   Barra do
Garças

donópolis
364

163   *Correntes*

Goiânia

ão   Pedro Gomes

Paraíso
Cassilândia

Camapuã   **MATO**

nedo   **GROSSO**
DO SUL   Inocência

Aparecida
do Tabuado

✈ CAMPO   Água Clara
❽ GRANDE

Sidrolândia
262

Três Lagoas
São Paulo

267

ju   Rio Brilhante   Bataguaçu

Dourados   *São Paulo*

Ivinheima   *Paraná*

orã

Navirai

nambai
163

Iguatemi

Clear water of the Rio Sucuri at Bonito

GETTING AROUND

Distances are huge in these states and there are
few paved roads. However, the capital cities –
Campo Grande in Mato Grosso do Sul and Cuiabá
in Mato Grosso have airports with good connections to the rest of Brazil. Alta Floresta also has an
airport. Corumbá, Bonito, and Miranda in Mato
Grosso do Sul are connected to Campo Grande by
fast, comfortable buses. Tour operators are based
in the capital cities and in Corumbá and Bonito.
Most can organize bookings through their websites.
Tours to the Pantanal are also organized, and
usually enter the Pantanal by road and spend a
couple of days exploring in canoes, motorboats,
or on horseback from a land base. Rented cars are
also a possibility, though visitors would be limited
to only a few tracks along the fringes.

KEY

═══	Highway
━━━	Major road
═══	Minor road
┅┅┅	Railroad
▨▨▨	International border
━━━	State border

0 km   100

0 miles   100

The spectacular vista of the Chapada dos Guimarães plateau, Mato Grosso

Cuiabá ❶

Mato Grosso. 🏙 483,400. ✈
🚌 ℹ️ Sedtur, (065) 3613 9300.
🎭 Festa de São Benedito (Jul).
www.cuiaba.mt.gov.br

Mato Grosso's capital and the
warmest city in Brazil sits
on a low, languid plain
at the foot of the
Chapada dos
Guimarães hills.
Situated on the banks
of the Rio Cuiabá, a
tributary of the Rio
Paraguai, the city has
some leafy squares
and is known as the Cidade
Verde or the Green City.
Cuiabá is also a good starting
point for excursions into the
Pantanal (see pp320–21).

**Kadiwéu pottery,
Museu Rondon**

Like Cidade de Goiás
(see p310) and Ouro Preto
(see pp126–7), Cuiabá was
originally a flourishing gold-
mining town, full of handsome buildings and fine
churches. Almost all were
demolished in a spate of
hasty modernization in the
late 1960s. The town has lost
most of the splendid works
of José Joaquim da Veiga
Valle (1806–74), one of the
country's great geniuses of
the Baroque. Fortunately,
some of his exquisite craftsmanship can still be seen in
the well-preserved, vast, rectangular interiors of the new
concrete Catedral do Bom
Jesus, which has an unusual
square, Moorish façade.

The most interesting of the
city's sights is the small
university-run **Museu do
Índio Marechal Rondon**. The
museum holds some exquisite
and priceless pieces of
indigenous art. These include
exhibits of the Xavante,
Bororo, and Karajá peoples.
The museum
houses some
beautiful, Bororo
and Rikbaktsa head-
dresses and superb
pieces of Kadiwéu
ceramics from Mato
Grosso do Sul.

🏛 **Museu do Índio
Marechal Rondon**
Av Fernando Correia da Costa.
Tel (065) 3615 8489. ⏰ 7:30–
11:30am & 1:30–5:30pm Tue–Fri,
1:30–5:30pm Mon. 🏷️ 📷

Chapada dos Guimarães ❷

Mato Grosso. 🏙 13,500. 🚌 from
Cuiabá. ℹ️ Secretaria de Turismo,
Rua Quinco Caldas, (065) 3301 1690.
🎫 Eco Turismo, Praça Dom
Wunibaldo 464, (065) 3301 1393.
🎭 Festival de Inervo (Jul). **www**.
chapadadosguimaraes.com.br

The town of Chapada dos
Guimarães is set on a plateau
of the same name. Said to
be about 500 million years
old, the majestic honey-
colored tablelands and
escarpments of the plateau
are among the oldest rock

formations in the world.
As the continent's geodesic
center, the tablelands of the
Chapada dos Guimarães are
reputedly imbued with ener-
gizing powers strong enough
to reduce the speed of a car
and said to be attractive to
UFOs. While the residents of
the Chapada claim this effect
has been documented, cynics
believe otherwise.

The little town has
numerous shops, cafés, and
spiritual centers devoted to
the New Age movement,
which is growing in Brazil.
Nature-lovers come here to
admire the scenery. The edge
of the Chapada offers sweeping vistas out over the patchy,
remnant *cerrado* forests of

**Véu de Noiva, the highest waterfall
in Chapada dos Guimarães**

the Mato Grosso plains.
There are several waterfalls
in the area, the most famous
and tallest of which is the
Véu de Noiva, or the Bridal
Veil Falls.

Although the Chapada has
seen far more aggressive
agricultural development
than its counterparts in Goiás
and Toacantins, many upland
bird species which are not
found either in the Pantanal
or the Amazonian forests
can be seen here. The high
cerrado forests, savannas, and
pasturelands of the Chapada
hold a special attraction for
bird-watchers, who
come here in
droves to catalogue
the variety of birds,
and perhaps to catch a
lucky glimpse of
mammals, such as
maned wolves,
ocelots, and black-
tailed marmosets.

**Red-capped
cardinal, Alta
Floresta**

Xingú ❸

Mato Grosso. 🚌 ❚ *Fundação
Nacional do Índio (Funai), Av C.P.A,
(065) 3644 1850, Cuiabá.* **www**.
funai.gov.br

By the end of the 19th
century, all of the great
Amazon tributaries had been
explored and colonized, and
their indigenous peoples
enslaved or completely wiped
out. The remote region of
Xingú, in the extreme northeast of Mato Grosso, was the
only indigenous settlement to
survive the onslaught and be
established as a preserve.

Home to one of the largest
areas of tribal lands in the
country, it sits as a huge
island of forest in a vast ocean
of soya plantations. These
tracts of land are concentrated
around the beautiful clear-
water Rio Xingú. Known to be
sophisticated, the indigenous
peoples flourishing in the
Xingú specialize in furniture-
making and basket-weaving,
among other things.

Tourism is extremely limited
here and visits to indigenous
villages can only be undertaken with prior permission
from Fundação Nacional
do Índio (Funai).

Alta Floresta ❹

Mato Grosso. 🏠 *43,000.* ✈ *to
Cuiabá, then bus.* ❚ *Anaconda
Pantanal Operators, (065) 33028
5990.* ❚ *Cristalino Jungle Lodge,
(066) 3512 7100.*

Situated in the extreme north
of Mato Grosso, Alta Floresta
sits on the edge of the
pristine southern Amazon
rainforest, and is a rapidly
growing frontier town. This
remote town is also a thriving
agricultural settlement. Its
surrounding areas are
considered some of the best
in the Brazilian Amazon for
spotting rare birds
and mammals. One
of the highlights of
Alta Floresta is the four-
star hotel, Floresta
Amazônica, which
serves as a base for
the **Cristalino Jungle
Lodge** *(see p385).*

The Cristalino Jungle
Lodge sits in the Cristalino
Forest Reserve deep in the
forest, north of Alta Floresta.
The lodge is situated on the
banks of the Rio Cristalino,
which is the black water
tributary of the Rio Tapajós,
whose blue waters flow into
the Amazon at Santarém *(see
p274).* The lodge is most
famous for the profuse birdlife surrounding it, as well
as an enormous variety of
butterflies and other insects,
reptiles, and mammals.

**A view out over the forests of
the Rio Cristalino preserve**

All the large Neotropical
rainforest mammals, including
the endangered white-nosed
bearded saki monkey, brown
titi monkey, giant river otter,
and three-toed sloth, as well
as jaguar, puma, and tapir
are present and can often be
spotted here. Facilities for
jungle walks and viewing
wildlife are excellent and
include English-speaking,
specialist guides, a 164-ft
(50-m) high canopy tower,
and a very good library
of decent field guides.

Other more challenging
outdoor adventure activities,
such as camping in the forest,
trekking, survival techniques,
rappeling, canyoning, and
canoeing, can also be
arranged through the
Cristalino Jungle Lodge.

Cristalino Jungle Lodge, in the Rio Cristalino Forest Reserve, Alta Floresta

Pantanal [5]

The world's largest wetland, the Pantanal provides a habitat for the greatest concentration of animals in the Western Hemisphere. Innumerable waterbirds gather toward the end of the dry season. There are plenty of reptiles and large mammals, including caimans, tapirs, giant anteaters, and all of Brazil's eight feline species. The secret to the vast numbers of animals lies in the diversity of habitats and the geography of the Pantanal, a gently sloping bowl which floods when nutrient-rich tributaries drain from the ancient sedimentary rocks of the Brazilian Shield and get trapped. Aquatic plants breed profusely and these provide ample food for fish and birds, who, in turn, feed the rest of the food chain.

Green and Rufous Kingfisher
The rarest of the Pantanal's five kingfishers, the green and rufous kingfisher is seen on the banks of small, undisturbed rivers.

Anhinga
The anhinga is a relative of the cormorant and is a common sight in the Pantanal. As it has no wax in its feathers, it must dry its wings in the sun after diving for fish.

Brahmin Cattle
The most common animals in the Pantanal are Brahmin cattle who are herded by local cowboys, or pantaneiros.

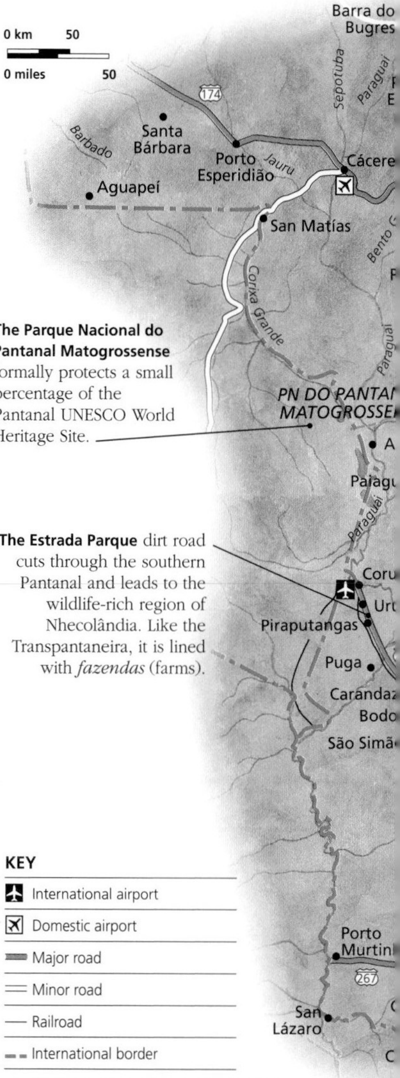

0 km 50
0 miles 50
Barra do Bugres
Sepotuba
Paraguai
174
Santa Bárbara
Barbado
Porto Esperidião
Jauru
Cácere
Aguapeí
San Matías
Bento
Corixa Grande
Paraguai
PN DO PANTA
MATOGROSSE
Paiagu
Paraguai
Coru
Urt
Piraputangas
Puga
Carandaz
Bodo
São Simã
Porto Murtin
267
San Lázaro

The Parque Nacional do Pantanal Matogrossense formally protects a small percentage of the Pantanal UNESCO World Heritage Site.

The Estrada Parque dirt road cuts through the southern Pantanal and leads to the wildlife-rich region of Nhecolândia. Like the Transpantaneira, it is lined with *fazendas* (farms).

KEY

- International airport
- Domestic airport
- Major road
- Minor road
- Railroad
- International border

STAR SIGHTS

★ Estrada Transpantaneira

★ Fazendas

For hotels and restaurants in this region see pp385–6 and pp409–10

★ Estrada Transpantaneira

The dirt road of Estrada Transpantaneira is lined with fazendas, many of which have accommodation for tourists. Wildlife viewing is excellent and the road is navigable in a normal car.

VISITORS' CHECKLIST

Mato Grosso & Mato Grosso do Sul. 🚂 Campo Grande & Corumbá. ✈ Caceres & Cuiabá. ℹ Rua Afonso Pena s/n, Campo Grande, (067) 3324 5830. 🗺 organized tours available in Campo Grande & Cuiabá. The dry season (Apr–May & Sep–Oct) is the best time to visit. Bird-watching ideal in Jul–Sep. Fishing best in Apr, but requires a permit from Ibama, (067) 3321 5053.

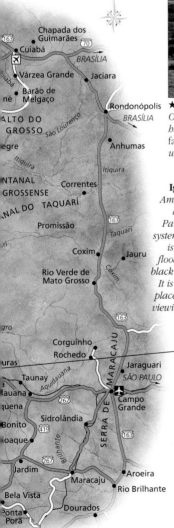

★ Fazendas

Originally built as cattle ranches, many fazendas have been converted into ranch-style hotels. The fazendas are connected by excellent bird-watching walkways throughout the Pantanal.

Igapó Forest

Among the most diverse of the Pantanal's eco-systems, the igapó is a seasonally flooded forest on black water rivers. It is a wonderful place for wildlife-viewing by canoe.

River Excursions

Fazendas near Miranda (see p322) offer boat trips on the various Pantanal rivers. Binoculars are essential for bird- and caiman-spotting.

Boats moored on the Rio Paraguai, Corumbá

Corumbá 6

Mato Grosso do Sul. 95,000.
along Rio Paraguai.
Secretaria de Turismo, (067) 3232
5221. Festa de Nossa Senhora
de Candelária (Oct).

On the banks of the Rio
Paraguai, Corumbá is a
small town surrounded by
the Pantanal region's unspoilt
beauty. Boat rides along the
river, as well as wetland
excursions form Corumbá's
major attractions. Sportfishing,
one of the main highlights, is
provided at the nature lodges,
floating hotels, and charming
fazendas in this area.

Corumbá was first explored
by Portuguese and Spanish
adventurers in search of
gold. By the 18th century,
the growing strategic importance of the Rio Paraguai led
to the construction of forts.
The **Forte Junqueira**, built
during the Paraguayan War
(see p53), is the only fort
still standing intact.

Another place worth a
visit is the **Casa do Artesão**,
a former prison housing
an interesting museum of
indigenous and local objets
d'art. The **Museu do Pantanal**
also has a small collection of
indigenous art.

🏛 Casa do Artesão
Rua Dom Corréa 405. 7:30–11am
& 1:30–5pm Mon-Fri, 8–11am Sat.

🏯 Forte Junqueira
Rua Cáceres 425. **Tel** (067) 3231
5828. 8–11am & 1:30–4:30pm
Mon-Fri.

🏛 Museu do Pantanal
Praça de República. **Tel** (067) 3231
5757. 7:30am–1:30pm Mon-Fri.

Miranda 7

Mato Grosso do Sul. 23,000.
Festa do Homem
Pantaneiro (Oct).

The tiny town of Miranda,
in the heart of the Pantanal,
hosts the region's liveliest
festival, the Festa do Homem
Pantaneiro. This grand celebration of the ranching and
cowboy way of life features
lasso contests (in the mornings for women, at night
for men), and rodeos. Live
sertanejo bands and dancing
carry on all night.

Miranda is an ideal base
for visiting the southern
Pantanal's various *fazenda*
ranches *(see pp385–6)*, many
of which lie on the outskirts
of town. The **Fazenda San
Francisco** is one of the best
locations in inland Brazil for
big cats, especially ocelot
and jaguar. The **Fazenda Baía
Grande** preserves a diverse
range of Pantanal habitats,
including a large caiman-filled

lake and extensive forest. The
Fazenda Meia Lua lies just on
the edge of town and is an
ideal soft adventure option.

Environs
Known for their distinctive
painted terra-cotta ceramics,
the Terena indigenous villages
surround Miranda. Tour operators in Miranda can arrange
trips to a Terena village, as
well as to the **Rio Salobrinho**,
a beautiful clear-water river
lined with gallery forest.
Expect to find rare bird species, including kingfishers and
black-crowned night herons.

Campo Grande 8

Mato Grosso do Sul. 665,000.
Centro Informação
Turistica e Cultural, (067) 3324 5830.

Mato Grosso do Sul's capital,
Campo Grande is also known
as Cidade Morena because
of its red earth. It is a prosperous, modern city devoted
far more to agro-business
than tourism. Yet most visitors
to the southern Pantanal
arrive here because the tourist
infrastructure is excellent.
Commerce, education, and
toursim are fast growing
industries here. The city
itself has few major
attractions, though there
are many good restaurants,
hotels, and bars, particularly
along and around Rua Barão
do Rio Branco. For those who
do not want to rough it out
with a Pantanal camping tour,
travel agencies sell packages
to pleasant farm hotels.

Rodeo at the Festa de Homem Pantaneiro

Rio Sucuri flowing near Bonito, reflecting the lush greenery around

Bonito **9**

Mato Grosso do Sul. 🏠 *17,000.*
🚌 ℹ️ *Setuma, (067) 255 1760.*
🚗 *Taika Tour, Pilad Rebuá 211, (067)*
3255 1354; Ygarapé Tours, Pilad
Rebuá 1853, (067) 3255 1159.

A one-street town, Bonito is lined with *pousadas*, restaurants, shops, and tour operators whose lifeline is tourism. It lies just beyond the Pantanal's southern extremities, in the Serra do Bodoquena, a low, *cerrado*-covered range of rugged hills busy with primates and birds, including the black-collared hawk. There are numerous sights around Bonito, all protected by regulations. Only Bonito-based tour agencies can organize trips and arrange permits.

Black-collared hawk

🏊 Aquário Natural Baía Bonita

4 miles (7 km) SE of Bonito.
Tel *(067) 255 1193.* 🕖 *7:30am–3:30pm daily.* 📷
One of the natural springs in the area, the Baía Bonita features a pristine aquarium, which contains 30 different varieties of fish. Facilities within the complex include a warm swimming pool and relaxation cabin. Snorkeling trips to the Rio Sucuri and Rio da Prata are offered by tour companies. Wetsuits and snorkels are also provided.

🏊 Rio Sucuri

12 miles (20 km) SW of Bonito.
This glassy river is broken by waterfalls and large pools filled with 3-ft (1-m) long *piraputanga* (ray-finned fish, typical of the Rio Paraguai basin) and silver dourado fish. Many pools are set in woodland cut with wildlife trails. The gentle flow of the Rio Sucuri and the excellent facilities draws a plethora of snorkelers and rafters, from morning to afternoon, mainly in the high season. Particularly popular are the flotation points where visitors begin a pleasant 1-mile (1.6-km) float downstream. Tour agencies provide meals and equipment.

🏊 Gruta do Lago Azul

12 miles (20 km) W of Bonito.
🕖 *7am–2pm daily.* 📷
The Serra do Bodoquena is dotted with caves, the most spectacular of which is the Gruta do Lago Azul. The main highlight is a radiant underground lake that shines as blue as a sapphire in the morning light. From the cave's spectacular mouth, a narrow path leads deep down through striking stalactite formations. At the bottom lies the lake, illuminated by ambient light that streams through the cave's opening.

🏊 Estância Mimosa

15 miles (24 km) NW of Bonito.
Tel *(067) 9986 4802.* 🕗 *8am–3pm daily.* 📷 🚗 www.estanciamimosa.com.br
Some of the best hiking opportunities are offered in the Estância Mimosa trail, which features rivers, natural pools, and as many as eight waterfalls. There are various bathing spots located in and around these natural features. The trail goes past the gorgeous riverside forest of the Rio Mimoso, with caves and a rich array of wildlife. The fauna includes a variety of birds and mammals, while various kinds of fern, orchid, and bromeliad are part of the lush vegetation found in this area. An optional horseback excursion is also available.

Lake and stalactites at the Abismo Anhumas cavern

🏊 Abismo Anhumas

16 miles (25 km) W of Bonito.
🕖 *7:30am–noon daily.*
A pothole that descends a vertical 240-ft (73-m) deep, the Abismo Anhumas is a cavern filled with a large, clear blue lake featuring vast stalagmites, stalactites, and many other cave deposits. It is possible to snorkel in the lake. The entrance to the cave is by rappel. The growing number of adventure activities include cave diving and canopy tours using rope bridges and zip lines. A group of 16 people are permitted in the cave on any given day. Book with Bonito tour agencies in advance as training is required.

SOUTHERN
BRAZIL

Introducing Southern Brazil

The states of Paraná, Santa Catarina, and Rio Grande do Sul form Southern Brazil – the only Brazilian region that lies entirely outside the tropics. Often dismissed as somehow not being truly Brazilian, this region is distinctive due to more than its temperate climate. Although there are vital indigenous, African, and Portuguese elements to the population, the region is largely associated with descendants of European immigrants. The landscape features tremendous contrasts – the pampas grasslands, mountains, and the highland plateau. The distinctive cultures that have emerged there, as along the equally varied coast, serve as reminders of Brazil's diversity.

BRAZIL

SOUTHERN
BRAZIL

Foz do Iguaçu (see pp340–43) *is one of South America's most impressive natural features. These spectacular waterfalls are shared by Brazil and Argentina, with each side offering unique perspectives. From Brazil, visitors enjoy a complete panorama, while the trails in Argentina allow visitors to see the falls close-up.*

RIO GRANDE DO
(see pp348–59

São Miguel das Missões (see p359) *is Rio Grande do Sul's best-preserved Jesuit ruin. This haunting place offers ample evidence of the sophistication of native Guaraní Baroque architecture that emerged in this remote region in the mid-17th century.*

◁ **Aerial view of wheat fields, Paraná**

Curitiba (see p336), *the capital of Paraná, is a pretty, well-planned town. Built during the city's cattle and coffee boom, today Curitiba has well-preserved historic buildings, less pollution and traffic than other Brazilian cities, plenty of green spaces, a great music scene, and several interesting sights.*

NTA CATARINA & PARANÁ
(see pp332–47)

Florianópolis (see pp346–7), *the vibrant capital city of Santa Catarina on Ilha de Santa Catarina, is surrounded by quiet fishing communities and excellent beaches. The sheltered north shore has the most developed beaches, while the east coast lures surfers attracted by giant Atlantic rollers.*

0 kilometers   150

0 miles   150

Porto Alegre (see pp352–3), *the capital of Rio Grande do Sul, has a host of Neo-Classical buildings dating from the 19th and early 20th centuries. The Palácio Municipal is one such expression of civic pride, built in 1898, when Porto Alegre was developing into a significant city.*

Multicultural Southern Brazil

Pysanky, Russian painted egg

More than anywhere else in the country, Southern Brazil has been shaped culturally and economically by immigrants. Unlike tropical Brazil to the north, this part was considered unsuitable for plantation agriculture, and instead immigrants were recruited for land colonization schemes. The legacy of its physical isolation from "mainstream" Brazilian society is reflected in the languages and cultures of the immigrants. The architectural heritage has become increasingly valued, festivals showcase traditional music and dance, while handicrafts and local products are sold in villages and on farms.

An illustration of European immigrants aboard a ship bound for Brazil

AZOREANS

In the 18th century, Azoreans settled along the coast of Southern Brazil, bringing with them fishing, farming, and lace-making skills. Villages were created, in particular on the island of Santa Catarina, whose white-and-blue buildings resemble those of the Portuguese mid-Atlantic islands.

Fishing, the main economic activity of the Azorean community in Santa Catarina

Azorean lace-making *is one of the important traditions that have been maintained by women in villages on the island of Santa Catarina.*

GERMANS

Germans were the first non-Portuguese immigrants to settle in Southern Brazil, in the 1850s. They were drawn to the highlands of Rio Grande do Sul and the river valleys of northeastern Santa Catarina. Their dialects and traditions continue in many rural areas, while German architectural styles are apparent in cities such as Blumenau and Nova Hamburgo.

Old-world architecture *still dominates in the areas of Southern Brazil settled by German immigrants. Many buildings are exact replicas of ones found in towns in southern Germany. In the countryside, distinctive half-timbered farmhouses, built by pioneer immigrants, remain a common sight.*

German-Brazilian celebration of Oktoberfest

ITALIANS

The first Italian immigrants settled in Rio Grande do Sul in 1875, with tens of thousands arriving there, and in Santa Catarina and Paraná, over the next 50 years. The vast majority came from the northern Italian provinces of Veneto and Trento, introducing rich culinary traditions and the ability to cultivate lucrative grape vines on the steepest of hillsides.

Vineyards in the Serra Gaúcha (see p355) *have become as much a part of the landscape as they are in Italy. These endless stretches of lush greenery form the center-stage for the region's wine production, known both in and outside Brazil.*

SLAVS

Paraná is the state most closely associated with Slavic immigrants from Central and Eastern Europe, with Poles settling in and around Curitiba from 1869, Ukrainians in the south-center of the state from 1895, and Russians around Ponta Grossa in the early 1960s. The Ukrainians have been especially successful in maintaining their ethnic identity.

São Josafat, *a typical Byzantine-style church in Prudentópolis, is easily recognizable by its onion dome features. The Ukrainian Catholic church is pivotal in maintaining Ukrainian identity in Brazil.*

A log cabin, *housed in the Museu da Imigração Polonesa in Curitiba, is one of the structures that were built by Polish immigrants in the 19th and 20th centuries.*

OTHER COMMUNITIES

At the beginning of the 20th century, Jews from Eastern Europe founded agricultural communities in Rio Grande do Sul. They later moved to Porto Alegre, establishing Brazil's third largest Jewish community. In the 1920s and 1930s, many Japanese immigrants relocated to Paraná from São Paulo, setting up coffee and soya farms. Immigrants from other ethnic backgrounds were too few to leave legacies. Some exceptions are the Austrians who settled in central Santa Catarina in the 1930s, and the Dutch who came to Paraná after World War II.

Praça Ministro Andreas Thaler, *in Treze Tílias, is named for the then Austrian Minister of Agriculture, who founded the city in 1933 for Austrian immigrants.*

Castrolanda, *a Dutch settlement thriving on dairy and agricultural products, mainly soya, continues to celebrate its past in the traditional folk dances of the Netherlands.*

The Gaúcho Life

The *gaúcho* culture developed in colonial times in what is now northeastern Argentina, Uruguay, and Southern Brazil. In Rio Grande do Sul, the natives of the state – whether urban or rural, and regardless of their ethnic origin – are called *gaúchos*. Traditionally, *gaúchos* were semi-nomadic people who lived by hunting wild cattle. With the introduction of fencing and border agreements, they were reduced to being ranch hands. Nonetheless, their legacy continues to be strongly visible in the distinct *gaúcho* culture of today. In the interior of the state, in the grasslands of both the pampas and *serra*, the heirs of the traditional *gaúcho* employ their skills as tough horsemen on cattle *estancias* (ranches).

Old *estancia* Sobrado, a traditional ranch, Rio Grande do Sul

CLOTHING

Traditional *gaúcho* attire remains commonplace among the rural population of the pampas and highlands of Southern Brazil. On special occasions, city dwellers also don *gaúcho* clothing, an outward sign of the distinctiveness of Rio Grande do Sul society.

Gaúcho dress is worn with immense pride. "Gaúcho pants" (*bombachas*), a linen shirt, kerchief, poncho, rimmed felt-hat, and pleated boots with fancy spurs are essential components of traditional *gaúcho* clothing.

A silver knife, delicately carved, is an important *gaúcho* tool, handy weapon, and eating implement.

Parade celebrating *gaúcho* culture in Argentina

CENTRO DE TRADIÇÕES GAÚCHAS

The worldwide Brazilian-*gaúcho* organization, Centro de Tradições Gaúchas, (Center for Gaúcho Traditions) was founded by eight Porto Alegre students in 1948, to preserve and promote *gaúcho* traditions. Today, it has more than 4,500 affiliate clubs that stage rodeos, *gaúcho* dances, parades, barbecues, and other social events. A *centro* can now be found wherever *gaúchos* live, both within Rio Grande do Sul and as far afield as Bolivia, Japan, and Portugal. The *centros* are perhaps the most convenient way for an outsider to observe *gaúcho* traditions, which are emerging as a part of popular culture even in non-*gaúcho* areas. Local tourist offices and hotels will be able to provide information on upcoming events.

WAY OF LIFE

The *gaúcho* way of life was originally a nomadic one, with the horsemen wandering the pampas, hunting wild cattle for their hides. Working as cattle hands today, *gaúchos* still cling to many of the traditions.

Rodeos, *often lasting several days, test the skills of cattlemen, serve as social events for local townsfolk, and help break the isolation of rural inhabitants.*

Cattle drives *by* gaúchos *on horseback are common sights en route to Rio Grande do Sul's extensive grassland regions.*

DANCE & MUSIC

Dance performances are integral to social gatherings. The music originates from a mixing of Portuguese, Spanish, Basque, African, German, and Italian cultures, with lyrics typically about local tales. Polkas and marches form the basis of traditional *gaúcho* dance.

A colorful kerchief is part of a *gaúcho*'s typical dress.

Bombachas, or loose-fitting trousers belted with a *tirador* (sash), are traditionally worn by the *gaúchos*.

Accordion music *first came to Southern Brazil with Portuguese colonists, but was transformed by exposure to other influences. The accordion and acoustic guitar are the most common folk instruments.*

FOOD & DRINK

Meat, especially beef, is central to the traditional *gaúcho* diet. While the *gaúcho* grill is legendary, rice, usually cooked with *charque* (jerked beef), is also a staple. Pumpkin and other varieties of squash are often incorporated into stews.

Chimarrão, a *sugarless* chá mate *tea, is the characteristic and most popular drink of Rio Grande do Sul. The caffeinated herbal tea is sipped through a bomba (a silver straw) from a* cuia *(gourd). The same* cuia *is generally used by a group of* chimarrão *drinkers.*

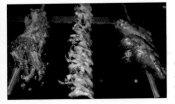

Churrasco, *barbecued beef popular throughout Brazil, is cooked on metal or wood skewers rested on a support or stuck into the ground, and roasted over a charcoal or firewood flame.*

SANTA CATARINA & PARANÁ

*B*razil's southern states are a delight for nature-lovers, with Paraná's spectacular Iguaçu Falls surrounded by lush rainforest and lovely beaches fringing the coast of tiny Santa Catarina. The region's long history of immigration from Europe has created a unique cultural identity that is visible even today.

During the 17th and 18th centuries, military garrisons were established all along the coast of Southern Brazil to guard against possible Spanish encroachment, and immigrants from the Portuguese mid-Atlantic islands of the Azores were brought in to establish farming and fishing settlements. Over time, these settlements grew into important towns, and Curitiba – on the trade route between Rio Grande do Sul and Minas Gerais – transformed into one of Brazil's most dynamic cities.

From 1840 to the mid-1900s, the interiors of Paraná and Santa Catarina were opened to immigration, with waves of European and other settlers staking out small farms. The newcomers settled along ethnic lines, with the Polish concentrated around Curitiba, Ukrainians in southern Paraná, Germans in Santa Catarina's Itajaí Valley, and Italians in the southern part of the state. The physical and cultural isolation of ethnic groups has resulted in distinct identities being maintained in rural areas to this day. The towns of Paranaguá, Antonina, and Morretes in Paraná, and Laguna, Florianópolis, and São Francisco do Sul in Santa Catarina also retain visible characteristics of their European origins.

The main destination for visitors to Paraná are the Iguaçu Falls and the surrounding rainforest. The state's coast has escaped the excesses of development despite the natural beauty of Ilha do Mel, Guaraqueçaba, and Superaguï Island. Visitors to Santa Catarina make straight for the beaches of Florianópolis. The mountainous interior around São Joaquim and Lages is worth visiting for its spectacular scenery.

Turquoise waves hitting Florianópolis beach, Santa Catarina

◁ Litorina, the tourist train running between Paranaguá and Morretes in Paraná

Exploring Santa Catarina & Paraná

Although the uncontested highlights of this region are Paraná's magnificent Iguaçu Falls and Santa Catarina's island resort of Florianópolis, these two states have much more to offer. Santa Catarina's 310-mile (500-km) coast features sheltered coves and long expanses of beach, while in Paraná, the Atlantic forest preserves of the Parque Nacional Ilha de Superagüi encompass dense virgin forest. Ilha do Mel, at the mouth of Paranaguá Bay, is a popular beach resort, and just across the bay on the mainland is the scenic port of Paranaguá. Inland, both states have a robust agricultural industry. Vast soya farms dominate large parts of Paraná, while small family holdings are characteristic of Santa Catarina. Descendants of European immigrants continue their traditions in these states, such as the Austrians in Treze Tílias.

SIGHTS AT A GLANCE

Towns & Cities
Curitiba ❶
Florianópolis & Ilha de Santa Catarina pp346–7 ❼
Paranaguá ❸

National Parks, Islands & Areas of Natural Beauty
Foz do Iguaçu pp340–43 ❻
Ilha do Mel ❹
Ilha de Superagüi ❺
Serra da Graciosa p337 ❷

SEE ALSO

Façade of the Mercado Público in Florianópolis, Santa Catarina

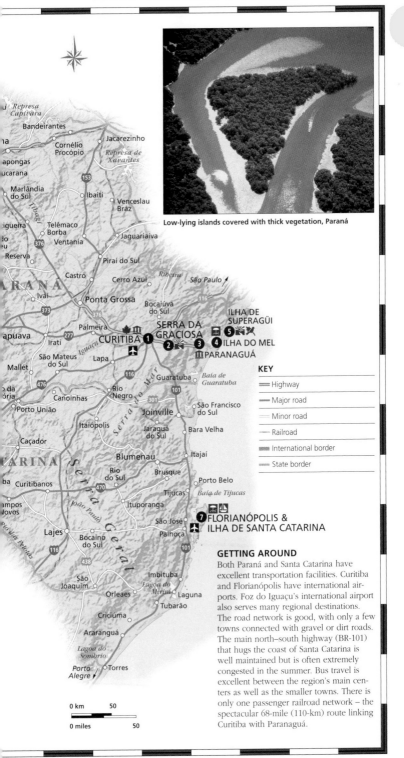

Low-lying islands covered with thick vegetation, Paraná

KEY

═══	Highway
───	Major road
────	Minor road
───	Railroad
▬▬▬	International border
▬▬▬	State border

GETTING AROUND

Both Paraná and Santa Catarina have excellent transportation facilities. Curitiba and Florianópolis have international airports. Foz do Iguaçu's international airport also serves many regional destinations. The road network is good, with only a few towns connected with gravel or dirt roads. The main north–south highway (BR-101) that hugs the coast of Santa Catarina is well maintained but is often extremely congested in the summer. Bus travel is excellent between the region's main centers as well as the smaller towns. There is only one passenger railroad network – the spectacular 68-mile (110-km) route linking Curitiba with Paranaguá.

Colorful shops and restaurants around Praça Garibaldi

Curitiba ❶

Paraná. 🏛 *1,730,000.* ✈
🚉 *from Paranaguá.* 🛈 *Rua da Glória 362, (041) 3352 8000.*
www.viaje.curitiba.pr.gov.br

Founded in 1693 as a gold mining encampment, Curitiba developed to become the largest city in Southern Brazil. It emerged from being a minor administrative, commercial and agro-processing center to grow into one of Brazil's most dynamic cities. Since the early 1990s, Curitiba has rivalled São Paulo as a location for corporate investment, in large measure attracted by the city's quality of life and public services, which are an example to the rest of the country.

The Largo da Ordem marks the heart of Curitiba's oldest quarter and features many well-preserved historic buildings. Dating from 1737, the Igreja da Ordem is the city's oldest church and the finest example of Portuguese ecclesiastical architecture in the state. The plain, white-washed, structure is decorated inside with typically Portuguese blue-and-white tiles and Baroque altars. Alongside the church is the **Museu de Arte Sacra** with a small but well-presented collection of relics gathered from churches in Curitiba. On the same side of the square is the **Igreja do Rosário**, originally serving Curitiba's slave population. First built in 1737, the church was completely reconstructed in the 1930s but retains its original Portuguese

colonial style. Across the square is the early 18th-century Casa Romário Martins, Curitiba's oldest surviving house and now a cultural center featuring exhibitions on the history of the city.

Up the hill from here, virtually adjoining the Largo da Ordem are Garibaldi and João Cândido squares. The squares are surrounded by brightly painted late 19th- and early 20th-century houses, now used as art galleries, antique shops, and restaurants. The grandest building, however, is the Palácio São Francisco, built in 1929 and later serving as the state governor's official residence. Renovated and extended in 2002, the building is now the **Museu Paranaense**, its displays

Detail outside Museu Paranaense

Façade of Igreja do Rosário on Largo do Ordem

concentrating on Paraná's archaeology, anthropology, and history.

The city's commercial center extends along Rua XV de Novembro. Rua das Flores is the pedestrianized section lined with early 20th-century pastel-colored shops. This area's one truly distinctive building is the magnificent former city hall at Praça José Borges, just across from the flower market. Built in 1916, the French-style Art Nouveau structure was later used as the Museu Paranaense until the opening of the new site.

To celebrate the contributions of European immigrants to the city's development, parks have been built in their honor. The best example of these is the **Bosque Papa João Paulo II Memorial Polonês**, where log cabins built in the 1880s by Polish immigrants have been re-erected. The buildings – including a farmhouse, chapel, and barns, are set amid a small araucaria preserve, pine trees that originally dominated the landscape. Bordering the Bosque Papa João Paulo II and representing modern Curitiba is the **Museu Oscar Niemeyer**. Popularly referred to as "The Eye" after the construction's central feature, the building is considered one of Oscar Niemeyer's greatest architectural achievements.

🌿 **Bosque Papa João Paulo II Memorial Polonês**
Av Mateus Leme/ Rua Wellington Oliveira Vianna (Centro Cívico). **Tel** (041) 3313 7194. ⏰ 10:30–6pm Mon, 9am–7:30pm Tue–Sun. ♿

🏛 **Museu de Arte Sacra**
Largo da Ordem s/n. **Tel** (041) 3321 3265. ⏰ 9am–noon & 1–6pm Tue–Fri, 9am–2pm Sat & Sun. 📷 ∅

🏛 **Museu Oscar Niemeyer**
Rua Marechal Hermes 999 (Centro Cívico). **Tel** (041) 3350 4400. ⏰ 10am–6pm Tue–Sun. 📷 ♿

🏛 **Museu Paranaense**
Rua Kellers 289. **Tel** (041) 3304 3320. ⏰ 9:30am–5:30pm Tue–Fri, 11am–3pm Sat & Sun. 📷 ♿

Serra da Graciosa ❷

The mountain range that separates Paraná state's coast from its interior is known as the Serra do Mar. Its southern extension, Serra da Graciosa, is one of the largest remaining areas of Mata Atlântica (Atlantic forest) in Southern Brazil. The Serra is rich in flora and fauna, ranging from lowland sub-tropical to cloud forest varieties. The road and railroad linking Morretes and Curitiba are amazing feats of 19th-century engineering, zigzagging through some of the most spectacular terrain in the country. The area is often shrouded with mist or fog, the result of cool air from the highlands colliding with the warm air of the subtropical coast. The forest thrives on such precipitation.

VISITORS' CHECKLIST

Paraná. 🚋 from Curitiba.
🛈 Largo Dr José Pereira 43,
Morretes, (041) 3462 1024.
🚢 in Morretes. **Parque
Estadual de Morumbi
Tel** (041) 3462 3598. ⏰ 6am–
7pm daily. **Litorina
Tel** (041) 3323 4007. Advance
booking required. **www.**
serraverdeexpress.com.br

Parque Estadual de Marumbi
*Usually shrouded with mist, trails
with stunning vistas crisscross
this vast expanse of
Mata Atlântica.*

The Estrada Graciosa
*Completed in 1873, the Estrada Graciosa
winds its way through the forbidding
terrain of the Serra do Mar.*

Morretes makes an excellent
base to explore the
surrounding region.

Taquari
Campina
Grande
do Sul
Antonina
Piraquara
Curitiba
Morretes
Baía de
Paranaguá
Paranaguá
Barro Preto
Alexandra

Serra do Mar, with its forest-
covered mountain range,
separates Paraná's coastal
plain and highland plateau.

| 0 meters | 150 |
| 0 yards | 150 |

KEY

━━ Major road

══ Minor road

── Railroad

The Litorina
*The remarkable Curitiba–Paranaguá
railroad line passes through 13 tunnels
and across 30 bridges. For much of the
route, the line clings to a seemingly sheer
mountainside from which, on clear
days, there are wonderful views across
untouched forest toward the coast.*

Colonial buildings along the waterfront in Paranaguá

Paranaguá ❸

Paraná. 🏠 142,000. 🚌 from Curitiba. 🚉 ℹ️ *Rua General Carneiro, (041) 3425 4542.* **www**.paranagua.pr.gov.br

Founded in 1585, Paranaguá is the oldest city in Paraná and is one of Brazil's most important ports today.

Paranaguá's historic center is small enough to explore on foot. The city's oldest buildings are located in the compact historic core on the shore of Paranaguá Bay. Most of these dilapidated, but distinguished-looking, 19th-century merchants' houses now serve as shops or inexpensive hotels. Also along the shore is the former Colégio dos Jesuítas, an imposing building that now houses the **Museu de Arqueológia e Etnologia**, with a rich collection relating to the region's indigenous inhabitants and popular culture.

Two churches in the historic center are worth seeking out. The **Igreja de Nossa Senhora do Rosário**, built between 1575 and 1578, has suffered considerable changes over the centuries, but the main structure retains a Portuguese colonial appearance. Built in 1784 for slaves, the **Igreja de São Benedito** is an excellent example of popular colonial

architecture. The simple, whitewashed building has undergone renovation in recent years and contains a small collection of sacred art.

🏛 **Museu de Arqueológia e Etnologia**
Rua 15 de Novembro 575. **Tel** (041) 3422 8844. ☐ noon–6pm Tue–Sun. 🈺

Ilha do Mel ❹

Paraná. 🏠 1,200. 🚤 from Paranaguá. **www**.ilhadomelonline. com.br

The most beautiful of Paraná's islands, Ilha do Mel offers a combination of almost entirely undeveloped beaches, isolated coves, and sandy trails. The island guards the entrance to Paranaguá Bay and there are well-preserved ruins of the mid-18th century fort, **Fortaleza de Nossa Senhora dos Prazeres**, that was constructed to ward off English, French, and Spanish attacks. The **Farol das Conchas** (Conchas Lighthouse), imported from Glasgow and placed on the island's most easterly point in 1872, is the best place for a stunning panoramic view of the island, bay, and mountains.

Tourist development is low-key. Visitor numbers are controlled, and there are no roads or motor vehicles on the island. Building work is also strictly regulated. *Pousadas* are all small and very simple, but most are all the more charming for this. The Ilha do Mel attracts predominantly

Farol das Conchas lighthouse on the eastern tip of Ilha do Mel

A flock of migratory birds in the Parque Nacional de Superagüi, Ilha de Superagüi

young visitors and in the summer it transforms into a party island, with beachside bars open through the night. In spite of this, there can be few more peaceful spots on the southern Brazilian coast than on this island. The beaches, some with waves suitable for skilled surfers, others with warm, calm water ideal for swimming, are never overcrowded. Some of the best beaches, such as **Praia Grande** and **Praia da Fora**, are located on the eastern part of the island.

Ilha de Superagüi ❺

Paraná. 🚢 *from Paranaguá.* ⌂ *Pousada Superagüi, (041) 3482 7149.* **www**.pousadasuperagui.com.br

Just a few dozen people who make a living from fishing and tourism inhabit the island of Superagüi. The island is part of the **Parque Nacional de Superagüi**, the largest stretch of intact Atlantic rainforest, or Mata Atlântica *(see p109)*. The park is home to jaguars and parrots, and is known for its mangroves and salt marshes, where an amazing variety of orchids grow. The park is also part of the Atlantic forest reserves that were given UNESCO World Heritage listing in 1999. The island is reached by boat, most easily from Paranaguá, although arrangements can also be made from Ilha do Mel. Most of the low-lying island is covered with shrub forest and mangrove. Very basic accommodation is available at **Barra de Superagüi**, a village located on the southeast of the island. The only other part of the island that is accessible to visitors is **Praia Deserta**, a glorious 24-mile (38-km) long expanse of white sand. The island attracts various migrating birds, but the flocks of rare, red-faced parrot (*Amazona brasiliensis*) are endemic. Visitors can observe them during the early hours of the evening.

Ⅹ Parque Nacional de Superagüi
Barra de Superagüi. 🕐 *24 hrs.* 📷
🛏 *arranged at Pousada Superagüi.*

Barreado, a regional specialty of Paraná

BARREADO

In Paraná's coastal towns, *barreado* is listed on the menu of most restaurants. Now available throughout the year, *barreado*, considered a poor man's meal, used to be eaten during Carnaval. *Barreado* is a dish that can provide food for several days and requires little attention while cooking. The dish is made of beef, bacon, tomatoes, onion, cumin, and other spices. Traditionally these ingredients are placed in layers in a large clay urn, covered, and then sealed with a paste of ash and *farinha* (manioc flour), before being cooked in a wood-fired oven for up to 15 hours. Today, pressure cookers are sometimes used, and gas or electric ovens are substituted for wood-fired ones. *Barreado* is served with *farinha*, which is spread on a plate; the meat and gravy is placed on top, and eaten with banana and orange slices.

Foz do Iguaçu ⑥

Blue butterfly

Iguaçu Falls rate as one of South America's great natural sights. The falls are formed by a succession of 275 interlinking cataracts up to 246 ft (75 m) in height cascading over a 1.8-mile (3-km) wide precipice. The falls owe their origins to several successive volcanic layers of rock built up over 110 million years. Shared between Brazil and Argentina, the falls are completely surrounded by nature preserves. The two preserves of Brazil's Parque Nacional do Iguaçu and Argentina's Parque Nacional Iguazú contain one of the largest surviving tracts of Atlantic forest in South America.

Estación Cataratas is the starting point of most of the trails. The station also has a rest area and a food court.

★ Garganta do Diabo
At the Garganta do Diabo (Devil's Throat), the river falls into the depths below with immense power, producing a thick cloud of misty spray.

Porto Canoas Restaurant, with its outdoor deck, has a wonderful view of the upper falls.

Estrada Velha de Guarapuava

| 0 meters | 50 |
| 0 yards | 50 |

Walkway
The walkway snaking along one tier of the falls is where visitors can peer into the depths of the magnificent, multiple cascading falls.

STAR SIGHTS

★ Garganta do Diabo

★ Tropical das Cataratas

★ Wildlife

★ Tropical das Cataratas
This majestic 1958 hotel (see p388) is the only one that lies in the Brazilian national park.

Tren Ecológia
Access to the trails leading to the falls in the Argentinian park is by a miniature train which runs on natural gas. The train stops at three stations along the way.

VISITORS' CHECKLIST

Paraná. ✈ Aeroporto Internacional do Foz do Iguaçu, (045) 3521 4200. 🚌 Rodoviária Internacional, 4 miles (6 km) NE from town. ℹ Av Jorge Schimmelpfeng, Foz; (045) 3522 1027. **Parque Nacional do Iguaçu Tel** (045) 3521 4400. ◯ 9am–6pm daily. 🎫 🚻
Note: The best time to visit is during the rainy season between April and July.

The railroad track runs through vast expanses of lush forest where wildlife and bird sightings are common.

Isla San Martín Surroundings
Walkways lead up to views of seven cascading waterfalls, including the powerful Salto San Martín.

Pasarelas de la Isla San Martín

Powerboat Trips
The falls can be experienced from close up in hired powerboats that skim the rapids to the very foot of the falls.

★ Wildlife
The forests around Foz do Iguaçu host many wildlife species, including jaguars, birds, and butterflies.

THE ARGENTINA FALLS

Although the Brazilian side is the best place for panoramic views of the falls, it is easier to get closer to both the main cataracts as well as a series of smaller ones from the network of trails on the Argentinian side. The Argentinian forest preserve is larger than the Brazilian one, with good walkable trails, requiring more time to explore. There is also a greater likelihood of being able to spot wildlife on the Argentinian side.

The Sheraton Internacional Iguazú, close to the falls

Exploring Iguaçu

The spectacular falls are located near the Brazilian city of Foz do Iguaçu and the sleepy Argentinian town of Puerto Iguazú. Thanks to excellent roads and tourist facilities, the huge numbers of visitors do little to detract from this majestic sight. Both sides are flanked by lush national parks, abundant with wildlife, and offering sweeping views of the falls, as well as options to go closer to the falls by boat. The region of Iguaçu, meaning "Great Waters" in Tupi-Guaraní *(see p47)*, was declared a UNESCO World Heritage Site in 1986.

The ground-dwelling red-winged tinamou at Parque das Aves

KEY

🛩 International airport

━━ Major road

═══ Minor road

-•- International border

--- Park boundary

Foz do Iguaçu

400 miles (639 km) W of Curitiba. ✈ 🚌 ℹ *Av Jorge Schimmelpfeng, (045) 3522 1027.* **Itaipu Binacional** Av Tancredo Neves 6702. **Tel** *(045) 3520 6999.* ⏰ *8am, 9am, 10am, 2pm, 3pm & 3:30pm daily.* 📷 💳 *mandatory.* ♿ **www**.itaipu.gov.br

Foz do Iguaçu, also referred to as just Foz, was a sleepy little border town until the 1970s, when construction work began on the nearby **Itaipu Binacional**, the world's largest hydroelectricity plant. Today, Foz is a base to visit

the city's main attraction, the spectacular waterfalls located to the east. Foz also boasts a wide range of accommodations, as well as reasonably good bars and restaurants.

♣ Parque das Aves

Rodovia das Cataratas Km 17. **Tel** *(045) 3529 8282.* ⏰ *8:30am–5:30pm daily.* 📷 ♿ **www**. parquedasaves.com.br

Located close to the main entrance to the **Parque Nacional do Iguaçu**, the Parque das Aves serves as

an excellent introduction to Brazilian birdlife. The park consists of over 40 acres (16 ha) of forest. The park has large aviaries housing some 180 species of birds from different Brazilian eco-systems and include macaws, parrots, toucans, red-winged tinamous, and flamingos. Apart from a butterfly habitat and a reptile exhibit, the park also has a successful breeding program that concentrates on Brazilian endangered species.

🛩 Parque Nacional do Iguaçu

Tel *(045) 3521 4400.* ⏰ *1–5pm Mon, 8am–5pm Tue–Sun* 📷 💳 ♿ **www**.cataratasdoiguacu.com.br

Created in 1939, Brazil's first national park is today one of the most visited sights in the country. Public and tour buses leave visitors at the visitors' center near the park's entrance where they transfer onto electric-powered, open-topped buses for the falls, located 6 miles (10 km) into the park. The bus stops at the Estação Macuco Safari, where visitors can (for an additional charge) transfer onto a smaller electric-powered vehicle that takes them along a forest trail to the Rio Iguaçu. There, inflatable powerboats carry visitors across rapids toward the Garganta do Diabo (Devil's Throat) and to virtually the foot of the falls.

Along the way are various rest points from where there are spectacular panoramic views of the main series of falls. At the trail's lowest point there is a secure walk-way that leads to a platform where one can peer into the stunning Garganta do Diabo, a deep gorge into which the fierce, cascading waters of the falls plummet.

Jungle Explorer trucks transporting visitors to the falls

For hotels and restaurants in this region see pp386–8 and pp410–12

Exploring the Argentinian Side

The Argentinian side of Iguaçu has a larger share of the waterfalls, and offers an intimate experience with a greater variety of perspectives. The quiet little town of Puerto Iguazú is a good place to make a base.

✖ Parque Nacional Iguazú

Tel (054) 3757 4232. ☐ Dec–Mar: 7:30am–6:30pm daily, Apr–Jul: 8am–6pm daily. 🎫 🅿 🅐 **www.** iguazuargentina.com

Whereas the Brazilian park's great attractions are the spectacular panoramic views of the falls, the Argentinian park has an extensive network of forest and waterside trails with close-up views of the smaller falls. As well as the Passeio Garganta do Diablo, there are trails to the Passeio Inferiores and the Passeio Superiores.

From the park's excellent visitors' center, a miniature railroad takes visitors to the Estación Central where the Passeio Inferiores and Passeio Superiores circuits begin. From the Passeio Superiores, visitors can look down onto and across dozens of cataracts. This circuit has concrete catwalks going behind the falls, which used to lead to the Garganta do Diablo until the floods swept them away.

A rainbow arcs above the Rio Iguazú, Parque Nacional Iguazú, Argentina

The Passeio Inferiores is a short circuit offering even more spectacular views of the falls from below. This circuit takes a little over an hour and involves climbing up and down stairs. Especially remarkable are the parts of the trail across catwalks allowing amazing views over cascading water. At the lowest point, boats make the short crossing to the **Isla San Martín**, an island located in the heart of the falls. Walking on the island also requires a high level of fitness, as it involves clambering up steep slopes and across some jagged rock formations. The Passeio Garganta do Diablo catwalk begins at a quiet point upstream, passing several small islands before reaching its final, majestic destination.

Puerto Iguazú

6 miles (10 km) S of Foz do Iguaçu. ✖ 🚌 🅐 Av Víctoria Aguirre 369, (037) 574 20800. **www.** iguazuturismo.gov.ar

Traveling between Foz and the Argentinian park by public transport involves changing buses in the Argentinian town of Puerto Iguazú. Although Puerto Iguazú boasts few sights, its quiet, tree-lined streets make for attractive wandering, with wooden, rather than concrete, buildings predominating.

A short walk along Puerto Iguazú's main artery, Avenida Victoria Aguirre, leads to the Hito Tres Fronteras (Triple Borders Landmark). From here there are superb views of the Rio Iguaçu and Rio Paraná rivers and across the rivers to Brazil and Paraguay.

Capucin monkey, Parque Nacional Iguazú

Coati, one of the most commonly spotted mammals in the park

WILDLIFE IN THE IGUAÇU REGION

The extent of native flora and fauna that the parks offer is varied. Over 2,000 species of flora have been identified, including ferns, bromeliads, orchids, and many large species of trees that serve as support for an equally large variety of climbing plants. In turn, this serves as a habitat for a similarly varied range of wildlife, lured by fruit, nesting spots, and dens. Although there are 450 varieties of bird amid this forested area, by far the most likely place to spot many of these is the Parque das Aves. With a practiced eye, birds can also be spotted within the forests and clearings of the national parks; the best time for bird-watching is early in the morning and at dusk when toucans, parrots, and hummingbirds abound. Some 80 kinds of mammals, with five varieties of feline, including jaguars and pumas, also rove the forest. Early morning and evening are the best time to see animals, with monkeys sometimes seen drinking from pools in the Argentinian park, or swinging overhead through the forest's canopy. The most commonly sighted mammal is the coati. One of the great joys of Iguaçu during the warm summer months is the immense quantity and variety of colorful butterflies that flutter about.

Florianópolis & Ilha de Santa Catarina ●

Sign of Box 32 bar

Santa Catarina's capital, Florianópolis, is one of South America's hippest destinations. A gateway to the Ilha de Santa Catarina, the sprawling urban center of Florianópolis is also the transport hub for the rest of the island. The industrial zone occupies the mainland, while the colonial center sits across the bay on the island. The island's north shore has pretty beaches and warm, tranquil waters that are popular with families. The Atlantic rollers of the east coast have made the island one of the world's great surfing centers. In the daytime, Praia Mole and Praia Joaquina are crowded, while the bars of the town of Centro da Lagoa bustle until early morning.

Colorful fishing boats moored in the village of Riberão da Ilha

Canasvieras

During the summer, the warm water and safe swimming of the resort of Canasvieras especially attract families from São Paulo and Argentina.

Inglese do Rio Vermelho

Praia dos Ingleses

Cachoeira do Bom Jesus

Ponta das Canas

Praia Grande/ Moçambique

São João do Rio Vermelho

Praia de Canasvieras

Canasvieras

(403)

Vargem Grande

Praia da Barra da Lagoa

(40

Rio Ratones

Praia de Jurerê

(402)

Praia de Daniela

Costa La

(401)

Forte de São José

Santo Antônio de Lisboa

Praia do Forte

Sambaqui

BAÍA NORTE

Cacupé

★ **Santo Antônio de Lisboa**

This charming little village, with the church as its focal point, is the best preserved of the island's 18th-century Azorean settlements. Fishing provides the community's basic livelihood.

FLORIANÓPOL

Biguaçu

(10

STAR SIGHTS

★ Santo Antônio de Lisboa

★ Florianópolis

★ Praia Mole

★ **Florianópolis**

The attractions of Florianópolis include Mercado Público, which features upbeat bars, as well as some 150 stands with fruits, vegetables, seafood, and handicrafts.

(407)

Angelina

VISITORS' CHECKLIST

Santa Catarina. ✈ 7 miles
(12 km) S of Florianópolis, then
bus or taxi. 🚌 for all beaches:
Rua Antônio Ruz, Florianópolis.
🚗 Latina Rent a Car, (048) 3236
2009. ℹ Praça XV de
Novembro, (048) 3223 7796.
🎭 🎻 Festa do Divino (May,
Jun & Jul)

Barra da Lagoa
*This pleasant fishing village and beach sits at the mouth
of the Rio Barra. Lined with a choice of accommodations
and restaurants, it is particularly lively in the summer
season. The clear river water is perfect for swimming.*

★ Praia Mole
*Surfers and
hang-gliding
enthusiasts favor
the laid-back Praia
Mole to showcase
their talents. A
number of pleasant
beach bars and
eateries line the
relaxed beach.*

Praia Joaquina
*Brazil's famous surfing
center is backed by huge
dunes. The cold water and
the rough sea make it fit only
for the strongest of swimmers.*

Centro da Lagoa, an
important fishing center,
is primarily known for its
lively nightlife, stylish
bars, and restaurants.

Campeche is
renowned for
some of the
finest beaches
on the island.

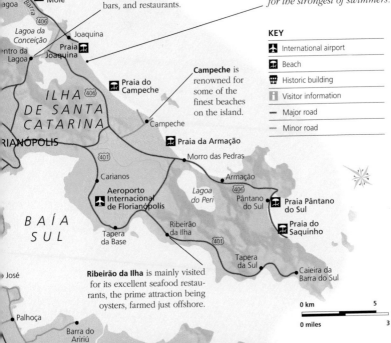

KEY

✈	International airport
🏖	Beach
🏛	Historic building
ℹ	Visitor information
—	Major road
—	Minor road

Ribeirão da Ilha is mainly visited
for its excellent seafood restaurants, the prime attraction being
oysters, farmed just offshore.

0 km   5

0 miles   3

RIO GRANDE DO SUL

The vast rolling pampas, rugged landscape, and fertile valleys of the Serra Gaúcha range are the dominant physical features of Rio Grande do Sul. A distinctive regional identity emerged with the semi-nomadic gaúcho, whose culture is still most apparent here. Although arable farming is important, the area is dominated by large, sprawling cattle estancias *or ranches.*

In 1494, even before Brazil was officially "discovered," the Treaty of Tordesillas divided South America between Portugal and Spain. An imaginary line was drawn through the continent with land to its west awarded to Spain and that to its east to Portugal. Although Brazil was Portuguese, the area that is now Rio Grande do Sul was Spanish. Neither power, however, controlled this frontier region.

Even after Brazil's independence in 1822, only a few military garrisons and small coastal settlements existed here until the mid-1800s. Apart from its obvious strategic significance, the economic potential of this sparsely populated province was gradually being recognized. Until the mid-19th century, indigenous Guaraní people and *gaúchos* inhabited the pampas, largely the preserve of wild cattle.

The forested highlands had an even smaller population. European immigrants settled here on small farms in the mid-18th century. These agricultural, wine-producing colonies grew rapidly and soon transformed the Serra's landscape and economy. By the early 19th century, Rio Grande do Sul had become synonymous with beef. The *charque* (dried beef) industry developed around the southern town of Pelotas. The introduction of railroads and refrigeration gave a further boost to the industry.

Beautiful mountain resorts and extraordinary hiking can be found around the canyons of Parque Nacional dos Aparados da Serra. Both *gaúcho* and European influences have instilled a distinct cultural identity in this state, offering a unique Brazilian experience.

Pastoral scene of cows grazing in Rio Grande do Sul

◁ *Gaúcho* riding through expansive fields of swaying pampas

Exploring Rio Grande Do Sul

The pampas that characterize the interior of southern and western Rio Grande do Sul are the state's economic heartlands. Porto Alegre, the state's capital, is a bustling city which is culturally rich and ethnically diverse. The windswept coast is for the most part unrelentingly bleak, and is fringed by lagoons and sand bars, making it one of the world's longest beaches. The araucaria pine forests, immense canyons, and terraced vineyards of Bento Gonçalves and Flores da Cunha in the northeast make perfect backdrops for charming country hotels, wineries, and mountain resorts. In the far west, the ruins of São Miguel das Missões are a haunting reminder of the Jesuit legacy in Brazil.

RIO GRANDE DO SUL

KEY

◼ Area illustrated

SIGHTS AT A GLANCE

Towns & Cities
Antônio Prado ❾
Bento Gonçalves ❻
Canela ❹
Caxias do Sul ❼
Flores da Cunha ❽
Gramado ❸
Nova Petrópolis ❷
Porto Alegre pp352–3 ❶

National Parks & Beach Resorts
Parque Nacional dos Aparados da Serra ❿
Torres ⓫

Churches
São Miguel das Missões p359 ⓬

Tours
Vale dos Vinhedos p355 ❺

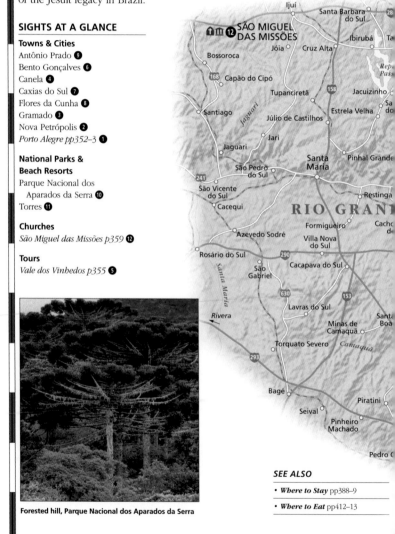

Forested hill, Parque Nacional dos Aparados da Serra

(Map labels:) Ijuí · Santa Barbara do Sul · 28 · 🏠 🏛 ⓬ SÃO MIGUEL DAS MISSÕES · Ibirubá · Ta· · Jóia · Cruz Alta · Bossoroca · 168 Capão do Cipó · Rep· Pass· · Tupanciretã · 158 · Jacuizinho · Santiago · Estrela Velha · Sa· do· · Júlio de Castilhos · Jaguari · Jari · Jaguari · Santa Maria · Pinhal Grande · São Pedro do Sul · 241 · São Vicente do Sul · Cacequi · Restinga · RIO GRAN· · Formigueiro · Cach· d· · Azevedo Sodré · Villa Nova do Sul · Rosário do Sul · 290 · São Gabriel · Cacapava do Sul · Santa Maria · Rivera · 630 · Lavras do Sul · 153 · Sant· Boa · Minas de Camaquã · Torquato Severo · Camaquã · 293 · Bagé · Piratini · Seival · Pinheiro Machado · Pedro O·

SEE ALSO

• *Where to Stay* pp388–9

• *Where to Eat* pp412–13

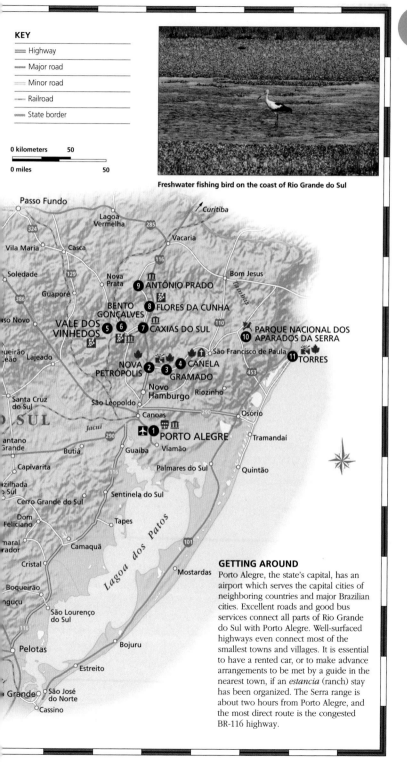

KEY

═══ Highway

──── Major road

┅┅┅ Minor road

╾╼╾╼ Railroad

═══ State border

0 kilometers 50

0 miles 50

Freshwater fishing bird on the coast of Rio Grande do Sul

Passo Fundo

Lagoa Vermelha

Curitiba

Vila Maria

Casca

Vacaria

324

285

116

Soledade

129

Nova Prata

Bom Jesus

9 **ANTÔNIO PRADO**

Guaporé

386

BENTO GONÇALVES

8 **FLORES DA CUNHA**

so Novo

VALE DOS VINHEDOS

5 **6**

110

PARQUE NACIONAL DOS APARADOS DA SERRA

10

ueirão eão

Lajeado

7 **CAXIAS DO SUL**

São Francisco de Paula

NOVA PETRÓPOLIS

2 **3** **4** **CANELA**

11 **TORRES**

Santa Cruz do Sul

São Leopoldo

GRAMADO

Novo Hamburgo

Riozinho

453

O SUL

Jacuí

Canoas

290

Osório

antano rande

Butiá

Guaíba

Viamão

1 **PORTO ALEGRE**

Tramandaí

Capivarita

116

Palmares do Sul

Quintão

zilhada Sul

Cerro Grande do Sul

Sentinela do Sul

Dom Feliciano

Tapes

maral rador

Camaquã

Lagoa dos Patos

Cristal

Mostardas

Boqueirão

nguçu

São Lourenço do Sul

116

101

Pelotas

Bojuru

Estreito

Grande

São José do Norte

Cassino

GETTING AROUND

Porto Alegre, the state's capital, has an airport which serves the capital cities of neighboring countries and major Brazilian cities. Excellent roads and good bus services connect all parts of Rio Grande do Sul with Porto Alegre. Well-surfaced highways even connect most of the smallest towns and villages. It is essential to have a rented car, or to make advance arrangements to be met by a guide in the nearest town, if an *estancia* (ranch) stay has been organized. The Serra range is about two hours from Porto Alegre, and the most direct route is the congested BR-116 highway.

Porto Alegre ❶

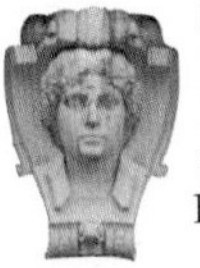

Detail, Museu de Arte do Rio Grande do Sul

Founded in 1755 on the right bank of the Rio Guaiba, Porto Alegre served as a Portuguese military garrison that guarded against Spanish encroachment into southern Brazil. Today, it is Rio Grande do Sul's capital and an important trading port. The city boasts some impressive public buildings and a lively street life. Most sights are located in the Cidade Baixa (Lower Town) and Cidade Alta (Upper Town) areas of downtown, while the best restaurants, bars, and hotels are increasingly concentrated in the suburbs.

🛒 Mercado Público

Praça XV de Novembro. 🕒 *9am–7pm Mon–Sat.* ♿

Dating back to 1869, the Neo-Classical-influenced Mercado Público has a vast collection of stalls selling household goods, fruit, vegetables, herbs, wine, meat, and fish. Characteristic of the region are the herb stalls selling *chá mate* (herbal tea) as well as *bombas* and *cuias* (silver straws and drinking gourds). Also of interest are the stalls devoted to *macumba* rituals, a reminder of the importance of Afro-Brazilian traditions in a part of the country associated primarily with European culture.

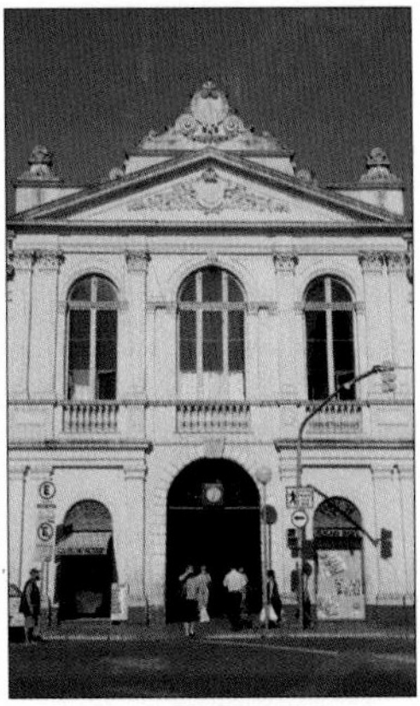

Façade of the Mercado Público, an excellent market for regional items

🏛 Praça da Matriz

Catedral Metropolitana ***Tel*** *(051) 3225 4980.* 🕒 *9am–noon & 2:30–6:30pm Mon–Fri, 9am–noon Sat.* ♿ **Museu Júlio de Castilhos** ***Tel*** *(051) 3221 3959.* 🕒 *10am–6pm Tue–Fri.* 📷 ♿ **Palácio Piratini** ***Tel*** *(051) 3210 4170.* 🕒 *9–11am & 2–5pm Mon–Fri.* 📷 ♿ **Teatro São Pedro** ***Tel*** *(051) 3227 5100.* 🕒 *noon–6pm Tue–Fri.* 📷

Designed by the renowned Italian architect Giovanni Giovenale, the 1772 **Catedral Metropolitana** features graceful classical columns, geometrically-perfect designs, and a large hemispherical dome. The present structure dates from 1921. There are a number of fine 19th- and early 20th-century buildings around Praça da Matriz.

Just off the square is the **Museu Júlio de Castilhos**, with an interesting collection of artifacts relating to the region's history. The imposing **Palácio Piratini**, just west of the cathedral, serves as the Governor's residence. It was built in 1909 in a fascinating mix of Neo-Classical, Baroque, and Rococo styles. To the square's north, the grand Neo-Classical **Teatro São Pedro** is the city's prestigious concert and

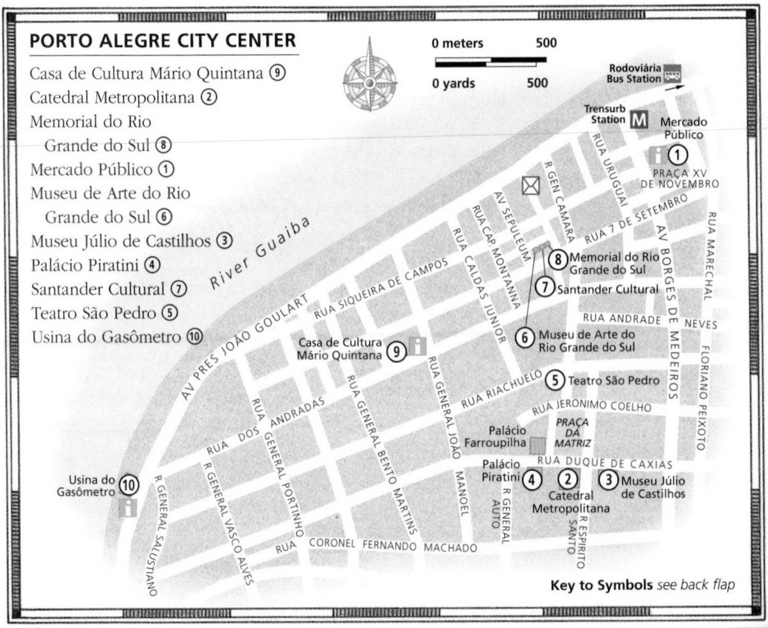
PORTO ALEGRE CITY CENTER
Casa de Cultura Mário Quintana ⑨
Catedral Metropolitana ②
Memorial do Rio Grande do Sul ⑧
Mercado Público ①
Museu de Arte do Rio Grande do Sul ⑥
Museu Júlio de Castilhos ③
Palácio Piratini ④
Santander Cultural ⑦
Teatro São Pedro ⑤
Usina do Gasômetro ⑩
0 meters 500
0 yards 500
Rodoviária Bus Station
Trensurb Station
Mercado Público
PRAÇA XV DE NOVEMBRO
River Guaiba
RUA URUGUAI
R GEN CAMARA
AV SEPULEUM
RUA CAP MONTANNA
RUA CALDAS JUNIOR
RUA 7 DE SETEMBRO
AV BORGES DE MEDEIROS
RUA MARECHAL FLORIANO PEIXOTO
Memorial do Rio Grande do Sul
Santander Cultural
RUA ANDRADE NEVES
Museu de Arte do Rio Grande do Sul
RUA SIQUEIRA DE CAMPOS
AV PRES JOÃO GOULART
Casa de Cultura Mário Quintana
Teatro São Pedro
RUA RIACHUELO
RUA JERONIMO COELHO
PRAÇA DA MATRIZ
Palácio Farroupilha
RUA DUQUE DE CAXIAS
Palácio Piratini
Catedral Metropolitana
Museu Júlio de Castilhos
RUA DOS ANDRADAS
RUA GENERAL PORTINHO
RUA GENERAL BENTO MARTINS
RUA GENERAL JOÃO MANOEL
R GENERAL AUTO
R ESPIRITO SANTO
Usina do Gasômetro
R GENERAL SALUSTIANO
R GENERAL VASCO ALVES
RUA CORONEL FERNANDO MACHADO
Key to Symbols see back flap

Ornate foyer of the Neo-Classical Teatro São Pedro

theater hall. Built in 1858, it is a popular venue for lunch and tea.

🏛 Museu de Arte do Rio Grande do Sul

Praça da Alfândega. **Tel** (054) 3227 2311. ⬤ 10am–7pm Tue–Sun. 📷 www.margs.org.br

Late 20th-century works by local artists are prominently displayed in this museum. More absorbing, however, is the small section devoted to 19th-century art. The museum also hosts a number of interesting traveling exhibitions.

🏛 Santander Cultural

Praça da Alfândega. **Tel** (051) 3287 5500. ⬤ 10am–7pm Mon–Fri & 11am–7pm Sat & Sun. ♿

This vibrant arts complex has an impressive repertoire featuring art, music, and cinema. The Neo-Classical building originally served as a bank between 1927 and 1932. Despite extensive renovations, it retains many of its original features including stained-glass windows.

VISITORS' CHECKLIST

🏘 1,416,400. ✈ 4 miles (6 km) N of city. 🚌 Mercado do Bom Fim, Loja 12, Parque Farroupilha, (0800) 517 686. 🎭 Semana Farroupilha (Sep). www.portoalegre.rs.gov.br/turismo

🏛 Memorial do Rio Grande do Sul

Praça da Alfândega. **Tel** (054) 3224 7210. ⬤ 10am–6pm Tue–Sat. ♿ www.memorial.rs.gov.br

The memorial features well-presented exhibits relating to the state's social and political history. It also houses the state archives and an oral history center.

🏛 Casa de Cultura Mário Quintana

Rua dos Andrades 736. **Tel** (054) 3221 7147. ⬤ 9am–9pm Tue–Fri, noon–9pm Sat & Sun. ♿ www.ccmq.rs.gov.br

This Neo-Classical building was designed as a hotel in 1923 by German architect Theo Wiedersphan. For many years, it was also the home of Mário Quintana, one of the state's foremost poets. Today, it hosts exhibitions relating to modern art and literature.

🏛 Usina do Gasômetro

Av Presidente João Goulart 551. **Tel** (051) 3212 5979. ⬤ 9am–9pm Tue–Sun.

Built in 1928 as a thermo-electrical power station, the Usina opened in 1991 as a cultural center hosting theater and art exhibitions. It also houses a wine museum and an art-house cinema. The west-facing terrace offers spectacular views of the sunset over the river. There are daily boat trips from the adjacent pier.

The picturesque Parque Aldeia do Imigrante, Nova Petrópolis

Nova Petrópolis ❷

66 miles (106 km) N of Porto Alegre. 🏘 18,700. 🚌 🏠 ℹ Parque Aldeia do Imigrante, (054) 3281 1398. 🎭 Festa do Folklore (Jul), Oktoberfest (Oct). www.novapetropolis.rs.gov.br

German immigrants arriving in the 1820s were the first to settle in the rolling hills north of Porto Alegre. The town of Nova Petrópolis, founded in 1858, remained relatively isolated until the mid-20th century and retains a strong German character even today.

Stretching along Avenida 15 de Novembro, the town's commercial center features a number of German-style buildings. Midway along the avenue is the interesting **Parque Aldeia do Imigrante**, which pays tribute to the region's early settlers. Set within an araucaria forest, the park houses a collection of beautifully reconstructed, half-timbered buildings dating between 1870 and 1910. The Lutheran church, houses, school, smithy, and cemetery help re-create the atmosphere of a 19th-century German hamlet. The park also hosts festivals and concerts and features a large bandstand and beer hall.

The hamlets and farmsteads surrounding Nova Petrópolis also have a distinctly German flavor. Here, German is still the dominant language and old-world traditions, such as music and dance, thrive.

♣ Parque Aldeia do Imigrante

Av 15 de Novembro 1966. **Tel** (054) 3281 1245. ⬤ 8am–6pm daily. 📷 ♿

Works on display at the Museu de Arte do Rio Grande do Sul

Swiss-style chalet, a common sight in Gramado

Gramado ❸

👥 32,000. 🚌 from Porto Alegre.
ℹ️ Av Borges de Medeiros 1674,
(054) 3286 1475. 🎫 Festival de
Gramado (Aug), Natal Luz (Nov 15–
Jan 15). www.gramadosite.com

Brazil's best-known mountain resort, Gramado does all it can to mimic a central European village. Although there are no Alpine peaks, the hilly landscape, reaching just 2,706 ft (825 m) around Gramado, is quite dramatic and the views are fantastic. The flower-filled **Parque Knorr** and the **Lago Negro**, an artificial lake bordered by pine trees imported from Germany's Black Forest, allow for pleasant strolls.

"Swiss chalet" is the dominant architectural style and, with the profusion of geranium-filled window boxes, chocolate shops, and restaurants specializing in cheese fondues, one is encouraged to believe that Gramado has connections with Switzerland. This is entirely an affectation as only a very tiny minority of the population is of Swiss origin and beneath its veneer, Gramado has more in common with an American shopping mall.

Gramado survives almost entirely on tourism. During the first two weeks in August, the city hosts the Festival de Gramado, one of Brazil's most prestigious film festivals, which also attracts an international crowd.

Environs

Just 4 miles (6 km) north from Gramado's main avenue is the **Vale do Quilombo**. Approached by a steep dirt road, much of the valley's original dense Mata Atlântica (Atlantic rainforest) remains and the climate is warmer and more humid. The **Refúgio Familia Sperry** supports an abundance of fauna including coati, toucans, and howler and capuchin monkeys. Forest trails pass magnificent waterfalls that enhance the valley's scenic splendor.

The valley floor is cultivated and picturesque. Half-timbered farm buildings, which were built by German immigrants in the 19th-century, are to be seen alongside the road.

🌿 **Refúgio Familia Sperry**
Vale do Quilombo. **Tel** (054) 3504
1649. ⏱ by appointment only.
🏞️ 📷

Canela ❹

👥 38,000. 🚌 from Porto Alegre.
ℹ️ Central de Informações, Lago
da Fama 227, (054) 3282 1510.
www.canelaturismo.com.br

Chilly winters, refreshing summers, and unspoilt nature attract visitors to Canela, once a stop-off point for cattle being herded across Rio Grande do Sul's grasslands. The town is dominated by the Igreja Matriz Nossa Senhora de Lourdes, an imposing stone church built in 1953 in English Neo-Gothic style, with other buildings in an eclectic mix of local and European styles. Thanks to the presence of students attracted to highly regarded tourism colleges, the town has a vibrant feel to it.

Environs

Most of the forests of the Serra were devastated in the 19th century in the quest for araucaria pine. Today, some of this forested area is being preserved. Approximately 5 miles (8 km) north of Canela is the **Parque do Caracol**, a forest reserve with a 429-ft (131-m) waterfall. A highlight here is the 927-step stairway leading to the base of the cascade from where visitors can best appreciate its force and the surrounding forests. A farther 3 miles (5 km) north along the road from Caracol is the **Parque da Ferradura**, a forest reserve notable for the dramatic views of the horseshoe-shaped Rio Caí and of the Arroio Caçador canyon and waterfall.

The area is a popular destination for adventure tourism, with rafting along the fast-flowing Rio Paranhana. Rappeling down its gorge allows for close-up views of the terrain.

🌿 **Parque da Ferradura**
Estrada do Caracol. **Tel** (054) 9969
6785. ⏱ 9am–5:30pm daily. 📷

🌿 **Parque do Caracol**
Estrada do Caracol. **Tel** (054) 3278
3035. ⏱ 8:30am–6pm Sat &
Sun. 📷

Majestic waterfall, Parque do Caracol, near Canela

Tour of Vale dos Vinhedos [5]

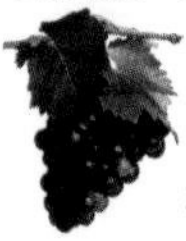

A bunch of black grapes

Some of the best wine in Brazil is produced in Vale dos Vinhedos. The majority of inhabitants here originate from Veneto, Italy, and life in the Vale dos Vinhedos follows a pattern very similar to that in the corner of Northeast Italy. In an area of virtual monoculture, grape is central to the year's activity, while the Catholic chapels are cornerstones for the maintenance of Italian traditions.

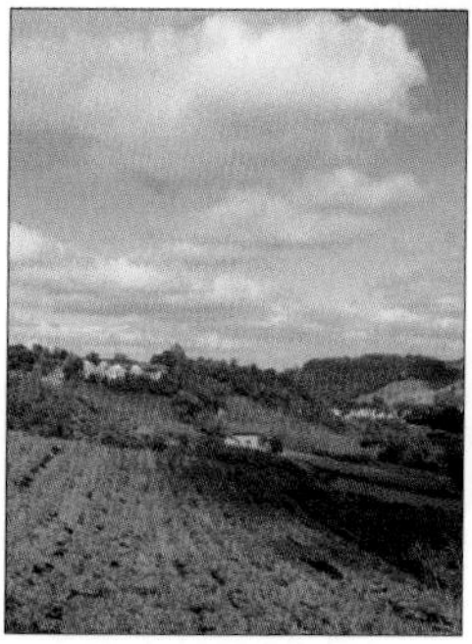

Picturesque vineyard in the Vale dos Vinhedos.

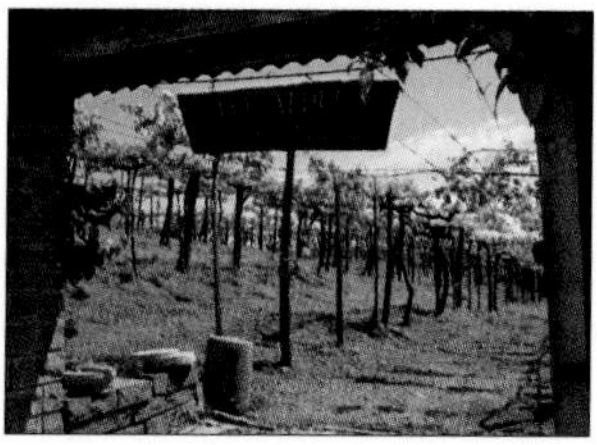

Casa Valduga [6]
Comfortable guest rooms and excellent food is offered by this pioneer of the production of high quality Brazilian wines and agritourism.

Capela das Neves [7]
Built in 1907, this is the earliest surviving chapel in Vale dos Vinhedos.

Vinícola Pizzato [5]
Still small-scale producers, the Pizzato family offer tastings and sell an extensive range of wines.

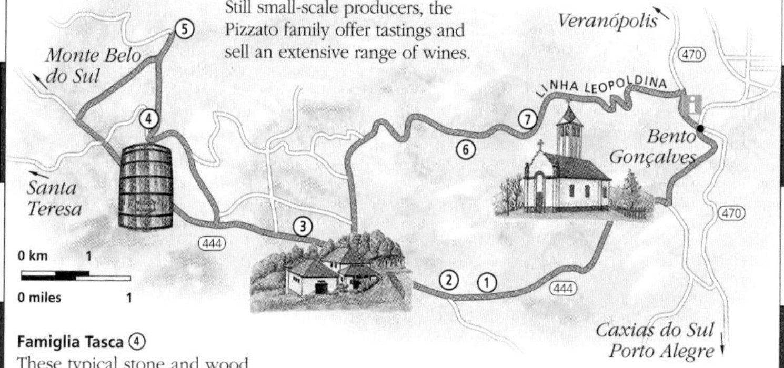
Monte Belo do Sul
Santa Teresa
Veranópolis
Linha Leopoldina
Bento Gonçalves
Caxias do Sul
Porto Alegre
444
470
0 km 1
0 miles 1

Famiglia Tasca [4]
These typical stone and wood farm buildings are amongst the oldest wineries in the valley.

Memorial do Vinho [2]
This small, fascinating exhibition charts the development of the local wine production from 1875 to present.

Capela das Graças [1]
Honoring Our Lady of Grace, this *capela* is one of the many Catholic chapels that are central to the valley's Italian immigrants.

KEY

- Tour route
- Other road
- [i] Visitor information

TIPS FOR DRIVERS

Starting point: *Bento Gonçalves (see p356).*
Length: *Allow a full day to visit several wineries and a stop for lunch.*
Driving conditions: *The main road is paved while the side roads have good-quality gravel surfaces.*

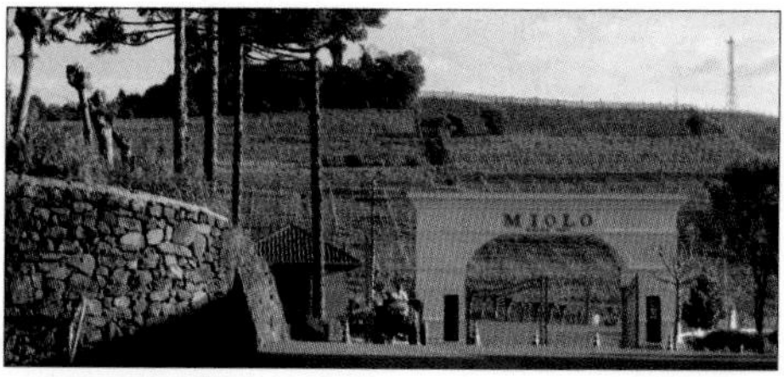
MIOLO

Vinícola Miolo [3]
The largest vineyard in the valley, Vinícola Miolo produces some of Brazil's best wine. The visitors' center tells the story of Miolo's development and allows tastings.

Vinhos Salton, one of the many wineries in Bento Gonçalves

Bento Gonçalves ❻

🏚 101,000. 🚌 ℹ️ Rua Mal Deodoro 70, (054) 3453 6934. www.bentogoncalves.com.br

Examine a bottle of Brazilian wine and, in all likelihood, the label will indicate Bento Gonçalves as its place of origin. Bento, as the city is usually called, is one of the largest producers of wine in Brazil, with virtually every patch of land outside the city growing vines. The city's economy relies solely on grapes and wine production, as a result of which Bento's vintners dominate the Brazilian market.

Bento was one of the earliest Italian communities established in the Serra Gaúcha in 1875. However, the rapid growth of the city's urban center in recent decades has left few traces of Italian influence during the early years of immigration. The **Museu do Imigrante** has a rich collection of artifacts relating to Bento's pioneer settlers with rooms focusing on the arrival of the immigrants and the central role of the Catholic church in the community and farming, in particular viticulture.

Wine is still produced in town by large commercial operations. The **Cooperativa Vinícola Aurora** is the best known, and Aurora is the most prominent wine producer in Brazil, with a membership of some

1,300 families, most of whom farm in the valley. Visitors to the cooperative are shown the entire production process from the crushing of grapes to bottling. Tours culminate with tastings. There are also numerous *cantinas* (wine cellars) dotting the town center which also offer free tours and tastings.

Smaller producers also produce fine wines. These are located just a short distance from downtown Bento, indeed vines extend right up to the city limits and through the beautiful Vale dos Vinhedos, the Valley of Vineyards (see p355).

Wine produced in Bento Gonçalves

Cooperativa Vinícola Aurora
Rua Olavo Bilac 500, Cidade Alta. **Tel** (054) 3455 2000. ⬜ 8:15am–5:15pm Mon, 8:30–11:30am Sun. ▢ ⬤

🏛 Museu do Imigrante
Rua Erny Hugo Dreher 127, (Planalto). **Tel** (054) 3451 1773. ⬜ 8–11:15am & 1:30–5:15pm Tue–Fri, 1–5pm Sat, 9am–noon Sun. ▢

Environs

Garibaldi, a small town just 12 miles (20 km) south of Bento Gonçalves, is known for its surprisingly good champagne-style sparkling wines. Part of the attraction of getting to this little town is the ride on the steam engine known as Maria Fumaça, or "Smoking Mary," a name commonly given to tourist steam trains *(see p440)*.

Passing through the landscape's patchwork of vineyards, the 15-mile (23-km) route is covered in an hour and a half. The high point of the journey is the stop at an observatory overlooking the Rio das Antas at the point where the route curves in a horseshoe shape.

Caxias do Sul ❼

🏚 396,000. ✈️ 🚌 ℹ️ Praça Dante Alighieri, (054) 3222 1875. www.visitecaxias.com.br

Founded in 1875 Caxias do Sul – or simply Caxias, as it is usually called – along with Bento Gonçalves, was one of the earliest Italian *colonias* to be established in the Serra. Like its neighboring settlements, commercial activity at first revolved entirely around wine production, but over the next century other agro-processing industries, as well as textiles, developed. Today, Caxias is Rio Grande do Sul's second largest city after Porto Alegre.

Although tower blocks and other concrete buildings have overtaken much of Caxias, some visible traces of the city's heritage survive.

Maria Fumaça, plying between Bento Gonçalves and Garibaldi

Artifacts displayed in Museu Casa de Pedra in Caxias do Sul

The **Museu Municipal**, built in 1880 as a private residence, documents the history of Caxias, starting with the arrival of the first immigrants from Veneto. The museum's permanent collection includes objects, documents, and photographs charting the development of the city.

The **Museu Casa de Pedra**, housed in a carefully preserved stone farmhouse built in 1878, sheds light on the lives of the pioneer settlers with interesting displays of tools, furniture, and photographs.

🏛 **Museu Casa de Pedra**
Rua Matteo Gianella 531, Bairro Santa Catarina. *Tel (054) 3221 2423.* ☐ *8:30am–5pm Tue–Sun.* 📷

🏛 **Museu Municipal**
Rua Visconde de Pelotas, 586. *Tel (054) 3221 2423.* ☐ *9am–5pm Tue.* 📷 📷

Flores da Cunha ⑧

🏚 *27,000.* 🚌 *from Caxias do Sul.* **www.**floresdacunha.com.br

The fact that Flores da Cunha boasts one of the highest concentrations of wineries in Rio Grande do Sul will come as little surprise to visitors. Just about every available patch of land in the municipality is given to grape vines and *cantinas*, ranging from small artisan wine producers to huge cooperatives.

The town of Flores da Cunha itself is unremarkable, but the surrounding villages and hamlets could easily be mistaken for simple northern Italian farming communities, even maintaining the Venetian dialect of their immigrant forbears, making it the most Italian of Brazilian towns.

Environs
Located in a fertile and picturesque valley, **Otávio Rocha**, 8 miles (13 km) southwest of Flores da Cunha, is especially striking, with vines extending down to the main streets. The village has become a popular place to eat and there is good choice of restaurants specializing in simple, but tasty, northern Italian country fare.

Another 4 miles (7 km) west of Otávio Rocha is **Nova Pádua**, another wine-producing *município*, whose inhabitants are descended from Venetian immigrants. The village's focal point is the church, characteristically Italian in style with a bell tower set slightly to the side of the main structure. A short distance farther west, there are breathtaking views below onto the fast flowing Rio das Antas and a landscape of the Antas Valley, a mix of vineyards and primary forest.

Antônio Prado ⑨

🏚 *14,000.* 🚌 🛈 *Praça Garibaldi 57, (054) 3293 1500.* **www.**antonioprado.com

The last of the major settlements, Antônio Prado was established in the Italian colonial zone in 1886. Located in the zone's northern extreme and, until recently, with poor links to other centers, Antônio Prado failed to make the transition from farming community to industrial town.

The lack of development is one of the reasons why the town was declared a National Heritage Site in 1989. Its particular attraction is its concentration of wooden, stone-base buildings erected by Italian immigrants.

Clustered around the town's central square, **Praça Garibaldi**, and the roads that extend immediately off it, some 48 historic buildings are protected and perfectly maintained. Most of the brightly painted clapboard structures with their unchanged interiors have been turned into shops or small government offices. One of these buildings is now the town hall on Praça Garibaldi. Also located on Praça Garibaldi, the **Museu de Antônio Prado** offers a useful historical overview of the development of the town.

🏛 **Museu de Antônio Prado**
Rua Francisco Maracantônio 77. *Tel (054) 3293 1277.* ☐ *8:30am–12:30pm & 1:30–5pm Tue–Fri, 1–5pm Sat, 11am–5pm Sun.*

Colorful stone-base wooden houses in Antônio Prado

Araucaria pine trees above the Cânion do Itaimbezinho, Aparados da Serra

Parque Nacional dos Aparados da Serra ⑩

🚌 from Canela to Cambará do Sul, then taxi. 📞 (054) 3251 1262.
🕐 9am–5pm Wed–Sun. 🎫

The highland plateau of southern Brazil emerged from the accumulation of layer upon layer of ocean sediment, with the resulting rock formations lifted up to form the Brazilian Shield. Some 150 million years ago, lava poured onto the shield to create a thick layer of basalt rock. Cracks emerged at the edge of the plateau, taking the form of narrow, but deep, canyons. It is around one of the largest of these canyons – **Canion do Itaimbezinho** – that the Parque Nacional dos Aparados da Serra, one of Brazil's first national parks, was created in 1959.

Canion do Itaimbezinho is a 2,360-ft (720-m) deep, 4-mile (6-km) long canyon featuring several ecosystems merging into one another with transition zones between them. The plateau around Itaimbezinho is mainly given over to cattle pasture, while dense Mata Atlântica (see p109) covers Itaimbezinho's lower reaches. The abundant flora ranges from lichens and mosses to orchids and other flowering plants and giant araucaria pines. Trails around the edge of the canyon are well marked, varying in length between 1 mile (2 km) and 4 miles (6 km), with observatories

enabling visitors to view the canyon in all directions. The longest trail, Trilha do Rio do Boi, can be challenging for unseasoned hikers. It is closed in the rainy season due to the danger of flooding.

The best season to visit the park is in winter (May to August), when visibility stretches to the base of the canyon and toward the coast. September is the worst time to come here, with low cloud and heavy rainfall. During the rest of the year, fog often obscures views, though it can lift very quickly.

Torres ⑪

🏙 34,000. 🚌 from Porto Alegre.
ℹ Av Barão do Rio Branco, (051) 3626 1937. **www**.clictorres.com.br

The main highlight of the long coastline of Rio Grande do Sul is Torres, located near the border with the neighboring state of Santa Catarina. Torres is named for a series of huge basalt rocks, or "towers," that jut into the ocean and break the otherwise seemingly unending beach. The towers are located in the **Parque da Guarita**, on the southern perimeter of town. Between the sea cliff towers are sandy coves offering protection from fierce Atlantic rollers. Stairs lead to caves on the cliffs facing the open sea, which were formed over the course of millions of years by the force of the ocean. From a hill at the southern edge of the park, visitors can enjoy tremendous views of the beautifully rugged coastline or trek through the dunes of 2-mile (4-km) long Praia de Itapeva. The water at Itapeva is tranquil and favorable for swimming.

Waves lapping against the cliffs, Parque da Guarita

THE RISE AND COLLAPSE OF JESUIT MISSIONS

Santa Cecilia, wood sculpture

For much of the 17th and 18th centuries, the Guaraní Indians of what is now north-western Rio Grande do Sul, as well as parts of Argentina and Paraguay, were controlled by the Jesuits. The first *redução* (community) was established in 1610; 30 others followed, including Brazil's São Miguel, which was founded in 1632. Over time, Guaraní-influenced Baroque music, architecture, painting, and sculpture began to flourish. The Spanish and Portuguese authorities became increasingly concerned about the power of the Jesuits, while Rome was worried that the order was too independent of papal authority. In 1756, Spanish and Portuguese forces expelled the Jesuits. The missions were razed to the ground or abandoned to nature.

São Miguel das Missões ⑫

Surviving through centuries of neglect, the São Miguel Mission presents a fine example of the Guaraní-Baroque style, a blend of Iberian and indigenous architectural elements. These influences are visible in architectural details, particularly in the carved stonework and in the wooden sculptures housed in the museum. The mission was designated a UNESCO World Heritage Site in 1984. Although the area around São Miguel has been given over to farmland, the mission retains an air of isolation.

Wooden sculpture

VISITORS' CHECKLIST

São Miguel. 🚌 from Porto Alegre to Santo Ângelo, then bus. 🛈 (055) 3664 1291. 🌐
📷 Festa do Gaúcho (some Sunday afternoons). **www**.rotamissoes.com.br **Museu das Missões** Rua São Nicolau s/n.
⏰ 9am–noon & 2–6pm daily (winter), 9am–noon & 2–7pm daily (summer). ♿ 📷 🏛
Sound & Light Show 7pm (winter), 9pm (summer) daily. 📷

The Bell
The mission's bell was not only rung as a call to prayers, but also to warn of attacks by roving gangs hunting for slaves.

Inner Corridors
A network of corridors give a sense of the extent of the original mission site, which at its height housed 4,000 people.

The façade is a replica of Il Gesù, the Jesuits' mother church in Rome. Only one of the two original towers remains intact.

Brick and stonework, made from local materials, was mainly used in the mission's construction.

Entrance

Museu das Missões
Designed in 1937 by Lúcio Costa, this early Modernist building was inspired by Jesuit-Baroque architecture. The museum houses statues and other relics excavated locally.

Ruins of Jesuit Buildings
Little remains of the workshops, school rooms, cloisters, and living quarters of the Jesuit mission. However, it is still possible to make out their distinct areas in the ruins.

TRAVELERS' NEEDS

WHERE TO STAY

Given the size and diversity of Brazil, it is no surprise that the country offers an excellent selection of accommodations to suit every taste and pocket. Large cities have a wide range of business hotels that comprise everything from budget brands, deluxe international properties such as Grand Hyatt and Orient-Express, to privately owned, cutting-edge boutique hotels such as

Pousada dos Quatro Cantos sign *(see p378)*

the Fasano and Unique in São Paulo. In tourist areas, the options include large, fancy, all-inclusive, internationally known resort properties, as well as Brazilian owned chain and individual hotels. There are also small, privately owned establishments, or *pousadas,* that may only have two or three rooms and are either very simple and basic or very sophisticated.

BOOKING

As Brazil is one of the most active Internet countries in the world, the majority of hotels, *pousadas,* and lodges have their own websites through which it is possible to make reservations. Many larger properties also appear on international booking engines and travel sites such as **Expedia** and **Last Minute**. In places where there is an English-speaking staff, it is also possible to make telephone and fax reservations.

In the age of the Internet, it is important for the traveler to check how financially protected they are if they do book directly and the property they choose goes out of business. Under European regulations, any company based in the EU

that sells a "package" (a combination of flight, hotels, car hire, among others) must be bonded through an approved body that will protect the client's financial security; this will probably not be the case if the traveler books direct.

During the high season, and especially during Carnaval and the Christmas to New Year period, many hotels and *pousadas* in Brazil will expect guests to stay for a minimum number of nights. This will need to be taken into consideration as one- or two-night stays may be difficult to find if you want to move around. Book in advance during high season, as good rooms are not easy to come by last minute. Weekends can also get quite crowded.

PRICES & PAYMENTS

Just as travelers want financial security, so do hotel and *pousada* owners. A deposit will certainly be required, whereas many smaller properties may require payment in advance to cover the entire duration of the stay, especially in high season or for weekend specials.

It is also normal for hotels in Brazil to ask the client to send a fax or photocopy of the credit card used to make the reservation. The reason for this is due to the increasing number of travelers who change their travel plans and then try to deny they ever made the reservation. A copy of the credit card – if not reported stolen – does tend to prove that the person

A swanky new Serhs Natal Grand Hotel on Via Costeira, Natal

◁ **Bags of spices and herbs at the *fiera livre* (open-air market) in Tijuca, Rio de Janeiro.**

Plush lobby of Hotel Bourbon Curitiba, one of Curitiba's premium hotels

did make the reservation. Credit cards are accepted as payment at most properties, especially in bigger cities.

Only the larger hotels in bigger cities will handle traveler's checks. Checks drawn on Brazilian banks are generally acceptable, as is cash. Many places accept payment in US dollars, but they will set the exchange rate, which will often be high.

When booking, it is important to check what taxes are included in the price. These may include a 10 percent service tax, a 5 percent sales tax and, in some areas of Brazil, a nightly tourist tax.

Prices throughout Brazil vary greatly and it is rare that any traveler should ever need to pay the rack rate as advertised by the hotels. Like airlines, hotels often make special offers available even through their own websites. Some hotels, normally smaller, privately owned properties, still think they can charge different prices for Brazilian travelers and foreign visitors, so it is worth checking the rates on the Portuguese language version of the website.

In Brazil, the price often reflects not only the quality of accommodation, but also the location. A traveler on a budget needs to decide if the priority is a beachfront location or a better quality hotel a couple of blocks back from the beach. There will also be notably different rates for rooms at the front of a beachfront property and those at the side or behind.

TIPPING

It is customary and much appreciated if guests leave a tip for the staff that have served them well during their stay. This could be the chambermaid, the bellboy, or the barman. Many of the people who serve visitors will be earning the minimum wage of around US$150 per month, so any tips can make a real difference.

CHILDREN

Many Brazilian families travel with their nanny in tow, and are quite happy taking their children with them wherever

Children's playroom, a feature in many Brazilian hotels

they go. Children are always welcome at most hotels with only a very few smaller, normally romantic *pousadas* having any restrictions, which will be clearly stated on their websites, or at the time of booking. The vast majority of hotels and *pousadas* in Brazil are child-friendly. Larger properties will have high chairs and possibly cots, and many resorts also have special child-friendly areas, playrooms, and even separate kitchens for mothers needing to prepare food for babies and smaller children. Many large hotels can also organize babysitters.

Warn the hotel of the age of your children and any special requirements you may need for them in advance. If the hotel does not have it already, it may be willing to get it by the time you arrive.

DISABLED TRAVELERS

The situation for disabled travelers in Brazil has greatly improved over the years but not all accommodation options, especially the smaller properties with narrow lifts or those in the remoter areas of the country, can offer wheelchair access or the facilities that disabled travelers may require. Brazilians by nature, however, will do everything they can to assist, so do not hesitate to ask.

The lush gardens of Pousada do Sol, Morro de São Paulo

CHAIN HOTELS

Until the 1990s, there were few foreign hotel chains operating in Brazil. The largest chains were Brazilian, and included **Othon**, **Tropical**, and **Luxor**, all of which are still in operation today. However, several hundreds of modern hotels throughout Brazil operate under different brands, such as the **Accor** and **Bristol** groups.

Brazilian hoteliers have not been left behind with the introduction of **Blue Tree**, the **Atlântica Hotels** group, and **Transamérica** that operates as Radisson, Clarion, Quality, Comfort Suites, Four Points, and Sleepy Inn.

The majority of chain hotels, which vary greatly in terms of price, infrastructure and quality, tend to be targeted at Brazilian and South American business travelers unless they are in obvious tourist destinations.

Only the properties in the tourist areas are likely to consider adding a Brazilian or tropical flavor to the surroundings or decorations.

APART-HOTELS

Though not strictly for budget travelers, apart-hotels, in most of the main Brazilian cities, offer good value for money. These come with one, two, or more bedrooms, a living area, and a kitchen. Some will have restaurants and cafés, as well as swimming pools and gyms.

One of the main chains with properties throughout Brazil is Accor's Parthenon group, while in São Paulo, Transamérica Flats is a very prominent brand.

Apart-hotels are the most convenient self-catering option in Brazil. Most houses and apartments are rented individually, and it may be easier to organize the rental through a local agency.

POUSADAS

Outside of the main city and town centers, the majority of accommodations on offer are smaller, privately owned properties. *Pousadas* vary dramatically in terms of cost, quality, and facilities offered. Some will be very basic, but certainly clean, while others will be extremely sophisticated and can be considered world-class boutique hotels set in lovely locations. *Pousadas* are usually charming, offer good value, and give a real flavor of Brazil.

It is a good idea to visit the website of an individual *pousada* to see the pictures of the property and what it has to offer. Most good tour operators know the best *pousadas* in each category and area. **Roteiros de Charme**, a network of outstanding *pousadas*, is also very useful.

Sign of Pousada dos Artistas, Praia do Forte

RESORTS

World-class resorts are a relatively new concept in Brazil, but are rapidly growing in popularity and in terms of what is on offer.

Aerial view of the Marriott Resort in Costa do Sauípe, Bahia

Brazil's largest resort is the **Costa do Sauípe**, just north of Salvador, which has a mixture of resort properties such as SuperClubs, Sofitel, and Marriott, as well as *pousadas*. With the success of Sauípe, SuperClubs is building a number of properties along the Brazilian coast, as are Club Med. Blue Tree is the main Brazilian resort brand, while the **Praia do Forte Eco Resort**, in Bahia, is the country's most famous resort, which introduced the concept of eco-resorts to Brazil.

Camping in the Serra dos Órgãos National Park

BUDGET OPTIONS

In the main areas visited by tourists, there are many *pousadas* that can be considered budget accommodation. In the cities, however, good budget accommodation is, by and large, offered by simpler hotels. There is also a good network of hostels in Brazil for those on a really tight budget. Reputable hostels will be members of the **Federação Brasileira de Albergues da Juventude** (Brazilian Hostel Federation). The federation's website has a full list of hostels in Brazil that are approved by the organization.

MOTELS

Motels in Brazil have nothing in common with the ones to be found in North America or in Europe. In Brazil, these tend to be "love hotels" and

rent rooms out to couples by the hour. Guests are not normally encouraged to spend more than one night at these establishments.

CAMPING

Brazil offers a massive number of places where it is possible to camp. However, campers should make sure they have not wandered on to private property or into a restricted area. Security, too, is an issue, and not just from miscreants, but also from Brazilian wildlife.

If not an experienced camper, the visitor should stick to official campsites, the majority of which are run and organized by the **Camping Clube do Brasil**. If using one of the national parks, check first with the park authorities where camping is permitted. Having your

own tent, or hiring one, is useful in ecotourist regions, such as the Amazon and the Pantanal.

LODGES

The majority of wildlife lodges that will help visitors to see and enjoy some of the remoter parts of Brazil are located in the Amazon *(see p383)* and the Pantanal *(see pp385–6)*. While there may be some exceptions, the infrastructure and home comforts of many of these lodges may be quite basic, as visitors are more keen on exploring the surrounding countryside, flora, and fauna.

It is recommended for travelers to consider traveling light, leaving the bulk of their belongings back in the main hotel, an airport locker, or at the city office of the lodge prior to transfer.

DIRECTORY

BOOKING

Expedia
www.expedia.com

Last Minute
www.lastminute.com

CHAIN HOTELS

Accor
Tel (0800) 703 7000.
www.accor.com.br

Atlântica Hotels
Tel (0800) 55 5855.
www.atlanticahotels.com.br

Blue Tree
Tel (0800) 150 500.
www.bluetree.com.br

Bristol
Tel (0800) 411 816.
www.bristolhoteis.com.br

Luxor
Tel (0800) 282 2070.
www.luxor-hotels.com

Othon
Tel (0800) 785 0505.
www.othonhotels.com.br

Transamérica
Tel (0800) 012 6060.
www.transamerica.com.br

Tropical
Tel (0800) 701 2670.
www.tropicalhotel.com.br

POUSADAS

Roteiros de Charme
Tel (021) 2287 1592.
www.roteirosdecharme.com.br

RESORTS

Costa do Sauípe
Tel (071) 2104 8470.
www.costadosauipe.com.br

Praia do Forte Eco Resort
Tel (0800) 718 888.
www.praiadoforte.com.br

BUDGET OPTIONS

Federação Brasileira de Albergues da Juventude
Tel (021) 2286 0303.
www.hostel.org.br

CAMPING

Camping Clube do Brasil
Tel (021) 3479 4200.
www.campingclube.com.br

Choosing a Hotel

The hotels in this guide have been selected across a wide price range for their good value and excellent location. The chart below lists hotels in Brazil, area by area. Hotels within the same price category are listed alphabetically. For map references, see pages 98–101 for Rio de Janeiro City and pages 156–9 for São Paulo City.

PRICE CATEGORIES
These price bands are for a standard double room per night (not per person), including tax and service charges.
$ Under $35
$$ $35–75
$$$ $75–120
$$$$ $120–175
$$$$$ Over $175

RIO DE JANEIRO CITY

AIRPORT Luxor Aeroporto $$$

Aeroporto Internacional, Galeão, 21941 570 **Tel** *(021) 2468 8998* **Fax** *(021) 3398 3983* **Rooms** *64*

Located right in the airport terminal, the Luxor Aeroporto is a convenient choice for travelers arriving late at the airport, as well as for those who are not planning to go into the city center. The hotel also offers rooms for shorter periods, which are ideal for freshening up or resting before a flight. **www.luxor-hotels.com**

BARRA DA TIJUCA Royalty Barra $$$

Av do Pepé 690, 22620 170 **Tel** *(021) 24835 373* **Fax** *(021) 2493 0482* **Rooms** *249*

Since its inauguration in 2000, the Royalty Barra has offered quality accommodation in one of the most sought-after areas of the Barra beach. It offers a sizable sundeck and swimming pool. Guests will probably need a car to explore Rio, and will have to use taxis to get around in Barra itself. **www.royaltyhotel.com.br**

BARRA DA TIJUCA Inter-Continental Rio $$$$

Av Prefeito Mendes de Moraes 222, 22610 095 **Tel** *(021) 3323 2200* **Fax** *(021) 3323 2295* **Rooms** *429*

A major resort property with large pool area, tennis courts, and leisure and recreational activities, this hotel is an excellent choice for business travelers. Many of the rooms have views over the Gavea Golf Course, the beach, or Pedra da Gavea, the beautiful mountain that is home to the city's hang-gliders. **www.ichotelsgroup.com**

BARRA DA TIJUCA Trypp Barra $$$$

Av das Américas 7897, 22793 081 **Tel** *(021) 2438 8800* **Fax** *(021) 2438 8801* **Rooms** *422*

Part of the fast-expanding Sol Melia group, the Trypp Barra is popular with visiting business executives. The hotel's proximity to RioCentro *(see p87)* adds to its attraction. Though not located on the beachfront, it offers a shuttle bus to the beach. In addition, it has its own pool. **www.solmelia.com**

BARRA DA TIJUCA Windsor Barra $$$$

Av Sernambetiba 2630, 22620 170 **Tel** *(021) 2195 5000* **Fax** *(021) 2195 5050* **Rooms** *338*

Opened for business at the end of 2005, the Windsor Barra is a modern, purpose-built hotel belonging to the Windsor Hotel group. The hotel offers modern, well-equipped rooms with views over Barra and the beach, a rooftop sundeck, pool, and convention center. **www.windsorhoteis.com**

BARRA DA TIJUCA Sheraton Barra $$$$$

Av Lucio Costa 3150, 22630 010 **Tel** *(021) 3139 8000* **Fax** *(021) 3139 8085* **Rooms** *292*

Inaugurated in 2003, the Sheraton Barra is the first luxury resort property to come up on the beachfront in Barra. While many European and North American visitors have yet to discover Barra, this hotel is in high demand by Brazilian and other Latin American visitors, who favor this state-of-the-art property. **www.starwoodhotels.com**

CENTRO Guanabara Palace $$$

Av Presidente Vargas 392, 22071 000 **Tel** *(021) 2195 6000* **Fax** *(021) 2516 1582* **Rooms** *485*　　　　**Map** *5 D3*

The largest hotel in the Windsor Hotel group, the 1950 Guanabara Palace has been totally modernized with a brand-new exterior. Located in the heart of downtown Rio, the hotel is popular with business executives. It features a good rooftop sun terrace and pool with views over the bay and Centro. **www.windsorhoteis.com**

CENTRO Serrador Palace $$$

Praça Mahatma Gandhi, 20031 000 **Tel** *(021) 2195 6000* **Fax** *(021) 2516 1582* **Rooms** *350*　　　　**Map** *5 E5*

Situated in a historic, listed building that dates from 1936, the Serrador Palace has a privileged location just off the Cinelândia end of Avenida Rio Branco, offering pleasant views from the rooms. A new rooftop sun terrace, pool, sauna, and fitness center were recently added. **www.windsorhoteis.com**

COPACABANA & LEME Bandeirantes $$

Rua Barata Ribeiro 548, 22040 002 **Tel** *(021) 2548 6252* **Fax** *(021) 2547 6703* **Rooms** *96*　　　　**Map** *3 D2*

The Bandeirantes offers clean and comfortable budget accommodation with few frills. In the bustling heart of Copacabana and just three blocks from the beach, the hotel is located close to the city's main theaters, cinemas, and nightclubs. **www.hotelbandeirantes.com.br**

Key to Symbols *see back cover flap*

COPACABANA & LEME Benidorm Palace

Rua Barata Ribeiro 547, 22040 001 **Tel** *(021) 2548 8880* **Fax** *(021) 2256 6396* **Rooms** *77*

Map 3 D2

$$

Opposite the Bandeirantes, on busy Rua Barata Ribeiro, the Benidorm Palace offers similar comfortable budget accommodation. The rooms at this hotel are simply appointed, but other features include a small rooftop sun terrace, dip pool, and fitness center. **www.benidorm.com.br**

COPACABANA & LEME Lancaster Othon Travel

Av Atlântica 1470, 22021 000 **Tel** *(021) 2106 0200* **Fax** *(021) 2521 7782* **Rooms** *69*

Map 3 F1

$$

Belonging to the budget range of the Othon group, the Othon Travel is one of the largest and most traditional of the Brazilian hotel chains that dominated Copacabana in the 1960s and the next two decades. This is a good choice for those looking for cozy budget accommodation right on the beachfront. **www.hoteis-othon.com.br**

COPACABANA & LEME Oceano

Rua Hilário de Gouveia 17, 22040 020 **Tel** *(021) 2548 4260* **Fax** *(021) 2235 3644* **Rooms** *90*

Map 3 E2

$$

Built in 1995, the Oceano offers modern rooms in the heart of Copacabana, a stone's throw from the beachfront. As an added bonus, the hotel also has a rooftop sun terrace and small pool, while rooms at the front have balconies with partial views of the beach. **www.oceanohotel.com.br**

COPACABANA & LEME Acapulco

Rua Gustavo Sampaio 854, 22010 010 **Tel** *(021) 2275 0022* **Fax** *(021) 2275 3396* **Rooms** *122*

Map 3 F1

$$$

Tucked away behind Le Meridien, the Acapulco is set just one block back from the beach. It was opened in 1971, but has since been modernized and refurbished. The hotel is popular with business travelers who work in, or go to, the city center, and still want to stay in and around the action in Copacabana. **www.acapulcocopacabana.com.br**

COPACABANA & LEME Califórnia Othon Classic

Av Atlântica 2616, 22041 001 **Tel** *(021) 2106 0200* **Fax** *(021) 2521 7782* **Rooms** *113*

Map 3 D3

$$$

Built at the end of the 1940s, the California Othon Classic is part of the Othon group's range of hotels. The chain reflects traditional architecture through intimate accommodation. Some beachfront rooms at this hotel offer balconies. **www.othonhotels.com**

COPACABANA & LEME Luxor Regente

Av Atlântica 3716, 22070 001 **Tel** *(021) 2525 2070* **Fax** *(021) 2267 7693* **Rooms** *236*

Map 3 D3

$$$

Considered to be the best of the three hotels offered in Copacabana by Luxor, a small traditional Brazilian chain, the beachfront Luxor Regente offers comfortable accommodation and good facilities. A rooftop sun terrace and small dip pool are also available. **www.luxor-hotels.com**

COPACABANA & LEME Orla Copacabana

Av Atlântica 4122, 22070 002 **Tel** *(021) 2525 2425* **Fax** *(021) 2287 9134* **Rooms** *115*

Map 3 D4

$$$

Opened in 2001, the Orla offers reasonably priced contemporary beachfront accommodation at the Ipanema end of Copacabana. The on-site rooftop sundeck, dip pool, and fitness center offer spectacular views along nearly the entire length of the beach to Sugar Loaf *(see pp76–7)* in the distance. **www.orlahotel.com.br**

COPACABANA & LEME Ouro Verde

Av Atlântica 1456, 22021 000 **Tel** *(021) 2543 4123* **Fax** *(021) 2543 4776* **Rooms** *64*

Map 3 F1

$$$

For most of the 1950s and 60s, the Ouro Verde was considered one of the world's great small hotels, a forerunner of today's boutique hotels. Though it has lost some of its former glory, this establishment offers good value for people who want to stay in more traditional and sedate surroundings on the beachfront. **www.dayrell.com.br**

COPACABANA & LEME Plaza Copacabana

Av Princesa Isabel 263, 22011 010 **Tel** *(021) 2195 5500* **Fax** *(021) 2549 9373* **Rooms** *237*

Map 3 F1

$$$

The Plaza is one of a number of Rio hotels belonging to the Windsor Hotel group that have been totally refurbished and modernized. It is particularly popular with Japanese tourists and offers a number of special services for them. There is a rooftop sundeck and pool with views over Copacabana and the beach. **www.windsorhoteis.com**

COPACABANA & LEME South American Copacabana

Rua Francisco Sá 90, 22080 010 **Tel** *(021) 2227 9161* **Fax** *(021) 2267 0748* **Rooms** *99*

Map 2 C4

$$$

Situated in a residential area and conveniently located within a short walk of both Copacabana and Ipanema beaches, the South American Copacabana opened for business in 1995. It offers contemporary, yet unfussy, budget accommodation, with a rooftop sundeck, pool, and fitness center. **www.southamericanhotel.com.br**

COPACABANA & LEME Excelsior Copacabana

Av Atlântica 1800, 22021 001 **Tel** *(021) 2195 5800* **Fax** *(021) 2257 1850* **Rooms** *233*

Map 3 F2

$$$$

Although built in 1950, the Excelsior is unrecognizable after being completely modernized and given a facelift at the end of the 1990s. It is a popular choice for business and leisure travelers. Rooms are functional, with many offering good views over Copacabana beach. There is a rooftop sundeck and pool. **www.windsorhoteis.com**

COPACABANA & LEME Pestana Rio Atlântica

Av Atlântica 2964, 22070 000 **Tel** *(021) 2548 6332* **Fax** *(021) 2255 6410* **Rooms** *217*

Map 3 D3

$$$$

Another modern Copacabana beachfront hotel, the Pestana Rio Atlântica is as popular with visiting business executives as it is with the tourists. Rooms are attractively decorated and furnished, and all have balconies. It offers a sizable rooftop sundeck and pool with stunning panoramic views over the beach. **www.pestana.com**

COPACABANA & LEME Portinari

🎇 🍴 🖳 🗐 P ♿ W $$$$

Rua Francisco Sá 17, 22080 000 **Tel** *(021) 3222 8800* **Fax** *(021) 3222 8800* **Rooms** *66*   **Map** *2 C4*

Well-priced and contemporary, the Portinari lies a short distance off Copacabana beach. Rooms are spread over 11 floors, with each floor offering a different style of room conceptualized by leading Brazilian designers. Guests have the choice of selecting a design and atmosphere that suits them best. **www.hotelportinari.com.br**

COPACABANA & LEME Rio Internacional

🎇 🗄 🍴 🗐 P ♿ W $$$$

Av Atlântica 1500, 22021 000 **Tel** *(021) 2546 8000* **Fax** *(021) 2542 5443* **Rooms** *117*   **Map** *3 E2*

This trendy business and tourist hotel is located on the Copacabana beachfront. Standard rooms all have balconies and sea views, while the deluxe rooms offer an option of large beachfront balconies or wall-to-wall windows with panoramic views down and across the beach. **www.riointernacional.com.br**

COPACABANA & LEME Rio Othon Palace

🎇 🗄 🍴 🗐 P ♿ W $$$$

Av Atlântica 3264, 22070 001 **Tel** *(021) 2106 1500* **Fax** *(021) 2521 7782* **Rooms** *602*   **Map** *2 C3*

Built in 1976, this 30-story hotel is a flagship of the Othon Hotel group. It is a landmark along the sweep of Copacabana and offers spectacular views from many of its rooms. Facilities include a rooftop pool and sundeck. Due to its size, the Othon is popular with groups and for events. **www.hoteis-othon.com.br**

COPACABANA & LEME Copacabana Palace

🎇 🗄 🍴 🗐 P ♿ W $$$$$

Av Atlântica 1702, 22021 001 **Tel** *(021) 2548 7070* **Fax** *(021) 2235 7330* **Rooms** *225*   **Map** *3 E2*

Opening its doors for the first time in 1923, this hotel is now a part of the Orient-Express group. Its old-fashioned glamor has attracted world leaders, royalty, and Hollywood stars. The huge pool and surrounding area are stunning, while the poolside Cipriani restaurant *(see p395)* is one of the city's finest. **www.copacabanapalace.com.br**

COPACABANA & LEME JW Marriott

🎇 🗄 🍴 🗐 P ♿ W $$$$$

Av Atlântica 2600, 22041 001 **Tel** *(021) 2545 6500* **Fax** *(021) 2545 6555* **Rooms** *245*   **Map** *3 D2*

The newest luxury hotel along the Copacabana beachfront, this Marriott flagship opened in 2001. Offering well-appointed rooms, it is favored by American business executives and tourists. The beach-facing rooms and suites are more popular. It has a small rooftop pool and sundeck. **www.marriottbrasil.com**

COPACABANA & LEME Le Meridien

🎇 🗄 🍴 🗐 P ♿ W $$$$$

Av Atlântica 1020, 22010 000 **Tel** *(021) 3873 8850* **Fax** *(021) 3873 8788* **Rooms** *496*   **Map** *3 F1*

Towering 37 floors over Copacabana Beach, Le Meridien marks the spot where Copacabana becomes Leme. The hotel is very popular with French visitors, though it has built up a global following since opening in 1975. Its flagship restaurant, Le Saint Honoré *(see p395)*, is excellent. **www.rio.lemeridien.com**

COPACABANA & LEME Sofitel Rio de Janeiro

🎇 🗄 🍴 🗐 P ♿ W $$$$$

Av Atlântica 4240, 22070 002 **Tel** *(021) 2525 1232* **Fax** *(021) 2525 1200* **Rooms** *388*   **Map** *3 D5*

The Rio flagship of the Accor group, the Sofitel was originally opened in 1979 by Frank Sinatra. Since becoming part of Accor in the late 1990s, the hotel has been totally refurbished to the highest international standards. The spacious rooms all have balconies, most with memorable views of Copacabana. **www.accorhotels.com**

FLAMENGO & BOTAFOGO Botafogo Easy Hostel

🗄 🗐 W $

Rua Bambina 158, Botafogo, 22251 050 **Tel** *(021) 2527 4536* **Fax** *(021) 2535 3788* **Rooms** *14*

A clean and safe budget option, this friendly hostel is located in the heart of Botafogo, not far from Botafogo metro station. It offers a mixture of dorms, four-bed private rooms, and double rooms with en suite bathrooms. Buffet breakfast is included in the tariff, and there is even a barbecue and pool area. **www.botafogohostel.com**

FLAMENGO & BOTAFOGO Rio Hostel

🍴 W $

Rua General Dionisio 63, Botafogo, 22271 050 **Tel** *(021) 2586 0303* **Fax** *(021) 2286 5652* **Rooms** *12*

Comfortable, well-maintained, and exuding warmth, this neighborhood hostel offers great value for money. Guest rooms vary in size, from double rooms with en suite bathrooms to 12-bunk dorms. The Rio Hostel has its own restaurant and a terrace area. **www.riohostel.com.br**

FLAMENGO & BOTAFOGO Argentina Hotel

🍴 🗐 W $$

Rua Cruz Lima 30, Flamengo, 22230 010 **Tel** *(021) 2558 7233* **Fax** *(021) 2285 4573* **Rooms** *80*

One of the most traditional budget hotels in Rio, this 1933 hotel offers excellent value for money for travelers who do not insist on being on the beachfront. Located close to a metro station, it has easy access to the city center and Copacabana. Though a bit dated, the double rooms and four-bed rooms are cozy. **www.argentinahotel.com.br**

FLAMENGO & BOTAFOGO Imperial

🎇 🗄 🍴 🗐 P ♿ W $$

Rua da Catete 186, Catete, 20011 000 **Tel** *(021) 2556 5212* **Fax** *(021) 2558 5815* **Rooms** *98*

Another great-value option for the budget traveler, the Imperial lies in historic Catete. Its proximity to the metro station gives it rapid access to both Copacabana and the city center. The tariff includes an excellent buffet breakfast that is served in its on-site restaurant. **www.imperialhotel.com.br**

FLAMENGO & BOTAFOGO Caesar Business Botafogo

🎇 🗄 🍴 🗐 P ♿ W $$$

Rua da Passagem 39, Botafogo, 22220 001 **Tel** *(021) 2131 1212* **Fax** *(021) 2131 1200* **Rooms** *127*

This Caesar flagship, located in one of Rio's busiest business areas, offers business executives modern rooms and facilities to match. As the name suggests, business rather than leisure is the focus of this property, so the leisure traveler may be able to get good weekend rates and packages. **www.caesarbusiness.com**

Key to Price Guide *see p366* **Key to Symbols** *see back cover flap*

FLAMENGO & BOTAFOGO Glória $$$
Rua do Russel, Glória, 22210 010 **Tel** *(021) 2555 7272* **Fax** *(021) 2555 7282* **Rooms** *630*

The Glória, which first opened in 1922, once rivaled the Copacabana Palace for the title of Rio's premier hotel and is still the city's largest. It offers fantastic value for money, with the infrastructure of a grand hotel in terms of accommodation, restaurants, and a hotel swimming pool, one of the city's best. **www.hotelgloriario.com.br**

IPANEMA & LEBLON Rio Hostel Ipanema $
Rua Barão da Torre 175, Ipanema, 20004 000 **Tel** *(021) 2247 7269* **Fax** *(021) 2268 0565* **Rooms** *9* **Map** *2 B4*

Located three blocks from the beach in Rio's most prestigious and upmarket quarter, this establishment offers bargain accommodation for visitors on a tight budget in shared dorms for four and six people. The hostel offers four additional rooms in another building in the same street. **www.geocities.com/hostelipanema/**

IPANEMA & LEBLON Mar Ipanema $$$
Rua V. de Pirajá 539, Ipanema, 22410 003 **Tel** *(021) 3875 9191* **Fax** *(021) 3875 9192* **Rooms** *77* **Map** *1 C4*

Small, yet modern, the Mar Ipanema offers affordable accommodation on Ipanema's busiest and most important shopping street. The decor features very few obvious frills, although rooms are comfortable and equipped with a minibar and an individual safe. Only two blocks from Ipanema beach. **www.maripanema.com.br**

IPANEMA & LEBLON Parthenon Queen Elizabeth $$$
Av Rainha Elizabeth 440, Ipanema, 22081 030 **Tel** *(021) 3222 9100* **Fax** *(021) 3222 9387* **Rooms** *51* **Map** *2 C5*

Belonging to the Parthenon apart-hotel brand of the Accor group, the largest hotel group operating in Brazil, this hotel offers excellent value in modern, quality apartments for a longer stay. There is a playground for children and a business center, as well as on-site pools and coffee shops. **www.accorhotels.com.br**

IPANEMA & LEBLON Praia Ipanema $$$
Av Vieira Souto 706, Ipanema, 22420 000 **Tel** *(021) 2540 4949* **Fax** *(021) 2239 6889* **Rooms** *105* **Map** *1 C5*

Despite opening in 1979, the Praia Ipanema remains one of Rio's best-kept hotel secrets. Located on the Ipanema beachfront, the hotel has rooms with balconies and sea views, while the rooftop is home to a sun terrace, small pool, fitness center, and the upbeat Bossa Nova bar. **www.praiaipanema.com**

IPANEMA & LEBLON Sol Ipanema $$$
Av Vieira Souto 320, Ipanema, 22420 000 **Tel** *(021) 2525 2020* **Fax** *(021) 2247 8484* **Rooms** *90* **Map** *2 A5*

Similar to, but not as modern as the Praia Ipanema, the Sol Ipanema is one of the few beach-front hotels in Ipanema and is a good choice if the larger deluxe hotels do not fit the budget. A rooftop sundeck and pool with views over Ipanema are on offer. **www.solipanema.com**

IPANEMA & LEBLON Everest Rio $$$$
Rua P. de Morais 1117, Ipanema, 22420 041 **Tel** *(021) 2525 2200* **Fax** *(021) 2521 3198* **Rooms** *156* **Map** *2 A5*

This traditional hotel is tucked one block back from the beach, close to the bars, restaurants, and shops of Ipanema. Though not on the beach, it features a rooftop sundeck and pool with panoramic views over Ipanema and the beach and offers a high quality of accommodation and service. **www.everest.com.br**

IPANEMA & LEBLON Ipanema Plaza $$$$
Rua F. de Amoedo 34, Ipanema, 22420 202 **Tel** *(021) 3687 2000* **Fax** *(021) 3687 2001* **Rooms** *140* **Map** *2 B5*

Since opening in 2000, the Ipanema Plaza has quickly built up a following among regular visitors to Rio. Stylish, well-priced, and contemporary accommodation is supported by superb facilities. The hotel has a lovely pool and sundeck with views over the beach and Ipanema to Corcovado and the Lagoa. **www.ipanemaplaza.com.br**

IPANEMA & LEBLON Ipanema Tower $$$$
Rua P. de Morais 1008, Ipanema, 22420 040 **Tel** *(021) 2247 7033* **Fax** *(021) 2247 7033* **Rooms** *28* **Map** *2 A4*

Small and well-appointed boutique apart-hotel in the heart of Ipanema. Most of the flats offer a tastefully decorated family room, dining area, veranda, and one or two bedrooms. Located one block back from the beach, the Ipanema Tower has its own pool and fitness center and offers a breakfast service. **www.ipanematower.com.br**

IPANEMA & LEBLON Caesar Park $$$$$
Av Vieira Souto 460, Ipanema, 22420 000 **Tel** *(021) 2525 2525* **Fax** *(021) 2521 6060* **Rooms** *223* **Map** *2 A5*

Inaugurated in 1978, this top-notch hotel attracts both business and leisure travelers. The service is excellent and the decor exudes class. Rooms and surroundings are discreetly luxurious. Dining options are limited, but there are plenty of restaurants located close by. Tasteful rooftop sun terrace and dip pool. **www.caesar-park.com**

IPANEMA & LEBLON Marina All Suites $$$$$
Av Delfim Moreira 696, Leblon, 22441 000 **Tel** *(021) 2172 1100* **Fax** *(021) 2172 1010* **Rooms** *38* **Map** *1 A5*

This beachfront property has eight signature suites created by leading designers. While these vary from traditional to contemporary avant-garde, the hotel boasts a further 30 modern, comfortable suites, each with a separate lounge and home theater. There is also a small dip pool and sun terrace. **www.marinaallsuites.com.br**

IPANEMA & LEBLON Sheraton Rio Hotel & Towers $$$$$
Av Niemeyer 121, Leblon, 22450 220 **Tel** *(021) 2274 1122* **Fax** *(021) 2239 5643* **Rooms** *559*

Located on its own beach on the coast road between Leblon and São Conrado, this hotel is considered Rio's premier resort property. Amenities featured are on par with the world's very best Sheratons and include one of the largest pool areas in Rio, tennis courts, fitness club, and great dining and bar options. **www.sheraton-rio.com**

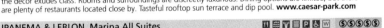

RIO DE JANEIRO STATE & ESPÍRITO SANTO

ANGRA DOS REIS (Rio de Janeiro State) Pestana Angra

$\$\$\$\$\$$

Estrada do Contorno 3700, Retiro **Tel** *(024) 3364 2005* **Rooms** *27*

With bungalows set in tropical gardens on a forested peninsula, this private beach resort provides a very high level of comfort. There are fantastic views over the sea, making this place a perfect choice for a beach vacation. Also on offer are conference facilities and a good restaurant, the Cais da Ribeira. **www.pestana.com**

ARRAIAL DO CABO (Rio de Janeiro State) Capitão n'Areia Pousada

$\$\$$

Rua Santa Cruz 7, Praia dos Anjos **Tel** *(022) 2622 2720* **Rooms** *32*

Located on the main town beach, this family-friendly seafront hotel draws a loyal clientele for its splendid views. There is a good range of chalets and rooms to choose from, all equipped with modern conveniences, as well as a sea-facing café and the pleasant Porto das Delícias Restaurante. **www.capitaopousada.com**

BÚZIOS (Rio de Janeiro State) Brigitta's Guest House

$\$\$$

Rua das Pedras 131, Centro **Tel** *(022) 2623 6157* **Rooms** *4*

Brigitte Bardot stayed in this *pousada* at the time when her presence in Búzios put the fishing village on the map. Named for its celebrity guest, the small guesthouse stands on what is now the main shopping street, overlooking the water. Rooms are decorated with arty bric-à-brac, and the ambience is laid-back and friendly.

BÚZIOS (Rio de Janeiro State) Hibiscus Beach

$\$\$\$$

Rua 1, 22 Quadra C, Praia de João Fernandes, 28950 000 **Tel** *(022) 2623 6221* **Fax** *(022) 2623 6221* **Rooms** *13*

One of the best-value hotels in the area, this British-run *pousada* overlooks Praia de João Fernandes, one of the peninsula's prettiest and liveliest beaches. The surrounding luxuriant tropical gardens create a calm ambience. Accommodation is in cabanas, all of which have sea views. **www.hibiscusbeach.com**

BÚZIOS (Rio de Janeiro State) Abracadabra

$\$\$\$\$$

Alto do Humaita 13, 28950 000 **Tel** *(022) 2623 1217* **Rooms** *16*

The pool and breakfast area and the most preferred rooms in this tastefully decorated mock-Mediterranean hotel have some of the best views in Búzios. The oceanfront hotel bar is known to serve fantastic *caipirinha*. Good beaches are a five-minute car ride away. **www.abracadabrapousada.com.br**

BÚZIOS (Rio de Janeiro State) Casas Brancas

$\$\$\$\$\$$

Alto do Humaitá 10, Búzios, 28950 000 **Tel** *(022) 2623 1458* **Fax** *(022) 2623 2147* **Rooms** *32*

Considered to be one of Brazil's best boutique hotels, the Casas Brancas has created a series of Mediterranean-inspired rooms with breathtaking views of the Morro do Humaita. The hotel restaurant serves superb modern Brazilian-Mediterranean fusion cuisine. There is a first-class on-site spa. **www.casasbrancas.com.br**

CABO FRIO (Rio de Janeiro State) La Plage

$\$\$$

Rua dos Badejos 40, Praia do Peró **Tel** *(022) 2647 1746* **Rooms** *32*

The principal suites at this beachfront hotel all come with a stunning ocean view. All suites are appointed with basic amenities, and are tastefully decorated. There is also a small play area for children. The hotel can organize trips to the nearby sand dunes. **www.laplage.com.br**

CABO FRIO (Rio de Janeiro State) Pousada do Leandro

$\$\$\$\$$

Avenida Peçanha 333, Praia do Forte **Tel** *(022) 2645 4658* **Rooms** *17*

Owned by famous ex-Flamengo footballer José Leandro Souza Ferreira, this intimate, brightly colored *pousada* is located a short stroll from the town center on the area's busiest beach, Praia do Forte. All suites come with a veranda and are equipped with modern amenities. **www.pousadaleandro.com.br**

GUARAPARI (Espírito Santo) Enseada Verde

$\$\$$

Rua Duarte Mattos 27, Enseada Verde, Praia do Meaípe **Tel** *(027) 3272 1376* **Fax** *(027) 3272 0421* **Rooms** *20*

Set in rainforest overlooking Praia do Meaípe, one of Guarapari's most popular beaches, the reasonably priced Enseada Verde has pretty apartments. The pool here is very popular and the on-site restaurant has unforgettable views of the lush tropical surroundings. **www.enseadaverde.com.br**

ILHA GRANDE (Rio de Janeiro State) Pousada Ancoradouro

$\$\$$

Rua da Praia, Vila do Abraão **Tel** *(024) 3361 5153* **Rooms** *8*

One of several *pousadas* in the picturesque Vila do Abraão, the Ancoradouro is located right on the beach, in the quiet part of the village. There are eight minimalistically decorated, but very well kept, apartments offering basic amenities, including a TV and a small refrigerator.

ILHA GRANDE (Rio de Janeiro State) Sítio do Lobo

$\$\$\$\$\$$

Enseada das Estrelas, Ilha Grande **Tel** *(024) 3361 4438* **Rooms** *9*

A luxury boutique hotel run by Julinha Serrado, a famous Brazilian interior designer, the Sítio do Lobo lies on a peninsula reachable only by boat from either the mainland or Abraão town. Activities include hiking, kayaking, yoga, and tai chi. Rooms are tastefully done, though the cheaper rooms are boxy. **www.sitiodolobo.com.br**

ITATIAIA (Rio de Janeiro State) Hotel Donati

Estrada Parque Nacional Km 9.5 **Tel** *(024) 3352 1110* **Rooms** *25*

The most comfortable of the hotels within Itatiaia's Parque Nacional Itatiaia, Hotel Donati has chalets set in tropical woodland with trails leading directly into town. The hotel has a sauna, children's play area, and sports facilities, and can also organize guides for park visits. **www.hoteldonati.com.br**

ITATIAIA (Rio de Janeiro State) Pousada Esmeralda

Estrada Parque Nacional Km 4 **Tel** *(024) 3352 1643* **Rooms** *14*

With 12 Swiss-style chalets and two cheaper apartments set in tropical gardens, this *pousada*-style hotel offers good value for money. One of the two swimming pools is fed by spring water. Other attractions include guided walks, horse-riding, sauna, and a children's play area. **www.pousadaesmeralda.com.br**

ITAÚNAS (Espírito Santo) Pousada Bemtevi

Rua Adolpho Pereira Duarte 41 **Tel** *(027) 3762 5012* **Rooms** *17*

Deriving its name from bem-te-vi (translated as "nice to see you"), a bird commonly found in Brazil, the Pousada Bemtevi lies just off the town's sandy main square. Clustered around the swimming pool, the suites come with a refrigerator and TV. Solar energy is used to provide hot water. **www.pousadabemtevi.com**

PARATY (Rio de Janeiro State) Arte Colonial

Rua da Matriz 292, Centro Histórico **Tel** *(024) 3371 7231* **Rooms** *7*

Housed in a colonial building right in the center of town, this French-owned *pousada* has a serene ambience. The best rooms are on the upper floors and have views out over the terra-cotta-tiled historic center of town. All rooms have a TV and a mini-refrigerator. **www.paraty.com.br/artecolonial**

PARATY (Rio de Janeiro State) Bromelias

Rodovia Rio-Santos Km 562 **Tel** *(024) 3371 2791* **Rooms** *10*

In the heart of the Mata Atlântica rainforest, the family-friendly Bromelias has chalets beautifully set amid natural swimming pools, waterfalls, and lush tropical gardens. The hotel also provides first-rate spa treatments and bird-watching. **www.pousadabromelias.com.br**

PARATY (Rio de Janeiro State) Coxixo

Rua do Comércio 362, Centro Histórico **Tel** *(024) 3371 1460* **Rooms** *33*

Located on the pretty cobblestone street of Paraty's historic center, this colonial *pousada* is owned by famous Brazilian theater and film personality, Maria Della Costa, now in her 80s. Rooms are simply appointed, yet exude elegance. The best rooms are the upper-floor suites. **www.hotelcoxixo.com.br**

PARATY (Rio de Janeiro State) Pousada Pardieiro

Rua do Comércio 74, Centro Histórico **Tel** *(024) 3371 1370* **Fax** *(024) 3371 1139* **Rooms** *27*

Considered to be one of the best in Brazil, this *pousada* is favored for its serene ambience, first-rate service, and comfortable rooms and suites. Its bougainvillea-filled gardens are visited by hummingbirds and tufted-eared marmosets. A complimentary Continental breakfast is served in the Café da Manhã. **www.pousadapardieiro.com.br**

PARATY (Rio de Janeiro State) Pousada do Sandi

Largo do Rosário 1, Centro Histórico **Tel** *(024) 3371 1236* **Fax** *(024) 3371 2100* **Rooms** *26*

Part of an 18th-century building, this *pousada* is decorated with local arts and crafts. Spacious, high-ceilinged rooms are done up with colonial bric-à-brac and colorful upholstery. Pleasant and comfortable public areas and an excellent on-site restaurant and bar. **www.pousadadosandi.com.br**

PEDRA AZUL (Espírito Santo) Pousada Peterle

Rodovia Br 262 Km 88, 29278 000 **Tel** *(027) 3248 1171* **Rooms** *15*

Set in gardens on a hill, the Pousada Peterle offers scenic views of Pedra Azul. Large mock-Swiss chalets and apartments, built with eucalyptus logs, come with a living room with fireplace, one bedroom, and a veranda. Some of the stone-built rooms have pleasant rustic decor. **www.pousadapeterle.com.br**

PETRÓPOLIS (Rio de Janeiro State) Hotel Casablanca Imperial

Rua da Imperatriz 286, Centro, 25610 320 **Tel** *(024) 2242 6662* **Rooms** *42*

Close to the Museu Imperial (see p114), the city's main attraction, the Casablanca is housed in a handsome colonial building with public balconies. All rooms have a high ceiling and are decorated with mock-colonial furniture and antiques. A very good choice for budget travelers. **www.casablancahotel.com.br**

PETRÓPOLIS (Rio de Janeiro State) Solar do Império

Av Koeler 376, Centro **Tel** *(024) 2103 3000* **Rooms** *16*

The most luxurious hotel in Petrópolis is housed in a mansion on its grandest avenue. The standards of comfort and service match the opulence of the hotel's interiors and public spaces. Services include spa and massage, an excellent on-site restaurant, and indoor and outdoor pools. **www.solardoimperio.com.br**

SERRA DOS ÓRGÃOS (Rio de Janeiro State) REGUA

Caixa Postal 98112, Cachoeiras de Macacu, 28680 000 **Tel** *(021) 2745 3998* **Rooms** *4*

REGUA (Reserva Ecologica de Guapi Assu), funded mainly by the UK, aims to protect the Atlantic rainforest in the area. Its large villa comes with several rooms set in primary rainforest. Guided walks are offered into the Serra dos Órgãos on the reserve's private land, which has a variety of birds, mammals, and orchids. **www.regua.co.uk**

SERRA DOS ÓRGÃOS (Rio de Janeiro State) Serra dos Tucanos 🍴 🏊 ❄ [P] $$$

Caixa Postal 98125, Cachoeiras do Macacu, 28680 000 ***Tel*** *(021) 2649 1557* ***Rooms*** *10*

Favored by naturalists, this lodge was started by keen bird-watchers, Cristina and Andy Foster. An expert guide takes visitors on nature walks and bird-watching expeditions. The lodge offers comfortable accommodation in a resplendent Atlantic rainforest setting. **www.serradostucanos.com.br**

TERESÓPOLIS (Rio de Janeiro State) Hotel Rosa dos Ventos 🍴 🏊 🏋 ❄ [P] [W] $$$$

Km 22, Estrada Teresópolis, Nova Friburgo, 25977 400 ***Tel*** *(021) 2644 9900* ***Fax*** *(021) 2644 9948* ***Rooms*** *42*

One of the two members of Relais et Chateaux in Brazil, this *fazenda*-style hotel offers diverse luxurious accommodation in mock-Alpine chalets. Activities include horse-riding, cycling, fishing, and mountain-biking. Children under the age of 14 are not allowed. **www.hotelrosadosventos.com.br**

TRINDADE (Rio de Janeiro State) Agua do Mar [P] $$

Rua das Flores, Praia de Fora ***Tel*** *(024) 3371 5120* ***Rooms*** *17*

Among the many modest *pousadas* in the region, the simple beachfront Agua do Mar is a two-minute stroll from Praia de Fora, a beach renowned for its natural beauty. While some of the rooms come with a TV and refrigerator, five superior suites come with verandas offering splendid sea views.

VITÓRIA (Espírito Santo) Hotel Ilha do Boi 🍴 🏊 🏋 ❄ [P] ♿ [W] $$$

Rua Braúlio Macedo 417, Ilha do Boi ***Tel*** *(027) 3345 0111* ***Fax*** *(027) 3345 0115* ***Rooms*** *95*

This is a large beachside hotel complex with a range of different hotel environments and beautiful views over the bay. Facilities include a business center, sauna, piano bar, and an excellent restaurant serving regional specialties and Continental cuisine. Round-the-clock room service is available. **www.hotelilhadoboi.com.br**

MINAS GERAIS

BELO HORIZONTE Hotel Wimbledon 🍴 🏊 ❄ $$$

Av Afonso Pena ***Tel*** *0800 318383* ***Rooms*** *70*

With a convenient location in the heart of town, this modest hotel meets the requirements of the frequent traveler. Although small and with no frills, the rooms are furnished tastefully. The Garden's Restaurant serves cuisine typical to Minas Gerais. The Wimbledon also has a convention center and a small pool. **www.wimbledon.com.br**

BELO HORIZONTE Liberty Palace Hotel 🍴 🏊 🏋 ❄ [P] ♿ [W] $$$$

Rua Paraíba 1465, Savassi ***Tel*** *(031) 2121 0900* ***Fax*** *(031) 3282 0808* ***Rooms*** *94*

A well-appointed, modern business hotel located in a tower, the Liberty Palace is one of the most expensive in the Savassi area. Rooms are luxuriously appointed. Facilities include a sauna, 24-hour room service, and broadband internet in all rooms. Close to the best restaurants in the city. **www.libertypalace.com.br**

CONGONHAS Colonial Hotel 👪 🏊 [P] $

Praça da Basílica 76 ***Tel*** *(031) 3731 1834* ***Rooms*** *8*

Next to the Basílica do Nosso Senhor Bom Jesus de Matosinhos *(see pp130–31)*, a long way from the main tourist sights, this well-maintained hotel offers the best accommodation in town, with spacious rooms. While somewhat dated, it retains its past glory in its huge hallways and high ceilings. **www.hotelcolonialcongonhas.com.br**

DIAMANTINA Pousada Montanhas de Minas 🏊 ❄ $

Rua da Romana 264 ***Tel*** *(038) 3531 3240* ***Rooms*** *13*

Housed in a mock-colonial building near the town center, this attractive *pousada* is a perfect choice for travelers on a budget. Minimalist rooms, which overlook a pool and the surrounding mountains, promise pretty views. Great value for money. **www.grupomontanhasdeminas.com.br**

DIAMANTINA Jardim da Serra 👪 🍴 🏊 ❄ [P] $$

Estrada do Cruzeiro Luminoso 3 km, 39100 000 ***Tel*** *(038) 3531 2987* ***Rooms*** *20*

A converted *fazenda* set in the mountains overlooking Diamantina, the Jardim de Serra has wonderful views of the town from many of the rooms and the bar. The hotel has a spring-water swimming pool. The town's best restaurants are only 2 miles (3 km) away. **www.jardimdaserra.com.br**

DIAMANTINA Relíquias do Tempo ❄ $$

Rua Macau de Baixo 104, Centro ***Tel*** *(038) 3531 1627* ***Rooms*** *18*

A beautifully restored 19th-century colonial house, the Relíquias do Tempo is located in the center of town. The interior features period furnishings and antiques, and a range of simple, but elegant, wooden-floored suites are offered. Excellent breakfast is included in the tariff. **pousadareliquiasdotempo.com.br**

DIAMANTINA Tijuco 🍴 ❄ [P] $$

Rua Macau do Meio 211 ***Tel*** *(038) 3531 1022* ***Rooms*** *27*

This hotel is housed in a building designed by renowned architect Oscar Niemeyer *(see p295)* at the start of his career, before he started work on Brasília. Beautifully restored to its original early 1960s look, the Tijuco has the best rooms on its second floor. **www.hoteltijuco.com.br**

MARIANA Pousada Solar dos Corrêa

Rua Josafá Macedo 70 **Tel** *(031) 3557 2080* **Rooms** *14*

A simple *pousada* in a converted colonial townhouse, this property is situated very close to the Igreja da Sé. The decor is minimalistic, though full of character. While every room is individually decorated, those on the first floor are preferred for their splendid views. **www.pousadasolardoscorrea.com.br**

OURO PRETO Estalagem das Minas Gerais

Rodovia dos Inconfidentes Km 87, 35400 000 **Tel** *(031) 3551 2122* **Fax** *(031) 3551 2709* **Rooms** *142*

A vast mock-colonial converted *fazenda* with a range of rooms, from plain standard apartments to more luxurious chalets. Facilities include horse-riding, tennis courts, a play area for children, a relaxing swimming pool, sauna, and live music at weekends. **www.sescmg.com.br/hospedagem/ouropreto.asp**

OURO PRETO Pousada do Mondego

Largo de Coimbra 38 **Tel** *(031) 3551 2040* **Fax** *(031) 3351 3094* **Rooms** *24*

The best rooms in this converted mid-18th-century colonial house have views out over the adjacent Igreja de São Francisco de Assis *(see p128)*. The hotel is beautifully done up with period furniture. All rooms are well-maintained; some of them come with a balcony. **www.mondego.com.br**

OURO PRETO Pousada Solar da Opera

Rua Conde de Bobadela 75 **Tel** *(031) 3551 6844* **Rooms** *15*

The hotel offers well-appointed and tastefully decorated modern rooms in a converted Portuguese town house in the historical town center. The best have balconies with views out over the street, though it can be noisy in high season. There is a good restaurant, bar, and café. **www.hotelsolardaopera.com.br**

OURO PRETO Solar Nossa Senhora do Rosário

Rua Getúlio Vargas 270 **Tel** *(031) 3551 5200* **Fax** *(031) 3551 4288* **Rooms** *46*

Spacious apartments with polished wooden floors housed in a 19th-century colonial mansion in the heart of the historic town. The decor is sumptuous, with spacious communal areas. The pool and other facilities are in a separate modern annexe. The hotel restaurant is one of the best in the city. **www.hotelsolardorosario.com.br**

SÃO JOÃO DEL REI Pousada Beco do Bispo

Rua Beco do Bispo 93 **Tel** *(032) 3371 8844* **Rooms** *13*

A newly-opened hotel, close to the Igreja de São Francisco de Assis, the Beco do Bispo offers bright, colorful rooms and helpful English-speaking staff. All rooms are equipped with a minibar and TV. The living room comes with a fireplace. **www.becodobispo.com.br**

PARQUE NACIONAL DA SERRA DA CANASTRA Fazenda Mirante

2 miles (3 km) from the park entrance, São Roque de Minas **Tel** *(037) 9983 6565* **Rooms** *10*

Very simple, spartan rooms are available in this rustic modern building with a view out over the lush *cerrado*. Some can accommodate as many as eight people. Breakfast and afternoon tea are included in the tariff. This is an ideal base for exploring the national park. **www.hotelfazendamirante.com.br**

PARQUE NACIONAL DA SERRA DO CIPÓ Cipó Veraneio

Rodovia MG-10 Km 95, Jaboticatubas, Serra do Cipó, 33400 **Tel** *(031) 3718 7000* **Rooms** *32*

This family-run *pousada*, located on the banks of a mountain river, offers a range of rooms, from simple en suite rooms to more luxurious family rooms. Children under the age of four years can stay for free. All meals are included in the tariff, and there are good restaurants and a café. **www.cipoveraneiohotel.com.br**

PARQUE NACIONAL DA SERRA DO CIPÓ Fazenda Toucan Cipo

Tel *(021) 2512 3895* **Rooms** *5*

Set in the heart of the national park, this super-luxurious eco-hotel and private home promises superb wildlife viewing and bird-watching. Naturalists can study the flora and fauna within a broad radius of the estate. All food and drinks, including alcohol, are included in the price, as are guided trips. **www.toucancipo.com**

TIRADENTES Pousada Três Portas

Rua Direita 280A **Tel** *(032) 3355 1444* **Rooms** *9*

Done up with hard wood and furnished with grandfather clocks, antiques, and four-poster beds, this attractive little colonial *pousada* in the historic center was voted among the top six hotels in Brazil by *Viagem e Turismo*, the country's leading travel magazine. **www.pousadatresportas.com.br**

TIRADENTES Solar da Ponte

Praça das Mercês **Tel** *(032) 3355 1255* **Rooms** *18*

This beautiful restored colonial mansion is set in its own walled garden in the heart of the colonial town. Rooms are furnished with antiques and four-poster double beds. Its afternoon tea, made by the English owner (and included in the price), is legendary throughout Minas. **www.solardaponte.com.br**

TIRADENTES Hotel Pequena Tiradentes

Av Governador Israel Pinheiro 670 **Tel** *(032) 3355 1262* **Rooms** *62*

The newly-opened mock-colonial Pequena Tiradentes blends old-world charm with ultra-modern facilities. Though on the outskirts of town, the hotel is just a ten-minute ride from the historic center. Rooms are spacious and well-appointed and the breakfasts generous. **www.pequenatiradentes.com.br**

SÃO PAULO CITY

CENTRO Othon Classic $$

Rua Líbero Badaró 190 **Tel** *(011) 2106 0202* **Rooms** *150* **Map** *1 C3*

The only reasonably well-kept hotel in the city center, the Othon Palace is housed in one of the city's oldest skyscrapers, close to the Teatro Municipal and Anhangabaú. However, visitors to this area need to be careful after dark. Parking is limited. There are good off-season discounts on offer. **http://othonhotels.com**

JARDINS & AVENIDA PAULISTA Pousada Dona Zilah $$

Alameda Franca 1633, Jardins, 01422 001 **Tel** *(011) 3062 1444* **Fax** *(011) 3061 5413* **Rooms** *18* **Map** *4 D2*

A pleasant B&B, the Dona Zilah is located in a small converted town house in the heart of fashionable Jardins. It offers one of the most attractive deals in this expensive area, and is close to the best restaurants, bars, cinemas, shops, and art galleries. Parking is limited. **www.zilah.com**

JARDINS & AVENIDA PAULISTA Maksoud Plaza $$$$

Alameda Campinas 150, Jardins, 01404 900 **Tel** *(011) 3145 8000* **Fax** *(011) 3145 8001* **Rooms** *416* **Map** *4 F3*

Just off Avenida Paulista, the Maksoud Plaza is an old-fashioned but well-kept business hotel with superb views out over the city from the upper floors. A limousine service is available on request to and from Congonhas Domestic Airport and Guarulhos International Airport. **www.maksoud.com.br**

JARDINS & AVENIDA PAULISTA Emiliano $$$$$

Rua Oscar Freire 384, Jardins **Tel** *(011) 3068 4399* **Fax** *(011) 3068 4399* **Rooms** *57* **Map** *4 D3*

One of the city's finest designer hotels, the Emiliano mixes opulence with refinement. Suites have thick carpets, leather sofas, and luxurious beds covered in rich Egyptian cotton sheets. Fittings are by famous designers, including the Campana brothers, Fernando and Humberto. Valet parking is available. **www.emiliano.com.br**

JARDINS & AVENIDA PAULISTA Fasano $$$$$

Rua Vittorio Fasano 88, Jardins, 01414 020 **Tel** *(011) 3896 4000* **Fax** *(011) 3896 4155* **Rooms** *64* **Map** *4 D3*

The most understated and sophisticated of the city's luxury hotels, the Fasano feels like a gentleman's club for the new millennium. It boasts one of Brazil's finest Italian restaurants, Fasano *(see p399)*. All rooms come as suites. Valet parking is available. **www.fasano.com.br**

JARDINS & AVENIDA PAULISTA Hotel Unique $$$$$

Av Brigadeiro Luís Antonio 4700, Jardins **Tel** *(011) 3055 4700* **Fax** *(011) 3055 4700* **Rooms** *95* **Map** *4 E5*

The most self-consciously designer hotel in Brazil, the Unique is a giant half-orange on stilts, with 7-ft (2-m) wide porthole windows and a splendid cavernous lobby *(see p146)*. The tail-end suites have floors that curve up to meet the ceiling. Sky, the rooftop bar with good views, serves wonderful cocktails. **www.hotelunique.com**

JARDINS & AVENIDA PAULISTA L'Hotel $$$$$

Alameda Campinas 266, Bela Vista **Tel** *(011) 2183 0500* **Fax** *(011) 2183 0505* **Rooms** *79* **Map** *4 F3*

Mock-New York meets mock-European in this hotel with sober antique and classical furniture. A quiet atmosphere prevails throughout and the service is impressive. All rooms are tastefully decorated, and there is a respectable on-site restaurant. Valet parking is available. Convenient for Avenida Paulista. **www.lhotel.com.br**

JARDINS & AVENIDA PAULISTA Renaissance $$$$$

Rua Alameda Santos 2233, Jardins **Tel** *(011) 3069 2233* **Fax** *(011) 3064 3344* **Rooms** *452* **Map** *4 E2*

A popular business hotel near Jardins and Avenida Paulista with conference rooms and excellent communication and business facilities. What the rooms lack in character they make up for with comfort. It may be a better idea to dine in one of the nearby places than in the on-site restaurant. **www.hoteis.marriott.com.br/renaissance-sao-paulo**

SERRA DA CANTAREIRA Unique Garden $$$$$

Estrada Laramara 3500, Mairiporã **Tel** *(011) 4486 8700* **Rooms** *25*

One of South America's great spa hotels, this place has beautifully designed individual bungalows set in a rainforest in the Serra da Cantareira mountains, a 40-minute ride from the city center. Superb facilities, treatments, and food are on offer. Children are not allowed. **www.uniquegarden.com.br**

THE NEW CENTER Grand Hyatt $$$$$

Av das Nacoes Unidas 13301, Brooklin **Tel** *(011) 6838 1234* **Fax** *(011) 6838 1235* **Rooms** *470*

This is the best business hotel in the city and convenient for the new business center around Avenida Luis Carlos Berrini. The top-floor suites are carefully designed and have magnificent views, and the excellent spa, restaurants, and bars attract fashionable São Paulo residents. **http://saopaulo.grand.hyatt.com**

THE NEW CENTER Hilton São Paulo Morumbi $$$$$

Av das Nacoes Unidas 12901, Brooklin **Tel** *(011) 6845 0000* **Fax** *(011) 6845 0001* **Rooms** *485*

The business-like modern apartments at this upscale hotel come stylishly equipped with a separate living room, kitchenette, en suite bathroom, and executive lounge access. Continental breakfast and refreshments are complimentary. On-site dining options include the Canvas Bar & Grill, Sol & Sombra, and Caffè Cino. **www.hilton.com**

SÃO PAULO STATE

CANANÉIA Pousada Caropá ▤ [$]

Praça Martim Afonso de Sousa 13, Centro **Tel** *(013) 3851 1601* **Rooms** *14*

Very minimally-appointed, clean rooms are available at this *pousada* near the waterfront in a restored 19th-century Portuguese town house. The friendly staff can help organize boat trips to the Ilha do Cardoso, an ecological preserve with fine beaches. The *pousada* is one of the best-value options in the area.

IGUAPE Pousada dos Martins ▨ [P] [$]

Rua Antonio Ferreira Aguiar 8, Centro **Tel** *(013) 3841 4260* **Rooms** *15*

This well-maintained family-run *pousada* offers motel-like rooms in the heart of Iguape, which is also an ideal base for exploring the Estação Ecológico Juréia-Itatins. The welcoming staff will happily answer questions about visiting this state park, which showcases the flora and fauna of the Atlantic rainforest.

IGUAPE Solar Colonial ▨ [$]

Praça da Basilica 30 **Tel** *(013) 3841 1591* **Rooms** *10*

Small, simple, but very well-kept rooms are available in this affordable B&B housed in a refurbished Portuguese colonial building, right in the heart of town. The best rooms, which look out on to the main square, are the most preferred. Generous breakfasts and warm service make the stay memorable.

ILHABELA Canto da Praia Ilhabela ≋ ▤ [P] [$][$][$][$]

Av Força Expedicionária Brasileira 793, Santa Tereza **Tel** *(012) 3896 1194* **Fax** *(012) 3896 6415* **Rooms** *4*

Sitting right above a narrow beach, with its own beautiful terrace, garden, and pool, this tiny *pousada* is a favorite location for Brazilian fashion shoots. All four apartments are embellished with rustic chic and there is plenty of shade from the palms and covered sundecks. **www.cantodapraiailhabela.com.br**

ILHABELA Maison Joly 🍴 ≋ ▤ [P] [$][$][$][$]

Rua Antônio Lisboa Alves 278, Centro **Tel** *(012) 3896 1201* **Rooms** *10*

A tastefully designed boutique hotel, the tiny Maison Joly is dotted with carefully chosen stylish arts and crafts. Each room comes with a private terrace providing a splendid view out over Ilhabela, the Atlantic, and the Serra do Mar mountains. Book well ahead for weekend stays. Children not allowed. **www.maisonjoly.com.br**

MARESIAS Brig Maresias 🍴 ≋ 🍸 ▤ [P] [$][$][$][$]

Av Francisco Loup 1158, 11620 000 **Tel** *(012) 3865 6527* **Rooms** *22*

At this hotel visitors can choose from a range of chalets and rooms, from spartan doubles to well-furnished bungalows decorated in mock-Oriental style. Facilities include a 24-hour reception and enormous complimentary breakfasts. The beach is just a stroll away. **www.brig.com.br**

MARESIAS Maresias Beach Hotel 🍴 ≋ 🍸 ▤ [P] [W] [$][$][$][$]

Av Francisco Loup 1109, São Sebastião, 11620 000 **Tel** *(012) 3891 7500* **Fax** *(012) 3891 7509* **Rooms** *93*

Located on one of the most beautiful beaches in the area, this sprawling family hotel provides comfortable rooms. Other amenities include games for children, babysitting, tennis courts, and an enormous pool. Special low-season deals are on offer. The hotel can be very noisy in high season. **www.maresiashotel.com.br**

SANTOS Mendes Plaza 🍴 ≋ ▤ [P] [W] [$][$][$]

Av Floriano Peixato 42 **Tel** *(013) 3289 4243* **Fax** *(013) 3284 8253* **Rooms** *104*

A huge beachfront business hotel built in the 1980s, the Mendes Plaza is a great accommodation choice, with air conditioning and TV in every room. Other features include sauna, massage, and sport facilities. The staff are efficient and there is a decent on-site restaurant. **www.grupomendes.com.br**

SANTOS Parque Balneário 🍴 ≋ ▤ [P] [W] [$][$][$]

Av Ana Costa 555, Praia do Gonzaga **Tel** *(013) 3289 5700* **Fax** *(013) 3284 0475* **Rooms** *119*

A fully refurbished 1970s beachfront luxury hotel, the Balneário has a grand marble lobby. The rooms have good ocean views, especially from the upper floors. The property also has a rooftop pool convention center and decent business facilities. Beach service is offered. **www.parquebalneario.com.br**

UBATUBA Refúgio do Corsário 🍴 ≋ 🍸 ▤ [P] [$][$][$][$]

Trilha do Corsário 10, Praia da Fortaleza **Tel** *(012) 3848 9229* **Rooms** *21*

A wonderful setting on the tip of a peninsula in the heart of the forest sets this hotel apart. Modest, though comfortable, chalets are set on a lawn in front of a sculpted pool and a small beach. Simpler apartment rooms are also on offer. Many fine beaches are located nearby. **www.corsario.com.br**

UBATUBA Pousada Piçinguaba 🍴 ≋ [P] [$][$][$][$][$]

Rua G 130, Vila Piçinguaba **Tel** *(012) 3836 9105* **Fax** *(012) 3836 9103* **Rooms** *10*

A luxury boutique hotel located in a converted convent, the Piçinguaba is situated in a small fishing village halfway between Ubatuba and Paraty. Rooms are simple, though very tastefully decorated. Wonderful views, kayaking, boat rides, and forest walks are on offer. Parking is limited. **www.picinguaba.com**

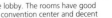

BAHIA

COSTA DO SAUÍPE Mariott Resort & Spa
 $$$$$

Rodovia BA-99 Km 76 s/n, Costa do Sauipe, 48280 000 **Tel** *(071) 2104 7000* **Fax** *(071) 2104 7001* **Rooms** *256*

A grand sprawling resort built in tropical colonial style, this Marriott property features large rooms with king-size beds and balconies. The extensive leisure areas include three pools, a pair of jacuzzis, saunas, and spa treatments. The best part of the hotel, however, is its location right on the beach. **www.marriott.com.br**

COSTA DO SAUÍPE Sofitel Suites Costa do Sauípe
 $$$$$

Costa do Sauipe s/n, 48280 000 **Tel** *(071) 2104 8000* **Fax** *(071) 2104 8001* **Rooms** *198*

Built in the style of an old cocoa plantation, this resort has an intimate feel. All suites have verandas and come with a spacious sitting area with sofa-bed, separated from the master bedroom. The pool area is magnificent and leisure activities include golfing, boating, horse-riding, and cultural presentations. **www.costadosauipe.com.br**

ILHA DE BOIPEBA Pousada Santa Clara
$$

Boca da Barra s/n, 45410 000 **Tel** *(075) 3653 6085* **Rooms** *9*

The pleasant Santa Clara provides a tropical hideaway just steps from the beach. Each room is unique in size and style and is colorfully decorated. The *pousada* also has a cozy sitting room and reading lounge. The Santa Clara restaurant is Boipeba's best dining option. Complimentary gourmet breakfast. **www.santaclaraboipeba.com**

ILHA DE BOIPEBA Pousada Vila Sereia
$$

Boca da Barra s/n, 45410 000 **Tel** *(075) 3653 6045* **Fax** *(075) 3653 6045* **Rooms** *4*

The Vila Sereia has four lovely bungalows with wide front decks and hammocks, facing the gorgeous, largely empty beach of Ilha de Boipeba. A satisfying Bahian-style breakfast is served on the balcony that comes with every bungalow. **www.amabo.org.br/en/vilasereia.html**

ILHÉUS Ilhéus Tropical
$$

Rodovia Ilhéus-Olivença Km 2, Jardim Atlântico, 45655 170 **Tel** *(073) 3632 7214* **Fax** *(073) 3632 7194* **Rooms** *28*

A small walk from Praia do Sul, this new *pousada* is located 2 miles (3 km) from the historic center. The no-frills apartments are clean and comfortable. The leisure area includes a games room and playground for children. There is a decent restaurant on the grounds. **www.ilheustropical.com.br**

ILHÉUS Pousada Praia Bela
$$

Rodovia Ilhéus-Olivença Km 2.5, Praia dos Milionários, 45655 170 **Tel** *(073) 3632 7022* **Rooms** *16*

Set on the Milionários beach, this small *pousada* offers pleasant accommodation. Rooms are decorated in bright colors and have verandas facing either the ocean or the lush garden. The leisure area includes a children's pool, beach soccer, and volleyball court. **www.praiabela.com.br**

ITACARÉ Itacaré Ecoresort
 $$$$$

Rodovia BA-001 Km 64, 45530 000 **Tel** *(073) 3251 3133* **Fax** *(073) 3251 3133* **Rooms** *25*

The resort is located off a small beach and set amid beautiful Atlantic rainforest. The apartments are spacious and elegantly furnished in light colors. Breakfast and dinner are included in the tariff. A complimentary shuttle service connects the beach to the village of Itacaré. **www.ier.com.br**

ITACARÉ Txai Resort
$$$$$

Rodovia Ilhéus Itacaré km 48, 45530 000 **Tel** *(073) 2101 5000* **Fax** *(073) 2101 5000* **Rooms** *26*

This full-service resort features spacious airy bungalows spread out through a 247-acre (100-ha) coconut plantation on the edge of the Itacarézinho beach. Numerous activities are offered, including tennis, horse-riding, beach safaris, hiking, canoeing, and a spa for those looking for relaxation. **http://www.txairesort.com.br/**

LENÇOIS Canto das Aguas
$$

Av Sr Dos Passos 1, 46960 000 **Tel** *(075) 3334 1154* **Fax** *(075) 3334 1154* **Rooms** *44*

Set close to the main square, this pleasant hotel looks over to the Rio Lençois. The best rooms are those in the new wing. Bright and spacious, these feature a queen-size bed and fold-out sofa, a sitting area, and veranda. The hotel restaurant is striking with a colorful interior. **www.lencois.com.br**

LENÇOIS Estalagem Alcino
 $$

Rua Tomba Surrão 139, 46960 000 **Tel** *(075) 3334 1171* **Fax** *(075) 3334 1171* **Rooms** *7*

This cozy *pousada* is housed in a replica of a 19th-century colonial house. A scrumptious breakfast is served in the tranquil, well-kept garden. The rooms are intimate and decorated with antique furniture. The only downside is that the bathrooms are shared. The hotel also boasts a good collection of books for browsing.

MORRO DE SÃO PAULO Pousada Puerto Beach
$$

Quarta Praia, 45400 000 **Tel** *(075) 3652 2136* **Rooms** *16*

Located far from the village on a largely empty beach, the Puerto Beach hotel features small self-contained chalets and comfortable rooms in a garden-like setting. The hotel has an outdoor leisure area with a jacuzzi, two small pools, a bar, and numerous hammocks and deck chairs. **www.hotelpuertobeach.com.br**

Key to Price Guide *see p366* **Key to Symbols** *see back cover flap*

MORRO DE SÃO PAULO Vila Guaiamú

Terceira Praia s/n, 45400 000 **Tel** *(075) 3652 1035* **Fax** *(075) 3483 1073* **Rooms** *22*

Set on a quiet beach, the Vila Guaiamú consists of 22 cabins scattered among a lush garden. Simply furnished with a double and single bed, each cabin comes with a private bathroom and veranda with hammock.The hustle and bustle of the main village is only a 20-minute stroll away. **www.vilaguaiamu.com.br**

PORTO SEGURO Porto Seguro Praia Hotel

Av Beira Mar s/n, 45810 000 **Tel** *(073) 3288 9393* **Fax** *(073) 3679 2069* **Rooms** *149*

Located on the pretty beach of Praia Curuípe, this full-service resort offers fine dining, tennis, two pools, and an outstanding view of the ocean. Rooms are spacious, comfortable, and modern. Besides a good on-site restaurant, there is the popular Nau Cabral Bar. Ideal for business as well as leisure travelers. **www.psph.com.br**

PORTO SEGURO Xurupita Resort

Caixa Postal 189, 45810 000 **Tel** *(073) 2105 9500* **Fax** *(073) 2105 9501* **Rooms** *16*

This resort is perfect for families traveling with children. Each apartment has two rooms and sleeps four people comfortably. A small kitchen is equipped with a stove, fridge, and microwave. The resort has a large leisure area. The main swimming pool includes a hydro-massage facility and a bar. **www.xurupita.com**

PRAIA DO FORTE Pousada Porto da Lua

Praia do Forte s/n, 48280 000 **Tel** *(071) 3676 1372* **Fax** *(071) 3676 1446* **Rooms** *26*

A short stroll from the Projeto Tamar *(see p207)*, the Porto da Lua is set right on the beach. Most of the apartments look out over the ocean. Only the lower-floor rooms have air conditioning, as the upper floor gets a steady sea breeze. The hotel's tropical architecture is by well-known architect Wilson Reis Netto. **www.portodalua.tur.br**

PRAIA DO FORTE Praia do Forte Eco Resort

Av Do Farol s/n, 48280 000 **Tel** *(071) 3676 4000* **Fax** *(071) 3673 1112* **Rooms** *250*

This sprawling resort is set in gorgeous gardens near the beach. All apartments are spacious and well-appointed. The resort offers a large number of sports and recreation activities, including snorkeling, windsurfing, kayaking, and nature walks. Breakfast and dinner are included in the rate. **www.ecoresort.com.br**

SALVADOR Ibis Rio Vermelho

Rua Fonte do Boi 215, Rio Vermelho, 41940 360 **Tel** *(071) 3330 8200* **Fax** *(071) 3330 8201* **Rooms** *252*

The no-frills Ibis brand specializes in tidy, comfortable rooms. Prices are low because the hotel does not offer services such as dry-cleaning, buffet breakfast, or valet parking. For the most memorable Ibis experience, request an ocean-view room when reserving. **www.accorhotels.com.br**

SALVADOR Pousada Beija-Flor

Rua D. de Santo Antônio 259, Centro Histórico, 40301 280 **Tel** *(071) 3241 7085* **Fax** *(071) 3241 2472* **Rooms** *7*

The rooms in this unpretentious *pousada* are on the small side, although most come with a veranda and offer fabulous views of the Salvador harbor and the Baía dos Todos os Santos (Bay of All Saints). Breakfast is served on the bright patio. A short stroll from the Pelourinho *(see pp186–7)*. **www.beijaflorpousada.com.br**

SALVADOR Pousada Redfish

Ladeira do Boqueirão 1, 40301 280 **Tel** *(071) 3243 8473* **Fax** *(071) 3326 2544* **Rooms** *8*

A crumbling heritage building on the edge of the historic center, the Redfish was bought and renovated by English owners into a comfortable inn. Rooms are simple but spacious, high-ceilinged, and flooded with light. The ground floor of the *pousada* contains a gallery of local art. **www.pousadaredfish.com.br**

SALVADOR Monte Pascoal Praia

Av Oceânica 591, Barra, 40170 010 **Tel** *(071) 2103 4000* **Fax** *(071) 3245 4436* **Rooms** *83*

This excellent-value hotel provides recently renovated rooms with comfortable king-size beds or two single beds. Every room features a balcony with either a full or partial view of the ocean. Close to Salvador's best restaurants, bars, museums, and shopping areas. **www.montepascoal.com.br**

SALVADOR Pousada do Boqueirão

Rua D. de Santo Antônio 48, Centro Histórico, 40301 280 **Tel** *(071) 3241 2262* **Fax** *(071) 3241 8064* **Rooms** *15*

A pretty *pousada* in the historic center of Salvador with high-ceilinged rooms that have period furnishings, but lack modern amenities such as TV or Internet. The best room is a split-level apartment with a separate sitting area and a large private terrace. The restaurant faces the sea. **www.pousadaboqueirao.com.br**

SALVADOR Pousada do Pilar

Rua D. de Santo Antônio 24, Centro Histórico, 40301 280 **Tel** *(071) 3241 2033* **Fax** *(071) 3241 3844* **Rooms** *12*

Set in a heritage building, this *pousada* has received a complete overhaul to meet modern standards. Rooms are spacious and pleasantly decorated with bright splashes of colour. Seven of the rooms have a veranda and look out over the port and the ocean. Breakfast is served on the rooftop patio. **www.pousadadopilar.com**

SALVADOR Pestana Bahia

Rua Fonte do Boi 216, Rio Vermelho, 41940 360 **Tel** *(071) 2103 8000* **Fax** *(071) 2103 8066* **Rooms** *430*

Sitting on an outcrop overlooking the ocean at the Rio Vermelho, the Pestana is one of Salvador's top luxury hotels. The modern rooms are spacious and decorated in a bright, funky style. The hotel's leisure area includes an outdoor pool and sundeck overlooking the beach and a top-notch fitness center. **www.pestanahotels.com.br**

TRANCOSO Pousada Mundo Verde

$$

Rua de Telgrafo 43, 4581 8000 **Tel** *(073) 36681 279* **Fax** *(073) 3668 1279* **Rooms** *11*

A small *pousada* set in a large garden, the Mundo Verde offers a tremendous clifftop view looking out over the nature preserve and beach in the distance. Rooms are in small bungalows, and feature double beds with mosquito canopies, tile floors, and large verandas with hammocks. **www.pousadamundoverde.com.br**

TRANCOSO Pousada Estrela d'Água

$$$$

Estrada do Arraial s/n, 4581 0000 **Tel** *(073) 36681 030* **Fax** *(073) 3575 1032* **Rooms** *27*

A beautiful high-end resort on Praia dos Nativos, this *pousada* has its own beachside pools and jacuzzi. Rooms are large, comfortable, and tastefully decorated. Guests can enjoy a range of activities, including bike rental and massage, as well as access to a nearby seaside golf course. **www.estreladagua.com.br**

SERGIPE, ALAGOAS & PERNAMBUCO

ARACAJU (Sergipe) Pousada Praia e Mar

$$

Av Santos Dumont 433, Praia de Atalaia, 49035 730 **Tel** *(079) 3243 4520* **Rooms** *14*

This inexpensive B&B is right across the street from Praia de Atalaia. The rooms are plain but very clean, and all come with a private bathroom. The reception staff are available 24 hours a day. The on-site restaurant serves authentic Northeastern cuisine. **www.pousadapraiaemar.com.br**

ARACAJU (Sergipe) Quality

$$$

Av Delmiro Gouveia 100, Corao do Meio, 49035 810 **Tel** *(079) 3234 7000* **Fax** *(079) 3234 7001* **Rooms** *109*

Reputedly Aracaju's best hotel, Quality offers very comfortable rooms with queen-size beds, a desk, a large TV, and wireless Internet. Women travelers can request a room on the women-only floor. The only drawback is the hotel's location far from the beach next to a mall. **www.atlanticahotels.com.br**

FERNANDO DE NORONHA (Pernambuco) Pousada do Vale

$$$$

Rua Pescador Sérgio Lino 18, Jardim Elizabeth, 53990 000 **Tel** *(081) 3619 1293* **Fax** *(081) 3619 1881* **Rooms** *5*

Within walking distance of the village, this *pousada* is set amid striking natural beauty. One of the nicer rooms is the Marlim, which has a great balcony. The cheerful decor features hand-crafted furniture. Although there is no swimming pool, the beach is only a five-minute walk away. **www.pousadadovale.com**

FERNANDO DE NORONHA (Pernambuco) Solar dos Ventos

$$$$

Estrada do Sueste s/n, 5399 0000 **Tel** *(081) 36191 347* **Fax** *(081) 3619 1253* **Rooms** *8*

Overlooking the Baía do Sueste, the self-contained bungalows at the Solar dos Ventos feature a double and two single beds, a sitting area, and a balcony with a hammock. The only drawback is the hotel's location at the far end of the island's restaurants and services. **www.solardosventos.com.br**

FERNANDO DE NORONHA (Pernambuco) Pousada Maravilha

$$$$$

BR-363 s/n, Sueste, 5399 0000 **Tel** *(081) 36190 028* **Fax** *(081) 3619 0162* **Rooms** *8*

Accommodation is either in independent bungalows or in the main building. The bungalows feature a spacious veranda with hammock, a king-size four-poster bed, and a huge bathroom. Rooms in the main building are smaller and less luxurious, but also feature king-size beds and good bathrooms. **www.pousadamaravilha.com.br**

FERNANDO DE NORONHA (Pernambuco) Pousada Zé Maria

$$$$$

Rua Nice Cordeiro 1, 5399 0000 **Tel** *(081) 36191 258* **Fax** *(081) 3619 1258* **Rooms** *20*

A luxury *pousada* on a hilltop with a panoramic view of the islands, Zé Maria offers newly-built self-contained bungalows, with queen-size beds, wide decks, and solar showers. Many bungalows feature private jacuzzis. There is a relaxing pool, gorgeous old mango trees, and an on-site spa. **www.pousadazemaria.com.br**

MACEIÓ (Alagoas) Ibis Maceió Pajuçara

$$

Av Dr. Antônio Gouveia 277, Praia de Pajuçara, 57030 170 **Tel** *(082) 2121 6699* **Fax** *(082) 3327 6711* **Rooms** *99*

One of the best budget options in Maceió, the rooms in this modern Ibis hotel feature comfortable beds, desks with laptop plug, and spotless bathrooms. All rooms, except for four on the first floor, boast ocean views. The hotel has a decent restaurant, A Boa Mesa, and a good coffee shop, Menu Express. **www.accorhotels.com.br**

MACEIÓ (Alagoas) Jatiúca Flat & Resort

$$$$

Lagoa da Anta 220, 57035 180 **Tel** *(082) 2122 5757 (Flat), 2122 2000 (Resort)* **Fax** *(082) 2122 2020* **Rooms** *179*

The Jatiúca Flat and Resort are set side by side on a lagoon right on Praia da Jatiúca. Both offer oustanding accommodation within walking distance of all the seaside entertainment and restaurants. There is a good selection of on-site restaurants and bars. Parking available in resort only. **www.hoteljatiuca.com.br**

OLINDA (Pernambuco) Pousada dos Quatro Cantos

$$

Rua Prudente de Morais 441, 53020 170 **Tel** *(081) 3429 0220* **Fax** *(081) 3429 1845* **Rooms** *17*

Set in the heart of Olinda, this *pousada* is housed in a beautiful heritage building. The recently refurbished deluxe rooms look plush and feature a jetted tub. One of the nicest rooms is the Veranda Suite, a spacious chamber overlooking the garden. All of Olinda's sights are an easy stroll away. **www.pousada4cantos.com.br**

Key to Price Guide *see p366* **Key to Symbols** *see back cover flap*

OLINDA (Pernambuco) Hotel 7 Colinas $$$

Ladeira de São Francisco 307, 53120 070 **Tel** *(081) 3493 7766* **Fax** *(081) 3493 7766* **Rooms** *39*

Surrounded by resplendent greenery, this hotel has the best leisure area in Olinda, with a large outdoor pool and play area. Rooms face the pretty garden and are decorated in rustic style, with tile floors and dark wood furniture. There is a small on-site museum and an English-speaking staff. **www.hotel7colinas.com.br**

OLINDA (Pernambuco) Pousada do Amparo $$$$

Rua do Amparo 199, 53020 170 **Tel** *(081) 3439 1749* **Fax** *(081) 3429 6889* **Rooms** *11*

Consisting of two renovated 18th-century heritage houses, the Amparo is one of Olinda's most beautiful *pousadas*. Rooms vary widely in size and configuration. Most have balconies, hammocks, and period furnishings. The views of Olinda and Recife from the leafy green common areas are spectacular. **www.pousadadoamparo.com.br**

PORTO DE GALINHAS (Pernambuco) Pousada Beira Mar $$

Av Beira Mar 12, 55590 000 **Tel** *(081) 3552 1052* **Fax** *(081) 3552 1052* **Rooms** *12*

This *pousada* is right on the beach, in the heart of the village. The best rooms are on the upper floor and come with a large private terrace. The eight standard-size rooms lack a terrace, but are still quite comfortable. Activities include swimming, snorkeling, diving, body-surfing, riding, and volleyball. **www.pousadabeiramar.com.br**

PORTO DE GALINHAS (Pernambuco) Tabajuba $$$

Praia Pontal do Cupe s/n, 55590 000 **Tel** *(081) 3552 1049* **Fax** *(081) 3552 1006* **Rooms** *24*

Just a few steps from Praia Pontal do Cupe, one of the finest beaches in Northeastern Brazil, the Tabajuba has cheerful, brightly-colored rooms with queen-size beds and balconies. The *pousada* also features a pool, leisure area, and an on-site restaurant. Children under 12 are not permitted. **www.tabajuba.com**

PORTO DE GALINHAS (Pernambuco) Tabapitanga $$$$

Praia Pontal do Cupe, 55590 000 **Tel** *(081) 3552 1049* **Fax** *(081) 3552 1037* **Rooms** *43*

A small inn, the Tabapitanga offers luxurious accommodation on the beach just 3 miles (5 km) from the village. The modern rooms are spacious, with bright, elegant decor and king-size beds and large flat-screen TVs. All of them come with an atmospheric veranda or a deck. **www.tabapitanga.com.br**

RECIFE (Pernambuco) Beach Class Suites $$$

Av Boa Viagem 1906, Boa Viagem, 51011 000 **Tel** *(081) 2121 2626* **Fax** *(081) 2121 2600* **Rooms** *140*

Considered to be the best accommodation option in Boa Viagem, this brand-new hotel features generously-proportioned rooms with modern furniture. Some rooms come equipped with a small kitchen. The hotel also offers a women-only floor, ideal for women traveling alone. **www.atlanticahotels.com.br**

RECIFE (Pernambuco) Hotel Jangadeiro $$$

Av Boa Viagem 3114, Boa Viagem, 51020 001 **Tel** *(081) 3465 3544* **Rooms** *93*

The Jangadeiro reputedly offers the best value in Boa Viagem. All rooms have been recently renovated and are bright and spotless. Reserve ahead as this hotel fills up quickly. The ocean-view rooms are worth the extra money, as they offer fabulous views of the beach along Boa Viagem. **www.jangadeirohotel.com.br**

RECIFE (Pernambuco) Recife Palace $$$$

Av Boa Viagem 4070, Boa Viagem, 51021 000 **Tel** *(081) 3464 2500* **Fax** *(081) 3465 2525* **Rooms** *295*

The five-star Recife Palace is just across from the Boa Viagem beach. All rooms, even the standard ones, are huge and decorated with modern blond-wood furniture and soft colors, while the bathrooms boast bathtubs. The superior rooms offer partial views of the ocean. Deluxe rooms have full views. **www.lucsimhoteis.com.br**

PARAÍBA, RIO GRANDE DO NORTE & CEARÁ

CAMPINA GRANDE (Paraíba) Hotel Village Campina Grande $$

Rua Otacílio Nepomuceno 1285, 58104 575 **Tel** *(083) 3310 8000* **Fax** *(083) 3310 8002* **Rooms** *85*

Campina Grande's top hotel mainly attracts a business crowd. Rooms are elegantly appointed and feature a work desk and Internet access. Hotel facilities include a sauna, games room, business center, and concierge service. The on-site restaurant, Le Chateau, serves continental cuisine. **www.hoteisvillage.com**

CANOA QUEBRADA (Ceará) Pousada Aruanã $$

Rua dos Bugueiros, Praia de Canoa Quebrada s/n, 62800 000 **Tel** *(084) 3421 7154* **Rooms** *12*

Inaugurated in 2005, this small *pousada* provides one of the most affordable accommodation options in town. The rooms are bright and spotless, and nicely furnished. Overlooking Praia de Canoa Quebrada, the hotel has breath-taking sea views. There is an impressive swimming pool with a swimmer's bar. **www.pousadaaruana.com.br**

CANOA QUEBRADA (Ceará) Pousada Chatteletta $$

Praia de Canoa Quebrada s/n, 62800 000 **Tel** *(084) 3421 7200* **Fax** *(084) 3421 7169* **Rooms** *18*

In an attractive location, just a five-minute stroll from the beach, this simple *pousada* offers chalets arranged around a pool. All chalets come with rooms that can sleep up to six people and have an attached terrace and hammocks facing the pool. The on-site bar serves memorable *caipirinhas*. **www.pousadachataletta.com.br**

CANOA QUEBRADA (Ceará) Pousada Long Beach   ⊞▤▤ P w $$$
Rua Long Beach s/n, 62800 000 **Tel** *(084) 3421 7404* **Fax** *(084) 3421 7407* **Rooms** *42*

The highlight of this *pousada* is its large oval swimming pool, which offers a panoramic view of Canoa Quebrada. The 20 self-contained chalets feature king-size beds and verandas with hammocks. Some of the chalets have spectacular views. Rooms, too, feature king-size beds, but lack the views. **www.longbeachvillage.com.br**

FORTALEZA (Ceará) Ibis Fortaleza   ▯▤▤▤ P ௯ w $$
Rua A. Barbosa de Lima 660, Iracema, 60060 370 **Tel** *(085) 3219 2121* **Fax** *(085) 3219 0000* **Rooms** *171*

According to the Ibis standard, this flagship hotel offers clean, quality accommodation at bargain rates. Rooms are sizable and inviting with sophisticated decor. The hotel is within easy walking distance of the beach and the Iracema nightlife area. The Ibis has a good restaurant and bar. **www.accorhotels.com.br**

FORTALEZA (Ceará) Othon Palace Fortaleza   ▯▤▯▤ P ௯ w $$$
Av Beira Mar 3470, Meireles, 60165 121 **Tel** *(021) 2016 0200* **Fax** *(085) 3466 5501* **Rooms** *115*

This elegant modern hotel has one of the best beachfront locations between Meireles and Mucuripe. Decorated in cheerful yellow and blue, the rooms are furnished with good quality beds and linen. The spacious bathrooms are tastefully done in marble. The hotel is close to Fortaleza's stylish bars and nightlife. **www.othon.com.br**

FORTALEZA (Ceará) Hotel Luzeiros   ▯▤▯▤ P ௯ w $$$$
Av Beira Mar 2600, Meireles, 62800 000 **Tel** *(085) 4006 8585* **Fax** *(085) 4006 8587* **Rooms** *202*

One of Fortaleza's best hotels, the Luzeiros has the look and feel of a boutique hotel. The rooms are beautifully appointed in elegant gold tones with dark wood furniture. All rooms have balconies and even the standard rooms offer a partial ocean view. A fully-equipped convention center and four meeting rooms. **www.luzeiros.com.br**

GENIPABU (Rio Grande do Norte) Pousada Villa do Sol   ▯▤▤▤ P $$
Enseada do Genipabu Km 5, 59575 000 **Tel** *(084) 3225 2132* **Fax** *(084) 3225 2037* **Rooms** *20*

Located 2 miles (3 km) north of town, this *pousada* offers 20 affordable, yet extremely attractive, chalets. Five of the chalets come with stunning views of the river. There is a decent pool and the service is pleasant. The *pousada's* friendly American owner is a good source of local information. **www.villadosol.com.br**

JERICOACOARA (Ceará) Pousada Recanto do Barão   ▤▤ P w $$
Rua do Forró 433, 62598 000 **Tel** *(088) 3669 2149* **Rooms** *20*

A great location, right in the heart of the village, adds to the appeal of this affordable *pousada*. Rooms come either with a double or single bed, or two or three twin beds. The apartments in the back are quieter. A Continental breakfast is included in the rate, and there is an impressive pool area with bar service. **www.recantodobarao.com**

JERICOACOARA (Ceará) Mosquito Blue   ▯▤▯▤ P w $$$
Rua do Forró, 62598 000 **Tel** *(088) 3669 2027* **Fax** *(088) 3669 2027* **Rooms** *44*

One of Jericoacoara's finest hotels, Mosquito Blue has the feel of a sprawling Mediterranean villa. The apartments look out over the lush gardens or towards the ocean. The rooms are elegantly decorated with pretty linen and curtains. The village and the beach are both within easy walking distance. **www.mosquitoblue.com.br**

JOÃO PESSOA (Paraíba) Tropical Tambaú   ▯▤▯▤ P ௯ w $$$
Av Alm. Tamandaré 229, Tambaú **Tel** *(083) 2107 1900* **Fax** *(083) 3247 3672* **Rooms** *175*

Standing on the sands of Praia do Tambaú, this unique circular hotel offers an almost resort-like setting. The recently renovated rooms are very pleasant with ample storage space, a breakfast table, and a spacious bathroom. Plush suites, such as Garden and Seaview, are also available. **www.tropicalhotel.com.br**

NATAL (Rio Grande do Norte) Soleil   ▯▤▤ P w $$$
Rua Elia Barros 70, Ponta Negra, 59090 140 **Tel** *(084) 3219 5959* **Fax** *(084) 3219 5959* **Rooms** *31*

Just three blocks off the Ponta Negra beach, the Soleil provides affordable accommodation. There is a wide range of suites to choose from. All are equipped with modern facilities that include a kitchenette unit with fridge, hot plate, and utensils, plus a balcony. There is an on-site business center. **www.soleilhotel.com.br**

NATAL (Rio Grande do Norte) Manary Praia Hotel   ▯▤▤ w $$$$$
Rua Francisco Gurgel 9067, Ponta Negra, 59090 050 **Tel** *(084) 3204 2900* **Fax** *(084) 3204 2908* **Rooms** *25*

This luxurious Spanish *hacienda*-style B&B is set right on the Ponta Negra beach. The rooms are luxurious and feature king-size beds and a balcony with ocean views. Rooms in the superior category have a romantic ambience, ideal for couples. The sea-facing hotel restaurant serves an outstanding breakfast buffet. **www.manary.com.br**

NATAL (Rio Grande do Norte) The Ocean Palace   ▯▤▯▤ P ௯ w $$$$$
Av Vía Costeira Km 11, Praia de Ponta Negra, 59090 001 **Tel** *(084) 3220 4144* **Fax** *(084) 3220 4144* **Rooms** *343*

Located on the seaside Via Costeira, this luxury hotel offers a variety of suites, bungalows, and apartments. It boasts its own beach and a fabulous leisure area that includes a multi-level pool complex, a children's play room, saunas, a spa, a top-quality weight room, and a tennis and squash court. **www.oceanpalace.com.br**

PRAIA DE PIPA (Rio Grande do Norte) Mirante de Pipa   ▤▤ P $$$
Rua do Mirante 1, 59178 000 **Tel** *(084) 3246 2251* **Rooms** *9*

Set on the bluff above Praia da Pipa, this *pousada* consists of pretty chalets in a wooded area. Ideal for families or small groups, several chalets have two bedrooms and sleep four to six people comfortably. Smaller units are for couples only. The village is only a short stroll away. **www.mirantedepipa.com.br**

Key to Price Guide *see p366* **Key to Symbols** *see back cover flap*

PRAIA DE PIPA (Rio Grande do Norte) Sombra e Água Fresca · 🄸 🛏 🄴 🄿 ⓦ · $$$$

Rua Praia do Amor 1000, 59178 000 **Tel** *(084) 3246 2258* **Fax** *(084) 3246 2376* **Rooms** *19*

Spectacularly located on a clifftop overlooking Praia do Amor, this hotel features comfortable rooms, five of which are suites. The suites all have vaulted wood ceilings, king-size beds, private jacuzzis, and vast picture windows. The rooms either look out over the ocean or offer garden views. **www.sombraeagua.com.br**

PRAIA DE PIPA (Rio Grande do Norte) Toca da Coruja · 🄸 🛏 🆅 🄴 🄿 · $$$$$

Av Baia dos Golfinhos 464 s/n, 59178 000 **Tel** *(084) 3246 2226* **Fax** *(084) 3246 2226* **Rooms** *15*

This exclusive *pousada* is perfect for a romantic getaway. The deluxe chalets are decorated in rustic-colonial style with super king-size beds and clawfoot bathtubs. Amenities include a pool, sauna, and reading room. The beach is close by. Children under 12 are not allowed. **www.tocadacoruja.com.br**

TIBAU DO SUL (Rio Grande do Norte) Ponta do Madeiro · 🄸 🛏 🄴 🄿 ⓦ · $$

Rota do Sol Km 3, 59178 000 **Tel** *(084) 3502 2377* **Fax** *(084) 3243 2243* **Rooms** *32*

While the rooms at this resort are well-kept but basic, the location is simply exceptional. It is set in a large grassy garden on a headland high above Praia do Madeiro, with a private staircase leading down to the sand. The view from the pool is spectacular. The hotel restaurant serves fine regional cuisine. **www.pontadomadeiro.com.br**

TIBAU DO SUL (Rio Grande do Norte) Marinas Tibau Sul · 🄸 🛏 🆅 🄴 🄿 ⓦ · $$$

Av Governador Aluisio Alves 301, 59178 000 **Tel** *(084) 3246 4111* **Fax** *(084) 3221 5548* **Rooms** *33*

A full-service resort with a remarkable beach setting. Accommodation is in self-contained seaside bungalows, with queen-size beds and balconies with hammocks. The resort offers a wide range of activities, including riding, boat and Land Rover excursions, sportfishing, tennis, volleyball, and swimming. **www.hotelmarinas.com.br**

PIAUÍ & MARANHÃO

BARREIRINHAS (Piauí) Pousada Encantes do Nordeste · 🄸 🄴 🄿 · $$

Rua Boa Vista s/n, 65590 000 **Tel** *(098) 3349 0288* **Rooms** *10*

Just on the outskirts of town, this charming *pousada* offers small chalets set on a green hillside that slopes down to the river. The staff can organize excursions to the Delta do Parnaíba and Parque Nacional Lençóis Maranhenses *(see p250–51).* Tours include pick-up and drop-off at the *pousada.* **www.encantesdonordeste.com.br**

PARQUE NACIONAL DE SERRA DA CAPIVARA (Piauí) Serra da Capivara · 🄸 🛏 🄴 🄿 · $$

PI-140 Km 0, Santa Luzia **Tel** *(086) 3582 1760* **Fax** *(086) 3582 1389* **Rooms** *18*

Its proximity to Parque Nacional de Serra da Capivara makes this hotel an excellent choice. Rooms are no-frills with a rustic interior, but equipped with basic modern amenities, including TV and a minibar. The helpful staff can arrange guides and provide information about the national park.

PARQUE NACIONAL DE SETE CIDADES (Piauí) Fazenda Sete Cidades · 🄸 🛏 🄴 🄿 · $$

Access via BR-222 Km 63 **Tel** *(086) 3232 3996* **Fax** *(086) 3276 2222* **Rooms** *37*

Located at the entrance of Parque Nacional de Sete Cidades, this *fazenda* offers budget accommodation of a reasonable standard. Besides providing amenities such as a decent restaurant and pool, the hotel also offers a regular shuttle into the park for guests, as well as outsiders. **www.portopreguicas.com.br**

SÃO LUÍS (Maranhão) Pousada Portas da Amazônia · 🄴 ⓦ · $$

Rua do Giz 129, Praia Grande, 65010 680 **Tel** *(098) 3222 9937* **Fax** *(098) 3221 4193* **Rooms** *28*

This *pousada* offers one of the nicest accommodation options in the historic city. The best rooms are the spacious master suites, featuring tall colonial windows looking out on the small cobblestone square. The on-site coffee shop, Café Amazônia, serves a range of tropical salads and sandwiches. **www.portasdaamazonia.com.br**

SÃO LUÍS (Maranhão) Brisa Mar · 🄸 🛏 🆅 🄴 🄿 ♿ ⓦ · $$$

Av São Marcos 12, Praia da Ponta d'Areia, 65077 310 **Tel** *(098) 2106 0606* **Fax** *(098) 3212 1212* **Rooms** *113*

Located at Ponta D'Areia, the Brisa Mar conveniently lies between the historic center and the beaches of Calhau and Olho d'Agua. The rooms are bright and spacious and come with either a queen-size bed or two singles. The hotel boasts an impressive swimming pool. **www.brisamar.com.br**

TERESINA (Piauí) Luxor Piauí · 🄸 🛏 🆅 🄴 🄿 ♿ ⓦ · $$

Praça Marechal Deodoro 310, 64000 160 **Tel** *(021) 3222 9700* **Rooms** *83*

With an excellent location close to the city center and only 3 miles (5 km) from the airport, this recently renovated hotel is one of the best bargains in town. The modern rooms boast elegant decor. The on-site restaurant serves international and regional dishes. Complimentary breakfast and 24-hour room service. **www.luxorhoteis.com**

TERESINA (Piauí) Metropolitan · 🄸 🛏 🆅 🄴 🄿 ♿ ⓦ · $$$

Av Frei Serafim 1696, 64001 020 **Tel** *(086) 3216 8000* **Fax** *(086) 3216 8011* **Rooms** *124*

Geared towards the business traveler, the Metropolitan offers efficient and attentive service. All rooms feature verandas and are equipped with desk space, good lighting, Internet access, and an electronic room safe. The hotel has two restaurants and three bars. **www.metropolitanhotel.com.br**

PARÁ & AMAPÁ

ALGODOAL (Pará) Bela Mar

Av Beira Mar, Praia da V. do Algodoal **Tel** *(091) 3854 1128* **Rooms** *16*

A small but popular hotel, right on the beach at Algodoal, the Bela Mar offers fabulous value. Cheaper rooms come without bathrooms. The hotel restaurant serves simple, well-cooked meals. It is recommended to book in advance, particularly during high season. **www.belamar.hpgvip.com.br**

ALTER DO CHÃO (Pará) Beloalter

Rua Pedro Teixeira 38 **Tel** *(093) 3527 1230* **Rooms** *26*

The Beloalter is a fairly new accommodation complex located by the beach at the Lago Verde on the banks of the Rio Tapajos. A couple of eco-cabins, one built into a tree, can also be rented. The service is flawless. Exciting tropical garden setting, with several bird species and small monkeys. **www.beloalter.com.br**

BELÉM (Pará) Hotel Machado's Plaza

Rua Henrique Gurjao s/n **Tel** *(091) 4008 9800* **Rooms** *36*

Centrally located, but off the main drag, the newly-built Machado's Plaza is a very reasonable mid-range choice of accommodation. Tastefully decorated rooms come with a private bathroom, TV, and a personalized minibar. Laundry service is available, as is a fully-equipped fitness room and an events hall. **www.machadosplazahotel.com.br**

BELÉM (Pará) Hilton Belém

Av Presidente Vargas 882 **Tel** *(091) 4006 7000* **Fax** *(091) 3225 2942* **Rooms** *361*

The most luxurious hotel in town, the Hilton Belém is located in the heart of the city, close to all the action. A modern hotel, it offers all the usual comforts of five-star accommodation. It also has a popular bar, Amazon. The foyer has some shops selling useful items and local crafts. Complimentary breakfast buffet. **www.hilton.com**

ILHA DE MARAJÓ (Pará) Paracauary Eco Pousada

Av Prado 6, Bairro Novo, Soure **Tel** *(091) 3222 6442* **Rooms** *8*

A small but attractive *pousada*, the Paracauary is preferred for its uplifting ambience and breathtaking vistas. The unpretentious apartments make up for their lack of character by providing basic comforts. Bicycles can be hired and fishing trips can be arranged. The service is efficient. **www.paracauary.com.br**

ILHA DE MARAJÓ (Pará) Pousada dos Guarás

Av Beira Mar s/n Km 3, Praia Grande **Tel** *(091) 3765 1133* **Rooms** *50*

Located on a fine beach, this *pousada* offers log cabin apartments, each appointed with modern comforts, including TV and a minibar. In addition to a good pool, recreational areas include play area, sport court, and soccer camp. Motorbikes can be hired and horse-riding is also offered. **www.pousadadosguaras.com.br**

MACAPÁ (Amapá) Atalanta

Av Coarary Nunes 1148 **Tel** *(096) 3223 1612* **Rooms** *36*

A medium-size hotel offering high levels of comfort, the Atalanta offers the added luxury of a sauna room. With subtle colors and subdued lighting, the rooms exude refinement. Service is good and the food served in its restaurant is delicious. There is also a decent café. **www.atalantahotel.com.br**

MACAPÁ (Amapá) Macapá Hotel

Rua Francisco Azarias Neto 17 **Tel** *(096) 3217 1350* **Rooms** *20*

One of the better mid-range hotels in town, the Macapá offers rooms with a spacious terrace and view, in addition to the regular interior rooms. Other features include a sauna room, a children's play area, and tennis courts. All rooms are ample in size, well-maintained, and have a pleasant bathroom.

SALINÓPOLIS (Amapá) Paraiso do Atlântico

2 miles (3 km) from town, Rua 17 Quadra 123, Lote 15 **Tel** *(091) 3423 2030* **Rooms** *63*

Though quite far from the town center, the Paraiso do Atlântico is a new hotel close to the river and beach. It offers most modern conveniences and is reasonably priced. The bar is good and there is also a children's play area. The best feature of the hotel, however, is the splendid view of the beach.

SANTARÉM (Amapá) Rio Dourado

Rua Floriano Peixoto 799 **Tel** *(093) 3522 0298* **Rooms** *30*

Refurbished recently, the Rio Dourado is favored for its excellent central location. Clean accommodation and good service are provided at quite affordable rates. The beds are comfortable and the bathrooms fitted with hot showers. All rooms come with TVs and fridge bars. The staff are warm and courteous.

SANTARÉM (Amapá) Santarém Palace Hotel

Av Rui Barbosa 726 **Tel** *(093) 3523 2820* **Rooms** *44*

A stylish hotel, the Santarém Palace was built in 1980. Relatively cheap for the standards of comfort and service that it offers, it is a popular place with Brazilian and foreign visitors. Rooms are a bit on the small side, but furnished with modern facilities. Reasonably priced river tours can be arranged by the hotel.

AMAZONAS, RORAIMA, ACRE & RONDÔNIA

BOA VISTA (Roraima) Euzébio's
Rua Cecília Brasil 1107 **Tel** *(095) 3623 0300* **Rooms** *10*

This popular hotel offers comfortable rooms, all equipped with basic amenities. The standard rooms are cheaper, though a bit on the small side. The cheerfully decorated bigger rooms come with hot water, minibar, and telephone. The hotel provides a free shuttle service to the airport.

BOA VISTA (Roraima) Aipana Plaza
Praça Centro Cívico 53 **Tel** *(095) 3224 4800* **Rooms** *87*

One of the few hotels in town with both a nice pool and a decent restaurant, the Aipana Plaza offers excellent value. The large rooms have glass showers and cozy beds. There are sculptures in the hallway, while the grand lobby, too, is replete with fascinating sculptures and polished stone floors. **www.aipanaplaza.com.br**

MAMIRAUÁ RESERVE (Amazonas) Uakari Floating Lodge
Accessed by plane to Tefé, then by boat **Tel** *(097) 3343 4160* **Rooms** *5 cabins*

Located up the Rio Solimões, this floating lodge is in an area of relatively untouched, seasonally flooded vegetation. A fleet of boats make it possible to explore from the Uacari, which is a comfortable base within the reserve. The lodge was the winner of the Conde Nast Best Ecotourism Destination 2003. **www.amazontravel.com**

MAMORI (Amazonas) Amazon Gero's Lodge
Dez de Julho 679, Centro **Tel** *(092) 3232 4755* **Rooms** *10*

A new lodge offering a wide range of comforts in individual and family cabins, plus hammock space for more basic accommodation. Located on the Lago Arara, just off the Paraná do Mamori, it is surrounded by beautiful rainforest and lakes. Pink dolphins can usually be seen swimming nearby. **www.amazonjungletour.com**

MAMORI (Amazonas) Dolphin Lodge
Rua Dr. Odilon 16a **Tel** *(092) 3613 4683* **Rooms** *8 apartments*

Comfortable and attractive, this rustic jungle lodge has a central circular restaurant and bar, with wooden double bedrooms running off along a wooden walkway. Located on the Paraná do Mamori, the Dolphin Lodge is ideal for bird-watching and exploring wildlife in the surrounding forest. **www.maiaexpeditionstur.com.br**

MANAUS (Amazonas) Hospedaje 10 de Julho
10 de Julho 679 **Tel** *(092) 3232 6280* **Rooms** *40*

A stone's throw from Teatro Amazonas *(see p282–3)* in an up-and-coming part of the town center, this fairly cozy mid-range hotel is immensely popular with overseas travelers. The generously-proportioned rooms come with TV and a good shower. Views tend to be restricted, even on the upper floors. **www.hoteldezdejulho.com**

MANAUS (Amazonas) Ana Cassia Palace Hotel
Rua dos Andradas 14 **Tel** *(092) 3622 3637* **Rooms** *88*

Known for its stupendous views across the city from the rooftop breakfast space, the Ana Cassia is an exceptional mid-range option. Rooms are comfortable and very clean, and all of them are provided with a fridge-bar and TV. Service is reasonable. Ana Cassia is close to the port area. **www.hotelanacassia.com.br**

MANAUS (Amazonas) Best Western Lord Manaus
Rua Marcílio Dias 217 **Tel** *(092) 3622 2844* **Rooms** *102*

A fairly well-maintained hotel, this Best Western property was built in 1959. It has comfortable beds, good air conditioning, and decent bathrooms. The Ristorante Fiorentina *(see p408)* offers a wide range of Italian dishes. The location is central to the business district and close to the port and Teatro Amazonas. **www.bestwestern.com.br**

MANAUS (Amazonas) Taj Mahal Continental Hotel
Av Getúlio Vargas 741 **Tel** *(092) 3627 3737* **Rooms** *170*

The smartest and most expensive hotel in downtown Manaus, the Taj Mahal offers great service and a range of high-quality rooms and suites. Its revolving restaurant has stunning views of the Rio Negro and Teatro Amazonas. The hotel's own travel agency service is located inside.

MANAUS (Amazonas) Tropical Manaus
Av Coronel Teixeira 1320, Ponta Negra **Tel** *(092) 2123 5000* **Rooms** *594*

Located right out of town at Ponta Negra, the Tropical is very upmarket, sometimes serving as a conference center for high-level politics. It offers top-quality comfort, food, and service, right on the edge of the rainforest. It has a great pool, a sauna, five bars with live music, and even an archery field. **www.tropicalhotel.com.br**

PORTO VELHO (Rondônia) Central
Rua Terreiro 2472 **Tel** *(069) 2181 2500* **Fax** *(069) 3224 5114* **Rooms** *78*

A modern hotel within easy walking distance of downtown and the riverside and museums, the Central has been recently refurbished. Though somewhat lacking in character, the rooms are spacious and clean. Most have full views over the city. Service is consistently good. **www.enter-net.com.br/central**

PORTO VELHO (Rondônia) Samauma

 $$

Rua D. Pedro II 1038 **Tel** *(069) 3224 5300* **Rooms** *33*

This moderately-proportioned hotel offers small cabin-like rooms, all of which open quite close to the street. A good mid-range choice, ideal for staying one or two nights, the Samauma provides modern amenities, including a fridge-bar in every room. In addition to a restaurant, there is a decent on-site bar.

PORTO VELHO (Rondônia) Vila Rica

$$$

Av Carlos Gomes 1616 **Tel** *(069) 3224 3433* **Rooms** *115*

Reputed to be the most luxurious hotel in town, the Vila Rica has a grand entrance. Rooms are adequate, well-kept, and thoughtfully furnished with modern comforts. There are scenic views from the top floors. Service is first-rate. The pool is relatively large, while the restaurant has a good reputation. **www.hotelvilarica.com.br**

PRESIDENTE FIGUEIREDO (Amazonas) Iracema Falls

$$$

7 miles (12 km) from town, access road at Km 115 of BR-174 Hwy **Tel** *(092) 3234 5500* **Rooms** *92*

With its own natural swimming spot, the Iracema Falls enjoys a beautiful countryside setting. Cozy apartments, a fine restaurant, bar, and good sports facilities are offered at this charming lodge. Service is quick and parking ample. There are separate swimming pools for children and adults. **www.iracemafalls.com.br**

RIO BRANCO (Acre) Terra Verde

$$

Rua M. Deodoro 221 **Tel** *(068) 2106 6000* **Rooms** *29*

Recently built and furnished, this plush hotel offers all modern conveniences, including a fridge-bar and cable TV in every room. Bright walls and cheerful decor liven up the spacious rooms. A wide buffet selection is available at breakfast. Service is exceptionally good. **www.terraverdehotel.com.br**

RIO BRANCO (Acre) Pinheiro Palace

$$$

Rua Rui Barbosa 450 **Tel** *(068) 3223 7191* **Rooms** *60*

Conveniently located in the city center, this relatively upscale hotel is one of the best and largest in Rio Branco. Rooms are fairly modern, and the lobby airy and spacious. Most of the upper-story rooms have splendid views over the city. The restaurants are good and the service impeccable. **www.irmaospinheiro.com.br**

BRASÍLIA, GOIÁS & TOCANTINS

BRASÍLIA Blue Tree Park

 $$$$

SHTN, Trecho 01, Lote 1B – Bloco C, 70800 200 **Tel** *(061) 3424 7000* **Fax** *(061) 3424 7001* **Rooms** *394*

This is a large business and family hotel overlooking Lago do Paranoá, close to the Brazilian President's residence in the Palácio do Alvorado. Top-notch services include a spa and massage, saunas, and tennis courts. A complimentary shuttle service to the town center is on offer. Close to Brasília International Airport. **www.bluetree.com.br**

BRASÍLIA Kubitschek Plaza

 $$$$$

SHTN, Quadra 2, Bloco E, 70702 904 **Tel** *(061) 3329 3333* **Rooms** *243*

A business hotel elegantly decorated in homage to the founder of Brasília, President Kubitschek *(see p58–9)*. The best of its well-equipped rooms come with a balcony and superb views. There is a relaxing swimming pool, a business center, a café, a lobby bar, and two elegant diners, the Diamantina and Vila Rica. **www.kubitschek.com.br**

CHAPADA DOS VEADEIROS (Goiás) Casa Rosa

$$

12 miles (18 km) SE of park, Rua Gumercindo 233, Alto Paraíso de Goiás **Tel** *(062) 3446 1319* **Rooms** *13*

Comfortable chalets and modest apartments are set in a garden on the edge of Alto Paraíso. Close to many of the region's numerous waterfalls, Casa Rosa is a convenient base for exploring the natural reserve of the Chapada dos Veadeiros and works closely with one of the area's good tour operators. **www.pousadacasarosa.com.br**

CHAPADA DOS VEADEIROS (Goiás) Pousada Fazenda São Bento

$$

Estrada para São Jorge Km 8 **Tel** *(062) 3459 3000* **Fax** *(062) 9967 8265* **Rooms** *20*

A converted *fazenda* on the edge of the national park, the São Bento offers a series of rustic chalets with terra-cotta roofs and stone walls set in the *cerrado* (grassland). Excellent for bird-watching. Trails lead to waterfalls and tours to the park can be organized. The on-site restaurant serves decent food. **www.pousadasaobento.com.br**

CHAPADÃO DO CÉU (Goiás) Pousada das Emas

$

17 miles (27 km) S of Parque Nacional das Emas, Rua Ipê, Qd. 17, Lote 1 **Tel** *(062) 3634 1382* **Rooms** *19*

Located in Chapadão das Céu, which is a convenient base for the Parque Nacional das Emas, this unpretentious *pousada* is popular with budget travelers. All rooms come with TV and a clean bathroom. Although no fine-dining option is available, there is a no-frills snack bar.

CIDADE DE GOIÁS (Goiás) Casa de Ponte

$

Rua Moretti Foggia s/n **Tel** *(062) 3371 4467* **Fax** *(062) 3371 4467* **Rooms** *38*

A recently refurbished hotel in the center of town, the Casa de Ponte is a perfect choice for travelers on a budget. Very simple, but well-maintained and adequately appointed with basic conveniences, rooms are housed in a large colonial building overlooking a tiny river. The staff are courteous and service fairly prompt.

JALAPÃO (Tocantins) Korubo Safari Camp $$$$

Between Parque Estadual do Jalapão & Ecological Station **Tel** *(011) 5083 6968* **Rooms** *10*

This Botswana-style safari camp with very comfortable tents can be found next to the fast-flowing Novo Rio. The area is visited by fascinating wildlife, including the Brazilian merganser, one of the world's rarest birds. The price includes meals, guided trips around Jalapão, and transfer from the main town, Palmas. **www.korubo.com.br**

PALMAS (Tocantins) Pousada dos Girassóis 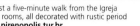 $$

Av NS 1, 103 Sul, Conj. 03, Lote 44, 77163 070 **Tel** *(063) 3219 4500* **Fax** *(063) 3215 2321* **Rooms** *74*

Small, but well-kept, this standard three-star hotel offers rooms just next to the central Praça dos Girassóis. The Palazzo restaurant is one of the finest in town. Korubo, the best-known among the Jalapão-based operators, picks up travelers from the *pousada*. **www.pousadadosgirassois.com.br**

PIRENÓPOLIS (Goiás) Pousada o Casarão  $$

Rua Direita 79, Centro Histórico **Tel** *(062) 3331 2662* **Rooms** *8*

A charming colonial house in a quiet street, the Pousada do Casarão is just a five-minute walk from the Igreja Nossa Senhora do Rosário Matriz *(see p308)*. It offers a range of spacious rooms, all decorated with rustic period furniture. Superb complimentary breakfasts are offered. **www.ocasarao.pirenopolis.tur.br**

MATO GROSSO & MATO GROSSO DO SUL

ALTA FLORESTA (Mato Grosso) Cristalino Jungle Lodge  $$$$$

Rio Cristalino **Tel** *(066) 3512 7100* **Fax** *(066) 3521 2221* **Rooms** *8*

One of the best Amazon jungle lodges in South America, the Cristalino Jungle Lodge has superb, tastefully designed luxury bungalows, in addition to a range of cheaper accommodation. The main draw, however, is the first-class wildlife viewing and the guided tours. **www.cristalinolodge.com.br**

BONITO (Mato Grosso do Sul) Zagaia Eco-Resort  $$$$

Rodovia Bonito-Três Morros, 79290 000 **Tel** *(067) 3255 5500* **Fax** *(067) 3255 5602* **Rooms** *100*

A large resort-style family hotel, the Zagaia is set in expansive grounds next to the forest. While the apartments are a bit plain, the chalets are quite comfortable. Facilities include horse-riding, a play area for children, tennis courts, two pools, and saunas. Breakfast and dinner are included in the tariff. **www.zagaia.com.br**

CAMPO GRANDE (Mato Grosso do Sul) Jandaía $$$

Rua Barão do Rio Branco 1271, 79002 174 **Tel** *(067) 3316 7700* **Fax** *(067) 3316 7700* **Rooms** *140*

A modern, well-appointed business hotel in the heart of Campo Grande, the Jandaia is one of the most luxurious options in town. It has two elegant restaurants, Jandaía Plaza and Imperium. Service is first-rate and there are scenic views from the upper floors. **www.jandaia.com.br**

CHAPADA DOS GUIMARÃES (Mato Grosso) Pousada Penhasco $$$

Av Penhasco s/n, 78195 000 **Tel** *(065) 3301 1555* **Rooms** *7*

This is a small English-run *pousada* in an old colonial house on the edge of town. Guests can choose from a variety of rooms, ranging from single to those sleeping up to four people. Breakfast and afternoon tea are complimentary. The on-site observatory has stunning views of the Chapada dos Guimarães area. **www.penhasco.com.br**

CORUMBÁ (Mato Grosso do Sul) Nacional Palace $$

Rua America 936, Corumbá **Tel** *(067) 3234 6000* **Rooms** *98*

A standard three-star town hotel, the Nacional Palace offers extraordinary value for money. Rooms are plush with classy decor. The interior features contemporary furniture. There is an attractive pool and a recreation area. The on-site restaurant is reputed to be one of the best in town. **www.hnacional.com.br**

CUIABÁ (Mato Grosso) Amazon Plaza $$$

Av Presidente Getúlio Vargas 600, Centro, 78050 840 **Tel** *(065) 2121 2000* **Rooms** *120*

A converted business hotel with a florid Amazon theme, the Amazon Plaza is adorned with paintings of tropical forests, while lush plants decorate the public areas. The rooms are modest but well-kept. Upper floors have good views. The hotel restaurant boasts rustic decor and offers regional delicacies. **www.hotelamazon.com.br**

MIRANDA (Mato Grosso do Sul) Pousada Aguas do Pantanal $$

Afonso Pena Avenue 367 **Tel** *(067) 3242 1314* **Rooms** *20*

One of the best town-based options in the region, the Aguas do Pantanal offers a range of simple, comfortable rooms and several excellent tour operators, who can help travelers plan imaginative trips to the Pantanal *(see p320–21)* and Bonito *(see p323)*. **www.aguasdopantanal.com.br**

MIRANDA (Mato Grosso do Sul) Fazenda Baía Grande $$$

Estrada Miranda-Aldeia Lalima Km 18, Southern Pantanal **Tel** *(067) 3382 4223* **Rooms** *6*

The enthusiastic young grandson of a former jaguar hunter runs this small farm. The most spectacular wildlife viewing is possible at dawn around the farm's huge private lake. The rate covers meals and rides, accompanied by a guide. Nature walks, piranha-fishing, and night excursions are available. **www.fazendabaiagrande.com.br**

MIRANDA (Mato Grosso do Sul) Cacimba de Pedra 🔢🏊📋🅿️ $$$$

Reino Selvagem, BR-262 Km 17, Southern Pantanal **Tel** *(067) 3382 1555* **Rooms** *12*

Newly-built motel-like rooms are provided in one of the Pantanal's few caiman farms. Hearing them hiss and gurgle as the owner throws them meat, is unforgettable. Stays also include tours into the Pantanal. The enormous swimming pool and mesmerizing sunsets add to the visit. **www.cacimbadepedra.com.br**

MIRANDA (Mato Grosso do Sul) Fazenda Meia Lua 🔢🏊📋🅿️🅆 $$$$

BR-262 Km 10, Southern Pantanal **Tel** *(067) 9981 1066* **Rooms** *6*

An intimate, family-run *fazenda*, the Meia Lua offers weekend and day packages, ideal for exploring the stunning wildlife of the Pantanal. The pool area, friendly staff, and light tours make it perfect for families. The best accommodation is in the self-contained house set in gardens next to the swimming pool. **www.fazendameialua.com.br**

MIRANDA (Mato Grosso do Sul) Fazenda San Francisco 🔢🏊📋🅿️ $$$$

BR-262 Km 30, Rua Calarge 349, Vila Glória, Southern Pantanal **Tel** *(067) 3325 6606* **Rooms** *5*

With very functional accommodation, this *fazenda* is known to provide the best chances of spotting the amazing Pantanal wildlife, including jaguars and ocelots. The bird-watching guides are acclaimed. The farm also runs an interesting jaguar conservation project. **www.fazendasanfrancisco.tur.br**

MIRANDA (Mato Grosso do Sul) Refúgio Ecológico Caiman 🔢🏊📋🅿️♿🅆 $$$$$

Estrada para Agachi Km 37, Southern Pantanal, 01452 000 **Tel** *(011) 3706 1800* **Rooms** *29*

The most luxurious accommodation in the Pantanal, this hotel sits in the heart of a wild preserve replete with animals and has its own conservation programs. Guided tours, which are included in the price along with full board, are timetable strict. The hotel has a good restaurant and bar. **www.caiman.com.br**

POCONÉ (Mato Grosso) Pouso Alegre 🔢🅿️ $$$

Transpantaneira Km 33, Northern Pantanal **Tel** *(065) 9968 6101* **Rooms** *14*

In the frontier town of Poconé, which is the primary entry point into the northern Panatanal for those heading south from Cuiabá, this rustic *pousada* focuses mainly on wildlife viewing. Guided tours can be best organized by the owner, or a specialist bird-watching guide. The surroundings are breathtaking. **www.pousalegre.com.br**

POCONÉ (Mato Grosso) Araras Lodge 🔢🏊📋🅿️🅆 $$$$

Transpantaneira Km 29, Northern Pantanal **Tel** *(065) 3682 2800* **Fax** *(065) 3682 1260* **Rooms** *19*

One of the best lodges on the Transpantaneira and popular with Europeans. The wildlife viewing is excellent, especially at dawn, from the treehouse over the lake. Activities, such as trekking, canoeing, riding, truck safaris, and night tours, can be organized by expert bilingual naturalist guides. **www.araraslodge.com.br**

NHECOLÂNDIA (Mato Grosso do Sul) Fazenda Rio Negro 🔢📋🅿️♿ $$$$$

Rua Paraná 32, Jd. dos Estado, Southern Pantanal (plane access only), 79021 220 **Tel** *(067) 3326 0002* **Rooms** *13*

This converted 19th-century ranch house also functions as the main office of the Centro de Pesquisa para Conservação (Conservation Research Center). Wildlife viewing is superb and guiding competent. The VIP suite has some of the best accommodation in the area. Rate includes full board and tours. **www.fazendarionegro.com.br**

SANTA CATARINA & PARANÁ

CURITIBA (Paraná) Elo Hotel 🔢🏊📋🅿️♿ $

Rua Amintas de Barros 383, 80060 200 **Tel** *(041) 3028 9400* **Fax** *(041) 3028 9404* **Rooms** *38*

Located next to the Federal University in the city center, this inexpensive hotel is slightly dated, but offers remarkable value. The standard rooms are quite small but the suites, only a little more expensive, are very spacious. Unusually for a hotel in this price range, a sauna and rooftop pool are offered. **www.hoteiselo.com.br**

CURITIBA (Paraná) Ibis Centro Cívíco 📋🅿️♿ $$

Rua Mateus Leme 358, 80510 190 **Tel** *(041) 3324 0469* **Fax** *(041) 3323 3404* **Rooms** *80*

A few minutes' walk from Curitiba's historic center, this budget hotel consists of an old German-style house (the reception area) linked to a modern tower block that has the guest rooms. The rooms are compact, but comfortable, and the service efficient. Pre-book for weekday stays. **www.accorhotels.com.br**

CURITIBA (Paraná) Full Jazz Hotel 🔢📺📋🅿️♿🅆 $$$

Rua Silveira Peixoto 1297, Batel, 80060 200 **Tel** *(041) 3312 7000* **Rooms** *76*

Jazz pervades every aspect of this hotel, from the ambient music, DVD library, and decoration to its upbeat Restaurante New Orleans and Full Jazz Bar. With modern rooms and live jazz, it is popular with musicians visiting the city. The surrounding streets have some of Curitiba's best bars and restaurants. **www.hotelslaviero.com.br**

CURITIBA (Paraná) Hotel Nikko 🔢📺📋🅿️♿🅆 $$$

Rua Barão do Rio Branco 546, 80010 180 **Tel** *(041) 2105 1808* **Fax** *(041) 2105 1838* **Rooms** *74*

Located midway between the bus and train station and the city center, the hotel is tastefully furnished in modern Japanese style. The guest rooms are decorated in neutral colors and all have a minibar, cable TV, and wireless Internet. There is a pretty Japanese courtyard garden and a restaurant. **www.hotelnikko.com.br**

Key to Price Guide *see p366* **Key to Symbols** *see back cover flap*

CURITIBA (Paraná) Four Points Sheraton

$$$$

Av 7 de Setembro 4211, Batel, 8006 0200 **Tel** *(041) 3340 4000* **Fax** *(041) 3340 4001* **Rooms** *165*

One of Curitiba's newest luxury hotels catering mainly to business travelers, this Sheraton flagship boasts spacious recreation areas, comfortably furnished rooms, and an extremely helpful multilingual staff. The hotel is located in upmarket Batel, with excellent bars and restaurants nearby. **www.starwood.com**

FLORIANÓPOLIS (Santa Catarina) Ibis

$$

Av Rio Branco 37, 8801 5010 **Tel** *(048) 3216 0000* **Fax** *(048) 3216 0001* **Rooms** *198*

An extremely efficient, large city-center hotel with young helpful staff, the Ibis is a ten-minute walk from the main square and near many good restaurants. Rooms, all en suite, are compact, with new, comfortable furniture. Reservations are advised, as it is very popular with both business visitors and tourists. **www.accor.com.br**

FLORIANÓPOLIS (Santa Catarina) Pousada Bizkaia

$$

Estrada Geral da Praia da Joaquina 682, 8806 2600 **Tel** *(048) 3232 5273* **Rooms** *16*

This small, friendly *pousada* enjoys a quiet location near Cento da Lagoa, one of Florianópolis's liveliest nightlife spots, and convenient for Joaquina, Mole, and other east coast beaches. Rooms are simple, attractively furnished, and most have a large balcony. **www.bizkaia.com.br**

FLORIANÓPOLIS (Santa Catarina) Quintal da Sol

$$

Rodovia Gilson da Costa Xavier 1562, Sambaqui **Tel** *(048) 3235 2334* **Rooms** *4 cabins*

Located across the road from the beach between Santo Antônio de Lisboa and Sambaqui, two pretty fishing villages on the quiet west coast of the island. Accommodation is in cabins that sleep up to seven people. All have a separate living room, bathroom, and small kitchen. The owners are welcoming and helpful. **www.quintaldasol.com.br**

FLORIANÓPOLIS (Santa Catarina) Hotel São Sebastião da Praia

$$$

Av Campeche 1373, 8806 3300 **Tel** *(048) 3338 2020* **Rooms** *74*

A short stroll from the unspoiled Campeche beach, this hotel stands on a beautifully landscaped property with a mix of lawns, original trees, and flowering bushes. Rooms, all with balconies, are cool and simply furnished. All have minibars and air conditioning, while some have separate sitting areas. **www.hotelsaosebastiao.com.br**

FLORIANÓPOLIS (Santa Catarina) Majestic Palace Hotel

$$$

Av Rubens de Arruda Ramos 2746, 8801 5010 **Tel** *(048) 3231 8025* **Rooms** *259*

The largest, newest, and most luxurious hotel in downtown Florianópolis, the Majestic Palace offers good value for money. There are large, comfortably furnished rooms and huge suites, most of which have sea views. There is a business center, restaurants, fitness center, and a large pool with great sea views. **www.majesticpalace.com.br**

FLORIANÓPOLIS (Santa Catarina) Pousada Alemdomar

$$$

Rua Lagoa do Peri 403, Armação, 8806 6000 **Tel** *(048) 3237 5000* **Rooms** *6*

This pretty *pousada* lies a short distance from the Armação beach and Lagoa do Peri, in the south of the island. Set amid original forest and beautiful gardens, it offers guests personalised attention and a peaceful atmosphere, and has simple but very comfortable rooms, all with a terrace or balcony. **www.alemdomar.com.br**

FLORIANÓPOLIS (Santa Catarina) Pousada Vila Tamarindo

$$$

Av Campeche 1836, Praia do Campeche, 8806 3000 **Tel** *(048) 3237 3464* **Rooms** *15*

Vila Tamarindo is located a short walk from the Campeche beach in the southeast of the island. Rooms, all with a terrace or balcony and most with sea views, are light, airy, and painted in bright colors. A large garden, cozy sitting areas, and a small pool create a very relaxed atmosphere. Staff are helpful. **www.tamarindo.com.br**

FLORIANÓPOLIS (Santa Catarina) Pousada da Vigia

$$$$

Rua Conêgo W. Castro 291, Praia da Lagoinha de Ponta das Canas, 8805 6770 **Tel** *(048) 3284 1789* **Rooms** *10*

At the extreme northeast tip of the island, this small building was the private residence of a former governor of Santa Catarina state. The *pousada* is beautifully positioned above a rocky stretch of the coast, next to sheltered beaches with forest behind. Most of the rooms have balconies and sea views. **www.pousadavigia.com.br**

FOZ DO IGUAÇU (Paraná) Paudimar Hostel

$

Rodovia das Cataratas 12.5, Remanso Grande, 8585 3000 **Tel** *(045) 3529 6061* **Rooms** *80 beds*

Located roughly midway between the city center and Parque Nacional do Iguaçu (see p342), the Paudimar is Brazil's best-equipped youth hostel. Dorms and private doubles are available. Leisure facilities, including a large pool, are excellent, and good, inexpensive meals are served. **www.paudimar.com.br**

FOZ DO IGUAÇU (Paraná) Continental Inn

$$

Av Paraná 1089, 85852 000 **Tel** *(045) 2102 3000* **Rooms** *124*

The inn has a quiet city-center location. Rooms are tastefully furnished and the suites, with separate sitting area and views across the city, are huge and especially good value. Attractive pool area in a central patio. The en suite bathrooms come with jacuzzi, douche, separate bathtub, and hair dryer. **www.continentalinn.com.br**

FOZ DO IGUAÇU (Paraná) Hotel Nadai

$$

Av República Argentina 1332, 8585 2000 **Tel** *(045) 3521 5050* **Rooms** *82*

Located in the heart of the city of Foz do Iguaçu, the Nadai is a popular choice with budget-conscious tour groups. The rooms are bright, newly furnished, and comfortable, although a bit on the small side. Service is extremely efficient. The hotel is close to the main tourist attractions. **www.hotelnadai.com.br**

FOZ DO IGUAÇU (Paraná) Pousada Evelina Navarrete

Rua Irlan Kalichewski 171, 85853 190 **Tel** *(045) 3574 3817* **Rooms** *25*

A firm favorite among foreign travelers, this modern family-run *pousada* in the city has a friendly multilingual owner and staff. Rooms are small and simply furnished, but comfortable. There is a pool and a pleasant sun terrace. Transfers to the parks can be arranged. **www.pousadaevelina.com.br**

FOZ DO IGUAÇU (Paraná) Hotel San Martin

Rodavia das Cataratas Km 17, 85863 000 **Tel** *(045) 3529 8088* **Rooms** *142*

Located alongside the Parque das Aves and across from the park's visitor center, this hotel has comfortable and well-equipped rooms. What makes the hotel special is its well-tended tropical garden (with an attractive pool) and the trails through the forest that has been preserved on the property. **www.hotelsanmartin.com.br**

FOZ DO IGUAÇU (Paraná) Tropical das Cataratas

Rodovia das Cataratas Km 28, Parque Nacional do Iguaçu, 85853 000 **Tel** *(045) 3521 7000* **Rooms** *203*

The only hotel in the Parque Nacional, the Tropical das Cataratas lies in a sprawling, colonial-style building. The service is impersonal and the rooms are remarkably simple, but there is a large pool and a very good restaurant. Transfers to the Argentine park can be arranged. **www.tropicalhotel.com.br**

ILHA DE SUPERAGÜI (Paraná) Sobre as Ondas

Barra do Superagüi, Guaraqueçaba **Tel** *(041) 3482 7118* **Rooms** *13*

Simple, but very neat, this hotel has extremely basic clapboard cabins, four of which come with private bathrooms. Arrangements can be made to collect guests in Paranaguá or Ilha do Mel. Boat trips are offered to outlying parts of the island as well as to other islands. Fishing trips are available. **www.superagui.net**

ILHA DO MEL (Paraná) Pousada das Meninas

Praia das Conchas, Caixa Postal 10, 83251 000 **Tel** *(041) 3426 8023* **Rooms** *9*

A pretty and cozy *pousada* with a very friendly and relaxed atmosphere. The rustic rooms and cabins (with or without private bathrooms) sleep two to five guests. Reservations are always advisable. Boat trips to other islands can be arranged. **www.pousadadasmeninas.com.br**

ILHA DO MEL (Paraná) Pousadinha Farrol das Conchas

Praia do Farol, 83251 000 **Tel** *(041) 3426 8026* **Rooms** *16*

With simple rooms sleeping two to seven people, the Pousadinha attracts mainly young people who enjoy its lively atmosphere. The beach setting and proximity to the bars of Nova Brasília fishing village adds to its appeal. The on-site restaurant serves good, very reasonably priced Italian food. **www.pousadinha.com.br**

MORRETES (Paraná) Nhundiaquara Hotel

Rua General Carneiro 13, 83350 000 **Tel** *(041) 3462 1228* **Rooms** *15*

A simple, but characterful, old hotel in the center of town, this Nhundiaquara property is situated alongside the picturesque Rio Nundiaquara. Rooms are on the small side, though it is worth paying more for one overlooking the river. The hotel restaurant serves well-cooked regional food. Very popular with budget travelers.

MORRETES (Paraná) Santuário Nhundiaquara

Estrada das Prainhas Km 02, Porto de Cima **Tel** *(041) 3462 1938* **Rooms** *8*

In a park-like setting near the base of the Serra do Mar off Graciosa Road, the Nhundiaquara is one of the best budget hotels in the area. All rooms have ceiling fans, as well as balconies overlooking the gardens. There are nature trails through the forest to waterfalls and a natural swimming pool. **www.nhundiaquara.com.br**

PARANAGUÁ (Paraná) San Rafael

Rua Júlia da Costa 185, 83203 060 **Tel** *(041) 3423 2123* **Rooms** *45*

Despite an unremarkable mirror-glass front, San Rafael enjoys a central location and offers a good range of facilities, including a well-equipped business center. The apartments and suites in this modern hotel are all comfortably furnished and there is a decent on-site restaurant. **www.sanrafaelhotel.com.br**

RIO GRANDE DO SUL

BENTO GONÇALVES Pousada Don Giovanni

VRS 805, Linha Amadeu 28 Km 12, Pinto Bandeira, 95717 000 **Tel** *(054) 3451 4129* **Rooms** *6*

Surrounded by vineyards, this imposing early 20th-century Italian-style farmhouse lies on the outskirts of town. Rooms feature a mix of antique and contemporary furniture, and have central heating for the winter. The on-site Italian restaurant is good and the estate's own, quite respectable wines are served. **www.dongiovanni.com.br**

BENTO GONÇALVES Pousada Valduga

Rodovia RS-470 Km 68.5, Linha Leopoldina, Caixa Postal 579, 95700 000 **Tel** *(054) 2105 3154* **Rooms** *20*

A very comfortable guesthouse run by one of the foremost producers of quality wine in the Vale dos Vinjedos. Rooms range in quality (and price) from rustic but comfortable to large and lavishly furnished. Guests are invited to participate in a three-hour tasting course and can wander the hillside vineyards. **www.casavalduga.com.br**

CANELA Pousada Quinta dos Marques

Rua Gravataí 200, 95680 000 **Tel** *(054) 3282 9812* **Rooms** *13*

Located close to the town center, this large wood-and-stone farmhouse in typical highland style dates back to the 1930s. The general feel of the *pousada* is rustic chic, dominated by polished wood and neutral tones. It is beautifully set amid native pine forest. **www.quintadosmarques.com.br**

CANELA Pousada Cravo & Canela
Rua Tenente Manoel Corrêa 144, 95680 000 **Tel** *(054) 3282 1120* **Rooms** *11*

An imposing Bavarian-style chalet in the center of town, the Cravo & Canela was built in the 1950s. Rooms are sumptuously furnished and there is an indoor heated pool. Excellent complimentary breakfast and a full afternoon tea. The large gardens are filled with native trees and flowering bushes. **www.pousadacravoecanela.com.br**

CAXIAS DO SUL Reynolds International
Rua Dr Montaury 1441, 95020 190 **Tel** *(054) 3223 5844* **Rooms** *47*

Considered to be the best among the more expensive hotels in town, the Reynolds is especially geared towards the needs of business visitors, with an impressive business center and conference facilities. Guest and public rooms are all elegantly furnished. Free transfer to the airport is offered. **www.reynolds.com.br**

GARIBALDI Hotel Casacurta
Rua Luíz Rogério Casacurta 510, 95720 000 **Tel** *(054) 3462 2166* **Rooms** *31*

Built in 1952 in the Art Deco style, this hotel boasts a recently refurbished interior, pleasantly embellished in pastel colours, chintz, and lace. The rooms are all very comfortable, but on the small side. The hotel has an outstanding Italian restaurant and a fine wine cellar. **www.hotelcasacurta.com.br**

GRAMADO Gramado Parque Hotel
Rua Leopoldo Rosenfeldt 818, 95670 000 **Tel** *(054) 3286 2588* **Rooms** *33*

Housed in a large Bavarian-style chalet, this 1940s establishment is one of the oldest hotels in Gramado. The rooms in the main building feature period furniture and wood paneling. Most rooms are in small, newer chalets set in a delightful garden with lots of hydrangeas and a small, sparkling lake. **www.gramadoparquehotel.com.br**

GRAMADO Estalagem St Hubertus
Rua da Carriere 974, 95670 000 **Tel** *(054) 3286 1273* **Rooms** *26*

Overlooking the Lago Negro, this property seems to be styled on an exclusive European lake-resort hotel. Guest rooms have floral patterns on furnishings and wallpaper. Lounges combine comfortable modern furniture with a classical country look. The manicured gardens abound with flowers and bushes. **www.sthubertus.com**

NOVA PETRÓPOLIS Recanto Suíça
Avenida 15 de Novembro 2195, 95150 000 **Tel** *(054) 3281 1229* **Rooms** *15*

A delightful inn that seems to belong in a Swiss village. Most rooms are in private cabins in the forested garden. While all are very simple, the wood-paneled rooms in the main building are especially cozy. The owner offers attentive service and local advice. Breakfast and other meals by arrangement. **www.recantosuico.com.br**

PORTO ALEGRE Comfort Porto Alegre
Rua Loureiro da Silva 1660, 90050 240 **Tel** *(051) 2117 9000* **Rooms** *75*

An efficient, new, city-center hotel, the Comforto Porto Alegre is popular with business travelers. The no-frills rooms are comfortable, offering a minibar and cable TV. Substantial weekend discounts are available. The on-site restaurant serves decent international cuisine. **www.atlanticahotels.com.br**

PORTO ALEGRE Plaza São Rafael
Av Alberto Bins 514, 90030 140 **Tel** *(051) 3220 7000* **Rooms** *283*

Much less expensive than the more modern, but characterless, luxury hotels elsewhere in Porto Alegre, the Plaza is by far the best city-center hotel. Though all rooms are comfortably and tastefully furnished, the ones on upper floors facing the lagoon are preferred for the fantastic views. Staff are helpful. **www.plazahoteis.com.br**

PORTO ALEGRE Sheraton Porto Alegre
Rua Olavo Barreto Viana 18 **Tel** *(051) 2121 6000* **Rooms** *173*

A new, luxury, business-oriented hotel above a small, upmarket shopping mall in Porto Alegre's fashionable Moinhos de Vento suburb, this Sheraton flagship is close to the city's best restaurants. The guest rooms and suites, all painted in tropical colors, exude sophistication. **www.starwood.com**

SÃO MIGUEL DAS MISSÕES Pousada das Missões

Rua São Nicolau 601, 98865 000 **Tel** *(055) 3381 1202* **Rooms** *30*

A youth hostel located right next to the Jesuit ruins, the Pousada das Missões welcomes guests of all ages. Rooms, all with a private bathroom, sleep one to four people. There is a large lounge area, garden, and a relaxing pool. This is excellent value for money. **www.albergues.com.br/saomiguel**

SÃO MIGUEL DAS MISSÕES Wilson Park

Rua São Miguel 664, 98865 000 **Tel** *(055) 3381 2000* **Rooms** *78*

Located alongside the Jesuit ruins, this large, sprawling property is popular with tour groups. The rooms are modern and comfortably furnished. Amenities include a large pool and tennis courts. The hotel restaurant, serving Brazilian and international cuisine, is the most popular in São Miguel. **www.wilsonparkhotel.com.br**

WHERE TO EAT

As a melting pot of races and influences, Brazil boasts a rich diversity of regional culinary styles *(see pp178–9* and *pp392–3).*

Although the term "haute cuisine" does not strictly apply to Brazilian fare, the art of eating well, or *arte do comer bem*, is known to all Brazilians. A light breakfast, a hearty lunch that can last from noon to 3pm, and a late afternoon snack are followed by a frugal dinner of soup. Sunday

Sign of Camamo Beijupirá restaurant

lunches are an elaborate, extended family affair. Everywhere in Brazil it is easy to get well-cooked, filling meals. For light snacks, there are umpteen *lanchonetes*, or corner snack bars. For lunch, a *botequin*, or working man's pub, can be fun, while dining at a formal *rodizío* is enjoyable. Famous for offering the widest varieties of cuisine, São Paulo is seen as the best place for a true Brazilian culinary experience.

RESTAURANTS & BARS

In Brazil, restaurants and bars come in every shape and size. From the corner *botacos* (pubs) and beach bars to elegant world-class restaurants, Brazil has it all. There is a good range to suit every budget. Even dining in top-notch restaurants offers excellent value for money in comparison to anywhere in Europe or North America.

LOCAL EATING HABITS

Visitors will recognize that many Brazilian eating habits have been influenced by European countries. People eat leisurely and throughout the day, although those who want to snatch a quick bite will not be disappointed. As several restaurants are open all through the day, the lunch hour is spread over many hours.

Brazilians generally eat dinner late, most of them preferring to start at 10pm or later. However, unlike the Spanish big late-night meal, the Brazilian dinner is generally a very light affair. At the weekend, numerous restaurants in the bigger cities, such as Rio de Janeiro and São Paulo, take orders well after midnight. It is not unusual to see Brazilians retreating to the bar if they have to wait for a table. Most restaurants take reservations, and this is often necessary at the bigger restaurants, especially those in the larger cities.

Inside the restaurant in Renaissance Costa do Sauípe Resort

Due to the many different culinary styles, it is virtually impossible to say what a typical Brazilian meal will be, although rice and beans will probably make an appearance at some point. Breakfast can be a meal in itself, and in most cases it will be a hearty spread of fruits, cold meats, cheeses, and breads.

DRESS CODE

The easygoing Brazilian nature is also reflected in the dress code. In corner bars, one can walk in wearing casuals. In Rio and other coastal areas, it is not unusual to see women in bikinis at beach bars. Dress codes, usually more relaxed and tropical in the north, tend to become formal in the south.

A collar and tie for men may be the norm only in restaurants in the business quarter of cites, or in Brasília, where the politicians and civil servants prefer formal dressing.

PAYING & TIPPING

The majority of restaurants take credit cards. By far the most widely accepted credit cards are MasterCard and Visa. Amex and Diners Club cards are also useful. However, it is recommended to check first, especially at the more expensive restaurants

Inside the Box 32 bar *(see p411)* in Florianópolis

where you might not have the cash to cover the bill. If you do get stuck in a "no credit card" situation, do remember that you can probably get cash out of the local ATM machine on your credit card.

Technically, restaurants are not meant to add a 10 percent service charge to the bill. However, in many places, it will be expected as a tip for the staff. If the service charge has not been added, the waiter will normally let you know. It is ideal to leave 10 to 12 percent or, if the service charge has been included, simply round up the bill to the next suitable number. Given the average wage of the staff, tips, however small, are always welcome.

Paying by credit card, in one of the street cafés in São Paulo City

FOOD HYGIENE

As most of Brazil is hot and tropical, every Brazilian knows the importance of keeping food fresh and well refrigerated. Food poisoning, even among visitors, is rare.

The majority of restaurants use ice cubes made from filtered water. However, in small backstreet bars, it is best to avoid ice.

ALCOHOL & DRINKS

On the whole, Brazilians are not great alcohol drinkers. Beer, however, is extremely popular. It is the most preferred alcoholic beverage, and the majority of Brazilian beer is a refreshingly cold light lager that comes in bottles (*cerveja*) or on tap (*chopp*). Also common, and much stronger, are a wide variety of drinks containing *cachaça*, a sugar-based spirit. The

Drinks kiosk on one of the beaches in Morro de São Paulo

most notable and well known of these is the *caipirinha* with fresh lime.

Though Scotch is regarded as a status symbol, wine is rapidly growing in popularity. Brazil already produces some excellent table wines. Brazilians also like soft drinks, especially Guaraná, which is as omnipresent as Coca-Cola. Most bars and restaurants will have bottled water *com* (with) and *sem* (without) gas.

A bottle of *cachaça*

SMOKING

There are regulations about smoking in Brazil, but don't expect anyone to obey or follow them in a restaurant. If you have a real problem with people smoking around you, let the restaurant know before you sit down, so they can seat you away from the smokers.

CHILDREN

Brazil is a child-friendly country. Most restaurants, however sophisticated or simple, will welcome children. Staff will normally go out of their way to entertain them. If they don't have a suitable chair, they will almost certainly try and improvise something. Do not be shocked by young children eating out late with their parents. That is considered quite normal in Brazil.

VEGETARIANS

Vegetarian options are extremely limited in Brazil. However, there are a few specialized restaurants offering dishes suitable for vegetarians, ranging from basic to highly innovative.

CHURRASCARIA RODIZÍO/POR KILO

There are two styles of eating out in Brazil that can take visitors by surprise. The first is the *churrascaria rodízio*, or large barbecue houses found throughout the country. Here, one fixed price covers the starter and main course. The only extras will be for the drinks and dessert. Go to a *churrascaria rodízio* when you are really hungry, as they will keep bringing you succulent pieces of grilled meat. Many offer a "traffic light system" where each diner will have a small card. Leave the green side up if you want more food. Turn over to red and they will stop. The *por kilo* type are self-service restaurants with a buffet of varying degrees of sophistication and a variety of dishes. You can choose from salads to an assortment of hot and cold courses. What you pay for at the check-out, as far as the food is concerned, will be based on exactly what the food on your plate weighs. Hence the name, *por kilo*, or "by-the-kilo."

Por kilo self-service buffet at the Mangai restaurant *(see p406)*

The Flavors of Brazil

Brazil offers a vast range of regional cuisines. Climate and geography influence ingredients, from the exotic tropical fruits and spices in Northern Brazil to Bahian seafood (see p179) and the heavy meat dishes of the southern states. Cultural heritage plays a part as well. In Amazônia, the diet is based on fruits and fish native to the forest and the rivers, with many dishes adapted from indigenous recipes. Farther south, settlement by Portuguese and, later, Italian and German immigrants put a distinctly European stamp on the cooking.

Brazilian coffee

Freshly caught Bonito tuna on sale at a coastal fish market

MEAT

Brazil is a nation that truly enjoys its meat and the wide variety of ways in which beef, chicken, and pork are prepared. The ability to devour large quantities of succulent Brazilian beef is considered a mark of manliness. The family barbecue (*churrasco*) is a Sunday tradition, but for visitors the best way to enjoy Brazil's superb beef is at a *churrascaria rodízio* (barbecue house). Waiters bring large skewers of freshly barbecued beef and other meats, and slice off cuts directly onto the plate. You can state your preference for *mal passado* (rare), *ao ponto* (medium), or *bem passado* (well done), or you can just point to the part that looks good. Cuts include *filet mignon* (tenderloin), *fraldinha* (bottom sirloin), *picanha* (sirloin), *alcatra* (top sirloin), and *maminha* (sirloin tip). *Cupim* is the soft floppy hump on a cow's shoulders. This tender beef, mixed heavily with fat, is an acquired taste and may not necessarily be liked by all.

FISH & SEAFOOD

Brazilians inherited a love of fish from their Portuguese forbears. Cod, a Portuguese staple, is sold dried and

Papaya Limes Pineapple Mangoes Coconuts Bananas

Part of Brazil's lush harvest of ripe tropical fruits

BRAZILIAN DISHES & SPECIALTIES

Now considered Brazil's national dish, *feijoada* was not always the chic cuisine it is today. The rich black bean stew traces its humble origins in the kitchens of the country's slave quarters. To make a meal with the leftovers from their masters' tables, the slaves improvised by combining the cast-off bits of meat into a hearty stew with black beans, flavored with garlic, onion, and bay leaves. Nowadays, a full *feijoada completa* spread is typically eaten for lunch on Wednesdays and Saturdays. In addition to the black beans, the stew contains several kinds of meat, including sausage, bacon, and sun-dried beef. Side dishes include rice, roasted cassava flour (*farofa*), sautéed kale, and slices of orange. A *batida de limão* (*cachaça* with ice shavings and lime) is served before the *feijoada*.

Black beans

Salgados, *such as deep-fried pastries stuffed with cheese or meat, are popular Brazilian snacks.*

Table laid out with all the elements that make up a *feijoada completa*

of which have no English name. In Rio and parts of Southern Brazil, one finds small, tart *jaboticaba*, and red *acerola* berries, often mixed in juices with other fruits. Farther north are vast orchards of cashew (*caju*) – not the nut, but the large fruit that grows above. In the Amazon, there are *taperaba*, *cupuaçu*, and the queen of Amazon berries, *açaí*. These are often puréed with *guaraná* berry powder or syrup and can be mixed with banana for a high-nutrition smoothie.

heavily salted in grocery stores, while cod balls (*bolinhos de bacalhau*) or cod fillets are found on many menus. For fresher fare, Brazil's long coastline offers a bounty of excellent fish and seafood. The colder waters off Santa Catarina offer the country's best oysters. Ilhabela, off São Paulo's green coast, is known for its cold-water jumbo shrimp (*camarão*). Farther north are mollusks, squid, octopus, crab, lobster, shrimp, and, of course, fish. Some of Brazil's best fish come not from the ocean but from the fresh waters of the Pantanal and the

The celebrated Brazilian *caipirinha*

Amazon rainforest. The Pantanal's prize fish is the *dourado*, a fish with firm flesh that is delicious when grilled. Other popular and tasty fish include the *pacú* and *pintado*. In the Amazon, the astounding variety of freshwater fish includes the *tambaqui*, *aruanã*, and *tucanaré*. They are often served grilled, or in soups with local herbs. Another Amazon freshwater favorite is *caldo de piranha* (piranha broth).

BRAZILIAN FRUITS

Along with tropical staples, there are regional fruits, most

WHAT TO DRINK

Brazil's best-known drink is almost certainly the *caipirinha*, made with nothing but lime, sugar, ice, and *cachaça* (sugar-cane liquor). A better choice for quenching thirst, however, are the wide variety of tropical fruit juices. Brazil's most popular soft drink is the domestically produced *guaraná*. This fizzy drink is prepared with wild *guaraná* berries from Amazônia. Also enormously popular is *chope*, or draft beer, served ice-cold after a hot day on the beach. *Chá mate*, herbal tea, is usually consumed hot in Southern Brazil, but in the rest of Brazil, it is served cold as iced tea. Although Brazil is very much a cold beverage country, the exception is the ubiquitous *cafézinho*, strong filter coffee. Most Brazilians drink it very sweet and consider that almost any time of the day is the right time for a *cafézinho*.

Camarão na Moranga *is a stew of large, juicy prawns cooked in coconut milk and served in a pumpkin.*

Picanha steak *is a sirloin steak and usually comes served with only a dusting of coarse salt.*

Pudim de Leite, *a traditional Portuguese dessert, is made from eggs, condensed milk, and caramelized sugar.*

Choosing a Restaurant

The restaurants in this guide have been selected, as far as possible, for the quality of the food and atmosphere. However, in some parts of Brazil where few restaurants can be recommended, places have been suggested that offer good value. Map references are given on pages 96–101 for Rio de Janeiro City and 154–9 for São Paulo City.

PRICE CATEGORIES
These price bands are for a two-course meal and non-alcoholic drinks for one person, plus service charges. Alcoholic drinks are not included in the price.
Ⓢ Under $10
ⓈⓈ $10–$20
ⓈⓈⓈ $20–$30
ⓈⓈⓈⓈ $30–45
ⓈⓈⓈⓈⓈ Over $45

RIO DE JANEIRO CITY

BARRA DA TIJUCA Bistro Montagu
Ⓐ🍴🍷📺Ⓥ   ⓈⓈⓈ
Av Armando Lombardi 800, Barra da Tijuca **Tel** *(021) 2493 5966*

A comfortable and cozy French bistro that has been generously applauded by Rio's gastronomic critics and enjoys a good reputation among residents for the high quality of its food. The house specialties include baked duck thighs served with sweet potato mousseline and orange-cointreau sauce.

BARRA DA TIJUCA Hard Rock Café
Ⓐ🏠🍴🍷🎵Ⓥ   ⓈⓈⓈ
Av das Americas 700, Citta América **Tel** *(021) 2132 8000*

A must on most visitors' lists, the Rio branch of Hard Rock Café boasts three bars, a restaurant, terrace, and dance floor. The highlight of the café, however, is the rock memorabilia on display, associated with such music legends as Elvis and Madonna. The menu features delightful starters, salads, burgers, sandwiches, and pizzas.

BARRA DA TIJUCA Fratelli
Ⓐ🍴🍷📺Ⓥ   ⓈⓈⓈⓈ
Av Pepe 2916 **Tel** *(021) 2494 6644*

This spacious and stylish Italian restaurant has established itself as one of the best places to dine in Barra. When it comes to the cost, Fratelli is a bit steep on the pocket, but makes up with the sumptuous fare on offer. The pizza with great mozzarella cheese topping and ravioli stuffed with duck are favorites.

CENTRO Albamar
🍴🍷Ⓥ   ⓈⓈⓈ
Praça Marechal Âncora 184 **Tel** *(021) 2240 8428*   **Map** *5 E3*

The last remaining tower of the old municipal market in the historic quarter of downtown Rio, this simple and unpretentious restaurant first opened for business in 1933 and offers wonderful atmosphere with great views across Guanabara Bay. Signature seafood options range from fish fillet to Spanish-style octopus.

CENTRO Atrium Del Rey
Ⓐ🍴🍷Ⓥ   ⓈⓈⓈ
Paço Imperial, Praça XV **Tel** *(021) 2220 0193*   **Map** *5 E3*

What sets this place apart is its location in the old Palácio Imperial *(see pp114–15)* allowing the visitor to enjoy a meal in a setting that has witnessed many key events in Brazilian history. Popular with business executives, the Atrium offers a small but eclectically modern menu of international and Brazilian dishes.

CENTRO Cais do Oriente
Ⓐ🏠🍴🍷🎵Ⓥ   ⓈⓈⓈ
Rua Visconde de Itaboraí 8 **Tel** *(021) 2233 2531*   **Map** *5 E3*

Set in an old warehouse that dates from 1878, Cais do Oriente is an eclectic mix of restaurant, bar, and a lounge, which is the venue for jazz and *bossa nova* performances at night. The restaurant has an extensive menu, offering European and Asian platters, as well as traditional Brazilian cuisine.

COPACABANA & LEME Shirley
🍴Ⓥ   ⓈⓈ
Rua General Sampaio 610, Caju **Tel** *(021) 2542 1797*

This small 38-cover outlet, one of Rio's first Spanish eateries, upholds its culinary status even after many decades. The Spanish dishes, including a fine paella, are complemented with an excellent selection of seafood at very accessible prices. Shirley doesn't take reservations, so expect to queue for a table.

COPACABANA & LEME Don Camillo
Ⓐ🏠🍴🍷📺Ⓥ   ⓈⓈⓈ
Av Atlântica 3056, Copacabana **Tel** *(021) 2549 9958*   **Map** *3 D3*

One of the many beachfront restaurants along Copacabana *(see p78)*, with tables laid out on the terrace as well as a more formal indoor dining area, Don Camillo has consistently stood out for the quality of its Italian and seafood dishes. Try the baked mix of lobster, shrimp, squid, mussels, tomato, potato, and the fresh fish of the day.

COPACABANA & LEME Marius
Ⓐ🍴🍷Ⓥ   ⓈⓈⓈ
Av Atlântica 290, Leme **Tel** *(021) 2104 9000*

A typical Brazilian *churrascaria rodízio*, or revolving barbecue, this sizable restaurant is among the best and most innovative. A little expensive, Marius serves as many as 30 kinds of grilled meats. A superb salad bar with tasty vegetable combinations offers interesting options for vegetarians.

Key to Symbols *see back cover flap*

COPACABANA & LEME Da Brambini
Av Atlântica 514, Leme **Tel** *(021) 2275 4346*

A pleasant change from the boisterous restaurants in Copacabana, this cozy little bistro with the feel of an Italian trattoria features cuisine from Northern Italy. Dishes include polenta with fresh mushrooms or gorgonzola cheese as an appetizer and *osso buco* (veal shanks braised in wine) as the main course. A good selection of Italian red wines.

COPACABANA & LEME Marius Crustáceos
Av Atlântica 290, Leme **Tel** *(021) 2104 9002*

Located next door to its popular steakhouse Marius, this outlet, decorated with maritime memorabilia, is renowned for its seafood preparations of prawns, oysters, and crabs. Popular Brazilian treats from the region of Bahia include *moqueca* (seafood stew) and *vatapá* (fish stew).

COPACABANA & LEME Cipriani
Av Atlântica 1702, Copacabana Palace, Copacabana **Tel** *(021) 2545 8747*   **Map** *3 E2*

Offering the best of Northern Italian cuisine, Cipriani has been lauded since its opening in 1994 as one of Brazil's best and most elegant restaurants. Housed in the legendary Copacabana Palace *(see p78)*, diners can look out over the hotel's pretty pool. Noted for freshly prepared pasta entrées and authentic Italian risotto.

COPACABANA & LEME Le Saint Honoré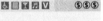
Le Méridien, Av Atlântica 1020, Copacabana **Tel** *(021) 3879 8880*   **Map** *3 F1*

Located 37 floors up on the top of Le Méridien *(see p368)*, Le Saint Honoré offers stunning views of Sugar Loaf *(see pp76–7)* and Corcovado *(see pp82–83)*. The menu of intricate, contemporary French cuisine, which uses fresh Brazilian herbs and fruits, complements the views along Copacabana beach.

FLAMENGO & BOTAFOGO Lamas
Rua Marquês de Abrantes 18, Flamengo **Tel** *(021) 2556 0799*

A gastronomic institution frequented by well-known politicians, writers, and artists, this traditional restaurant offers good unpretentious food for all palates. Recommended for its steaks, the restaurant is also famous for its cod fishcakes, best savored with cold draught beer.

FLAMENGO & BOTAFOGO Miam Miam
Rua General Góes Monteiro 34, Botafogo **Tel** *(021) 2275 7855*

Offering creative and innovative "comfort" food in attractive surroundings, Miam Miam draws an eclectic, cosmopolitan crowd. The 1890s house belonged to the chef's grandmother and is decorated with furniture and artifacts from the 1950s, 60s, and 70s, all for sale.

FLAMENGO & BOTAFOGO Yorubá
Rua Arnaldo Quintella 94, Botafogo **Tel** *(021) 2541 9387*

While the location is informal, critics tend to agree that Yorubá is Rio's best Brazilian restaurant, especially when it comes to cuisine from the state of Bahia. Diners willing to be adventurous will find that an evening spent at Yorubá is a great introduction to one of the world's greatest cuisines, relatively unknown outside its native Brazil.

FLAMENGO & BOTAFOGO Porcão
Av Infante Dom Henrique, Attero do Flamengo **Tel** *(021) 3461 9020*

This flagship branch in Flamengo Park, with striking views of Sugar Loaf, not only serves outstanding barbecued meats, but the buffet alone offers nearly 50 varieties of regional dishes and salads. If you can't get to this restaurant, Porcão maintains the same high standards in other outlets at Ipanema, Barra, and other locations around Rio.

FLORESTA DA TIJUCA Os Esquilos
Estrada D' Escragnole s/n **Tel** *(021) 2492 2197*

Off the beaten track, located in the heart of the Tijuca Forest *(see p88)* in an old colonial house that has operated as a restaurant since 1945, this dining place offers a small menu of Brazilian and international favorites including *feijoada* (a bean and meat stew) at the weekend.

IPANEMA & LEBLON Alessandro e Frederico Pizzaria
Rua Garcia D'Ávila 151, Ipanema **Tel** *(021) 2522 5415*   **Map** *1 C5*

Rio has a number of pizza parlors that vary from the traditional Pizza Guanabara in Leblon and Gattopardo on the Lagoa to this two-story house in Ipanema, which specializes in pizzas that even a Paulista would approve of. The pizzeria also boasts an impressive wine list.

IPANEMA & LEBLON Lã Mole
Rua Dias Ferreira 147, Leblon **Tel** *(021) 2294 0699*   **Map** *1 A4*

This, the first branch of the Lã Mole chain, opened its doors back in 1958 as an ice cream and pizza parlor. Over the years, salads, risotto, and desserts have been added to the menu, building its reputation for excellent, value-based Italian dining. Today, there are more than 15 Lã Mole restaurants across Rio and Niterói.

IPANEMA & LEBLON Carlota
Rua Dias Ferreira 64, Leblon **Tel** *(021) 2540 6821*   **Map** *1 A4*

Listed by *Conde Nast Traveller* as one of the 50 most exciting restaurants in the world, this small, attractive, laid-back bistro dishes out innovative and classical risotto, ravioli, Peking duck and the like from its small and ever-changing menu to provide a relaxing and enjoyable dining experience.

IPANEMA & LEBLON Plataforma ♿ ▤ 🍸 ♫ [V] $$$

Rua Adalberto Ferreira 32, Leblon ***Tel*** *(021) 2274 4022* ***Map*** *1 B2*

This large barbecue house offers a watered-down version of Brazilian culture, with high quality meats served in the main restaurant. The late musician and composer, Tom Jobim, was a regular here. Additional attractions include Bar do Tom, with live Brazilian musical acts, and the comedy club, Caso do Riso.

IPANEMA & LEBLON Esplanada Grill ♿ ▤ 🍸 $$$$

Rua Barão da Torre 600, Ipanema ***Tel*** *(021) 2512 2970* ***Map*** *1 C4*

For decades, this formal dining place has been Rio's most stylish grill, offering quality meats at bargain prices. Esplanada Grill has little in common with the more frantic *churrascaria rodízios*, and its restful atmosphere makes it popular with business clientele, although there is nothing stiff about the atmosphere.

IPANEMA & LEBLON Madame Butterfly ▤ 🍸 [V] $$$$

Rua Barão da Torre 472, Ipanema ***Tel*** *(021) 2267 4347* ***Map*** *2 A5*

A Japanese restaurant that has firmly established itself on the evolving Brazilian gastronomic scene, Madame Butterfly provides a good selection of both classical and innovative Japanese dishes in cozy surroundings. Highlights include traditional *umewan* soup (sweet red bean soup with cherry blossom) and other Japanese dishes with a Brazilian twist.

IPANEMA & LEBLON Margutta ♿ ☂ ▤ 🍸 [V] $$$$

Rua Henrique Dumont 62, Ipanema ***Tel*** *(021) 2259 3718* ***Map*** *1 C4*

Hailing from a family of traditional chefs, Paolo Neroni arrived in Rio from Italy in 1982 and married a Brazilian, Conceição, in 1985. Together they opened this stylish and chic 70-cover restaurant in 1994. Traditional Italian cuisine and seafood are the strengths of this elegant dining option.

IPANEMA & LEBLON Satyricon ♿ ▤ 🍸 [V] $$$$

Rua Barão da Torre 192, Ipanema ***Tel*** *(021) 2521 0627* ***Map*** *2 B4*

An elegant, stylish choice that has seen celebrities such as Madonna and her entourage stroll through its door for dinner, used to be split between serving sophisticated Italian fare and seafood. Today, the focus is firmly on creative and outstanding seafood, including sushi.

IPANEMA & LEBLON Antiquarius ♿ ▤ 🍸 [V] $$$$$

Rua Aristides Espínola 19, Leblon ***Tel*** *(021) 2294 1049* ***Map*** *1 A5*

Often billed as Rio's best Portuguese restaurant, Anitquarius has been very consistent in its offerings since it first opened in 1975. *Perna de cordeico* (leg of lamb) is the most popular dish on the menu. A remarkable wine list, including Portuguese gourmands, complements the menu. Service is attentive and discreet.

IPANEMA & LEBLON Gero ♿ ▤ 🍸 [V] $$$$$

Rua Aníbal de Mendonça 157, Ipanema ***Tel*** *(021) 2239 8158* ***Map*** *1 C4*

One of the most fashionable restaurants in Rio, with the impeccable pedigree of being part of the Fasano family that has been exciting Paulista palates for decades with its sophisticated Italian cuisine, Gero is the place to be seen along with the rich and the beautiful.

LAGOA & JARDIM BOTÂNICO Bar Lagoa ♿ ☂ 🍸 [V] $$

Av Epitácio Pessoa 1674, Lagoa ***Tel*** *(021) 2523 1135* ***Map*** *2 A4*

This Art Deco bistro has been around since 1934. German dishes figure heavily on the extensive menu, which offers meals and snacks for every taste. Excellent steaks and a signature sausage with potato salad accompanied by ice cold beer are on offer. Waiters are legendary for their bad humor and enjoy playing up to this reputation.

LAGOA & JARDIM BOTÂNICO Guimas ♿ ☂ 🍸 [V] $$$

Rua José Roberto Macedo Soares 5, Gavea ***Tel*** *(021) 2259 7996* ***Map*** *1 A2*

An adventurous bistro with a relaxed atmosphere, Guimas has been a popular haunt of artists and the bohemian community since opening in 1981. The menu mixes old favourites with exciting innovative combinations. An informal restaurant, it offers good quality food at reasonable prices.

LAGOA & JARDIM BOTÂNICO Olympe ♿ ▤ 🍸 [V] $$$$$

Rua Custódio Serrão 62, Jardim Botânico ***Tel*** *(021) 2539 4542* ***Map*** *2 A1*

Owner Claude Troisgros, one of the most recognized chefs in Brazil, continues to create culinary delights using the best in Brazilian ingredients combined with his grounding in traditional French cuisine. The passionfruit crêpe soufflé is a favorite dessert. Reservations are required.

RIO DE JANEIRO STATE & ESPÍRITO SANTO

ILHA GRANDE (Rio de Janeiro) Sushi Leblon ☂ $$$

Ilha de Itanhangá, Baía da Ilha Grande ***Tel*** *(024) 3369 3558*

Rio de Janeiro's most famous Japanese restaurant caters to an island-hopping crowd during the high season. Located on an island, you need a boat to get here. Lunch here can be combined with an island cruise or a stop-off at one of the Ilha do Itanhanga's many beautiful beaches.

Key to Price Guide *see p394* **Key to Symbols** *see back cover flap*

BÚZIOS (Rio de Janeiro) Satyricon

$$$

Av José Bento Ribeiro Dantas 500, Centro **Tel** *(024) 2623 1595*

Miro Leopardo's Satyricon has been serving the best seafood in Rio de Janeiro for over 20 years. The restaurant is especially known for its oven-baked fish, served with rock salt and accompanied by lightly fried vegetables. A good selection of wine is available.

BÚZIOS (Rio de Janeiro) Sawasdee

$$$

Av José Bento Ribeiro Dantas 422, Centro **Tel** *(022) 2623 4644*

This seafront restaurant serves Brazilian versions of simple Thai dishes. The restaurant's *pad thai* is made from egg noodles fried with *myashi* sauce, baby squid, mussels, and prawns and garnished with coriander, lemon, and grated peanuts. The grilled salmon comes with a sliced mango, sweet and sour sauce, mint, and black pepper.

BÚZIOS (Rio de Janeiro) Casas Brancas

$$$$

Pousada Casas Brancas, Morro do Humaitá 10 **Tel** *(022) 2623 1458*

This open-air restaurant and bar on the Morro do Humaitá offers sweeping views out over the bay. Popular with couples, the atmosphere is rendered romantic when the bar and the handful of tables are lit with candles in the evening. The highlight is light Mediterranean seafood and simple, elegant Italian dishes.

CABO FRIO (Rio de Janeiro) Restaurante La Gondole

$$$

Rua Almirante Barrosa 247, Passagem **Tel** *(022) 2643 5264*

The best seafood restaurant in Cabo Frio, Restaurante La Gondole is run by Swiss chef André Cabrini, who trained in France. House specialties include *feuilleté de la mer,* filo pastry filled with seafood and accompanied by stuffed mussels and saffron risotto.

GUARAPARI (Espírito Santo) Guaramare

$$$$

Rodovia do Sol 65, Rodovia para Anchieta **Tel** *(027) 3272 1300*

Located between a busy main road and the beach resort of Guarapari, this restaurant, with its mock-farmhouse dining room and rustic ambience, is a haven of peace and at its most magical in the evenings. Highly recommended for its sumptuous seafood. Chef Vitor Bojovski has received numerous stars from *Guia Quatro Rodas* magazine.

PARATY (Rio de Janeiro) Catimbau

$$

Baía de Paraty **Tel** *(024) 9222 8954*

Strikingly built between two giant boulders on a tiny island in the bay by local fisherman, Caca, and his Dutch wife, this restaurant and bar serves simple but superb fresh seafood amid great views. The *caipirinhas,* cocktails made with lime, sugar, and *cachàca,* are chilled and strong.

PARATY (Rio de Janeiro) Merlin O Mago

$$

Rua do Comércio 376, Centro Histórico **Tel** *(024) 3371 2154*

This little rustic restaurant, tucked away in a forest just behind Paraty town, is a big draw not only for the delicious light Italian fare on offer, but for its tropical garden that attracts giant electric blue morpho butterflies, emerald hummingbirds, and flame red tanagers, who flutter through the restaurant's open sides to the delight of diners.

PARATY (Rio de Janeiro) Punto Divino

$$

Rua da Matriz 129, Praça da Matriz, Centro Histórico **Tel** *(024) 3371 1348*

Paraty's best seafood restaurant is run by an Italian scuba diver who fell in love with the bay of Ilha Grande on a visit here some decades ago. Their Italian pizza, lighter on cheese than customary in Brazil, is a good choice. Classy live acoustic music plays during high season. There is an excellent wine list.

PARATY (Rio de Janeiro) Vila Verde

$$

Estrada para Cunha km 7 **Tel** *(024) 3371 7808*

This little rustic restaurant, tucked away in a forest just behind Paraty town, is a big draw not only for the delicious light Italian fare on offer, but for its tropical garden that attracts giant electric blue morpho butterflies, emerald hummingbirds, and flame red tanagers, who flutter through the restaurant's open sides to the delight of diners.

PARATY (Rio de Janeiro) Le Gite d'Indaiatiba

$$$$

Rodovia Rio-Santos km 562, Graúna **Tel** *(024) 9999 9923*

In the heart of the Atlantic rainforest, next to the Bromelias spa *(see p371),* is one of Brazil's finest restaurants. Classic French cuisine is combined with Brazilian tropical ingredients to create culinary delights. The fantastic meals are accompanied by excellent wines and jazz performances set amid the sweeping rainforest.

PETRÓPOLIS & TERESÓPOLIS (Rio de Janeiro) Locanda della Mimosa

$$$$

Alameda das Mimosas 30, Vale Florido **Tel** *(024) 2242 5405*

One of the most distinguished restaurants and hotels, set in a colonial mansion in the forested hills near Petrópolis and Teresópolis, Locanda della Mimosa has won many accolades. Inspired by French nouvelle cuisine, the hearty meals are served in Brazilian-sized portions. There are plenty of Italian choices too. The wine list is superb.

VITÓRIA (Espírito Santo) Lareira Portuguesa

$$$

Av Saturnino de Brito 260 **Tel** *(027) 3345 0329*

This is the best of a handful of Portuguese restaurants in Vitória. The cooking and the service are directed by an owner and chef from Guarda in central Portugal and dishes like *bacalhau* (codfish) are served by black-tie and aproned waiters in a bustling dining room.

MINAS GERAIS

BELO HORIZONTE Splendido

$$$

Flat Volpi Residence, Rua Levindo Lopes 251, Savassi **Tel** *(031) 3227 6446*

One of the best restaurants in the city lies in the heart of the fashionable Savassi nightlife district. The menu and the bright atmosphere are light Mediterranean. Excellent pasta entrées are on offer and the wine list is respectable, with some imported wines from Tuscany.

BELO HORIZONTE Aurora

$$$$

Rua Expedicionário Mário Alves de Oliveira 421, São Luis, Pampulha **Tel** *(031) 3498 7567*

The large, airy dining room overlooks a little private garden close to Oscar Niemeyer's Pampulha *(see p125)*. The cuisine is Brazilian-Oriental fusion, with delectable items like steak with *jabuticaba* sauce and tiger prawns in wasabi sauce with wild rice and grated mango.

BELO HORIZONTE Vecchio Sogno

$$$$

Rua Martim de Carvalho 75, Santo Agostinho **Tel** *(031) 3292 5251*

This bustling Italian restaurant has been named Belo Horizonte's best restaurant of the year in *Veja* magazine seven times over. Chef Ivo Faria da Costa learnt his trade from Frenchman Lucien Iltis at the Copacabana Palace in Rio, and is celebrated for his pastas and steaks. The wine list and sommeliers are excellent.

DIAMANTINA Cantina do Marinho
$$

Rua Direita 113 **Tel** *(038) 3531 1686*

One of the handful of restaurants in the area, Cantina do Marinho has a formal atmosphere, with a dining room decorated with assorted bottles of wine. The filling *prato feito* (buffet lunch) includes a drink. Try the delicious traditional *lombo com feijão tropeiro* (pork with beans).

MARIANA Lua Cheia
$

Rua Dom Viçoso 23, Centro **Tel** *(031) 3557 3232*

This busy restaurant serves typical Minas Gerais food *por kilo* (by weight), or all-you-can-eat the buffets, with plenty of choices of salads, vegetable dishes for the vegetarians, various cuts of meat from the *churrascaria*, and generous amounts of desserts.

OURO PRETO O Passo

$$

Rua São José 56, Centro **Tel** *(031) 3552 5089*

Housed in a Portuguese colonial town house, this upmarket pizzeria offers pizzas made in a traditional Italian wood-fired oven, served either in the dining area, or the adjacent veranda which has sweeping views out over the town. At weekends there is live music and dancing.

OURO PRETO Triumpho

$$

Rua Donato da Fonseca 02, Largo do Rosário **Tel** *(031) 3552 6774*

This local favorite is housed in a cozy cellar bar right next to the Igreja do Rosário. The menu comprises Minas Gerais cuisine, which is heavy on meat and vegetables like manioc and squash. Food comes accompanied by live acoustic music from guitarists and singer-songwriters, and there is a reasonable wine list.

OURO PRETO Le Coq D'Or

$$$

Rua Getulio Vargas 270, Largo do Rosário **Tel** *(031) 3551 5200*

The restaurant occupies a formal dining area inside the colonial Solar Nossa Senhora do Rosário hotel *(see p373)* and in a separate covered annex lit by natural light. The menu is largely Portuguese, focusing on fish, meat, and pasta. There is a modest wine list. The service is prompt and attentive.

SÃO JOÃO DEL REI Quinto do Ouro

$$

Praça Severiano de Rezende 4 **Tel** *(032) 3371 7577*

Although it has plenty of cafés and *por kilo* options, São João, unlike neighboring Tiradentes, does not have many upmarket restaurants. The Quinto do Ouro offers the best Minas Gerais cooking in town, well-prepared regional food at reasonable prices.

PARQUE NACIONAL DA SERRA DA CANASTRA Zagaia
$

Av Tancredo Neves 10 **Tel** *(037) 3433 1323*

This is the best of limited food choices available in Serra da Canastra, serving traditional local cuisine such as *galinha caipira* (stewed wild rooster), excellent *pão de queijo* (cheese rolls), and on select days, the Brazilian specialty, *feijoada* (black beans and pork stew).

PARQUE NACIONAL DA SERRA DO CIPÓ Parador Nacional

$$$

Alameda das Orquídeas, Parque Nacional Serra do Cipó **Tel** *(031) 9984 3278*

This stylish, romantic restaurant set in a rustic 18th-century colonial house is surrounded by picturesque tropical gardens, which are beautifully lit at night, setting the tone for a delightful meal. Chef Laurents blends Mediterranean cuisine with the regional Minas style of cooking to create an interesting menu. The wine list is respectable.

Key to Price Guide *see p394* **Key to Symbols** *see back cover flap*

TIRADENTES Quartier Latin

$$$

Rua São Francisco de Paula 46, Praça de Rodoviária **Tel** *(032) 3355 1552*

This restaurant, just across the river from the center of town, hosts the annual gastronomic festival *(see p43)*. The French-trained chef offers a menu of Franco-Brazilian cuisine, as well as Italian fare and good seafood. Their own cultivated organic vegetables are used to make great salads, and there is a decent wine list.

TIRADENTES Tragaluz

$$$

Rua Direita 52 **Tel** *(032) 3355 1979*

Housed in an 18th-century colonial town house in the city center, Tragaluz has a menu offering a modern interpretation of traditional Mineira cuisine. Sumptuous dishes include smoked freshwater catfish in garlic crumbs and sweet potato. The restaurant is known for its desserts, especially the *goiabada* (guava paste).

TIRADENTES Theatro da Vila

$$$$

Rua Padre Toledo 157 **Tel** *(032) 3355 1275*

In the heart of the town, this intimate restaurant occupies a converted colonial house. The dining room is rustic chic, decorated with local art and crafts, and offers a sweeping view out over a little garden and the mountains beyond. The meals are Franco-Brazilian. The little garden theater hosts performances in summer.

SÃO PAULO CITY

JARDINS & AVENIDA PAULISTA A Figueira Rubaiyat

$$$

Rua Haddock Lobo 1738, Jardins **Tel** *(011) 3063 3888*   **Map** *4 D3*

The flagship outlet of the Rubaiyat group, this serves some of the best Brazilian beef in the city. The Figueira has an extensive menu with remarkable seafood, including fresh *cananéia* oysters from the oyster bar. Steaks remain the best choice on the menu. Tables sit under an enormous tropical fig tree and the ambience is informal-chic.

JARDINS & AVENIDA PAULISTA D.O.M

$$$$

Rua Barão de Capanema 549, Jardins **Tel** *(011) 3088 0761*   **Map** *4 D3*

Among the most celebrated chefs in Brazil, Alex Atala has been voted chef of the year numerous times by *Veja* magazine. His innovative cooking fuses Brazilian ingredients with French and Italian styles, creating fantastic meals such as the Brazilian fish *filhote* with tapioca or heart of palm fettuccine carbonara.

JARDINS & AVENIDA PAULISTA East

$$$$

Alameda Jaú 1303 **Tel** *(011) 3081 1160*   **Map** *4 E2*

East introduced São Paulo to vodka martini cocktails and authentic East Asian cuisine. The martinis come with a tropical twist, flavored with a gamut of sumptuous tropical ingredients such as *maracuja* (passionflower) and pink basil. The simple and sumptuous meals range from Thai curry to Korean grills.

JARDINS & AVENIDA PAULISTA Gero

$$$$

Rua Haddock Lobo 1629, Jardins **Tel** *(011) 3064 0005*   **Map** *4 D3*

Rogerio Fasano's other Italian restaurant in Jardins is the polar opposite of the eponymous Fasano, a highly regarded gourmet restaurant. Gero is a restaurant to be seen in, a favorite with celebrities, the fashionable set, and the young crowd. Diners wait at the long bar before dining on light Italian fare such as black polenta with baby squid.

JARDINS & AVENIDA PAULISTA Fasano

 $$$$$

Rua Vitório Fasano 88, Jardins **Tel** *(011) 3896 4000*   **Map** *4 D3*

The flagship of the Fasano chain is the finest, most formal dining place in the city, with discreet dimly-lit booths. Sardinian chef Salvatore Loi dishes out excellent Italian and French creations with special emphasis on seafood. The wine list is among the best in the country. Live music plays in the adjacent cigar bar, Baretto.

CENTRO Ponto Chic

$

Largo do Paiçandu 27 **Tel** *(011) 3222 6528*   **Map** *1 C2*

This small corner restaurant is a lunchtime institution. The Brazilian equivalent of the hamburger – the *bauru* – was invented here in the 1930s. The sandwich comprises a thick slab of yellow cheese, salad, and finely cut, rare roast beef held together in a crusty French roll. A photograph of Casemiro Pinto Neto, creator of the *bauru*, adorns the wall.

CENTRO La Casserole

 $$$$

Largo do Arouche 346, Vila Buarque **Tel** *(011) 3331 6283*   **Map** *1 B2*

An intimate French restaurant and local institution founded in 1954, the dining room bustles at lunchtime and has a fixed menu. It is quieter and more romantic in the evenings, with a French-influenced menu that has changed little over the decades. Bouillabaisse and lamb shanks are popular choices.

CENTRO Terraço Itália

$$$$

Av Ipiranga 344, Edifício Itália **Tel** *(011) 3257 6566*   **Map** *1 B2, 1 B3*

While some diners come here for the mock-Mediterranean food, most people are drawn by the spectacular view from the observation deck out over Oscar Niemeyer's Edifício Copan and the vast sprawl of São Paulo. Come for a light soup, or try the grilled *dourado* fish with oyster if you want to dine.

FARTHER AFIELD Grazie a Dio $$$

Rua Girassol 67, Vila Madalena **Tel** *(011) 3031 6568*

One of the best small venues for emerging Brazilian bands, the restaurant has hosted acts such as Clube do Balanco, Seu Jorge, and Tutti Bae, who played here on their journey to fame. The food is mock-Mediterranean, but the after-dinner performances and the cocktails are always great.

FARTHER AFIELD Capim Santo $$$$

Rua Min Rocha Azeredo 471, Vila Madalena **Tel** *(011) 3068 8486*

Capim Santo began as an informal fish restaurant in Trancoso. Once the town was discovered by international celebrities, the restaurant became one of the most fashionable places to dine. It recreates Bahian informality with tables set in a tropical garden and Bahian music in the background. The menu is predominantly seafood.

HIGIENÓPOLIS Carlota $$$$

Rua Sergipe 753 **Tel** *(011) 3661 8670*

This New York-inspired deli is now a favorite with food-loving intellectuals from São Paulo's Zona Sul. The atmosphere is chic rustic, the dining room buzzes with conversation, and the menu offers delicious Asian-Mediterranean cuisine utilizing Brazilian ingredients. The puddings are legendary.

PARQUE DO IBIRAPUERA & AROUND Prêt no MAM $$

Portão 3 **Tel** *(011) 5549 9688*

This upmarket café in the Museu de Arte Moderna *(see p147)* serves an excellent lunchtime buffet consisting of light, healthy Mediterranean-inspired dishes and salads. The dining area is a bright, elongated room with its outer wall made almost entirely of glass. Excellent coffee is served.

IBIRAPUERA PARK & AROUND JAM Warehouse $$$

Rua Lopes Neto 308, Itaim **Tel** *(011) 3079 4259*

JAM is an acronym for Japanese food, art, and music, all of which are presented in a tastefully designed, modern space. The food is classical Japanese, the art contemporary Brazilian, and the music ranges from *samba* rock to *bossa nova* and jazz. The bar is a great spot for pre-dinner cocktails, and the crowd usually young and fashionable.

IBIRAPUERA PARK & AROUND 348 Parilla Porteña $$$$

Rua Comendador Miguel Calfat 348, Vila Olimpia **Tel** *(011) 3849 0348*

Owned and run by Argentinian Eduardo Santaller, this restaurant is said to serve better cuts than are available in Buenos Aires, and they come with all the traditional Argentinian acoutrements, right down to the *chimichurri* sauce. The wine list boasts some of the finest Argentinian reds.

IBIRAPUERA PARK & AROUND Kosushi $$$$

Rua Viradouro 139, Itaim Bibi **Tel** *(011) 3167 7272*

Kosushi is one of a string of new restaurants in the Itaim neighborhood where the dining space is as important as the food. The city's young and rich flock here to eat at the sparse designer tables offset against an enormous backdrop of light wood and white stone. The food is classical Japanese and is renowned for its sushi and sashimi.

IBIRAPUERA PARK & AROUND Le Coq Hardy $$$$$

Rua Jerônimo da Veiga 461, Itaim Bibi **Tel** *(011) 3079 3344*

With the closure of Café Antique, Le Coq Hardy has established itself as the best fine-dining French restaurant in São Paulo. The dining room is formal and resplendent in white. As ever with Brazilian-run French restaurants, there are plenty of Italian options on the menu, alongside dishes like lamb Provençale and superior foie gras.

LIBERDADE Kinoshita $$$

Rua da Glória 168, Liberdade **Tel** *(011) 3241 3586*   **Map** 1 C4

One of the pioneer Japanese fusion restaurants in São Paulo, Kinoshita has a convivial atomsphere, with a long bar sitting opposite low Japanese tables with room for up to four diners. Owner and chef Tsuyoshi Murakami has traveled extensively to introduce flavors from other regions of the world. Service is efficient and attentive.

LIBERDADE Sushi Yassu $$$

Rua Tômas Gonzaga 98, Liberdade **Tel** *(011) 3288 2966*   **Map** 1 C4

One of the most traditional Japanese restaurants in Liberdade is known to connoisseurs for its excellent sushi and sashimi. For the more adventurous diner, there is exotic eel sautéed with soy sauce and sake. Dining is at one of the handful of tables, at the long sushi bar, or in private booths.

THE NEW CENTER Vicolo Nostro $$$

Rua Jataituba 29, Brooklin **Tel** *(011) 5561 5287*

This expansive restaurant has a series of different rooms and outdoor areas, each of which attempts to bring a taste of Tuscany, Sicily, and Sardinia to the concrete that dominates the area. The menu is as large as the restaurant and is inspired by regional Italian home cooking.

THE NEW CENTER Govinda $$$$

Av Roque Petroni Júnior 1089 **Tel** *(011) 5092 4816*

This is an upmarket restaurant decorated with Indian art and with a large bar area beloved of cigar smokers. The menu is excellent, with *naan* (Indian bread) and a series of chutneys. The curries, although tasty, are underspiced in deference to the European palate.

Key to Price Guide *see p394* **Key to Symbols** *see back cover flap*

PINHEIROS Mani $$$$

Rua Joaquim Antunes 210 **Tel** *(011) 3085 4148* **Map** *3 B3*

The latest star on São Paulo's dining scene is owned by a famous television actress and a Formula 1 driver. The atmosphere is rustic chic, with tables positioned for people-watching. The food, from two former Michelin-starred chefs, is a light, healthy fusion of Mediterranean techniques and Brazilian ingredients.

SÃO PAULO STATE

ILHABELA Viana $$$$

Av Leonardo Reale 1560, Praia de Viana **Tel** *(012) 3896 1089*

The best seafood restaurant on the island is tucked away north of the main town of Ilhabela on Viana Beach. It is celebrated for its fresh fish, grilled with heart of palm, capers, and mushroom, and its red crab with mango risotto. Open weekends only outside the summer months.

SANTOS Bolsa e Café do Museu $

Rua XV de Novembro 95, Centro **Tel** *(013) 3219 5585*

This little café within Museu do Café (*see pp168–9*) in São Paulo state serves one of the best cups of coffee in the country. Patrons can choose their own beans or blend, and there is a small menu of indulgent sweet and savory snacks and pastries. The café has Internet access for customers.

SANTOS Pier One $$

Av Almirante Saldanha de Gama s/n, Ponta da Praia **Tel** *(013) 3261 6121*

This seafood restaurant sits over the water at the end of the peninsula where Santos lies. It is most popular for sunset *caipirinha* cocktails or dinners. A popular choice is the *meca santista*, a filet of fish served with manioc and banana and accompanied by heart of palm risotto.

SÃO SEBASTIÃO Acqua $$$

Estrada de Camburi 2000, Camburi **Tel** *(012) 3865 2388*

This newly opened restaurant offers the most spectacular view of the entire Brazilian coast out over the forest, the Atlantic, and the broad crescent of Camburí beach. The menu combines light seafood with wood-fired pizzas and pasta dishes, and the wine list is respectable.

SÃO SEBASTIÃO Manacá $$$$

Rua de Manacá, Camburizinho **Tel** *(012) 3865 1566*

A boardwalk cuts through the rainforest behind the beach at Camburi, in southern São Sebastião, province to reveal a little moonlit glade furnished with tables filled with some of the state's most beautiful beachgoers. The menu changes with the season and focuses on seafood. The spiced fish steak wrapped in banana leaf is popular.

UBATUBA Solar das Águas Cantantes $$$

Estrada Saco da Ribeira s/n, Praia do Lázaro **Tel** *(012) 3842 0288*

This hotel restaurant sits on Praia do Lázaro, one of the prettiest beaches in Ubatuba province, divided by a forested promontory of land. The hotel, like the beach, is popular with families and the restaurant is celebrated for its light *moquecas* (seafood stews made with coconut milk) and filet of *badejo* with squid.

BAHIA

CACHOEIRA Beira Rio $

Rua Paulo Filho 19, Centro **Tel** *(075) 3425 5050*

This small restaurant overlooking the river Paraguaçu and the town of São Félix serves up excellent lunches. The menu includes chicken stew, fish *moqueca*, and *vatapá* (fish stew) served with rice and *farofa* (a manioc flour sautéed in butter).

ILHÉUS Bar Vesuvio $$$

Praça Dom Eduardo, Centro **Tel** *(073) 3634 4724*

Facing the architecturally marvelous Catedral Basílica San Marino, and made famous by noted writer Jorge Amado (*see p31*) in his works of fiction, this atmospheric but expensive Swiss-owned restaurant is an ideal place to enjoy a glass of beer and some outstanding Arabic food at the outdoor tables.

ILHÉUS Marostica $$

Av 2 de Julho 966 **Tel** *(073) 3634 5691*

Located in the historic center of the town, this cozy, no-fuss restaurant offers excellent Italian dining. The kitchen prepares delicious pastas with classic sauces, and stuffed pastas such as ravioli and lasagnes. A climatized cellar displays more than 50 different labels.

ITACARÉ Casa Sapucaia

Rua Londônio Almeida 84 **Tel** *(073) 3251 3091*

Housed in a charming old colonial house with a beautiful garden in front that is candlelit at night, this cozy restaurant offers casual dining. The wide-ranging menu leans towards Mediterranean cuisine. Try the sumptuous king prawns caramelized with ginger.

ITACARÉ Dedo de Moça

Rua Plinio Soares 26 **Tel** *(073) 3251 3372*

One of Bahia's outstanding stylish restaurants, the menu offers fresh and contemporary Brazilian cuisine with a tropical twist. Noted chef Vagner Aguiar prepares interesting dishes that include the *bobó de camarão* (prawn stew in yuca cream with coconut rice) and the grilled *cavala* fish with pineapple and mango compote.

LENÇOIS Neco's Bar

Praça Clarim Pacheco 15 **Tel** *(075) 3334 1179*

Renowned for serving the best regional fare in town, Neco's bar offers a good sampling of regional specialties such as salted beef, flavored with strong, traditional spices. For special meals orders must be placed a day in advance. Kitchen closes at 10pm.

LENÇOIS Picanha na Praça

Praça do Coreto 62 **Tel** *(075) 3334 1080*

An outdoor terrace restaurant in town popular for grilled steaks. Dishes at Picanha na Praça are done to perfection and arrive sizzling hot at the table on their own grill. The portions are generally large, and even the half portions can feed up to two persons.

PORTO SEGURO Bistrô da Helô
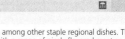

Travessa Assis Chateaubriand 26 **Tel** *(073) 3288 3940*

An elegant bistro, this is a good choice for a gourmet meal. This pleasant restaurant is known for its signature shrimp dishes, but also serves a variety of meat, fowl, and pasta entrées. The balsamic glazed shellfish with basil risotto is recommended.

PORTO SEGURO Tia Nenzinha

Av Portugal 170 **Tel** *(073) 3288 1846*

This simple restaurant specializes in local seafood and traditional Brazilian dishes such as fish *moqueca* stew, accompanied by salad, rice, and *pirão* (fish broth gravy thickened with mandioca). The outstanding service adds to the dining experience.

PRAIA DO FORTE Sabor da Vila

Al do Sol s/n **Tel** *(071) 3676 1156*

This pleasant and no-fuss restaurant is famous for its crab *moqueca*, among other staple regional dishes. The menu also offers other appetizing seafood and fish options, along with a range of nicely flavored meat and chicken preparations.

SALVADOR Jardim das Delicias

Rua João de Deus 12, Pelourinho **Tel** *(071) 3322 1449*

An elegant restaurant and antique shop with a lovely garden patio, this is a perfect place to visit for a snack, drink, or wonderful desserts. Bahian and international cuisine is served both indoors and outside in the tropical garden. The fresh salads are particularly good. Live music is played in the evenings.

SALVADOR Pereira

Av Sete de Setembro 3959, Porto da Barra **Tel** *(071) 3264 6464*

With a contemporary look and modern decor, Pereira is a mix of restaurant and bar. The menu has lots to offer, and includes a wide variety of tapas, hearty appetizers, as well as tasty pastas, traditional steaks, and beef, pork, or chicken grilled over an open fire.

SALVADOR Soho

Av Lafayete Coutinho 1010 **Tel** *(071) 3322 4554*

The city's best Japanese restaurant is located right on the water, inside the Bahia Marina hotel. The extensive menu includes a variety of creative sushis and stir fries, which are a big draw for food-lovers. Like the other dining places in Brazil, portions are generous.

SALVADOR Sorriso da Dadá

Rua Frei Vicente 5, Pelourinho **Tel** *(071) 3321 9642*

Dadá, one of Salvador's most celebrated chefs, prepares excellent Bahian food at this intimate dining place, located at the historic center of the city. The regional cuisine focuses on traditional stews and seafood appetizers. Make sure to try the *negão do Dadá* dessert, a delicious rich and creamy chocolate concoction.

SALVADOR Yemanjá

Av Otavio Mangabeira 4655, Praia Jardim Armação **Tel** *(071) 3461 9008*

A large, bustling, family-style restaurant, this is considered by local food critics as one of the great places in town for a Bahian meal. The rich *moquecas* (seafood stew) serve even two people generously. The most popular dishes are the prawn or soft-shell (*siri mole*) crab *moqueca*.

Key to Price Guide *see p394* **Key to Symbols** *see back cover flap*

SALVADOR Maria Mata Mouro $$$$

Rua Inácio Acciole 8, Pelourinho **Tel** *(071) 3321 3929*

One of the few elegant dining options in Pelourinho, this beautiful restaurant offers an international menu with a variety of dishes such as pasta, grilled lamb, steak, and paella. The restaurant is very busy at weekends, and it is advisable to book a table in advance.

SALVADOR Trapiche Adelaide $$$$

Av Contorno, Praça dos Tupinambás 2, Cidade Baixa **Tel** *(071) 3326 2211*

An elegant upscale dining option with sweeping views of the bay, the Trapiche Adelaide serves up sophisticated Brazilian cuisine with a French touch. The signature dish is quail with a manioc, onion, and raisin stuffing, served in a sweet-and-sour grape sauce.

TRANCOSO Capim Santo $$$

Praça São João s/n **Tel** *(073) 3668 1122*

This restaurant, with a lovely outdoor patio, serves up excellent contemporary Brazilian cuisine. Signature dishes include fresh fish in a cashew nut crust and prawns with plantain. Classic desserts with a tropical twist, such as guava crème brûlée, are all-time favorites.

TRANCOSO O Cacau $$$

Praça São João s/n **Tel** *(073) 3668 1266*

The leafy outdoor ambience adds to the charm of this tastefully decorated restaurant that specializes in Bahian cooking with an Oriental twist. The *moqueca* is the signature dish, but their seafood is equally good. Passion-seafood salad or fish with saffron, white wine, mash, and kale are some of the interesting food choices.

SERGIPE, ALAGOAS & PERNAMBUCO

ARACAJU (Sergipe) Carro de Bois $

Rua Niceu Dantas 1040, Atalaia **Tel** *(079) 3243 4800*

A cozy restaurant with an old-style atmosphere, Carro de Bois features solid furniture and dark wood paneling. A wide variety of succulent beef dishes are served in simple, hearty ways. Menu items include a beef filet served with demi-glacé sauce, *carrero* rice, and fried potatoes.

ARACAJU (Sergipe) Cariri $$

Passarela do Caranguejo s/n **Tel** *(079) 3243 1379*

The large menu at this lively restaurant boasts a variety of regional seafood and meat dishes. Worth trying are the *pitu moqueca* and *pitu à Sergipe*, made with freshwater prawns from the São Francisco river, stewed with coconut, garlic, onion, parsley, pepper, and tomato. Live *forró* music is played from Tuesday to Saturday.

FERNANDO DE NORONHA (Pernambuco) Café Com Arte $

Terminal Turistico **Tel** *(081) 3619 1634*

A relaxed little café in the main village, Café Com Arte is the perfect place to sit back and enjoy coffee or a light lunch. The menu offers crêpes, hearty sandwiches, and desserts. There are also small art pieces for sale, some made from recycled items originally used by the café.

FERNANDO DE NORONHA (Pernambuco) Ecologikus $$

Estrada Velha do Sueste (access via the airport) **Tel** *(081) 3619 1807*

One of the best dining options on the island, this simple restaurant specializes in delicious fresh seafood. The highly recommended house special is the Sinfonia Ecologiku, a spicy, delectable hotpot of fish, octopus, shrimp, and sweet lobster, all in a rich seafood broth. Ecologikus also serves fish platters for large groups.

FERNANDO DE NORONHA (Pernambuco) Trattoria di Morena $$

Rua Nice Cordeiro 2600 **Tel** *(081) 3619 1142*

For excellent Italian food, visit the Trattoria di Morena. This pleasant intimate restaurant inside the Pousada da Morena serves great pasta with a variety of seafood ingredients. The wine list offers excellent choices, as well as a few options by the glass.

MACEIÓ (Alagoas) Divina Gula $$

Rua Eng. Paulo Brandão Nogueira 85, Jatiúca **Tel** *(082) 3235 1016*

This large bustling restaurant is one of the most popular gathering places in Maceió. The kitchen cooks up excellent regional dishes such as the tender marinated lamb dish, grilled fish with grape sauce or chicken with okra, and other specialities of the Northeast. The bar offers 50 different kinds of *cachaça*.

MACEIÓ (Alagoas) O Peixarão $$

Av Dr Júlio Marques Luz 50, Jatiúca **Tel** *(082) 3325 7011*

Overlooking the large Lagoa Mundaú, this simple restaurant draws locals who come here for the tasty seafood stews made with local clams, fresh and saltwater crabs, and oysters. The portions are generous and the price is right. It is also a popular sunset spot.

MACEIÓ (Alagoas) Wanchako

Rua São Francisco de Assiss 93, Jatiúca **Tel** *(082) 3377 6024*

One of Brazil's few Peruvian restaurants, Wanchako is known as one of the finest restaurants in the city. It offers a great variety of typical dishes. The most popular one is the *ceviche* made with tender chunks of fresh fish and seafood cured in lemon juice.

OLINDA (Pernambuco) Don Francesco

Rua Prudente de Morais 358 **Tel** *(081) 3429 3852*

Located in the old part of the city, this restaurant is tucked away among the cobblestoned streets. Run by Francesco and his wife, the kitchen specializes in fresh and simple Italian cooking. The herbs and many of the vegetables come from the couple's organic garden, and the pastas and bread are all home-made.

OLINDA (Pernambuco) Oficina do Sabor

Rua do Amparo 335 **Tel** *(081) 3429 3331*

Oficina do Sabor is a well-known restaurant and is the place in Olinda to try the famous *jerimum* (pumpkin) dishes. The restaurant's signature dish is the *jerimum recheado com camarão ao maracuja*, a baked pumpkin filled with prawn and passionfruit sauce. The terrace offers beautiful views of the city.

OLINDA (Pernambuco) Goya

Rua do Amparo 157 **Tel** *(081) 3439 4875*

The works of local artists decorate this creative space, which fills the interior and terrace of a renovated colonial mansion. The inventive menu gives a regional twist to local seafood dishes, which are creatively served, and include such preparations as shrimp or fish served inside a green coconut.

OLINDA (Pernambuco) Kwetu

Av Manuel Borba 338, Praça do Jacaré **Tel** *(081) 3439 8867*

Situated in a beautiful house on the waterfront, Kwetu offers excellent Belgian cuisine along with standard regional favorites. Try the steamed mussels in white wine or the rabbit stew. On Sundays, the kitchen cooks up a fabulous paella for two.

PENEDO (Alagoas) Forte da Rocheira

Rua da Rocheira 2 **Tel** *(082) 3551 3273*

Overlooking the São Francisco river, Forte da Rocheira, one of the better restaurants in Penedo, is known for its interesting local dishes such as fish stew made with *surubim* fish or *pitu* (freshwater prawns), both found in the local river. For the more adventurous diner, there are alligator meat dishes.

PORTO DE GALINHAS (Pernambuco) Peixe na Telha

Av Beira Mar s/n **Tel** *(081) 3552 1877*

Located just above the seawall, this restaurant offers one of the best ocean views. Although not as well known as Beijupirá, the other restaurant in town, the kitchen serves up delicious fresh seafood and fish. The house specialty, and namesake of the restaurant, is *peixe an telha*, grilled fish served in a clay roof pan.

PORTO DE GALINHAS (Pernambuco) Beijupirá

Rua Beijupirá s/n **Tel** *(081) 3552 2354*

Part of the attraction is the restaurant itself, with its playful, eclectic decorations and its romantic, candlelit atmosphere. However, the food is outstanding as well. The menu blends fresh seafood or chicken with tropical ingredients such as grilled bananas, coconut milk, tangy *pitanga* fruit, and cashew nuts.

RECIFE (Pernambuco) Assucar

Rua da Alfândega 35, Paço Alfândega **Tel** *(081) 3419 7582*

Located on the top floor of the Paço Alfândega shopping center, Assúcar offers great views of the Capibaribe river. The fun and creative menu serves up seafood risottos, regional dishes such as *carne-de-sol* (salted, sundried beef), and grilled fish with banana and carrot purée.

RECIFE (Pernambuco) Bargaço

Av Boa Viagem 670, Praia de Pina **Tel** *(081) 3465 1847*

Specializing in Bahian cuisine, this pleasant restaurant is the best place in town to enjoy a *moqueca*, a fish or shrimp stew that is cooked with coconut milk, or *vatapá*, a type of stew made with shrimp, coconut milk, palm oil, and nuts.

RECIFE (Pernambuco) Leite

Praça Joaquim Nabuco 147, Santo Antônio **Tel** *(081) 3224 7977*

One of Recife's oldest, best, and most traditional restaurants, Leite has been around since 1882. The menu includes some excellent cod fish dishes as well as steak, king prawns grilled in butter, and grilled fish. A taste of the regional dessert *cartola* (banana topped with a slice of cheese, baked with sugar and cinnamon), is a must.

RECIFE (Pernambuco) Tasca

Rua Dom José Lopes 165, Boa Viagem **Tel** *(081) 3326 6309*

The best of Recife's traditional Portuguese restaurants, small and cozy Tasca is done up with beautiful Portuguese decor. Dishes not to miss include oven-baked cod with potatoes, octopus with rice and wine sauce, and lobster grilled in butter.

Key to Price Guide *see p394* **Key to Symbols** *see back cover flap*

RECIFE (Pernambuco) Yolanda

Rua Francisco da Cunha 881, Boa Viagem **Tel** *(081) 3325 5395*

Modern and trendy, Yolanda is well known for its fresh and contemporary cuisine, such as grilled prawns in tamarind sauce with coconut rice. Make sure to try some of the home-made ice creams, a special creation of the restaurant's chef, made with delicious tropical fruit and other ingredients.

PARAÍBA, RIO GRANDE DO NORTE & CEARÁ

CAMPINA GRANDE (Paraíba) Tábua de Carne

Av Manoel Tavares 1040, Alto Branco **Tel** *(083) 3341 1008*

The local specialty of this simple eatery is the *carne-de-sol* (sun-dried beef), made from a variety of prime beef cuts. The beef is sautéed in butter or grilled and generally served with beans, vegetables, manioc, and *pirão*, (fish broth gravy thickened with mandioca).

CANOA QUEBRADA (Ceará) Costa Brava

Rua Dragão do Mar 2022 **Tel** *(088) 3421 7088*

This is a fun and lively restaurant that serves up great Spanish seafood. The paella dishes come in an only-seafood variety or in the traditional combination of pork, chicken, and seafood. Other menu options include grilled steak, pasta, or grilled fish.

CANOA QUEBRADA (Ceará) Natural Bistrô

Rua Dragão do Mar 52 **Tel** *(088) 3421 7162*

The bistro is known for its excellent salads, grilled fish, seafood, and chicken dishes. Healthy alternatives include quality whole-grain pasta with seafood sauce or fish in yogurt sauce. Simple and rustic outdoor seating lend it a laid-back ambience.

FORTALEZA (Ceará) Santa Clara Café

Rua Dragão do Mar 81 **Tel** *(085) 3219 6900*

This great little café located inside Fortaleza's prime cultural center, Centro Cultural, is always bustling with activity. It serves a whole range of delicious organic coffees, desserts, and is a great place to stop for snacks or a light bite. The café is closed on Mondays.

FORTALEZA (Ceará) La Bohème

Rua dos Tabajaras 380, Praia de Iracema **Tel** *(085) 3219 3311*

La Bohème combines an art gallery with restaurant and large outdoor patio. The menu offers mostly seafood, such as grilled lobster, *moqueca* (fish stew with a variety of ingredients), or octopus simmered in traditional Bahian style, with coconut milk and red palm oil.

FORTALEZA (Ceará) Moana

Av Beira Mar 4260, Murucipe **Tel** *(085) 3263 4635*

Located inside the Parthenon Hotel, this restaurant is elegant, modern, and surprisingly affordable. Dishes come with a tropical twist such as the chicken in mango sauce with savory crêpes or the duck in an orange Cointreau sauce. The chocolate desserts are delicious.

FORTALEZA (Ceará) Al Mare Marisco

Av Beira Mar 2821, Praia de Meireles **Tel** *(085) 3263 3888*

Set right on the water, Al Mare offers excellent seafood and fish. A delicious appetizer is the *lula á milanesa* (fried calamari). Main courses include seafood pastas, grilled fish, and the pièce de résistance – the seafood combination, a huge platter of grilled lobster, prawns, fish, octopus, and squid.

GENIPABU (Rio Grande do Norte) Bar 21

Av Beira Mar s/n, Praia Genipabu **Tel** *(084) 3224 2484*

This simple thatched-roof restaurant has a spectacular setting, set on stilts above the high tide line, at the bottom of a large sand dune. The best dish on the menu is the catch of the day. The whole fish is served delicately grilled and coarsely salted. Side dishes include salad and fries.

JERICOACOARA (Ceará) Da Izabel

Rua do Forró s/n **Tel** *(088) 3669 2127*

This simple oceanfront restaurant with a great view specializes in local seafood. Try the *peixada cearense*, a tasty, hearty stew made with fish, vegetables, and coconut milk, which is their specialty. Recommended for lunch. Kitchen closes at 9pm.

JERICOACOARA (Ceará) Leonardo Da Vinci

Rua Principal 40 **Tel** *(088) 3669 2222*

A romantic outdoor Italian restaurant, Leonardo da Vinci is perfect for al fresco dining on balmy evenings. The menu focuses on Italian cuisine and seafood. The penne pasta with crab in a vodka sauce or spaghetti with prawns in creamy curry are favorites. Dishes comfortably serve two people.

JOÃO PESSOA (Paraíba) Mangai $

Av Gen. Edson Ramalho 696, Manaira **Tel** *(083) 3226 1615*

The large buffet at Mangai offers a true cornucopia of Nordestino dishes. Try some grilled goat meat, the delicious *carne-de-sol* (sun-dried beef), or stewed chicken. Vegetarian diners could try the okra or several different dishes prepared with manioc.

JOÃO PESSOA (Paraíba) Ippon $$

Rua Prof. Maria Sales 314, Tambaú **Tel** *(083) 3214 8000*

A sophisticated and modern Japanese restaurant, Ippon attracts João Pessoa's well-heeled. One of the more interesting dishes is the salmon roll with shiitake mushrooms flambéed in *cachaça*. Also on the menu are excellent miso soup, sashimi, and sushi.

NATAL (Rio Grande do Norte) Camarões $$

Av Eng. Roberto Freire 2610, Ponta Negra **Tel** *(084) 3209 2424*

For all things shrimp, there is no better place than Camarões (which means shrimp in Portuguese). The house favorite is the *papa jerimum* (prawns served in a pumpkin). Also worth trying is the dish of champagne prawns sautéed with butter in a champagne-apple sauce. Most dishes are sufficient for two.

NATAL (Rio Grande do Norte) Tábua de Carne $$

Av Senador Dinarte Mariz 229, Ponta Negra **Tel** *(084) 3202 5838*

Not ideal for vegetarians, Tábua de Carne specializes in grilled lamb, pork chops, and the traditional favorite, *carne de sol* (salted sun-dried beef). To sample a little of everything, go for the Tábua platter. Dishes here are made to serve two, and depending on appetite, even three.

NATAL (Rio Grande do Norte) Manary $$$

Rua Francisco Gurgel 9067, Ponta Negra **Tel** *(084) 3219 2900*

The Manary is one of Natal's best seafood restaurants, in a wonderful setting overlooking the beach at Ponta Negra. The signature dish is the *misto fritti di mare*, a scrumptious platter of grilled lobster, shrimp, octopus, mussels, fish, and vegetables.

TIBAÚ DO SUL (Rio Grande do Norte) Camamo Beijupirá $$$$

Estrada Tibaú-Goianinha **Tel** *(084) 3246 4195*

One of the most exclusive and remarkable dining experiences in Northeast Brazil. Guests are met by the host and chef, led to the tables that extend on to the picturesque veranda, and served a leisurely, inventive, and delicious six-course meal. Open only for dinner. Reservations are a must.

PIAUÍ & MARANHÃO

BARREIRINHAS (Piauí) Restaurante Porto Preguiças Resort $$

Estrada do Carnaubal Velho **Tel** *(098) 3349 1220*

The restaurant in the Porto Preguiças Resort is perfect for an elegant night out. The *peixada* fish stew with sea bass is delicious and served in very generous portions. If possible, call a few hours ahead and order the tender juicy lamb simmered in coconut milk.

PRAIA DA PIPA (Piauí) Sorveteria Real de 14 $

Av Baía dos Golfinhos s/n, Shopping Vila Mangueira **Tel** *(084) 3246 2113*

This is a brand-new ice cream parlour located in a small shopping gallery serving old-fashioned cold desserts. For a delicious treat, try the home-made ice creams, milk shakes and fruit smoothies made with a mélange of tropical fruits, coconut milk, and other exotic ingredients.

PRAIA DA PIPA (Piauí) La Provence $$

Rua Gameleira 111 **Tel** *(084) 3246 2280*

One of the only restaurants offering French country cooking in the far reaches of Brazil. Menu highlights include duck prepared with various sauces, including duck breast with plum sauce, foie gras in shallot sauce, and a good wine list with reasonably priced reds.

PRAIA DA PIPA (Piauí) Pacifico $$

Av Baia dos Golfinhos 758 **Tel** *(084) 3246 2585*

The menu at this small bistro is inspired by Mediterranean and Californian cuisine. Dishes are made with fresh fish and seafood, grilled to perfection and served with caper sauce or herb butter, accompanied by organic vegetables and roasted potatoes.

SÃO LUÍS (Maranhão) Antigamente $$

Rua Estrela 220 **Tel** *(098) 3232 3964*

One of the prettiest restaurants in the historic city, Antigamente's large bustling patio offers musical entertainment every night. The menu includes *picanha* (cut of sirloin beef eaten fresh from the grill). The pasta and pizza are also decent. Alternatively, just enjoy a snack and take in the atmosphere.

Key to Price Guide *see p394* **Key to Symbols** *see back cover flap*

SÃO LUIS (Maranhão) Cabana do Sol

 $$

Rua João Damasceno 24, Farol de São Marcos **Tel** *(098) 3235 2586*

This is the place where locals come to enjoy a traditional meal. The best-selling dish is the barbecued *carne-de-sol* (salted, sun-dried beef) served with rice, beans, mashed manioc, and grilled bananas. Known for its huge portions, a single dish serves three to four persons.

SÃO LUIS (Maranhão) Kitaro

$$

Av São Marcos 8, Ponta do Farol **Tel** *(098) 3227 2416*

Overlooking the lake, Kitaro offers excellent Japanese food in a pleasant setting. The menu lists all the usual fare like sushi and sashimi, as well as hot dishes such as *yakisobas* and tempuras. On Friday and Saturday, the kitchen stays open until 3am.

SÃO LUIS (Maranhão) Por Acaso

$$

Av Ana Jansen, Ponta do Farol **Tel** *(098) 3233 5837*

This lively restaurant and bar is buzzing almost every night of the week. The large antipasto self-service buffet allows you to put together your own plate, choosing from the excellent variety of grilled vegetables, cheeses, cold cuts, fresh dips, breads, and salads.

TERESINA Vivenda do Caranguejo

 $

Av Aviador Irapuã Rocha 2071, Jóquei **Tel** *(086) 3233 6228*

Although Teresina is a long way from the sea, Vivenda do Caranguejo offers excellent seafood in a lovely outdoor setting, with tables shaded by overhanging trees. House specialties include sumptuous crab dishes. The restaurant plays live music on Fridays. Closed on Mondays.

TERESINA (Piauí) Carnaúba

 $$

Av Jóquei Clube 1662, Jóquei **Tel** *(086) 3233 6829*

Carnaúba is a pleasant restaurant featuring some of the region's best known dishes such as the *carne-de-sol* (sun-dried beef), grilled lamb, home-made sausage, and *tambaqui* fish, flavored with fresh cilantro, green onions, and fresh bell peppers.

PARÁ & AMAPÁ

ALGODOAL (Amapá) Jardim do Eden

 $

Praia do Farol **Tel** *(091) 9967 9010*

One of the better places to eat on the Algodoal island, Jardim do Eden combines Brazilian and French influences, serving a delectable range of seafood and vegetarian dishes. The seafood is exceptional, and all other dishes are also excellent.

BELÉM (Pará) Remanso do Peixe

$

Trapiche Barao do Triunfo 2590, Casa 64, Marco **Tel** *(091) 3228 2477*

Arguably one of the best restaurants for fish delicacies in the city, the Remanso do Peixe is the place to try one of the excellent local lobsters. Remanso do Peixe is located in a residential mansion with no obvious sign on the door and is only open at weekends.

BELÉM (Pará) La Em Casa

 $$

Av Gov. Jose Malcher 247, Nazaré **Tel** *(091) 3223 4222*

Located in the trendy Nazaré sector, this popular restaurant serves the very best in local Pará cuisine. There is an open-air veranda attached to this restaurant. The dishes are creatively prepared using quality Amazon ingredients. The duck in *tucupi* (cassava) sauce is excellent.

BELÉM (Pará) Restô das Docas

 $$

Boulevard Castilhos Franca **Tel** *(091) 3212 3737*

A trendy, relatively new restaurant located down in the dock area by the Estacao das Docas, this place serves a varied range of local and international dishes. Open through the week until midnight, this popular spot attracts a loyal clientele, who come here for a well-made drink.

MACAPÁ (Amapá) Trapiche Restaurante

$

Rua Azaria Neto 64 **Tel** *(096) 3225 2665*

Located at the end of the Trapiche Eliezer Levy pier *(see p271)*, the Trapiche Restaurante is a great place to come for an afternoon beer. Known for its spectacular view across the Amazon river, especially during the rainy season, this restaurant serves a variety of tasty fish dishes, as well as meat and chicken.

SANTAREM (Pará) Restaurante O Mascote

$

Praça Pescadores 10 **Tel** *(093) 3523 2836*

Offering both indoor and outdoor seating with good views of the Amazon river, O Mascote serves excellent fish dishes. Worth trying is the *tucunaré ao molho de camarão* (peacock bass in shrimp sauce). The restaurant also serves a reasonable lunch buffet.

AMAZONAS, RORAIMA, ACRE & RONDÔNIA

BOA VISTA (Roraima) Tropical Peixada
Rua Ajuricaba & Rua Pedro Rodrigues **Tel** *(095) 3224 6040*

One of Boa Vista's popular restaurants, with an airy outdoor seating area, is a favorite lunch spot. This simple place is highly recommended for its great variety of fish, prepared in every way possible – from hearty Portuguese fish stews to fried and spicy Bahian treats.

MANAUS (Amazonas) Canto da Peixada
Rua Emílio Moreira 1677, Praça 14 **Tel** *(092) 3234 3021*

The best known of fish restaurants in Manaus, Canto da Peixada is the place to try one of the local river specialty dishes. *Tucanaré* and *pirarucu* are among the popular fish dishes eaten here. *Tucupi* (cassava) soup, with a manioc base, is rich in traditional flavors.

MANAUS (Amazonas) Scarola Pizzaria
Rua 10 de Juhlo, at corner of Av Getúlio Vargas **Tel** *(092) 3232 6503*

This popular place is a lively corner café, largely outdoor but with some roof cover for when it rains. Specializing in pizzas, it also offers a good value *comida por kilo* (pay-by-weight) buffet at lunch time, comprising fresh vegetables, rice and beans, and grilled meat and fish.

MANAUS (Amazonas) Churrascaria Bufalo
Av Joaquim Nabuco 628 **Tel** *(092) 3633 3773*

Very popular with locals and tourists alike, Churrascaria Bufalo is somewhere where you can eat as much as you like for a set price. Argentinian-style cuts of meat are brought to your table in large, generous portions. There is also a wide selection of salads, pastas, fish, and other dishes to choose from.

MANAUS (Amazonas) Himawari
Rua10 de Julho 618 **Tel** *(092) 3233 2208*

This is the best of the growing number of Japanese restaurants in Manaus. Well located on a corner opposite the majestic Teatro Amazonas, this distinctive restaurant serves very tasty sushi and traditional Japanese dishes in its spartan, clean white interior.

MANAUS (Amazonas) O Larajinha
Estrada Ponta Negra 10675 **Tel** *(092) 3658 6666*

One of the larger and better known restaurants, O Larajinha has a great bar, and presents interesting musical shows on its outdoor stage. The atmosphere is lively with lots of music and dancing. The food is fine, and the service great, but people come here mainly for fabulous drinks and entertainment. Best after 10pm.

MANAUS (Amazonas) Ristorante Fiorentina
Rua José Paranaguá s/n, Praça da Policia **Tel** *(092) 3215 2233*

A very pleasant Italian restaurant in the Best Western Lord Manaus hotel *(see p383)*, this serves a good range of pasta and spaghetti dishes with meat, vegetables, or fish. Salads combine Italian and Amazon ingredients, and include such dishes as freshly grated *palmito* (heart of palm). The wine is good and the service excellent.

PORTO VELHO (Rondônia) Caravelo do Madeira
Rua José Camacho 104 **Tel** *(069) 3221 6641*

As well as being one of the more upmarket places in town, Caravelo do Madeira is known as the very best of all the many good fish restaurants in Porto Velho. Specializing in river fish, the restaurant offers dishes such as grilled piranha, as well as a variety of fish dishes served in a creamy Brazil nut sauce. Service is good.

PORTO VELHO (Rondônia) Miyoshi
Av Amazonas 1280 **Tel** *(069) 3224 4600*

An excellent fine-dining restaurant offering Far Eastern cuisine, Miyoshi combines Amazon ingredients with traditional Chinese and Japanese recipes to produce delicious meals. Regular Japanese dishes include sushi, sashimi, and tempura. The service is excellent.

PRESIDENTE FIGUEIREDO (Amazonas) Terra Nostra
BR-174, Av Padre Caleri **Tel** *(092) 3324 1597*

A restaurant offering a wide variety of dishes at great prices. Italian pastas are a specialty but Terra Nostra also serves standard Brazilian grilled meat dishes accompanied by beans, rice, and vegetables, as well as excellent fish. The service is very good. Closed on Mondays.

RIO BRANCO (Acre) Point do Pato
Rua Palmeiras 613 **Tel** *(068) 3223 3070*

A popular and trendy restaurant with the locals, young and old alike, Point do Pato specializes in regional dishes but also cooks a range of international meals, such as pastas and pizzas. Among the local specialties, the alligator steaks are surprisingly tender.

Key to Price Guide *see p394* **Key to Symbols** *see back cover flap*

BRASÍLIA, GOIÁS & TOCANTINS

BRASÍLIA Oca da Tribo
 $$

SCES Trecho 2, opposite Agepol **Tel** *(061) 3226 9880*

Housed in a mock Indian log house or *oca*, this restaurant specializes in whole food – natural and unprocessed foods. It has a wide choice of vegetarian dishes, especially at the buffet lunch. There is meat too, and in the evenings, an à la carte menu with Asian and Arabic vegetarian options from Dutch Cordon Bleu trained chef Gabriel Fleijsman.

BRASÍLIA La Torreta
$$$

SCLS 402, Bloco A, Loja 9 **Tel** *(061) 3321 2516*

This is one of the best Spanish restaurants and tapas bars in Brazil. The food, prepared by Spanish Moroccan Isaac Corcias who learnt his trade in Barcelona, is strong on seafood and – in homage to the Brazilian central west – steaks. The wine list has some respectable Spanish bottles.

BRASÍLIA Porcão
$$$$

SCES Trecho 2, Conjunto 35, Lote 2B **Tel** *(061) 3223 2002*

Porcão is Brazil's most upmarket *churrascaria* (steakhouse) chain. All of their restaurants serve enormous quantities of the finest Brazilian meats hot off the barbecue spit. These come with a buffet of salads, vegetables, and a large selection of fresh juices and beers.

BRASÍLIA Alice
$$$$$

SHIN, Qi 11, Conjunto 9, Casa 17, Lago Norte **Tel** *(061) 3368 1099*

The capital's favorite restaurant serves French and Brazilian-French fusion cooking in a large, glass-walled dining room set in tropical gardens. Chef Alice de Castro has won *Veja's* coveted restaurant and chef of the year awards numerous times. The wine list is excellent. Reservations are required.

BRASÍLIA Piantella
$$$$$

SCLS 202, Bloco A, Loja 34, **Tel** *(061) 3224 9408*

Piantella is almost as old as the city, and since its early days has been a favorite of senior politicians. The menu is varied, with traditional Brazilian dishes like *feijoada* (a rich stew of beans and pork), Italian options such as prawn fetuccine, steaks, and river fish. The wine list is excellent.

CHAPADA DOS VEADEIROS (Goiás) Casa da Mama
$$

Rua São José Operário, Alto Paraíso **Tel** *(062) 3446 1362*

An intimate indoor restaurant, Casa da Mama holds a seating capacity for as many as 100 people. Well-prepared regional cuisine, mainly comprising chicken and fish, is served. A variation from the traditional Brazilian fare, pastas also feature on the menu. Decent service.

CIDADE DE GOIÁS (Goiás) Flor do Ipê
 $

Rua Boa Vista 32 **Tel** *(062) 3372 1133*

The most popular restaurant in Cidade de Goiás sits in a small garden next to the river just above the Igreja do Rosário. The motherly owner serves a huge lunchtime buffet spread and à la carte dishes at night. The cooking is typical of Goiás, with plenty of stewed vegetables, meats, and sweet desserts.

PALMAS (Tocantins) Trattoria Toscana
$$

ACSE-2 & Av NS 04 **Tel** *(063) 3028 2795*

An understated bistro-like eatery that stays open till midnight, the trattoria dishes out fine Italian pasta, such as salmon linguine served piping hot, and a few other chicken and beef options. Desserts are highly recommended, such as the divine *petit gâteau di cioccolato*.

PIRENÓPOLIS (Goiás) Caffe e Tarsia
 $$

Rua do Rosário 34 **Tel** *(062) 3331 1274*

Located on the busiest of Pirenópolis's few streets, this restaurant serves a mix of Mediterranean cooking à la carte and generous buffets with cold meats, stews, salads, and home-made bread and pastries at lunchtime. The bar is lively on Fridays and Saturdays when visitors from Brasília gather to drink *cachaças*, dine, and enjoy the live music.

MATO GROSSO & MATO GROSSO DO SUL

BONITO (Mato Grosso do Sul) Cantinho do Peixe
$$

Rua 31 de Março 1918 **Tel** *(067) 3255 3381*

Bonito's best fish restaurant cooks fresh river fish catches from the clearwater rivers that surround the town and from the Pantanal. *Dourado* and *surubim* (catfish) are popular choices, either as grilled filets or cooked in a variety of different sauces.

CAMPO GRANDE (Mato Grosso do Sul) Fogo Caipira   📋 $$
Rua José Antonio 145, JD Piracicaba **Tel** *(067) 3324 1641*

This is the best restaurant in the city for regional food, which is served in generous portions. The menu is meat- and fish- oriented and includes *surubim* (catfish) with tomato and banana, caiman and manioc *moqueca* soup, and huge filets of beef. À la carte dishes can take up to 30 minutes to prepare.

CHAPADA DOS GUIMARÃES (Mato Grosso) Morro dos Ventos $$
Estrada para Campo Verde, Chacara Morro dos Ventos **Tel** *(065) 3301 1030*

The food in this little restaurant, which is hidden away in a private condominium, is very standard Brazilian fare mainly comprising meats, beans, and rice. But the views out over the cliffs at the edge of the Chapada to the interminable plains of Mato Grosso are spectacular and well worth a visit. An entrance fee is charged.

CORUMBÁ (Mato Grosso do Sul) Avalom $
Rua Frei Mariano 499 **Tel** *(067) 3231 4430*

A bustling restaurant bar popular with Corumbá's growing young middle class, Avalom is especially lively after 9pm on Fridays and Saturdays. Draught beer, river fish, pasta, and wood-fired pizzas are served to a busy crowd. There is occasional live music on weekends.

CUIABÁ (Mato Grosso) Al Manzul $$$
Av Arquimedes Pereira Lima, Antiga Estrada do Moinho, Cachoeira das Garças **Tel** *(065) 3663 2237*

Cuiabá has one of the largest communities of ethnic Lebanese and Syrians in Latin America, and this is their favorite restaurant, serving some of the best Arabic food in the country. Dishes include an excellent mezze with *falafel*, *baba ghanoush* and stuffed vine leaves, and good couscous and tagine.

SANTA CATARINA & PARANÁ

CURITIBA (Paraná) Kawiarnia Krakowiak $
Travessa Wellinton de Oliveira Vianna 40 **Tel** *(041) 3026 7462*

Located by the entrance to the Bosque João Paulo II and its Museu Polonês on the Linha de Turismo bus route, this rustic Polish café offers authentic savory dishes and an excellent selection of cakes, making it a popular place for afternoon tea.

CURITIBA (Paraná) Estrela da Terra $$
Rua Jaime Reis 176, Largo do São Francisco **Tel** *(041) 3222 5007*

On offer is a lunchtime buffet of typical dishes from the state of Paraná, including *barreado (see p339)*, a coastal specialty, and rice, beans, pork, and *charque* or jerked beef, the traditional food of cattle drivers, as well as dishes representing the state's various immigrant communties.

CURITIBA (Paraná) Schwarzwald (Bar do Alemão) $$
Rua Claudino dos Santos 63, Largo da Ordem **Tel** *(041) 3223 2585*

Located in the historic center, this perpetually crowded bar and restaurant is equally popular for the range and quality of its beers as for its German food. Sausages and other pork dishes are the mainstays, but the roast duck is also excellent.

CURITIBA (Paraná) Carolla Pizza $$$
Alameda Dom Pedro II 24, Batel **Tel** *(041) 3225 4346*

Baked in wood-fired ovens in front of diners, the pizzas here are excellent, made with top-quality ingredients such as buffalo mozzarella. Along with pizza, there's a varied choice of salads, pasta, and risotto dishes. A very pleasant and informal atmosphere.

CURITIBA (Paraná) Durski $$$
Rua Jaime Reis 254, Largo do São Francisco **Tel** *(041) 3225 7893*

Located in a tastefully renovated late 19th-century building in the historic center, the Durski is the best place in Curitiba to sample Polish and Ukrainian dishes. All the standard dishes are served, such as *borscht, pierogi,* or dumplings, and smoked meats and fish. The food is good and attractively presented, and the service is pleasant.

CURITIBA (Paraná) Barolo Trattoria $$$$
Av Silva Jardim 2487 Água Verde **Tel** *(041) 3243 3430*

An excellent Italian restaurant, Barolo Trattoria is not afraid to occasionally introduce a few Brazilian ingredients such as heart of palm into its recipes. Meat dishes dominate the menu but vegetarians will find plenty of salads and fine pasta dishes to choose from.

CURITIBA (Paraná) Boulevard $$$$
Rua Voluntários da Pátra 539 **Tel** *(041) 3023 8244*

One of Curitiba's best restaurants, Boulevard serves French dishes with Italian accents aimed at Brazilian tastes. The beef dishes in particular are superb. It boasts an outstanding wine list. Formal yet light, airy and with a comfortable environment, Boulevard has consistently been rated as one of the city's top ten places to eat.

CURITIBA (Paraná) Famiglia Caliceti (Bologna) $$$$$

Alameda Dr. Carlos de Carvalho 1367, Batel **Tel** *(041) 3223 7102*

Fresh pasta, made on the premises, is a specialty of this sophisticated Italian restaurant. The *carpaccio de carne* uses beef of the highest quality, and there's an outstanding choice of tortellini and other filled pasta. The Monday to Friday lunch menu is especially good value.

CURITIBA (Paraná) Zea Maïs $$$$$

Rua Barão do Rio Branco 354 **Tel** *(041) 3232 3988*

Creative Brazilian and Mediterranean cooking is served in a contemporary yet comfortable setting. Herbs and fresh-tasting sauces feature prominently in the beautifully-presented dishes. Although some dishes include meat, there are more salads and other vegetarian options on the menu than is typical for a Brazilian restaurant.

FLORIANÓPOLIS (Santa Catarina) Bar do Arante $$

Rua Abelardo Otacilio Gomes 254, Praia do Pântano do Sul **Tel** *(048) 3237 7022*

This bar and restaurant is an important beachside fixture, always crowded at weekends and on summer evenings. It offers reliable fish dishes, including some very tasty Azorean-style stews. A very reasonably priced shellfish buffet is served daily in January and February and on weekends from March to December.

FLORIANÓPOLIS (Santa Catarina) Box 32 $$

Mercado Público Municipal, Centro **Tel** *(048) 3224 5588*

A traditional after-work meeting point for journalists and politicians, this market stall offers drinks and light meals throughout the day from Monday to Saturday. Especially good are the oysters, mussels, and prawns. Savory pastries and salami are also served, accompanied by excellent draught beer and juices.

FLORIANÓPOLIS (Santa Catarina) Ostradamus $$$

Rodovia Baldicero Filomeno 7640, Ribeirão da Ilha **Tel** *(048) 3337 5711*

Harvested from the oyster beds just offshore from the restaurant, Ostradamus specializes in oysters, served steamed, baked, grilled, and raw with a delectable array of sauces and side dishes. Other shellfish are available, as are fish dishes.

FLORIANÓPOLIS (Santa Catarina) Restinga Recanto $$$

Rodovia Rafael da Rocha Pires 2759, Praia de Sambaqui **Tel** *(048) 3235 2093*

With a terrace right on the seashore, the Recanto is one of the most inviting Portuguese and Azorean restaurants in the area. The shellfish are sourced from the house's own oyster and mussel beds. Apart from the shellfish, traditional Azorean fish stews and fresh grilled fish are the house specialties. The dining area exhibits works by local artists.

FLORIANÓPOLIS (Santa Catarina) Chez Altamiro $$$$

Rodovia João Gualberto Soares 7742, Rio Vermelho **Tel** *(048) 3269 7727*

A little piece of France in a quiet rural corner of the north of the island of Santa Catarina, Chez Alatamiro serves good, traditional French food. Options include foie gras, quail, and pheasant, but the seafood dishes are the best choice and the guava soufflé is mouth watering. Reservations are advisable.

FLORIANÓPOLIS (Santa Catarina) Villa Maggione $$$$$

Rua Canto da Amizade 273, Lagoa da Conceição **Tel** *(048) 3232 6859*

Florianópolis's best restaurant, attractively located in a pretty house by the lagoon. The menu is based on Italian dishes but includes influences of Mediterranean cuisines. The Moroccan salad includes a delicious mix of fruity and savory flavors, while the pasta dishes are all fairly good. Reservations are required.

FOZ DO IGUAÇU (Paraná) Bier Kastell $

Av Jorge Schimmelpfeng 362 **Tel** *(045) 3574 5493*

Bier Kastell is a downtown tree-shaded beer garden serving ice cold draught beer (*chope*) and simple German food along the lines of bratwurst, sauerkraut, and potato salad. The restaurant is always lively, and especially popular late into the evenings.

FOZ DO IGUAÇU (Paraná) Clube Maringá $$

Rua Dourado 111, Porto Meira **Tel** *(045) 3527 9683*

Located on the grounds of the local yacht club but open to the public, this restaurant specializes in giant freshwater fish from the Iguaçu and Paraná rivers. The fixed-price buffet of hot and cold Brazilian dishes is excellent value and for a little extra you can request a plate of sashimi. Views of the Iguaçu and Paraná rivers are stunning.

FOZ DO IGUAÇU (Paraná) Empório da Gula $$

Av Brasil 1441 **Tel** *(045) 3574 6191*

One of the-well frequented restaurants located on a beautiful avenue, Empório da Gula offers a variety of cuisine from traditional Brazilian fare to Italian signature dishes. Visit this place for excellent meat, straight from the grill, and regional fish preparations. Reservations are recommended.

FOZ DO IGUAÇU (Paraná) Búfalo Branco $$$

Rua Rebouças 530 **Tel** *(045) 3523 9744*

Located in the heart of downtown Foz, one of the city's best *churrascarias* attracts local residents and visitors alike. The restaurant somehow succeeds in being elegant yet relaxed. There is an all-you-can-eat *rodizio* – the beef is superb – and chicken and local fish are also served. There is also an excellent salad bar.

FOZ DO IGUAÇU (Paraná) Tropical das Cataratas

$$$$

Rodovia das Cataratas Km 24.5, Parque Nacional do Iguaçu **Tel** *(045) 3521 7000*

Based in the hotel of the same name in Iguaçu (see p388), this is the only restaurant worth going out of the way for. There are two distinct rooms, a very varied buffet of hot and cold Brazilian and international dishes, and a grill specializing in à la carte barbecue offerings, usually accompanied by traditional *gaúcho* music.

MORRETES (Paraná) Armazém Romanus

$$

Rua Visconde do Rio Branco 141 **Tel** *(041) 3462 1500*

The best restaurant in Morretes to sample *barreado*, a tasty and rather heavy beef-based dish cooked for many hours in a sealed clay urn, the typical regional dish. A low-fat version is also served, as is fresh, grilled fish served with vegetables.

PARANAGUÁ (Paraná) Danúbio Azul

$$

Rua 15 de Novembro 95 **Tel** *(041) 3423 3255*

Right on the water's edge, this restaurant specializes in fish – and it could hardly be more fresh. There are many choices, ranging from simply grilled to Bahian-style *moquecas*. The restaurant is quite simple and a pleasant place to watch the activity out in the bay beyond the huge glass window.

RIO GRANDE DO SUL

ANTÔNIO PRADO Nostra Cantina

$$

RS-122 para Flores da Cunha Km 122 **Tel** *(054) 3293 4057*

Authentic food of Italian immigrant descendents can be found in this restaurant on the outskirts of Antônio Prado. Simple and hearty fare like roast chicken, salad, polenta, and pasta are made very well. Wine produced by the restaurant's owner is also quite delicious.

BENTO GONÇALVES Casa Valduga

$$$

Linha Leopoldina, Caixa Postal 579 **Tel** *(054) 2105 3122*

One of the foremost producers of quality wine in the Vale dos Vinhedos, Casa Valduga serves typical local-style Italian food such as roast pork and chicken, pasta, polenta, and salads. A bottle of Valduga wine is an essential accompaniment. Reservations are required.

BENTO GONÇALVES Giuseppe

$$$

RS-470 para Porto Alegre Km 221 **Tel** *(054) 3463 8505*

Located in a lovely old stone farmhouse on the road leading to Garibaldi, Giuseppe serves typical regional food, an all-you-can-eat *galeteria*, specializing in *galeto* (the regional dish of roast chicken), polenta, and pasta. The delightful dining room is decorated with pictures and mementos of the Italian immigrants that settled in the area.

CAXIAS DO SUL La Vindima

$$

Rua Borges de Madeiros 446 **Tel** *(054) 3221 1696*

La Vindima is the oldest and best *galeteria* in town. Here, the sage-flavored chicken is roasted in charcoal ovens, which gives them an additional delicate flavor, and are served with radicchio salad, accompanied by bacon, polenta, and other Italian country dishes.

GRAMADO Coelho Café Colonial

$$

Av das Hortênsias 5433 **Tel** *(051) 3286 2538*

A stay in Gramado is incomplete without enjoying this café, which offers colonial high tea featuring salami, cheese, cakes, bread, and fruity jams produced by local German and Italian farmers and bakers. This café is one of the largest in Gramado and offers a particularly large choice of items – all you can eat at a single price.

GRAMADO Mamma Mia

$$$

Av das Hortênsias 3400 **Tel** *(054) 3286 1991*

A well-established *galeteria*, Mamma Mia is a restaurant serving typical food of the nearby Italian farmers. Grilled chicken forms the heart of the meal, but the all-you-can-eat menu includes a range of salads, soups, pastas, and polenta.

GRAMADO Chez Pierre

$$$$

Av Borges de Medeiros 3022 **Tel** *(054) 3286 2057*

This romantic little restaurant has a cozy mock-Swiss atmosphere and does offer cheese fondues, but a far more delicious dish is the fondue bourguignonne (meat fondue) served with a selection of tasty dips. This is a popular item in Rio Grande do Sul where fondue is especially appreciated. Raclettes and fresh trout are also served.

GRAMADO La Caceria

$$$$$

Av Borges de Medeiros 3166 **Tel** *(054) 3286 2057*

An elegant restaurant in the style of a German hunting lodge , La Caceria is located in Hotel Casa da Montanha. The specialty here is game such as boar, wild duck, partridge, pheasant, and rabbit. Fruit-based sauces are typically served with the flavorsome meat. The wine list – including Brazilian and foreign wines – is one of the best in town.

NOVA PETRÓPOLIS Opa's Kaffeehaus

Rua João Leão 96 **Tel** *(054) 3281 1273*

Located in a quiet old house, Opa serves what in Southern Brazil is called Café Colonial – a high tea based on ingredients and traditional recipes of the immigrant-descended local farmers. For a fixed price, a huge meal is presented, consisting of over 45 items, such as smoked sausage and ham, breads, jams, and German-style cakes.

PORTO ALEGRE Via Vêneto

Rua José de Alencar 501, Menino Deus **Tel** *(051) 3233 1400*

Via Vênato is a large, inexpensive *galeteria* with a lively, informal atmosphere. The restaurant serves the typical Italian food of Rio Grande do Sul. For a fixed price a huge meal is on offer, including roast chicken, fried polenta, soup, salads, and pasta.

PORTO ALEGRE Baumbach

Av Pará 1324, São Geraldo **Tel** *(051) 3346 4322*

Baumbach is one of Porto Alegre's best German restaurants. Recipes from German communities in the interior of the state have been adapted for more sophisticated big-city tastes. The range of duck dishes is especially good, but *eisbein* (pork knuckle), *bockwurst*, and other pork dishes are also delicious.

PORTO ALEGRE Galpão Crioulo

Parque Mauricio Sirotsky Sobrinho s/n **Tel** *(051) 3226 8194*

Waiters wearing typical *gaúcho* garb serve the all-you-can-eat (*rodizio*) round of meat, mainly cuts of beef but also chicken, lamb, and pork. A particular attraction of this downtown *churrascaria*, located in a huge barn-like structure, are the lunch and dinner performances by a traditional *gaúcho* dance ensemble.

PORTO ALEGRE Na Brasa

Rua Ramiro Barceles 389, Floresta **Tel** *(051) 3225 2205*

Although ordinary-looking, Na Brasa is widely considered one of the best *churrascarias* in Porto Alegre. All-you-can-eat (*rodizio*) meat of all kinds, with 20 different cuts of grilled meat and a superb *por kilo* salad bar (pay by weight), and dozens of other hot and cold dishes.

PORTO ALEGRE Polska Restauracja

Rua João Guimarães 377, Santa Cecilia **Tel** *(051) 3333 2589*

This cozy Polish restaurant is attractively decorated with old photographs, antiques, and handicrafts from Poland. The roast duck is cooked to perfection and other standard Polish dishes such as *bigos* (a stew of cabbage and meat) are on the menu. Hearty food that is perfect for a cold Porto Alegre winter's evening.

PORTO ALEGRE Sálvia Pizza

Rua Comendador Caminha 338, Moinhos de Vento **Tel** *(051) 3268 0000*

The thin-crust pizzas baked in wood-fired ovens at Sálvia Pizza are are some of the best in Porto Alegre. The toppings are prepared with the finest of ingredients. Live local bands perform every evening, and the place is especially popular with young people.

PORTO ALEGRE Sanduíche Voador

Praça Mauricio Cardoso 23, Moinhos de Vento **Tel** *(051) 3395 4717*

A contemporary bistro with an attractive terrace, this has a central location in the fashionable Moinhos de Vento suburb. Beautifully presented sandwiches and salads are its mainstays, but the seasonal menu also includes light hot dishes. Excellent also for quality ice creams and cakes.

PORTO ALEGRE Al Dente

Rua Mata Bacelar 210, Auxiliadora **Tel** *(051) 3343 1841*

A wonderful, intimate, and very friendly restaurant serving Northern Italian fare. Freshly made pasta is the staple, but gnocchi and risotti are also served, and there is a strong emphasis on dairy produce, with a delectable array of cheese.

PORTO ALEGRE Koh Pee Pee

Rua Schiller 83, Moinhos de Vento **Tel** *(051) 3333 5150*

A stylish and remarkably authentic Thai restaurant. The food here is cooked in an open, central position, with the colours and activity creating quite an exciting spectacle. Koh Pee Pee offers very good vegetarian options and all the dishes are delicious and beautifully presented. Reservations are advisable.

PORTO ALEGRE Puppi Baggio

Rua Dinarte Ribeiro 36, Moinhos de Vento **Tel** *(051) 3346 3630*

A charming Italian restaurant with a rustic-looking interior designed to be reminiscent of an immigrant's home. The baked polenta with bacon is fresh, and the pasta and gnocchi are served with a choice of equally fresh sauces, such as red pepper and prawn, and garlic and white wine.

PORTO ALEGRE Chez Philippe

Av Independência 1005, Independência **Tel** *(051) 3312 5333*

Situated in an imposing early 20th-century mansion with an elegant interior, Chez Philippe offers contemporary French cuisine, opting, where possible, for distinctly local ingredients, giving many of the dishes an unapologetically Brazilian accent. The fish in tomato, coconut, and heart of palm sauce is delicious and the beef dishes are all good.

SHOPPING IN BRAZIL

The most exciting aspect of shopping in Brazil is that it never fails to surprise visitors with its amazing variety. Major cities, such as Rio *(see pp90–91)* and São Paulo *(pp150–51)*, boast expansive, world-class shopping centers that have everything from sophisticated boutiques to high-tech items. Craft centers, artisans' houses, and *ateliers* (workshops) showcase the unique, attractive products manufactured by the local people. Colorful street markets and *camelódromos* offer a truly exhilarating Brazilian shopping experience. The prices are, by and large, reasonable, and large items can be shipped home. In most state capitals and tourist areas the opening hours are extended for convenience.

OPENING HOURS

Business hours are normally from 8am until 6pm on weekdays and from 8am to 1pm on Saturdays. In large cities, tourist areas, and resorts, opening hours are more flexible. Stores in central areas extend their opening hours until 7 or 8pm on weekdays and 4pm on Saturdays. Shopping centers are open from 10am to 10pm from Monday to Saturday. In resorts and tourist areas, even small stores are open daily until midnight during the high season.

HOW TO PAY

Major credit cards are accepted in most stores in large cities and resorts, though there may be a minimum spend value (about R$50). US dollars are sometimes accepted in tourist areas, but in small towns it is best to pay in cash using the *real (see p431)*.

Interior of an upmarket clothing store in Jardins, São Paulo

SHOPPING CENTERS & HYPERMARKETS

More convenient than street stores and offering much more than shopping alone, shopping centers have multiplied in the last few years. Fast-food chains and restaurants, department stores and boutiques, clothes repair, cobblers, and other services can all now be found within one complex. A combination of supermarket and department store, hypermarkets are often located on main roads and the outskirts of towns. Apart from the ubiquitous local chain, Extra, foreign names such as Wal-Mart and Carrefour also have a formidable presence in Brazil.

In resorts, smaller shopping centers sell souvenirs and fashionable items. Department stores such as C&A and Casas Pernambucanas have found their way into shopping centers, although they exist more prominently as street shops in the large city centers.

MARKETS & CAMELÓDROMOS

Almost every medium-size city in Brazil has its own special market, some located in beautiful historical buildings. Lively and picturesque, these markets sell an array of fresh products from meat and fish to fruit and cheese. Authentic regional food, typical sweets, and crafts

Ver o Peso, Belém's picturesque waterfront *mercado* (market)

can also be found here. Ver o Peso market in Belém *(see p268)* and public markets in Olinda (Pernambuco), as well as Porto Alegre (Rio Grande do Sul) are good examples.

Everywhere in Brazil, street traders or *camelôs* sell goods on improvised stands, or at places called *camelódromos*. A wide range of items, from clothes to electronics of fairly decent quality, are sold at reasonably reduced prices.

It is possible for shoppers to bargain at open-air markets. Vendors will often start at double the price of products, but with a little skill and some charm on the part of the buyer, this can be reduced. Be on guard in crowded street markets, as pickpockets are not uncommon. Be discreet when taking out money to pay.

Traditional musical instruments and masks for sale in Bahia

ART & CRAFTS

Every region in Brazil has its own distinctive handicrafts. The use of specific raw materials makes every piece of work unique. The best way to buy these pieces is to go directly to the *ateliers*. Tourist information offices can provide the addresses. Craft centers, where artists can be seen at work, offer lower prices than the upmarket souvenir shops.

Typical Amazonian crafts include indigenous masks, jewelry, plume helmets, basketwork, and bows and arrows in Manaus, Belém, and Santarém. Attractive replicas of Marajoara pottery are sold in Belém and the Ilha de Marajó. Delicate lacework

is found in all northeastern states, while Pernambuco and Bahia are famed for their fine ceramics.

Woven items, hand-crafted furniture, and Arraiolo tapestry are popular in Minas Gerais. In the south, Santa Catarina's crystalware is exceptional. In the state of Rio Grande do Sul, it is worth looking for good-quality woolen items in Gramado and Caxias do Sul.

GEMS

Brazil has 60 percent of the world's gem reserves. It is the world's largest exporter of rough-cut gems and the sixth largest exporter of worked gems. The variety and quantity of precious stones are spectacular. Amethyst, citrine, diamond, emerald, opal, and royal topaz are just a few of the gems that Brazil is famous for. Rough and worked pieces can be bought in the cities of Ouro Preto (Minas Gerais), Cuiabá (Mato Grosso), Salvador and Chapada Diamantina (Bahia), and Porto Alegre. Designed jewelry can also be found in these places, as well as in São Paulo and Rio de Janeiro.

Although gems are largely sold in open-air markets, it is best to buy them at stores offering origin warranty certificates, which gives the weight (in carats), quality, origin, and – in the case of readymade jewelry – the characteristics of any precious metal used.

Salesman displaying gems, Howard Stern Jewellers, Ipanema

FOOD & DRINK

Brazil is known for its rich variety of conserves, dried fruits, and cakes *(see pp392–3)*. Another favorite is fruit – figs, citron ciders, pineapples, and oranges – crystallized in compôte. These delicacies can be bought at public markets, craft centers, and confectioners' shops, found everywhere in Brazil.

An immensely popular beverage, *cachaça* (sugarcane liquor) is produced all over the country and locally distilled *(see p393)*. The best *cachaça* comes from Minas Gerais, Rio de Janeiro, Bahia, Pernambuco, and Ceará. It can also be bought at craft centers, local bars, and in hypermarkets in the larger cities.

Excellent coffee and gourmet blends are easily available in all big cities in Brazil. Look out for the ABIC seal on the packets, as this certifies the coffee quality.

Cachaça **emporium in Paraty, with a large array of different types for sale**

ENTERTAINMENT IN BRAZIL

Entertainment in Brazil varies according to the region and the city, but one thing is certain – Brazilians love going to bars, cafés, or *botecos* (a kind of bar with snacks and an old-fashioned atmosphere) to meet with friends and drink cold beer. This usually happens before and after other activities such as watching movies, plays, and shows. Dancing is another popular

DJ Zod playing in a nightclub

activity with Brazilians. In a country known for the richness of its rhythms, there are venues catering to all kinds of music and dancing, from *forró*, *samba*, and *axé* to techno and electronic music. Outdoor activities, such as soccer and volleyball, are national pastimes. Water parks, beaches, and public gardens are also good places to enjoy the warm weather and outdoor activities.

INFORMATION & BOOKING

Most Brazilian shows, such as plays and operas, do not run for very long and tickets must be booked quickly. Rio and São Paulo have specific magazines with a good listing of events and entertainment *(see p95 & p153)*. In most other Brazilian cities, local newspapers are the best way to find out what's on. They usually come with special sections or supplements on Fridays or on weekends showing cinema, theater, and other entertainment listings.

Only the most active theaters and concert houses provide listings on a website on the Internet. In some big cities, shows can also be booked via Ticketmaster using Visa, MasterCard, and American Express, for a small additional service fee. Hotel concierges can often be helpful and informative when it comes to finding out what shows are on and booking them as well.

DISCOUNT TICKETS & FREE EVENTS

In general, students and seniors (over 60) get a 50 percent discount for most events. The conditions for students vary from state to state. In Rio de Janeiro, any person under the age of 21 gets a discount. In other cities, students must show their university identity card. There are many free events at museums and cultural centers, but as they always become crowded quickly, arriving early is wise.

Almost every city has one or more cultural centers. Supported by the government or by private companies, they often offer cheap tickets or free access to a variety of events, such as plays, dance, and art exhibitions, performed by professional or amateur companies.

PERFORMING ARTS

Theater and dance shows are popular in bigger cities in Brazil, where the theaters feature regular shows. At some resorts, dance or musical performances take place during the high season, or during specific summer or winter festivals. Most plays run only for a season. There is a fair amount of traditional and experimental theater, many dance performances, and

chamber and classical music recitals to attend. Some performances have become annual traditions, such as *The Passion of Christ* play staged during the Passion Week at an open-air theater in Nova Jerusalém *(see p223)* in the state of Pernambuco. Another big performance takes place every January in São Vicente *(see p169)*, retelling the story of the foundation the town.

Musical shows are as prolific in Brazil. They take place at venues ranging from bars and theaters to sophisticated cultural centers. During music festivals, concerts are held in open-air areas, such as squares, public parks, or beaches. The really big and famous acts, which can be costly, usually perform in the stadia and require advance booking of tickets.

A view of the private boxes in the Teatro Amazonas, Manaus *(see pp282–3)*

Inside Rio City's world-famous soccer stadium, Estádio Maracanã *(see p84)*

CINEMA

In larger cities, modern multiplex cinemas, most of which are located in shopping centers, mainly feature recent Hollywood and European, as well as good Brazilian films. There are also a few good cineclubs, especially in Rio and São Paulo, that screen feature- and short-film festivals, often screening films with English subtitles. There are three main cinema chains operating in Brazil – United Cinemas International (UCI), Cinemark, and the Brazilian Playarte. They offer facilities for disabled people and sell tickets in advance via the Internet or at the box office.

BARS, CAFÉS & BOTECOS

Nightlife is always exciting in large cities, resorts, and tourist areas. Bars are open through the week, usually after 6pm until 1 or 2am (some continue until sunrise, especially those on the beaches); some are open 24 hours. Most cities offer a wide variety of bars to visit – dance bars, bars with live music, and in the bigger cities, gay and lesbian bars. *Botecos* – traditionally *carioca* bars known for their simplicity and good snacks – have now been adopted by many cities and have increased in popularity and sophistication.

Happy hour is an institution in many of the larger cities. It begins at 6pm and extends until 9 or 10pm, after which many people carry on at all-night bars.

Bars and kiosks on and near the beaches are often crowded and buzzing with activity, through the week, and especially on weekends. Cities without beaches generally make do with tables and chairs spread over the sidewalks with impromptu cafés sprouting up outside restaurants.

SOCCER MATCHES

Soccer is a national passion – across Brazil there are 800 soccer clubs, 13,000 amateur teams, and 300 stadia, including Rio City's Estádio Maracanã *(see p84)*, one of the largest in the world. There are many championships through the year, with matches taking place on Wednesdays, Thursdays, and weekends.

It is not always easy to get a ticket for these games, and very often there are immense queues to purchase tickets. Clubs and stadia do not sell tickets on the Internet. There are some websites that sell tickets online, provided this is done well in advance. Most travel agencies would be able to provide information on this.

GARDENS & THEME PARKS

Public gardens and parks are always crowded on weekends. Many of them offer jogging tracks, roller-skating rinks, sports courts for playing soccer, volleyball, basketball, tennis, and other games.

Theme parks are becoming increasingly popular everywhere in Brazil. Nowadays, most of these parks include some form of outdoor activity, such as swimming pools, water slides, water tobogganing, horse-riding, and roller-coasters.

Live music in the popular Carioca da Temin, Lapa district, Rio de Janeiro

SPECIALIZED HOLIDAYS & OUTDOOR ACTIVITIES

The climate and great variety of landscapes – mountains, flatlands, waterfalls, and forests – make Brazil an outstanding outdoor destination. This ecological paradise offers great opportunities to observe its fascinating flora and fauna, or to indulge in adventure sports that allow close contact with the environment. Visitors can choose from a range of thrilling activities such as rappeling down cliffs, canyoning, or climbing peaks in spectacular settings. However, the infrastructure varies from region to region. It is best to get in touch with reputed tour operators licensed by Embratur, a government tourism agency. Other interesting activities may involve learning to dance to the beautiful rhythms of *forró* and *samba*, performing the legendary *capoeira*, or even joining a game of soccer.

ECOTOURISM

Brazil's rich and varied ecosystem has much to offer, and ecotourism is becoming a popular a form of tourism. Visitors can capture on film the splendor of the Amazon rainforest near Manaus, or enjoy excursions into the forest organized by jungle lodges. Similar eco-tours can also be undertaken from Belém or Santarém (Pará). **Amazon Explorers** and **Selvatur** are the two agencies based in Manaus; in Belém contact **Paratur**.

Serra da Capivara (see pp248–9) and Sete Cidades parks (Piauí) (see p249) offer amazing rock formations, while Chapada Diamantina in Bahia (see pp204–205) and Chapada dos Veadeiros (see pp312–13) in Goiás have good trekking trails, forested areas, and scenic waterfalls. National parks such as Serra dos Órgãos (see p115), Parque Nacional do Itatiaia (see p111) and Aparados da

Serra (see p358), and natural reserves such as Ilha do Cardoso (see p171) offer a broad range of biodiversity. Look for **Fazenda Palomas** or contact **Fellini Turismo** for special rural tours in Rio Grande do Sul.

BIRD-WATCHING & SAFARIS

Home to almost a fifth of the world's bird population, Brazil offers a surfeit of bird-watching excursions. **Birding Brasil Turismo**, based in Manaus, provides good deals. **Iara Turismo** conducts special programs. **Estação Ecológica Santa Lúcia**, run by renowned naturalist Augusto Ruschi, organizes regular bird-watching. **Reserva Natural da Vale do Rio Doce** offers about 400 species of birds and more than 1,500 types of butterflies. Ornithologist **Edson Endrigo** organizes tours to Parque Nacional Itatiaia (see p111) and Ubatuba. A typical safari can be experienced at Jalapão State Park (see p310–11). The travel agency **Korubo Expedições** uses a truck with hatches for professional photo equipment.

Spectacular golden sand dunes in Jalapão

OFF-ROAD DRIVING

Many beautiful sites in Brazil are accessible only by off-road vehicles. The Transpantaneira road (Pantanal) and the Estrada Park road are attractions in themselves, allowing passengers to leisurely observe the flora and fauna. The Transpantaneira extends 93 miles (149 km) from Poconé to Porto Jofre in Mato Grosso and has 126 wooden bridges to cross. Many inns and farms receive visitors along this road. Stretching 73 miles (117 km), the Estrada Park road links Corumbá to Buraco

The rare and striking scarlet ibises that inhabit the Ilha de Marajó (see p270)

das Piranhas (Piranha's Hole) in the state of Mato Grosso do Sul. Another enjoyable road experience is to cross Jalapão State Park, a wonderful contrast of golden dunes and gushing waterfalls. **Korubo Expedições** offers week-long packages leaving from Palmas. The Northeast region's off-road adventure *Rota das Dunas* (Dunes Route) runs from Fortaleza (Ceará) to São Luís (Maranhão), passing through Jericoacoara Beach and Delta do Parnaíba (a group of 80 islands) and Parque Nacional dos Lençóis Maranhenses *(see pp250–51)*. For bookings contact **Dunnas Expedições** and **Jeri Off-Road**.

CYCLING & BIKING

Cycling and mountain biking have been attracting increasing numbers of enthusiasts to Brazil. Many tour operators rent bikes, and provide necessary equipment, food, and accommodation. Trancoso (Bahia) is the starting point of the Discovery Route – a crossing that passes through wonderful beaches. Contact **Sampa Bikers** and **Natural Cicloturismo** for details.

Mountain biking is an interesting way to discover the attractions of Florianópolis (Santa Catarina). There are 30 trails that traverse its 42 beaches, lakes, and stunning landscape. These and other options in the state can be found at **Caminhos do Sertão**

Ecotourism by bicycle, Parque Nacional dos Lençóis Maranhenses

and **Ecos da Serra**. Cycling tours near the Parque Nacional Aparados da Serra covering the cities of Gramado, Canela, and the Vale dos Vinhedos *(see p355)* are organized by **Casa da Montanha Adventures**. Accommodation can be found at the Parador Casa da Montanha, a kind of luxurious camping site.

WATER SPORTS

Vast stretches of beach, and an abundance of rivers, lakes, and waterfalls make water sports widely available and accessible in Brazil. Fernando de Noronha (Pernambuco) and Itacaré (Bahia) are hot destinations for water sports such as snorkeling, surfing, and wind surfing. Búzios and Rio (Rio de Janeiro), and Ubatuba and Guarujá (São Paulo) are easier, while Praia

Joaquinas and other beaches in Florianópolis pose more challenging water sports options *(see pp346–7)*.

The country has many scuba diving options. **PDIC Brasil** (Professional Diving Instructor's Corporation) is a good place to contact. Rio de Janeiro state, Cabo Frio, Angra dos Reis, Paraty, and Ilhabela in São Paulo are outstanding places for diving and exploring shipwrecks. Beaches in the Northeast are a snorkeler's paradise.

Among the sail sports, kitesurf reigns in Ceará's beaches and lakes near Jericoacoara. **Kite Club Preá** provides facilities for intermediate to advanced kiters.

Rafting and canoeing enthusiasts should head to Brotas and Socorro, in São Paulo; Três Rios, in Rio de Janeiro; Domingos Martins, in Espírito Santo; Jaguariaíva and Tibagi, in Paraná; Apiúna, in Santa Catarina; and Rio Cristlino, in the Amazon rainforest of Mato Grosso.

Cascading and canyoning can be challenging, but highly enjoyable, in the waterfalls of Chapada dos Veadeiros in Goiás and Cipó mountains, in Minas Gerais where visitors can get in touch with **ABETA (Brazilian Adventure Travel Association)**. Other agencies to contact for water sports include **Artmarina** and **Tropical Port Turismo Náutico**.

For those who enjoy fishing, **Clube de Pesca Cananéia** helps organize expeditions. This club can also make arragements for the obligatory fishing license.

Canoeing on the Rio Cristalino near Cristalino Jungle Lodge *(see p319)*

LANGUAGE & CULTURE

Almost 70 universities in the country offer Portuguese classes to foreign students. Many of these courses are now open to visitors. Some language schools also offer flexible Portuguese courses, which can stretch from one week to many months. These lessons may include lectures on Brazilian culture and guided tours of museums and galleries. Some of them prepare for the Portuguese Proficiency Certificate (CELPE-Bras), the Portuguese language qualification granted by the **Ministério da Educação**. **Excellence Idiomas**, **Idiomas to Go**, and **Diálogo Language School** are some of the better private school options.

MUSIC & DANCE

The sensuous dance forms of Brazil have evoked a lot of interest worldwide. With their natural hospitality Brazilians are easily motivated to teach dance steps at bars, dance houses, parties, and local performances. But you can also arrange to take professional dancing classes in the cities. In Rio de Janeiro, it is possible to learn with the famous dancer Carlinhos de Jesus at **Casa de Dança**. In

Couples dancing the *forró* on a festive occasion

São Paulo, one can visit **Avenida Club** and take *samba* lessons from professional dancers. Diálogo Language School conducts workshops on dancing and singing to Brazilian rhythms, which may be tied in with Portuguese language classes. These lessons are a good way to familiarize oneself with the most representative artists of Brazilian popular music.

SOCCER

It is possible to arrange day and residential soccer camps, as well as team and individual training sessions or family packages. The coaching programs vary from a week to several months and may include friendly games and tournaments for players between 6 and 18 years of

age. Some good options are **Central de Intercambio** in São Paulo City, **Cruzeiro Esporte Clube** in Belo Horizonte (Minas Gerais), and **Athletic Center Football Club**, a soccer academy located in Poços de Caldas (Minas Gerais). The Athletic Center also organizes special tours involving visits to famous clubs and stadia.

CAPOEIRA CLASSES

The amalgam of acrobatic movements, rhythm, music, and song make *capoeira* (see p199) a big draw. Almost every city has an academy. **Zebra & Pepi** take lessons on the Itacaré beaches. In Salvador, **Filhos de Bimba** is one of the best and most famous *capoeira* schools. With several branches outside Brazil, it strives to keep alive the regional spirit of *capoeira*.

VOLUNTEER PROGRAMS

Volunteers can work in non-profit organizations contributing in the field of education, child welfare, health, ecology, and the environment. This is a good way of getting to know local people, and at the same time making a social contribution. These programs are open to adults of any age, and may include homestay with a Brazilian family. The program duration commonly varies from two to ten months. To enroll contact **Diálogo Language School**, **World Study**, **AFS Intercultura Brasil**, or **BIL Intercâmbios**. For all such programs, a basic knowledge of Portuguese is required.

A rigorous soccer training session, Ipanema beach, Rio de Janeiro City

DIRECTORY

ECOTOURISM

Amazon Explorers
Av Djalma Batista 2100, Sala 10, Manaus, Amazonas. *Tel (031) 3261 5707.* www.abeta.com.br

Fazenda Palomas
BR-158 Santana do Livramento, Rio Grande do Sul. *Tel (055) 3242 2551.* www.fazendapalomas.com

Fellini Turismo
Rua Gen Bento Martins, 24 Conj. 401, Porto Alegre, Rio Grande do Sul. *Tel (051) 3228 6388.*

Paratur
Praça Maestro Waldemar Henrique, Belém, Pará. *Tel (091) 3212 0669.* www.paratur.pa.gov.br

Selvatur
Rua Floriano Peixoto 17, Sala 1, Manaus, Amazonas. *Tel (092) 3622 1191, 3622 2577.* www.selvatur.com.br

BIRD-WATCHING & SAFARIS

Birding Brasil Turismo
Conjunto Acariquara 214, Manaus, Amazonas. *Tel (092) 3638 4540.* www.birdingbraziltours.com

Edson Endrigo
Rua Antonio Aggio 1296/11, São Paulo. *Tel (011) 3742 8374.* www.avesfoto.com.br

Estação Ecológica Santa Lúcia
Av José Ruschi 4, Museu Mello Leitão, Santa Teresa, Espírito Santo. *Tel (027) 3259 1182.*

Iara Turismo
Rua Jerônimo Pimentel 82, Belém, Pará. *Tel (091) 4006 3850.*

Korubo Expedições
Rua Traipu 260, São Paulo. *Tel (011) 3667 5053.*

Reserva Natural da Vale do Rio Doce
BR-101 Km 120, Linhares, Espírito Santo. *Tel (027) 3371 9797.* www.cvrd.com.br/linhares

OFF-ROAD DRIVING

Dunnas Expedições
Av Desembargador Moreira 2001, Fortaleza, Ceará. *Tel (085) 3264 2514.*

Jeri Off-Road
Rua Principal 208, Jericoacoara, Ceará. *Tel (088) 3669 2268.* www.jeri.tur.br

CYCLING & BIKING

Caminhos do Sertão
Rua Caminho do Arvoredo 169, Rio Vermelho, Florianópolis, Santa Catarina. *Tel (048) 3234 9527.* www.caminhosdosertao.com.br

Casa da Montanha Adventures
Estra do Faxinal/Morro Agudo, Cambará do Sul, Rio Grande do Sul. *Tel (054) 3295 7575.* www.paradorcasadamontanha.com.br

Ecos da Serra
Rua Presidente Lincoln 76, Lages, Santa Catarina. *Tel (049) 9972 9672.* www.ecosdaserra.com.br

Natural Cicloturismo
Praça do Bosque, Trancoso, Bahia. *Tel (073) 3668 1955.*

Sampa Bikers
Rua Baluarte 672, São Paulo. *Tel (011) 3045 2722.* www.sampabikers.com.br

WATER SPORTS

ABETA (Brazilian Adventure Travel Trade Association)
Rua Sergipe 1333, Belo Horizonte, Minas Gerais. *Tel (031) 3261 5707.* www.abeta.com.br

Artmarina
Av Cel. Augusto Carvalho 37, Canavieiras, Bahia. *Tel (073) 3284 1262.* www.artmarina.com.br

Clube de Pesca Cananéia
Rua João Maciel, Porto Cubatão, Cananéia, São Paulo. *Tel (013) 3851 6117.* www.pescacananeia.com.br

Kite Club Preá
Preá Villa, Jericoacoara, Ceará. *Tel (088) 3669 2359.* www.kiteclubprea.com

PDIC Brasil (Professional Diving Instructors Corporation)
Av Presidente Vargas 446, Grupo 1006, Rio de Janeiro. *Tel (021) 2263 8068.* www.pdic.com.br

Tropical Port Turismo Náutico
Rua Desembargador Sampaio, 40/102, Praia do Canto, Vitória. *Tel (027) 2123 0937.* www.tropicalport.com.br

LANGUAGE & CULTURE

Diálogo Language School
Rua João Ponde 240, Barra, Salvador, Bahia. *Tel (071) 3264 0007.* www.dialogo-brazilstudy.com

Excellence Idiomas
Av Rio Branco 181, Sala 103, Rio de Janeiro. *Tel (021) 2533 0065.* www.excellenceidiomas.com.br

Idiomas to Go
Al Jauaperi 1020, São Paulo. *Tel (011) 5052 4802.* www.idiomastogo.com.br

Ministério da Educação
Esplanada dos Ministérios, Bloco L, Sala 227, Brasília. *Tel (061) 2104 8006.* www.mec.gov.br/sesu

MUSIC & DANCE

Avenida Club
Av Pedroso de Moraes 1036, São Paulo. *Tel (011) 3814 7383.* www.avenidaclub.com.br

Casa de Dança
Rua Álvaro Ramos 11, Botafogo, Rio de Janeiro. *Tel (021) 2541 6186.* www.carlinhosdejesus.com.br

SOCCER

Athletic Center Football Club
Rua Antonio Benedito Silvério 40, Poços de Caldas, Minas Gerais. *Tel (035) 3714 3617.*

Central de Intercambio
Praça Charles Miller 152, São Paulo. *Tel (011) 3677 3600.* www.ci.com.br

Cruzeiro Esporte Clube
Av Otacílio Negrão de Lima 7100, Bairro Bandeirante, Belo Horizonte. www.cruzeiro.com.br

CAPOEIRA CLASSES

Filhos de Bimba
Rua Gregório de Mattos 51, Pelourinho, Salvador, Bahia. *Tel (071) 3322 5082.*

Zebra & Pepi
Rua Pedro Longo 385, Pituba, Itacaré, Bahia. *Tel (073) 3251 2354.*

VOLUNTEER PROGRAMS

AFS Intercultura Brasil
Av do Ouvidor, Rio de Janeiro. *Tel (021) 2224 4464.*

BIL Intercâmbios
Rua do Orfanato 760, São Paulo. *Tel (011) 6161 7799.* www.bil.com.br

World Study
Av do Contorno 4480, Sala 1509, Belo Horizonte, Minas Gerias. *Tel (031) 3224 4293.* www.worldstudy.com.br

SURVIVAL GUIDE

PRACTICAL INFORMATION

Tourism is one of the fastest growing industries in Brazil, and for the past decade, the country has been investing heavily in new airports, hotels, and other facilities designed to make the country more attractive to visitors. Brazil offers a variety of travel experiences for all ages and tastes. The sheer size of Brazil makes air travel almost a necessity for those interested in exploring beyond

Tourist information sign

just one region. All major tourist destinations are very well set up to receive international visitors. English and Spanish are generally spoken by those who work in the tourism industry. However, very few other Brazilians speak English. Fortunately, the friendliness and outgoing nature of the people more than makes up for these challenges and Brazilians overall are very helpful in assisting foreigners.

WHEN TO GO

High season in Brazil runs from Christmas to Carnaval (held in February or early March). Many musical and cultural events take place in these months. Although not as busy, a second peak season is during July and August when schools and universities have their winter break and many Europeans and North Americans visit on their summer holidays. The best times of year for lower prices and fewer travelers are the low seasons from March to May and September to November.

WHAT TO TAKE

Dress standards in Brazil seem largely a matter of personal taste. A sarong or sheet sleeping bag is invaluable for use as a towel, a bedsheet, or beach towel. Bring a first-aid kit, raincoat, sun hat, penknife, flashlight, wax earplugs, insect repellent,

A local travel agency with Internet facilities, Morro de São Paulo

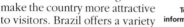
◁ **Carnaval in Rio City in 2006**

eye mask for sleeping on buses, and a chain for securing luggage to bus or train seats. For a jungle trip, a hammock is a good idea.

VISAS & PASSPORTS

All travelers to Brazil must have a valid passport. Holders of European Union or New Zealand passports do not require a visa. Those with US, Canadian or Australian passports need to apply for a visa at the Brazilian embassy or consulate in their country of residence. Passport holders of other nationalities should check with the nearest Brazilian embassy.

Upon arrival, visitors receive a 90-day entry stamp, which can be extended for another 90 days by the **Polícia Federal**, up to a maximum of 180 days per year. Visitors are also required to fill out an entry card that they must keep with their passport at all times. It must be surrendered when leaving Brazil. Failure to produce this slip of paper may lead to a fine, and will certainly result in a hassle.

The 90 days are added on the day of renewal. There may not be a requirement to get an extension much before the expiry date. An expired visa cannot be extended.

The Polícia Federal may request to see an outbound ticket and proof of sufficient funds for the remainder of your stay. Those who outstay their visa term will be fined upon departure.

Map of Canoa Quebrada in one of its streets to assist tourists

TOURIST INFORMATION

All international and domestic airports in Brazil have tourist information booths that offer maps, brochures, and general information. These are usually run by either the state or city's tourist office.

Embratur Overseas Offices, the national tourist office, with its headquarters in Brasília, is run by the Ministry of Tourism. It has several overseas offices, including those in the United Kingdom, the United States, France, Germany, Spain, Portugal, and Japan.

Polícia Federal badge

LANGUAGE

The language of Brazil is Portuguese, but it is quite different in style and pronunciation from the Portuguese spoken in Portugal. The language has quite a few similarities with Spanish. In major tourist areas, the staff will speak some English and/or Spanish. However, in general, English is not widely spoken and often Brazilians will only have a basic intermediate knowledge of the language.

RELIGION

Brazil is often called "the largest Catholic country on earth," although, to be accurate, one should probably call it the "largest and least devout" of Catholic nations. Many Brazilians consider themselves culturally Catholic, without being regular church-goers. In recent years, the influence of the Church has greatly diminished. Traditional Afro-Brazilian religions are still followed, especially in the North and Northeast, with the religious ceremonies and practices gaining more acceptance over the years.

TIME

Brazil has four time zones. Most of the country is three hours behind GMT (known as the Brasília Time Zone). Both Rio de Janeiro and São Paulo, as well as all of Southern and Northeast Brazil and Pará and Amapá states are three hours behind GMT. The island group of Fernando de Noronha is two hours behind GMT. The states of Mato Grosso, Mato Grosso do Sul, Amazônia, Rondônia, and Roraima are four hours behind GMT. The state of Acre, in the far western corner, is five hours behind GMT. During daylight saving hours it gets a little bit more complicated. The southern states set their clocks back an hour, but the states in the north and northeast do not.

ELECTRICITY

There is no uniform voltage across Brazil. Some states are 110 volts, others 220 volts. Rio de Janeiro and São Paulo are both 110 volts. Brasília is 220 volts. Hotels will often have plugs for both volt-ages and are good at labeling the outlets. Adapters for laptops and cellphone chargers can normally handle the full range of voltage, but it is always better to check the specifications of your equipment to be sure.

Local tour guide with a group of tourists in Cachoeira

ETIQUETTE

Brazilians are very friendly and outgoing, even when meeting someone for the first time. When introduced, men will greet each other with a handshake and a friendly slap on the shoulder. Good friends usually embrace. When introduced to a woman, it is customary to greet her with a handshake and a kiss on the cheek (one kiss in São Paulo and the South, two kisses in Rio, the North, and Northeast). When introduced to a group of people, every-body has to kiss or shake hands with everybody else.

WOMEN TRAVELERS

A woman alone, especially at night, will attract some form of attention. It usually depends on where you are. Steer clear of areas around train stations, since it is likely to be a red-light area at night. The trans-port terminals themselves, though, are usually policed and fairly safe at all hours.

SPECIAL NEEDS

Wheelchair parking sign

Travelers with mobility problems will find Brazil a very challenging country. Although it is relatively easy to find wheelchair-accessible hotels and restaurants, very few public places are accessible or wheelchair-friendly. Older buildings may still lack elevators or ramps, and streets and sidewalks are often uneven or broken.

The metro system in Rio has electronic wheelchair ele-vators, but these are not always operational. For short distances, buses are not the best option for disabled travelers to get around. Taxis are better, and plentiful in most cities. For long distances, however, buses are generally comfortable, with special services offering fully reclining seats. Wheelchairs are available at all main airports.

TRAVELING WITH CHILDREN

Those traveling with small children will find Brazilians very child-friendly and accommodating. There are virtually no places that do not welcome children. Brazilians themselves think nothing of bringing their children to restaurants, theaters, cafés, concerts, or other events.

PUBLIC TOILETS

Public toilets are not that hard to find in Brazil, but vary greatly in cleanliness. Clean toilets can usually be found in hotel lobbies, shopping centers, and in public locations such as bus stations, parks, or beaches. A fee is sometimes charged. Note that toilet paper is sometimes dispensed from a central dispenser outside the stalls. It is a good idea to carry a roll of toilet paper.

Directory

VISAS & PASSPORTS

Policia Federal
Map 5 D2. Av Venezuela 2, Centro, Rio de Janeiro. **Tel** (021) 3213 1400. **www**.dpf.gov.br

TOURIST INFORMATION

Embratur Overseas Offices
UNITED KINGDOM
18 Greyhound Road, Hammersmith, London.
Tel (044) 207 396 5551.
www.braziltour.com

USA
1230 Avenue of the Americas, 7th floor, New York. **Tel** (01) 212 997 3360. **www**.braziltour.com

Health & Medical Matters

Brazil has a free national public healthcare system. Even foreign tourists will receive medical attention in any of the public hospitals, should they require it. Unfortunately, the public health system is overloaded and inadequately funded, especially in the rural areas of Brazil. Queues can be long and tedious, and facilities are not always up to European or North American standards. However, Brazil's private hospitals and clinics, though not free, offer world-class medical facilities. A good travel insurance policy will give access to these private facilities in an emergency, but remember to read the fine print carefully. Overall, hygiene standards in Brazil are high. Normal care is required with food and drink, and with preventive vaccinations, particularly when visiting the most remote parts of the country.

mosquitoes, and there is no vaccine to prevent it. It is much more common in the summer months, from December to March. Symptoms include high fever, joint pain, and headaches (especially behind the eyes). The illness usually runs its course in a week or 10 days, but a check-up is recommended to avoid any complications.

Cholera occasionally occurs in remote areas, but is mostly preventable by taking proper hygiene precautions such as drinking filtered water and washing and peeling fruit and vegetables. The most important precaution is to wash hands frequently.

PHARMACIES

For minor ailments, travelers can turn to Brazil's *farmácias*, or pharmacies. These can be found everywhere, are always well supplied, and are often open late. Every city will have at least one that is open 24 hours. Many medications that in other countries are available only by prescription can be bought over the counter in Brazil. Take care to remember the generic name of a medication taken regularly. A trained pharmacist is normally on hand to recommend the appropriate medication for common ailments such as diarrhoea, allergies, rashes, or infections. It is possible to get injections and free medical advice in pharmacies all over Brazil.

A fire brigade ambulance parked outside a fire control office

VACCINATIONS

It is a good idea to consult a travel clinic or family doctor for an International Certificate of Vaccinations, an up-to-date list of the required vaccinations. The ones most commonly recommended are a DTP (diphtheria, tetanus, and polio) booster, as well as for typhoid and hepatitis A.

A yellow fever vaccination is also required. This disease is endemic to many parts of South America, including Brazil. Officially, all visitors to Brazil are required to show proof of yellow fever vaccination. Although the requirement is not regularly enforced for visitors coming from North America or Europe, it is compulsory for those from other countries in South America. Entry can be denied upon failure to show proof of vaccination. Anti-malarial tablets may be advisable for those visiting some of the more remote parts of the Amazon.

TROPICAL DISEASES

Visitors to Brazil's major tourist destinations rarely have to worry about tropical diseases. The one tropical disease that can occur anywhere in the country, even in urban areas, is dengue fever. It is a viral infection that prevails throughout South America. The disease is transmitted by

A well-stocked pharmacy in São Paulo

Holiday-makers relaxing under umbrellas on the beach

PRIVATE HOSPITALS

Brazil does not offer the best medical facilities in its public hospitals. Foreign visitors, in particular, may find it difficult getting a bed, unless it is an infectious disease. In most public hospitals, the level of health care will not match European or US standards.

Private hospitals, however, offer world-class facilities. Though good medical care may be rare to find in rural areas, in the larger cities you will never be far from a decent private hospital. In many big cities, local tourist offices and some good hotels can provide a list of doctors who can speak English, French, and German.

For medical emergencies in a remote area, an air ambulance service offers a pick-up within 24 hours of calling. However, it is advisable to contact the travel insurance company before requesting for this service.

Though fairly affordable by international standards, private treatment in Brazil may turn out to be expensive. Many doctors and hospitals do not accept travel-health insurance, and insist on payment in cash.

HEALTH PRECAUTIONS

A visit to Brazil, by and large, does not require special health precautions. Impure water and contaminated food are usually the reasons for most diseases. However, hygiene standards of food and drink are high, especially in major tourist areas. Water is usually filtered or bottled and ice cubes are made from filtered water. Even in the most remote parts, mineral water is easily available. As long as fruit, vegetables, and meat are handled properly, they can be eaten safely.

A local drink seller on a Rio de Janeiro beach

SUN PROTECTION

Visitors from the northern hemisphere should take extra care with Brazil's intense tropical sun, especially for the first few days in the country. Brazil basks in almost year-round sunshine, making adequate sun protection absolutely crucial. Avoid exposure between 11am and 3pm and apply sunscreen to all exposed parts of the body. Wear sunblock (minimum SPF 30) and limit tanning to a only few hours. Pharmacies and grocery stores sell a variety of national and international sunscreen brands. Those sold on the beach itself, or in street markets, are best avoided. The contents may either be fake, or have been kept in storage for a long time, which causes the active ingredients to deteriorate.

DIRECTORY

EMERGENCY NUMBERS

Ambulance
Tel 192.

PRIVATE HOSPITALS

Rio de Janeiro
Hospital Samaritano,
Rua Bambina 98, Botafogo.
Tel (021) 2537 9722.
Copa d'Or, Rua Figueiredo de Magalhães 875, Copacabana.
Map 3 D1. *Tel (021) 2545 3600.*
www.rededor.com.br

Hospital Ipanema, Rua Antônio Parreiras 67, Ipanema.
Map 2 C4. *Tel (021) 2287 2322.*

São Paulo
Hospital Albert Einstein, Av Albert Einstein 627–701, Morumbi.
Tel (011) 3747 1233.
For ambulance: *(011) 3747 0200.*
www.einstein.br

Hospital Sírio-Libânes, Rua da Adma Jafet 91, Bela Vista.
Map 4 F2. *Tel (011) 3155 0200.*

Safety for Travelers

Brazil is known to have a higher crime rate than anywhere in North America and Europe. However, in reality, the kind of violence that affects travelers is mostly limited to the bigger cities, and is usually restricted to crimes that target valuables such as cameras, credit cards, cell phones, or cash. Such assaults are rare in the countryside and smaller towns. While some parts of Brazil can truly be regarded as violent and dangerous, travelers can be assured of personal security by using common sense and observing some very basic precautions.

A Guarda Municipal policewoman patrolling on a bicycle, Rio City

Local showing the way to visitors, Salvador

PERSONAL SAFETY

The large cities, especially Rio de Janeiro, São Paulo, and Salvador, are generally considered more prone to violence than the rest of Brazil. Statistically, crime rates in these cities are significantly higher than in cities in Europe or the US. However, much of the violent crime is confined to poorer neighborhoods in parts of the city where travelers rarely venture. The crime that visitors are most likely to be susceptible to is theft or robbery. The most basic precaution is not to carry anything worth stealing and to avoid empty beaches and nearly-empty streets after dark. Avoid ostentatious behavior such as walking around with expensive equipment; instead keep it in a plain bag.

When sightseeing, keep all belongings in a bag that can be placed in a money-belt. Never carry large amounts of cash. Credit cards are widely accepted and can be used for purchases in most hotels and stores. Keep a few small bills handy in a pocket so that when making small purchases, the wallet doesn't have to be pulled out in a busy area. Public transport is safe in the daytime, but in the evenings taxis are a better option. If you get robbed, just hand over your valuables, as robbers are often armed with a gun or a knife. Streets and public places can be unsafe at times. A very common technique is to distract the victim by spraying something on their shoulder. An accomplice may then offer to clean the mess, while the thief will make off with your belongings. The best and safest way is to politely turn down any such offer.

It is always best to exercise caution when someone unknown offers a drink, or even cigarettes. Instances of drugging, or spiked drinks are not uncommon in Brazil.

POLICE

Brazil has several different types of police that travelers are likely to encounter. Known to be the most efficient by far, the **Polícia Federal** (see p424) is responsible for passport control at airports and border crossings. Dressed in plain clothes, they deal with visas and their extensions.

Dressed in gray uniforms and caps, the **Polícia Militar** are responsible for public safety and can be seen patrolling the streets, beaches, and highways. These policemen often carry out "blitzes" (traffic checks) along major streets or roads. These can appear a little intimidating as the Polícia Militar come out in full gear, carrying automatic weapons. If you are driving a car, slow down, turn on the interior light, and roll down the windows.

A few cities with a strong tourist presence, such as Rio and Salvador, also have **Polícia de Turismo**,

A brightly painted tourist police station in Olinda

or tourist police, who offer assistance in case of any difficulty. Unfortunately, many of them do not speak English. A special Delegacia do Turista (tourist department) is available for those who require further help or wish to report a crime.

The state-controlled **Polícia Civil** handle local laws and investigate more serious crimes. When there is no tourist police post in the vicinity, thefts are reported to these policemen. Rio City has an unarmed guard force, **Guarda Municipal** (Municipal Civil Guards), to complement state police patrolling of parks and beaches.

REPORTING A CRIME

If you have been the victim of a crime, it can be reported at the nearest police station or tourist police office. This should be done within 24 hours of the crime. To obtain a report of the incident or theft for insurance purposes, insist that you receive a copy of the *boletim de ocorrência*. There may be nobody at the police station who speaks English, so it may be useful to request a hotel employee or tour guide to accompany you if you need to file a report. Missing credit cards should be reported to the

Polícia Militar booth in São Paulo, responsible for traffic checks

relevant company *(see p430)*. In case you have lost or damaged your passport, it is recommended that you contact your nearest consulate or embassy.

IDENTIFICATION

It is mandatory in Brazil to carry some form of photo identification. Often you will be asked to show some form of ID when entering an office building or government agency, or sometimes even a museum or library. To avoid carrying around a passport, keep a photocopy, and carry some other form of less valuable ID such as a student card, or a health card that has your picture, name, and date of birth.

DIRECTORY

POLICE

Guarda Municipal
www2.rio.rj.gov.br/gmrio

Polícia Civil
Tel 197.

Polícia Militar
Tel 190.

Polícia de Turismo
RIO DE JANEIRO
Rua João Bento do Campos 315,
Leblon. **Map** 1 B4.
Tel (021) 2511 5112.

SALVADOR
Praça São Francisco 14,
Pelourinho. *Tel (071) 3322 1188.*

SÃO PAULO
Av São Luíz 91, Centro.
Map 1 B3. *Tel (011) 3214 0209.*

CONSULATES

Australia
Av Presidente Wilson 231,
Centro, Rio de Janeiro.
Map 5 E4. *Tel (021) 3824 4624.*

Canada
Av Atlântica 1130, 5th Floor,
Copacabana, Rio de Janeiro.
Map 3 F1. *Tel (021) 2453 3004.*
Av Nações Unidas 12901,
São Paulo. *Tel (021) 2543 3004.*

Ireland
Rua 24 de Maio 347,
Raichuelo, Rio de Janeiro.
Tel (021) 2501 8455.

Av Paulista 2006, Conjunto 514,
São Paulo. **Map** 4 E2.
Tel (011) 3287 6362.

New Zealand
Alameda Campinas 579,
São Paulo. **Map** 4 F3.
Tel (011) 3148 0616.

UK
Praia do Flamengo 284,
Rio de Janeiro.
Tel (021) 2555 9600.

Rua Ferreira de Araújo 741,
Pinheiros, São Paulo.
Tel (011) 3094 2700.

USA
Av Presidente Wilson 147,
Rio de Janeiro. **Map** 5 E5.
Tel (021) 2292 7117.

Rua Henri Dunant 500, São
Paulo. *Tel (011) 5186 7000.*

Polícia Federal car

Guarda Municipal car

Banking & Local Currency

Brazil provides a range of accessible banking facilities and money exchange services. Except for the US dollar, foreign currencies are rarely accepted outside of major tourist regions. Exchange rates for cash transactions are usually not very good, and the best rates can be obtained on credit card or *caixa automática* (automated teller machine) transactions. Credit cards, widely accepted in most establishments, can be used to withdraw local currency (*real*), giving a more favorable exchange rate, and are by far the most convenient. Traveler's checks can be changed in banks and *casas de câmbio* (exchange offices).

BANKING HOURS

HSBC has a number of banks that are open from 9am to 5pm on all weekdays. Most other banks, including **Banco do Brasil**, are also open on weekdays, but only from 10am to 4pm. Hours for changing money or traveler's checks are even more limited, usually falling between 11am and 2pm. Automated teller machines (ATMs) have more flexible hours but are not always open 24 hours.

Automated teller machine (ATM) at a branch of Banco do Brasil

ATMS

The easiest way of getting cash in big cities is by using ATMs (*caixa automática*), which are widely found and accept foreign cards. Check with your bank prior to traveling to Brazil whether your ATM card can be used internationally for cash withdrawals and that you have the appropriate PIN (*numero de identificao*). In addition to ATM cards, most bank machines will also give a cash advance on a credit card. Banco do Brasil, HSBC, Citibank, Bradesco, and Banco 24 Horas have reliable networks that work with international cards.

Bank machines are often updated and adjusted so other banks may join the network. For safety reasons, bank machines are not always open 24 hours. ATMs may close at 8 or 10pm, or be programmed to dispense only

DIRECTORY

CREDIT CARDS

AmEx
Tel (0800) 787 070.

Diners Club
Tel (0800) 4001 4444.

MasterCard
Tel (0800) 891 3294.

Visa
Tel (0800) 891 3680.

BANKS

Banco do Brasil
Av Paulista 2163, São Paulo.
Map 4 E2. *Tel (011) 3066 9322.*
Rua Joana Angélica 124,
Ipanema, Rio de Janeiro.
Map 2 A4. *Tel (021) 2522 1442*
www.bb.com.br

HSBC
Av Paulista 949, São Paulo.
Map 4 E2. *Tel (011) 3146 8500.*
Nossa Senhora de Copacabana
583, Rio de Janeiro.
Map 3 E2. *Tel (021) 3816 8100.*
www.hsbc.com.br

a small amount of money. It is also good to plan ahead on weekends or statutory holidays when machines sometimes run out of cash. Keep in mind that some small towns and islands do not have ATMs, so plan ahead.

CREDIT CARDS

Credit cards are widely accepted in Brazil. The most commonly used cards are **AmEx**, **MasterCard**, and **Visa**. **Diners Club** is less widely used. Credit cards can be used in almost all establishments. Street markets and kiosks, of course, only take cash. When you pay by credit card the cashier will usually ask "*débito ou credito*" (debit or credit). It is important to state "*credito*" as most international credit cards do not work as debit cards. Credit cards with a PIN can also be used to make cash withdrawals from ATMs at banks. The service fee is higher for using a credit card instead of a regular ATM card.

Branch of Banco do Brasil with *caixa automática* (ATMs)

It is a good idea to instruct your bank that you will be using your card in Brazil, so as to avoid any transaction problems at a later stage.

TRAVELER'S CHECKS

Very few banks will cash traveler's checks, and at those that do, there is a high fee and a long wait. The Banco do Brasil, for example, charges a flat fee of US$20 per transaction. Some hotels and some tour operators will accept traveler's checks, but

the exchange is always bad. American Express will cash AmEx traveler's checks for free, but they only have offices in a few major cities in Brazil. It is more convenient to use a credit card for major expenses incurred at hotels and on excursions.

CURRENCY

The currency of Brazil is the *real* (R$, plural *reais*). All bank notes come with a print of a Brazilian animal. The smallest R$1 and R$2 notes

are green and blue, respectively, featuring a hummingbird and sea turtle. The purple R$5 and the red R$10 have pictures of a heron and a macaw respectively. The yellow R$20 notes feature the endangered *mico-leão dourado* (golden lion tamarin) monkey. The brown R$50 notes come with a picture of a jaguar. R$100 bills, featuring the endangered dusky grouper fish, are often impossible to break at small shops, so stock up on change at drugstores and grocery stores.

Banknotes
Brazilian reais bills come in denominations of 1, 2, 5, 10, 20, 50, and 100. Brazilian bank notes are bright, with each denomination coming in a different color.

1 real

2 reais

5 reais

10 reais

50 reais

20 reais

100 reais

Coins
Coins come in the following denomination: 1, 5, 10, 25, 50 centavos and 1 real. 100 centavos make up 1 real.

5 centavos

10 centavos

25 centavos

50 centavos

1 real

Communications

Internet café sign

Brazil has an efficient communication system. Telecommunication systems are reasonably advanced and mobile phones are widely used. Postal networks, with a variety of services, including registered post and express mail, are quite reliable. Most hotels subscribe to a digital or satellite television service with international channels. Although there are no foreign language Brazilian newspapers, foreign newspapers are available in all major cities, mostly in the main airports, business districts, and tourist centers.

PUBLIC PHONES

Public telephones (*orelhôes,* or "big ears") are plentiful all over Brazil. Pay phones do not take coins. You must purchase a phone card (*cartão telefonico*), available at newsstands, drugstores, and post offices. To make overseas collect calls from a pay phone you have to contact the operator (dial 21) to complete the call for you. Local or long-distance collect calls within Brazil can be made by dialing 9090 before the number.

USING THE PHONE

Almost all telephone numbers in Brazil are now eight digits. Unfortunately, phone listings are not always updated right away. If you do come across a seven-digit number, it is

Public telephones, easily available all over Brazil

best to confirm if it is still correct. Local calls do not require an area code, whereas long-distance calls do. This consists of two digits. All long-distance calls (within Brazil and international) also require the use of a

long-distance service provider (*prestadora*). The two-digit code of the *prestadora* needs to be dialed before the area code. In listings, long-distance numbers often look like this – 0-XX-11-3455-3288. The two-digit *prestadora* number is inserted in place of the "XX." Customers have several options, depending on the region and prices. Embratel (Brazil's largest tele-communications company) phonecards work everywhere in Brazil. If using Embratel, the number would look like this – 0-21-11-3455-3288. This can sometimes be confusing because some *prestadora* codes are the same as some area codes.

MOBILE PHONES

Mobile phones are common all over Brazil, and are generally used in most public places, including in restaurants. Most tri-band GSM phones will work in Brazil. You can purchase a local SIM chip upon arrival and obtain a local number. Some phones need to be unlocked before they can be used in a foreign country. Check with your phone company before leaving home. If your service provider has a roaming agreement with Brazil, you can use your regular number.

DIALING CODES

- A local call requires only the seven or eight digit number without the area code.
- To phone Brazil from overseas, dial the international access code, followed by Brazil's country code (55), followed by the two-digit area code and local number.
- To call abroad from Brazil, dial 00, then the *prestadora* code, followed by the country code, area code, and phone number.
- Contact Embratel at 0800 703 2100 to ask for collect calls or international calls.

USING A PHONECARD TELEPHONE

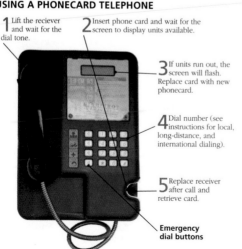

1 Lift the reciever and wait for the dial tone.

2 Insert phone card and wait for the screen to display units available.

3 If units run out, the screen will flash. Replace card with new phonecard.

4 Dial number (see instructions for local, long-distance, and international dialing).

5 Replace receiver after call and retrieve card.

Emergency dial buttons

The distinct blue and yellow colors of a post office in Rio de Janeiro

POST OFFICES

The Brazilian postal service is quite efficient. Post offices (*correios*) are open from 9am to 5pm Monday to Friday. Large shopping centers and airports will have branches with longer opening hours, including Saturdays. Regular delivery service within Brazil takes two to four days and overseas 6 to 12 days. For guaranteed or registered delivery, the *correios* offers the excellent *sedex* (domestic Brazilian express mail) service, which functions like a courier service. In larger cities, there are also several international couriers for express overseas delivery.

Post box

COURIER

For international courier services, it is best to use an international courier company such as **DHL** or **FedEx**. Drop-off points are mostly in Rio de Janeiro and São Paulo, and a few in other cities, but wherever available, both companies will schedule convenient pick-ups and provide all the documentation required for an international delivery. Do remember, delivery from Brazil to the main cities and towns in the US or Europe normally takes 48 hours.

INTERNET

Internet service is widely available in Brazil and usually quite cheap. If traveling with a laptop, ask about the hotel's in-room Internet access rates. Cyber cafés are the most inexpensive options for accessing the Internet. These are usually found in shopping centers, and large bookstores. Some of the bigger Internet cafés inlude **FNAC Centro Cultural** and **Sebo Paulista**, in São Paulo, and **Telerede Internet Café** and **ICafé**, in Rio.

ADDRESSES

Most addresses are fairly straightforward, giving the street name first, followed by the number. Landmark buildings or houses in small towns may be listed as s/n (*sem número* or without number). Other common abbreviations in addresses include *lj* or *loja* (shop), *sl* or *sobreloja* (first floor or mezzanine), and *apt* or *apartamento* (apartment).

NEWSPAPERS & MAGAZINES

Brazil does not have any English language daily newspapers or magazines. The main Brazilian dailies are *O Globo* and the *Folha de São Paulo*. The Friday editions include a cultural and entertainment section with detailed information on shows, concerts, plays, movies and

Local publications, São Paulo

exhibitions. The bestselling weekly news magazines are *Època*, *Veja*, and *IstoÉ*. On weekends, in Rio de Janeiro and São Paulo, the *Veja (see p152)* edition includes a separate magazine and listings related to cultural events.

Foreign newspapers and magazines can be purchased in large cities, in the tourist areas or business districts. These are also available at all major airports.

Newspapers and magazines are most commonly sold at a newsstand (*banca de jornal*). Newsstands in Ipanema in Rio and Praca de Republica in São Paulo have a good range of international newspapers. Supermarkets and bookstores also sell them, but often carry a smaller selection.

DIRECTORY

POST OFFICES

Av Nossa Senhor de Copacabana 540, Copacabana, Rio de Janeiro. **Map** 3 D2, 3 E2. *Tel (021) 2256 1439.*

Rua Pamplona 1083, Jardim Paulista, São Paulo. **Map** 4 F3. *Tel (011) 3283 1500.*

COURIER

DHL
Tel (011) 3618 3200 (in São Paulo).

FedEx
Tel (011) 5641 7788 (in São Paulo), (0800) 703 3339 (elsewhere in Brazil).

INTERNET

ICafé
Rua Prudente de Morais 167b, Ipanema, Rio de Janeiro. *Tel (021) 2247 2394.*

FNAC Centro Cultural
Av Pedroso de Morães 858, São Paulo. **Map** 3 A3. *Tel (011) 4501 3000.*

Sebo Paulista
Av Paulista 1919, São Paulo. **Map** 4 E2. *Tel (011) 3285 2443.*

Telerede Internet Café
Rua Nossa Senhora de Copacabana 209, Copacabana, Rio de Janeiro. **Map** 3 E2. *Tel (021) 2275 3148.*

TRAVEL INFORMATION

ost travelers arrive in Brazil by plane. There are regular scheduled flights from Europe and North and South America. Travelers from Asia or Africa will most likely have to connect elsewhere before continuing to Brazil. Several airlines offer stopovers to or from Brazil at no extra cost. Almost all direct flights land at São

Directional sign at airport

Paulo's international airport or in Rio de Janeiro. There are a few regular flights to Salvador and Recife. However, most direct flights to these and other destinations in the Northeast, such as Fortaleza or Natal, are European charter flights. Air travel within Brazil is quite efficient, and even the most remote locations are accessible by plane.

ARRIVING BY AIR

Most direct international flights land either in Rio de Janeiro or São Paulo. Convenient connections are available for those continuing to other domestic destinations. Travelers will clear customs at the airport where they first enter Brazil.

INTERNATIONAL AIRLINES

Most major European and North and South American airlines operate regularly scheduled flights to Brazil. Delta, American Airlines, Continental Airlines, KLM, Lufthansa, Air France, British Airways, Alitalia, Iberia, Tap, and others offer non-stop flights to Rio de Janeiro and São Paulo. The largest Brazilian airlines, **Varig**, **TAM**, and **Gol**, also fly overseas. Varig covers a much larger number of destinations, and also codeshares

Modern, well-equipped Belém International Airport

with Air Canada, United, Lufthansa, and a number of other leading airlines. It also offers good discounts on transfers and hotel tariffs, as part of its stopover program.

ON ARRIVAL

All tourists are expected to fill out a *cartao de entrada/saida* (entry/exit card). Immigration officials will keep half and return the other to you. This card is important. It serves as

proof of stay in Brazil and will be checked upon departure. Loss of the card may result in a major hassle and possibly a fine *(see p424)*. Officials will also stamp your passport, and in case they are not granting you the usual 90-day stay in Brazil, the number of days will be written beneath the word *Prazo* on the stamp in your passport. For an extension of the 90-day entry stamp, contact the Polícia Federal *(see p424–5)*.

A Gol aircraft at the Deputado Luíz E. Magalhães International Airport, Salvador

Taxis waiting outside Internacional de Guarulhos, São Paulo City

CUSTOMS REQUIREMENTS & DUTY FREE

All international travelers are allowed to purchase up to US$500 at the Brazilian duty-free shop in the arrival hall. Purchases must be made prior to exiting the customs area. Visitors may bring items for their personal use, including electronics. Expensive gadgets, such as cameras or laptops, may need to be registered upon arrival to ensure that they will be taken out of the country again. Gifts up to a value of US$500 can be brought in without additional duties; Brazilian duty-free purchases are not included in this amount.

GETTING FROM AIRPORTS

In Rio City, taxis can be a rip-off. Instead, go for the **Real Auto Bus**, which runs an efficient half-hourly bus service. São Paulo City offers excellent air-conditioned shuttles known as the "Airport Service." These run every 30 minutes, and depart from the

arrivals terminal. Taxis, too, are easily available at a fixed price. Salvador's international airport is linked to the city center by an hourly shuttle express bus service.

TRAVEL AGENCIES & PACKAGES

European residents have access to some attractive package deals to Northeast Brazil. Packages typically include hotel and airfare to a popular destination such as Fortaleza, Natal, or Recife. Though affordable, these package tours do not offer a lot of flexibility. Independent travelers, who wish to visit several destinations, must book their own airfare and hotels. Confirm hotel prices with travel operators, as Brazilian hotels often reserve their best prices for agencies.

A number of travel agencies, such as **Brazil Nuts**, offer customized tours or programs, including activities for seniors, youths, gay travelers, or for those interested in cultural activities. **Journey Latin**

America, a UK-based travel agency, offers tailor-made tours across Brazil. Based in Miami, **Brol** (BR Online Travel) is the first American online travel company to specialize in Brazil.

DIRECTORY

INTERNATIONAL AIRLINES

Gol
Tel *(0300) 789 2121.*
www.voegol.com.br

TAM
Tel *(0800) 570 5700.*
www.tam.com.br

Varig
Tel *4003 7000.*
www.varig.com.br

AIRPORT SHUTTLES

Real Auto Bus
Tel *(0800) 3424 0850.*

TOUR OPERATORS

Brazil Nuts
1854 Trade Center Way,
Suite 101 Naples, USA FL 34109.
Tel *(800) 553 9959.*
www.brazilnuts.com

Brol
100 N Biscayne Blvd, Suite 703
Miami, USA FL 33132. *Tel* *(0305)*
379 0005. www.brol.com

Journey Latin America
12 & 13 Heathfield Terrace,
Chiswick, London, UK W4 4JE.
Tel *(020) 8747 3108.*
www.journeylatinamerica.co.uk

AIRPORT	INFORMATION	DISTANCE TO CITY CENTER	AVERAGE TAXI FARE	AVERAGE JOURNEY TIME
Internacional de Guarulhos	(011) 6445 2945	São Paulo City 17 miles (28 km)	US$30	40 minutes
International Airport Tom Jobim	(021) 3398 5050	Rio de Janeiro City 12 miles (20 km)	US$25	45 minutes
Deputado Luíz E. Magalhães	(071) 3204 1010	Salvador 17 miles (28 km)	US$35	40 minutes
Internacional dos Guararapes	(081) 3462 4960	Recife 11 miles (18 km)	US$20	20 minutes
Eduardo Gomes	(092) 3652 1212	Manaus 10 miles (16 km)	US$25	25 minutes
Internacional Salgado Filho	(051) 3358 2903	Porto Alegre 4 miles (6 km)	US$10	15 minutes

Domestic Air Travel

Varig logo

The sheer size of Brazil makes air travel the preferred mode of transportation. The country has an excellent network of airlines and most airports have recently been modernized. Air travel is an important means of transportation to reach remote areas in Amazônia and the interior of Brazil. All towns in the country have at least an airstrip, and all cities have an airport, usually some distance from the city, or located fairly centrally, as in the case with São Paulo City and Rio City.

Gol Linhas Aereas Inteligentes aircraft taxi at Congonhas airport, São Paulo

DOMESTIC AIRLINES

Domestic air travel within Brazil is a well organized and efficient form of transportation. There are currently two major airlines that fly both international and domestic routes – TAM and Varig (see p435). Domestic bargain airlines include **Rio Sul** and **Nordeste** (both allied to Varig), **Gol** and **Trip**. Smaller airlines, such as **Pantanal**, operating flights between São Paulo and Mato Grosso do Sul, have recently built up a wide and inexpensive network throughout the Amazon region.

CHECKING IN

Check-in for domestic flights is normally 60 minutes prior to departure. A valid ID is required, and foreigners are required to show their passport upon check-in. Make sure to keep the luggage claim tags handy upon arrival, as airport staff will check for those when exiting the baggage claim area.

AIRPASS

Non-residents of Brazil who arrive on an international flight are entitled to buy an airpass with TAM or Varig, making long-distance flights within Brazil quite affordable. Both airlines sell the pass for US$479, for which you are allowed four domestic flights within a 21-day period. Additional segments can be purchased. No direct return flights are allowed. For example, Rio–Manaus–Rio–Salvador is not allowed but Rio–Manaus–Salvador–Rio is.

A travel agent can explain the detailed terms and conditions, or else, check the airline's website for more information.

HIGH SEASON

High season for domestic air travel corresponds with the major holidays and vacation periods in Brazil. The peak season is in the Brazilian summer, from the week of Christmas until Carnaval in mid-February or early March. The month of July is also peak season when schools and universities are off on their winter break. Other popular periods are Easter, Corpus Christi, and Independence Day (September 7).

Both TAM and Varig offer significant discounts for those who take night flights. As unpleasant as departures and arrivals in the wee hours may be, the savings can be significant. It is also advisable to book well ahead of time when flying Friday evening or Monday morning between major cities.

AIR TAXI

Many parts of Brazil, and particularly Amazônia, feature air taxi companies. Air taxis, known locally as *teco-tecos,* are not the most reliable form of transportation. Before taking one, be aware that the airstrips are often dangerous. These small planes routinely fly overloaded, and are very often in questionable condition. There are no checks made on the qualifications of pilots, so taking an air taxi is at the traveler's own risk.

Teco-teco (air taxi) in the Amazon region

A Varig flight landing at Fortaleza airport

RESERVATIONS & CANCELLATIONS

Flights tend to be booked in advance so book your tickets as far ahead as possible. The only exception to this is the Rio–São Paulo shuttle, where you can purchase tickets on the spot. Flights at the beginning and end of working days and on weekends are usually quite crowded.

Confirm onward flights a day or two in advance. This can be done over the phone, as most airlines have English-speaking staff.

If you have an airpass and you happen to change your flight, remember to cancel the original flight.

If you don't do so, the computer will flag you as a no-show, and all your other airpass reservations will also be canceled. Similarly, if you miss a flight, reconfirm all onward flights on your airpass. If you don't, all your other flights will be canceled.

DOMESTIC AIRPORTS

Along with domestic airports, such as **Aeroporto de Congonhas** in São Paulo, and **Aeroporto Santos Dumont** in Rio de Janeiro, there are small domestic airports all over Brazil, including Recife, Belo Horizonte, Cuiabá, Campo Grande, Curitiba, Fernando de Noronha, Florianópolis, and Fortaleza.

Both Congonhas and Santos-Dumont airports are close to the commercial areas. The shuttle services to the city centers take around 50 minutes.

DIRECTORY

DOMESTIC AIRLINES

Gol
Tel (0300) 789 2121.
www.voegol.com.br

Nordeste
Tel (0800) 4003 7000.
www.voenordeste.com.br

Pantanal
Tel (0800) 125 883.
www.pantanal-airlines.com.br

Rio Sul
Tel (0800) 4003 7000.
www.rio-sul.com.br

Trip
Tel (0300) 789 8747.
www.airtrip.com.br

DOMESTIC AIRPORTS

Aeroporto de Congonhas
Tel (011) 5090 9000.

Aeroporto Santos Dumont
Tel (021) 3814 7070.

FLIGHT DURATION CHART
1:15 = Duration in hours:minutes

RIO DE JANEIRO	SÃO PAULO	FLORIANÓPOLIS	BRASÍLIA	MANAUS	BELÉM	SÃO LUÍS	FORTALEZA	RECIFE	SALVADOR	BELO HORIZONTE
0:45	SÃO PAULO									
2:30	1:00	FLORIANÓPOLIS								
1:30	1:35	2:17	BRASÍLIA							
3:00	2:55	6:00	2:45	MANAUS						
3:35	5:25	4:40	2:20	1:00	BELÉM					
4:00	5:45	5:25	2:27	4:20	1:00	SÃO LUÍS				
3:00	2:30	0:55	2:30	4:25	2:50	1:10	FORTALEZA			
2:45	3:00	6:18	2:20	7:30	4:20	2:45	1:10	RECIFE		
1:50	0:45	5:10	1:55	7:30	7:45	4:35	1:40	1:10	SALVADOR	
0:50	1:00	3:00	1:10	7:00	5:00	4:45	4:00	3:55	1:35	BELO HORIZONTE

GETTING AROUND
Due to the size and distances across Brazil, the fastest and easiest way to travel around the country is by air. All big cities, smaller towns, and even more remote areas across the country have airports, or at least an air strip of some sort. Domestic flights are available to and from just about any major city across Brazil.

Bus & Car Travel

Bus and car travel is a challenge in Brazil, both because of the distances, and because of the often poor quality of the roads. Brazil possesses a total of 932,000 miles (1.5 million km) of federal, state, and local roads but only 49,000 miles (79,000 km) are paved and in decent condition. Intercity bus travel is well organized and most routes offer efficient and comfortable express services. Though car rentals are widely available, given the distances and the high cost of gasoline, a car is not really advisable for longer trips, but it is a convenient way to explore attractions closer to the city.

Busy *rodoviária* (central bus terminal) in São Paulo

BUSES

Brazil has an excellent network of long-distance buses which makes traveling around the country easy and economical. Intercity buses leave from a central station, called a *rodoviária*, usually built on the outskirts of the city. Buses are operated by numerous private companies, but prices are standardized, and very reasonable. Several categories of buses operate on longer routes. Regular buses (*ônibus comum*) sometimes do not have air conditioning, so ask. *Comum com ar* are regular buses with air conditioning. The *executivo* bus is more comfortable, its chairs wider and equipped with footrests. The best buses for overnight trips are known as *semi-leito* or *leito*. *Semi-leito* have seats that recline almost horizontally and have large footrests. *Leito* buses offer a fully horizontal bed-like seat. Both normally offer onboard refreshments, blankets, and pillows. Nearly all buses have onboard bathrooms. Buy your tickets from the *rodoviária* ahead of time, especially on holidays.

CAR RENTALS

All major cities and most smaller cities and towns offer car rental services, such as **Avis** and **Localiza**. Car rental offices, known as *locadoras*, can be found at every airport and in most towns. Foreigners need to show a valid driver's license from their home country, state, or province, their passport, and a major credit card. It is also a good idea to carry an International Driver's Permit (IDP). A wide variety of cars are available in Brazil, from small economy models with no air conditioning, to large air-conditioned 4WDs. Rental agreements can be with full or partial insurance, with unlimited driving or with a per kilometer charge. In terms of price, a 4-door mid-size sedan with air conditioning, unlimited driving, and full insurance will cost about R$150 (US$75) per day in a larger city. In smaller towns and remote areas, prices go up by 50 to 100 percent. It is a good idea to check with locals about the condition of the roads you plan on taking.

GAS STATIONS

Cars in Brazil run on either gasoline or alcohol, but car rental agencies normally rent only gasoline models. Service stations selling gasoline are more common, especially in remote areas. On long-distance road trips, service stations may be few and far between, so ensure that the car is in good condition. Always be well prepared with some cash, water, enough car fluids, a good spare tyre with tools, and a flashlight.

DRIVING IN TOWNS

Driving in Brazilian towns and cities can sometimes be a frustrating experience. Anytime after about 9pm, especially in Rio and São Paulo, drivers begin to treat red lights as strictly optional. Be especially alert at intersections at night (even as a pedestrian). Often the driver running the red light won't even slow down, because of the risk of robberies at isolated intersections.

Estação de gás (gas station) in Rio de Janeiro

On highways and secondary roads, drivers tend to be fearless overtaking other vehicles, even when they can't see what's around the bend.

Parking in cities can be a bit tricky. It is worth paying extra for a hotel with a lock-up garage facility. Do not leave valuables in the car. It is also worth paying a few *reais* to self-appointed "guards" who may approach you to watch over your car.

Parking sign

RULES OF THE ROAD

Officially, the rules of the road are much the same as in Continental Europe or the United States. Drive on the right side of the road; unlike the USA, right turns on red lights are not allowed. Roundabouts are common only in Brasília. The right of way is always with the car already in the roundabout, or to the left.

However, it is the application of these rules – or lack thereof – that sets Brazil apart. Most Brazilians are aggressive and impatient drivers. They tend to drive fast, overtake often, either on the right or left, and when they cannot, they hang impatiently on your back bumper. Do not expect the large bus driving next to you to stay in its lane. Drivers switch lanes constantly, for no apparent reason, normally without signaling.

Things have improved significantly over the past few years as a result of the use of photo radar. Seatbelt laws are also rigorously enforced. But in larger cities such as São Paulo, Rio, and Salvador, traffic is still very chaotic. In case of an emergency, it is best to call the Polícia Militar *(see pp428–9)*. Road accidents should be reported to the department of transport, **Detran**, in the respective state.

ROAD NETWORK

Brazil's intercity road network is made up of state and federal highways. Federal highways are denoted by the initials BR followed by the number of the highway (BR-163). State roads are indicated by the state initials (RJ for Rio de Janeiro, PA for Pará, and so on) followed by the highway number (PA-150). Toll roads have become more common recently. Most are run by private companies. They are usually well maintained and offer roadside assistance.

Most other state and federal highways are undivided 2-lane blacktops, with occasional passing lanes. Care is required when driving

DIRECTORY

CAR RENTALS

Avis
Tel (011) 2155 2847 (São Paulo) or (0800) 725 2847.
www.avis.com.br

Localiza
Tel (0800) 992 000
www.localiza.com.br

EMERGENCY

Detran
Tel (021) 3550 9744 (Rio de Janeiro).

on these roads. Generally speaking, the roads in southern states such as Rio and São Paulo are much better than in northeastern or Amazônian states such as Bahia or Rondônia. Even in the south, roads in bad condition are not uncommon.

Traveling by night is best avoided. With very few exceptions, highways in Brazil are poorly lit, and completely lacking in reflective paint, reflective signage, and the road-side reflectors that show the edge of the road.

The best compilation of national road maps come bundled with the *Guia Quatro Rodas*, a publication brought out by a Brazilian motoring organization of the same name, available at newsstands, bookstores, and magazine stalls.

Road sign meaning "slow down" on a highway near Goiás

Train & Boat Travel in Brazil

Train travel is not a common mode of transportation in Brazil. While large parts of the country have never seen train tracks, in other areas, many routes have been deactivated in favor of roads. Today, the few remaining routes are of more interest to train aficionados, and are often of great scenic beauty. In some parts of Brazil, boat travel is still the only mode of transportation. With few roads connecting the major cities, particularly in the Amazon and along the northern coast, locals depend entirely on boats to get around. On the Rio Paraguay, on the western edge of the Pantanal, boats are used for multi-day fishing charters.

The interior of a Maria Fumaça steam locomotive train

Trains waiting at the Luz railroad station in São Paulo

TRAIN TRAVEL

Although Brazil does not have a large train network, there are a few specific routes that can be useful for travelers and are good for a scenic ride. The Minas-Vitória train journey is an excellent day trip, and perfect for those traveling between the cities of Belo Horizonte, in the heartland of Minas Gerais, and Vitória on the Espírito Santo coast.

The quickest and most comfortable way to travel between São Luís and the interior of Pará, in Northern Brazil, is the São Luís Carajás railroad. In the state of Amapá, also in Northern Brazil, a passenger and cargo train runs from the port of Santana, 124 miles (200 km) inland, to the former mining town of Serra de Navio. Its passenger cars, though old and in need of maintenance, are still functional.

Brazil offers a few charming, short historic routes. Steam locomotive trains, lovingly called Maria Fumaça, or "Smoking Mary," run on these routes. One of the journeys this unique steam engine makes is a regular 7-mile (12-km) run on weekends between São João del Rei and Tiradentes (see p132), historic towns in Minas Gerais. An appealing short trip is offered along the route between the beautiful, historic mining town of Ouro Preto, one of Brazil's best preserved colonial towns, and Mariana, also in Minas. Even though the towns are only 7 miles (12 km) apart, the route buzzes with history, as gold miners and gem hunters in the days of the gold rush used to travel through these hills. Contact the **Estação Ferroviária** for further details.

Another spectacular route is the Curitiba-Paranaguá train ride through the Atlantic rainforest of the Serra do Mar. The most unforgettable stretch is between Curitiba and Morretes (see p337). For information, contact the **Curitiba Ticket Office**.

BOAT TRAVEL

In many parts of Brazil, boats are a vital form of transport. The network is extensive, and services are regular, although the facilities largely depend on the type of boat chosen for traveling.

In the Amazon, rivers are still the major highways, and old-style wooden river boats are an important part of the transportation system. The most common and popular route runs between Manaus and Belém. The journey takes four days downstream and five days upstream. On this route, there are also several larger and more modern boats, which feature air-conditioned cabins and even enclosed air-conditioned hammock spaces. Continuing right up to Tefé, **AJATO** runs a speedboat service every Wednesday and Saturday, with airplane-style seating.

On most other routes, the boats are the older, smaller traditional type, with small wooden cabins, and two

A picturesque view of one of the Maria Fumaça steam trains

Cruise ship Iberostar moored on the Manaus harbor

open decks – upper and lower – where passengers sling their hammocks. Meals and water are provided.

Boats of the old style ply dozens of routes throughout the Amazon basin. The most common routes run between Manaus and Porto Velho, Manaus, Tabatinga, and São Gabriel de Cachoeira, near the borders of Peru and Columbia, respectively, and Manaus and Santarem, halfway to Belém. The Manaus-Santarem route also has a high-speed catamaran which makes the journey in a single day. Those more keen on tours than transportation can go for one of the comfortable boats for charter in Manaus, such as **Viverde**, that take passengers on a personal exploration of the Amazon River. For information on buying tickets in advance, contact **Amazonastur**, the state tourism agency.

The Rio Paraguay on the western edge of the Pantanal has a large fleet of boats, most of which are outfitted for multi-day sport fishing cruises. These boats depart from both Corumbá in Mato Grosso do Sul and Caceres in Mato Grosso.

On the Northeast coast, an absence of roads connecting the Maranhão and Piauí coast makes boat travel the only alternative to long detours inland. The most scenic option is to travel from Parnaíba in Piauí through the islands and inlets of the Delta da Parnaíba to Tutóia, one of the gateways to the Lençóis Maranhenses.

CRUISE TRAVEL

A very leisurely way to travel the Brazilian coast is on board a cruise ship. Several companies offer three- to five-day cruises, most typically between Santos, Rio de Janeiro as far as Salvador, or other Northeastern cities. Another route starts in Recife and travels to Fernando de Noronha. There is now also a regular cruise ship, the **Iberostar Grand Amazon**, that departs from Manaus on three- and four-day cruises on the Amazon. **Tropical Cruises**, which leaves from Rio de Janeiro City, offers very good trips along the Atlantic Coast. The old-style **Amazon Clipper Cruises** can be excellent for a tour of the Rio Negro.

DIRECTORY

TRAIN TRAVEL

Curitiba Ticket Office
Tel (041) 3323 4007.
www.serraverdeexpress.com.br

Estação Ferroviária
Praça Cesário Alvim 102, barra,
Ouro Preto. *Tel* (031) 3371 8485.
www.mariafumacamg.com

BOAT TRAVEL

AJATO
Rua Bares 3, Centro, Manaus
Tel (092) 622 6047.

Amazonastur
Tel (092) 2123 3819.
www.amazonastur.am.gov.br

Viverde
Rua dos Cardeiros 26, Manaus
Tel (092) 248 9988.
www.viverde.com.br

CRUISE TRAVEL

Amazon Clipper Cruises
Tel (092) 3656 1246.
www.amazonclipper.com.br

Iberostar Grand Amazon
www.iberostar.com

Tropical Cruises
Tel (021) 2487 1687.
www.tropicalcruises.com.br

Yachts at anchor near Ubatuba beach, São Paulo state

Getting around Brazilian Towns

Public transportation in Brazil varies greatly from city to city and region to region. Large cities such as São Paulo and Rio de Janeiro have modern metro systems that offer quick access to many parts of the city and decent bus systems. However, in most cities and towns, the main mode of transportation is the bus and its variations, such as minivans and minibuses. Taxis are plentiful and quite affordable. In very small communities where there is little in the way of regular public transportation, people often use motorcycle taxis (moto-taxis). It is a cheap and fast one-person ride.

Moto-taxi stand in Camamu with moto-taxi drivers

Visitors exploring the town of Búzios on foot

ON FOOT

Visitors to Brazil often seem preoccupied with street crime. What they should really worry about is traffic. Pedestrians get little or no respect. It is safest to assume that cars have the absolute right of way everywhere at all times. Even when the pedestrian has the right of way, such as when crossing with a green light, extreme care should be exercised at all times.

After dark, or when traffic is light, or when police are absent, cars tend to run red lights. Also, when making a right turn, cars rarely give preference to pedestrians trying to cross. Pedestrians should also be aware of bikes or motorcycles that may go down the wrong way on a one-way street. Always look both left and right.

Motorcyclists often weave in and out between the cars at high speeds. Be very careful when walking in between stopped or slow moving traffic.

TAXIS & MOTO-TAXIS

Taxis are affordable and a quick mode of transportation. Prices generally run 50 to 70 percent lower than in Europe or North America. Most taxis work on the meter. When starting the ride, make sure that the meter is cleared and shows "tariff 1" except from 11pm to 6am, Sundays, and in December when "2" is permitted. Drivers sometimes "forget" to start the meter and end up charging a flat rate.

The only taxis allowed to charge a flat rate are radio taxis or cooperatives at airports, bus stations, or other specific locations. The price will be set before the passenger gets in. Rates are typically 30 to 40 percent higher than regular metered taxis, but you know what the final price will be. Although these pre-paid taxis are not a bargain, they may be good value when taking a taxi from the international airports in Rio de Janeiro and São Paulo (see p435), where taxi drivers have developed the unfortunate habit of taking advantage of tourists who don't speak Portuguese and aren't familiar with Brazil.

In most cities, taxis can be hailed on the street or at numerous taxi stands. Renting a taxi for the day is an inexpensive alternative to renting a car. The price is negotiated with the driver. Taxis in small towns do not have meters, so it is best to agree upon a price in advance.

Another option in smaller towns is the moto-taxi, or motorcycle-taxi. The driver carries an extra helmet and the passenger just hops on the back and rides pillion after fixing a price.

METRO

The metro is the safest form of public transport in Rio and São Paulo. Both cities have metro systems that are very convenient for visitors, as they offer quick and reliable transportation to a number of

Yellow Rio taxis, plentiful and relatively inexpensive

Passengers waiting to board the bus at a city bus stand in Paraná

interesting sites. It is much easier and faster to take the metro to the stop closest to your destination and then take a taxi, rather than figure out a complicated and often slow bus system.

In Rio de Janeiro, the metro runs from 5am to midnight Monday through Saturday, and from 7am to 11pm on Sundays and holidays. During Carnaval, the metro runs non-stop for the five days of the festival. The metro has two main lines, both of which are clean and safe, even in the evenings. The main line from Siqueira Campos in Copacabana to Sãens Peña has 17 stops. The line splits at Estácio, with one line continuing west, while the secondary line goes north to São Cristóvão and beyond. The stops of most interest to visitors are downtown and along the southern beach neighborhoods, as well as the first few stops along the northern line to the Maracanã Stadium and Boã Vista Palace. Rio's metro now also offers a series of integrated metro-bus routes, which offer connections on air-conditioned buses to many of the city's attractions that are off the metro system, such as Santa Teresa, Sugar Loaf, and Ipanema. Passengers must request a special integrated ticket (*integração*) at the time of purchase.

São Paulo's metro system covers quite a large part of the city. It runs from 4:40am to midnight on all days of the week and is also clean, efficient, and safer than the buses.

For both systems, one-way (*unitário*), round-trip (*duplo*), or 10-ride (*múltiplo*) tickets are available. However, no discounts are offered for multiple-ride tickets. Transfers between lines are allowed. Free metro maps are available at most ticket booths of both metro systems.

BUSES

Buses are plentiful in the big cities. Most buses list their destination in large letters on their front window, while another sign with smaller lettering lists key landmarks along the route. Buses in Rio and São Paulo run 24 hours a day, but with fewer circulating in the middle of the night.

In Rio, most buses going from the south to the center will go to Copacabana. Keep in mind that buses are often crowded, and get stuck in terrible time-consuming traffic snarls. They are also often the sites of many of the city's robberies. To avoid pickpockets, try to sit at the front of the bus.

In São Paulo, a couple of the main bus transfer points are at Praça da Republica and the busy Terminal Bandeira, where it is also possible to catch different buses to far-off destinations within the city.

Tickets are sold on the bus by a ticket-seller who sits at a turnstile. Keep small change handy. Brazilian bus drivers can drive fast, so hold on at all times and be alert for sudden stops when standing. It is safer to take buses in the daytime. In the evenings, it is advisable to take taxis.

São Paulo Metro arriving in the Barra Funda station

General Index

Acknowledgments

Dorling Kindersley would like to thank the many people whose help and assistance contributed to the preparation of this book.

Main Contributors
Shawn Blore, a Rio de Janeiro-based journalist, publishes travel and investigative articles in magazines and newspapers in Canada, the USA, the UK, and elsewhere.

Dilwyn Jenkins has been traveling in South America since 1976. Anthropologist, sustainable development expert, and travel writer, he has made documentaries for television for 30 years.

Oliver Marshall has been visiting Brazil regularly since 1982. Specializing in travel and history, he has written extensively on Latin America.

Christopher Pickard has lived in Brazil for nearly 20 years and written widely about the country. He is vice-chairman of the Latin American Travel Association.

Alex Robinson is a travel writer and photographer with a client list that includes *Conde Nast Traveller*, *Wanderlust*, *Footprint*, BBC, and Channel 4.

Neiva Augusta Silva writes for Brazilian travel guides and magazines, as well as on adventure sports and rural tourism.

Fact Checker Stephen Wingrove

Proofreader Word-by-Word

Indexer Jyoti Dhar

Design and Editorial
Publisher Douglas Amrine
Publishing Managers Jane Ewart, Scarlett O'Hara, Anna Streiffert
Senior Designer Paul Jackson
Senior Cartographic Editor Casper Morris
Editorial Assistance Alexandra Farrell, Fay Franklin
DTP Designer Natasha Lu
Picture Researcher Ellen Root
Production Controller Shane Higgins
XML Coordinator Bulent Yusuf

Additional Photography
Geoff Brightling, Geoff Dann, Barnabus Kindersley, Cyril Laubscher.

Additional Illustrations
Chapel Design and Marketing Ltd.

Cartography credits
Base mapping for São Paulo derived from Netmaps, and assistance from Ed Merrit.

Special Assistance
Dorling Kindersley would like to thank José Mayrink, Sônia Lúcia da Costa Conrado, Leonardo A. P. Silva, and Adriana Teixeira for their assistance.

Picture Credits
t=top; tc=top centre; tr=top right; cla=centre left above; ca=centre above; cra=centre right above; cl=centre left; c=centre; cr=centre right; clb=centre left below; cb=centre below; crb=centre right below; bl=bottom left; bc=bottom centre; br=bottom right; ftl=far top left; ftr=far top right; fcla=far centre left above; fcra=far centre right above; fcl=far centre left; fcr=far centre right; fclb=far centre left below; fcrb=far centre right below; fbl=far bottom left; fbr=far bottom right.

Every effort has been made to trace the copyright holders, and we apologize in advance for any unintentional omissions. We would be pleased to insert the appropriate acknowledgments in any subsequent edition of this publication.

The Publisher would like to thank the following for their kind assistance and permission to photograph their establishments:

Alta Floresta: Cristalino Jungle Lodge; Belém: Basílica de Nossa Senhora de Nazaré, Teatro da Paz; Brasília: Catedral Metropolitana Nossa Senhora Aparecida, Santuário Dom Bosco; Caxias do Sul: Museu da Casa de Pedra; Congonhas: Basílica do Senhor Bom Jesus de Matosinhos; Curitiba: Hotel Burbon; Diamantina: Igreja Nossa Senhora do Carmo; Itamaracá Island: Projeto Peixe Boi; João Pessoa: Igreja de São Francisco; Manaus: Teatro Amazonas; Olinda: Convento de São Francisco, Mosteiro de São Bento; Ouro Preto: Casa dos Contos, Igreja de São Francisco de Assis, Matriz de Nossa Senhora da Conceição de Antônio Dias, Museu do Aleijadinho; Paraty: Casa de Cadeia, Igreja de Nossa Senhora do Rosário e São Benedito; Petrópolis: Museu das Cavalhadas, Palácio de Cristal; Porto Alegre: Museu de arte de Rio Grande do Sul, Teatro São Pedro; Recife: Casa da Cultura, Oficina Cerâmica Francisco Brennand, Kahal Zur Israel Synagogue; Rio de Janeiro: Barra Shopping, Blue Man, Confeitaria Colombo, H. Stern, Museu do Índio, Museu Nacional de Belas Artes, Nossa Senhora da Candelária, Rio Scenarium Bar; Salvador: Catedral Basílica, Fundação Casa de Jorge Amado, Igreja e Convento de São Francisco, Memorial das Conquistas do Santos, Museu Afro-Brasileiro, Museu Tempostal; Santos: Bolsa e Museu do Café; São Paulo City: Igreja São

Francisco de Assis, Jacaré do Brasil, Mosteiro de São Bento de São Paulo, Museu de Arte Contemporânea, Museu de Arte de São Paulo, Museu de Arte Sacra de São Paulo, Museu de Arte Moderna de São Paulo, Vila Madalena; Tiradentes: Igreja Matriz de Santo Antônio.

Works of art have been reproduced with the kind permission of the following copyright holders:

Alfredo Volpi, *Composição* (1976) 140tr; José Pancetti, *Serie Bahia Musa da Paz* 141cl; Anita Malfatti, *Tropical* 141tc, Almeida Júnior, *Caipira Picando Fumo* 141cra; Tomie Ohtake, *Pintura* (1969) 141crb.

ALAMY: 1Apix 417t; AM Corporation 145tr; Arco Images 18tl, 20br, 321tc; Graham Bailey 260tl; BrazilPhotos, Ricardo Beliel 26tr, 27tl, 39br; Felipe Goifman 244, 254tl, 419tr; Nando Neves 289cb; Marco A. Rezende 33tr; Ricardo Siqueira 103b; George Brewin 238b; Gerrit Buntrock 312tl; Cristiano Burmester 249cr; Cephas Picture Library 355cla, 355br; Gary Cook 177br, 256-7, 283cr; David Crausby 58bc; David Davis Photoproductions 85br, 392cl; Danita Delimont 320tr; Redmond Durrell 261bc; Dynamic Graphics Group, Creatas 178cl; Chad Ehlers 60-61, 77br; Julio Etchart 37cb; Eye Ubiquitous 24cl; Robert Fried 104cl, 111br, 261cla, 343tr; Mike Goldwater 263crb, 263bl; Andrew Holt 56tr; ImageState 155br; IML Image Group Ltd 417br; James Davis Photography 302tr; Jacques Jangoux 109cla; Jon Arnold Images 261tl; Wolfgang Kaehler 77cr; Brian Kelly 258cla; David Laudien 33br; Look Die Bildagentur der Fotografen GmbH 11tr; Alex Maddox 177cra; Mary Evans Picture Library 173c; Mediacolor's 38-9c, 233bl, 436br; David Muenker 180; David Muscroft 77tl; Network Photographers 282cla; Beren Patterson 193bl; Natalie Pecht 26-7c; Peter Adams Photography 102; Pictorial Press Ltd 57tl, 76clb; Fabio Pili 346br, 347tl; Popperfoto 36br, 37bl, 37bc, 55bc, 57tr, 168bl; Douglas Pulsipher 2-3; Richard Wareham Fotografie 341crb; Robert Harding Picture Library Ltd 262crb; Kevin Schafer 25bl; Sdbphoto Brasil 331cr; Andre Seale 175b, 195cl, 224br, 297cb; David South 174bl; StockBrazil 8c, 117cl, 204br, 205cl, 365tr; Sue Cunningham Photographic 26cl, 179c; Angel Terry 83cr; Travelstock44 27bl, 92b; Peter Treanor 21t, 39bl, 64bl, 78tl; Genevieve Vallee 248c, 293tr, 297cr, 311tc; Mireille Vautier 6-7, 176br; Visual Arts Library (London) 52bc, 61c; Peter M. Wilson 120; Andrew Woodley 79tl; Worldwide Picture Library 133tr, 263cr; Noel Yates 79tr.
MARCIO CABRAL: 204c.
SÔNIA LÚCIA DA COSTA CONRADO: 187crb.
CORBIS: Alinari Archives 54Abc; Theo Allofs 261crb, 315b; Archivo Iconografico, S.A. 50crb, 52crb; Ricardo Azoury 93tr, 116clb, 249br, 360-1; Yann Arthus Bertrand 22bc, 22br, 37cra, 341br; Bettmann 32tr, 54cl, 55tc, 55cb, 56br, 56-7c, 58cb,

75cr, 291c, 295crb; Barnabas Bosshart 272-3; Tom Brakefield 261cr, 296cl, 312bl; João Luiz Bulcão 420bl; Pierre Colombel 47bc; Corbis KIPA/Rault Jean François 33tl; Corbis Sygma/262cl, 262cra, 262br; Bernard Bisson 34bl; Whitemore Hank 263cla; Collart Herve 59br, 222bl, 257c, 262bl, 276; Manchete 82clb; Le Segretain Pascal 21cl; Ecoscene, Joel Creed 341cra; Paul Edmondson 10b; EPA, Caetano Barreira 43br; Eye Ubiquitous/James Davis 191br, 340br; Paulo Fridman 59bl, 295cra; Gallo, Martin Harvey 296br; Farrell Grehan 295tc; Darrell Gulin 109br; Martin Harvey 24cb, 260bl; Eric and David Hosking 109tc, 109 clb; Wolfgang Kaehler 260clb, 283tl; Kuba 415br; Lawrence Manning 48tr; Stephanie Maze 324-325, 415tr; Joe McDonald 261fcra; Diego Lezama Orezzoli 253tl; Fabio Polenghi 36tr; José Fuste Raga 67b; Reuters/Sergio Moraes 275tr; Kevin Schafer 109bl, 296bl, 297br; Torleif Svensson 234-5; Staffan Widstrand 22cl, 261ca, 290-1; Peter M. Wilson 16.
COSTA DO SAUÍPE MARRIOTT RESORT & SPA: 364b, 390c.
MARTIN M. CRESPO: 9b.
DK IMAGES: Andy Crawford, Courtesy Football Museum; Preston 36clb; Ian O'Leary 178, 392-393.
GETTY IMAGES: AFP 31tr; Hulton Archives/ Evans 57cr, 57bl, 57br; Iconica/Wild Pics 347cr; Lonely Planet images, John Maier Jr. 346tr; Photographer's Choice, Fernando Bueno 82cla; SambaPhoto, Eduardo Barcellos 179tl, Cassio Vasconcellos 66; Stone/Orion Press 344-5, /Will & Deni McIntyre 177bl; Time Life Pictures 58tl, /Leonard McCombe 56cl.
IMAGEM BRASIL: Gentil Barreira 23tl, 40cr, 250clb; Francisco Chagas 11bc; Alex Uchôa 9t, 172-3, 202-3, 251bl, 314; Flávio Veloso 34cl.
LATIN PHOTO: Biosfera 263tl, 263br; Carlos Ortiz Fragalá 330bl.
LONELY PLANET IMAGES: Guy Moberly 150tc.
MARY EVANS PICTURE LIBRARY: 49bl, 56bl, 324c, 423c.
MASTERFILE: Mark Leibowitz 28tr; F. Lukasseck 25crb; David Mendelsohn 17b, 19t; Brian Sytnyk 39tr; Jeremy Woodhouse 1c, 20tl, 25cr.
MUSEU IMPERIAL: 114tr, 114cl, 114cb, 115tl, 115ca, 115cb.
PAUL MOWATT: 286tl.
OLHAR IMAGEM: Aristides Alves 197bl, 204tl; Daniel Augusto Jr. 33c, 194cr; Ricardo Azoury 28clb, 65br, 70clb, 109crb, 177tr, 258cl, 258bl, 279tr; Flávio Bacellar 287br; Cynthia Brito 195tr; Fausto Pires de Campos 166-7; Maristela Colucci 224clb; Salomon Cytrynowicz 42tl, 227b; Adri Felden 353tr; Iolanda Huzak 328cl; Marcos Issa 206bl, 233cla, 333b; Zig Koch 23cr, 296-7c, 298, 313cr; Stefan Kolumban 176-7c; Delfim Martins 25tc, 170b; Juca Martins 27tr, 27cr, 30bc, 34crb, 35tr, 38cl, 106cl, 111t, 119b, 144tl, 174cl, 195cl, 233br, 233cr, 268br, 286b, 288t, 321cra; Renata Mello 23br, 208; Sonia Oddi 339t; Saulo Petean 35br; Rogério Reis 32bl, 176bl, 254br, 327cr; Zaida

Siqueira 260cla; Monica Vendramini 275b; Luciana Whitaker 117bl, 289tr.
PA PHOTOS: Peter Robinson 37tl.
PHOTOGRAPHERS DIRECT.COM: Chris Fairclough Worldwide 250br; David Davis Photoproductions 39c; Jahan Images 281cl; Marcelo Krause Photography 117br.
PHOTOLIBRARY: JTB Photo 330-1c, 393tl; Robert Harding Picture Library Ltd 10tr.
POPPERFOTO: 36ca, 36cl, 36bc, 37br.
PETER PRICE: 296cb.
PRIVATE COLLECTION: 31br, 51b, 294cl.
PULSAR IMAGENS: Nelson Almeida 59tc; Ricardo Azoury 41tl, 64-65c, 209b, 252tr, 252br, 299b, 320clb; J. L. Bulcão 181b; Armando Catunda 109c; Daniel Cymbalista 141bl, 439b; Adriano Gambarini 24crb, 241t; Artur Keunecke 25bc, 318br; Stefan Kolumban 348; Marcio Lourenço 24bl; Delfim Martins 29br, 42b, 118t, 118bl, 134, 230cla, 237cla, 237cr, 247br, 297tc, 434b, 438cl; Juca Martins 26bl, 29cl, 196t, 285t, 443br; Manoel Novaes 24cr, 25cb, 306-7; Rogério Reis 24bc, 43tl, 116tr; André Seale 8br, 24tr, 201br, 225br, 261br; Paula Simas 19br; Mauricio Simonetti 25tl, 25tr, 25cl, 62ca, 123tr, 133b, 236bl, 318t, 420tr; Luciana Whitaker 89bl; Palê Zuppani 321cr.
REUTERS: 263cra; Alexandra Beier 37fbr; Andrea Comas 33cb, 176cl; Alex Grimm 36-37c; Lucas Jackson 32bc; Sergio Moraes 40b; Jose Patricio 26br; STR New 135b; Paulo Whitaker 32-33c, 145br, 153tr, 262tr, 436cl.
OCTAVIO CAMPOS SALLES: 285bl.
SOFITEL HOTELS & RESORT: 184cl, 187tc, 363bc, Christian Knepper 186clb, 414cl.
LORI STILGER: 296cla.
THE BRIDGEMAN ART LIBRARY: *Botocudos Family*, Rio Grande, Brazil, from *Le Costume Ancien et Moderne*, Volume II, plate 37, by Jules Ferrario, published c.1820s-30s (colour litho) (see also 84784), Gallina, Gallo (1796-1874) / Private Collection, The Stapleton Collection 49tr; *The Slave Hunter* (oil on canvas), Debret, Jean Baptiste (1768-1848) / Museu de Arte, São Paulo, Brazil, Giraudon 50tl; Cross-section of a model of a slave ship, late 18th century (wood), French School, (18th century) / Bibliothèque de L'Arsenal, Paris, France, Archives Charmet 50br; *Independence or Death, the Shout of Ipiranga on the 7th September 1822* (oil on canvas), Américo, Dom Pedro di

Figueredo (1843-1905) / Museu Historico Nacional, Rio de Janeiro, Brazil, Index 52tl; *The Surrender of Uruguaiana, Brazil*, 1865 (oil on canvas), Lopez, Candido (1840-1902) / Museu Historico Nacional, Buenos Aires, Argentina, Index 53tr; *The Dinner, a white couple being served and fanned by black slaves*, from *Voyage Pittoresque et Historique au Brésil*, published in 1839 (color litho), Debret, Jean Baptiste (1768-1848) (after) / Bibliotheque Nationale, Paris, France, Archives Charmet 53bc; *The Funeral of the Emperor of Brazil: The Carriage*, from *Le Petit Journal*, 26th December 1891 (color litho), Meyer, Henri (1844-99) / Private Collection, Giraudon 54tc.
THE GRANGER COLLECTION, NEW YORK: 7c, 31cl, 46, 47c, 48cla, 48-9c, 48bl, 49tl, 49cl, 51t, 53c, 328tr, 361c.
TYBA PHOTOGRAPHIC AGENCY: J.R. Couto 76cl, 84bl, 86bl; Alberto Ferreira 294clb, 294-5c, 294bc, 295bl; Antonio Gusmão 32clb; Paulo Jares 32ca, 295tl; Marcello Lourenço 277b, 288br; Ciro Mariano 206t; L.C. Marigo 287tl; Claus Meyer 131cr, 295cr, 331tr; O Brito News 294tr; Rogério Reis 64cb, 87tl, 94tr, 232clb, 239br, 245b; Ricardo Ribas 329br; David Santos Júnior 205bl; André Valentim 278cl; Flávio Vidigal 347cl.
ALEX SANDRO DO AMARAL UCHÔA: 205br, 225cr, 240tr.
WIKIPEDIA: Public Domain 49clb, 82tr, 294bl.

Front Endpaper: ALAMY: BrazilPhotos/ Felipe Goifman tc, David Muenker fcra, Peter Adams Photography cr, Peter M. Wilson fbr; CORBIS: Collart Herve fcl; GETTY: Sambaphoto/Cassio Vasconcellos fcr; IMAGEM BRASIL: Alex Uchôa cl; OLHAR IMAGEM: Zig Koch bc, Renata Mello ftr; PULSAR IMAGEM: Stefan Kolumban fbl, Delfim Martins br.

Jacket images: Front: Alamy Images: Elvele Images / Fritz Poelking clb; Getty Images: Photographer's Choice / Tim Thompson. Back: Corbis: Frans Lanting cla; José Fuste Raga tl; DK Images: Demetrio Carrasco clb; Alex Robinson: bl. Spine: DK Images: Linda Whitwam b; Getty Images: Photographer's Choice / Tim Thompson.

All other images © Dorling Kindersley
For further information see: www.dkimages.com

SPECIAL EDITIONS OF DK TRAVEL GUIDES

DK Travel Guides can be purchased in bulk quantities at discounted prices for use in promotions or as premiums. We are also able to offer special editions and personalized jackets, corporate imprints, and excerpts from all of our books, tailored specifically to meet your own needs.

To find out more, please contact:
(in the United States) **SpecialSales@dk.com**
(in the UK) **Sarah.Burgess@dk.com**
(in Canada) DK Special Sales at **general@tourmaline.ca**
(in Australia)
business.development@pearson.com.au

Phrase Book

The Portuguese spoken in Brazil differs in various ways from the Portuguese spoken in Portugal. In general, Brazilian pronunciation tends to omit far fewer sounds, especially the sounds at the end of words, and rarely runs two words together, both of which are common practice in Portugal. One feature of Brazilian Portuguese, particularly in the Rio de Janeiro area, is that an "r" sound can be spoken like an "h." So *carro* (car) may sound like "ka-hoo." Another difference lies in the ways of saying "you." The Portuguese form of placing the definite article in front of a person's name (*o João*, *a Cristina*), as a way of saying "you," does not exist in Brazil, where *você* and *vocês* are the most common words for "you." The Portuguese *tu* is not used much in Brazil. A huge number of other vocabulary differences exist, many at the level of everyday speech: train is *trem* in Brazil, *comboio* in Portugal; breakfast is *café da manhã* in Brazil, *pequeno almoço* in Portugal; bathroom is *banheiro* in Brazil, *casa de banho* in Portugal; goalkeeper is *goleiro* in Brazil, *guarda-redes* in Portugal; to drive is *dirigir* in Brazil, *conduzir* in Portugal. The sound indicated by "ï" in the phrase book is like the "i" in English word "hi." "J" sounds like the "s" in the word "pleasure."

In an Emergency

Help!	**Socorro!**	*sookorroo*
Stop!	**Pare!**	*pahree*
Call a doctor!	**Chame um médico!**	*shamih oong mehjikoo*
Call an ambulance!	**Chame uma ambulância!**	*shamih ooma amboolans-ya*
Where is the hospital?	**Onde é o hospital?**	*ohnd-yeh oo oshpital*
Police!	**Polícia!**	*poolees-ya*
Fire!	**Fogo!**	*fohgoo*
I've been robbed	**Fui assaltado**	*fwee asaltadoo*

Communication Essentials

Yes	**Sim**	*seeng*
No	**Não**	*nowng*
Hello	**Olá**	*ohla*
How are you?	**Como vai?**	*kohmoo vi*
How is it going?	**Tudo bem/ tudo bom?**	*toodoo bayng/ toodo bong*
Goodbye	**Tchau**	*tshow*
See you later	**Até logo**	*ateh logoo*
Excuse me	**Com licença**	*kong lisaynsa*
I'm sorry	**Desculpe**	*dishkoolp*
Thank you	**Obrigado (if a man is speaking)/ obrigada (if a woman is speaking)**	*obrigadoo/obrigada*
Good morning	**Bom dia**	*bong jeea*
Good afternoon	**Boa tarde**	*boh-a tarj*
Good evening/ night	**Boa noite**	*boh-a noh-itsh*
Pleased to meet you	**Muito prazer**	*mweengtoo prazayr*
I'm fine	**Estou bem/ tudo bem**	*shtoh bayng/ toodoo bayng*
Today	**Hoje**	*ohJ*
Yesterday	**Ontem**	*ohntayng*
Tomorrow	**Amanhã**	*aman-yang*
What?	**O que?**	*oo kay*
When?	**Quando?**	*kwandoo*
How?	**Como?**	*kohmoo*
Why?	**Por que?**	*poorkay*

Useful Phrases

On the left/right	**À esquerda/direita**	*a-shkayrda/jirayta*
I don't understand	**Não entendo**	*nowng ayntayndoo*
Please speak slowly	**Fale devagar por favor**	*falee Jivagar poor favohr*
What's your name?	**Qual é seu nome?**	*kwal eh say-oo nohm*
My name is...	**Meu nome é...**	*may-oo nohm eh*
Go away!	**Vá embora!**	*va aymbora*
That's fine	**Está bem**	*shtah bayng*
Where is...?	**Onde está/fica...?**	*ohnj shtah/feeka*
When does the bus leave/arrive?	**A que horas sai/ chega o ônibus?**	*a kih orash si/ shayga oo ohniboosh*
Is this the way to the...?	**Este é o caminho para...?**	*aysht-yeh oo kameen-yoo pra*

Useful Words

big	**grande**	*granj*
small	**pequeno**	*pikaynoo*
hot	**quente**	*kayntsh*
cold	**frio**	*free-oo*
bad	**mau**	*mow*
good	**bom**	*bong*
enough	**suficiente**	*soofis-yayntsh*
open	**aberto**	*abehrtoo*
closed	**fechado**	*fishadoo*
dangerous	**perigoso**	*pirigohzoo*
safe	**seguro**	*sigooroo*
full	**cheio**	*shay-oo*
empty	**vazio**	*vazee-oo*
straight on	**reto**	*rehtoo*
under	**debaixo**	*dibïshoo*
over	**em cima**	*ayng seema*
in front of	**em frente de**	*ayng frayntsh ji*
behind	**atrás de**	*atraj jih*
first floor	**primeiro andar**	*primayroo andar*
ground floor	**térreo**	*tehrryoo*
lift	**elevador**	*elevadohr*
toilet	**banheiro**	*ban-yayroo*
men's	**dos homens**	*dooz ohmaynsh*
women's	**das mulheres**	*dash mool-yebrish*
quick	**rápido**	*rapidoo*
soon	**cedo**	*saydoo*
late	**tarde**	*tarj*
now	**agora**	*agora*
more	**mais**	*mïsh*
less	**menos**	*maynoosh*
a little	**um pouco**	*oong pohkoo*
a lot	**muito**	*mweengtoo*
too much	**demais**	*dimïsh*
entrance	**entrada**	*ayntrada*
exit	**saída**	*sa-eeda*
passport	**passaporte**	*pasaportsh*

Post Offices & Banks

bank	**banco**	*bankoo*
bureau de change	**(casa de) câmbio**	*(kaza jih) kamb-yoo*
exchange rate	**taxa de câmbio**	*tasha jih kamb-yoo*
post office	**correio**	*koorray-oo*
postcard	**cartão postal**	*kartowng pooshtal*
postbox	**caixa de correio**	*kïsha jih koorray-oo*
ATM	**caixa automática**	*kïsha owtoomatshika*
stamp	**selo**	*sayloo*
cash	**dinheiro**	*jeen-yayroo*
withdraw money	**tirar dinheiro**	*tshirar jeen-yayroo*

Shopping

How much is it?	**Quanto é?**	*kwantweh*
I would like...	**Eu quero...**	*ay-oo kehroo*
clothes	**roupa**	*rohpa*
This one	**Esta**	*ehshta*
That one	**Essa**	*ehsa*
market	**mercado**	*merkadoo*
supermarket	**Supermercado**	*soopermerkadoo*
Do you accept credit cards?	**Aceitam cartão de crédito?**	*asaytowng kartowng jih krehditoo*
expensive	**caro**	*karoo*
baker's	**padaria**	*padaree-a*
butcher's	**açougue**	*asohgee*
chemist's	**farmácia**	*farmas-ya*

Sightseeing

museum	**museu**	*moozay-oo*
art gallery	**galeria de arte**	*galiree-a jih artsh*
national park	**parque nacional**	*parkee nas-yoonal*
beach	**praia**	*prï-a*
park	**parque**	*parkee*
river	**rio**	*ree-oo*
church	**igreja**	*igray-Ja*
cathedral	**catedral**	*katidrow*
district	**bairro**	*bïrroo*
garden	**jardim**	*Jardeeng*
tourist office	**informações turísticas**	*infoormasoyngsh tooreeshtsheekash*
guide	**guia**	*gee-a*
guided tour	**excursão com guia**	*shkoorsowng kong gee-a*
ticket	**bilhete/ingresso**	*bil-yaytsh/ingrehsoo*
map	**mapa**	*mapa*

Transport

bus	ônibus	obniboosh
boat	barco	barkoo
train	trem	trayng
airport	aeroporto	a-ayroopobrtoo
airplane	avião	av-young
flight	vôo	vob-oo
bus station	rodoviária	roodobvyar-ya
bus stop	ponto de ônibus	pobntoo j-yobniboosh
train station	estação de trem	stasoung jih trayng
ticket	passagem	pasajayng
taxi	táxi	taxee
subway	metrô	metrob

Health

I feel bad/ill	Sinto-me mal/doente	seentoomih mow/dwayntsh
I need to rest	Preciso descansar	priseezoo jishkansar
diarrhoea	diarréia	j-yarreb-ya
pharmacy	farmácia	farmas-ya
headache	dor de cabeça	dohr jih kabaysa
medicine	remédio	rimebd-yoo
sanitary towels/tampons	absorventes/tampões	absoorvayntsh/tampoyngsh
mosquito repellent	repelente de mosquito	ripelayntsh dih mooshkeetoo
doctor	médico	mebjikoo
condom	camisinha	kamizeen-ya

Staying in a Hotel

hotel	hotel	obteb-oo
boutique hotel	pousada	pobzada
guesthouse	pensão	paynsowng
hostel	albergue	owbebrgee
Do you have a room?	Tem um quarto?	tayng oong kwartoo
I have a reservation	Tenho uma reserva	tayn-yoo ooma risebrva
single/double (room)	(quarto de) solteiro/casal	(kwartoo jih) sooltayroo/kazow
shower	chuveiro	shoovayroo
sheet	lençol	laynsob
bed	cama	kama
pillow	travesseiro	travisayroo
towel	toalha	twal-ya
toilet paper	papel higiênico	papeb-oo iJ-yebnikoo

Eating Out

I want to reserve...	Quero reservar...	kebroo rizirvar
Do you have...?	Tem...?	tayng
The bill, please	A conta, por favor	a kobnta, poor favobr
menu	cardápio/menu	kardap-yoo/maynoo
wine list	lista de vinhos	leesbta de veen-yoosb
glass	copo	kopoo
bottle	garrafa	garrafa
fork	garfo	garfoo
knife	faca	faka
spoon	colher	kool-yebr
restaurant	restaurante	rishtourantsh
breakfast	café da manhã	kafeb da man-yang
lunch	almoço	owmobsoo
dinner/supper	jantar	Jantar
(mineral) water	água (mineral)	agua (minerow)
vegetarian	vegetariano	vigitar-yanoo
Is service included?	O serviço está incluído?	oo sirveesoo shtab inklweedoo

Menu Decoder

açúcar	asookar	sugar
alho	al-yoo	garlic
arroz	arrobsh	rice
azeite	azaytsh	olive oil
bebida	bibeeda	drink
bem passado	baymg pasadoo	well done
bife	beefee	steak
café	kafeb	coffee
cerveja	sirvayJa	beer
chá	sba	tea
churrasco	shoorrashkoo	barbecue
feijão (preto)	faylowng (praytoo)	(black) beans
frango	frangoo	chicken
fruta	froota	fruit
lanche	lansbee	snack
leite	laytsh	milk
pão	powng	bread
pimenta	pimaynta	pepper
mal passado	mow pasadoo	rare
refrigerante	rifrigirantsh	soft drink
sal	sow	salt
suco	sookoo	fruit juice
vinho	veen-yoo	wine
ao ponto	ow pobntoo	medium
feijoada	faylwada	bean and meat stew
sorvete	sobrvaytsh	ice cream
manteiga	mantayga	butter
ovo cozido	obvoo koozeedoo	hard-boiled egg
grelhado	gril-yadoo	grilled
batatas fritas	batatasb freetasb	chips
carne	karnee	beef
peixe	paysbee	fish
pastel de carne	pasbteb-oo jih karnee	puff-pastry patty filled with mince
pastel de queijo	pasbteb-oo jih kay-Joo	puff-pastry patty filled with cheese
pão de queijo	powng jih kay-Joo	cheese cookie
farofa	farofa	dish based on manioc/cassava meal
quindim	keenjeeng	coconut and egg sweet
muqueca de peixe	mookebka jih paysbee	fish stew with coconut milk

Time

minute	minuto	minootoo
hour	hora	ora
half an hour	meia hora	may-a ora
next week	na próxima semana	na prosima simana
last month	no mês passado	noo maysb pasadoo
Monday	segunda-feira	sigoonda fayra
Tuesday	terça-feira	tayrsa fayra
Wednesday	quarta-feira	kwarta fayra
Thursday	quinta-feira	keenta fayra
Friday	sexta-feira	saysbta fayra
Saturday	sábado	sabadoo
Sunday	domingo	doomeengoo
January	janeiro	Janayroo
February	fevereiro	feverayroo
March	março	marsoo
April	abril	abree-oo
May	maio	mī-oo
June	junho	Joon-yoo
July	julho	Jool-yoo
August	agosto	agobsbtoo
September	setembro	sitaymbroo
October	outubro	obtoobroo
November	novembro	noovaymbroo
December	dezembro	dizaymbroo

Numbers

1	um/uma	oong/ooma
2	dois/duas	dob-isb/doo-asb
3	três	traysh
4	quatro	kwatroo
5	cinco	seenkoo
6	seis	saysb
7	sete	sebt
8	oito	ob-itoo
9	nove	novee
10	dez	debsh
11	onze	obnzee
12	doze	dobzee
13	treze	trayzee
14	catorze	katobrzee
15	quinze	keenzee
16	dezesseis	dizesaysb
17	dezessete	dizesebtee
18	dezoito	dizob-itoo
19	dezenove	dizenovee
20	vinte	veentee
21	vinte e um	veentib-oong
30	trinta	treenta
40	quarenta	kwaraynta
50	cinqüenta	sinkwaynta
60	sessenta	sesaynta
70	setenta	setaynta
80	oitenta	ob-itaynta
90	noventa	nobvaynta
100	cem, cento	sayng/sayntoo
1000	mil	mee-oo

FOR PEACE OF MIND ABROAD
we've got it covered **wherever you are**

For an **instant quote** on quality worldwide travel insurance visit **www.dk.com/travel-insurance** or call:

— **USA** 1 800 749 4922 (Toll Free)
— **UK** 0800 258 5363
— **Australia** 1300 669 999
— **New Zealand** 0800 55 99 11
— **Canada** www.dk.com/travel-insurance
— **Worldwide** +44 870 894 0001

Cover provided to residents of over 46 countries for virtually every kind of trip

Please quote our ref: Eyewitness Travel Guides

Insurance is arranged through and provided by Columbus Travel Insurance Services Ltd (trading as Columbus Direct), Advertiser House, 19 Bartlett St, Croydon, CR2 6TB . Columbus Direct is authorised and regulated by the Financial Services Authority.

RIO DE JANEIRO TRANSIT MAP

SÃO PAUL

Belford Roxo

Saracuruna,
Vila Inhomirim

Pavuna [2]

Costa Barros

Eng. Rubens Paiva

Vigário Geral

Vigário

Barros Filho

Acari/Fazenda
Botafago

Lucas

Honório Gurgel

Cohelo Meto

Cordovil

Rocha Miranda

Colégio

Braz de Pina

Mercadão de
Madureira

Irajá

Penha Circular

Cavalcante

Penha

Tomás Coelho

Vicente de Carcalho

Olaria

Pilares

Tomás Coelho

Ramos

Del Castilho

Eng. da Rainha

Bonsucesso

Jacarezinho

Inhaúma

Manguinhos

Itapevi,
Amador Bueno

[B] Osasco
[C] Pres.
Altino

Imper
Leope

Del Castilho

Maria da Graça

Triagem

Central

Ceasa

Pres. Vargas

Santa Cruz,
Campo Grande

Uruguaiana

Maracanã

São
Cristóvão [2]

Praça Onze

Jaguaré

Estácio

Carioca

Alfonsa Pena

Cinelândia

Cidade
Universitaria

[1]

São Francisco Xavier

Glória

Pinhei

Saens Peña

Catete

[4] Morun

GETTING AROUND

Rio's comfortable and efficient metro
network is limited to two lines. The
main line, Linha 1, which has 17 stops,
runs from Siqueira Campos, north
through Central, out to the Saens Peña
station. Linha 2 comes in from Pavuna
to the city center and goes via the
Maracanã to meet Linha 1 at Estácio,
by Dom Pedro II metro station. The
commuter line Supervia connects
downtown Rio to its suburbs, but is
not commonly used for commuting.

Largo do Machado

Flamengo

Botafogo

Vila Sônia

Capão
Redondo
[5]

Campo
Limpo

KEY

— Linha 1

— Linha 2

— Supervia

Cardeal Arcoverde

Siqueira Campos [1]

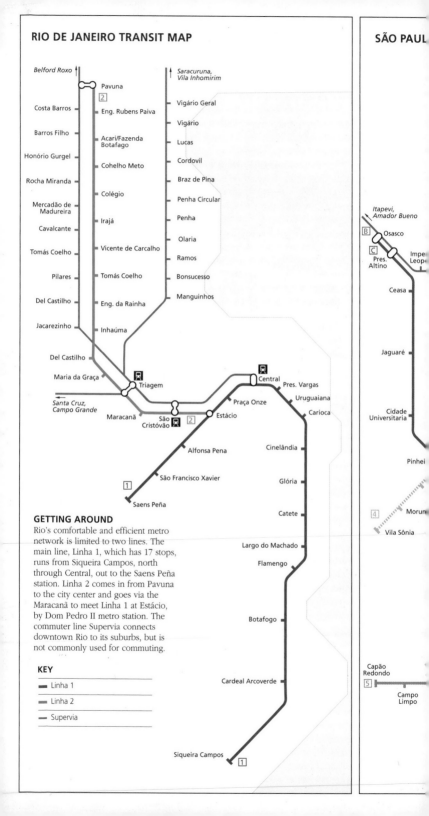